Guide to Biometric Reference Systems and Performance Evaluation

Dijana Petrovska-Delacrétaz • Gérard Chollet
Bernadette Dorizzi
Editors

Guide to Biometric Reference Systems and Performance Evaluation

with a Foreword by Professor Anil K. Jain, Michigan State University, USA

Springer

Dijana Petrovska-Delacrétaz, PhD
Electronics and Physics Department,
TELECOM SudParis,
France

Gérard Chollet, PhD
Centre National de la Recherche
Scientifique (CNRS-LTCI),
TELECOM ParisTech,
France

Bernadette Dorizzi, Professor
Electronics and Physics Department,
TELECOM SudParis,
France

ISBN: 978-1-84800-291-3 e-ISBN: 978-1-84800-292-0
DOI: 10.1007/978-1-84800-292-0

Library of Congress Control Number: 2008940851

Printed on acid-free paper

Springer Science+Business Media
springer.com

Foreword

With the pioneering studies of Galton and Henry on fingerprint-based human identification over a hundred years ago, biometrics recognition is now permeating many sectors of our society. Even though the origins and the most frequent use of biometrics, primarily fingerprints, have been in forensics and law enforcement applications, biometric recognition is now needed to address a number of societal problems related to security risks, terror threats and financial fraud. In some situations, for example, detecting duplicate enrolments (for issuing official documents such as passports and driver licenses), biometrics is the only method to confirm that an applicant has not been previously enrolled in the database. In addition to fingerprints, new anatomical and behavioral traits, viz., face, iris, voice and hand shape have also become popular.

Biometrics recognition is an excellent proving ground for pattern recognition. While pattern recognition systems have been available for document imaging, speech recognition, medical image analysis, remote sensing and variety of inspection tasks, no other application domain offers as many challenges as the biometrics domain. Some of these challenges include (i) sensing the biometric traits of a very large number of individuals of different ages and profession and with diverse cultural and religions backgrounds, (ii) large number of pattern classes (millions in applications such as biometric-enabled national ID card), (iii) large intra-class and inter-class variations, (iv) accuracy, cost and throughput requirements, (v) integration of biometrics with existing security infrastructure, and (vi) securing the biometric system itself so that user's privacy is preserved. While there are no perfect solutions that match the requirements of all the applications, the number of deployed biometric systems is steadily increasing. With continued research and development, particularly in areas related to biometric system performance and system security, users will become more comfortable using this technology, resulting in even broader adoption of biometrics.

This book, edited by three leading researchers in biometrics, Gérard Chollet, Bernadette Dorizzi and Dijana Petrovska-Delacrétaz, is a valuable addition to the growing body of knowledge in biometrics. The value of this book lies in providing complete source code for matching major biometric traits (2D face, 3D face, fingerprints, iris, hand, voice and online signature). Additional chapters on multimodal biometrics and benchmarking methodology, along with reference databases, will be of great value to young researchers and for training future biometric researchers. All the chapter authors are active researchers in biometrics and they formed the core of the very successful European Union BioSecure Network of Excellence. I am confident that this book will serve as a valuable reference book and will enable in advancing the state of the art in biometric recognition.

Michigan State University April 13, 2008 *Anil K. Jain*

Preface

This book would never have existed without the BioSecure Network of Excellence (NoE). This European project, launched in 2004 and that ended in 2007, was partly supported by the European Commission. It grouped 30 partners (all academic but one) from eight countries. Its main objective was to federate the biometric research conducted independently in different laboratories, as well as to give visibility to the European research in biometrics.

With the goal to continue to exploit the achievements of the BioSecure project, the "Association BioSecure" was created to handle the property rights and legal issues related to the distribution of biometric databases, as well as to assure the maintenance of the reference systems. The Association is also eager to organize further open evaluation campaigns in order to continue to exploit the biometric databases acquired during the BioSecure project.

When starting this project, it seemed obvious to us that one of the main obstacles to the progress of research in this domain was the lack of facilities for evaluation, considering the large number of modalities that can be encountered, without speaking of the emergence either of new modalities or of the interest in multimodality.

At that time the National Institute of Standards and Technologies (NIST) was conducting yearly speaker recognition evaluations, as well as the first face recognition competitions, putting databases, experimental protocols and baseline software at the disposal of researchers for comparative evaluations. The Fingerprint Verification Competitions (FVC) offered an independent evaluation for fingerprints every two years. But what about hand, iris, online handwritten signature or multimodality?

Our efforts were therefore focused on providing new evaluation tools for different modalities such as 2D and 3D face, iris, speaker, talking faces, hand, fingerprints, and online handwritten signature. Taking advantage of the multisite repartition of the Network, three large databases were gathered, including modalities recorded in different application conditions (mobility, access control and Internet communications). Open source reference systems were also produced for each modality, as well as assessment protocols for benchmarking.

During the First Residential Workshop organized in August 2005 within the BioSecure NoE[1], following the model of John's Hopkins University[2], we put the premises of the design of an evaluation framework, including publicly available databases, assessment protocols, and reference systems. They allowed a preliminary comparative evaluation of the algorithms developed by the BioSecure partners in their own laboratories.

During the 2005 Residential Workshop, the idea of this book was initialized, and it took us two more years to complete the drafted tasks, namely to complement and test the ten open source reference systems available at the companion URL site of this book[3]. In the meantime, the acquisition of the upper-mentioned databases was completed, and the BioSecure Multimodal Evaluation Campaign (BMEC'2007) took place in September 2007. Unfortunately, due to lack of time and data distribution obstacles, this evaluation was not open largely outside BioSecure.

Content This book is composed of eleven chapters. In Chap. 1, a short introduction about biometrics is provided. The proposed benchmarking methodology and its basic terminology are presented in Chap. 2. The next eight chapters (Chaps. 3–10), dedicated to iris, fingerprint, hand, online handwritten signature, speech, 2D and 3D face, and talking face modalities, follow a common structure. First, the state of the art and current issues and challenges are addressed. The existing databases and evaluation campaigns are next summarized. Then, the Biometric Evaluation Framework for the specific modality is introduced. Research systems are presented after, with experimental results according to the benchmarking protocols. Because for each modality all experiments presented follow the benchmarking protocol, the presented research results could be compared. Chapter 11 presents the experimental results from the mobile scenario of the BioSecure Multimodal Evaluation Campaign (BMEC'2007).

Intended audience This book, with it's unique combination of state-of-the-art research on common benchmarking experimental protocols and practical evaluation tools, is intended for graduates, researchers and practitioners in the fields of Biometrics and Pattern Recognition.

Conclusions and Perspectives This book may not answer all the questions set forth in Chap. 1! At least some methodological suggestions are put forward to improve the performance and comparability of biometric systems:

- Open source reference software can be uploaded for a number of modalities.
- For each of the presented modalities, publicly available databases are used to define the benchmarking experimental protocols.
- The benchmarking results, obtained with the open source reference systems, benchmarking databases, and protocols are fully reproducible (How-to documents are also available on the companion URL.[3])

---

[1] http://www.biosecure.info

[2] http://www.clsp.jhu.edu/workshops/

[3] http://share.int-evry.fr/svnview-eph/

What is missing? What needs to be improved?

- Reference systems should be maintained and improved.
- Reference systems should be developed for emerging modalities, such as palm prints, hand vein, DNA, ear, teeth, etc. State-of-the-art classification and statistical modeling technique should be made compatible with the existing and new reference systems.
- Existing reference systems need to be improved and submitted to standardization organizations (such as ISO, CEN, W3C, etc.) to facilitate interoperability and comparability. A similar approach has proven quite successful for speech, audio and video coders. It should also be profitable for biometrics.
- More databases should be recorded in diverse conditions, with new sensors, over a long time span, with a huge number of subjects, etc.
- Evaluation protocols must be defined and published as soon as databases are available. Databases (and particularly multimodal data) should be made anonymous to protect privacy.
- Multimodal biometrics, revocability of biometric data, spoofing, privacy, and user acceptance are major issues that require further research and experimentation.
- Sequestered evaluation campaigns need to be organized regularly.

Acknowledgments

We would like first to thank all the authors of the different chapters for their hard work, cooperation, and for the time they spent to re-run their experiments with the benchmarking databases and protocols. Thanks are also due to several authors and members of the BioSecure Network who participated in the review process.

Special thanks to Aurélien Mayoue for his dedicated efforts to maintain, document, and test the reference systems.

The assistance of Danielle Paes de A. Camara for the LaTeX version is gratefully acknowledged.

Thanks to all the BioSecure partners and in particular to the participants to the BioSecure Residential Workshop and to the BMEC'2007 Evaluation Campaign.

Dijana Petrovska-Delacrétaz, Institut TELECOM, TELECOM SudParis
Gérard Chollet, Institut TELECOM, TELECOM ParisTech
Bernadette Dorizzi, Institut TELECOM, TELECOM SudParis
August 2008

Contents

Contributors

Lale AKARUN
Boğaziçi University, Computer Engineering Dept. Bebek, TR-34342, Istanbul, Turkey
e-mail: akarun@boun.edu.tr

José-L. ALBA-CASTRO
TSC Department ETSE Telecomunicación, Campus Universitario de Vigo, 36310, Vigo, Spain
e-mail: jalba@gts.tsc.uvigo.es

Albert ALI SALAH
Formerly with Boğaziçi University, Computer Engineering Dept., Currently with Centre of Mathematics and Computer Science (CWI), Kruislaan 413, 1090 GB Amsterdam, The Netherlands
e-mail: a.a.salah@cwi.nl

Lorène ALLANO
TELECOM SudParis (ex GET-INT), 9 rue Charles Fourier – 91011 Evry, France
e-mail: lorene.allano@it-sudparis.eu

Fernando ALONSO-FERNANDO
Formerly with UPM – Universidad Politecnica de Madrid, currently with ATVS/Biometric Recognition Group., Escuela Politecnica Superior, Univ. Autonoma de Madrid, Avda. Francisco Tomas y Valiente 11, 28049 Madrid, Spain
e-mail: fernando.alonso@uam.es

Mohamed ANOUAR-MELLAKH
TELECOM SudParis (ex GET-INT), 91011 Evry, France
e-mail: mohamed.anouar_mellakh@it-sudparis.eu

Manuele BICEGO
Universitá degli Studi di Sassari, Piazza Universitá 21, 07100 Sassari, Italy
e-mail: bicego@uniss.it

Josef BIGUN
Halmstad University, Box 823, SE-30118, Halmstad, Sweden
e-mail: josef.bigun@ide.hh.se

Jean-François BONASTRE
Laboratoire d'Informatique d'Avignon (LIA), France
e-mail: jean-francois.bonastre@lia.univ-avignon.fr

Hervé BREDIN
CNRS-LTCI, TELECOM ParisTech (ex GET-ENST), 46 rue Barrault – 75013 Paris, France
e-mail: herve.bredin@aist.enst.fr

Gérard CHOLLET
CNRS-LTCI, TELECOM ParisTech (ex GET-ENST), 46 rue Barrault – 75013 Paris, France
e-mail: gerard.chollet@telecom-paristech.fr

Jérôme DARBON
LRDE-EPITA: Ecole pour l'Informatique et les Techniques Avancées, Paris, France
e-mail: jerome.darbon@lrde.epita.fr

Bernadette DORIZZI
TELECOM SudParis (ex GET-INT), 9 rue Charles Fourier, 91011 – Evry Cedex, France
e-mail: bernadette.dorizzi@it-sudparis.eu

Jean-Luc DUGELAY
Institut Eurecom, CMM, 2229 route des Crêtes, B.P. 193, F-06904 Sophia Antipolis, Cedex, France
e-mail: jean-luc.dugelay@eurecom.fr

Helin DUTAĞACi
Boğaziçi University, Dept. Electrical-Electronics Engineering, Bebek, Istanbul, Turkey
e-mail: dutagach@boun.edu.tr

Asmaa EL HANNANI
Computer Science Department, Sheffield University, UK
e-mail: a.elhannani@sheffield.ac.uk

Remy ETHEVE
Institut Eurecom, CMM, 2229 route des Crêtes, B.P. 193, F-06904 Sophia Antipolis, Cedex, France
e-mail: remy.etheve@eurecom.fr

Benoît FAUVE
Speech and Image group, Swansea University, Wales, UK
e-mail: b.g.b.fauve.191992@swansea.ac.uk

Julian FIERREZ
Formerly with UPM – Universidad Politecnica de Madrid, currently with ATVS/Biometric Recognition Group., Escuela Politecnica Superior, Univ. Autonoma de Madrid, Avda. Francisco Tomas y Valiente 11, 28049 Madrid, Spain
e-mail: julian.fierrez@uam.es

Geoffroy FOUQUIER
LRDE-EPITA: Ecole pour l'Informatique et les Techniques Avancées, Paris, France
e-mail: geoffroy.fouquier@lrde.epita.fr

Hartwig FRONTHALER
Halmstad University, Box 823, SE-30118, Halmstad, Sweden
e-mail: hartwig.fronthaler@ide.hh.se

Sonia GARCIA-SALICETTI
TELECOM SudParis (ex GET-INT), 9, rue Charles Fourier 91011 Evry, France
e-mail: sonia.salicetti@it-sudparis.eu

Berk GÖKBERG
Boğaziçi University, Computer Engineering Dept. Bebek, TR-34342, Istanbul, Turkey
e-mail: gokberk@boun.edu.tr

Daniel GONZÀLEZ-JIMÉNEZ
TSC Department ETSE Telecomunicación, Campus Universitario de Vigo, 36310, Vigo, Spain
e-mail: danisub@gts.tsc.uvigo.es

Jean HENNEBERT
University of Fribourg, Ch. du Musée 3 – 1700 Fribourg, Switzerland
e-mail: jean.hennebert@unifr.ch

Nesma HOUMANI
TELECOM SudParis (ex GET-INT), 9 rue Charles Fourier, 91011 – Evry Cedex, France
e-mail: nesma.houmani@it-sudparis.eu

Klaus KOLLREIDER
Halmstad University, Box 823, SE-30118, Halmstad, Sweden
e-mail: klaus.kollreider@ide.hh.se

Emine KRICHEN
TELECOM SudParis (ex GET-INT), 9, rue Charles Fourier 91011 Evry, France
e-mail: emine.krichen@it-sudparis.eu

Laurence LIKFORMAN-SULEM
TELECOM ParisTech (ex GET-ENST), 46 rue Barrault – 75013 Paris, France
e-mail: lauli@enst.fr

Bao LY-VAN
TELECOM SudParis (ex GET-INT), 9 rue Charles Fourier, 91011 – Evry Cedex, France
e-mail: bao.ly-van@it-sudparis.eu

John MASON
Speech and Image group, Swansea University, Wales, UK
e-mail: j.s.d.mason@swansea.ac.uk

Aurélien MAYOUE
TELECOM SudParis (ex GET-INT), 9 rue Charles Fourier, 91011 – Evry Cedex, France
e-mail: aurelien.mayoue@it-sudparis.eu

Javier ORTEGA-GARCIA
Formerly with UPM – Universidad Politecnica de Madrid, currently with ATVS/Biometric Recognition Group., Escuela Politecnica Superior, Univ. Autonoma de Madrid, Avda. Francisco Tomas y Valiente 11, 28049 Madrid, Spain
e-mail: javier.ortega@uam.es

Dijana PETROVSKA-DELACRÉTAZ
TELECOM SudParis (ex GET-INT), 9 rue Charles Fourier, 91011 – Evry Cedex, France
e-mail: dijana.petrovska@it-sudparis.eu

Daniel RICCIO
Universita di Salerno, 84084 Fisciano, Salerno, Italy
e-mail: driccio@unisa.it

Bülent SANKUR
Boğaziçi University, Dept. Electrical-Electronics Engineering, Bebek, Istanbul, Turkey
e-mail: bulent.sankur@boun.edu.tr

Tobias SCHEIDAT
Otto-Von-Guericke University of Magdeburg, School of Computer Science, Dept. ITI, Universitaetsplatz 2, 39016 Magdeburg, Germany
e-mail: tobias.scheidat@iti.cs.uni-magdeburg.de

Zhenan SUN
Center for Biometrics and Security Research 12th Floor, Institute of Automation Chinese Academy of Sciences, P.O. Box 2728 Beijing 100080 P.R. China
e-mail: znsun@nlpr.ia.ac.cn

Tieniu TAN
Center for Biometrics and Security Research 12th Floor, Institute of Automation Chinese Academy of Sciences, P.O. Box 2728 Beijing 100080 P.R. China
e-mail: tnt@nlpr.ia.ac.cn

Massimo TISTARELLI
Universitá degli Studi di Sassari, Piazza Universitá 21, 07100 Sassari, Italy
e-mail: tista@uniss.it

Florian VERDET
University of Fribourg, Ch. du Musée 3 – 1700 Fribourg, Switzerland
e-mail: florian.verdet@unifr.ch

Claus VIELHAUER
Otto-Von-Guericke University of Magdeburg, School of Computer Science, Dept. ITI, Universitaetsplatz 2, 39016 Magdeburg, Germany
e-mail: claus.vielhauer@iti.cs.uni-magdeburg.de

Erdem YÖRÜK
Boğaziçi University, Dept. Electrical-Electronics Engineering, Bebek, Istanbul, Turkey
e-mail: yoruk.erdem@gmail.com

Acronyms

3D-RMA	3D face database
3D-FRRS	3D Face Recognition Reference System
ALISP	Automatic Language Independent Speech Processing
ALIZE	Open-source software for speaker recognition
BANCA	Audio-video database
BECARS	Open-source software for speaker recognition
BIOMET	Multimodal database
BioSec	Multimodal database
BioSecure	Multimodal database
BioSecurID	Multimodal database
BMDP	Open-source data analysis software
BMEC'2007	BioSecure Multimodal Evaluation Campaign
BU	Boğaziçi University
CANCOR	Canonical Correlation Analysis
CASIA v1	Iris database
CASIA	Chinese Academy of Sciences, Institute of Automation
CBS	CASIAv2 + BioSecure iris database
CI	Confidence Intervals
CMC	Cumulative Match Score
CMOS	Complementary Metal-Oxide-Silicon
CMS	Cepstral Mean Substraction
CMU PIE	2D face database
CoIA	Co-Inertia Analysis
DARPA	Defense Advanced Research Products Agency
DCF	Decision Cost Function
DCT	Discrete Cosine Transform
DET	Detection Error Trade-off curve

DFFS	Distance From Face Space
DTW	Dynamic Time Warping
EBM	Elastic Graph Matching
EER	Equal Error Rate
ENST	Ecole Nationale Supérieure des Télécommunications
FA	Factor Analysis
FAR	False Acceptance Rate
FERET	2D face database
FFT	Fast Fourier Transform
FLD	Fisher's Linear Discriminant optimization criterion
FNMR	False NonMatch Rate
FMR	False Match Rate
FpVTE2003	NIST Fingerprint Vendor Technology Evaluation
FRGC	Face Recognition Grand Challenge + database
FRR	False Rejection Rate
FRVT	Facial Recognition Vendor Test, organized by NIST
FVC	Fingerprint Verification Competition
GDA	General Discriminant Analysis
GET	Groupement des Ecoles de Télécommunication
GMM	Gaussian Mixture Model
GPL	Open-source software license
GSL	GMM Supervector Linear kernel
GSS	Global Similarity Score
HH	Halmstad University in Sweden
HMM	Hidden Markov Model
HTER	Half Total Error Rate
HTK	Open-source automatic speech recognition software
ICA	Independent Component Analysis
ICE	Iris Challenge Evaluation
ICP	Iterative Closest Point algorithm
INT	Institut National de Télécommunication
IV^2	Multimodal database
JULIUS	Open-source automatic speech recognition software
KFDA	Kernel Fisher Discriminant Analysis
KLT	Karhunen-Loève Transform
LDA	Linear Discriminant Analysis
LFCC	Linear Frequency Cepstral Coefficients

LFS	Line Spectral Frequencies
LGPL	Open-source software license
LPC	Linear Prediction Coding
LPCC	Linear Predictive Cepstral Coefficients
LSS	Local Similarity Score
M2VTS	Multimodal database
MBGC	Multiple BioMetric Grand Challenge
MCYT	Multimodal database
MFCC	Mel Frequency Cepstral Coefficients
MINEX	NIST Minutia Interoperability Exchange Test
MINDTCT	Minute extraction package, part of the NFIS2 software
MSU	Michigan State University Fingerprint Database
MLOF	MultiLobe Ordinal Filter
MLP	MultiLayer Perceptron
NAP	Nuisance Attribute Projections
NoE	Network of Excellence
NIR	Near InfraRed
NIST	National Institute of Standards and Technology
NFIS2	NIST Fingerprint Image Software
NMF	Nonnegative Matrix Factorization
OSIRIS	Open Source for IRIS
PC	Personal Computer
PCA	Principal Component Analysis
PDA	Personal Digital Assistant
PIN	Personal Identification Number
PLP	Perceptual Linear Prediction
PSR	Peak to Slob Ratio
RASTA	RelAtive SpecTrA
RGB	Red Green Blue
SAS	Open-source data analysis software
SDGJ	Subject-specific face verification via Shape-Driven Gabor Jets
SFinGe	Synthetic Fingerprint Generator
SIFT	Scale Invariant Feature Transform
SMS	Similarity Measure Score
SPHINX	Open source automatic speech recognition software
SVC	Signature Verification Competition
SVM	Support Vector Machine

TNorm	Test Normalization
TORCH	Open-source machine learning software
TPS	Thin Plate Spline warping algorithm
UAE	United Arab Emirates
UAM	Universidad Autonoma de Madrid, in Spain
UBM	Universal Background Model
UPM	Universidad Politecnica de Madrid, in Spain
WEKA	Open-source machine learning software
WER	Weighted Error Rate
XOR	Exclusive OR
ZNorm	Zero normalization

Symbols

α, β	Standard deviation of the Gabor wavelet of polar dimension
$\Lambda(X)$	$= \frac{p(X\|\lambda_S)}{p(X\|\lambda_{\bar{S}}}$; Likelihood ratio
ω	$= 2\pi f$ radial frequency
$\Psi_m(x)$	1D Gabor filter
σ, β	Standard deviation of the elliptic Gaussian along the x an y axis
Σ_{XY}	Covariance matrix of two random variables X and Y
Θ	Threshold applied to $S(X)$
$C(u,v)$	Cross-correlation at pixel (u,v) between a reference image and a test image
$D(i,j)$	Cumulative DTW distance, computed at coordinates (i,j) with constants w_{ins}, w_{rep} and w_{del} corresponding to insertion, repetition and deletion penalties and the $d(i,j)$ local distance
$G(x,y)$	2D Gaussian kernel function modulated by a complex sinusoidal function
h_n	$= (x+iy)^n \cdot g$ Spatial filter with a Gaussian Kernel g
$H(X)$	Entropy
$\mathrm{I}(\rho,\phi)$	Intensity value at the polar coordinates (ρ,ϕ)
$I(x,y)$	Greyscale pixel value at point (x,y)
$I_t(x,y)$	Greyscale pixel value of the region of interest at point (x,y)
$\{\mathcal{J}_{\mathbf{p}_i}\}_m$	$m-^{th}$ coefficient of the Gabor jet at point $\mathbf{p}_i$
$\log p(X\|\lambda)$	$= \sum_{t=1}^{T} \log p(x_t\|\lambda$ The log-likelihood of an observation sequence X, computed as the sum (assuming independence) of T log pdfs (probability density functions)
$MI(X,Y)$	Mutual Information
$p(x_t\|\lambda)$	$= \sum_{n=1}^{N} w_n \mathcal{N}(x_t, \mu_n, \Sigma_n)$; The probability density function $p(x_t\|\lambda)$ (x_t is the observation and λ is the model) is approximated as a Gaussian Mixture with N components
$p(z\|\lambda)$	Probability distribution that an observation sample z could be generated by a model λ
$P(X,Y)$	Plausibility of two sequences X and Y

r_0, Θ_0	Location of the Gabor wavelets in polar coordinates
$R(X,Y)$	Pearson's product-moment coefficient
s	$= \frac{1}{N_s} \log p(O/\lambda)$, log-likelihood score of an observation sequence O of length N_s given a model λ
$S(X)$	$= \log \lambda\ (X)$ Verification score that an observation sequence X could be explained by model λ_s rather than $\lambda_{\bar{S}}$
S_b	Between class scatter value
S_w	Within class scatter value
S_c	Synchrony measure
z	$= (f_x + i f_y)^2$ Orientation tensor of an image

Chapter 1
Introduction—About the Need of an Evaluation Framework in Biometrics

Gérard Chollet, Bernadette Dorizzi, and Dijana Petrovska-Delacrétaz

Abstract How can scientific progress be measured? How do we know if a pattern recognition algorithm performs better on average than another one? How much data is needed to claim with confidence that one system performs better than another one? Is it possible to predict performance on a different data set? How will the performance rates achieved under laboratory conditions compare to those in larger populations?

These are some of the questions that are central to this book. Biometrics is the application domain under concern. For applications related to verification, a person claims an identity. The system has in memory some training data for this identity claim (or a statistical model of it) and performs a comparison (or computes a likelihood) with the test data. The output is a score that is compared to a threshold to take a decision: accept or reject the identity claim. For applications related to identification, the system has in memory a list of identities and their training data. When a person presents biometric data, the system has to find out to whom the data belong. These two tasks, verification and identification, are grouped under the term of biometric recognition throughout this book.

1.1 Reference Software

It is argued in this book that the distribution of open-source reference software is an efficient means to improve the performance of biometric systems, to avoid duplication of efforts, to distribute state-of-the-art reusable modules, to benchmark other systems, to calibrate databases, to facilitate interoperability, to measure robustness, etc. Such an approach has been used with success in many other domains.

In automatic speech recognition [10] open-source software is available, such as HTK [17], SPHINX [28] and JULIUS [20]. Open-source data analysis software also exists (SAS [26], BMDP [8]), as well as machine learning open-source software (WEKA [31], TORCH [29]). Open-source software has also been tested in

D. Petrovska-Delacrétaz et al. (eds.), *Guide to Biometric Reference Systems and Performance Evaluation*, DOI 10.1007/978-1-84800-292-0_1,

evaluation campaigns. NIST (National Institute for Standards and Technology) was a pioneer with open-source software for fingerprints and face. Open-source speaker verification software (ALIZE [1] and BECARS [2]) has been available for years. They are described in Chaps. 7 and 10 related to speaker and talking faces. The BioSecure Network of Excellence (NoE) [7] has also supported the development of reference software for online handwritten signature, 2D and 3D face, iris, hand and talking faces. These developments and their applications are also described in the corresponding chapters.

A major issue in research, development and standardization is the reproducibility of results [21]. For a field to qualify as a science, it is important first and foremost that published work be reproducible by others. In recent years, *reproducible research* has been championed by Jon Claerbout and David Donoho [9, 30]. The reproducibility of experiments requires having the complete software and full source code for inspection, modification and application under varied parameter settings. Donoho summarizes Claerbouts insight in a slogan:

> An article about computational science in a scientific publication is not the scholarship itself, it is merely advertising of the scholarship. The actual scholarship is the complete software environment and the complete set of instructions which generated the figures.

Claerbout and his colleagues have developed a discipline for building their own software, so that from the start, they expect it to be made available to others as part of the publication of their work. Specifically, they publish CD-ROMs (available from Stanford University Press) which contain the text of their books along with a special viewer that makes those books interactive documents, where as one reads the document, each figure is accompanied by the possibility of pop-up windows which allow interactions with the code that generated the figure, to "burn" the illustration (i.e., erase the postscript file supplied with the distribution), and to rebuild the figure from scratch performing all the signal and image processing in the software environment that the CD-ROM makes available on one's own machine. By following the discipline of planning to publish in this way from the beginning, they maintain all their work in a form that is easy to make available to others at any point in time. Unfortunately, reproducible research has not spread widely among the biometrics research community, nor has a standard technology emerged. Why? And do other potential user communities exist that would benefit even more from a similar technology? What are their needs? And would they potentially be more capable in adopting such a technology? Is there a business case out there?

Frequent scientific practice consists in comparing a new approach to a previously existing one, and in evaluating the new method in terms of (relative) improvement [5]. This practice can be understood as a way to calibrate the difficulty of the task under test by some kind of reference technique. Desirable properties of a reference system are its relative efficiency and robustness, its easy implementation, its modularity, and its absolute reproducibility (from an algorithmic point of view). From a practical point of view, the calibration of a given database for a given task by a reference system is relatively easy to implement.

This philosophy was adopted by the BioSecure Network of Excellence. As a result, all reference software described in this book is available in source code from [6]. Major biometric modalities are concerned: iris, finger, hand, signature, speech, 2D and 3D face, and talking face. For each modality, a reference system is described. A development and an evaluation database are associated with each system. Biometric modalities belong to two broad categories

1. Physiological modalities are under no (or very limited) control of the subject; such as fingerprint, iris, and face modalities.
2. Behavioral modalities allow a greater degree of freedom to the individual. They include speech and signature modalities.

It should be mentioned that a reference system could also be a group of human experts accomplishing the same task as the automatic systems under test. This was experimented for the NIST Speaker Recognition Evaluation campaign in 1998 [27]. It was shown that human listeners do not perform any better than automatic systems for speaker verification. In any case, a human reference system does not fulfill the requirements such as cost, reproducibility, and distribution.

1.2 Biometrics

A number of recent books [11, 19, 25] provide many details about this technology. These books, together with reports from the BioVisioN and BioSecure European projects, are the sources of the following paragraphs.

Biometric applications relate to the recognition of individuals in four possible ways:

- Verification of identity, confirming that a person is who he claims to be.
- Non-identification, checking that a user has not been previously enrolled into a database.
- Closed-set identification, recognizing a person by his characteristics being the closest match to a person on a master database of such characteristics.
- Open-set identification, either rejecting an impostor or performing closed-set identification.

For each biometric method (e.g., speaker verification, facial recognition, etc.), there are a number of different implementations. These may use different sensors; each will certainly use different algorithms to process the signals captured by the sensor; and the interface presented to the individuals being authenticated will vary between implementations. In addition, performance will depend to a large extent on the way the biometric is deployed in a specific application or service. Therefore, it makes little sense to compare the performance of biometric methods in general (e.g., fingerprint against facial recognition).

A new client of a biometric system must go through an initial enrollment stage. This stage may involve confirmation of the identity of the individual though presentation of trustworthy documentation (a passport, identity card or driving license) and/or through corroboration of identity by a trusted individual. During enrollment, a number of biometric samples of data are collected. The quality of these samples are of paramount importance in assuring the optimal performance of the biometric method in subsequent, operational uses. Many systems set a quality threshold to enforce a repeat enrollment should the processing fail to provide a sufficiently good sample. However, a significant proportion of the population may be unable to make use of a biometric at all, and this failure to enroll rate is an important limitation to the application of biometric systems.

In operational applications, an individual claims an identity and presents his biometric to a sensor, which captures the signal and processes it using a feature extraction *algorithm* into a form that allows comparison with the reference (enrollment) data. Since a person's submission of a biometric to a sensor is subject to variability (e.g., different positioning of a finger on a fingerprint reader, changes in orientation or illumination of a face in front of a camera, or suffering a viral infection to modify the characteristic of a speaker voice), a perfect match with enrollment data is unlikely. One of the key determinants in the successful operation of a biometric system is the setting of a *threshold* for acceptable *matching* of the test and enrollment data. Demanding too close a match risks *false rejection* of the enrolled individual, while widening the tolerance allows the possibility of *false acceptance* by someone with similar characteristics. *Testing* of a prototype system under conditions similar to the proposed deployment is a prerequisite for a successful application—with tests being a realistic preview of the performance in the field provided that the subjects' population is representative of the end user group (both in demographics and in motivation) and that sufficient numbers are tested over a sufficiently long period.

1.3 Databases

How much data is needed to develop and evaluate a biometric system? How many clients? Which clients? How many samples per client? When should these samples be collected? Under which conditions? How should impostor samples be collected? Given the huge variety of the targeted population (including variations in gender, age, race, health condition, motivation, etc.), the variability due to the use of different sensors and data types—single capture or data stream, sampling rate, number of bits per sample, compression, etc.—and all possible application scenarios (indoor and outdoor environments, static or moving subjects, natural or controlled illumination, etc.) it is rather difficult to gather a data set that covers all possible situations, still including enough subjects to ensure a statistically significant test. Nevertheless, several biometric databases have been acquired over time to test algorithms related to single and multi modalities. Most of them still do not include the required level of variability to cover all issues of interest. Depending on the application scenario, development and evaluation data could be more or less difficult and costly to acquire as illustrated in the examples of the next section.

1.4 Risks

Let us consider three applications: access to a nuclear power plant, border control and e-banking.

- The verification of identity to access a nuclear power plant is a high risk situation, but the number of employees is limited and well known. The risk is that an employee gets through verification under the threat of a terrorist (who therefore gets access to the plant). Simple means of detection of such an intrusion were found [13]. The terrorist could also try to look like, sound like, show the image of the iris or come with a gummy finger [23] of the target employee. He may well succeed (he is a deliberate impostor). Random imposture tests do not really make sense in this situation. What is important is to measure the intraemployee variability of the chosen biometrics to adjust a threshold according to a target operating point which could be as low as 0.1% False Rejection Rate (FRR). Such a database could be collected during the development phase of the system (under the supervision of an operator).
- For border control, the target population is potentially the entire planet. The owner of a passport will not give a lot of training data over a long period. An impostor will again make every effort to look like the true owner of the passport. Under these circumstances, biometric applications at the border are difficult to assess. It could just be a facility for frequent fliers or cross-border workers (a limited population with facilities to acquire many samples of their biometric data). The first biometric-based border crossing system in the world was installed at Schiphol Airport in 1992 (an early fingerprint based deployment), and a new system using iris recognition started operation in December 2001. Since then, border crossing facilities that use biometrics for frequent fliers have been experimented within many other airports.
- In e-banking, a person's identity should be verified to allow some transactions. A person whose credit card has been stolen is unaware of it, and the thief will make every effort to look like the person. He will make a mask of the person's face, a gummy copy of his fingerprint [23], use voice transformation techniques to sound like the person, etc. The thief will empty the bank account but the bank and/or the person will discover the problem and will stop the process. The risk for the society is far less than in the power plant example. In any case, biometric verification in banking is an add on to existing controls (Personal Identification Number — PIN codes) but is of limited deployment due to cost and user acceptance.

These three application scenarios have clearly different costs associated with the risks of false acceptance and false rejection. False acceptance on a nuclear power plant (a criminal gets in) may have much greater consequences for the society than letting a thief access your bank account! On the other hand, a bank may lose the clients who are frequently rejected by the authentication system.

1.5 Biometric "Menagerie"

Parametric variability (over time, recording conditions, subject behavior, etc.) and sample quality are major issues in biometric applications. Human beings have different capacities to control this variability. Doddington et al. [14] have introduced a taxonomy of subjects:

- *Sheep* are easy to recognize (Correct Acceptance Rate is high for them) possibly because their intrapersonal variability is low.
- *Goats* are difficult to recognize (False Rejection Rate is high for them) possibly because their intrapersonal variability is high.
- *Lambs* are easily imitated (False Acceptance Rate is high for them).
- *Wolves* have good abilities to imitate others (deliberate impostors are in this category).

Although this classification was initially proposed for speakers, similar findings have been reported for face [32]. Manual workers are often "goats" for a fingerprint system.

1.6 Spoofing

Spoofing (forgery) is a major issue in biometrics. In the past, random impostures were used for evaluation in best cases. This is not realistic. Deliberate impostors will make every effort to look and sound like their targeted clients. However, in most situations, it is difficult to imagine the collection of data from dedicated impostors. The exceptions could be signature and speech. Signers could be trained to imitate the signature of somebody else (particularly if this signature is simple). The consequences on performances are reported in Chaps. 6 and 11, related to handwritten signature and to the BioSecure Multimodal Evaluation Campaign (BMEC'2007). Voice imitation is quite feasible (with limited success) and voice transformation is a real threat to speaker verification systems. The NIST's Speaker Recognition Evaluation activity did not yet develop an interest on these aspects probably because the financial organizations are more interested in "Echelon-like" applications! The animation of a photo of the target client is quite a threat for talking-face verification systems as demonstrated in Chaps. 10 and 11, related to talking faces and to the BioSecure Multimodal Evaluation Campaign (BMEC'2007).

1.7 Evaluation

Assuming a database has been collected, what is the best use that could be made of it? First: a part should be set aside for evaluation. The evaluation set should have training and testing samples from clients. Impostor samples (at least as many as testing samples) should also be available. It is always dangerous to use other clients as impostors. It all depends how the training samples are used. The rest of the data is the development set. No client or impostor should belong to both development and evaluation sets. Re-sampling [15] and cross-validation techniques should be used to estimate confidence intervals, parameter distributions, etc. The main goal is to ensure that performance could be correctly predicted for a different data set.

Performance of a biometric system could be measured with several indicators. The output of a test is a similarity score (such as the likelihood that the test sample comes from the claimed identity). Comparing this score to a threshold leads to an accept/reject decision. This decision could be erroneous in two ways: *false acceptance* if an impostor is accepted or *false rejection* if a genuine client is rejected. False Acceptance Rate (*FAR*) and False Rejection Rate (*FRR*) are estimated on a test that should have a sufficient number of client and impostor trials. If all the scores are normalized in such a way that a unique threshold is applied to all clients, then the relation between FRR and FAR is obtained by varying this threshold. A plot of the FRR as a function of the FAR takes the name of Detection Error Trade-off (*DET*) [22] if the axes are on a normal deviate scale or Receiver Operating Characteristic (*ROC*) if other scales are used [4]. If performance needs to be summarized with a single number, the operating point where $FAR = FRR$, called the Equal Error Rate (EER) is a common candidate. Another more operational measure combines FAR and FRR into the so-called decision cost function (DCF) as follows:

$$DCF = C_{FR} P_{tar} FRR + C_{FA} P_{imp} FAR \tag{1.1}$$

where C_{FR} is the cost of false rejection, C_{FA} is the cost of false acceptance, P_{tar} is the a priori probability of targets and P_{imp} is the a priori probability of impostors.

A particular case of the DCF is known as the half total error rate (HTER) where the costs are equal to 1 and the probabilities are 0.5 each:

$$HTER = (FAR + FRR)/2 \tag{1.2}$$

Numerical results have no meaning if confidences in these numbers are not given. In many instances, results are given with two decimal points! What confidence could we have in these numbers? It is impossible to infer confidence intervals if one does not have access to the data. The number of tests performed is only partial information because many of these tests could be correlated and most estimators of confidence intervals assume independence of the tests [3].

1.8 Evaluation Campaigns

The U.S. National Institute of Standards and Technology (NIST) is the leader of biometric evaluation activities.

NIST has been coordinating Speaker Recognition Evaluations since 1996. Each evaluation campaign begins with the announcement of the official evaluation plan, which clearly states the rules and tasks involved with the evaluation. The evaluation culminates with a follow-up workshop, where NIST reports the official results and where researchers share their findings. The NIST protocols and databases used in the 2005 Speaker Recognition Evaluations are part of the BioSecure Benchmarking Framework for speaker verification, described in Chap. 7, related to text-independent speaker verification.

NIST is also quite active on fingerprints. Besides the organization of evaluation campaigns since 2003, they also regularly improve and maintain open-source reference software for this modality. More details are reported in Chap. 4, related to fingerprint recognition.

Face recognition evaluation activities were boosted as early as 1993 by the availability of the FERET [12] database sponsored by the Defense Advanced Research Products Agency (DARPA). This activity was transferred to NIST who organized the first Facial Recognition Vendor Test (FRVT) in 2000. The Face Recognition Grand Challenge (FRGC) was then conducted to facilitate research on this technology. Continuous progress was achieved over years on FRVT. Details are reported in Chaps. 8 and 9, related to 2D and 3D face recognition.

NIST organized the first Iris Challenge Evaluation (ICE) in 2006 [24]. It consisted of a large-scale, open, independent technology evaluation of iris recognition technology.

NIST is launching the Multiple Biometric Grand Challenge (MBGC) in 2008. Iris and face are concerned. Only still images were used in previous NIST evaluations. MBGC exploits video sequences.

But NIST is not the only organization involved in biometric evaluation. Fingerprint Verification Competitions (FVC) were organized by the University of Bologna every two years since 2000. European projects such as M2VTS and BANCA provided data to organise Face Verification Contests and Competitions in the framework of international conferences (ICPR, ICBA, ICB).

The BioSecure Network of Excellence supported the data collection, software development and infrastructure necessary to conduct the BioSecure Multimodal Evaluation Campaign in 2007 [6]. The last chapter of this book is devoted to these activities.

French Research Ministry and the Ministry of Defense are also sponsoring evaluations. In the Technovision Program, with the "Identification par l'Iris et le Visage via la Vidéo"-IV^2 [18] project. Within this project a multimodal database, including 2D, 3D face images, audio-video sequences and iris data, was acquired. An evaluation package has been defined, allowing new experiments to be reported with the protocols defined in this package.

1.9 Outline of This Book

Most biometric papers provide some experimental results, but it is quite rare that enough information is given to be able to reproduce such results. This book is an attempt to modify this situation. First, an extensive benchmarking methodology is detailed in the next chapter. This methodology is then implemented as best as possible in all the following chapters. In particular, reference algorithms are described in detail (with a link to source code). Results are obtained from publicly available databases using well-defined protocols. The benchmarking results can be easily reproduced with the detailed instructions that can be found on the companion URL [16] of this book.

Acknowledgments

Thanks to J. Darbôn who pointed out to us the adoption by S. Mallat of the *reproducible research* philosophy of Stanford University.

References

1. ALIZE. http://old.lia.univ-avignon.fr/heberges/alize/.
2. BECARS. http://www.tsi.enst.fr/becars.
3. S. Bengio, C. Marcel, S. Marcel, and J. Mariéthoz. Confidence measures for multimodal identity verification. *Information Fusion*, 3, 2002.
4. J. O. Berger. *A Statistical Decision Theory*. Springer-Verlag, 1980.
5. F. Bimbot and G. Chollet. *Handbook of Standards and Resources for Spoken Language Systems*. Mouton de Gruyter, 1998.
6. BioSecure Mutimodal Evaluation Campaign 2007 (BMEC'2007). http://www.biometrics.it-sudparis.eu/BMEC2007/.
7. BioSecure NoE. http://biosecure.info.
8. BMDP. http://www.statsol.ie/html/bmdp/bmdphome.html.
9. J. B. Buckheit and D. L. Donoho. *WaveLab and Reproducible Research*. Stanford University, Stanford CA 94305, US.
10. G. Chollet and C. Gagnoulet. On the evaluation of speech recognizers and databases using a reference system. *ICASSP*, 38(1):2026–2029, 1982.
11. R. J. Connell, S. Pankanti, N. Ratha, and A. Senior. *Guide to Biometrics*. Springer, 2003.
12. FERET database. Url: http://www.itl.nist.gov/iad/humanid/feret.
13. G. Doddington. Speaker recognition – identifying people by their voices. In *Proc. of the IEEE*, 1985.
14. G. Doddington, W. Ligget, A. Matrin, M. Przybocki, and D. Reynolds. Sheeps, goats, lambs, and wolves: A statistical analysis of speaker performance in the nist 1998 speaker recognition evaluation. In *Proceedings of ICSLP*, 1998.
15. B. Efron and R. J. Tibshirani. *An Introduction to the Bootstrap*. Chapman & Hall/CRC, 1993.
16. BioSecure Benchmarking Framework. http://share.int-evry.fr/svnview-eph/.
17. HTK. http://htk.eng.cam.ac.uk/.
18. IV2: Identification par l'Iris et le Visage via la Vidéo. http://iv2.ibisc.fr/PageWeb-IV2.html.
19. A. K. Jain, P. Flynn, and A. A. Ross. *Handbook of Biometrics*. Springer-Verlag, 2008.
20. Julius. http://julius.sourceforge.jp/en/.
21. S. Mallat. *A Wavelet Tour of Signal Processing*. Academic Press, 1999.
22. A. Martin, G. Doddington, T. Kamm, M. Ordowski, and M. Przybocki. The det curve in assessment of detection task performance. *Proc. Eurospeech*, 1997.
23. T. Matsumoto. Impact of artificial gymmy fingers on fingerprint systems. In *Proceedings of SPIE – Optical Security and Counterfeit Deterrence Techniques IV*, volume 4677, January 2002.

24. P. J. Phillips, W. T. Scruggs, A. J. OToole, P. J. Flynn, K. W. Bowyer, C. L. Schott, and M. Sharpe. *FRVT 2006 and ICE 2006 Large-Scale Results (NISTIR 7408)*, March 2007.
25. N. K. Ratha and V. Govindaraju. *Advances in Biometrics: Sensors, Algorithms and Systems*. Springer-Verlag, 2007.
26. SAS. http://www.sas.com/software/.
27. A. Schmidt-Nielsen and T. H. Crystal. Speaker verification by human listeners: Experiments comparing human and machine performance using the nist 1998 speaker evaluation data. *Digital Signal Processing*, 10:249–266, 2000.
28. SPHINX. http://cmusphinx.sourceforge.net/html/cmusphinx.php.
29. Torch. http://www.torch.ch/.
30. wavelab. http://www-stat.stanford.edu/ wavelab/.
31. Weka. http://www.cs.waikato.ac.nz/ml/weka/.
32. M. Wittman, P. Davis, and P. J. Flynn. Empirical studies of the existence of the biometric menagerie in the frgc 2.0 color image corpus. In *Proceedings of the 2006 Conference on Computer Vision and Pattern Recognition Workshop*, June 2006.

Chapter 2
The BioSecure Benchmarking Methodology for Biometric Performance Evaluation

Dijana Petrovska-Delacrétaz, Aurélien Mayoue, Bernadette Dorizzi, and Gérard Chollet

Abstract Measuring real progress achieved with new research methods and pinpointing the unsolved problems is only possible within a well defined evaluation methodology. This point is even more crucial in the field of biometrics, where development and evaluation of new biometric techniques are challenging research areas. Such an evaluation methodology is developed and put in practice in the European Network of Excellence (NoE) BioSecure. Its key elements are: open-source software, publicly available biometric databases, well defined evaluation protocols, and additional information (such as How-to documents) that allow the reproducibility of the proposed benchmarking experiments. As of this writing, such a framework is available for eight biometric modalities: iris, fingerprint, online handwritten signature, hand geometry, speech, 2D and 3D face, and talking faces.

In this chapter we first present the motivations that lead us to the proposed evaluation methodology. A brief description of the proposed evaluation tools follows. The multiple possibilities of how this evaluation methodology can be used are also described, and introduce the other chapters of this book that illustrate how the proposed benchmarking methodology can be put into practice.

2.1 Introduction

Researchers working in the field of biometrics are confronted with problems related to three key areas: sensors, algorithms and integration into fully operational systems. All these issues are equally important and have to be addressed in a pertinent manner in order to have successful biometric applications. The issues related to biometric data acquisition and the multiple issues related to building fully operational systems are not in the scope of this book, but can be found in numerous articles and books. This book is focused on the area of algorithmic developments and their evaluation. The unique feature of this book is to present and compare in one place recent algorithmic developments for main biometric modalities with the proposed evaluation methodology.

D. Petrovska-Delacrétaz et al. (eds.), *Guide to Biometric Reference Systems and Performance Evaluation*, DOI 10.1007/978-1-84800-292-0_2,

Biometrics could be seen as an example of the pattern recognition field. Biometric algorithms are designed to work on biometric data and that point introduces a series of problems related to biometric databases. More data is always better from the point of view of pattern recognition. Databases are needed in the different phases of the design of classifiers. More development data usually leads to better classifiers. More evaluation data (leading to a bigger number of tests) gives statistically more confident results. Databases should be also acquired in relation to the foreseen application, so for each new system or application, new data have to be acquired.

But collecting biometric samples is not a straightforward task, and in addition to a number of practical considerations, it also includes issues related to personal data protection. The personal data protection laws are also different between countries, as explained in [14]. All these issues result in the fact that the collection and availability of relevant (multi site and multi country) biometric databases is not an easy task, as explained in [6].

Once the problem of availability and pertinence of the biometric databases is solved, other problems appear. Biometrics technologies require multidisciplinary interactions. Therefore collaborative work is required in order to avoid duplication of efforts. One solution to avoid duplication of efforts in developing biometric algorithms is the availability of open-source software. That is one of the concerns of our proposal for a research methodology based on the usage of open-source software, and publicly available databases and protocols, which will enable fair comparison of the profusion of different solutions proposed in the literature. Such a framework will also facilitate reproducibility of some of the published results, which is also a delicate question to address. These reproducible (also denoted here as benchmarking) experiments can be used as comparison points in different manners.

In this chapter we will introduce in more detail the proposed benchmarking framework using some hypothetical examples to illustrate our methodology. The benchmarking framework is designed for performance evaluation of monomodal biometric systems. It can also be used for multimodal experiments. In the following chapters, the proposed framework is put in practice for the following biometric modalities: iris, fingerprint, hand geometry, online handwritten signature, speech, 2D and 3D face, talking faces, and multimodality. The algorithms (also called systems) that are analyzed within the proposed evaluation methodology are developed in the majority of the cases by the partners of the European Network of Excellence (NoE) BioSecure [3]. The major part of the work related to this framework was realized in the framework of the BioSecure NoE supported to better integrate the existing efforts in biometrics.

2.2 Terminology

In order to explain our ideas we will first introduce some definitions that will be used through this book. Figure 2.1 is an illustration of a generic biometric experiment. Researchers first develop their biometric algorithms. In the majority of cases they need development data. A typical example for the need of development data is the need for face images to construct the face space with the Principal Component Analysis (PCA) method. Data are also needed to fix thresholds, to tune parameters, to build statistical models, or to learn fusion rules. Ideally, researchers should aim at developing systems that could have generalization capabilities. In this case these development data should be different from the data used for evaluation. But for new emerging biometrics it is not easy to have at disposal enough data for disjoint development and evaluation partitions.

The biometric data necessary for the development part are denoted here as *Development data*, or *Devdb*. The *biometric algorithms*, or *pattern recognition algorithms* for sake of simplicity are also denoted as *systems*, and have not to be taken in their more generic usage as a system designing the whole biometric application. The performance of these *systems* is measured (evaluated) on *Evaluation database and protocols* (abbreviated as *Evaldb*) and give a certain result, denoted as *Result System X*.

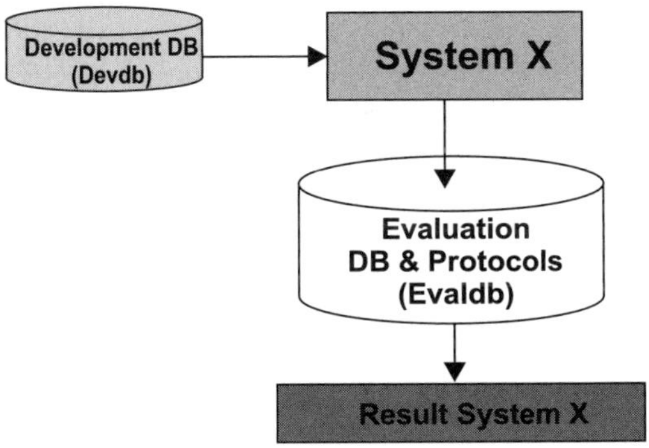

Fig. 2.1 Flow diagram of a generic biometric experiment. *Devdb* stands for Development database, *Evaldb* for Evaluation database and protocols. When *System X* uses this data for the development and evaluation part, it will deliver a result, denoted as *Result System X*

2.2.1 When Experimental Results Cannot be Compared

The majority of published work where researchers report their biometric experiments could not be compared to other published work in the domain. There are multiple reasons of this noncomparability of published work, such as:

- The biometric databases that underlie the experiments are private databases.
- The reported experiments are done using publicly available databases, but evaluation protocols are not defined, and everybody can choose his own protocol.
- The experiments use publicly available databases (with available evaluation protocols), but in order to show some particularities of the proposed system, the researchers use "only" their evaluation protocol, adapted to their task.

This situation is illustrated in Fig. 2.2 where the reported results of the three biometric systems are not comparable. This situation is found in the majority of current scientific publications regarding biometrics. Let us assume that there are three

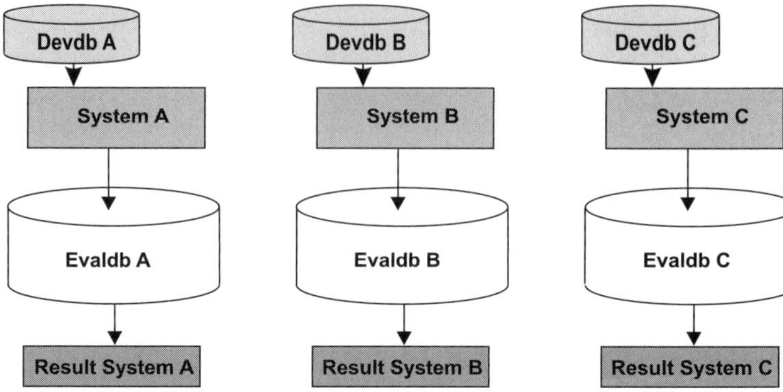

Fig. 2.2 Current research evaluation status with no common comparison point. *Devdb* stands for Development database and *Evaldb* for Evaluation database and protocols

research groups coming from three different institutions reporting results on their new algorithms that they claim provide the solution to the well known illumination problem for face verification. *Group A* has a long experience in the domain of image processing and indexing, and has on its hard disks a lot of private and publicly available databases. *Group B* has a lot of experience, but not as many databases, and *Group C* is just starting in the domain. All of them are reporting results in the same well known international conference and all of them claim that they have achieved significant improvements over a baseline experiment. Let us further assume that the baseline experiment that the three groups are using is their own implementation of the well known Principal Component Analysis (PCA) algorithm, with some specific normalizations of the input images. Let us further guess what the main characteristics of their systems are:

- *Group A* is comparing their new research results with a statistical method using Hidden Markov Models–HMMs (denoted as *System A*) in Fig. 2.2. They report results they obtained on an evaluation database and protocol (abbreviated here as *EvalDb A*). They report that the database (publicly available) is composed of 500 subjects, with different sessions with a maximum temporal variability of one year between the sessions, and with a certain kind of illumination variability (the illumination source is situated on the extreme left side of the face). They report that they are using some private databases (denoted as *Devdb A*) for their development part, more precisely to build their HMM representing their "world model." They report that no overlap of subjects is present between development and evaluation databases. They report 30% relative improvement over the baseline PCA based algorithm with their research *System A*. No precise details on the normalization procedure of the face images are given, aside from the fact that as a first step they use histogram equalization.
- *Group B* is trying to solve the problem in a different way. They are working on image enhancement methods. They use two publicly available development databases, and report results on their private database. Their database is not

publicly available, has 50 subjects, no temporal variability, and a huge variability of illumination. They report 40% of relative improvement over their baseline PCA-based implementation with their research *System B*. They do not give details if they use histogram equalization prior to their image enhancement method. The rest of their algorithms is the same as their baseline PCA system.

- *Group C* is claiming to have 60% relative improvement with their new method, that we call here *System C*. Their baseline is a proprietary PCA implementation, and their new research algorithm is based on the Support Vector Machine (SVM) method for the classification (matching) step. They use sub sets of two publicly available databases for development and evaluation with no details regarding the experimental protocols.

What conclusions could we make if we try to summarize their results and use their findings in order to understand which method is the best, or which part of their algorithms is responsible for the improvements that they report? Without being able to reproduce either of the experiments, the conclusion is that each of the above cited groups has made great improvements, but that their results cannot be compared among them. They have certainly developed better solutions tailored for their evaluation databases, but these experiments do not guarantee that the results could be used and/or generalized to another databases. A lot of questions arise:

- What if the PCA baseline method they have used is a quickly developed version which has a bad performance?
- What if one could also achieve improvements using a better tuning of the PCA baseline method?
- What if by using well-tuned baseline PCA algorithms with a simple histogram equalization in the pre-processing step we get almost as good of results as we do with the more complicated and computationally more expensive methods?
- What about the classification power of the SVM?
- What about the combination of the feature extraction step of *Group B* with the classification method of *Group C*?

Finally, the conclusion is that *Results A, B*, and *C* cannot be compared. We cannot conclude which is the best method or what the major contributions of each method are.

2.2.2 Reporting Results on a Common Evaluation Database and Protocol(s)

Hopefully, there are some common evaluations proposed and used in the field of biometrics. The basic scheme of such evaluation campaigns is depicted in Fig. 2.3. Let us suppose that the evaluation database and protocols are given to the participants, on the condition that they submit their results, and publish only their own results.

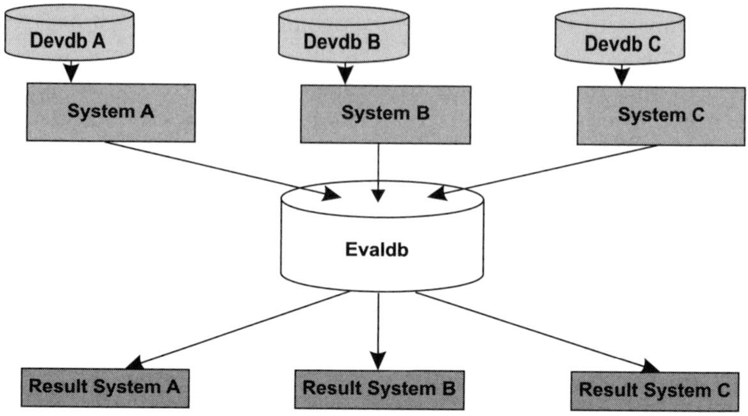

Fig. 2.3 Current research evaluation status with common evaluation database and protocols

We will continue to follow our hypothetical *Groups A, B*, and *C*. Let us further assume that they have submitted slightly modified versions of their *Systems A, B,* and *C* in another well-known conference (six months later), describing their submitted versions on the Evaluation Campaign, and each one in a separate paper. *Group A* is first, *Group B* holds the third position and *Group C* is in seventh place, among 10 participating institutions. But this ranking is only available to the participants of the campaign, and each institution can publish only their own results. Compared to their previous publications, this time they have used a common evaluation database and protocol, keeping secret their development databases. The evaluation database is a new database made available only to the participants of the evaluation campaign.

The researchers who have not participated in the evaluation campaign do not know what the best results obtained during this evaluation campaign are. What conclusions can be made when comparing their three biometric systems, through the three published papers? That using HMM modelling is best suited for solving the problem of illumination variability posed by this evaluation? Could these results be reproduced by another laboratory that does not have all the development databases that are owned by *Group A*? Or is it the normalization module of *Group B* that is mostly contributing to their good results? Or could it be that the image enhancement technique from *Group B*, when combined with the classification method of *Group C*, would give even better results? Or could it be that it is the HMM modelling method in combination with the image enhancement techniques that would give the best results?

The conclusion is that for that particular campaign, and only for institutions that have participated, they can say which institution has the best results. And their results are still dependent on the database and protocol.

There is also an ambiguity with the previously reported results of the same institutions. Are the systems described by *Group A* in different publications the same? In this case the difference in performance should be only related to the database. Or is it that they have modified some parts? And if yes do we know exactly which ones? Are the results reproducible?

2.2.3 Reporting Results with a Benchmarking Framework

Let us assume that some organization has prepared an evaluation package including a publicly available (at distribution cost) database, mandatory and auxiliary evaluation protocols, and a baseline open-source software. Let us also assume that the database is divided in two well-separated development and evaluation sets. We will denote this package as a *Benchmarking package*. The building components of this Benchmarking (or Reference) Framework (or Package) are schematically represented in Fig. 2.4.

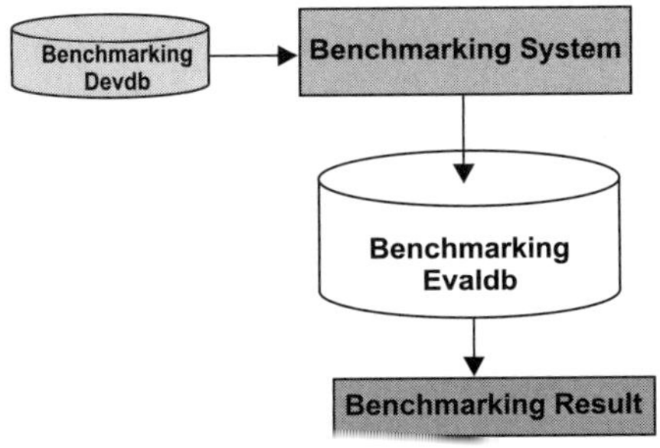

Fig. 2.4 Building components of a benchmarking framework (package)

If the default parameters of the software are well chosen and use the predefined development data, the results of this baseline system can be easily reproduced. In order to avoid using the baseline software with parameters that are not well chosen, leading to bad results, a How-to document could be of great help. Such benchmarking experiments could serve as a baseline (comparison point), and measure the improvements of new research systems.

The above cited components compose the benchmarking (also called reference) framework. Such a benchmarking or reference framework should be composed of

- Open-source software.
- Publicly available databases.
- Disjoint development and evaluation sets, denoted as *Devdb Bench* and *Evaldb Bench*.
- Mandatory evaluation protocols.
- How-to documents that could facilitate reproducibility of the benchmarking experiment(s).

The algorithms implemented in this benchmarking framework could be baseline or state-of-the-art algorithms. The distinction is rather subtle and is related to the maturity of the research domain. For mature technologies normally a method is found that has proven its efficiency and best performance. As such state-of-the-art algorithms we can mention the minutia based fingerprint systems, or the usage of Gaussian Mixture Models (GMM) for speaker verification. It should be noted that a distinction should be made between a method and its implementation. If the convergence point is not reached, then the systems are denoted as baseline, related to a well known algorithmic method (for example the PCA for face analysis). In the rest of our document the distinction is sometimes made between baseline and state-of-the-art algorithms, but in the majority of the cases the software implementations are denoted as comparison, reference or benchmarking software (algorithms or system).

Their purpose is to serve as a comparison point and should be based on principles that have proven their efficiency. They should be modular and be composed of the major steps needed in a biometric system, such as preprocessing, feature extraction, creation of models and/or comparison and decision making.

Our major concern when proposing, describing, illustrating and making available such a framework for the major biometric modalities is to make a link between different published work. This link is the benchmarking framework that is introduced and put in practice in this book. The main component of this evaluation methodology is the availability and definition of benchmarking experiments, depicted in Fig. 2.4. This benchmarking package should allow making a link between different publications in different ways.

It has to be noted that it is the methodology that we are mainly concerned with and not the software implementation. Therefore "framework" does not design an informatics environment with plug and play modules, but rather autonomous C or C++ software modules with well-defined input and output data. Results of modules could be easily combined with other software. This is necessary when dealing with research systems that have the potential to change very fast, and are not here to serve as a practical implementation of a well proven method.

Let us continue to follow our three groups that decided to use such a framework. Young researchers arriving in these groups could immediately be faced with state-of-the-art or debugged baseline systems and they could put all their efforts into implementing their new ideas, rather then trying to tune the parameters in order to obtain satisfactory results of the baseline systems. We will follow the new PhD student that just arrived in *Group A*, who would like to fully concentrate his work on a new feature extraction method in order to improve current feature extraction parameters used for speaker verification. He would like to investigate in the direction of replacing the spectral parameters that are widely used for speech and speaker recognition by using wavelets. Using a benchmarking framework should avoid any loss of time in developing all the components of a state-of-the-art system from scratch. For mature technologies developing such systems requires a lot of work, personnel, and experience, and could not be done in a short time.

Another new PhD student arrived in *Group B*, and it happens that he would like to work on the same problem as PhD A, but with another features. Using the same benchmarking framework would allow them to work together and to constructively share their newly acquired findings and to measure their results against a mature system.

Such a benchmarking framework is introduced in this book, for the major biometric modalities. It is not only described, but the open-source programs have been developed, tested and controlled by persons other than the developers. The benchmarking databases and protocols have been defined and results of the benchmarking framework (benchmarking results) made available, so that they could be fully reproduced. A short description of the benchmarking framework is given in the following section.

2.3 Description of the Proposed Evaluation Framework

The proposed framework was developed by the partners of the BioSecure NoE. The evaluation framework concerns eight biometric modalities. It is comprised of publicly available databases and benchmarking open-source reference systems (see Table 2.1). Among these systems, eight were developed within the framework of the NoE BioSecure. We also included the existing fingerprint and speech open-source software. The added value for those existing open-source software is the fact that we defined benchmarking databases, protocols and How-to documents, so that the benchmarking experiments could be easily reproduced.

Table 2.1 Summary of the BioSecure Evaluation Framework [8]. *ICP* stands for Iterative Closest Point, and *TPS* stands for Thin Plate Spline warping algorithm

Modality	System	Short description	Database(s)
Iris	BioSecure	Inspired by Daugman's algorithms [5]	CBS [8]
Fingerprint	NFIS2 [11]	Minutiae based approach	MCYT-100 [13]
Hand	BioSecure	Geometry of fingers	BioSecure [8], BIOMET [8]
Signature	BioSecure Ref1	Hidden Markov Model (HMM)	MCYT-100 [13], BIOMET [8]
Signature	BioSecure Ref2	Levenshtein distance measures	MCYT-100 [13], BIOMET [8]
Speech	ALIZE [1]	Gaussian Mixture Models (GMM)	BANCA [2], NIST'2005 [12]
Speech	BECARS [10]	Gaussian Mixture Models (GMM)	BANCA [2]
2D face	BioSecure	Eigenface approach	BANCA [2]
3D face	BioSecure	ICP and TPS warping algorithms	3D-RMA [4]
Talking-face	BioSecure	Fusion of speech and face software	BANCA [2]

The material related to this framework could be found on the companion URL [8]. This framework is also used for the experiments reported in the rest of the chapters of this book. Each chapter includes a section related to the benchmarking framework of the modality in question. In those sections more detailed description of the methods implemented in the benchmarking software are given, as well as reasons about the choice of the benchmarking database (with partitions including disjoint development and evaluation sets), including descriptions of the mandatory protocols that should be used as well as the expected results.

In the following paragraph, the collection of existing (at the time of writing) material [8] is enumerated.

1. **The Iris BioSecure Benchmarking Framework**: *the Open Source for IRIS (OSIRIS) v1.0 software was developed by TELECOM SudParis. This system is*

deeply inspired by Daugman algorithms [5]. The associated database is the CBS database [8]. The system is classically composed of a segmentation and classification steps. The segmentation part uses the canny edge detector and the circular Hough transform to detect both iris and pupil. The classification part is based on Gabor phase demodulation and Hamming distance measure.
2. **The Fingerprint BioSecure Benchmarking Framework**: *the open-source software is the one proposed by NIST [11], NFIS2–rel.28-2.2. The database is the bimodal MCYT-100 database [13], with two protocols (one for each sensor data).* It uses a standard minutiae approach. The minutiae detection algorithm relies on binarization of each grayscale input image in order to locate all minutiae points (ridge ending and bifurcation). The matching algorithm computes a match score between the minutiae pairs from any two fingerprints using the location and orientation of two minutiae points. The matching algorithm is rotation and translation invariant.
3. **The Hand BioSecure Benchmarking Framework**: *the open-source software v1.0 was developed by Epita and Boğaziçi University and uses geometry of fingers for recognition purposes [7]. The hand database is composed of three databases: BioSecure, BU (Boğaziçi University) and the hand part of the BIOMET [8], with protocols for identification and verification experiments.* The hand image is first binarized. The system searches the boundary points of the whole hand and then the finger valley points. Next, for each finger its major axis is determined and the histogram of the Euclidian distances of boundary points to this axis are computed. The five histograms are normalized and are thus equivalent to probability density functions. These five densities constitute the features used for the recognition step. Thus, given a test hand and an enrollment hand, the symmetric Kullback-Leibler distance between the two probability densities is computed separately for each finger. Only the three lower distance scores are considered and summed yielding a global matching distance between the two hands.
4. **The Online Handwritten Signature Benchmarking Framework**: *the signature part is composed of two open-source software Ref1 and Ref2, two databases (the signature parts of MCYT-100 [13] and BIOMET [8] databases, accompanied by six mandatory protocols).*

    a. *The first signature open-source software, denoted here as Ref1 v1.0 (or Ref-HMM) was developed by TELECOM SudParis.* It uses a continuous left-to-right Hidden Markov Model (HMM) to model each signer's characteristics [17]. 25 dynamic features are first extracted at each point of the signature. At the model creation step, the feature vectors extracted from several client signatures are used to build the HMM. Next, two complementary information derived from a writer's HMM (likelihood and Viterbi score) are fused to produce the matching score.
    b. *The second signature open-source software, denoted here as Ref2 v1.0 or Ref-Levenshtein, was developed by University of Magdeburg and it is based on Levenshtein distance measures [15].* First, an event-string modelling of features derived from pen-position and pressure signals is used to represent

each signature. In order to achieve such a string-like representation of each online signature, the sample signal is analyzed in order to extract the feature events (such as gap between two segments, local extrema of the pressure, pen-position in $x-axis$ and $y-axis$, and velocity) which are coded with single characters and arranged in temporal order of their occurrences leading to an event string (which is simply a sequence of characters). Then, the Levenshtein distance is used to evaluate the similarity between a test and a reference event string.

5. **The Speech Evaluation Framework**: *is composed of two open-source software ALIZE v1.04 [1] and BECARS v1.1.9 [10]. Both ALIZE and BECARS software are based on the Gaussian Mixture Model (GMM) approach. The publicly available BANCA [2] database (the speech part), and the NIST'05 database [12] are used for the benchmarking experiments.* The speech processing is done using classical cepstral coefficients. A bi-Gaussian modelling of the energy of the speech data is used to discard frames with low energy (i.e., corresponding to silence). Then, the feature vectors are normalized to fit a zero-mean and a unit variance distribution. The GMM approach is used to build the client and world models. The score calculation is based on the estimation of the log-likelihood between the client and world models.
6. **2D Face Benchmarking Framework**: *the open-source software v1.0 was developed by Boğaziçi University and it uses the standard eigenface approach [16] to represent faces in a lower dimensional subspace. The associated database are the extracted 2D images from BANCA [2]. The mandatory protocols are the P and Mc protocols.* The PCA algorithm works on normalized images (with the detected positions of the eyes). The face space is built using a separate training set (from the *Devdb*) and the dimensionality of the reduced space is selected such that 99% of the variance is explained by the Principal Component Analysis (PCA). At the feature extraction step, all the enrollment and test images are projected onto the face space. Then, the L_1 norm is used to measure the distance between the projected vectors of the test and enrollment images.
7. **3D Face BioSecure Benchmarking Framework**: *the open-source software v1.0 was developed by Boğaziçi University [9]. The 3D-RMA database is used for the benchmarking experiments.* The 3D approach is based on the Point Set Distance (PSD) technique and uses both Iterative Closest Point (ICP) and Thin Plate Spline (TPS) warping algorithms. A mean 3D face has to be constructed as a preliminary step. Then facial landmark coordinates are automatically detected on each face (using the ICP algorithm). Then using the TPS algorithm the landmarked points of each face move to the coordinates of their corresponding landmarks of the mean face. After that, the warped face is re-sampled so that each face contains equal number of 3D points. Finally, similarities between two faces are calculated by Euclidean norm between registered 3D point sets.
8. **The Talking Face BioSecure Benchmarking Framework**: *is a fusion algorithm for face and speech. The 2D Face BioSecure software is used for the face part, and for the speech part the same two open-source software as for the*

speech modality are chosen. The database is the audio-video part of the BANCA database [2]. The min-max approach is used to fuse the face and speech scores.

2.4 Use of the Benchmarking Packages

The evaluation packages can be found on a companion URL. A public access (for reading/downloading only) is available via a Web interface at this URL

`http://share.int-evry.fr/svnview-eph/`

The following material is available for the eight biometric modalities reported in the previous section. The source code of the reference systems described in Sect. 2.3, scripts, Read-mes, How-tos, lists of tests (impostor and genuine trials) to be done, and all the necessary information needed to fully reproduce the benchmarking results are available at this address. In the How-to documents more details about the following points are to be found:

- Short description of the reference database (and a link to this publicly available database).
- Description of the reference protocol.
- Explanation about the installation and the use of the reference system.
- The benchmarking results/performance (including statistical significance) of the reference system using the reference database in accordance with the reference protocol.

On the companion URL, additional open-source software can be found, which could be useful for running biometric experiments. This additional software is used, for example, for eye detection (when face verification algorithms require the position of the eyes), or they explain how to calculate the confidence intervals, or how to plot the results curves.

In practice, the user of our evaluation tool can be confronted with the following scenarios:

1. He wants to reproduce the benchmarking results to be convinced of the good installation and use of the reference system, and also do some additional experiments by changing some parameters of the system, in order to become familiar with this modality. He should

    - Download the reference system and the associated database.
    - Compile the source code and install the reference system.
    - Run the reference system on the reference database using the scripts and list of trials provided within the evaluation framework.
    - Verify that the obtained results are the same as the benchmarking results.
    - Run some additional test.

2. He wants to test the reference system on his own database according to his own protocol in order to calibrate this particular task. In this case, he has to process as follows:
   - Download the reference system from the SVN server.
   - Compile the source code and install the reference system.
   - Run the reference system using his own database and protocol (for this task, he is helped by the script files provided within the evaluation framework).
   - Compare the obtained results to those provided within the evaluation framework to evaluate the "difficulty" of these particular database and protocol.
3. He wants to evaluate his new biometric algorithm using the reference database and protocol to calibrate the performance of his algorithm. In this case, he has to process as follows:
   - Download the reference database.
   - Run the evaluated system on the reference database using the list of trials provided within the evaluation framework.
   - Compare the obtained results to the benchmarking results provided within the evaluation framework to evaluate the performance of the new algorithm.

These scenarios can also be combined. Running more experiments is time consuming, but the results of comparing a newly developed system within different evaluation scenarios is more valuable. In such a way the research system can not only be compared to the reference system, but also on other databases and with new experimental protocols. All these comparisons will give useful information about the behavior of this system in different situations, its robustness, how competitive it is compared to the reference system and to the other research systems that have used the same evaluation methodology.

2.5 Conclusions

This framework has been widely used in this book to enable comparisons of the algorithmic performances presented in each of the next nine chapters.

References

1. ALIZE: a free and open tool for speaker recognition. http://www.lia.univ-avignon.fr/heberges/ALIZE/.
2. E. Bailly-Baillière, S. Bengio, F. Bimbot, M. Hamouz, J. Kittler, J. Mariéthoz, J. Matas, K. Messer, V. Popovici, F. Porée, B. Ruiz, and J.-P. Thiran. The BANCA Database and Evaluation Protocol. In *4th International Conference on Audio-and Video-Based Biometric Person Authentication (AVBPA'03), volume 2688 of Lecture Notes in Computer Science*, pages 625–638, Guildford, UK, January 2003. Springer.

3. BioSecure Network of Excellence. http://biosecure.info/.
4. 3D RMA database. http://www.sic.rma.ac.be/~beumier/DB/3d_rma.html.
5. J. G. Daugman. High confidence visual recognition of persons by a test of statistical independence. *IEEE Trans. Patt. Ana. Mach. Intell.*, 15(11):1148–1161, 1993.
6. P. J. Flynn. Biometric databases. In A. Jain, P. Flynn, and A. Ross, editors, *Handbook of Biometrics*, pages 529–548. Springer, 2008.
7. G. Fouquier, L. Likforman, J. Darbon, and B. Sankur. The Biosecure Geometry-based System for Hand Modality. In *the Proceedings of 32nd International Conference on Acoustics, Speech and Signal Processing (ICASSP)*, Honolulu, Hawai, USA, april 2007.
8. BioSecure Benchmarking Framework. http://share.int-evry.fr/svnview-eph/.
9. M. O İrfanoğlu, B. Gökberk, and L. Akarun. Shape-based Face Recognition Using Automatically Registered Facial Surfaces. In *Proc. 17th International Conference on Pattern Recognition*, Cambridge, UK, 2004.
10. BECARS Library and Tools for Speaker Verification. http://www.tsi.enst.fr/becars/index.php.
11. National Institute of Standards and Technology (NIST). http://www.itl.nist.gov/iad/894.03/fing/fing.html.
12. NIST Speaker Recognition Evaluations. http://www.nist.gov/speech/tests/spk.
13. J. Ortega-Garcia, J. Fierrez-Aguilar, D. Simon, M. F. J. Gonzalez, V. Espinosa, A. Satue, I. Hernaez, J. J. Igarza, C. Vivaracho, D. Escudero, and Q. I. Moro. MCYT baseline corpus: A bimodal biometric database. *IEE Proceedings Vision, Image and Signal Processing, Special Issue on Biometrics on the Internet*, 150(6):395–401, December 2003.
14. M. Rejman-Greene. Privacy issures in the application of biometrics: a european perspective. volume Chapter 12. Springer, 2005.
15. S. Schimke, C. Vielhauer, and J. Dittmann. Using Adapted Levenshtein Distance for On-Line Signature Authentication. In *Proceedings of the ICPR 2004, IEEE 17th International Conference on Pattern Recognition, ISBN 0-7695-2128-2*, 2004.
16. M. Turk and A. Pentland. Eigenfaces for recognition. *Journal of Cognitive Neuroscience*, 3(1):71–86, 1991.
17. B. Ly Van, S. Garcia-Salicetti, and B. Dorizzi. On using the Viterbi Path along with HMM Likelihood Information for On-line Signature Verification. *IEEE Transactions on Systems, Man and Cybernetics-Part B: Cybernetics, Special Issue on Recent Advances in Biometric Systems*, 37(5):1237–1247, October 2007.

Chapter 3
Iris Recognition

Emine Krichen, Bernadette Dorizzi, Zhenan Sun, Sonia Garcia-Salicetti, and Tieniu Tan

Abstract Recognizing persons from their irises is not straightforward as different types of noise can be present in the image. Indeed, the iris is located behind the cornea, which is a highly reflective mirror; the resulting images could therefore be perturbed by illumination reflections. The iris is also covered by eyelids in both its upper and lower parts and partially by eyelashes. This noise is very hard to detect as it has a random form and location. Blur can also be present in the images in case of non controlled acquisition conditions. In this chapter, the state of the art in iris recognition research is presented. In order to allow future benchmarking, a new modular reference system called OSIRIS (Open Source for IRIS) based on Daugman's works is described. Our experiments show that the recognition module of OSIRIS v1.0 outperforms Masek, another open-source software. We have defined a benchmarking protocol on a multicultural—European and Chinese—iris database and compared OSIRIS v1.0, Masek and two other research systems using this benchmarking framework.

3.1 Introduction

Iris is the only internal organ available for acquisition. Its information richness and stability makes it a very suitable and efficient biometric modality. Indeed, it was reported in [35] that iris recognition is the most reliable biometrics for human recognition and is suitable for large scale identification purposes. Iris recognition is already used in government programs, border or restricted areas access control. Moreover, it is used in one of the largest national biometric deployments up to now. Indeed, the United Arab Emirates (UAE) are conducting a border control program in which they report that 3 billion comparisons per day are performed. According to the UAE Ministry of Interior, no false matching has been noticed [34].

A typical iris recognition system includes iris capture, localization, normalization, feature extraction and matching. Localization and normalization processes

D. Petrovska-Delacrétaz et al. (eds.), *Guide to Biometric Reference Systems and Performance Evaluation*, DOI 10.1007/978-1-84800-292-0_3,

correspond to the detection of both iris and pupil and to the transformation of the iris rim into a rectangular shape texture. This chapter is mainly focused on the feature extraction and matching steps.

In Sect. 3.2, the state of the art of iris recognition is presented. Section 3.3 details the current issue and challenges. The existing evaluation databases, campaigns and reference systems are summarized in Sect. 3.4. Then, we will present the BioSecure evaluation framework for iris recognition in Sect. 3.5. Finally, in Sect. 3.6, two iris verification systems are evaluated within the BioSecure evaluation framework.

3.2 State of the Art in Iris Recognition

John Daugman, the pioneer scientist who invented iris recognition, proposed the first successful algorithm used in the majority of today's commercial iris recognition systems, in both verification and identification modes.

3.2.1 The Iris Code

Daugman's approach is based on two major and original achievements: the use of two-dimensional Gabor filters as carrier waves coupled with four quadrant demodulation and of the Bernoulli trials techniques in order to fit the interclass distribution, a unique achievement in biometrics [9].

Daugman used 2D Gabor wavelet filters at different scales and different positions spanning three octaves. He was among the first to investigate the usage of 2D Gabor filters for images. Gabor filters are known to achieve the maximum possible joint resolution in the conjoint 2D visual space (pixel representation of an image) and 2D Fourier domains, minimizing the joint uncertainty of both domains as defined by the Gabor-Heinsenberg-Weyl uncertainty relation [7]. This property makes Gabor wavelets a performant tool for texture analysis and classification. Daugman has explicitly considered the fact that Gabor filters are expressed in the complex space by using phase encoding (since it was shown that phase carries the most useful part of information [29]). The 2D Gabor filter expression is given by:

$$\int_{\rho}\int_{\theta} e^{-i\omega(\theta_0-\phi)} e^{-(r_0-\rho)^2/\alpha^2} e^{-(\theta_0-\phi)^2/\beta^2} I(\rho,\phi)\rho d\rho d\theta \tag{3.1}$$

where ω is the frequency of the wavelet, α and β control the shape of the Gabor filters, θ_0 and r_0 are the localization parameters of the Gabor filter and I is expressed in polar coordinates. Once phase coefficients are obtained from different positions of the iris rim and under different resolutions and orientations, a phase demodulation process is performed according to the four quadrants principle. The trigonometric circle is decomposed in four quadrants; depending on which quadrant the phase belongs to, it is then coded into two bits and the iris texture is transformed into an iris code of 2,048 bits. Comparison between irises is made using the Hamming distance, in which iris codes are compared using XOR technique.

The second major achievement in this method relies on the ability to predict the interclass distribution behavior using statistical techniques, namely Bernoulli trials. Daugman has noticed that the iris code comparisons can be considered as coin tossing trials, as the probabilities to get 1 or 0 in the iris code are equal. To predict coin tossing, Bernoulli probability distributions are the most adequate. He supposed that, if N independent tosses are performed, then the distribution of getting n heads out of the N trials can be predicted by the binomial distribution. Adopting those hypotheses to the code comparisons is not straightforward. Although iris codes are 2048 bits long, it doesn't mean that each code comparison leads to 2048 independent XOR operations. Indeed, there is some correlation within the iris texture itself, especially along the angular direction, and this correlation leads to some dependence in Gabor coefficients. Besides, as Gabor filters have several resolutions and orientations at a given position, the resulting Gabor coefficients show further dependencies. To estimate the number of independent operations in codes comparison, Daugman performed all possible comparisons between irises belonging to different persons. He estimated the empirical mean and standard deviation as well as the closest binomial distribution of Hamming interclass distances. He obtained 240 degrees of freedom for the closest binomial distribution of phase sequence variation among different eyes in different databases [8, 9, 12]. To deal with problems that frequently occur in iris acquisition, Daugman proposed some simple techniques. For iris size variation and pupil dilation and contraction, he proposed using a rubber sheet model allowing the transformation of the iris rim into a normalized and fixed rectangular size texture image [9]. This rubber sheet normalization is used in almost all works. To deal with iris rotations, Daugman applies several rotations on the iris reference image, calculates the Hamming distance between codes provided by the same iris but under different rotations (seven rotations), and keeps the minimum Hamming distance obtained. Finally, eyelids and eyelashes occlusions are processed at the same time as the iris codes. This is done through an iris mask in which Daugman indicates whether the bits computed in the iris code belong to iris texture or not. Only those bits corresponding to iris texture are effectively used in the Hamming distance computation.

Besides Daugman's approach, several solutions have been proposed in the literature, especially since CASIA database was released for public use in 2002. In the following paragraph, we selected several research directions among the frequently used and promising ones. These directions include correlation-based approaches, minutia and texture-based methods. The two research systems presented and compared within the BioSecure Network of Excellence belong to correlation and texture-based methods.

3.2.2 Correlation-based Methods

Wildes [36] was among the first researcher to propose an alternative to Daugman's approach. He developed a correlation-based method suitable for iris verification, including an original acquisition platform and also an original (and since widely used) iris segmentation method using the Hough transform [18]. He proposed measuring the correlation between two images using four Laplacian filters. The fusion between the normalized scores at each resolution was done using a Fisher analysis.

Kumar et al. [20] proposed some new techniques for correlation filter design in the frequency space and adapted their methods to biometric data (face and iris modalities). Tests on the ICE database show encouraging results.

Krichen et al. [19] used a correlation method on local Haar decomposition subimages, using both peak position and value in order to handle rotation and dilation/contraction problems.

Miyazawa et al. [27] introduced the concept of phase correlation for iris verification in the frequency domain. They used a band limited phase correlation to detect whether frequencies are useful or not for matching. They adopted this method in order to deal with images containing eyelids, and proposed a scaling method to normalize the correlation scores.

3.2.3 Texture-based Methods

Iris recognition can be seen as a texture classification problem, therefore many widely used texture analysis methods have been adapted to iris recognition. Derived from Gabor filters, a bank of circular symmetric filters was designed to capture the discriminant information along the angular direction of the iris images [28]. In [1], the authors applied the 2D Haar wavelet transform four times in order to decompose the iris image and to construct a compact code from the high frequency coefficients.

3.2.4 Minutiae-based Methods

Similarly to fingerprints, iris patterns can be seen as a geometrical combination of different minutiae. Although it hasn't been proved that iris patterns present the same stable and discriminant sets of minutiae as fingerprints, several works had been done in this direction.

Local variations illustrate the most important properties of a transient signal. For this reason the intensity variations of local image regions (iris subimages), i.e.—the shape of the iris signal—always correspond to the intrinsic iris features. Using a class of quadratic 1D spline wavelets spanning two scales, Ma et al. [24] identified a local sharp variation point as a possible iris feature. The iris is then transformed into a 1D signal in which local extrema (minimum or maximum) are detected.

The positions of those extrema are coded depending on their nature into binary codes. The matching is performed using a normalized OR operator.

Mira et al. [26] used some morphological operators such as opening, closing and thinning to detect the iris special patterns present in the iris texture. After removing redundancy in the extracted pattern using hit or miss operation, they detected nodes and end points that are then considered as iris templates. The matching process simply consists of computing the nodes and end points that coincide with client and test templates.

A third way of detecting iris minutiae is to use the zero crossings of the wavelet transform which provide meaningful information on the image structures. Sanchez-Avila and Sanchez-Reillo [32] improved Boles et al.'s [1] method in two aspects: an iris annular region, rather than a single circle, was used for dyadic wavelet transform; and the Hamming distance was employed to measure the dissimilarity between two zero crossing representations. The results showed that the positions of zero crossings are more discriminant than their magnitudes for iris pattern representation.

3.3 Current Issues and Challenges

Besides a very competitive algorithm, the success of the Daugman's iris recognition system greatly relies on a fixed and strongly invasive iris capture protocol. So algorithms, sensors and user interfaces have to be designed and improved to be able to reduce the level of failure to enroll and failure to acquire rates. The intolerance of the commercial systems to poor image quality and reflections, variable user distance to the camera, low resolution and low signal to noise ratio make iris recognition not straightforward to use as a biometric modality.

The iris community needs to learn more about the intraclass variability. Some techniques to estimate or even predict this variability, like the nonlinear deformation due to pupil dilatation are needed. Moreover, tests are yet to be done on dependencies between performances and demographic indicators, like left/right eye, gender, race and eye colors.

Interoperability between sensors on one side, and sensors and systems on another side has also to be studied. Preliminary tests showed a great decrease in iris performances when sensors interoperability is tested. One explanation is the fact that different sensors use different near infrared wavelengths with different penetration properties that lead to a different iris pattern regarding the wavelength. Anyway, the iris community should overcome this difficulty in order to have efficient and reliable systems. Interoperability between systems and sensors or even systems themselves have not yet been tested, as Daugman enforced a monopole in the iris market up to now.

Some impostor scenarios have been proposed in the literature. Few tests have been made on iris recognition algorithm under these scenarios. For example, tests in the Schiphol Airport show performance of 98% of good rejection of fake irises.

Combining iris and cryptography is also a very promising field of investigation. Daugman et al. [17] have started a good but limited (in tests) work in this direction and there is still a lot of work to be done in order to comply cryptography necessities (a 100% correct identification) with iris realities (changes between two different templates).

Capturing irises from long distances and with less cooperation from the users became a main research topic in the iris community. Products proposed by Sarnoff [5] would be a first step toward iris recognition in a video surveillance context.

3.4 Existing Evaluation Databases, Campaigns and Open-source Software

3.4.1 Databases

In the earlier stage of iris recognition research (before 2000), iris image databases were not available because almost all iris imaging devices were developed for commercial use and did not allow storage of acquired images. This lack of iris data was a main obstacle to the development of research on iris recognition. Fortunately, this situation has recently changed and several iris image databases are now publicly available: CASIA [4], UPOL [14], UBATH [6], UBIRIS [2] and ICE'2005 [30].

The Chinese Academy of Sciences, Institute of Automation (CASIA) was the first institute that shared iris images with researchers, free of charge. Two versions of CASIA iris image databases have been released to more than 1,400 research groups from 70 countries or regions. CASIA v1 includes 756 iris images from 108 eyes. For each eye, seven images are captured in two sessions (three samples are collected in the first session and four in the second session). The image resolution of CASIA v1 is 320×280 pixels. CASIA v2 includes 2,400 iris images from 60 eyes, which compose the development set of the iris algorithm competition held in China. Some iris images with eyeglasses and visible lighting changes are also included into CASIA v2 in order to test iris recognition performance in real environment applications. The image resolution of CASIA v2 is 640×480. The iris images of the CASIA database are captured by three different sensors under Near Infra Red (NIR) illumination, and most of the subjects are Chinese.

UPOL iris database includes 384 iris images from 64 European persons. The irises were scanned by the TOPCON TRC50IA optical device connected with SONY DXC-950P 3CCD camera. The image quality is good and without occlusions of eyelids and eyelashes. The original images are stored in color with a resolution of 768×576.

The University of Bath has developed an iris capture system based on a high resolution machine vision camera. Two thousand iris images from 50 persons are freely available, including both European and Asian subjects. Because of a controlled capture interface and illumination, with highly cooperating volunteers, the quality of the database is good. The resolution of the images is 1280×960.

The UBIRIS iris database was developed to test the robustness of the iris recognition algorithms to different types of degradation. Many intraclass variations or image degradations (illumination, contrast, reflection, defocus, and occlusion) were therefore introduced in this database. It includes 1,877 greyscale images (resolution 400×300) from 241 persons, captured in two different sessions.

The National Institute of Standards and Technology (NIST) has made available the ICE'2005 iris database. 2,953 images from 132 subjects were captured by the LG2200 sensor. In most cases both left and right irises were acquired. Although some quality control was applied during the iris database collection, some "non-ideal" iris images are still present in the database, such as occlusion by eyelids and eyelashes, nonlinear deformation, defocus and skewed eyes.

Figure 3.1 shows some iris images from different databases.

3.4.2 Evaluation Campaigns

Daugman's algorithm has been tested intensively through all these years. Two reports of independent laboratory experiments are currently available. In the first one [10] carried out on iris images from 323 persons, results show no False Acceptances and no False Rejections. The same performance was reported in a second more important test [13] performed on around 1,500 persons. Unfortunately, in both reports, neither the protocol nor the nature of the benchmarking data (acquisition system used, resulting iris image quality, population chosen) is detailed. Daugman's algorithm has been introduced commercially worldwide through IriScan and Iridian. These commercial versions have been tested by the U.S. Department of Homeland Security using three different cameras (LG, OKI and Panasonic) [16]. The reported results show that at a null False Acceptance Rate (FAR), the False Rejection Rate (FRR) varies from 0.5% to 1.5%. Beyond these excellent results, the U.S. Department of Homeland Security also reports a very high Failure to Enroll Rate rising to 7%, and a non null Failure to Acquire Rate (0.69%) for some sensors. In fact, commercial versions of Daugman's algorithm impose to the user highly constrained acquisition conditions in order to obtain high quality iris images: the user has to be at a constant distance from the device, to open his/her eye enough to avoid partial occlusions by eyelids and eyelashes, among others.

Wildes's algorithm has also been tested [21]. A database of 40 persons has been acquired including some identical twins. In the reported results, the impostor and genuine distributions are well separated. Unfortunately, neither the database nor the details about the acquisition scenario are revealed.

As a joint event of the Chinese Conference on Biometrics in 2004 (ICBA'2004) and the International Workshop on Biometric Recognition System in 2005, two iris recognition algorithm competitions were held in China. The general evaluation protocol used for the iris recognition campaigns was similar to the one of Fingerprint Verification Competition (FVC). Parameters of each algorithm could be tuned on the development set, which was released in advance. Each iris image on the test set

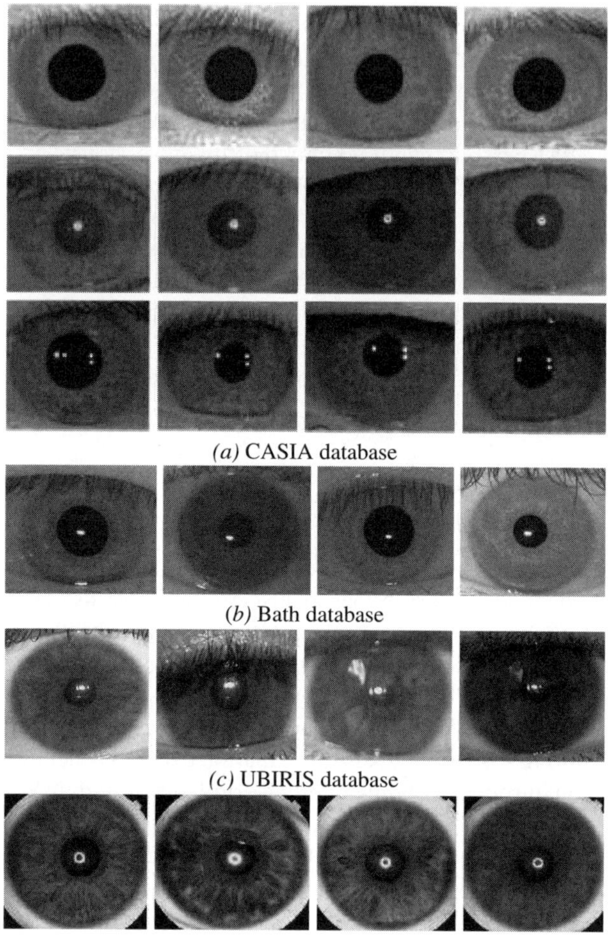

(a) CASIA database

(b) Bath database

(c) UBIRIS database

(d) UPOL database

Fig. 3.1 Examples of iris images from different databases (see insert for color reproduction of part (d) of this figure)

is compared to the other intraclass iris images so that the False NonMatch Rate (FNMR) is measured. The performance of each method is measured by EER (Equal Error Rate), FMR1000 (FNMR when FMR $= 1/1000$), Average Enrollment Time, Average Matching Time and Average Template Size.

The National Institute of Standards and Technology (NIST) organized in 2005 the Iris Challenge Evaluation (ICE), aiming at improving iris recognition research and development, and measuring state-of-the-art iris recognition performance on realistic environments [30]. The iris data was captured by the LG2200 camera, resulting in 2,953 images from 132 subjects. Although some quality control was applied during data collection, some "nonideal" iris images are still present in the database, such as occlusion by eyelids and eyelashes, defocus, off-angle images and motion blur. The first report on this competition shows a FRR varying from 30% (worst case) to around 0.2% for the best system, at 0.1% of FAR. Globally, five systems among 13 show a low FRR, below 0.7% at 0.1% of FAR. More recently, a second report describes an extended version of the database, called ICE'2006, containing 59,558 images of 240 persons [31], including very degraded images: off angle images, blurred images with highly dilated pupil, highly covered images by eyelids, or iris images taken with patterned contact lenses [11]. This report shows a degradation of the system's performance in general. Indeed, in ICE'2006 the FRR varies from 0.5% to 4% at 0.1% of FAR, whereas it varied from 0.1% to 0.7% at 0.1% of FAR in ICE'2005.

3.4.3 Masek's Open-source System

Libor Masek from the University of Western Australia has developed a modular and freely downloadable iris recognition system using the Matlab platform [25]. The system is composed of three modules corresponding to the main stages of any iris recognition process—segmentation, normalization, feature extraction, and matching.

The segmentation process uses the circular Hough transform [15] combined with a Canny edge detector [3]. In order to speed up the detection phase, iris images are downscaled by roughly a factor of two. Weak edges are eliminated using a Gamma transformation. In the original version, the iris is detected prior to the pupil inside a region defined by the position of the iris center. Liu et al. [23] showed that inverting the process allows a better detection.

The normalization process is done using the linear rubber sheet model proposed by Daugman [9]. The classification process is itself divided into two stages: feature encoding and matching. The first one relies on the use of a bank of Log Gabor wavelets convolved with a set of 1D signals extracted from the normalized iris image. Each signal corresponds to a particular circle extracted from the iris rim. Some enhancements are performed on the signals. Namely, the intensity values at known noise areas in the normalized pattern are set to the average intensity of surrounding pixels. This helps to prevent the influence of noise in the output of the filtering. As in the Daugman's algorithm, the resulting complex coefficients are transformed into a binary code using the four quadrant phase encoder and Hamming distance is used in the matching process. Masek incorporates noise masking, so that only significant bits are used in the Hamming distance computation between two irises.

The system has been tested on two different databases, CASIA v1 and Lion Eye Institute databases [25]. Results on CASIA v1 database show a good performance of 99.8% of verification rate at 0.005% of false acceptance rate. The experiment protocol specifies that all possible comparisons between images are made.

NIST has re written the Masek's system in C programming language and made it available to the participants to the ICE evaluation campaigns.

3.5 The BioSecure Evaluation Framework for Iris

In order to ensure a fair comparison of various iris recognition algorithms, a common evaluation framework has to be defined. First, we describe the reference system that can be used as a baseline for future improvements and comparisons. The databases used for the evaluation and the corresponding protocols are then described along with the associated performance measures.

3.5.1 OSIRIS v1.0 Open-source Reference System

OSIRIS v1.0 (Open Source for IRIS) is an open-source iris recognition system developed in the framework of the BioSecure Network of Excellence. The system is inspired by Daugman's approach (described in more detail in Sect. 3.2.1) and uses 2D phase demodulation instead of 1D analysis as in Masek's open-source system. The segmentation step is based on the Canny edge detector and the circular Hough transform to detect both iris and pupil. The classification part is based on Gabor phase demodulation and Hamming distance.

This reference system has several submodules, some of which are portable modules (re usable on any database) and some are non portable (shouldn't be used on a new database without spending some effort on optimization). These modules have been written for CASIA v1 database images. The system was written in such a way that the users can easily change the filters applied on images (form and localization). Figure 3.2 shows the connections between each module.

- **Iris Scan** Read the input iris image. In our case, we will read images in BMP format.
- **Iris Segmentation** Isolate the iris rim from the eye image. We need to localize both inner and upper boundaries of the iris rim by the Hough transform. This module was optimized for CASIA v1 database images.
- **Iris Normalization** This module normalizes the iris rim in terms of size and illumination.
- **Feature Extraction** This module performs a convolution operation between the normalized image and a set of filters at pre-fixed points. At the end of this step, we have at disposal a set of coefficients representing the iris.
- **Template Extraction** Each coefficient is coded depending on its sign, resulting in a binary code of fixed length.
- **Mask Extraction** We also define a mask code using the pre-processed image and the position of the 2D Gabor filters in order to define which bits are extracted from iris texture and which correspond to noisy data (eyelids, eyelashes, spot reflections).
- **Matching** Provides a comparison between two iris codes (CodeA using MaskA) and (CodeB using MaskB) using the Hamming distance.

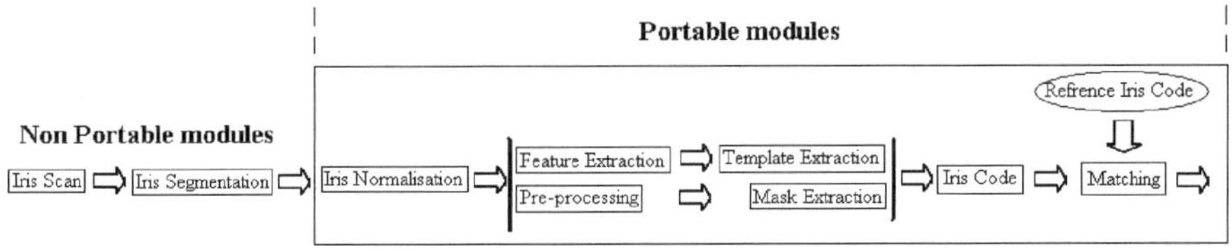

Fig. 3.2 Modules of the Reference System: Iris Segmentation, Iris Normalization, Feature Extraction, Preprocessing, Template and Mask Extraction, Iris Code and Matching

3.5.2 Benchmarking Databases

For benchmarking experiments, we have used two different databases (see Table 3.1) including the widely used CASIA v2 and the BioSecure v1 database, acquired during the 1st BioSecure Residential Workshop. These two databases are combined together in a common database called CASIA-BioSecure Iris Database (CBS). The BioSecure v1 was acquired following the same protocol as the one used for CASIA v2 in order to be able to combine the two databases. Therefore, in the CBS database, there are 120 eyes from 60 different subjects, with some intraclass variability including illumination, glasses, eyelids/eyelashes occlusions, and blurred images.

Two kinds of cameras were used to acquire the iris images. One is a handheld camera produced by OKI, whose small size is suitable for small-scale personal verification, such as PC login, e-commerce, or information security. The distance between the camera and the eye is about 4 cm. The other iris camera was developed by CASIA for physical access control to buildings or for border control. The distance between the camera and the eye is about 10 cm. This camera has a mirror in front of the lens and the user only needs to watch his eye in the mirror to assist self-positioning. An iris image quality assessment algorithm is used in order to automate the iris image capture procedure. For each person, 20 good quality iris images are selected automatically from a 35-second video. For subjects wearing eyeglasses, both the iris images with and without eyeglasses were captured.

The CASIA-BioSecure iris database has many special characteristics compared to the existing publicly available databases. First, it is the only iris image database with a comparable number of Asian and European subjects. Moreover, the possibility of personal categorization (Male/Female, Old/Young, etc.) based on iris features could be addressed in this combined database because those parameters were recorded. Second, it is the first iris database with irises captured by two devices, thus allowing sensor interoperability to be studied. Finally, the presence of eyelashes and other degradations above described allows testing new algorithms able to cope with these difficulties.

Table 3.1 Description of the reference databases

Databases	Devices	Number of Subjects	Number of Eyes	Number of Iris Images
CASIA v2	OKI	30	60 (2×30)	1200 (20×60)
	PATTEK	30	60 (2×30)	1200 (20×60)
BioSecure v1	OKI	30	60 (2×30)	1200 (20×60)
	PATTEK	30	60 (2×30)	1200 (20×60)

3.5.3 Benchmarking Protocols

The benchmarking protocol is closely related to the nature of the CASIA-BioSecure (CBS) database. Since the data was acquired with two different cameras (OKI and PATTEK), two separate benchmarking experiments are proposed:

- Benchmarking experiment with data acquired using the OKI device.
- Benchmarking experiment with data acquired using the PATTEK device.

For each experiment, data consists of 2,400 iris images from 120 eyes. The protocol for both experiments is the same. We divided the datasets into two different sets:

- Enrollment dataset composed of the first 10 images of one eye of each person.
- Test dataset composed of the remaining 10 images.

This protocol leads to test images acquired under different illumination settings and to comparisons of images acquired with and without eyeglasses. For intraclass comparisons, the 10 images of the enrollment dataset are compared to the 10 images of the test dataset. For interclass comparisons, the 10 images of the reference dataset are compared to 10 images which are randomly selected from other subjects, to be considered as impostors. The total number of genuine and impostor trials is the same and is equal to $10 \times 10 \times 120 = 12,000$ for each device.

3.5.4 Benchmarking Results

The results obtained with OSIRIS v1.0 Reference System on the benchmarking databases in accordance with the protocols described in Sect. 3.5.3 are presented in Fig. 3.3, and are reported in Table 3.2.

Table 3.2 shows that results on data captured with the OKI device are better than those obtained on data captured with the PATTEK device. It is due to the fact that the iris images obtained with the PATTEK sensor are of less quality compared to those captured with the OKI sensor. The latter is a commercial device while PATTEK is a research prototype.

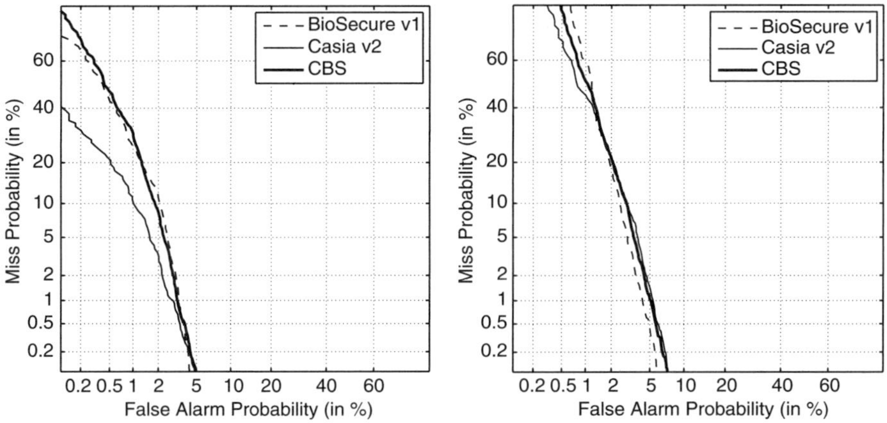

(a) OKI device (b) PATTEK device

Fig. 3.3 OSIRIS v1.0 performance (DET curves) on the benchmarking databases CASIA v2, BioSecure v1 and CBS

Table 3.2 OSIRIS v1.0 performance (EER (in %)) on CASIA v2, BioSecure v1 and CBS

Databases	OKI device	PATTEK device
BioSecure v1	2.83 [±0.35]	3.35 [±0.38]
CASIA v2	2.12 [±0.31]	4.01 [±0.42]
CBS	2.75 [±0.25]	3.72 [±0.28]

3.5.5 Experimental Results with OSIRIS v1.0 on ICE'2005 Database

We have also run some experiments on the ICE'2005 database using OSIRIS v1.0. This database, described in Sect. 3.4.1, is divided almost equally into right iris images and left iris images. Results are shown in Fig. 3.4 and are reported in Table 3.3.

Table 3.4 shows the FRR at 0.1% of FAR of OSIRIS v1.0 alongside other reported performance on the same database. It shows that the OSIRIS v1.0 outperformed the Masek system, but that it is outperformed by several other systems. Indeed, OSIRIS v1.0 performance is situated in the second group of systems. This can be explained by the fact that the OSIRIS v1.0 Reference System does not implement all the quality checks necessary to cope with the difficulties inherent to the ICE'2005 database [30].

3.5.6 Validation of the Benchmarking Protocol

In this section, we would like to justify the Benchmarking protocol described in Sect. 3.5.3 as it is not common in the iris community. Indeed, in the iris domain,

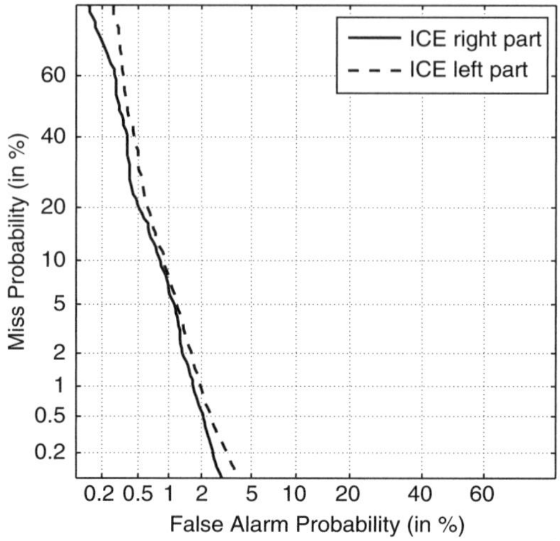

Fig. 3.4 OSIRIS v1.0 performance (DET curves) on the ICE'2005 database

Table 3.3 OSIRIS v1.0 performance on the ICE'2005 database

ICE'2005	EER (in %)
Right irises	1.52 [±0.12]
Left irises	1.71 [±0.12]

Table 3.4 Performance of different systems on the ICE'2005 database

System	FRR at Right Eye	FAR = 0.1% Left Eye
Sagem	0.1-0.2	1
CMU	0.4	0.9
Cam	0.5	1.7
Iritech	0.5	0.8
CASIA	2.2	1.5
WVU	2.2	3.2
Masek	15	15
Osiris	3	4

most authors adopt Daugman's protocol, which consists in making all possible comparisons between images in the database. The purpose of such a protocol is to get the highest possible number of comparisons to estimate in a precise way the decision threshold. This protocol is efficient only when the number of comparisons is very large (around millions). However, most researchers keep following Daugman's protocol even on small or medium size databases. But a major question holds: can Daugman's protocol be informative in verification mode with a small amount of data? In order to answer to such an essential question, we have compared system's results using both Daugman's and the proposed Verification Benchmarking Protocol.

To that purpose, we have performed all possible comparisons between the images of the test and the reference dataset for the OSIRIS v1.0 reference system, following Daugman's protocol. On the other hand, we ran 1,000 times the proposed verification Benchmarking Protocol on OSIRIS v1.0 with different randomly selected impostor trials and compared the behavior of the DET curves to those obtained under Daugman's protocol. Results are shown in Fig. 3.5. The thin curves correspond to our Benchmarking Protocol and the thick curve corresponds to the Daugman's protocol on CBS database. First, we notice that the DET curve corresponding to Daugman's protocol is situated into the "curves' cloud" of Benchmarking Protocol. In 1,000 trials, the EERs vary from 2.75% to 2.99% and it is equal to 2.85% for Daugman's protocol. The variation is smaller than the width of the confidence interval.

Given this result, in the following sections, systems' evaluation is performed with our verification benchmarking protocol. This methodological choice does not mean that Daugman's protocol is not useful to compare systems but rather that our protocol is considerably less demanding in terms of computation power and leads to similar results.

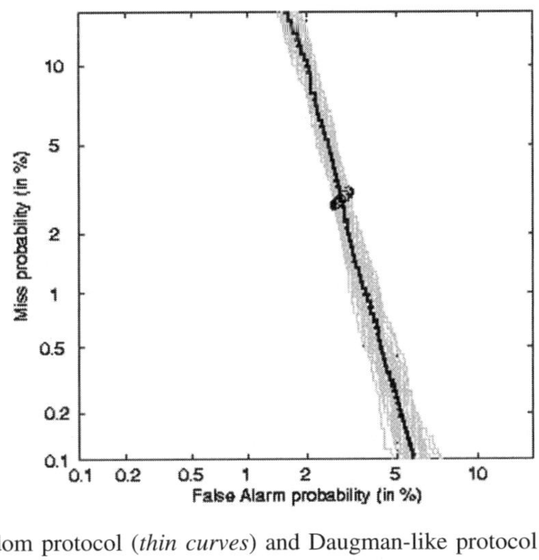

Fig. 3.5 1,000 Random protocol (*thin curves*) and Daugman-like protocol (*coarse curve*) using OSIRIS v1.0 reference system (BioSecure v1 & OKI device)

3.5.7 Study of the Interclass Distribution

Iris recognition operates successfully in identification mode because of the shape of the interclass or "impostors" distribution, that shows a very rapid decay in its tail. For this reason, an interesting question is whether the interclass distribution with OSIRIS v1.0 Reference System, as a function of the quality of the database, is stable. To tackle this question, we considered two databases of different quality, namely CASIA v1 and CBS database. Figure 3.6 shows the distribution of the interclass distances obtained with OSIRIS v1.0 Reference System on CASIA v1 and CBS. The two distributions have the same aspect, roughly the same mean (0.46 vs. 0.47), although the standard deviation of the distribution obtained on degraded data (CBS) is larger than that obtained on good quality data from CASIA v1 (0.045 vs. 0.037); indeed, the extremely rapid decay of the tail of the interclass distribution remains intact regardless of the important difference in image quality between the two databases.

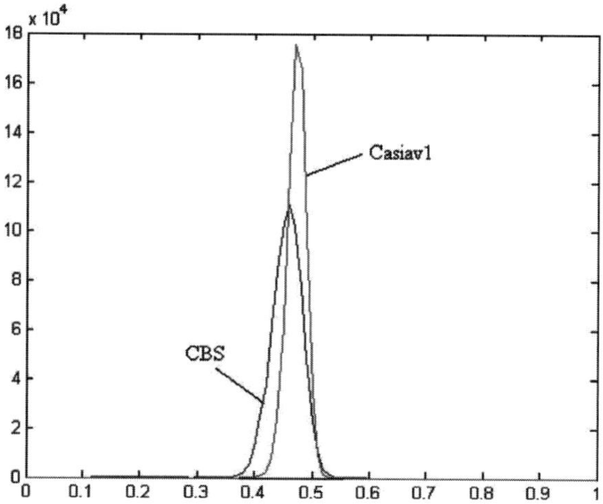

Fig. 3.6 Interclass distributions on the CASIA v1 database and CBS database

3.6 Research Systems Evaluated within the Benchmarking Framework

3.6.1 Correlation System [TELECOM SudParis]

The method is based on 2D Gabor phase correlations. In a previous work Krichen et al. [19] proposed a local correlation method based on a Haar phase decomposition, fusing correlation peak scores and their positions to take the final decision. The drawback of this system is that it relied on a high number of thresholds and also on a complicated method to normalize the scores between all images. That system was tested on CASIA v1 database and showed good results. CASIA v1 is considered as a very good quality database that besides does not contain variabilities which can be met in iris (occlusions, blur, reflections,...). Later tests made on CASIA v2 database showed lower results compared to those obtained on CASIA v1 database. Tests showed that this method had very little interoperability power, as it has to be optimized considerably related to databases. Finally, tests also showed that the method doesn't comply with the problems induced by the presence of eyelids. For these reasons, the initial method was strongly modified. The new method still relies on the fusion between correlation peaks and positions in a more generalized way, as we believe that it is suitable for iris recognition in degraded conditions. We use 2D Gabor phase decomposition instead of Haar transform as it offers more filtering options. We also use a normalized correlation process and different fusion techniques between the scores obtained at each resolution and orientation. A general weakness of correlation approaches is the need to normalize each iris image with respect to its texture energy. Indeed, when strong illumination is present, a correlation peak may be observed between iris images of different persons, and on the other hand, when there is a weak contrast in the image, the correlation peak amplitude may be attenuated even between irises from the same person. This problem does not exist if the phase-based approach is adopted. Samples of the Gabor phase images obtained for a given iris image are shown in Fig. 3.7, spanning four resolutions.

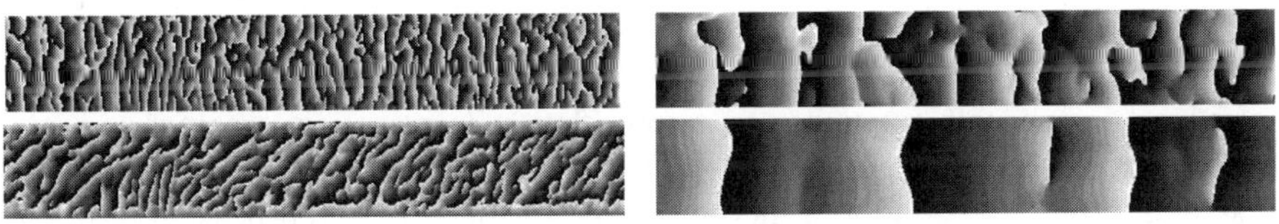

Fig. 3.7 Iris Gabor phase images under four different scales and orientations

We consider the normalized cross-correlation measure proposed in [22], given at pixel (u,v) by:

$$C(u,v) = \frac{\sum\limits_{x,y}\left[I(x,y)-\bar{I}_{u,v}\right]\left[J(x-u,y-v)-\bar{J}\right]}{\sum\limits_{x,y}\left[I(x,y)-\bar{I}_{u,v}\right]^2 \sum\limits_{x,y}\left[J(x-u,y-v)-\bar{J}\right]^2} \tag{3.2}$$

where I is the reference image, J the test image (that may be of a smaller or equal size) positioned at pixel (u,v) of I, $\bar{J}$ is the mean of J and $\bar{I}_{u,v}$ is the mean of I in a neighborhood of pixel (u,v) of size equal to that of J. If I and J belong to the same person, $Max_{u,v}C(u,v)$ is equal or close to 1. Then, we consider as measure of the peak amplitude the "Peak to Slob Ratio" (PSR) [2] which takes into account the mean value of the correlation matrix C and its standard deviation by the equation:

$$PSR = \frac{Max(C) - Mean(C)}{Std(C)} \tag{3.3}$$

In the following paragraphs, we will study two approaches: one in which the iris image is considered globally ("global correlation-based method"), and one in which correlation is applied locally to some regions of the image ("local correlation-based method"). Of course, I and J are phase images given at fixed filter resolutions and orientations.

1. *Local correlation-based method.* One of the most difficult source of variability in iris recognition is due to rotations. As explained previously, the iris rim is transformed into a normalized rectangular shape [9], in which rotations are transformed into translations in the horizontal direction. In the same way, the nonlinear stretch of iris texture due to pupil's dilation or contraction is represented as a translation in the vertical direction. In the literature, only the peak amplitude is used for matching, whereas we propose to exploit also the position of such correlation peak. Indeed, when genuine irises are matched, the observed translations are constant, while random translations characterize impostures. Our method is designed to handle these problems by combining the mean of correlation peak amplitudes and standard deviation of peak positions in subimages.

   The test iris image J is divided into several subimages $\{J_W\}$, each of size W, and the reference (enrollment) image I into another set of subimages $\{I_{W'}\}$ each of size $W' > W$ in order to be able to detect each test subimage J_W in $I_{W'}$. This choice is motivated by the necessity of a bigger window in the reference image to cope with rotations and pupil dilations/contractions transformed into translations after image unwrapping. Then we correlate each J_W with its corresponding $I_{W'}$ and store both the magnitude of the correlation peak in terms of $PSR(W)$ and peak position $PP(W)$. Finally, we compute the Local Similarity Score (LSS) between I and J as:

$$LSS(I,J) = \frac{Mean_W(PSR(W))}{Std_W(PP(W))} \tag{3.4}$$

   If I and J belong to the same person, a high $LSS(I,J)$ may be observed since the peak amplitude should be high and the standard deviation should be small simultaneously. On the contrary, if I and J do not belong to the same person, the peak position may be observed anywhere in the correlation matrix and is independent from one subimage to the next, thus presenting a high standard deviation. In this case, a lower $LSS(I,J)$ should be obtained compared to the one observed when I and J belong to the same person.
2. *Global correlation-based method.* We have chosen to consider a test image J of smaller size compared to that of the reference image I. We perform correlation between I and J in order to measure the Global Similarity Score ($GSS(I,J)$), equal to the PSR measure above defined. In this case, the peak position is not useful. In our implementations, we have used four resolution Gabor filters, and four orientations for each. From one image, we extract 16 filtered images (some examples are shown in Fig. 3.7), and for each comparison between two irises, we have therefore 16 matches to perform.

We recall that I and J are unwrapped iris images, and $I_{R,\theta}$ and $J_{R,\theta}$ are respectively their corresponding phase images, given both at fixed filter resolution R and orientation θ. First, we fuse separately the local scores $LSS(I_{R,\theta}, J_{R,\theta})$ and the global scores $GSS(I_{R,\theta}, J_{R,\theta})$ at each resolution level R by computing the mean values across the different orientations considered, as follows:

$$LSS_R(I,J) = \frac{\sum_{\theta} LSS(I_{R,\theta}, J_{R,\theta})}{4}$$

$$GSS_R(I,J) = \frac{\sum_{\theta} GSS(I_{R,\theta}, J_{R,\theta})}{4} \tag{3.5}$$

Then, at this stage, we have obtained eight scores, four local and four global, two per resolution. To combine these scores, a previous normalization process is required. Indeed, the images across resolutions are of different aspect: thin edges are visible at low resolutions, while coarse ones appear at higher resolutions as shown in Fig. 3.7. We thus apply to each local and global score a ZNorm normalization by considering the mean and variance of the interclass score distribution at resolution level R, as follows:

$$LSS(I,J) = \sum_{R} \frac{LSS_R - \mu_{LR}}{\sigma_{LR}}$$

$$GSS(I,J) = \sum_{R} \frac{GSS_R - \mu_{LR}}{\sigma_{LR}} \tag{3.6}$$

Finally, we average the two scores to define the Similarity Measure Score $SMS(I,J)$ between I and J:

$$SMS(I,J) = \frac{LSS(I,J) + GSS(I,J)}{2} \tag{3.7}$$

The system leading to the obtention of this score is called the Correlation System in the rest of this chapter.

3.6.2 Ordinal Measure [CASIA]

CASIA iris recognition algorithm encodes ordinal measures of iris images for feature representation, called "ordinal code." Ordinal measures were first proposed by Stevens in 1951 [33], as one of the four kinds of scale measurements (nominal measures, ordinal measures, interval measures, and ratio measures). In fact, ordinal measures come from a simple and straightforward concept that we often use. For example, we could easily rank or order the heights or weights of two persons, but it is hard to guess their precise differences. This kind of qualitative measurement, which is related to the relative ordering of several quantities, is defined as ordinal measures. In computer vision, the absolute intensity information associated with an object can vary because it can change under various illumination settings. However, ordinal relationships among neighborhood image pixels or regions, present some stability with such changes and reflect the intrinsic natures of the object. A simple illustration of ordinal measures is shown in Fig. 3.8 where the symbols "*p*" or "*f*" denote the inequality between the average intensities of two image regions. The inequality represents an ordinal relationship between two regions and this yields a symbolic representation of the relations. For digital encoding of the ordinal relationship, only a single bit is enough, e.g., "1" denotes "A^pB" and "0" denotes "A^fB".

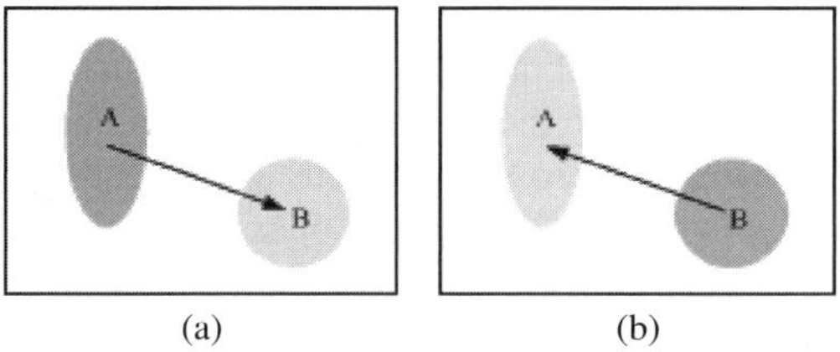

Fig. 3.8 Measure of relationship between two regions. An arrow points from the darker region to the brighter one. (a) Region A is darker than B, i.e. A^pB. (b) Region A is brighter than B, i.e. A^fB

Based on the concept of ordinal measures, we proposed a general framework of iris recognition. For an input iris image, the boundaries of pupil and limbus should be located firstly. After localization, the iris region is transformed into the polar coordinates [9]. In this example, the quantities used for ordinal encoding are the average intensities of iris image regions. Of course the effective ordinal relationship is not limited to intensity measurement, and other image features such as texture energy, contrast, wavelet features may be used. So the objective of intensity transformation is to obtain the special measurements of the normalized iris image, which are the input of ordinal comparison. Based on qualitative comparison between several image measurements, the ordinal results are generated. In practice, the transformation and ordinal comparison can be combined into one step via differential filtering. A novel concept of a differential filters for feature extraction of ordinal measures between several image regions, namely multilobe ordinal filter (MLOF, see Fig. 3.9) is proposed. The MLOF operator slides across the whole normalized iris image, and each nonlocal comparison is encoded as one bit, i.e., 1 or 0 according to the sign of the filtering result. The whole binary iris code constitutes a composite feature of the input iris image. The dissimilarity between two iris images is determined by the Hamming distance of their features. In order to complement the possible rotation difference between the two iris images, the input ordinal code is circularly rotated at different starting angles to match the template ordinal code. The minimum Hamming distance of all matching results is the measure describing the dissimilarity between the two iris images. Because the preprocessing has complemented the position and scale differences between two iris images, the whole procedure of iris matching is insensitive to iris data position, scale and rotation variance.

In conclusion, an iris feature based on a multilobe ordinal filter represents iris image contents in three levels of locality: each iris feature element (ordinal code) describes the ordinal information of an image patch covered by the MLOF which is localized by the central pixel of the image patch; and each ordinal measure is jointly determined by several regions' averaged intensities. At the end, all ordinal measures are concatenated to build a global description of the iris.

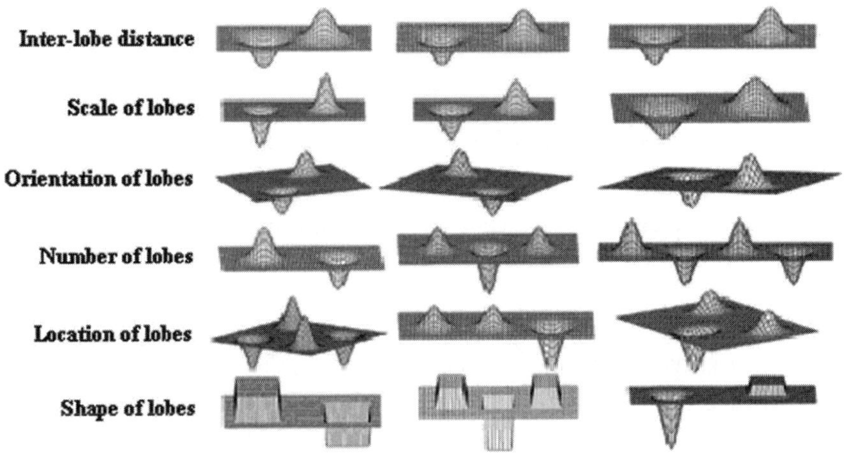

Fig. 3.9 Different kinds of multi-lobe ordinal filters

3.6.3 Experimental Results

3.6.3.1 Systems' Comparisons

We have tested the two research prototypes described above, using the benchmarking framework described in Sect. 3.5 (Database + Protocol + Reference Systems). In the following, tests were performed on the CBS database subset captured with the OKI device. Results on CBS database are reported using DET curves of all systems in Fig. 3.10.

Results show that the CASIA System outperforms the Correlation System, OSIRIS v1.0 and Masek at the EER functioning point. But at 0.1% of FAR, the Correlation System has better FRR performance (2%) compared to the CASIA System and OSIRIS v1.0 (2.8%). Masek performance is far behind the other systems (53%). This result shows that the Correlation System has a better behavior on challenging images.

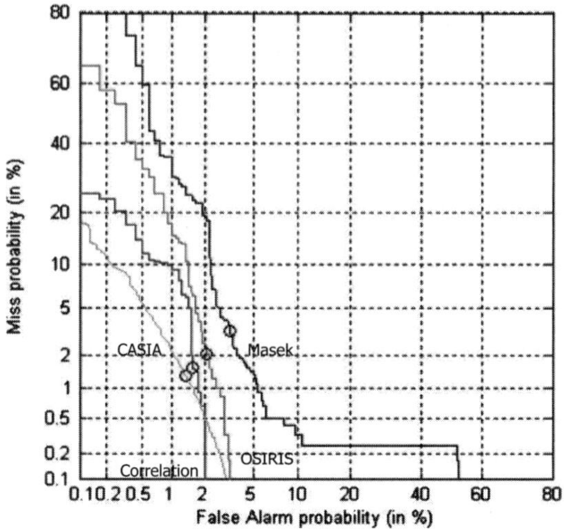

Fig. 3.10 DET curves on the CBS database for the CASIA System, the Correlation System, OSIRIS v1.0 and the Masek Reference Systems

3.7 Fusion Experiments

We considered the two best algorithms, the Correlation System and CASIA, and plotted the intraclass and interclass scores of both systems (see Fig. 3.11). We noticed that the two systems are very complementary. For example, the CASIA System has poor discriminatory power on images from Set1 (the bubble labeled by 1 in Fig. 3.11), while the Correlation System discriminates them easily. Conversely, images from Set2 are well separated from the interclass distribution using the CASIA System and they are not when using the Correlation System. Some errors remain using either the CASIA System or the Correlation System. Figure 3.11 suggests that, in case we apply an adequate fusion method, the resulting system will outperform each single system's performance.

To perform fusion, a prior score normalization is mandatory. Both scores have been normalized according to how far each of them is from the mean of their interclass distribution. Fusion is performed by computing the final score as the maximum between the two normalized scores. When the Correlation and the CASIA systems are fused, the new system reduces the error rate at least by a factor of two: it upgrades to an impressive 0.92% of FRR at FAR = 0.1%, a HTER of 0.5% and an EER of 0.67 on the CBS database (OKI device) with only one image as reference. Figure 3.12 shows a major improvement compared to each single system.

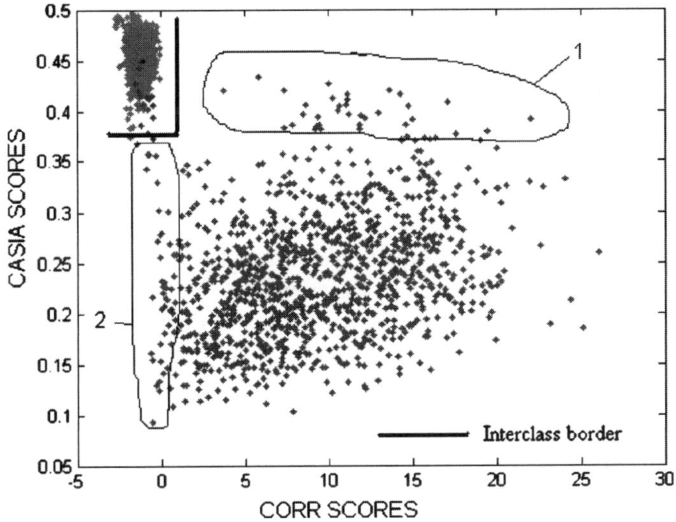

Fig. 3.11 Intraclass and interclass distances for the CASIA System (*Y axis*) and the Correlation System (*X axis*). The color version of this figure can be found in the color insert

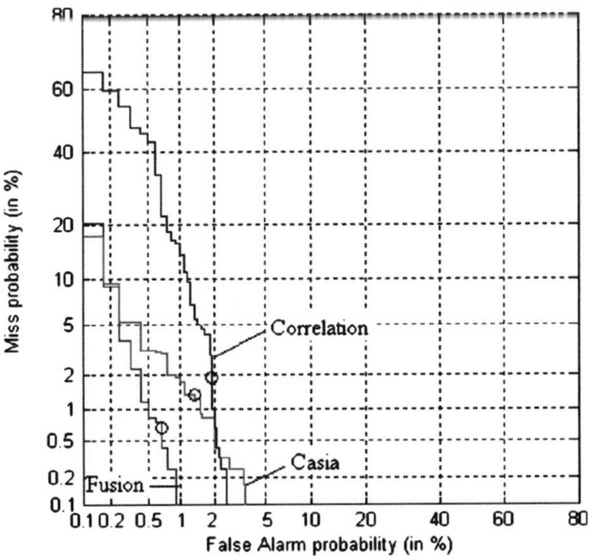

Fig. 3.12 DET curves of the fused Corr+CASIA systems, CASIA and Corr

3.8 Conclusions

In this chapter, we have presented a benchmarking protocol for iris verification, developed in the context of the Biosecure Network of Excellence. Indeed, in this framework, we have developed a new reference system called OSIRIS v1.0, which proves to be more performant than the Masek system used by the NIST. We also recorded a new database, the CASIA-BioSecure database (CBS), which has the particularities of both comprising an equal proportion of Asian and European subjects and of having been acquired with two different sensors. We also proposed a verification benchmarking protocol suitable for small size databases. Using this framework, we compared two iris verification systems, namely the CASIA System and the Correlation System developed by TELECOM SudParis, and showed their complementarity. This framework also offers an alternative to the evaluation framework released by the NIST for the ICE evaluations, as both the database and the protocols offer different challenges to the research community.

References

1. W.W. Boles and B. Boashash. A human identification technique using images of the iris and wavelet transform. *IEEE Trans. on Signal Processing*, 46(4):1185–1188, 1998.
2. H. Proença and L.A Alexandre. Ubiris: A noisy iris image database – http://iris.di.ubi.pt/, 2005.
3. J. Canny. A computational approach to edge detection. *IEEE Transactions on Pattern Analysis and Machine Intelligence, PAMI*, 8, 1986.
4. CASIA. Iris images database – www.sinobiometrics.com, 2002.
5. Sarnoff Corporation. Iris on the move – http://www.sarnoff.com/products/iris-on-the-move, 2006.
6. BATH database from Bath University. http://www.bath.ac.uk/elec-eng/pages/sipg/irisweb/index.htm, 2003.
7. J. Daugman. Complete discrete 2-d gabor transforms by neural networks for image analysis and compression. *IEEE Transactions on Acoustics, Speech and Signal Processing*, 36:1169–1179, 1988.
8. J. Daugman. High confidence visual recognition of persons by a test of statistical independence. *IEEE Transactions: Pattern Analysis and Machine Intelligence*, 15:1148–1161, 1993.
9. J. Daugman. How iris recognition works. In *Intl. Conf. on Image Processing, Vol. 1*, 2002.
10. J. Daugman. The importance of being random: Statistical principles of iris recognition. *Pattern Recognition*, 36(2):120–123, 2003.
11. J. Daugman. Flat roc curves, steep predictive quality metrics: Response to nistir-7440 and frvt/ice2006 reports, 2007.
12. J. Daugman and C. Downing. Epigenetic randomness, complexity and singularity of human iris patterns. *Proceedings of the Royal Society*, 268:1737–1740, 2001.
13. J.G. Daugman. Statistic richness of visual phase information: Update on recognizing persons by iris patterns. *Int. J. Computer Vision*, 45:25–38, 2001.
14. M. Dobe and L. Machala. Upol iris database – http://www.inf.upol.cz/iris/, 2003.
15. R.O. Duda and P.E. Hart. Use of the hough transformation to detect lines and curves in pictures. *Comm. ACM*, 15:11–15, 1972.
16. International Biometrics Group. Independent testing of iris recognition technology – http://biometricgroup.com/reports/public/reports/itirt_report.htm, 2005.

17. F. Hao, R. Anderson, and J. Daugman. Combining crypto with biometrics effectively. *IEEE Transactions on Computers*, pages 1081–1088, 2006.
18. J. Illingworth and J. Kittler. A survey of the hough transform. *Comput. Vision Graph. Image Process.*, 44(1):87–116, 1988.
19. E. Krichen, L. Allano, S. Garcia-Salicetti, and B. Dorizzi. Specific texture analysis for iris recognition. In *AVBPA*, 2005.
20. B.V.K Vijaya Kumar, C. Xie, and J. Thornton. Iris verification using correlation filters. In *Proceedings of the 4th International Conference on Audio- and Video-Based Biometric Person Authentication, AVBPA*, pages 697–705. J. Kittler and M.S. Nixon, 2003.
21. Miles Rsearch Laboratory. Iris imaging systems – www.milesresearch.com, 2005.
22. J.P. Lewis. Fast template matching. *Vision Interface*, pages 120–123, 1995.
23. X. Liu, K.W. Bowyer, and P.J. Flynn. Iris recognition and verification experiments with improved segmentation method. In *Proc. Fourth IEEE Workshop on Automatic Identification Advanced Techniques, AutoID*, pages 118–123, 2005.
24. L. Ma, T. Tan, Y. Wang, and D. Zhang. Personal identification based on iris texture analysis. *IEEE Trans. Pattern Analysis and Machine Intelligence*, 25(12):1519–1533, 2003.
25. Libor Masek. Recognition of human iris patterns – www.milesresearch.com, 2003.
26. J. Mira and J. Mayer. Identification of individuals through the morphological processing of the iris. In *ICIP*, pages 341–344, 2003.
27. K. Miyazawa, K. Ito, and H. Nakajima. A phased-based iris recognition algorithm. In *International Conference in Biometrics, ICB*, pages 356–365, 2006.
28. S. Noh, K. Bae, and J. Kim. A novel method to extract features for iris recognition system. In *Proceedings of the 4th International Conference on Audio- and Video-Based Biometric Person Authentication, AVBPA*, pages 838–844, 2003.
29. A.V. Oppenheim and J.S. Lim. The importance of phase in signals. *Proc. of the IEEE*, 69:529–541, 1981.
30. J. Philips. Ice – http://iris.nist.gov/ice/, 2005.
31. P.J. Phillips, W. Todd Scruggs, A.J. O'Toole, P.J. Flynn, K.W. Bowyer, C.L. Schott, and M. Sharpe. Frvt 2006 and ice 2006 large-scale results – http://iris.nist.gov/ice/frvt2006 andice2006largescalereport.pdf, 2007.
32. C. Sanchez-Avila and R. Sanchez-Reillo. Two different approaches for iris recognition using gabor filters and multiscale zero-crossing representation. *PR*, 38(2):231–240, February 2005.
33. S.S. Stevens. *Handbook of experimental psychology*. New York: John Wiley, 1951.
34. Iridian Technologies. Historical timeline – www.iridiantech.com/about.php?page=4, 2003.
35. J. Wayman, A. Jain, D. Maltoni, and D. Maio. *Biometric Systems: Technology, Design and Performance Evaluation*. London: Springer, 2005.
36. R.P. Wildes. Iris recognition: an emerging biometric technology. *Proceedings of the IEEE*, 85(9):1348–1363, September 1997.

Chapter 4
Fingerprint Recognition

Fernando Alonso-Fernandez, (in alphabetical order) Josef Bigun, Julian Fierrez,
Hartwig Fronthaler, Klaus Kollreider, and Javier Ortega-Garcia

Abstract First, an overview of the state of the art in fingerprint recognition is presented, including current issues and challenges. Fingerprint databases and evaluation campaigns, are also summarized. This is followed by the description of the BioSecure Benchmarking Framework for Fingerprints, using the NIST Fingerpint Image Software (NFIS2), the publicly available MCYT-100 database, and two evaluation protocols.

Two research systems are compared within the proposed framework. The evaluated systems follow different approaches for fingerprint processing and are discussed in detail. Fusion experiments involving different combinations of the presented systems are also given. The NFIS2 software is also used to obtain the fingerprint scores for the multimodal experiments conducted within the BioSecure Multimodal Evaluation Campaign (BMEC'2007) reported in Chap. 11.

4.1 Introduction

Finger-scan technology is the most widely deployed biometric technology, with a number of different vendors offering a wide range of solutions. Among the most remarkable strengths of fingerprint recognition, we can mention the following:

- Its maturity, providing a high level of recognition accuracy.
- The growing market of low-cost small-size acquisition devices, allowing its use in a broad range of applications, e.g., electronic commerce, physical access, PC logon, etc.
- The use of easy-to-use, ergonomic devices, not requiring complex user-system interaction.

On the other hand, a number of weaknesses may influence the effectiveness of fingerprint recognition in certain cases:

D. Petrovska-Delacrétaz et al. (eds.), *Guide to Biometric Reference Systems and Performance Evaluation*, DOI 10.1007/978-1-84800-292-0_4,

- Its association with forensic or criminal applications.
- Factors such as finger injuries or manual working, can result in certain users being unable to use a fingerprint-based recognition system, either temporarily or permanently.
- Small-area sensors embedded in portable devices may result in less information available from a fingerprint and/or little overlap between different acquisitions.

In this chapter, we report experiments carried out using the BioSecure Reference Evaluation Framework for Fingerprints. It is composed of the minutiae-based NIST Fingerprint Image Software (NFIS2) [83], the publicly available MCYT-100 database (described in [70], and available at [64]) and two benchmarking protocols. The benchmarking experiments (one with the optical sensor and the other one with the capacitive sensor) can be easily reproduced, following the How-to documents provided on the companion website [16]. In such a way they could serve as further comparison points for newly proposed biometric systems.

As highlighted in Chap. 2, the comparison points are multiple, and are dependent of what the researchers want to study and what they have at their disposal. The points of comparisons that are illustrated in this book regarding the fingerprint experiments are the following:

- One comparison point could be obtained if the same system (NFIS2 software in this case) is applied to a different database. In such a way the performances of this software could be compared within the two databases. The results of such a comparison are reported in Chap. 11, where the NFIS2 software is applied on fingerprint data from the BioSecure Multimodal Evaluation Campaign.
- Yet another comparison could be done that is related to comparing different systems on the same database and same protocols. In such a way, the advantages of the proposed systems could be pinpointed. Furthermore if error analysis and/or fusion experiments are done the complementarities of the proposed systems could be studied, allowing further design of new, more powerful systems. In this chapter, two research fingerprint verification systems, one minutiae-based and the other ridge-based, are compared to the benchmarking system. The three systems tested include different approaches for feature extraction, fingerprint alignment and fingerprint matching. Fusion experiments using standard fusion approaches are also reported.

This chapter is structured as follows. Section 4.2 continues with a review of the state of the art, including current issues and challenges in fingerprint recognition. Sections 4.3 and 4.4 summarize existing fingerprint databases and evaluation campaigns, respectively. Section 4.5 introduces the benchmarking framework (open-source algorithms, database and testing protocols). In Sect. 4.6, two research systems are described. Experimental results within the benchmarking framework are given in Sect. 4.7, including evaluation of the individual systems and fusion experiments. Conclusions are finally drawn in Sect. 4.8.

4.2 State of the Art in Fingerprint Recognition

This section provides a basic introduction to fingerprint recognition systems and their main parts, including a brief description of the most widely used techniques and algorithms. A number of additional issues that are not in the scope of this book can be found in [59].

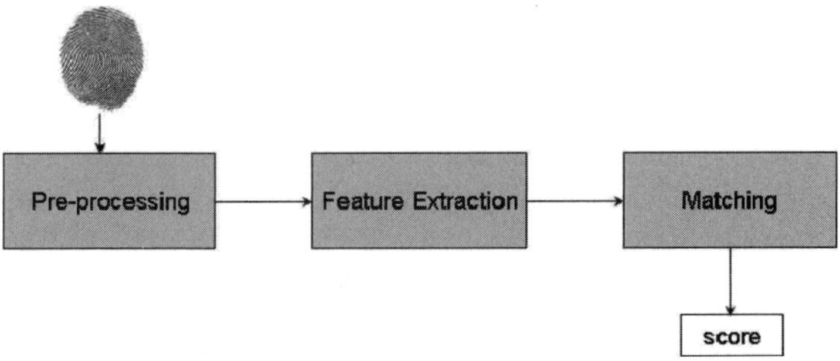

Fig. 4.1 Main modules of a fingerprint verification system

The main modules of a fingerprint verification system (cf. Fig. 4.1) are: *a) fingerprint sensing*, in which the fingerprint of an individual is acquired by a fingerprint scanner to produce a raw digital representation; *b) preprocessing*, in which the input fingerprint is enhanced and adapted to simplify the task of feature extraction; *c) feature extraction*, in which the fingerprint is further processed to generate discriminative properties, also called feature vectors; and *d) matching*, in which the feature vector of the input fingerprint is compared against one or more existing templates. The templates of approved users of the biometric system, also called clients, are usually stored in a database. Clients can claim an identity and their fingerprints can be checked against stored fingerprints.

4.2.1 Fingerprint Sensing

The acquisition of fingerprint images has been historically carried out by spreading the finger with ink and pressing it against a paper card. The paper card is then scanned, resulting in a digital representation. This process is known as *off-line* acquisition and is still used in law enforcement applications. Currently, it is possible to acquire fingerprint images by pressing the finger against the flat surface of an electronic fingerprint sensor. This process is known as *online* acquisition. There are three families of electronic fingerprint sensors based on the sensing technology [59]:

- *Solid-state* or silicon sensors (left part of Fig. 4.2): These consist of an array of pixels, each pixel being a sensor itself. Users place the finger on the surface

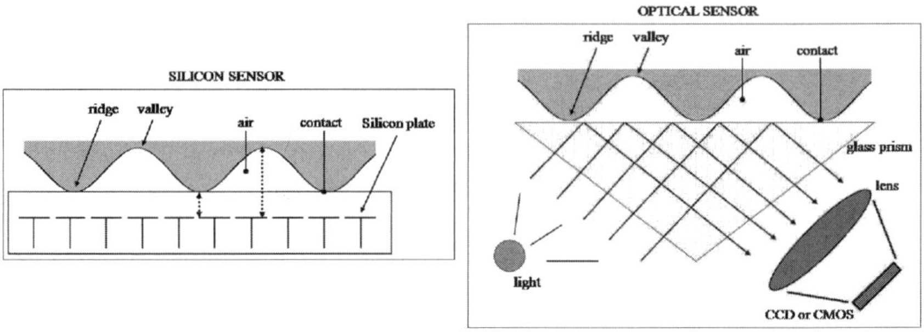

Fig. 4.2 Acquisition principles of silicon and optical sensors

of the silicon, and four techniques are typically used to convert the ridge/valley information into an electrical signal: capacitive, thermal, electric field and piezoelectric. Since solid-state sensors do not use optical components, their size is considerably smaller and can be easily embedded. On the other hand, silicon sensors are expensive, so the sensing area of solid-state sensors is typically small.

- *Optical* (right part of Fig. 4.2): The finger touches a glass prism and the prism is illuminated with diffused light. The light is reflected at the valleys and absorbed at the ridges. The reflected light is focused onto a CCD or CMOS sensor. Optical fingerprint sensors provide good image quality and large sensing area but they cannot be miniaturized because as the distance between the prism and the image sensor is reduced, more optical distortion is introduced in the acquired image.
- *Ultrasound*: Acoustic signals are sent, capturing the echo signals that are reflected at the fingerprint surface. Acoustic signals are able to cross dirt and oil that may be present in the finger, thus giving good quality images. On the other hand, ultrasound scanners are large and expensive, and take some seconds to acquire an image.

A new generation of touchless live scan devices that generate a 3D representation of fingerprints is appearing [22]. Several images of the finger are acquired from different views using a multicamera system, and a contact-free 3D representation of the fingerprint is constructed. This new sensing technology overcomes some of the problems that intrinsically appear in contact-based sensors such as improper finger placement, skin deformation, sensor noise or dirt.

4.2.2 Preprocessing and Feature Extraction

A fingerprint is composed of a pattern of interleaved *ridges* and *valleys*. They smoothly flow in parallel and sometimes terminate or bifurcate. At a global level, this pattern sometimes exhibits a number of particular shapes called *singularities*, which can be classified into three types: *loop*, *delta* and *whorl*. In Fig. 4.3 a, we can see an example of loop and delta singularities (the whorl singularity can be defined as two opposing loops). At the local level, the ridges and valleys pattern can exhibit a particular shape called *minutia*. There are several types of minutiae, but for practical reasons, only two types of minutiae are considered: ridge ending (Fig. 4.3 b) and ridge bifurcation (Fig. 4.3 c).

Singularities at the global level are commonly used for fingerprint classification, which simplifies search and retrieval across a large database of fingerprint images. Based on the number and structure of loops and deltas, several classes are defined, as shown in Fig. 4.4.

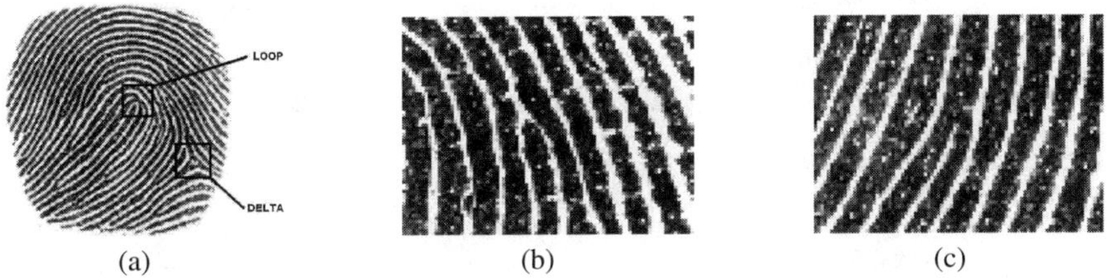

Fig. 4.3 Fingerprint singularities: (a) loop and delta singularities, (b) ridge ending, and (c) ridge bifurcation

The gray scale representation of a fingerprint image is known to be unstable for fingerprint recognition [59]. Although there are fingerprint matching techniques that directly compare gray images using correlation-based methods, most of the fingerprint matching algorithms use features which are extracted from the gray scale image. To make this extraction easy and reliable, a set of preprocessing steps is commonly performed: computation of local ridge frequency and local ridge orientation, enhancement of the fingerprint image, segmentation of the fingerprint area from the background, and detection of singularities.

The local ridge orientation at a pixel level is defined as the angle that the fingerprint ridges form with the horizontal axis [59]. Most of the algorithms do not compute the local ridge orientation at each pixel, but over a square-meshed grid (Fig. 4.5). The simplest approach for local ridge orientation estimation is based on the gray scale gradient. Since the gradient phase angle denotes the direction of the maximum pixel-intensity change, the ridge orientation is orthogonal to this phase angle. There are essentially two orientation estimation techniques: direction tensor sampling [13] and spectral tensor discretization [50] using Gabor filters. For its computational efficiency the method independently suggested by [13] is the most commonly used in fingerprint applications because the spectral approach needs more filtering. We refer to [12] for a detailed treatment of both approaches.

The local ridge frequency at a pixel level is defined as the number of ridges per unit length along a hypothetical segment centered at this pixel and orthogonal to the local ridge orientation [59]. As in the case of the local ridge orientation, the local ridge frequency is computed over a square-meshed grid. Existing methods [39, 56, 52] usually model the ridge-valley structure as a sinusoidal-shaped wave (Fig. 4.6), where the ridge frequency is set as the frequency of this sinusoid, and the orientation is used to angle the wave.

Fig. 4.4 The six major fingerprint classes: (a) arch, (b) tented arch, (c) left loop, (d) right loop, (e) whorl, and (f) twin-loop

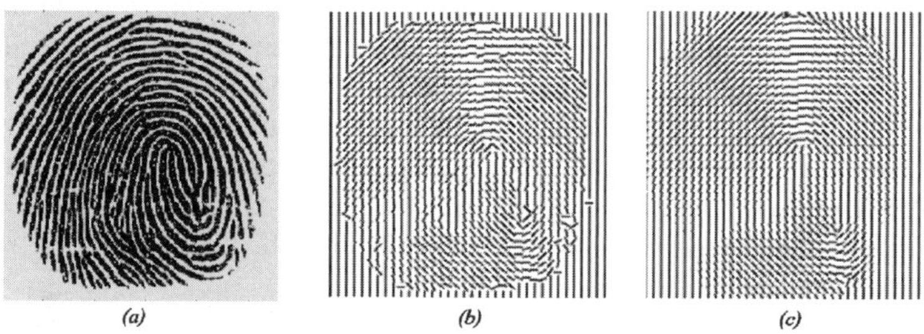

Fig. 4.5 Local ridge orientation of a fingerprint image computed over a square-meshed grid: (a) original image, (b) orientation image, and (c) smoothed orientation image. Each element of (b) and (c) denotes the local orientation of the ridges

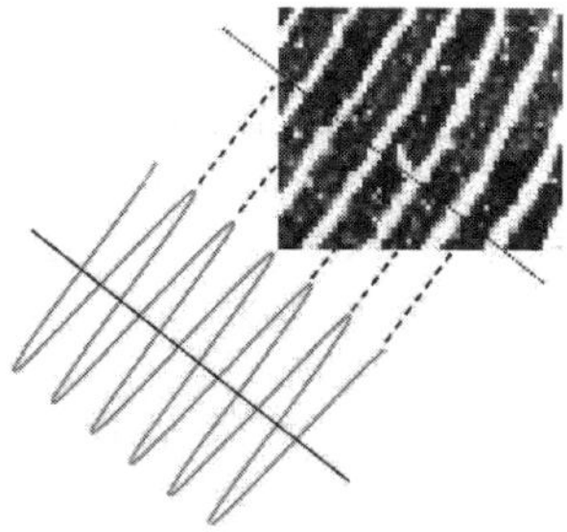

Fig. 4.6 Modeling of ridges and valleys as a sinusoidal-shaped wave

Ideally, in a fingerprint image, ridges and valleys flow smoothly in a locally constant direction. In practice, however, there are factors that affect the quality of a fingerprint image (cf., Fig. 4.7): wetness or dryness of the skin, noise of the sensor, temporary or permanent cuts and bruises in the skin, variability in the pressure against the sensor, etc. Several enhancement algorithms have been proposed in the literature with the aim of improving the clarity of ridges and valleys. The most widely used fingerprint enhancement techniques use *contextual filters*, which means changing the filter parameters according to the local characteristics (context) of the image. Filters are tuned to the local ridge orientation and/or frequency, thus removing the imperfections and preserving ridges and valleys (cf. Fig. 4.8).

Fig. 4.7 Fingerprint images with different quality. From left to right: high, medium and low quality, respectively

Fingerprint segmentation consists of the separation of the fingerprint area (foreground) from the background [59]. This is useful to avoid subsequent extraction of fingerprint features in the background, which is the noisy area. Global and local thresholding segmentation methods are not very effective, and more robust segmentation techniques are commonly used [65, 44, 55, 9, 79, 67]. These techniques exploit the existence of an oriented periodical pattern in the foreground and a nonoriented isotropic pattern in the background (Fig. 4.9).

As mentioned above, the pattern of ridges and valleys exhibits a number of particular shapes called *singularities* (Fig. 4.3 a). For the detection of singularities, most of the existing algorithms rely on the ridge orientation information (Fig. 4.5). The best-known algorithm for singularity detection is based on the *Poincaré* index [48, 47, 10]. Alternatively, detection of core and delta type singularities was shown to be efficient and precise using different filtering techniques.

Once the fingerprint image has been preprocessed, a feature extraction step is performed. Most of the existing fingerprint recognition systems are based on minutiae matching, so that reliable minutiae extraction is needed. Usually, the preprocessed fingerprint image is converted into a binary image, which is then thinned using morphology (Fig. 4.10). The thinning step reduces the ridge thickness to one pixel, allowing straightforward minutiae detection. During the thinning step, a number of spurious imperfections may appear (Fig. 4.11 a) and thus, a postprocessing step is sometimes performed (Fig. 4.11 b) in order to remove the imperfections from

Fig. 4.8 Examples of original and enhanced fingerprint images

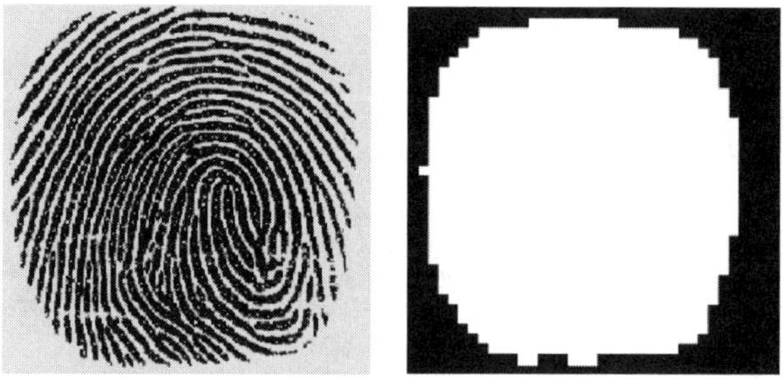

Fig. 4.9 Segmentation of fingerprint images: (**left**) original image and (**right**) segmentation mask

the thinned image. Several approaches for binarization, thinning and minutiae detection have been proposed in literature [59]. However, binarization and thinning suffer from several problems: *a*) spurious imperfections; *b*) loss of structural information; *c*) computational cost; and *d*) lack of robustness in low quality fingerprint images. Because of that, other approaches that extract minutiae directly from the gray scale image have been also proposed [53, 55, 54, 46, 20, 17, 31].

Fig. 4.10 Binarization and thinning of fingerprint images using contextual filters

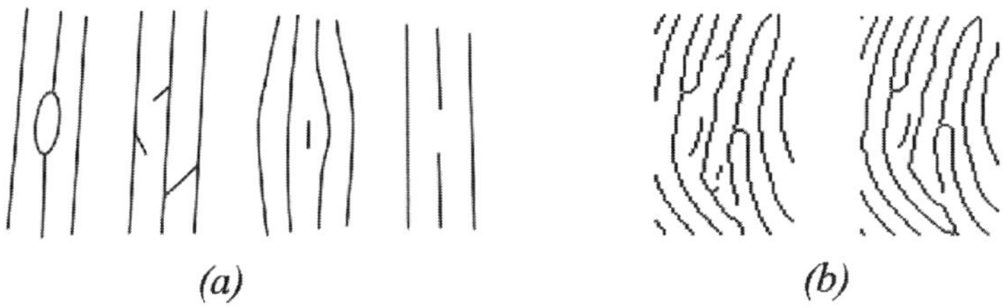

Fig. 4.11 Thinning step: (a) typical imperfections appeared during the thinning step, and (b) a thinned fingerprint structure before and after removing imperfections

4.2.3 Fingerprint Matching

In the matching step, features extracted from the input fingerprint are compared against those in a template, which represents a single user (retrieved from the system database based on the claimed identity). The result of such a procedure is either a degree of similarity (also called matching score) or an acceptance/rejection decision. There are fingerprint matching techniques that directly compare gray scale images (or subimages) using correlation-based methods, so that the fingerprint template coincides with the gray scale image. However, most of the fingerprint matching algorithms use features that are extracted from the gray scale image (see Sect. 4.2.2).

One of the biggest challenges of fingerprint recognition is the high variability commonly found between different impressions of the same finger. This variability is known as *intraclass* variability and is caused by several factors, including: *a*) displacement or rotation between different acquisitions; *b*) partial overlap, specially in sensors of small area; *c*) skin conditions, due to permanent or temporary factors (cuts, dirt, humidity, etc.); *d*) noise in the sensor (for example, residues from previous acquisitions); and *e*) nonlinear distortion due to skin plasticity and differences in pressure against the sensor. Fingerprint matching remains as a challenging pattern recognition problem due to the difficulty in matching fingerprints affected by one or several of the mentioned factors [59].

A large number of approaches to fingerprint matching can be found in literature. They can be classified into: *a*) correlation-based approaches, *b*) minutiae-based approaches, and *c*) ridge feature-based approaches.

In the correlation-based approaches, the fingerprint images are superimposed and the gray scale images are directly compared using a measure of correlation. Due to nonlinear distortion, different impressions of the same finger may result in differences of the global structure, making the comparison unreliable. In addition, computing the correlation between two fingerprint images is computationally expensive. To deal with these problems, correlation can be computed only in certain local regions of the image, which can be selected following several criteria. Also, to speed up the process, correlation can be computed in the Fourier domain or using heuristic approaches, which allow the number of computational operations to be reduced.

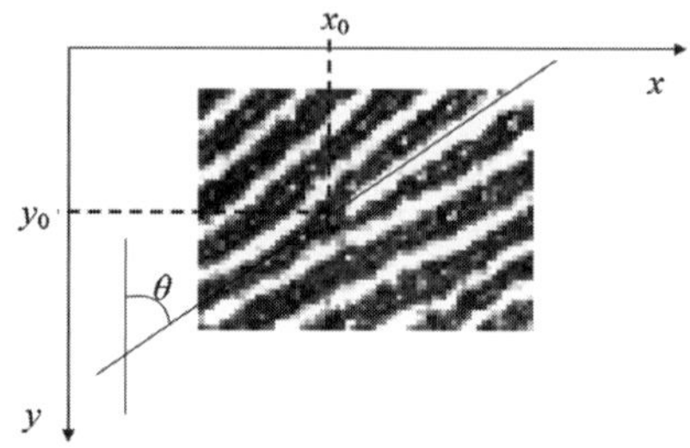

Fig. 4.12 Minutia represented by its spatial coordinates and angle

Minutiae-based approaches are the most popular and widely used methods for fingerprint matching, since they are analogous with the way that forensic experts compare fingerprints. A fingerprint is modeled as a set of minutiae, which are usually represented by its spatial coordinates and the angle between the tangent to the ridge line at the minutiae position and the horizontal or vertical axis (Fig. 4.12). The minutiae sets of the two fingerprints to be compared are first aligned, requiring displacement and rotation to be computed (some approaches also compute scaling and other distortion-tolerant transformations). This alignment involves a minimization problem, the complexity of which can be reduced in various ways [23]. Once aligned, corresponding minutiae at similar positions in both fingerprints are looked for. A *region of tolerance* around the minutiae position is defined in order to compensate for the variations that may appear in the minutiae position due to noise and distortion. Likewise, differences in angle between corresponding minutia points are tolerated. Other approaches use *local minutia matching*, which means combining comparisons of local minutia configurations. These kind of techniques relax global spatial relationships that are highly distinctive [59] but naturally more vulnerable to nonlinear deformations. Some matching approaches combine both techniques by first carrying out a fast local matching and then, if the two fingerprints match at a local level, consolidating the matching at global level.

Unfortunately, minutiae are known to be unreliably extracted in low image quality conditions. For this and other reasons, alternative features have been proposed in the literature as an alternative to minutiae (or to be used in conjunction with minutiae) [59]. The alternative feature most widely studied for fingerprint matching is texture information. The fingerprint structure consists of periodical repetitions of a pattern of ridges and valleys that can be characterized by its local orientation, frequency, symmetry, etc. Texture information is less discriminative than minutiae, but more reliable under low quality conditions [29].

4.2.4 Current Issues and Challenges

One of the open issues in fingerprint verification is the lack of robustness against image quality degradation [80, 2]. The performance of a fingerprint recognition system is heavily affected by fingerprint image quality. Several factors determine the quality of a fingerprint image: skin conditions (e.g., dryness, wetness, dirtiness, temporary or permanent cuts and bruises), sensor conditions (e.g., dirtiness, noise, size), user cooperation, etc. Some of these factors cannot be avoided and some of them vary along time. Poor quality images result in spurious and missed features, thus degrading the performance of the overall system. Therefore, it is very important for a fingerprint recognition system to estimate the quality and validity of the captured fingerprint images. We can either reject the degraded images or adjust some of the steps of the recognition system based on the estimated quality. Several algorithms for automatic fingerprint image quality assessment have been proposed in literature [2]. Also, the benefits of incorporating automatic quality measures in fingerprint verification have been shown in recent studies [28, 6, 32, 5].

A successful approach to enhance the performance of a fingerprint verification system is to combine the results of different recognition algorithms. A number of simple fusion rules and complex trained fusion rules have been proposed in literature [11, 49, 81]. Examples for combining minutia- and texture-based approaches are to be found in [75, 61, 28]. Also, a comprehensive study of the combination of different fingerprint recognition systems is done in [30]. However, it has been found that simple fusion approaches are not always outperformed by more complex fusion approaches, calling for further studies of the subject.

Another recent issue in fingerprint recognition is the use of multiple sensors, either for sensor fusion [60] or for sensor interoperability [74, 7]. Fusion of sensors offers some important potentialities [60]: *a*) the overall performance can be improved substantially, *b*) population coverage can be improved by reducing enrollment and verification failures, and *c*) it may naturally resist spoofing attempts against biometric systems. Regarding sensor interoperability, most biometric systems are designed under the assumption that the data to be compared is obtained uniquely and the same for every sensor, thus being restricted in their ability to match or compare biometric data originating from different sensors in practice. As a result, changing the sensor may affect the performance of the system. Recent progress has been made in the development of common data exchange formats to facilitate the exchange of feature sets between vendors [19]. However, little effort has been invested in the development of algorithms to alleviate the problem of sensor interoperability. Some approaches to handle this problem are given in [74], one example of which is the normalization of raw data and extracted features. As a future remark, interoperability scenarios should also be included in vendor and algorithm competitions, as done in [37].

Due to the low cost and reduced size of new fingerprint sensors, several devices in daily use already include embedded fingerprint sensors (e.g., mobile telephones, PC peripherals, PDAs, etc.) However, using small-area sensors implies having less information available from a fingerprint and little overlap between different acquisitions of the same finger, which has great impact on the performance of the recognition system [59]. Some fingerprint sensors are equipped with mechanical guides in order to constrain the finger position. Another alternative is to perform several acquisitions of a finger, gathering (partially) overlapping information during the enrollment, and reconstruct a full fingerprint image.

In spite of the numerous advantages of biometric systems, they are also vulnerable to attacks [82]. Recent studies have shown the vulnerability of fingerprint systems to fake fingerprints [35, 72, 71, 63]. Surprisingly, fake biometric input to the sensor is shown to be quite successful. Aliveness detection could be a solution and it is receiving great attention [26, 78, 8]. It has also been shown that the matching score is a valuable piece of information for the attacker [82, 73, 62]. Using the feedback provided by this score, signals in the channels of the verification system can be modified iteratively and the system is compromised in a number of iterations. A solution could be given by concealing the matching score and just releasing an acceptance/rejection decision, but this may not be suitable in certain biometric systems [82].

With the advances in fingerprint sensing technology, new high resolution sensors are able to acquire ridge pores and even perspiration activities of the pores [40, 21]. These features can provide additional discriminative information to existing fingerprint recognition systems. In addition, acquiring perspiration activities of the pores can be used to detect spoofing attacks.

4.3 Fingerprint Databases

Research in biometrics profoundly depends on the availability of sensed data. The growth that the field has experienced over the past two decades has led to the appearance of increasing numbers of biometric databases, either monomodal (one biometric trait sensed) or multimodal (two or more biometric traits sensed). Previous to the International Fingerprint Verification Competitions (FVC, see Sect. 4.4), the only large, publicly available datasets were the NIST databases [69]. However, these databases were not well suited for the evaluation of algorithms operating with live-scan images [59] and will not be described here. In this section, we present some of the most important publicly available biometric databases, either monomodal or multimodal, that include the fingerprint trait acquired with live-scan sensors. A summary of these databases with some additional information are shown in Table 4.1.

4.3.1 FVC Databases

Four international Fingerprint Verification Competitions (FVC) were organized in 2000, 2002, 2004 and 2006 [57, 58, 18, 33], see Sect. 4.4. For each competition, four databases were acquired using three different sensors and the SFinGE synthetic generator [59]. Each database has 110 fingers (150 in FVC2006) with eight impressions per finger (twelve in FVC2006), resulting in 880 impressions (1,800 in FVC2006). In the four competitions, the SFinGe synthetic generator was tuned to simulate the main perturbations introduced in the acquisition of the three "real" databases.

In FVC2000, the acquisition conditions were different for each database (e.g., interleaving/not interleaving the acquisition of different fingers, periodical cleaning/no cleaning of the sensor). For all the databases, no care was taken to assure a minimum quality of the fingerprints; in addition, a maximum rotation and a nonnull overlapping area were assured for impressions from the same finger.

In FVC2002, the acquisition conditions were the same for each database: interleaved acquisition of different fingers to maximize differences in finger placement, no care was taken in assuring a minimum quality of the fingerprints and the sensors were not periodically cleaned. During some sessions, individuals were asked to: *a*) exaggerate displacement or rotation or, *b*) dry or moisten their fingers.

The FVC2004 databases were collected with the aim of creating a more difficult benchmark because, in FVC2002, top algorithms achieved accuracies close to 100% [18]: simply more intraclass variation was introduced. During the different sessions, individuals were asked to: *a*) put the finger at slightly different vertical position, *b*) apply low or high pressure against the sensor, *c*) exaggerate skin distortion and rotation, and *d*) dry or moisten their fingers. No care was taken to assure a minimum quality of the fingerprints and the sensors were not periodically cleaned. Also, the acquisition of different fingers were interleaved to maximize differences in finger placement.

For the 2006 edition [33], no deliberate difficulties were introduced in the acquisition as it was done in the previous editions (such as exaggerated distortion, large amounts of rotation and displacement, wet/dry impressions, etc.), but the population is more heterogeneous, including manual workers and elderly people. Also, no constraints were enforced to guarantee a minimum quality in the acquired images and the final datasets were selected from a larger database by choosing the most difficult fingers according to a quality index, to make the benchmark sufficiently difficult for an evaluation.

4.3.2 MCYT Bimodal Database

In the MCYT database [70], fingerprints and online signatures were acquired. The fingerprint subcorpus of this database (MCYT Fingerprint subcorpus) includes ten-print acquisition of each of the 330 subjects enrolled in the database. For each individual, 12 samples of each finger were acquired using an optical and a capacitive sensor. With the aim of including variability in fingerprint positioning on the sensor, the 12 different samples of each fingerprint were acquired under human supervision and considering three different levels of control. For this purpose, the fingerprint core had to be located inside a size-varying rectangle displayed in the acquisition software interface viewer.

4.3.3 BIOMET Multimodal Database

In the multimodal BIOMET database [36], the fingerprint acquisitions were done with an optical and a capacitive sensor. During the first acquisition campaign, only the optical sensor was used, whereas both the optical and capacitive sensors were employed for the second and third campaigns. The total number of available fingerprints per sensor is six for the middle and index fingers of each contributor.

4.3.4 Michigan State University (MSU) Database

The MSU fingerprint database [45] was acquired within the Pattern Recognition and Image Processing Laboratory (PRIP) at Michigan State University. Data was acquired from nonhabituated cooperative subjects using optical and solid-state sensors connected to IBM Thinkpads. A live feedback of the acquired image was provided and users were guided to place their fingers in the center of the sensor and in upright position. Because of that, most of the fingerprint images are centered and no significant rotation is found. Some images were acquired while the subject was removing the finger from the sensor due to time lag in providing the feedback, resulting in partial fingerprints. It was also observed that subjects had greasier fingers during and after the lunch hour, whereas drier fingers were registered in the evening compared to the morning sessions.

With the aim of studying user adaptation within the fingerprint image acquisition process, a second database using the solid-state sensor was acquired. Eight subjects were asked to choose the finger that they felt most comfortable with and then use the same finger every day to give one fingerprint image during six consecutive weeks. The subjects were cooperative but unattended.

4.3.5 BioSec Multimodal Database

Among the five modalities present in the BioSec Database, recorded in the framework of an Integrated Project of the 6th European Framework Programme [14], fingerprints are also present. The baseline corpus [27] comprises 200 subjects with two acquisition sessions per subject. The extended version of the BioSec database comprises 250 subjects with four sessions per subject (about one month between sessions). Fingerprint data have been acquired using three different sensors.

4.3.6 BiosecurID Multimodal Database

The BiosecurID database [34] has been collected in an office-like uncontrolled environment (in order to simulate a realistic scenario). The fingerprint part comprises data from 400 subjects, with two different sensors and four sessions distributed in a four-month time span.

4.3.7 BioSecure Multimodal Database

One of the main integrative efforts of the BioSecure Network of Excellence was the design and collection of a new multimodal database [4], allowing to create a common and repeatable benchmarking of algorithms. Acquisition of the BioSecure Multimodal Database has been jointly conducted by 11 European institutions participating in the BioSecure Network of Excellence [15]. Among the three different datasets that are present in this database, fingerprints are captured in the *Data Set 2 (DS2)* and *Data Set 3 (DS3)*. Pending integration, the BioSecure database has approximately 700 individuals participating in the collections of DS2 and DS3. Fingerprint data in DS2 were acquired using an optical and a capacitive sensor. Fingerprint data in DS3 were acquired with a PDA, and they are considered degraded in acquisition condition with respect to DS2, since they were acquired while subjects were standing with a PDA in the hand.

4.4 Fingerprint Evaluation Campaigns

The most important evaluation campaigns carried out in the fingerprint modality are the NIST Fingerprint Vendor Technology Evaluation (FpVTE2003) [84] and the four Fingerprint Verification Competitions (FVC), which took place in 2000 [57], 2002 [58], 2004 [18] and 2006 [33]. A comparative summary of FVC2004, FVC2006 and FpVTE2003 is given in Table 4.2. An important evaluation is also the NIST Minutiae Interoperability Exchange Test (MINEX) [37].

4.4.1 Fingerprint Verification Competitions

The Fingerprint Verification Competitions (FVC) were organized with the aim of determining the state of the art in fingerprint verification. These competitions have received great attention from both academic and commercial organizations, and several research groups have used the FVC datasets for their own experiments later on. The number of participants and algorithms evaluated has increased in each new edition. Also, to increase the number of participants, anonymous participation was

Table 4.1 Summary of existing databases that include the fingerprint trait (where # S. denotes number of sessions)

Name	Type	Sensor	Image Size	Resolution	Subjects	# S.	Samples	Distributor
FVC2000	monomodal	Low cost optical (KeyTronic)	300 × 300	500 dpi	110	2	880	Univ. Bologna http://biolab.csr.unibo.it
		Low cost capacitive (ST Microelectronics)	256 × 364	500 dpi	110	2	880	
		Optical (Identicator technology)	448 × 478	500 dpi	110	2	880	
		Synthetic (SFinGe v2.0)	240 × 320	500 dpi	110	2	880	
FVC2002	monomodal	Optical (Identix)	388 × 374	500 dpi	110	3	880	Univ. Bologna http://biolab.csr.unibo.it
		Optical (Biometrika)	296 × 560	569 dpi	110	3	880	
		Capacitive (Precise Biometrics)	300 × 300	500 dpi	110	3	880	
		Synthetic (SFinGe v2.51)	288 × 384	500 dpi	110	3	880	
FVC2004	monomodal	Optical (CrossMatch)	640 × 480	500 dpi	110	3	880	Univ. Bologna http://biolab.csr.unibo.it
		Optical (Digital Persona)	328 × 364	500 dpi	110	3	880	
		Thermal sweeping (Atmel FingerChip)	300 × 480	512 dpi	110	3	880	
		Synthetic (SFinGe v3.0)	288 × 384	500 dpi	110	3	880	
FVC2006	monomodal	Capacitive (Authentec)	96 × 96	250 dpi	150	3	1800	http://biolab.csr.unibo.it http://atvs.ii.uam.es
		Optical (Biometrika)	400 × 560	569 dpi	150	3	1800	
		Thermal sweeping Atmel)	400 × 500	500 dpi	150	3	1800	
		Synthetic (SFinGe v3.0)	288 × 384	500 dpi	150	3	1800	
MCYT	multimodal (fingerprint, signature)	Capacitive (Precise Biometrics)	300 × 300	500 dpi	330	1	39600	ATVS (Biometric Recognition Group) http://atvs.ii.uam.es
		Optical (Digital Persona)	256 × 400	500 dpi	330	1	39600	
BIOMET	multimodal (audio, face, hand, fingerprint, signature)	Optical (SAGEM)	N/A	N/A	327	3	N/A	Association BioSecure http://biosecure.info
		Capacitive (GEMPLUS)	N/A	N/A	327	3	N/A	
MSU	monomodal	Optical (Digital Biometrics)	640 × 480	500 dpi	160	2	2560	MSU (Michigan State Univ.)
		Solid-state (Veridicom)	300 × 300	500 dpi	160	2	2560	
		Solid-state (Veridicom)	300 × 300	500 dpi	8	30	240	
Smartkom	multimodal (hand, signature, fingerprint, voice)	N/A	N/A	N/A	96	N/A	N/A	ELDA (European Language Resources Distribution Agency)
BioSec	multimodal (face, speech, fingerprint, iris)	Optical (Biometrika)	400 × 560	569 dpi	250	4	16000	ATVS (Biometric Recognition Group) http://atvs.ii.uam.es
		Thermal sweeping (Atmel)	400 × 500	500 dpi	250	4	16000	
		Capacitive (Authentec)	96 × 96	250 dpi	250	4	16000	
BiosecurID	multimodal (speech, iris, face, signature, hand, handwriting, fingerprints, keystroking)	Optical (Biometrika)	400 × 560	569 dpi	400	4	25600	ATVS (Biometric Recognition Group) http://atvs.ii.uam.es
		Thermal sweeping (Yubee)	400 × 500	5 dpi	400	4	25600	
BioSecure	multimodal (face, speech, signature, fingerprint, hand, iris)	Optical (Biometrika)	400 × 560	569 dpi	700	2	16800	Association BioSecure http://biosecure.info
		Thermal sweeping (Atmel)	400 × 500	500 dpi	700	2	16800	
		Thermal Sweeping (HP iPAQ hx2790 PDA)	300 × 470	96 dpi	700	2	16800	

allowed in 2002, 2004 and 2006. Additionally, the FVC2004 and FVC2006 were subdivided into: *a*) *open category* and *b*) *light category*. The light category aimed at evaluating algorithms under low computational resources, limited memory usage and small template size.

Table 4.2 Comparative summary between FVC2004, FVC2006 and FpVTE2003

	FVC 2004	**FVC 2006**	**FpVTE 2003**
Participants	43	53	18
Algorithms	Open Category: 41 Light Category: 26	Open Category: 44 Light Category: 26	Large Scale Test (LST): 13 Medium Scale Test (MST): 18 Small Scale Test (SST): 3
Population	Students	Heterogeneous (incl. manual workers and elderly people)	Operational data from U.S. Government sources
Fingerprint format	Flat impressions from low-cost scanners		Mixed formats from various sources
Perturbations	Deliberate perturbations	Selection of the most difficult images based on a quality index	Intrinsic low quality fingers and/or noncooperative users
Data collection	Acquired for the event	From the BioSec database	U.S. Government sources
Database size	4 databases, each containing 1800 fingerprints from 150 fingers		48105 fingerprints from 25309 subjects
Anonymous partic.	Allowed	Allowed	Not allowed
Best EER	2.07 % (avg, Open Category)	2.16 % (avg, Open Category)	0.2 % (MST, the closest to the FVC Open Category)

For each FVC competition, four databases are acquired using three different sensors and the SFinGE synthetic generator [59] (see Sect. 4.3.1). The size of each database was set at 110 fingers with eight impressions per finger (150 fingers with 12 impressions per finger in FVC2006). A subset of each database (all the impressions from 10 fingers) was made available to the participants prior to the competition for algorithm tuning. The impressions from the remaining fingers are used for testing. Once tuned, participants submit their algorithms as executable files to the evaluators. The executable files are tested at the evaluator's site and the test data are not released until the evaluation concludes. In order to benchmark the algorithms, the evaluation is divided into: *a*) genuine attempts: each fingerprint image is compared to the remaining images of the same finger, and *b*) impostor attempts: the first impression of each finger is compared to the first image of the remaining fingers. In both cases, symmetric matches are avoided.

The FVC2004 databases were collected with the aim of creating a more difficult benchmark compared to the previous competitions [18]. During the acquisition sessions, individuals were requested to: *a*) put a finger at slightly different vertical position, *b*) apply low or high pressure against the sensor, *c*) exaggerate skin distortion and rotation, and *d*) dry or moisten their fingers. Data for the FVC2006 edition were collected without introducing deliberate difficulties, but the population is more heterogeneous, including manual workers and elderly people. Also, the final datasets in FVC2006 were selected from a larger database by choosing the most difficult fingers according to a quality index. In Table 4.3, results of the best performing algorithm in each FVC competition are shown. Data in the 2000 and 2002 editions were acquired without special restrictions and, as observed in Table 4.3, error rates decreased significantly from 2000 to 2002, demonstrating in some sense the maturity of fingerprint verification systems. However, in the 2004 and 2006 editions, it is observed that error rates increase with respect to the 2002 edition due to the deliberate difficulties and/or low quality sources introduced in the data, thus revealing that degradation of quality has a severe impact on the recognition rates.

Table 4.3 Results in terms of Equal Error Rate (EER) % of the best performing algorithm in each of the four databases of the FVC competitions

Database	2000	2002	2004	2006
DB1	0.67	0.10	1.97	5.56
DB2	0.61	0.14	1.58	0.02
DB3	3.64	0.37	1.18	1.53
DB4	1.99	0.10	0.61	0.27
Average	**1.73**	**0.19**	**2.07**	**2.16**

4.4.2 NIST Fingerprint Vendor Technology Evaluation

The NIST Fingerprint Vendor Technology Evaluation (FpVTE2003) aimed at: *a*) comparing systems on a variety of fingerprint data and identifying the most accurate systems; *b*) measuring the accuracy of fingerprint matching, identification, and verification on actual operational fingerprint data; and *c*) determining the effect of a variety of variables on matcher accuracy. Eighteen different companies competed in the FpVTE, and 34 systems were evaluated.

Three separate subtests were performed in the FpVTE2003: *a*) the Large-Scale Test (LST), *b*) the Medium-Scale Test (MST), and *c*) the Small-Scale Test (SST). SST and MST tested matching accuracy using individual fingerprints, whereas LST used sets of fingerprint images. The size and structure of each test were designed to optimize competing analysis objectives, available data, available resources, computational characteristics of the algorithms and the desire to include all qualified participants. In particular, the sizes of MST and LST were only determined after a great deal of analysis of a variety of issues. Designing a well-balanced test to accommodate heterogeneous system architectures was a significant challenge.

Data in the FpVTE2003 came from a variety of existing U.S. Government sources (paper cards, scanners), including low quality fingers. 48,105 sets of flat, slap or rolled fingerprint sets from 25,309 individuals were used, with a total of 393,370 fingerprint images. The systems that resulted in the best accuracy performed consistently well over a variety of image types and data sources. Also, the accuracy of these systems was considerably better than the rest of the systems. Further important conclusions drawn from the FpVTE2003 included: *a*) the number of fingers used and the fingerprint quality had the largest effect on system accuracy; *b*) accuracy on controlled data was significantly higher than accuracy on operational data; *c*) some systems were highly sensitive to the sources or types of fingerprints; and *d*) accuracy dropped as subject age at time of capture increased.

4.4.3 Minutiae Interoperability NIST Exchange Test

The purpose of the NIST Minutiae Interoperability Exchange Test (MINEX) [37] is to determine the feasibility of using minutiae data (rather than image data) as the interchange medium for fingerprint information between different fingerprint matching systems, and to quantify the verification accuracy changes when minutiae from dissimilar systems are used for matching fingerprints. Interoperability of templates is affected by the method used to encode minutiae and the matcher used to compare the templates. There are different schemes for defining the method of locating, extracting, formatting and matching the minutiae information from a fingerprint image [59]. In the MINEX evaluation, proprietary template formats are also compared with the ANSI INCITS 378-2004 template standard [1].

The images used for this test come from a variety of sensors, and include both live-scanned and non live-scanned rolled and plain impression types. No latent fingerprint images are used. Participants submitting a system had to provide an algorithm capable of extracting and matching a minutiae template using both their *proprietary* minutiae format and the ANSI INCITS 378-2004 minutiae data format standard [1]. The most relevant results of the MINEX evaluation were:

- Proprietary templates are superior to the ANSI INCITS 378-2004 templates.
- Some template generators produce standard templates that are matched more accurately than others. Some matchers compare templates more accurately than others. The leading vendors in generation are not always the leaders in matching and vice-versa.
- Verification accuracy of some matchers can be improved by replacing the vendors' template generator with that from another vendor.
- Performance is sensitive to the quality of the dataset. This applies to both proprietary and interoperable templates. Higher quality datasets provide reasonable interoperability, whereas lower quality datasets do not.

4.5 The BioSecure Benchmarking Framework

In order to ensure a fair comparison of various fingerprint recognition algorithms, a common evaluation framework has to be defined. In this section a reference system that can be used as a baseline for future improvements and comparisons is first defined. The database and the corresponding protocols are then described along with the associated performance measures. The benchmarking experiments presented in this section can be easily reproduced using the material and relevant information provided on the companion site [16].

4.5.1 Reference System: NFIS2

[1]The reference system for the fingerprint modality in the BioSecure Network of Excellence is the minutiae-based NIST Fingerprint Image Software (NFIS2–rel.28–2.2) [83]. NFIS2 contains software technology, developed for the Federal Bureau of Investigation (FBI), designed to facilitate and support the automated manipulation and processing of fingerprint images. Source code for over 50 different utilities or packages and an extensive User's Guide are distributed on CD-ROM free of charge [83]. For the evaluations and tests with the NFIS2 software presented in this chapter, two packages are used: the minutiae extraction MINDTCT package and the fingerprint matching BOZORTH3 package. These two packages are described next.

4.5.1.1 Minutiae Extraction Using MINDTCT

MINDTCT takes a fingerprint image and locates all minutiae in the image, assigning to each minutia point its location, orientation, type, and quality. The architecture of MINDTCT is shown in Fig. 4.13 and it can be divided in the following phases: *a*) generation of image quality map; *b*) binarization; *c*) minutiae detection; *d*) removal of false minutiae (including islands, lakes, holes, minutiae in regions of poor image quality, side minutiae, hooks, overlaps, minutiae that are too wide, and minutiae that are too narrow-pores); *e*) counting of ridges between a minutia point and its nearest neighbors; and *f*) minutiae quality assessment. Additional details of these phases are given below.

Because of the variation of image quality within a fingerprint, NFIS2 analyzes the image and determines areas that are degraded. Several characteristics are measured, including regions of low contrast, incoherent ridge flow, and high curvature. These three conditions represent unstable areas in the image where minutiae detection is unreliable, and together they are used to represent levels of quality in the image. An image quality map is generated integrating these three characteristics. Images are divided into nonoverlapping blocks, where one out of five levels of quality is assigned to each block.

The minutiae detection step scans the binary image of the fingerprint, identifying local pixel patterns that indicate the ending or splitting of a ridge. A set of minutia patterns is used to detect candidate minutia points. Subsequently, false minutiae are removed and the remaining candidates are considered as the true minutiae of the image. Fingerprint minutiae marchers often use other information in addition to just the points themselves. Apart from minutia's position, direction, and type,

[1] Material from this section is reproduced with permission from Annals of Telecommunication; source [3].

MINDTCT computes ridge counts between a minutia point and each of its nearest neighbors.

In the last step, a quality/reliability measure is associated with each detected minutia point. Even after performing the removal step, false minutiae potentially remain in the list. A robust quality measure can help to manage this. Two factors are combined to produce a quality measure for each detected minutia point. The first factor is taken directly from the location of the minutia point within the quality map described before. The second factor is based on simple pixel intensity statistics (mean and standard deviation) within the immediate neighborhood of the minutia point. A high quality region within a fingerprint image is expected to have significant contrast that will cover the full grayscale spectrum [83].

4.5.1.2 Fingerprint Matching Using the BOZORTH3 Algorithm

The BOZORTH3 matching algorithm computes a match score between the minutiae from any two fingerprints to help determine if they are from the same finger. This matcher uses only the location and orientation of the minutia points to match the fingerprints. It is rotation and translation invariant. The algorithm can be described by the following three steps: *a*) construction of two IntraFingerprint Minutia Comparison Tables, one table for each of the two fingerprints; *b*) construction of an InterFingerprint Compatibility Table; and *c*) generation of the matching score using the InterFingerprint Compatibility Table. These steps are described in Fig. 4.13. The first step is to compute relative measurements from each minutia in a fingerprint to all other minutia in the same fingerprint. These relative measurements are stored in the IntraFingerprint Minutia Comparison Table and are used to provide rotation and translation invariance. The invariant measurements computed are the distance

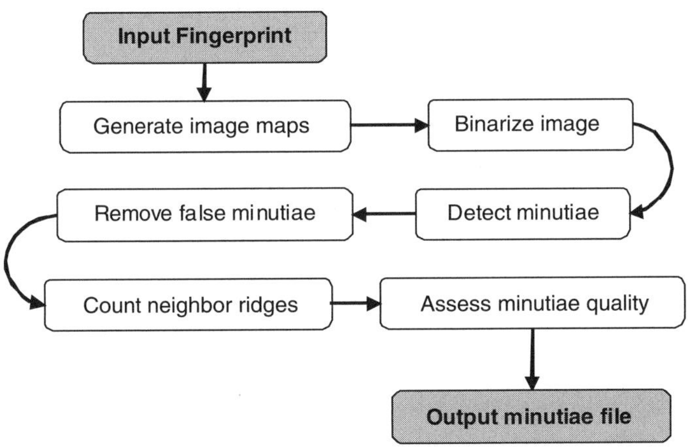

Fig. 4.13 System architecture of the MINDTCT package of the NIST Fingerprint Image Software 2 (NFIS2), [83]

between two minutiae and angle between each minutia's orientation and the intervening line between both minutiae. A comparison table is constructed for each of the two fingerprints.

The next step is to take the IntraFingerprint Minutia Comparison Tables from the two fingerprints and look for "compatible" entries between the two tables. Table entries are "compatible" if: *a*) the corresponding distances and *b*) the relative minutia angles are within a specified tolerance. An InterFingerprint Compatibility Table is generated, only including entries that are compatible. A compatibility table entry therefore incorporates two pairs of minutia, one pair from the template fingerprint and one pair from the test fingerprint. The entry into the compatibility table indicates that the minutiae pair of the template fingerprint corresponds to the minutiae pair of the test fingerprint.

At the end of the second step, we have constructed a compatibility table that consists of a list of compatibility associations between two pairs of potentially corresponding minutiae. These associations represent single links in a compatibility graph. The matching algorithm then traverses and links table entries into clusters, combining compatible clusters and accumulating a match score. The larger the number of linked compatibility associations, the higher the match score, and the more likely the two fingerprints originate from the same person.

4.5.2 Benchmarking Database: MCYT-100

A large biometric database acquisition process was launched in 2001 within the MCYT project [70]. For the experiments reported in this chapter, the freely available MCYT-100 subcorpus [64], which contains 100 individuals extracted from the MCYT database is used. The single-session fingerprint database acquisition was designed to include different types of sensors and different acquisition conditions. Two types of acquisition devices were used: *a*) a CMOS-based capacitive capture device, model 100SC from Precise Biometrics, producing a 500 dpi, 300×300 pixel image; and *b*) an optical scanning device, model UareU from Digital Persona, producing a 500 dpi, 256×400 pixel image. Some example images of the MCYT database acquired with the optical and the capacitive sensor are shown in Fig. 4.14.

With the aim of including variability in fingerprint positioning on the sensor, the MCYT database includes 12 different samples of each fingerprint, all of which were acquired under human supervision and with three different levels of control. For this purpose, the fingerprint core must be located inside a size-varying rectangle displayed in the acquisition software interface viewer. In Fig. 4.15, three samples of the same fingerprint are shown, so that variability in fingerprint positioning can be clearly observed. Depending on the size of the rectangle, the different levels of control will be referred to as: *a*) "low," with three fingerprint acquisitions using the biggest rectangle; *b*) "medium," with three fingerprint acquisitions; and *c*) "high," with six fingerprint acquisitions using the smallest rectangle. Therefore, each individual provides a total number of 240 fingerprint images for the database (10 prints $\times$ 12 samples/print $\times$ 2 sensors).

Fig. 4.14 Examples of MCYT fingerprints, of four different fingerprints (*one per column*); acquired with the optical (*top line*) or with the capacitive sensor (*bottom line*)

Fig. 4.15 Examples of the same MCYT fingerprint samples acquired at different levels of control

4.5.3 Benchmarking Protocols

For the experiments, data consist of 12,000 fingerprint images per sensor from the 10 fingers of the 100 contributors. We consider the different fingers as different users enrolled in the system, thus resulting in 1,000 users with 12 impressions per user. The experimental protocol is applied to each sensor separately.

We use one impression per finger with low control during the acquisition as a template. In genuine trials, the template is compared to the other 11 impressions available (two with low control, three with medium control and six with high control). The impostor trials are obtained by comparing the template to one impression with high control of the same finger of all the other contributors. The total number of genuine and impostor trials are therefore $1{,}000 \times 11 = 11{,}000$ and $1{,}000 \times 99 = 99{,}000$, respectively, per sensor.

4.5.4 Benchmarking Results

The minutiae-based NIST Fingerprint Image Software (NFIS2–rel.28–2.2) [83] was used to provide the benchmarking results, on the MCYT-100 database (see Sect. 4.5.2) according to the reference protocols (see Sect. 4.5.3). The benchmarking results obtained with both sensors (optical and capacitive) are presented in Table 4.4. Corresponding DET curves are displayed in Fig. 4.16.

Table 4.4 Fingerprint verification results (EER%) with Confidence Intervals [CI], obtained by applying the NIST Fingerprint Image Software (NFIS2–rel.28–2.2) [83] on the MCYT-100 database, according to the proposed benchmarking protocols, for the optical and capacitive sensors

	Optical (dp)	Capacitive (pb)
EER (in %)	3.18 [±0.18]	8.58 [±0.29]

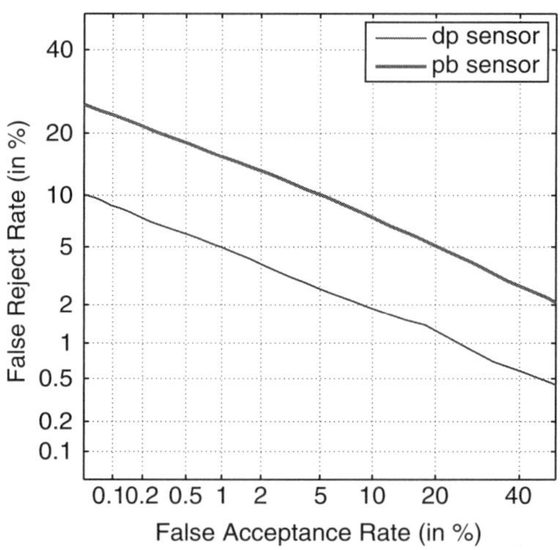

Fig. 4.16 DET plots for the benchmarking experiments obtained by applying the NIST Fingerprint Image Software (NFIS2–rel.28–2.2) [83] on the MCYT-100 database according to the proposed benchmarking protocols. The experiment with the fingerprint images acquired with the optical Digital Persona device is denoted as *db* and with the capacitive Precise Biometrics sensor is denoted as *pb*. The corresponding EER are 3.18% and 8.58%, respectively

4.6 Research Algorithms Evaluated within the Benchmarking Framework

We have also tested the minutiae-based fingerprint matcher developed by Halmstad University [HH] in Sweden [31] and the ridge-based fingerprint matcher developed by the ATVS/Biometric Recognition Group at Universidad Politecnica de Madrid [UPM], Spain [29].

4.6.1 Halmstad University Minutiae-based Fingerprint Verification System [HH]

[2]The fingerprint recognition software developed by Halmstad University [31] includes a novel way to detect the minutia points' position and direction, as well as ridge orientation, by using filters sensitive to parabolic and linear symmetries. The minutiae are exclusively used for alignment of two fingerprints. The number of paired minutiae can be low, which is advantageous in partial or low-quality fingerprints. After a global alignment, a matching is performed by distinctive area correlation, involving the minutiae's neighborhood. We briefly describe the four phases of the system: *a*) local feature extraction, *b*) pairing of minutiae, *c*) fingerprint alignment, and *d*) matching.

4.6.1.1 Local Feature Extraction

Two prominent minutia types, ridge bifurcation and termination have parabolic symmetry properties [67], whereas they lack linear symmetry [68]. The leftmost image in Fig. 4.17 shows a perfectly parabolic pattern. On the contrary, the local ridge and

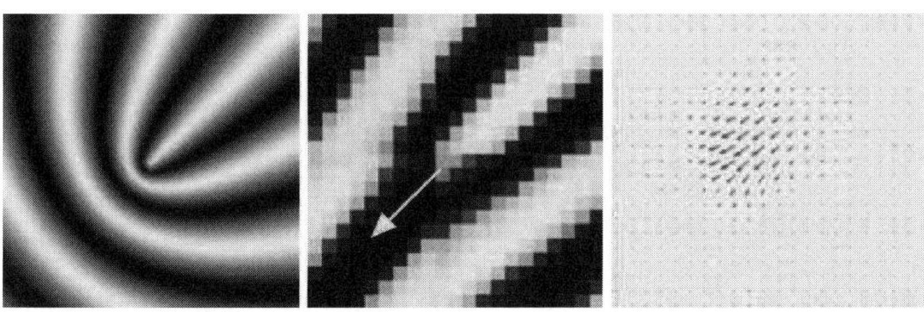

Fig. 4.17 (**Left-hand side**) perfectly parabolic pattern; (**center**) ridge bifurcation neighborhood with indicated minutia direction; (**right-hand side**) corresponding complex response of h_1 when convoluted with z

[2] Material from this section is reproduced with permission from Annals of Telecommunication; source [3].

valley structure is linearly symmetric. Perfect linearly symmetric patterns include planar waves, which have the same orientation at each point.

Averaging the orientation tensor $z = (f_x + if_y)^2$ of an image (with f_x and f_y as its partial derivatives) gives an orientation estimation and its error. A signal energy independent linear symmetry measure, *LS*, can be computed by dividing averaged z with averaged $|z|$. The result is a complex number, having the ridge orientation (in double angle) as argument and the reliability of its estimation as magnitude. Parabolic symmetry *PS* is retrieved by convolving z with a filter $h_n = (x+iy)^n \cdot g$ where g denotes a 2D Gaussian, with $n = 1$. The result is again a complex number, having the minutiae's direction as argument and an occurrence certainty as magnitude (compare Fig. 4.17). Note that h_0 can be used for the calculation of *LS*. All filtering is done in 1D involving separable Gaussians and their derivatives.

At the beginning, an image enhancement [24] is applied prior to the calculation of linear and parabolic symmetries. Some additional measures are then taken in order to reliably detect minutiae points. First, the selectivity of the parabolic symmetry filter response is improved, using a simple inhibition scheme to get $PSi = PS(1-|LS|)$. Basically, parabolic symmetry is attenuated if the linear symmetry is high, whereas it is preserved in the opposite case. In Fig. 4.18, the overall minutia detection process is depicted. The first two images show the initial fingerprint and its enhanced version, respectively. The extracted parabolic symmetry is displayed in image IV ($|PS|$), whereas the linear part is shown in image III (*LS*). The sharpened magnitudes $|PSi|$ are displayed in image V.

To avoid multiple detections of the same minutia, neighborhoods of 9×9 pixels are considered when looking for the highest responses in *PSi*. At this stage, *LS* can be reused to verify minutia candidates. First, a minimum $|LS|$ is employed to segment the fingerprint area from the image background. Second, each minutia is required to have full surround of high linear symmetry, in order to exclude spurious and false minutiae. Minutiae's coordinates and direction are stored in a list ordered by magnitude. In image VI of Fig. 4.18, its first 30 entries are indicated by circles.

In Fig. 4.18, the overall minutia detection process is depicted. The first two images show the initial fingerprint and its enhanced version, respectively. The extracted parabolic symmetry is displayed in image IV ($|PS|$), whereas the linear part is shown in image III (*LS*). The sharpened magnitudes $|PSi|$ are displayed in image V.

4.6.1.2 Pairing of Minutiae

In order to establish correspondences between two fingerprints, a local minutia matching approach inspired by triangular matching [51] is implemented. This approach essentially means establishing a connected series of triangles, which are equal with respect to both fingerprints and have corresponding minutiae as their corners.

For each minutia in a fingerprint, additional attributes are derived, which describe their within-fingerprint relation. For two arbitrary minutiae m_i and m_j of one fingerprint, the following attributes are derived: a) the distance $d_{ij} = d_{ji}$ between

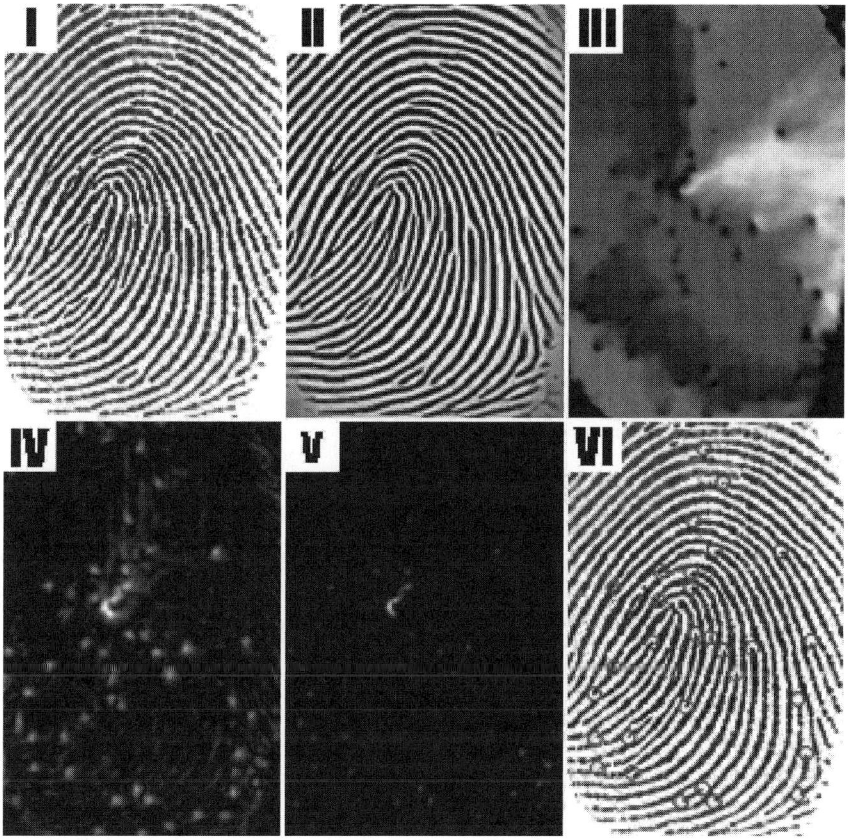

Fig. 4.18 Local feature extraction using complex filtering (HH system): (**I, II**) show the initial fingerprint and its enhanced version; (**III**) linear symmetry *LS*; (**IV**) parabolic symmetry *PS*; (**V**) sharpened magnitudes $|PSi|$; and (**VI**) the first ordered 30 minutiae; (see insert for color reproduction of this figure)

the two minutiae; and $b)$ the angles α_{ij} and α_{ji} of the minutiae with respect to the line between each other (compare Fig. 4.19). Next, corresponding couples in the two fingerprints are selected. Having two arbitrary minutiae m_k and m_l of the second fingerprint, the correspondence is fulfilled if $\left|d_{ij} - d_{kl}\right| < \lambda_{dist}$ and $\left(\left|\alpha_{ij} - \alpha_{kl}\right| + \left|\alpha_{ji} - \alpha_{lk}\right|\right) < \lambda_{angle}$. Thus, a corresponding couple means two pairs of minutiae, — e.g. $\{m_i, m_j; m_k, m_l\}$ — which at least correspond in a local scope.

Among all corresponding couples, we look for those that have a minutia in common in both of the fingerprints. Taking $\{m_i, m_j; m_k, m_l\}$ as a reference, it may be that $\{m_i, m_o; m_k, m_p\}$ and $\{m_j, m_o; m_l, m_p\}$ are corresponding couples as well. This is also visualized right, in Fig. 4.19. Such a constellation suggests m_o and m_p being neighbors to $\{m_i, m_j\}$ and $\{m_k, m_l\}$, respectively. To verify neighbors, we additionally check the closing angles γ_1 and γ_2 in order to favor uniqueness. In this way neighbors are consecutively assigned to the corresponding reference couples, the

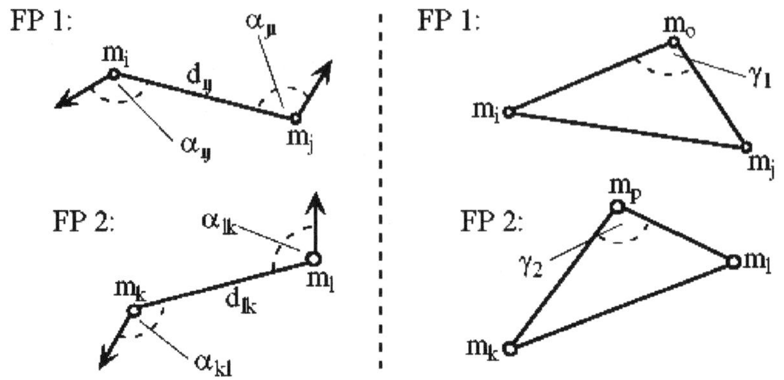

Fig. 4.19 Corresponding couples (**left-hand side**) and triangles (**right-hand side**) for two fingerprints; all angles are signed in order to be unambiguous

equivalent of establishing equal triangles with respect to both fingerprints sharing a common side. Each corresponding couple is taken as a reference once. The corresponding couple to which most neighbors can be found is considered for further processing. This couple and its mated neighbors are stored in a pairing list.

4.6.1.3 Fingerprint Alignment

Here, global alignment of two fingerprints is assumed to be a rigid transformation since only translation and rotation is considered. The corresponding parameters are computed using the established minutia pairs (list): translation is given by the difference of the position vectors for the first minutia pair. The rotation parameter is determined as the averaged angle among vectors between the first minutia pair and all others. Following the estimated parameters, the coordinate transformation for all points in *LS* is done, as the latter is needed for the final step. No further alignment efforts, e.g., fine adjustment, are performed.

4.6.1.4 Fingerprint Matching

Finally, a simple matching using normalized correlation at several sites of the fingerprint is performed (similar to [66]). Small areas in *LS* around the detected minutia points in the first fingerprint are correlated with areas at the same position in the second fingerprint. Only areas having an average linear symmetry higher than a threshold are considered. This is done to favor well-defined (reliable) fingerprint regions for comparison. The final matching score is given by the mean value of the single similarity measures.

4.6.2 UPM Ridge-based Fingerprint Verification System [UPM]

[3]The UPM ridge-based matcher uses a set of Gabor filters to capture the ridge strength. The image is tessellated into square cells, and the variance of the filter responses in each cell across all filtered images is used as feature vector. This feature vector is called FingerCode because of the similarity to previous research works [75, 25]. The automatic alignment is based on the system described in [76] in which the correlation between the two FingerCodes is computed, obtaining the optimal offset. The UPM ridge-based matcher can be divided in two phases: *a*) extraction of the FingerCode; and *b*) matching of the FingerCodes.

4.6.2.1 Feature Extraction (the FingerCode)

No image enhancement is performed since Gabor filters extract information that is in a specific (usually low-pass) band that is not affected by noise to the same extent as the original image is. The complete processing for extracting the feature vectors consists of the following three steps: *a*) convolution of the input fingerprint image with eight Gabor filters, obtaining eight filtered images F_θ; *b*) tessellation of the filtered images into equal-sized square disjoint cells; and *c*) extraction of the FingerCode. For each cell of each filtered image F_θ, we compute the variance of the pixel intensities. These standard deviation values constitute the FingerCode of a fingerprint image. A sample fingerprint image, the resulting convolved image with a Gabor filter of orientation $\theta = 0°$, the tessellated image and its FingerCode are shown in Fig. 4.20.

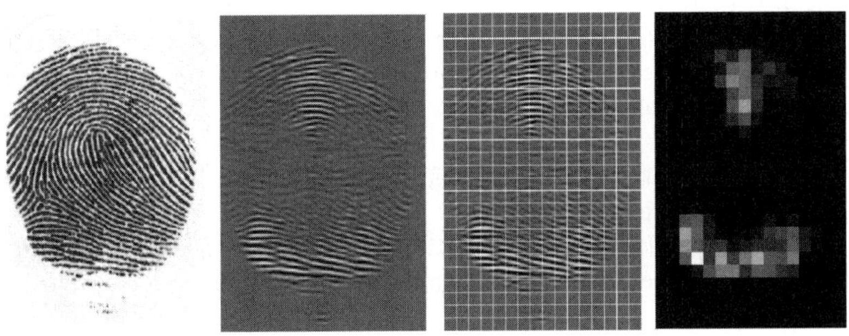

Fig. 4.20 Processing steps of the UPM ridge-based verification system

[3] Material from this section is reproduced with permission from Annals of Telecommunication; source [3].

4.6.2.2 Matching of FingerCodes

The complete sequence of stages performed is: *a*) alignment of the two fingerprints to be compared; and *b*) similarity computation between the FingerCodes. The matching score is computed as the Euclidean distance between the two FingerCodes.

To determine the alignment between two fingerprints, the 2D correlation of the two FingerCodes [76] is computed. Correlation involves multiplying corresponding entries between the two FingerCodes at all possible translation offsets, and determining the sum, which is computed more efficiently in the Fourier domain. The offset that results in the maximum sum is chosen to be the optimal alignment. Every offset is properly weighted to account for the amount of overlap between the two FingerCodes. It is worth noting that this procedure does not account for rotational offset between the two fingerprints. For the MCYT database used in this work, which is acquired under realistic conditions with an optical sensor, we have observed that typical rotations between different impressions of the same fingerprint are compensated by using the tessellation.

4.7 Experimental Results within the Benchmarking Framework

4.7.1 Evaluation of the Individual Systems

In Fig. 4.21 we show the verification results of the reference system and research systems described in Sects. 4.5.1 and 4.6. Furthermore, a general algorithmic description of these individual systems is given in Table 4.5. In Table 4.6 we also show the verification performance in terms of EER[4].

As expected, we can observe that minutiae-based matchers perform better than the ridge-based matcher. It is also supported by other findings that minutiae are more discriminative than other features of fingerprints, such as local orientation and frequency, ridge shape or texture information [59]. Regarding the technology of the sensor, we observe that the optical sensor performs better than the capacitive one. This could be because acquisition area is lower for the capacitive sensor, as can be seen in Fig. 4.14. Smaller acquisition surface implies less overlap between different acquisitions of the same finger and less amount of discriminative information in the fingerprint image [59].

By considering only minutiae-based approaches, HH algorithm results in the best performance. This result may be justified as follows:

- HH algorithm relies on complex filtering for minutiae extraction, considering the surrounding ridge information directly in the gray scale image. On the other

[4] The experimental protocol (individuals, enrollment and test images) for the results reported in this section is different from the one used for the experiments reported in [4].

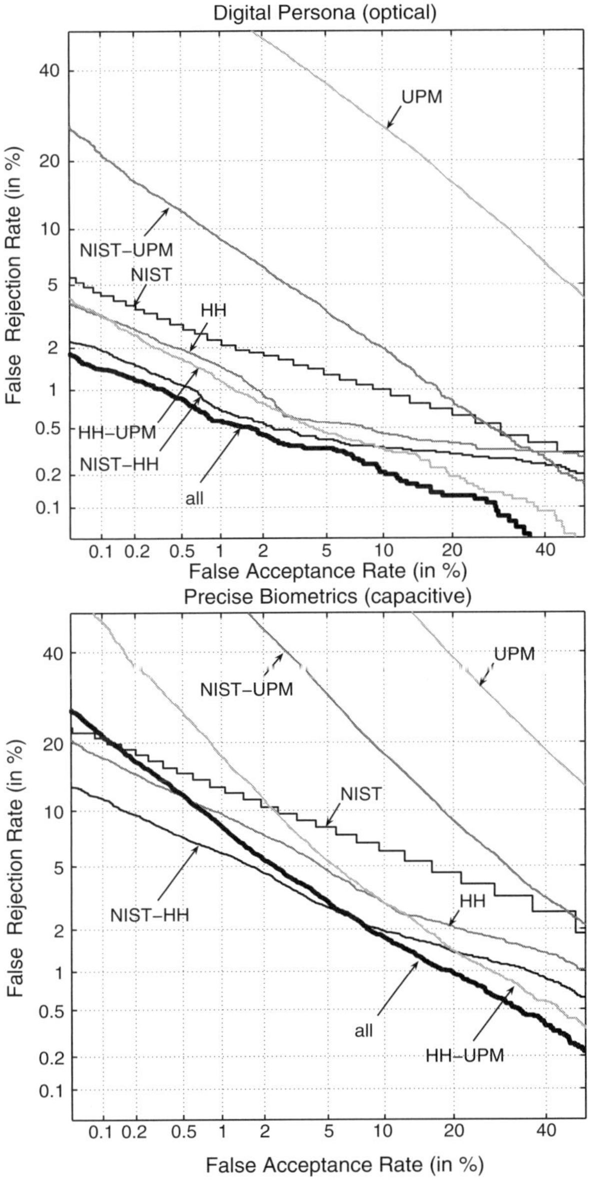

Fig. 4.21 Verification performance of the individual systems and of the fusion experiments carried out using the mean rule

hand, NIST algorithm relies on binarization and morphological analysis, which does not take the surrounding ridge information of the gray scale image into account, but only the information contained in small neighborhoods of the binarized image. Binarization-based methods usually result in a significant loss of information during the binarization process and in a large number of spurious minutiae introduced during thinning [59], thus decreasing the performance of the system.

- For fingerprint alignment, the NIST algorithm matches minutia pairs, whereas the HH algorithm performs triangular matching of minutiae. As the complexity of the alignment method increases, more conditions are implicitly imposed for a fingerprint to be correctly aligned, resulting in higher accuracy.
- In the same way, for fingerprint matching, the NIST algorithm looks for compatibility of minutiae pairs, whereas the HH algorithm does not perform minutiae matching but local orientation correlation of areas around the minutiae. Thus, the HH algorithm combines the accuracy of a minutiae-based representation with the robustness of a correlation-based matching, which is known to perform properly in low image quality conditions [59].

It should be noted that there are other reasons that justify significantly different performance between different implementations of systems that exploit the same features and use the same basic techniques. In the FVC experience [18], it was noted that commercial systems typically outperform academic approaches. Although they are based on the same ideas, commercial systems usually are strongly tuned and optimized.

Table 4.5 High-level description of the individual systems tested (reproduced with permission from Annals of Telecommunication; source [3])

	Segmentation (Y/N)	Enhancement (Y/N)	Features	Alignment: Translation Rotation	Alignment	Matching
NIST	Y	Y	Minutiae by binarization	TR	Minutiae-based by compatibility between minutiae pairs	Compatibility association between pairs of minutiae
HH	Y	Y	Minutiae by complex filtering (parabolic and linear symmetry)	TR	Minutiae-based by triangular matching	Normalized correlation of the neighborhood around minutiae
UPM	N	N	Ridge information by Gabor filtering and square tessellation	T	Correlation between the extracted features	Euclidean distance between extracted features

4.7.2 Multialgorithmic Fusion Experiments

We have evaluated two different simple fusion approaches based on the max rule and the mean rule. These schemes have been used to combine multiple classifiers in biometric authentication with good results reported [11, 49]. More advanced fusion rules currently form the basis of an intensive research topic. The use of these simple fusion rules is motivated by their simplicity, as complex fusion approaches may

Table 4.6 Verification performance in terms of EER of the individual systems and of the fusion experiments carried out using the mean and the max rule. The relative performance gain compared to the best individual matcher involved is also given for the mean rule

	Optical	Capacitive
NIST	1,73%	6,53%
HH	1,22%	4,67%
UPM	17,96%	28,39%

	Optical		Capacitive	
	MAX	MEAN	MAX	MEAN
NIST-HH	**1,00%**	**0,8% (-34,16%)**	**4,51%**	**3,37% (-27,79%)**
NIST-UPM	7,66%	4,07%	17,98%	13,69%
HH-UPM	7,58%	**1,1% (-15,39%)**	15,67%	5,18%
All	5,22%	**0,69% (-43,21%)**	13,91%	**3,72% (-20,29%)**

need training to outperform simple fusion approaches, which even then cannot be guaranteed, e.g., see [30].

Each matching score has been normalized to be a similarity score in the $[0,1]$ range using the tanh-estimators described in [41]:

$$s' = \frac{1}{2}\left\{\tanh\left(0.01\left(\frac{s-\mu_s}{\sigma_s}\right)\right)+1\right\} \tag{4.1}$$

where s is the raw similarity score, s' denotes the normalized similarity score, and μ_s and σ_s are respectively the estimated mean and standard deviation of the genuine score distribution.

In Table 4.6 we show the verification performance in terms of EER of the fusion experiments carried out using the max and mean rule. In addition, Fig. 4.21 depicts the DET plots only using the mean rule, which is the fusion rule that results in the best performance, based on the results of Table 4.6.

From Table 4.6, it is worth noting that an important relative improvement is obtained when fusing HH and NIST algorithms. Both of them use minutiae-based features, but they rely on completely different strategies for feature extraction (complex filtering vs. binarization) and matching (normalized correlation vs. minutiae compatibility), see Table 4.5. Fusing the three available systems results in an additional improvement for the optical sensor. For the capacitive one, however, improvement is obtained only for low FRR values (see Fig. 4.21). Interestingly enough, combining the ridge-based system (UPM) with minutiae-based systems does not always result in better performance, although they are systems based on heterogeneous strategies for feature extraction and/or matching. Only the combination of UPM and HH systems results in lower error rates for certain regions of the DET plot.

In terms of EER, the best combination of two systems (HH and NIST) results in a significant performance improvement. Subsequent inclusion of the third system (UPM) only produces a slight improvement of the performance or even no improvement, as it is the case of the capacitive sensor. Interestingly, the best combinations always include the best individual systems (HH and NIST). This should not be taken as a general statement because none of our fusion methods used training. Other studies have revealed that the combination of the best individual systems can be outperformed by other combinations [30], especially if the supervisor is data or expert adaptive.

4.8 Conclusions

In this work, we have reported on experiments carried out using the publicly available MCYT-100, database which includes fingerprint images acquired with an optical and a capacitive sensor. Three published systems [31, 83, 29] have been tested and the results discussed. The three systems implement different approaches for feature extraction, fingerprint alignment, and matching. Furthermore, several combinations of the systems using simple fusion schemes have been reported.

A number of experimental findings can be put forward as a result. We can confirm that minutiae have discriminative power but that complementary information, such as second and higher order minutiae constellation, local orientation, frequency, ridge shape or texture information encoding alternative features, improves the performance, in particular in low-quality fingerprints [59]. The minutiae-based algorithm that results in the best performance (HH) exploits both a minutiae-based correspondence and a correlation-based matching, instead of using only either of them. Moreover, the HH algorithm extracts minutiae by means of complex filtering, instead of using the classical approach based on binarization, which is known to result in loss of information and spurious minutiae [59].

When combining only two systems we generally obtain a significant performance improvement compared to including a third system. Though the latter combination produces the overall best EER of $\sim$0.69 for the optical sensor, it is not the scope of this work to work towards a perfect verification rate but to give an incentive to combine different methods within the same modality and reveal the fundamental reasons for such improvements.

In this study, which used untrained supervisors, the best combinations of two/three systems always included the best individual systems. Other studies have shown that however the performance of different individual systems can be influenced by database acquisition and the sensors [60]. This motivates us to extend the presented experiments to different databases and complementary method combinations to obtain compact and efficient systems.

Acknowledgments

This work was partially funded by the IST-FP6 BioSecure Network of Excellence. F. Alonso-Fernandez is supported by a FPI Scolarship from Consejeria de Educacion de la Comunidad de Madrid and Fondo Social Europeo. J. Fierrez is supported by a Marie-Curie Fellowship from the European Commission.

References

1. ANSI-INCITS 378, Fingerprint Minutiae Format for Data Interchange. American National Standard (2004)
2. Alonso-Fernandez, F., Fierrez, J., Ortega-Garcia, J., Gonzalez-Rodriguez, J., Fronthaler, H., Kollreider, K., Bigun, J.: A comparative study of fingerprint image quality estimation methods. IEEE Trans. on Information Forensics and Security **2**(4), 734–743 (2007)
3. Alonso-Fernandez, F., Fierrez, J., Ortega-Garcia, J., Fronthaler, H., Kollreider, K., Bigun, J.: Combining Multiple Matchers for fingerprint verification: a case study in BioSecure Network of Excellence. Annals of Telecommunications, Multimodal Biometrics, Eds. B.Dorizzi and C.Garcia-Mateo, Vol. 62, (2007)
4. Alonso-Fernandez, F., Fierrez, J., Ramos, D., Ortega-Garcia, J.: Dealingwith sensor interoperability in multi-biometrics: The UPM experience at the Biosecure Multimodal Evaluation 2007. Defense and Security Symposium, Biometric Technologies for Human Identification, BTHI, Proc. SPIE (2008)
5. Alonso-Fernandez, F., Roli, F., Marcialis, G., Fierrez, J., Ortega-Garcia, J.: Performance of fingerprint quality measures depending on sensor technology. Journal of Electronic Imaging, Special Section on Biometrics: Advances in Security, Usability and Interoperability (to appear) (2008)
6. Alonso-Fernandez, F., Veldhuis, R., Bazen, A., Fierrez-Aguilar, J., Ortega-Garcia, J.: On the relation between biometric quality and user-dependent score distributions in fingerprint verification. Proc. of Workshop on Multimodal User Authentication – MMUA (2006)
7. Alonso-Fernandez, F., Veldhuis, R., Bazen, A., Fierrez-Aguilar, J., Ortega-Garcia, J.: Sensor interoperability and fusion in fingerprint verification: A case study using minutiae- and ridge-based matchers. Proc. IEEE Intl. Conf. on Control, Automation, Robotics and Vision, ICARCV, Special Session on Biometrics (2006)
8. Antonelli, A., Capelli, R., Maio, D., Maltoni, D.: Fake finger detection by skin distortion analysis. IEEE Trans. on Information Forensics and Security **1**, 306–373 (2006)
9. Bazen, A., Gerez, S.: Segmentation of fingerprint images. Proc. Workshop on Circuits Systems and Signal Processing, ProRISC pp. 276–280 (2001)
10. Bazen, A., Gerez, S.: Systematic methods for the computation of the directional fields and singular points of fingerprints. IEEE Trans. on Pattern Analysis and Machine Intelligence **24**, 905–919 (2002)
11. Bigun, E., Bigun, J., Duc, B., Fischer, S.: Expert conciliation for multi modal person authentication systems by bayesian statistics. Proc. International Conference on Audio- and Video-Based Biometric Person Authentication, AVBPA **LNCS-1206**, 291–300 (1997)
12. Bigun, J.: Vision with Direction. Springer (2006)
13. Bigun, J., Granlund, G.: Optimal orientation detection of linear symmetry. First International Conference on Computer Vision pp. 433–438 (1987)
14. BioSec: Biometrics and security, FP6 IP, IST – 2002-001766 – http://www.biosec.org (2004)
15. BioSecure: Biometrics for secure authentication, FP6 NoE, IST – 2002-507634 – http://www.biosecure.info (2004)
16. BioSecure Benchmarking Framework. http://share.int-evry.fr/svnview-eph
17. Bolle, R., Serior, A., Ratha, N., Pankanti, S.: Fingerprint minutiae: A constructive definition. Proc. Workshop on Biometric Authentication, BIOAW **LNCS-2359**, 58–66 (2002)
18. Cappelli, R., Maio, D., Maltoni, D., Wayman, J.L., Jain, A.K.: Performance evaluation of fingerprint verification systems. IEEE Trans. on Pattern Analysis and Machine Intelligence **28**(1), 3–18 (2006)
19. CBEFF: Common Biometric Exchange File Format – http://www.itl.nist.gov/div893/biometrics/documents/NISTIR6529A.pdf (2001)
20. Chang, J., Fan, K.: Fingerprint ridge allocation in direct gray scale domain. Pattern Recognition **34**, 1907–1925 (2001)
21. Chen, Y., Jain, A.: Dots and incipients: Extended features for partial fingerprint matching. Proceedings of Biometric Symposium, Biometric Consortium Conference (2007)

22. Chen, Y., Parziale, G., Diaz-Santana, E., Jain, A.: 3d touchless fingerprints: Compatibility with legacy rolled images. Proceedings of Biometric Symposium, Biometric Consortium Conference (2006)
23. Chikkerur, S., Ratha, N.K.: Impact of singular point detection on fingerprint matching performance. Proc. IEEE AutoID pp. 207–212 (2005)
24. Chikkerur, S., Wu, C., Govindaraju, V.: A systematic approach for feature extraction in fingerprint images. Intl. Conf. on Bioinformatics and its Applications pp. 344–350 (2004)
25. Daugman, J.: How iris recognition works. IEEE Transactions on Circuits and Systems for Video Technology **14**, 21–30 (2004)
26. Derakhshani, R., Schuckers, S., Hornak, L., O'Gorman, L.: Determination of vitality from a non-invasive biomedical measurement for use in fingerprint scanners. Pattern Recognition **36**, 383–396 (2003)
27. Fierrez, J., Torre-Toledano, J.D., Gonzalez-Rodriguez, J.: BioSec baseline corpus: A multimodal biometric database. Pattern Recognition **40**(4), 1389–1392 (2007)
28. Fierrez-Aguilar, J., Chen, Y., Ortega-Garcia, J., Jain, A.: Incorporating image quality in multi-algorithm fingerprint verification. Proc. International Conference on Biometrics, ICB **LNCS-3832**, 213–220 (2006)
29. Fierrez-Aguilar, J., Munoz-Serrano, L., Alonso-Fernandez, F., Ortega-Garcia, J.: On the effects of image quality degradation on minutiae- and ridge-based automatic fingerprint recognition. Proc. IEEE Intl. Carnahan Conf. on Security Technology, ICCST pp. 79–82 (2005)
30. Fierrez-Aguilar, J., Nanni, L., Ortega-Garcia, J., Capelli, R., Maltoni, D.: Combining multiple matchers for fingerprint verification: A case study in FVC2004. Proc. Int Conf on Image Analysis and Processing, ICIAP **LNCS-3617**, 1035–1042 (2005)
31. Fronthaler, H., Kollreider, K., Bigun, J.: Local feature extraction in fingerprints by complex filtering. Proc. Intl. Workshop on Biometric Recognition Systems, IWBRS **LNCS-3781**, 77–84 (2005)
32. Fronthaler, H., Kollreider, K., Bigun, J., Fierrez, J., Alonso-Fernandez, F., Ortega-Garcia, J., Gonzalez-Rodriguez, J.: Fingerprint image quality estimation and its application to multi-algorithm verification. IEEE Trans. on Information Forensics and Security (to appear) (2008)
33. FVC2006: Fingerprint Verification Competition – http://bias.csr.unibo.it/fvc2006/default.asp (2006)
34. Galbally, J., Fierrez, J., Ortega-Garcia, J., Freire, M., Alonso-Fernandez, F., Siguenza, J., Garrido-Salas, J., Anguiano-Rey, E., Gonzalez-de-Rivera, G., Ribalda, R., Faundez-Zanuy, M., Ortega, J., Cardeoso-Payo, V., Viloria, A., Vivaracho, C., Moro, Q., Igarza, J., Sanchez, J., Hernaez, I., Orrite-Uruuela, C.: Biosecurid: a multimodal biometric database. Proc. MADRINET Workshop pp. 68–76 (2007)
35. Galbally-Herrero, J., Fierrez-Aguilar, J., Rodriguez-Gonzalez, J., Alonso-Fernandez, F., Ortega-Garcia, J., Tapiador, M.: On the vulnerability of fingerprint verification systems to fake fingerprint attacks. Proc. IEEE Intl. Carnahan Conf. on Security Technology, ICCST (2006)
36. Garcia-Salicetti, S., Beumier, C., Chollet, G., Dorizzi, B., les Jardins, J., Lunter, J., Ni, Y., Petrovska-Delacretaz, D.: BIOMET: A multimodal person authentication database including face, voice, fingerprint, hand and signature modalities. Proc. International Conference on Audio- and Video-Based Biometric Person Authentication, AVBPA p. 845853 (2003)
37. Grother, P., McCabe, M., Watson, C., Indovina, M., Salamon, W., Flanagan, P., Tabassi, E., Newton, E., Wilson, C.: MINEX – Performance and interoperability of the INCITS 378 fingerprint template. NISTIR 7296 – http://fingerprint.nist.gov/minex (2005)
38. Guyon, I., Makhoul, J., Schwartz, R., Vapnik, V.: What size test set gives good error rate estimates? IEEE Trans. on Pattern Analysis and Machine Intelligence **20**, 52–64 (1998)
39. Hong, L., Wan, Y., Jain, A.: Fingerprint imagen enhancement: Algorithm and performance evaluation. IEEE Trans. on Pattern Analysis and Machine Intelligence **20**(8), 777–789 (1998)
40. Jain, A., Chen, Y., Demirkus, M.: Pores and ridges: High resolution fingerprint matching using level 3 features. IEEE Trans. on Pattern Analysis and Machine Intelligence **29**(1), 15–27 (2007)

41. Jain, A., Nandakumar, K., Ross, A.: Score normalization in multimodal biometric systems. Pattern Recognition **38**(12), 2270–2285 (2005)
42. Jain, A., Ross, A., Pankanti, S.: Biometrics: A tool for information security. IEEE Trans. on Information Forensics and Security **1**, 125–143 (2006)
43. Jain, A., Ross, A., Prabhakar, S.: An introduction to biometric recognition. IEEE Transactions on Circuits and Systems for Video Technology **14**(1), 4–20 (2004)
44. Jain, A.K., Hong, L., Pankanti, S., Bolle, R.: An identity authentication system using fingerprints. Proc. IEEE **85**(9), 1365–1388 (1997)
45. Jain, A.K., Prabhakar, S., Ross, A.: Fingerprint matching: Data acquisition and performance evaluation". Tech. Rep. TR99-14, MSU (1999)
46. Jiang, X., Yau, W., Ser, W.: Detecting the fingerprint minutiae by adaptive tracing the gray level ridge. Pattern Recognition **34**, 999–1013 (2001)
47. Karu, K., Jain, A.: Fingerprint classification. Pattern Recognition **29**(3), 389–404 (1996)
48. Kawagoe, M., Tojo, A.: Fingerprint pattern classification. Pattern Recognition **17**, 295–303 (1984)
49. Kittler, J., Hatef, M., Duin, R., Matas, J.: On combining classifiers. IEEE Trans. on Pattern Analysis and Machine Intelligence **20**(3), 226–239 (1998)
50. Knutsson, H.: Filtering and reconstruction in image processing. Ph.D. thesis, Linköping University (1982)
51. Kovacs-Vajna, Z.: A fingerprint verification system based on triangular matching and dynamic time warping. IEEE Trans. on Pattern Analysis and Machine Intelligence **22**, 1266–1276 (2000)
52. Kovacs-Vajna, Z., Rovatti, R., Frazzoni, M.: Fingerprint ridge distance computation methodologies. Pattern Recognition **33**, 69–80 (2000)
53. Leung, M., Engeler, W., Frank, P.: Fingerprint image processing using neural network. Proc. IEEE Region 10 Conf. on Computer and Comm. Systems (1990)
54. Liu, J., Huang, Z., Chan, K.: Direct minutiae extraction from gray level fingerprint image by relationship examination. Proc. Int. Conf. on Image Processing **2**, 427–300 (2000)
55. Maio, D., Maltoni, D.: Direct gray scale minutiae detection in fingerprints. IEEE Trans. on Pattern Analysis and Machine Inteligence **19**(1), 27–40 (1997)
56. Maio, D., Maltoni, D.: Ridge-line density estimation in digital images. Proc. Int. Conf. on Pattern Recognition pp. 534–538 (1998)
57. Maio, D., Maltoni, D., Capelli, R., Wayman, J., Jain, A.: FVC2000: Fingerprint verification competition. IEEE Trans. on Pattern Analysis and Machine Intelligence **24**(3), 402–412 (2002)
58. Maio, D., Maltoni, D., Capelli, R., Wayman, J., Jain, A.: FVC2002: Second fingerprint verification competition. Proc. Intl. Conf. on Pattern Recognition, ICPR **3**, 811–814 (2002)
59. Maltoni, D., Maio, D., Jain, A., Prabhakar, S.: Handbook of Fingerprint Recognition. Springer, New York (2003)
60. Marcialis, G., Roli, F.: Fingerprint verification by fusion of optical and capacitive sensors. Pattern Recognition Letters **25**, 1315–1322 (2004)
61. Marcialis, G., Roli, F.: Fusion of multiple fingerprint matchers by single-layer perceptron with class-separation loss function. Pattern Recognition Letters **26**, 1830–1839 (2005)
62. Martinez-Diaz, M., Fierrez-Aguilar, J., Alonso-Fernandez, F., Ortega-Garcia, J., Siguenza, J.: Hill-climbing and brute-force attacks on biometric systems: A case study in match-on-card fingerprint verification. Proc. IEEE Intl. Carnahan Conf. on Security Technology, ICCST (2006)
63. Matsumoto, T., Matsumoto, H., Yamada, K., Hoshino, S.: Impact of artificial gummy fingers on fingerprint systems. Proc. of SPIE, Optical Security and Counterfeit Deterrence Techniques IV **4677**, 275–289 (2002)
64. MCYT multimodal database http://atvs.ii.uam.es
65. Mehtre, B.: Fingerprint image analysis for automatic identification. Machine Vision and Applications **6**, 124–139 (1993)
66. Nandakumar, K., Jain, A.: Local correlation-based fingerprint matching. Proc. of Indian Conference on Computer Vision, Graphics and Image Processing pp. 503–508 (2004)

67. Nilsson, K.: Symmetry filters applied to fingerprints. Ph.D. thesis, Chalmers University of Technology, Sweden (2005)
68. Nilsson, K., Bigun, J.: Using linear symmetry features as a pre-processing step for fingerprint images. Proc. International Conference on Audio- and Video-Based Biometric Person Authentication, AVBPA **LNCS-2091**, 247–252 (2001)
69. NIST special databases and software from the image group – http://www.itl.nist.gov/iad/894.03/databases/defs/dbases.html
70. Ortega-Garcia, J., Fierrez-Aguilar, J., Simon, D., Gonzalez, J., Faundez-Zanuy, M., Espinosa, V., Satue, A., Hernaez, I., Igarza, J., Vivaracho, C., Escudero, D., Moro, Q.: MCYT baseline corpus: a bimodal biometric database. IEE Proceedings on Vision, Image and Signal Processing **150**(6), 395–401 (2003)
71. Putte, T., Keuning, J.: Biometrical fingerprint recognition: dont get your fingers burned. Proc. IFIP TC8/WG8.8, Fourth Working Conf. Smart Card Research and Adv. App. pp. 289–303 (2000)
72. Ratha, N., Connell, J., Bolle, R.: An analysis of minutiae matching strength. Proc. International Conference on Audio- and Video-Based Biometric Person Authentication, AVBPA **LNCS-2091**, 223–228 (2001)
73. Ratha, N., Connell, J., Bolle, R.: Enhancing security and privacy in biometrics-based authentication systems. IBM Systems Journal **40**(3), 614–634 (2001)
74. Ross, A., Jain, A.: Biometric sensor interoperability: A case study in fingerprints. Proc. Workshop on Biometric Authentication, BIOAW **LNCS-3087**, 134–145 (2004)
75. Ross, A., Jain, A., Reisman, J.: A hybrid fingerprint matcher. Pattern Recognition **36**(7), 1661–1673 (2003)
76. Ross, A., Reisman, K., Jain, A.: Fingerprint matching using feature space correlation. Proc. Workshop on Biometric Authentication, BIOAW **LNCS-2359**, 48–57 (2002)
77. Schiel, F., Steininger, S., Trk, U.: The SmartKom multimodal corpus at BAS. Proc. Intl. Conf. on Language Resources and Evaluation (2002)
78. Schuckers, S., Parthasaradhi, S., Derakshani, R., Hornak, L.: Comparison of classification methods for time-series detection of perspiration as a liveness test in fingerprint devices. Proc. International Conference on Biometric Authentication, ICBA, **LNCS-3072**, 256–263 (2004)
79. Shen, L., Kot, A., Koo, W.: Quality measures of fingerprint images. Proc. 3rd International Conference on Audio- and Video-Based Biometric Person Authentication, AVBPA **LNCS-2091**, 266–271 (2001)
80. Simon-Zorita, D., Ortega-Garcia, J., Fierrez-Aguilar, J., Gonzalez-Rodriguez, J.: Image quality and position variability assessment in minutiae-based fingerprint verification. IEE Proceedings - Vis. Image Signal Process. **150**(6), 402–408 (2003)
81. Snelick, R., Uludag, U., Mink, A., Indovina, M., Jain, A.: Large-scale evaluation of multimodal biometric authentication using state-of-the-art systems. IEEE Trans. on Pattern Analysis and Machine Intelligence **27**(3), 450–455 (2005)
82. Uludag, U., Jain, A.: Attacks on biometric systems: a case study in fingerprints. Proc. SPIE-EI 2004, Security, Seganography and Watermarking of Multimedia Contents VI pp. 622–633 (2004)
83. Watson, C., Garris, M., Tabassi, E., Wilson, C., McCabe, R., Janet, S.: User's Guide to Fingerprint Image Software 2 – NFIS2 (http://fingerprint.nist.gov/NFIS). NIST (2004)
84. Wilson, C., Hicklin, R., Korves, H., Ulery, B., Zoepfl, M., Bone, M., Grother, P., Micheals, R., Otto, S., Watson, C.: Fingerprint Vendor Techonology Evaluation 2003: Summary of results and analysis report. NISTIR 7123, http://fpvte.nist.gov (2004)

Chapter 5
Hand Recognition

Helin Dutağacı, Geoffroy Fouquier, Erdem Yörük, Bülent Sankur,
Laurence Likforman-Sulem, and Jérôme Darbon

Abstract In this chapter, an overview of hand recognition is given first. We then describe the BioSecure Benchmarking Framework for hand modality, which is composed of open-source software, publicly available databases, and experimental protocols. For hand image-based person recognition, two methodologies are presented, namely geometry-based and appearance-based methods. The geometry-based method, with its C++ based open-source software, is part of the BioSecure Benchmarking framework for hand modality. Both methods use publicly available databases and follow the benchmarking protocols. For both systems the vital preprocessing operations involving the registration of deformable shapes are described and details of feature extraction schemes are discussed. The identification and verification results are given under a set of factors, such as population, enrollment, image resolution, time lapse and hand type. It is shown that hand modality is a user-friendly, robust and very effective biometric method, at least for populations of several hundred.

5.1 Introduction

Recognizing persons based on hand data is an attractive biometric modality, due to its unobtrusiveness, low cost, easy interface, and low data storage requirements. Some of the presently deployed access control schemes based on hand geometry range from passport control in airports to international banks, from parents' access to child daycare centers to university student meal programs, from hospitals and prisons to nuclear power plants [43]. There are also several patents using either geometrical features or hand profile data, as in [37, 38, 39, 40, 41].

Hand modality is developing rapidly as a viable biometric modality. Hand biometry has a number of advantages in that it is user-friendly, hand-imaging devices are not intrusive, and template storage costs are small. Briefly, the hand modality in biometry possesses some distinct advantages such as:

D. Petrovska-Delacrétaz et al. (eds.), *Guide to Biometric Reference Systems and Performance Evaluation*, DOI 10.1007/978-1-84800-292-0_5,

1. Among biometric technologies, it has the highest acceptance rate of all devices tested, according to the Sandia report [49] . Users view it as a nonthreatening and user-friendly technique.
2. Hand geometry features are exceptionally robust and can function in harsh environments, in the outside premises, in extreme temperatures ranging from subzero to high degrees, the latter potentially encountered in foundries. It is not affected by soiled or dirty hands, a situation that could occur in construction sites.
3. Hand data can be used in multiple ways, such as binary hand silhouette, textured hand, hand geometries in 2D and 3D, finger characteristics and palm texture, allowing fusion strategies at the data level, at the feature level or at the decision level.
4. Beyond stand-alone applications, hand biometry can play an important complementary role in multimodal schemes [22].

This chapter is organized as follows. First, an overview of the state of the art in hand modality is given in Sect. 5.2. The evaluation framework including the BioSecure reference system for hand recognition is presented in Sect. 5.3. In this section benchmarking hand databases, experimental protocols, and results are also given. More experimental results with the Reference system are shown in Sect. 5.4. In Sect. 5.5, the appearance-based hand recognition algorithm is presented along with the performance results. Finally, conclusions are drawn in Sect. 5.6.

5.2 State of the Art in Hand Recognition

Previous studies have addressed different aspects of hand data. A brief survey of these techniques is given. It is organized relative to the various features that can be extracted from hand data.

5.2.1 Hand Geometry Features

The algorithms that rely purely on hand geometry use a set of measurements, such as lengths and perimeters of fingers, and radii of inscribed circles within the palm. Typical examples of these features include finger lengths, finger widths and heights at the knuckle positions, palm width, finger perimeters and/or areas, largest inscribed circle area or radius within the palm, and aspect ratio of the palm to fingers. An illustrative case is given in Fig. 5.1 a.

Jain et al. [46] use 16 predetermined axes along the fingers and extracted grayscale profiles along these axes. These profiles are then modeled as steep profiles contaminated by Gaussian noise. Using this profile model, 15 geometrical features are extracted and tested for verification. Sanchez-Reillo et al. [48] propose the use of geometric features, such as the widths of the four fingers measured at different latitudes, the lengths of the three fingers, and the palm. The set also includes the distances between three finger valleys and the angles between the lines connecting these points. Wong and Shi [52], in addition to finger widths, lengths and interfinger baselines, employ the fingertip regions. The fingertip curves are extracted from the top one-eighth portion of the index, middle and ring fingers and are then aligned, resampled and compared via the Euclidean distance. Bulatov et al. [4] describe a system where a set of 30 geometrical measures is used. The radii of inscribing circles of the fingers and the radius of the largest inscribing circle of the palm are also incorporated into the set.

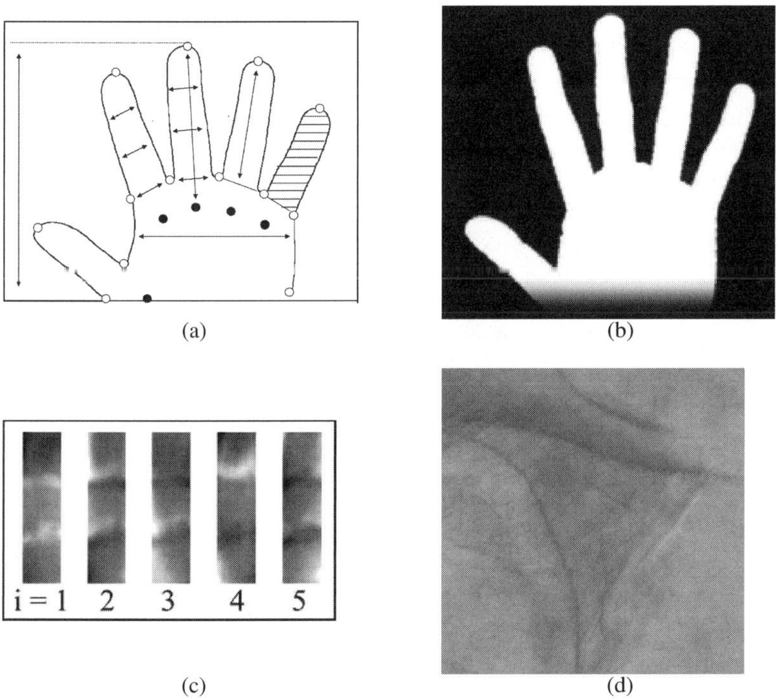

Fig. 5.1 Illustration of hand data representations: (**a**) hand geometric features; (**b**) hand silhouette; (**c**) little finger eigenfingers; (**d**) sample palmprint image

The geometrical features are not viewed as suitable for identification (one-to-many comparison) purposes, but instead are better suited to verification (one-to-one comparison) tasks [46]. Therefore, for more demanding applications one should extract more distinguishing features from the shape, appearance and/or texture of the hand images.

5.2.2 Hand Silhouette Features

In this case, the hand biometric data consist of the silhouette of the hand extending from fingers to the wrist line. Jain and Duta [23] were the first to propose deformable shape analysis, and they developed an algorithm where hand silhouettes are registered and compared in terms of the mean alignment error. More recent purely shape-based approaches use the Hausdorff measure [56], active shape modes [1, 10, 57], or resort to subspace techniques after the inside of the shape silhouette was filled in [55]. In an earlier work, Lay [30] has considered quad-tree decomposition of the hand surface. Figure 5.1 (b) shows a sample binary silhouette.

5.2.3 Finger Biometric Features

The fingers alone provide rich enough biometric evidence to enable person recognition. Oden et al. [35] represented fingers with implicit polynomials; Woodard and Flynn [53] considered the three-dimensional characteristics of the fingers using their curvature properties; while Ribaric and Fratric [44, 45] proposed an eigenfilter approach in terms of Karhunen-Loève transform (cf. Fig. 5.1 c). Since finger geometry alone was not sufficient, hand geometry features and palm features had to be considered, respectively, in [35, 42] and [44, 45]. Chang et al. [5] considered a multimodal scheme of 3D fingers and 3D face images jointly. Recently, Malassiotis et al. [34] considered 3D finger geometry to surmount some of the handicaps of the luminance image of hands.

5.2.4 Palmprint Biometric Features

Palmprints have recently attracted significant interest as evidenced by the profusion of papers [19, 24, 25, 28, 31, 32, 33, 50, 59, 60, 61, 62]. A challenging problem with the palmprint is the extraction of features such as line structures from the palmprint image. In fact, some of the proposed algorithms [13, 59, 61] have used ink markings for obtaining enhanced palmprint images.

Zhang and Shu [61] have used the main creases (such as heart line or life line) to align hands, while other authors used the not necessarily connected lines of the palm area to match hands [7, 13].

Instead of explicitly detecting palm lines, some authors use edge maps directly. Wu et al. [54] used a fuzzy directional element energy feature, which provides line structural information about palmprints via encoding the directions and energies of the edges. Han et al. [19] applied Sobel and morphological operators to the central part of the palm image and used the mean values of the grid cells as features. Similarly, Kumar et al. [29] used line detection operators consisting of four-orientation convolution masks. The output of these operators are merged in one single directional map. The standard deviation of pixels of overlapping blocks on the directional map are used as palmprint features.

Other researchers have used Gabor filters [27], wavelets [28], Fourier transform [31], and local texture energy [59]. Figure 5.1 (d) shows a typical palmprint image.

5.2.5 Palmprint and Hand Geometry Features

There are authors that couple hand geometry and palmprint or the print of the entire hand. Yörük et al. [57, 58] used a holistic view of the hand image, such that in their subspace projection method the geometry of the hand silhouette is merged with the overall handprint.

Kumar et al. [26, 29] joined the palm feature vector with the hand geometrical feature vector. Similarly, Han [20] uses wavelet features of both palmprint and of the finger profiles.

In order to characterize the palm, Kumar et al. [29] used line detection operators consisting of convolution masks, each of which is tuned to one of the four orientations. The output of these operators are merged in one single directional map, and standard deviation of pixels of overlapping blocks on the directional map are used as the palmprint features. In order to represent the shape, they have used 18 geometrical measures such as widths and lengths of the fingers and the palm. The palmprint and geometrical representations are fused at feature level and at score level via the max rule.

In order to enable comparison of published results, the BioSecure Network of Excellence [3, 8, 9] has been promoting since 2004 the development of biometric reference systems. The hand reference system includes both the collection of hand databases, which are intended to be available publicly, and the development of open-source software for hand-based person recognition systems. The University of Boğaziçi[1], ENST[2] and Epita[3] joined their efforts to provide a reference system based on hand modality. One can envision different uses of this reference system:

1. Adaptation to new user groups: The reference recognition system can be re-trained on new hand image databases to adapt them to alternate user groups or to accommodate new enrollments to the existing database.
2. Development of new hand biometric tools: New hand biometric tools can be explored by inserting them in the existing framework (cf. Fig. 5.2). Thus, new algorithms for preprocessing, registration, normalization of hands, extraction of the salient points of contours, new texture and shape features, feature-level or decision-level fusion methods can be grafted and tested on the BioSecure reference framework.

---

[1] `www.busim.ee.boun.edu.tr`

[2] `www.tsi.enst.fr`

[3] `www.lrde.epita.fr`

3. System performance comparisons: The BioSecure reference system, with its open-source software, will constitute a testbed against which new systems can be compared. In this respect, we expect that the accessibility to the BioSecure reference system in general, and to the hand biometric category in particular, will encourage the competitive development of improved biometric systems.

5.3 The BioSecure Evaluation Framework for Hand Recognition

In this section, the BioSecure Benchmarking Framework for the hand modality is presented. Its main components are open-source software, databases, and protocols. The results obtained within this framework can be fully reproduced with some additional information, such as How-to documents and lists of trials to be done. All the relevant material, with pointers to the software and databases, can be found on the companion URL site [2]. The BioSecure Hand Reference System v1.0, which uses geometry-based features, is detailed in the following section.

5.3.1 The BioSecure Hand Reference System v1.0

The approach uses the geometry of fingers for recognition purposes. We briefly present the system before describing each of its components in detail. The overall process is described in Fig. 5.2. First, the hand shape is extracted before segmenting each finger. Given a grayscale image, the image is binarized. Since the presence of rings may result in disconnected fingers, a robust approach based on generalized connectivity is used [47] to remove ring cuts. Then the boundary points of the whole hand are considered. We search for finger valley points using the boundary points. These valley points allow us to segment fingers. For each finger we find its major axis and compute the histogram of the Euclidian distances of the boundary points to this axis. The five histograms are normalized and are thus equivalent to probability density functions. These five densities constitute the features of the hand boundary. Given a test hand and one of the enrolled hands, the symmetric Kullback-Leibler distance between the two probability densities is computed, separately for each finger, and the distances are summed yielding a global matching distance between the two hands.

The five main steps present in the reference system are described in greater detail bellow.

Step 1: Binarization and Hand Referential Hand major axis are first found, in degrees of hand orientation. Then, the hand direction is determined, and only two directions are considered: upward and downward depending on finger positions. The image is thresholded using the Otsu algorithm [36] to get the hand silhouette. The resulting image still includes artifacts such as spurious small connected areas

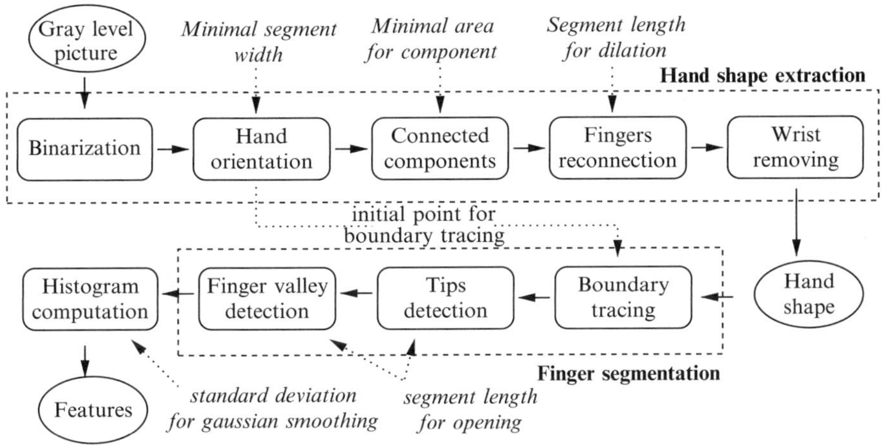

Fig. 5.2 Block diagram of the processing steps for extracting the geometry-based hand features. Boxes represent algorithmic steps, ellipses represent data and dashed lines represent parameter inputs. **Parameter's explanation**: *minimal segment width*–8% of image width, denotes the minimal width for a segment in picture to be recognized as a finger; *minimal area for component*—is given by $image\ height/8 \times image\ width/10$ and it is used to prune small components; *segment length for dilation*–3% of image width, and this dilation operator is used to reconnect fingers severed from a hand; **segment length for opening** is initialized at 200 and iteratively adapted until convergence with steps of 50. Standard deviation for Gaussian smoothing is set as 0.2, though the outcome is not very sensitive to this value. This figure, extracted from [16], is reprinted with permission from IEEE

due to noise, sleeves and rings to be removed in the following steps. Note that the Otsu algorithm corresponds to the K-means algorithm (with K = 2) when applied to the original grayscale image.

The hand major axis, which corresponds to the hand orientation, is computed through the eigenvectors of the inertia matrix. A line, orthogonal to hand major axis and crossing the fingers, presents alternate segments of background/object color. This behavior allows us to identify hand direction. We define the latitudinal axis as a line orthogonal to the major axis at the point where palm width is maximal. The latitudinal axis divides the hand in two parts (wrist or fingers) depending on hand direction, as shown in Fig. 5.3 c.

Step 2: Hand Shape Extraction Some fingers may be isolated and disconnected after hand thresholding because of the presence of rings. These fingers are detected by searching for large-enough connected components (minimal component area is deduced from image size). The biggest component is assumed to be the hand; the others correspond to potential disconnected fingers. We reconnect the selected components using a morphological dilation. The structural element is a linear segment parallel to the component major axis and in the direction of the palm. If this dilation does not reconnect this component with the palm, it is eliminated. The length of the structural element depends on image height (3%). Next, the wrist line is established:

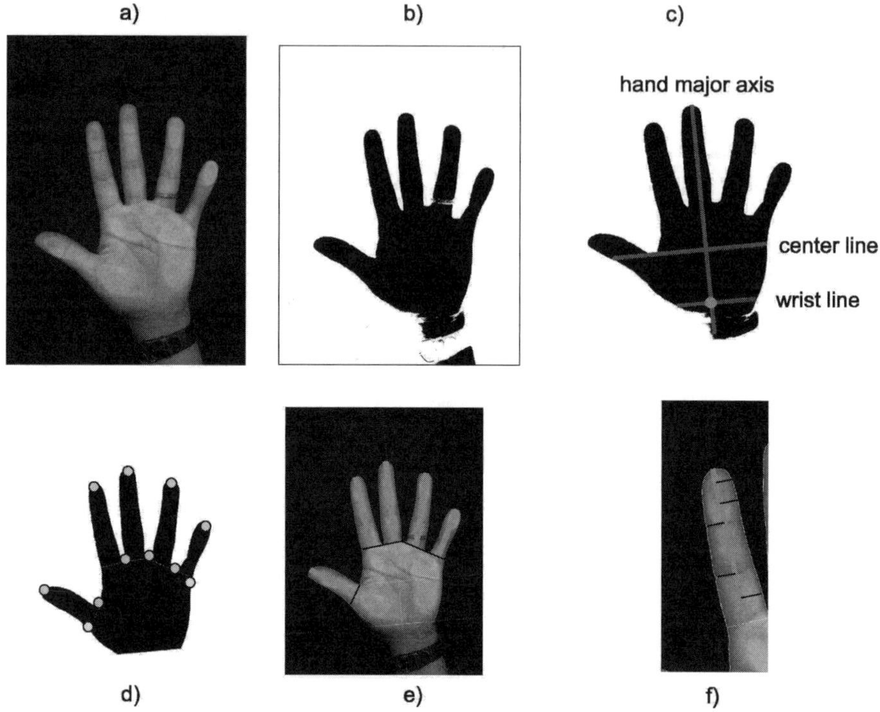

Fig. 5.3 Processing steps and feature extraction for the geometry-based reference system: (**a**) original image; (**b**) binarized hand with one finger disconnected; (**c**) hand component with reconnected finger, construction lines (hand major axis, centerline and wrist line) and contour starting point at the intersection of the wrist line and the hand major axis; (**d**) hand with removed wrist region, the five tip points, the four valley points extracted from the radial distance curve, and the two estimated valley points; (**e**) segmented fingers and finger major axes; and (**f**) distances from finger contour to finger axis are searched in order to get the distance distribution; (see insert for color reproduction of this figure)

starting from the latitudinal axis, whose associated segment is of length L (largest palm width), we consider the closest parallel line, whose segment length is less than $1/2L$, and we remove all points below it.

Step 3: Extraction of Fingers The contour of the hand shape is extracted through a boundary-tracing algorithm. The starting point is chosen at the intersection of the hand major axis and the wrist line. Then, the radial distance curve is computed with respect to this initial point (the radial distance is the Euclidian distance between each boundary point and the initial point). The positions of the finger tips are found from the radial distance curve by searching for their extrema. To avoid spurious local maxima, the radial distance curve is smoothed through a morphological opening. The structural element is a centered linear segment whose size is adaptively chosen so that only five extrema remain (one for each finger). The same analysis is done on the inverted radial distance curve to find the four finger valley points.

This approach allows us to find finger valley points that only live on local minima of the radial curve. The positions of the two remaining exterior valley points have still to be estimated (at the left of the thumb and at the right of the little finger). For each finger, the tips and at least one valley point is known. The Euclidian distance between those points is projected on the finger boundary to find the remaining point on the boundary. Once all finger valleys are found, we can easily segment fingers from hand and compute each finger's major axis.

Step 4: Feature Extraction For each finger, we project each boundary point on the finger major axis (cf. Fig. 5.3 f). The lengths of the projected segments are computed and we get a histogram of these lengths. The histogram is restricted to 100 quantified values and then normalized by the number of points of the finger, yielding a probability distribution of the lengths. Next, we smooth this distribution with a Gaussian kernel (standard deviation 0.2, selected into a range of tested values). The feature set consists of 5×100 features, including the five distributions.

Step 5: Hand Matching The hand classification relies on a global distance resulting from the comparison of the five finger distributions. The symmetric Kullback-Leibler distance is used to compare the histogram distribution of two fingers (the tested one, and the enrollment one). First, five individual finger-to-finger distances are computed. The global distance result corresponds to the summation of the three lowest distance scores. In this sense, we consider the one-sided trimmed mean of finger distances. Finally, for identification and verification tasks, the minimal distance between the test hand and the enrolled hand(s) is declared as the owner of the test hand.

5.3.2 The Benchmarking Databases

The reference database is a collection of three databases. The hand images were also collected at different sites. The hand images from the BIOMET database were collected from 2001 to 2003 during the BIOMET project [18], the BU hands were collected at Boğaziçi University from 2003 to 2005, and the ENST hands were collected in 2005. Figure 5.4 shows sample images from the three different sources. The scanning devices used for each set were of different makes and brands, though they were all set to 150 dpi resolution. In addition, the ENST set possesses hand images recorded at two other resolutions, namely 400 dpi and 600 dpi. As we will point out in Sect. 5.5, actually much lower resolutions (e.g., 45 dpi or less) suffice for recognition purposes. A substantially higher recording resolution was adopted to meet eventual needs, for example to enable joint finger print and hand biometry. 642 subjects of the Boğaziçi set have both left- and right-hand images. Finally, left-hand images of the 74-subject Boğaziçi set were recaptured after an interval of six months to provide time-lapse data.

The hand images consist of the palm side of hands lying in a flat position. All hand images are captured with scanning devices. Very few constraints are imposed upon subjects, the only constraint being that the subjects have to keep their fingers apart, but otherwise they can place their hands in any orientation, in relaxed and strained modes, with less or higher pressure, as they wished. Furthermore, subjects could keep hand accessories, such as rings or watches, and were not forced to pull up their sleeves. No pegs were used to position the hands. Moreover, the database contains large and unusual posture angles. In fact, this was done on purpose to obtain challenging registrations schemes.

The hand images from the BIOMET, BU, and ENST databases are grouped into two sets: a development database, denoted as *Devdb*, and an evaluation set, denoted as *Evaldb*. The *Devdb* can be used for example for model building and has left and right hands in it. The performance of different algorithms could be tested on the evaluation, which is also called the test set. Details about the databases are summarized in Table 5.1. The BIOMET, ENST, and part of the BU hands are reserved for model-building purposes. For example, the Independent Component Analysis (ICA) model of the appearance-based system described in Sect. 5.5 is built from this set, and the ICA vectors are estimated using these model-building sets. Note that the databases used for model building (development) and the database used for evaluation have no subjects in common.

Table 5.1 Hand sets in the reference database. Sources are Boğaziçi University-BU, Ecole Nationale Supérieure des Télécommunications-ENST, and BIOMET

Usage	Content	#Subjects	#Images/subject	Time lapse	Source
Devdb	Left hands	276	3	Short	BIOMET, BU
Devdb	Right hands	272	3	Short	ENST, BU
Evaldb	Left & right hands	642	6	Short	BU
Evaldb	Left hands	74	5	Six months	BU

Since collection of such a large hand database is a very time consuming task, the number of images per subject has been limited to three. This enables two options: a) partition *A*, where one image is used for enrollment and two for testing, and b) partition *B*, where two images are used for enrollment and one for testing.

5.3.3 The Benchmarking Protocols

We defined the following protocols to evaluate the performance of the algorithms. Verification (one to one) and identification (one to many) tasks are also defined, permitting evaluation of new systems with regard to these two tasks. The verification results are presented with a Detection Error Tradeoff (DET) curve, including the Equal Error Rate (EER) point. For the identification task, the Identification Rate (IR)

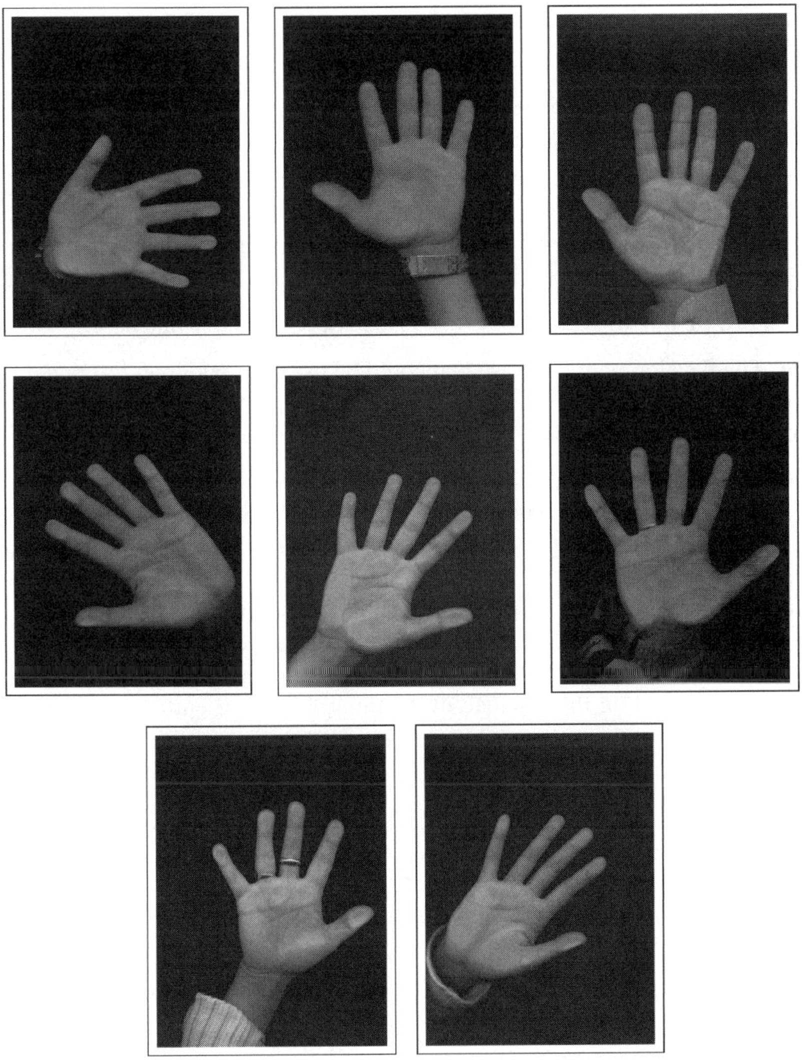

Fig. 5.4 Sample images of right and left hands from the BIOMET, BU and ENST databases (see insert for color reproduction of this figure)

is given, as the percentage of correctly identified test cases, as well as Cumulative Match Characteristics (CMC) curves. Confidence Intervals (CI) are also calculated, as described in the Annexe of Chap. 11, and with the programs being also given on the companion URL [2]. The benchmarking protocols for hand recognition are assembled in two groups, subdivided into development and evaluation parts.

Left-hand protocol Left hands from Boğaziçi and BIOMET database.

Devdb The development database that could be used for example, for model building for left hands, is composed of 276 individuals and three images per individual, leading to 828 images in total.

Evaldb The evaluation database for left hands uses only images from the Boğaziçi database, that are separated into enrollment and test images for each subject. For imposture tests, random impostures are considered (the other clients of the evaluation database).

Right-hand protocol Right hands from Boğaziçi and ENST database.

Devdb The development database that could be used for example, for model building for right hands, is composed of 272 individuals and three images per individual, leading to 816 images in total.

Evaldb The evaluation database for right hands uses only images from the Boğaziçi database, that are separated into enrollment and test images for each subject. For imposture tests, random impostures are considered (the other clients of the evaluation database).

These protocols clearly make the distinction between the development process from the evaluation (test) phase. Development images should be used for system development and tuning of different parameters. Once the system is developed, it should be evaluated on the separate evaluation part where enrollment and test trials are defined. In summary, four benchmarking experiments are defined. They are denoted as *Verif-Left*, *Verif-Right*, *Identif-Left*, and *Identif-Right* experiments in the rest of this chapter.

5.3.4 The Benchmarking Results

In this section, we give the benchmarking results obtained by the geometry-based BioSecure Hand Reference System v1.0. Table 5.2 and Fig. 5.5 present results for the two reference protocols.

Table 5.2 Verification and identification performances of the BioSecure Hand Reference System v1.0, with the reference protocols *Verif-Left*, *Verif-Right*, *Identif-Left*, and *Identif-Right*. Number of subjects is 642, resolution–150 dpi, one image used for enrollment, and Confidence Intervals [CI]

Hand type	Verification EER% CI[±]	Identification % reco
Left	6.31 [±0.58]	82.76
Right	8.87 [±0.68]	79.76

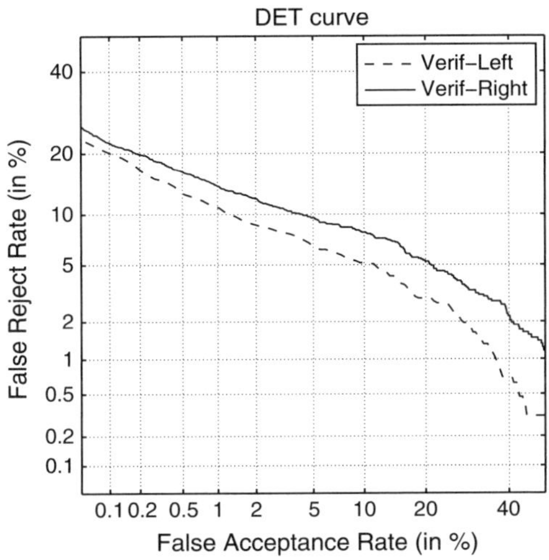

Fig. 5.5 DET curves for the verification reference protocols of Table 5.2, *Verif-Left* and *Identif-Right* experiments are illustrated with (*normal*), respectively (*bold line*)

5.4 More Experimental Results with the Reference System

We have extensively tested the performances of the reference hand-based person recognition system under more experimental conditions than those defined in the benchmarking framework (Sect. 5.3). These various conditions have been separated into the following components: population size, enrollment size, hand type, image resolution and time lapse between enrollment and test instances.

Identification and verification performances are functions of various parameters such as enrollment condition and population size. Each such factor is denoted with a code (*Ta*, *Po*, *En*, *Te*, *Re*, *Ha*) as summarized in Table 5.3. These two-character symbols denote, respectively, the factors of *Ta*sk type, *Po*pulation size, *En*rollment number, *T*ime *e*lapsed, *Re*solution of images, and *Ha*nd type.

- Task factor, *Ta*, switches between identification and verification. In verification, the system must accept or reject the claimed identity based on enrolled hands, while in identification one must recognize the person, obviously a more difficult task.
- Population factor *Po* defines the population size. In the following experiments, we ran the algorithms from a minimum population size of 100 to a maximum of 750.
- Enrollment, $En-K$ denotes enrollment with K hand images. The critical importance of enrollment size was proved in [56]. Though in principle the enrollment condition can be set to any K, it was limited to two in this protocol due to the tedious process of database building. Notice that when we state $En-k$, there are actually $(k+1)$ images, K images for enrollment and one for testing.

- Time lapse, *Te*, is a critical factor for commercial biometric systems. In all biometric systems, it is known that the shorter the time elapsed from enrollment, the more accurately one can identify or verify [22]. Protocol variable *Te* denotes the time, in months, elapsed between enrollment and test data acquisition. For example, $Te-6$, means that the test images were taken at least six months after the last enrolled training images, while $Te-0$ signifies that all images were taken on the same day.
- Hand type, Ha, denotes whether left hands, right hands, or both right and left hands are used. In [57], it was shown that cross referencing the hands (that is trying to test the right (left) hands on the training set of left (right) hands) was not a good idea, as there was some performance drop, though not necessarily dramatic.
- Resolution, *Re*, varies between 15 and 60 dpi. The studies in [56, 57] had already revealed that a much lower resolution level than 150 dpi registration resolution sufficed to extract geometrical and shape features.

Table 5.3 Hand identification and verification protocol description

Protocol	Description	**Value**
Ta	Task (identification, verification)	I, V
Re	Image resolution	15, 30, 45, 60, 90, 120, 150
Po	Population size (number of subjects)	200, 450, 600, 750
En	Enrolled hands/subject	1, 2
Te	Time lapse between enrollment and test	0, 6
Ha	Hand type (left, right, both)	l, r, l&r

The encoding of the factors describing the protocols is reflected by the alphanumeric character following the symbol. For example, the string $Ta-I, En-2$, $Po-642, Re-50, Ha-l, Te-0$ denotes an experiment with the goal of identification, with a population size of 642 subjects under the enrollment conditions of two sample images of their left hands in the database. Finally in this example, the resolution is 50 dpi and there is no time lapse between enrollment and test images.

For verification experiments protocol, $Ta-V$, an individual claims an identity. The system accepts this claim or rejects it. Client access is defined as the attempt of an individual claiming his correct identity. Impostor accesses is the attempt of an individual claiming other than his own identity. When one image per subject is enrolled, and two images are used for test, there are $2 \times Po$ possible client accesses and $2 \times Po \times (Po-1)$ possible impostor accesses. When enrolled hands become two and test hand per person is one, we have *Po* client accesses and $Po \times (Po-1)$ impostor accesses. These genuine-to-genuine and impostor-to-genuine comparisons lead to performance measures such as the DET curve and Equal Error Rate.

For identification experimental protocols, $Ta - I$, an individual presents his hand image without any claim of identity. The system always identifies the applicant, rightly or wrongly, as one of the enrolled subjects. For each access, the system tries to select the correct individual from the *Po* enrolled candidates.

The verification performance is reported via EER (Equal Error Rate) tables as well as in terms of Decision-Error Tradeoff (DET) curve. The Identification Performance (IP) is given as the percentage of correctly identified test cases, as well as in terms of Cumulative Match Characteristics (CMC) curves. In each case, the distance functions between the feature vector of the test hands and the feature vectors of the hands stored in the database are computed.

5.4.1 Influence of the Number of Enrollment Images for the Benchmarking Protocol

In this section, the influence of the number of enrollment images is studied within the benchmarking framework. The performances of the reference geometry-based system are tested on the left and right hand sets of the Reference database. For each user, there are three registered hands and two $En = 2$ or only one $En = 1$ of these hands are used as enrolled hands. The results are given here by averaging the rates of three-fold experiments. The EER and identification performance rate are given in Table 5.4. Corresponding DET curves are displayed in Fig. 5.6.

Table 5.4 Performances on the Reference database. Population is 642, resolution–150 dpi, enrollment is 1 or 2, 3-fold experiments

Hand type	En	Verification EER% CI[±]	Identification % reco
Left	1	6.91 [±0.35]	82.19
Left	2	4.69 [±0.41]	89.25
Right	1	7.66 [±0.37]	79.80
Right	2	5.01 [±0.43]	86.60

5.4.2 Performance with Respect to Population Size

We test the effect of increasing population size of subjects on performance. For each population size, eight sets are randomly built and the results averaged. The performance results are given in Table 5.5, and Figs. 5.7 and 5.8. The *En* parameter is set to two. We conclude that system performances are robust to the increase of population for the verification task.

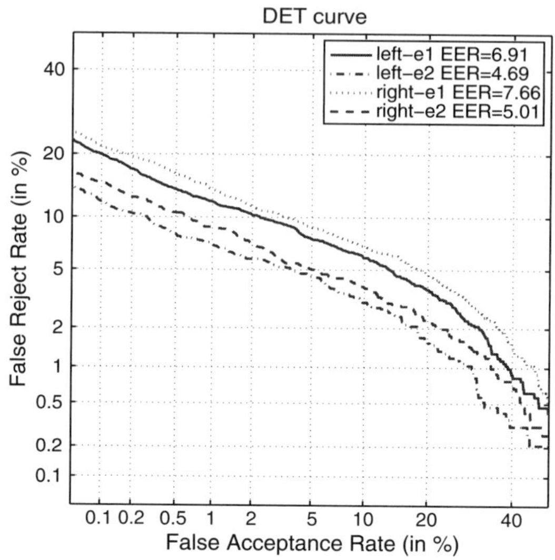

Fig. 5.6 DET curves of the experiments from Table 5.4

Table 5.5 Performances with respect to the population size. Resolution-150 dpi, $En = 2$, 3-fold experiments, left hands

Population	Verification EER% CI[±]	Identification % reco
200	4.28 [±0.26]	91.92
450	4.22 [±0.17]	89.94
600	4.34 [±0.15]	89.42
750	4.20 [±0.13]	88.92

5.4.3 Performance with Respect to Enrollment

We evaluate the effect of enrollment (number of enrolled hands) on system performance. For that purpose, we test the left-hand set of the Reference database. As three hands are registered per user, one of them is used for testing and the other two for training ($En = 2$), or two of them used for testing and one for training ($En = 1$). The verification and identification performance rates are given in Table 5.6. Corresponding DET curves are displayed in Fig. 5.9. Enrolling two hands rather than one hand always yields better performances in identification or verification. This yields higher system costs as the features corresponding to two hands rather than one are stored in memory, and comparisons are made twice.

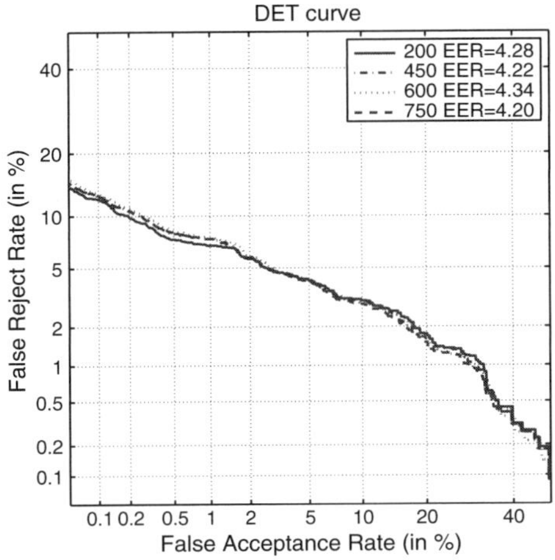

Fig. 5.7 DET curves for the Reference database. Performance with respect to population size. Resolution—150 dpi, $En = 2$, 3-fold experiments, left hands

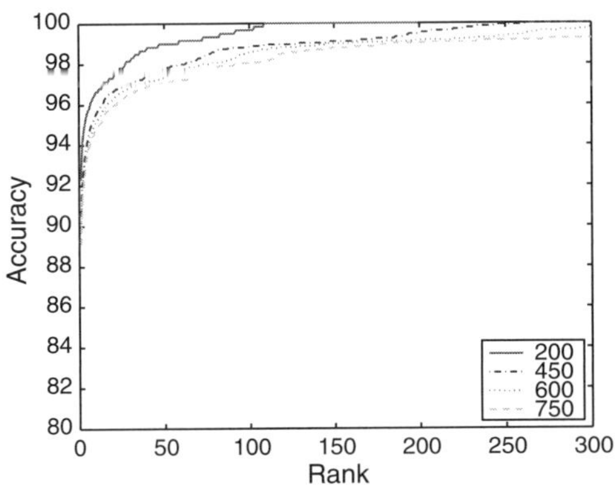

Fig. 5.8 CMC curve for the Reference database. Performances with respect to population size. Resolution—150 dpi, $En = 2$, 3-fold experiments, left hands

5.4.4 Performance with Respect to Hand Type

We compare here performances using only one type hand (left or right) or both hands using the left-and-right hand set. $En = 2$, i.e., two left or/and two right hands are used for enrollment, and the population parameter is $Po = 642$.

In the multihand scheme—that is when considering both left and right hands—feature fusion and decision fusion scheme are compared. The feature fusion scheme consists of using the five best fingers (the five finger/finger minimal distances)

Table 5.6 Verification and identification performances on the Reference database with respect to enrollment size. Population: 750, resolution: 150 dpi, 1-folds, left hands. Verification performance: Equal Error Rate (EER) and Confidence Interval (CI). Identification performance: recognition rate

Enrollment	Verification EER% CI[±]	Identification % reco
1	7.57 ± 0.82	75.83
2	5.20 ± 0.69	87.32

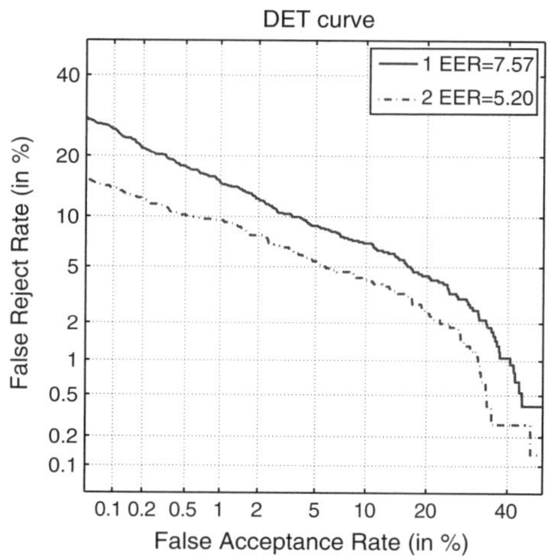

Fig. 5.9 DET curves for the Reference database. Performances with respect to enrollment size. Population: 750, resolution: 150 dpi, 1-folds, left hands

among the 10 fingers of the left and right hands. The decision fusion scheme consists of voting for the minimal distance given either by the right hand or the left hand. It corresponds to the min rule of score combination. Table 5.7 gives performances for the different hand types and fusion schemes. Corresponding DET curves are displayed in Fig. 5.10. One can observe that multiview matching yields better performances than single view, and feature fusion is more effective than decision fusion.

Table 5.7 Performances with respect to hand type (L: left hand, R: right hand, L&R: both hands)

Experiment	Verification EER% CI[±]	Identification % reco
Left hand	4.53 [±0.41]	88.84
Right hand	5.23 [±0.44]	83.85
L&R (feature fusion)	3.62 [±0.37]	92.47
L&R (decision fusion)	4.85 [±0.30]	92.16

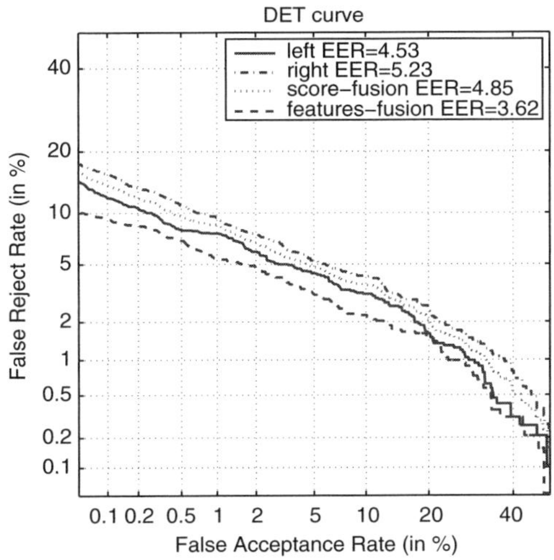

Fig. 5.10 DET curves for the Reference database. Performances with respect to hand type. Population—642, resolution—150 dpi

5.4.5 *Performance Versus Image Resolution*

We use the left hand set ($Po = 750$) with $En = 2$. The original images were downsampled to each lower resolution starting at 150 dpi with a step of 30 dpi. Performance is stable in the range of 90–150 dpi. Table 5.8 and Figs. 5.11 and 5.12 show the results obtained when varying image resolution. For the verification task, low-resolution images (as low as 30 dpi) are still efficient. The identification task benefits from higher resolutions, around 100 dpi.

Table 5.8 Performances with respect to image resolution. Population is 750, $En = 2$, 3-fold experiments, left hands

Resolution	Verification EER% CI[±]	Identification % reco
30 dpi	5.86 [±0.42]	77.81
45 dpi	5.13 [±0.39]	85.47
60 dpi	4.90 [±0.39]	87.23
90 dpi	4.28 [±0.36]	89.26
120 dpi	4.54 [±0.37]	89.26
150 dpi	4.19 [±0.36]	88.95

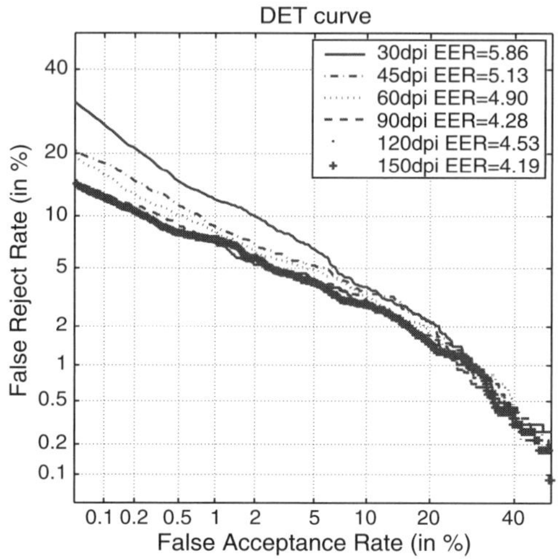

Fig. 5.11 DET curves for the Reference database. Performance with respect to image resolution. Population—750, $En = 2$, 3-fold experiments, left hands

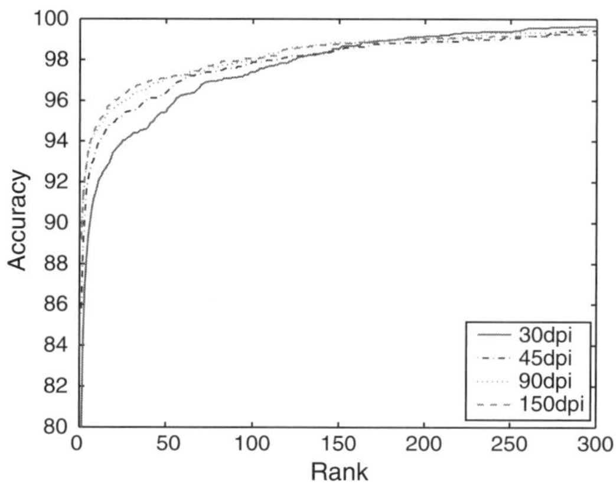

Fig. 5.12 CMC curves for different image resolutions. Population—750, $En = 2$, 3-fold experiments, left hands

5.4.6 Performances with Respect to Elapsed Time

We use the left hand set which includes images registered at different time lapse ($Po = 74, En = 2$). When parameter Te is set to 0, the third hand is tested against the two first (enrolled) hands within the same session. When $Te = 3 - 6$, the third hand of the first session is tested against the two hands captured within the second session. The performance results are shown in Table 5.9 and Fig. 5.13.

Table 5.9 Performances with respect to the time lapse. $Po = 74, En = 2$, resolution—150 dpi, left hands

Te	Verification EER% CI[±]	Identification % reco
Short	2.70 [±1.73]	98.64
3-6 months	20.44 [±4.30]	59.45

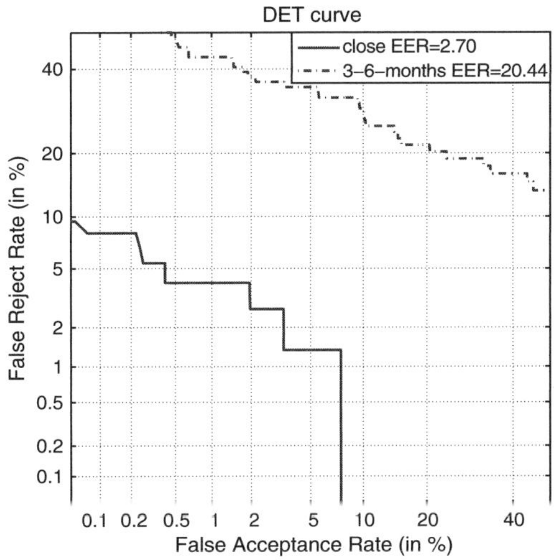

Fig. 5.13 DET curves for the Reference database. Performance with respect to image resolution. Population—750, resolution—150, $En = 2$, left hands

Performance drops considerably when varying the time lapse parameter. The geometry-based system is sensitive to the elapsed time between enrollment and testing.

5.5 Appearance-Based Hand Recognition System [BU]

In this section, we describe the appearance-based hand recognition system, which was developed at Boğaziçi University within the BioSecure Network of Excellence. The approaches of the Reference system described in both the previous section and the appearance-based system, have a somewhat complementary nature in that one of them is geometry-based while the other is holistic, or appearance-based. The geometric scheme bases its feature vectors on palm and finger geometry measurements, while the holistic approach views the scene containing the hand in its totality and extracts subspace-based features. The commonalities between the two algorithms are as follows:

1. They both have been developed for the left hands, and the mirror reflection of right hands needs to be taken.

2. The schemes assume a segmentation stage to delineate the hand from its background.
3. The hands can be in arbitrary postures and orientations as long as the fingers are not in contact with each other and the hand is lying flat. We emphasize again that there are no control pegs.
4. The hands can wear accessories such as rings and bracelets or the sleeves can partly occlude the palm. The recognition algorithms are capable of removing these artifacts.

The recognition system addresses the two related tasks of verification and identification. Verification means that the system must decide whether a test hand corresponds to the claimed identity within enrolled hands. The verification performance is documented in tabular form with the Equal Error Rate, as well as via DET curves. Identification means that the identity of an unknown test hand is to be recognized within the enrolled hand set. The identification performance is documented in tabular form as well as via CMC (Cumulative Match Count) curves.

In this appearance-based approach the whole scene, consisting of the global hand shape and its texture, is considered. In Sect. 5.5.1, more details about the registration part are given, while Sect. 5.5.2 deals with features extracted from appearance images.

5.5.1 Nonrigid Registration of Hands

The normalization of the non-rigid hand object is of paramount importance for any subsequent recognition task. The normalization process involves positioning of the hand and posturing of the fingers. In other words, the hand is translated and rotated to a reference frame and the fingers are forced to take a standard posture with preset orientations. The steps of the normalization algorithm, shown in the block diagram in Fig. 5.14 and illustrated in Fig. 5.15 are as follows.

Step 1: Hand Segmentation The hand segmentation is enacted via a two-class K-means clustering algorithm, followed by morphological operators to fill in holes and remove isolated foreground debris [56] (Fig. 5.15 b). The K-means clustering algorithm, run on both the grayscale pixels and the RGB color components gave very similar results; hence the simpler grayscale clustering was preferred. We find the largest connected components in the foreground, and then remove the debris, such as holes in the foreground and isolated blobs in the background by using respective size filters.

Step 2: Global Positioning Hand images are subjected to translation such that the centroid of the binary hand mass coincides with the coordinate origin, and then to a global rotation to align the orientation of the larger eigenvector of the inertia matrix to a fixed angle. Recall that that the inertia matrix is simply the 2×2 matrix of the second-order moments of the distances of binary hand pixel from their centroid.

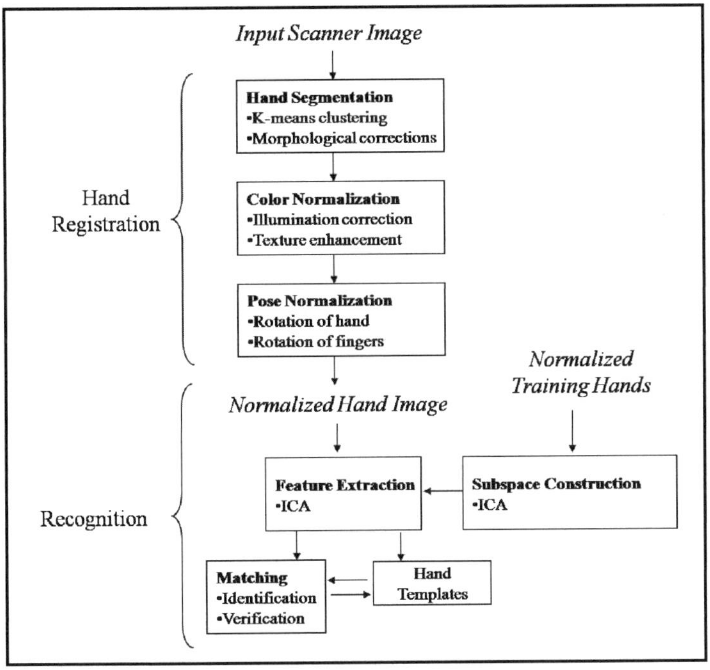

Fig. 5.14 Block diagram of the processing steps for appearance-based hand normalization

Step 3: Accessory Artifact Removal The presence of accessories may cause severance of the finger from the hand body or alternatively may create an isthmus-like distortion. The "ring removal" algorithm corrects for any distortions, like isthmuses in the finger due to rings (Fig. 5.15 f) [56]. The outcome is a binary image corresponding to the silhouette of the hand.

Step 4: Determination of Hand Extremities and Finger Pivots Hand extremities that correspond to finger tips and valleys are extracted by computing the radial distances with respect to a reference point around the wrist region. The resulting extrema are very stable, so that the definitions of the five fingertips and of the four valleys are not affected by segmentation artifacts on the contour (Fig. 5.15 e).

Step 5: Finger Pivots Each finger rotates around its pivot, which is the joint between proximal phalanx and the corresponding metacarpal bone, and they correspond to knuckle positions on the reverse side [4]. The pivot joints are somewhat below the line joining the inter-finger valleys. Therefore, the major axis of each finger is prolonged toward the palm by 20% in excess of the corresponding finger length as shown in Fig. 5.15 k. The ensemble of end points of the four fingers axes (index, middle, ring, little) establishes a line, called hand pivotal axis, which depends on the size and orientation of the hand. An alternative technique to estimate an actual pivot set by starting with a prototypical pivot set using a two-stage fine localization is described in [57].

Step 6: Texture Correction The hand texture, consisting of the wrinkles and crevices in the palm, as well as at and around the finger articulations, is corrected for nonuniform pressure and discolorations (see Fig. 5.15 a). If the hand texture information is to be included in recognition, then a number of preprocessing steps must be executed. First, we render the hand monochromatic by choosing the principal component color with the largest variance. Second, we compensate for the artifacts due to the nonuniform pressure of the hand applied on the platen of the imaging device. Such nonuniform pressure causes spurious grayscale variations due to withdrawal of the blood from capillaries, as often occurs on the thumb's metacarpal mount. Finally, the image is smoothed with a Gaussian kernel and subtracted from the original image. The tone corrected hand and its texture-enhanced version are shown in Fig. 5.15 c and d.

Step 7: Texture Blending The plastic deformation of the knuckle region of the palm ensuing from each finger's rotation around its metacarpal joint is corrected with texture interpolation. The texture blending is effected by a linear combination of the pixel value of the rotated finger and the palm pixel at the corresponding position as in Fig. 5.15 l, [57].

Step 8: Wrist Completion The hand contours in the wrist region can be irregular and noisy due to sleeve occlusion, to the different angles that the forearm can make with the platen, or due to the varying pressure exerted on the imaging device. In order to consistently create a smooth wrist contour for every hand image, the hand was guillotined at some latitude, that is, a straight line connected the two sides of the palm. It turned out that tapering off the wrist region with a cosinusoidal window starting to taper off from the half distance between the pivot line and the wrist line was the most effective approach in appearance-based recognition and verification tasks (Fig. 5.15 g and l).

5.5.2 Features from Appearance Images of Hands

A variety of features were investigated and their performance compared for different feature sizes, different populations in both recognition and identification scenarios. The considered features are listed below.

Principal Contour Components (active contours) [10] The set of 2D coordinates of the contour points are reorganized according to the eleven fiduciary reference points. These fiduciary reference points consist of the first and last contour elements, the five finger tips, and the four finger valleys. The contours are re-sampled in order to guarantee correspondence between contour elements of all hands, as shown in Fig. 5.16 a. Using the eigenvalue decomposition of the contour data, we obtain their principal components. Two illustrative cases are given in Fig. 5.16 b and c, where the average hand contour is perturbed with the distinct eigenvalues to show their impact on the hand shape synthesis. The features consist of the contour data projected upon

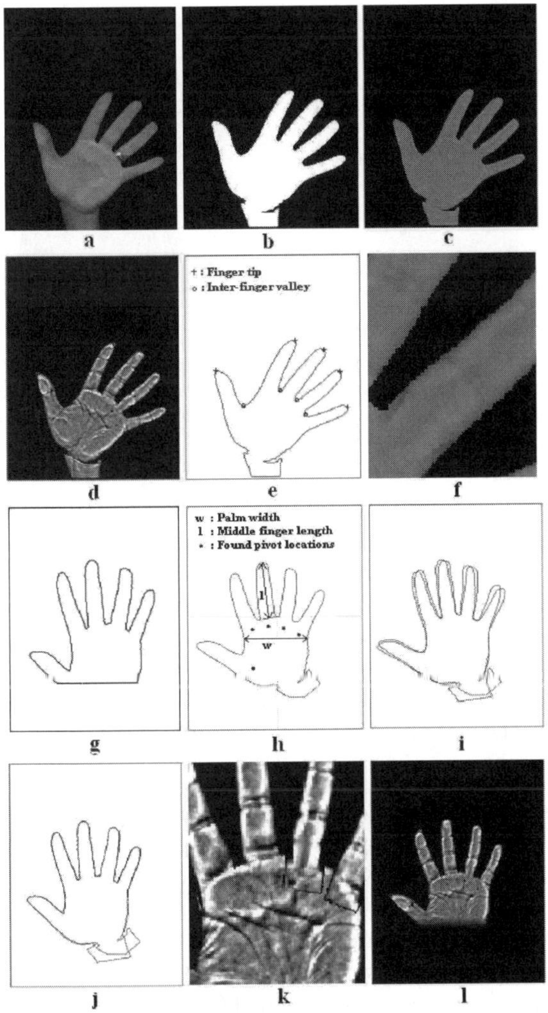

Fig. 5.15 Processing steps for hand normalization: (**a**) original hand image; (**b**) segmented hand image; (**c**) illumination corrected hand image (ring removed); (**d**) graylevel, texture enhanced hand image; (**e**) determination of finger tips and valleys; (**f**) finger after ring removal; (**g**) hand after wrist-completion; (**h**) initial global registration by translation and rotation: middle finger length and palm width for hand image scaling and derivation of the metacarpal pivots; (**i**) superposed contours taken from different sessions of the same individual with rigid hand registration only; (**j**) superposed contours taken from different sessions of the same individual after finger orientation normalization; (**k**) texture blending around pivot location for finger rotation; (**l**) final grayscale, normalized hand with cosine-attenuated wrist (see insert for color reproduction of this figure). Reprinted with permission from Elsevier Limited, source [58]

eigenvectors. Recently, an interesting approach for establishing salient points on the hand contours has been advanced by [1] using an incremental neural network and Hebbian learning.

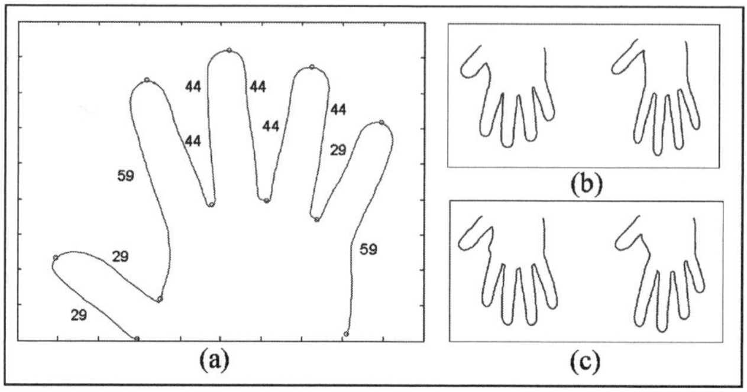

Fig. 5.16 Active hand contours: (**a**) the number of contour elements chosen between landmarks of the hand; (**b**) elongation of hands due to second mode perturbation; (**c**) relative lengths of the fingers due to third mode perturbation. Reprinted with permission from Elsevier Limited, source [58]

Principal Appearance Components [10] The hand texture information can also be expressed via the Principal Component Analysis (PCA). We have followed Coote's method [10] to decouple texture information from shape. To this effect each image is warped to make its landmarks match with those of some mean shape. Thin-plate splines are used for image warping as in Bookstein [6]. The resulting warped texture information is then expressed as a one-dimensional vector. Finally, PCA is applied to the texture vectors of the training hand examples to obtain modes of variation of the texture. The feature vector consists of the juxtaposition of the eigenvector projections of the contour and texture data.

Independent Components of Binary Hands Independent Component Analysis (ICA) is a technique for extracting statistically independent variables from a mixture of them, and it has found several applications in feature extraction and person authentication tasks [11, 14, 21]. We apply the ICA analysis tool on binary silhouette images to extract and summarize prototypical shape information. ICA assumes that each observed hand image is a mixture of a set of *N* unknown independent source signals. Notice also that, while in the PCA analysis we had considered only the contours of the hand, in the case of ICA, we consider the total scene image, which consists of its foreground and background. The ICA algorithm finds a linear transformation that minimizes the statistical dependence between the hypothesized independent sources.

There exist two possible architectures for ICA, called ICA1 and ICA2 [11], depending on whether one aims for independent basis images or for independent mixing coefficients. In a previous study [56], we found that the ICA2 architecture yielded superior performance. In the ICA2 architecture, the superposition coefficients are assumed to be independent, but not the basis images. The source and mixing coefficients are then obtained using the FastICA algorithm [21]. The synthesis of a hand in the data set from the superposition of hand "basis images" is illustrated in Fig. 5.17.

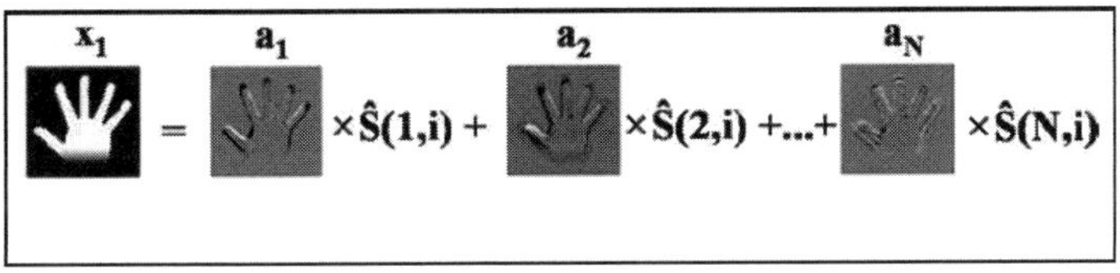

Fig. 5.17 Hand pattern synthesis using ICA2 basis functions. a_i, $i = 1,\ldots,N$ denote the N basis images, while the weighting coefficients $S(n,i), n = 1,\ldots,N$ for the hand i are statistically independent. Reprinted with permission from Elsevier Limited, source [58]

Independent Components of Texture and Silhouette We apply the ICA analysis tool as well on the appearance data, which is shape plus texture. To take into account the texture of images in the ICA formalism, we consider an image consisting of additive combination of the binary hand silhouette (foreground set to 1 and background to 0), and of the textured image, also normalized to $(0,1)$ interval. The image fed into the ICA2 algorithm is thus $I(i,j) = I_{shape}(i,j) + \alpha I_{texture}(i,j)$, where the tuning factor is $0 \leq \alpha \leq 1$. We have observed that increasing the texture-to-shape ratio α, from zero to 0.3, makes the performances significantly better, as expected, since discriminative texture also starts to play a role together with the pure shape information. However, for α beyond 0.5 we see a certain decrease in the overall identification rate. This decrease in performance can be attributed to the irrelevant skin texture other than palm prints, which appears more for larger values of α.

Axial Radial Transform of Contours and Appearances Angular Radial Transform (ART) is a complex transform defined on the unit disk. The basis functions are defined in polar coordinates as a product of two separable functions, an n'th order radial function and an m'th order angular function. With increasing order n, the basis functions vary more rapidly in the radial direction, whereas the order m expresses the variation in the angular direction. The angular radial transform of an image in polar coordinates is a set of ART coefficients $\{F_{nm}\}$ of order n and m, obtained by projecting the hand image upon the ART basis functions. After aligning the hand images and placing them in a fixed-size image plane, we take the center of the plane as the center of the unit disk. Furthermore, each pixel location is converted to polar coordinates and the radial coordinate is normalized with the image size to have a value between 0 and 1. We compute the ART coefficients both for the silhouette (binary) hands as well as for the shape plus texture appearance data, which includes palm and finger grayscale details.

5.5.3 Results with the Appearance-based System

Table 5.10 and Fig. 5.18 present results of the reference protocols obtained by the appearance-based system. In the following tables and figures, verification performance is given as an Equal Error Rate (ERR) and a Confidence Interval (CI). The results were obtained by training the ICA model using the model-building databases of size 276 and 272 subjects, for left and right hands, respectively. The dimension of the feature vectors were set to 275 for left hands and 271 for right hands, just one minus the number of training subjects. The 642 subjects in the evaluation database were not seen during the training phase. No parameters were adjusted during evaluation. These experiments are done with the benchmarking protocols described in Sect. 5.3.3.

Table 5.10 Performance of the appearance-based system on the Reference database with the Reference protocol. Population—642 and resolution—45 dpi

Hand type	*En*	Verification EER% CI[±]	Identification % reco
Left	1	0.85 [±0.22]	97.42
Left	2	0.47 [±0.23]	99.22
Right	1	1.80 [±0.32]	95.72
Right	2	0.93 [±0.33]	98.60

More experimental results with the shape and texture based system follow. The results are obtained using ICA Architecture II features, as this set of features yielded the best performance among the several other alternatives considered in Sect. 5.5.2 [57]. The ICA basis vectors are constructed using the model-building databases, which do not share any subjects with the evaluation set in common. This is the case when the ICA basis vectors are constructed on a given population and then these vectors are used on another platform where totally different subjects use the system. All the experiments in this work are conducted using this procedure.

Unless otherwise stated, the performance results are obtained under zero time lapse, $Te = 0$, with images at 45 dpi resolution $Re = 45$.

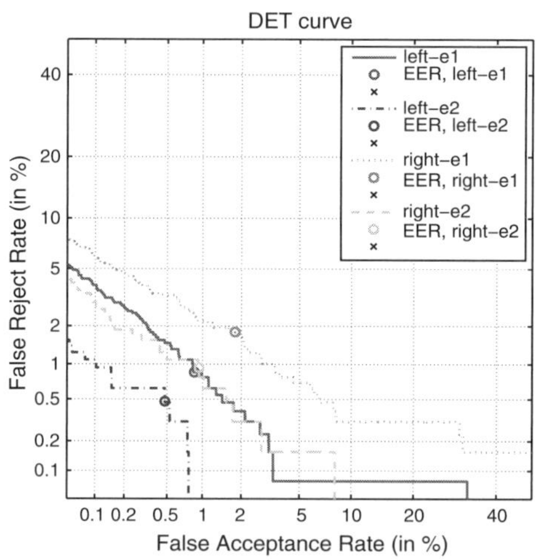

Fig. 5.18 DET curves for the appearance-based system on the Reference database with the Reference protocol. Population—642 and resolution—45 dpi

5.5.3.1 Performance with Respect to Population Size

We first report the identification and verification performance results as a function of population size in Table 5.11. The scores are the average of several experimental folds. Since the ICA-based feature extraction scheme needs a separate training database, we are left with a maximum of 642 subjects for evaluation. There exists a large number of ways of selecting subsets of hands from the total population of 642. We have randomly created several subsets (minimum five) from the database and, by altering the enrollment and test images, we performed three-fold experiments on each of the subsets. The identification and verification results are averaged over all the experiments performed with one population size. The full size of 642 can obviously support one unique "subset."

Table 5.11 Performance of the appearance-based system with respect to population size. Resolution—45 dpi, $En = 2$, left hands, three-fold experiments

Population	Verification EER% CI[±]	Identification % reco
100	0.51 [±0.44]	99.60
200	0.46 [±0.38]	99.80
450	0.48 [±0.27]	99.33
600	0.45 [±0.15]	99.30
642	0.47 [±0.23]	99.22

5.5.3.2 Performance with Respect to Enrollment

As expected, the enrollment size has a direct impact on the performance. Due to the tediousness of data collection, we have limited our experiments to enrollment sizes of 1 and 2, as in Table 5.12. We conjecture that the performance will still improve with higher enrollment numbers though the returns will be diminishing.

Table 5.12 Identification and verification performances of the appearance-based system relative to the enrollment size. Population—642, left hand, and ICA-II features

Enrollment	Verification EER% CI[±]	Identification % reco
1	0.85 [±0.22]	97.42
2 (hand-averaging)	0.59 [±0.27]	99.22
2 (two-representations)	0.47 [±0.23]	99.22

For double enrollment, there are two different enrollment approaches. In the hand-averaging scheme, we take the average of two normalized hand images for each person, and extract the ICA2 features from the average image. In the two-representations method we calculate the distances with respect to both hand samples, and then select the one with the maximum similarity (minimum distance). This simply corresponds to storing two feature vectors per subject.

The conclusion is that the poorer the performance of the feature type or the more the test case is difficult, the more multiple enrollment is useful.

5.5.3.3 Performance with Respect to Available Hand Type

We have obtained performance results with respect to the hand type, that is, left hands, right hands, both right and left hands. When both hands are available, there are three different types of fusion schemes: data level, feature level and score level. At the data level, the fusion consists of averaging the registered right and left hands in one image, and then one proceeds with feature extraction. At the feature level, the fusion consists in separately extracting features from left and right hands, and then merging the two vectors via some subspace method, such as principal component projection, or simply juxtaposing the two vectors in a double size feature vector. Finally, at the score level, we can use one of the fusion rules, such as choosing the maximum of the available decision scores. All the three fusion schemes are feasible for our appearance-based hand recognition system. In this work, we only report the results for score-level fusion with sum rule.

For this experiment, we have used the single enrollment case $En = 1$, since for the $En = 2$ case, the performance is too good (99% or more) to observe the impact of any fusion. Table 5.13 lists the EER verification and identification performances under single and double enrollments with single hands vis-à-vis single enrollment with double hands.

Table 5.13 Identification and verification performances of the appearance-based system as a function of hand type, with a population size of 642

Hand type	*En*	Verification EER% CI[±]	Identification % reco
Left	1	0.85 [±0.22]	97.42
Right	2	1.80 [±0.32]	95.72
Left	1	0.47 [±0.23]	99.22
Right	2	0.93 [±0.33]	98.60
Left and right[a]	1	0.47 [±0.23]	99.25

[a] score fusion

We have observed with some surprise that there exists some statistically significant difference between the right and left hands, especially since we had not conjectured any underlying physical reason. The reason of this discrepancy is that the right hands, being the working hand for the majority of people possess a more plump and "meaty" palm, which gets more easily deformed by pressure on the platen. An example is shown in Fig. 5.19. This suggests that hand images should be captured without any contact, for example, with hand positioned for palm facing up and with an overhead camera. We had also hypothesized that double enrollment with a single hand (two lefts) would be tantamount to a single enrollment with two hands (one right and one left). Indeed, the L+R fusion performance has come out to be equivalent to double left (L+L) enrollment. This implies that double enrollment of a single hand and single enrollment of both hands are interchangeable.

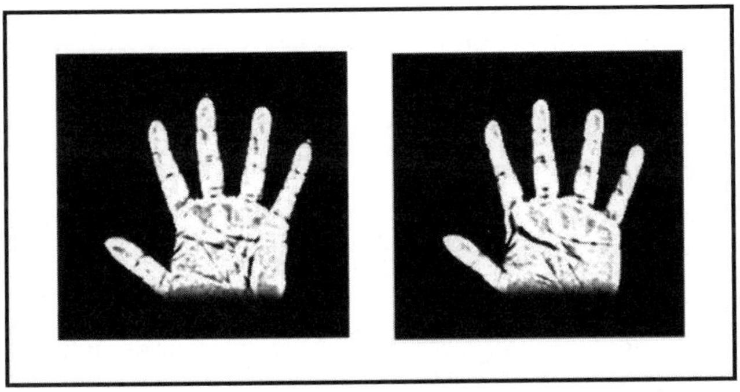

Fig. 5.19 The preprocessed and texture-enhanced images of the same subject. Note the sharp changes in palm due to folding and creasing of the palm texture

5.5.3.4 Performance with Respect to Image Resolution

The BioSecure hand database was collected with scanners operating at a resolution of 150 dpi, in principle to meet future eventualities. Actually, the reference systems can operate at much lower resolutions. In fact, all the shape-and-texture results presented so far, have been obtained with images at resolutions of 45 dpi. We have tested our results with 30 dpi and even 15 dpi where scores are shown in Table 5.14. With 30 dpi and 15 dpi, very few of the test images were not normalized, due to the fact that at very low resolutions fingers that are close to each other start to merge.

Table 5.14 Verification EER% with Confidence Intervals CI[±] and identification (I%) performance of the appearance-based system as a function of resolution. Left hands, $En = 2$

Resolution	# training subjects	# test subjects	EER% CI[±]	I%
15 dpi	275	637	2.20 [±0.42]	95.76
30 dpi	275	641	0.63 [±0.27]	98.75
45 dpi	276	642	0.47 [±0.23]	99.22

5.5.3.5 Performance with Respect to Time Lapse

In realistic environments, enrolled subjects can present themselves at arbitrary intervals. We wanted to test if the hand-biometry system can maintain its accuracy over larger lapses of time. From a subset of 74 subjects that we could track, we recorded hand images after an average interval of six months, with time lapses actually varying between 20 and 30 weeks.

We use the left hand set including images registered at different time lapse $Po = 74$. We set $En = 1$ and $En = 2$ when we compare the images acquired on the same day. When $Te = 3-6$, the new hands are compared against the first two or three gallery hands, which were acquired $3-6$ months before the test images. The performance results are reported in Table 5.15.

Table 5.15 Identification (I%) and verification (EER% with CI[±] performance of the appearance-based system with respect to time lapse. Resolution—45 dpi, left hands

Te	*En*	*Po*	# test images	# misclassified	I%	EER% CI[±]
short	1	74	148	2	98.65	0.68 [±0.62]
short	2	74	74	0	100.00	0.20 [±0.07]
3-6 months	2	74	148	5	96.62	2.02 [±1.06]
3-6 months	3	74	148	3	97.97	1.35 [±0.88]

5.5.3.6 Generalization Ability of ICA-based Scheme

In order to study the generalization ability of the ICA-based system, we conducted experiments with variable number of subjects present in the model-building set for the ICA training (denoted also as *Devdb*). We built different ICA-training sets with 50, 100, 200 and 300 subjects. The rest of the 400 different subjects present in the database was put in the evaluation *Evaldb* (also known as gallery) set). The results are given in Table 5.16. For these experiments for each ICA training set, five random combinations of the ICA model-training and evaluation data are used, and the identification performance is obtained by averaging over the five experiments. The results indicate that the ICA-based biometric system is completely generalizable.

Table 5.16 Identification performance (I%) with respect to the population size of the training set for building the ICA subspace (ICA-model building set), evaluated on a disjoint *Evaldb* set of 400 subjects

Population size of the ICA model-building set	Population size of the disjoint *Evaldb* set	Identification %	Number of misclassified images
50	400	96.35	15
100	400	98.45	6
200	400	98.95	4
300	400	99.28	3

In order to assess the generalization ability of the ICA-based system in a verification task, we divided the database as follows: a model-building set for the ICA training (denoted also as *Devdb*), and a disjoint evaluation *Evaldb* set, subdivided into impostors and genuine users. Table 5.17 gives the equal error rates. They are averaged over five-fold experiments where combinations of ICA model-training, genuine and impostor samples are selected randomly. The results confirm once more the generalization capability of the proposed appearance-based system.

Table 5.17 Verification performances with respect to the size of the training set for building the ICA subspace

Population size of the ICA model-building set	Population size of the *Evaldb* genuine set	Population size of the *Evaldb* impostor set	EER %
50	400	100	1.24
100	400	100	0.66

5.6 Conclusions

In this chapter, a benchmarking framework for hand modality developed within the BioSecure project has been presented. It includes a hand biometric database, reference system and protocols, which will, hopefully, serve as a testbed for hand biometric algorithms. The hand database is available with both raw original images as well as preprocessed and registered images. An appearance based system is also presented and compared within this framework.

Some results are also summarized in Table 5.18. The good results obtained highlight the efficiency of the hand modality for verification and identification tasks.

Table 5.18 Selected identification and verification results of the geometry-based Reference System and the shape and texture (appearance-based) system. *L* and *R* stands for left and right hands, *En* for enrollment, *Po* for population size, and *Re* for resolution in dpi

System	Hand Type	*En*	*Po*	*Re*	Identification %	EER%
Reference	L	2	642	150	89.25	4.69
	R	2	642	150	86.60	5.01
Appearance	L	1	642	45	97.42	0.85
	R	1	642	45	95.72	1.80
	L	2	642	45	99.22	0.47
	R	2	642	45	98.60	0.93

The very critical importance of a proper registration that takes into account the deformations not only in the shape but also in the texture of the hand is shown. Among several competitor features the Independent Component Analysis features are found to perform uniformly superior to all others considered. The attained performance of 99.22% correct identification, and of 0.47% EER verification for a population of 642 subjects is very encouraging and it indicates that hand-biometric devices can respond to the security requirements for populations of several hundred.

References

1. A. Angelopoulou, J.G. Rodriguez, and A. Psarrou, Learning 2D Hand Shapes Using the Topology Preservation Model GNG, European Conference on Computer Vision, ECCV06, Vienna, 2006.
2. BioSecure Reference Systems, http://share.int-evry.fr/svnview-eph/
3. BioSecure Web Page, http://www.biosecure.info/
4. Y. Bulatov, S. Jambawalikar, P. Kumar, and S. Sethia, Hand recognition using geometric classifiers, DIMACS Workshop on Computational Geometry, Rutgers University, Piscataway, NJ, November 14-15, 2002.
5. K.J. Chang, D.L. Woodard, P.J. Flynn, and K.W. Bowyer, Three dimensional face and finger biometrics, 12th European Conference on Signal Processing, EUSIPCO, Vienna, Austria, 2004.
6. F.L. Bookstein, Principal warps: thin-plate splines and the decomposition of deformations, IEEE Transactions on Pattern Analysis and Machine Intelligence 11 (1989) 567-585.
7. J. Chen, C. Zhang, and G. Rong, Palmprint recognition using creases, Int. Conf. on Image Processing, ICIP2001, 234-237.
8. G. Chollet, G. Aversano, B. Dorizzi, and D. Petrovska, The First BioSecure Residential Workshop, 4th International Symposium on Image and Signal Processing and Analysis, Zagreb (Croatia) September 2005.
9. G. Chollet, D. Petrovska, and B. Dorizzi, The BioSecure Network of Excellence, NIST Speaker Recognition Workshop, Montreal, Canada, June 2005.
10. T.F. Cootes, G.J. Edwards, and C.J. Taylor, Active appearance models, IEEE Transactions on Pattern Analysis and Machine Intelligence, 23 (2001) 681-685.
11. B.A. Draper, K. Baek, M.S. Bartlett, and J.R. Beveridge, Recognizing faces with PCA and ICA, Computer Vision and Image Understanding, 91 (2003), 115-137.
12. M.P. Dubuisson and A.K. Jain, "A modified Hausdorff distance for object matching," 12th International Conference on Pattern Recognition, 566-568, Jerusalem, 1994.
13. N. Duta, A.K. Jain, and K.V. Mardia, Matching of Palmprint, Pattern Recognition Letters, 23:4, 2002, pp. 477-485.
14. H.K. Ekenel and B. Sankur, Feature selection in the independent component subspace for face recognition, Pattern Recognition Letters, 25 (2004), 1377-1388.
15. G. Fouquier, J. Darbon, L. Likforman, B. Sankur, E. Yörük, and H. Dutagaci, Reference recognition systems for hand modality: source files, http://trac.lrde.epita.fr/hands
16. G. Fouquier, L. Likforman, J. Darbon, and B. Sankur, The Biosecure Geometry-based System for Hand Modality, In the proceedings of the 32nd IEEE International Conference on Acoustics, Speech, and Signal Processing (ICASSP'2007), vol I, 801-804, Honolulu, Hawaii, USA, 2007.
17. T. Funkhouser, P. Min, M. Kazhdan, J. Chen, A. Halderman, and D. Dobkin, A Search Engine for 3D Models, ACM Transactions on Graphics, vol. 22, No. 1, Jan. 2003.
18. S. Garcia-Salicetti, C. Beumier, G. Chollet, B. Dorizzi, J. Leroux les Jardins, J. Lunter, Y. Ni, and D. Petrovska-Delacrétaz, BIOMET: A Multimodal Person Authentication Database Including Face, Voice, Fingerprint, Hand and Signature Modalities, Lecture Notes in Computer Science, Volume 2688, Jan 2003, Pages 845-853.
19. C.C. Han, H.L. Cheng, C.L. Lin, and K.C. Fan, Personal authentication using palm print features, Pattern Recognition 36(2003), 371-381.

20. C.C. Han, A Hand-Based Personal Authentication Using a Coarse-to-Fine Strategy, Image and Vision Computing, vol. 22, pp. 909-918, 2004.
21. A. Hyvarinen and E. Oja, Independent component analysis: Algorithms and applications, Neural Networks 13 (2000), 411-430.
22. A.K. Jain, A. Ross, and S. Prabakar, An Introduction to Biometric Recognition, IEEE Trans. on Circuits and Systems for Video Technology, vol. 14, no. 1, 4-20, January 2004.
23. A.K. Jain and N. Duta, Deformable matching of hand shapes for verification, Proc. of Int. Conf. on Image Processing, October 1999.
24. D.G. Joshi, Y.V. Rao, S. Kar, V. Kumar, and R. Kumar, Computer-vision Based Approach to Personal Identification Using Finger Crease Pattern, Pattern Recognition, vol. 31, no. 1, pp. 15-22, 1998.
25. A. Wai-Kin Kong, D. Zhang, and W. Li, Palmprint feature extraction using 2-D Gabor filters. Pattern Recognition 36(10): 2339-2347, 2003.
26. A. Kumar, D. Wong, H. C. Shen, and A. Jain. Personal verification using Palmprint and Hand Geometry Biometric. AVBPA 2003: 668-678.
27. A. Kumar and H. C. Shen, Palmprint identification using Palm Codes, 3rd Int. Conference on mage and Graphics, ICIG20, Hong Kong, pp. 258-261.
28. A. Kumar and D. Zhang, Personal Authentication Using Multiple Palmprint Representation, Pattern Recognition, vol. 38, pp. 1695-1704, 2005.
29. A. Kumar, D.C.M. Wong, H.C. Shen, and A.K. Jain, Personal Authentication Using Hand Images, Pattern Recognition Letters, (to appear), 2006.
30. Y. L. Lay, Hand shape recognition, Optics and Laser Technology, 32(1), 1-5, Feb. 2000.
31. W. Li, D. Zhang, and Z. Xu, Palmprint Identification by Fourier Transform, Int. J. Pattern Recognition and Artificial Intelligence, vol. 16, no. 4, pp. 417-432, 2002.
32. W. Li, D. Zhang, and Z. Xu, Image Alignment Based on Invariant Features for Palmprint Identification, Signal Processing: Image Communication, vol. 18, pp. 373-379, 2003.
33. G. Lu, D. Zhang, and K. Wang, Palmprint Recognition Using Eigenpalm Features, Pattern Recognition Letters, vol. 24, nos. 9-10, pp. 1463-1467, 2003.
34. S. Malassiotis, N. Aifanti, and M.G. Strintzis, Personal Authentication Using 3-D Finger Geometry, IEEE Transactions on Information Forensics and Security, vol. 1, no. 1, 12-21, 2006.
35. C. Öden, A. Erçil, and B. Büke, Combining implicit polynomials and geometric features for hand recognition , Pattern Recognition Letters, 24 (2003), 2145-2152.
36. N. Otsu. A threshold selection method from grey-level histograms, IEEE Trans. Syst., Man, Cybern., Vol. SMC-1, pp. 62-66, Jan 1979.
37. R.H. Ernst, Hand ID System, U.S. Patent No. 3576537, 1971.
38. I.H. Jacoby, A.J. Giordano, and W.H. Fioretti, Personal Identification Apparatus, U.S. Patent No. 3648240, 1972.
39. D. Sidlauskas, 3D Hand Profile Identification Apparatus, U.S. Patent No. 4736203, 1988.
40. M. Gunther, Device for Identifying Individual People by Utilizing the Geometry of their Hands, European Patent No. DE10113929, 2002.
41. C.C. Han, B.J. Jang, C.J. Shiu, K.H. Shiu, and G.S. Jou, Hand Features Verfication System of Creatures, European Patent No. TW476917, 2002.
42. G. Zheng, C. Wang, and T.E. Boult, Personal Identification by Cross Ratios of Finger Features, Int. Conference on Pattern Recognition, Workshop on Biometrics, Cambridge, MA, Aug. 2004.
43. R.L. Zunkel, Hand Geometry Based Verification, pp. 87-101, in Biometrics, Eds. A. Jain, R. Bolle, and S. Pankanti, Kluwer Academic Publishers, 1999.
44. S. Ribaric and I. Fratric, A Biometric Identification System Based on Eigenpalm and Eigenfinger Features, IEEE Transactions on Pattern Analysis and Machine Intelligence, vol. 27, no. 11, pp. 1698-1709, November, 2005.
45. S. Ribaric and I. Fratric, An Online Biometric Authentication System Based on Eigenfingers and Finger-Geometry, Proc. 13th European Signal Processing Conference, Antalya, Turkey, September 2005.

46. A.K. Jain, A. Ross, and S. Pakanti, A prototype hand geometry based verification system, Proc. of 2nd Int. Conference on Audio- and Video-Based Biometric Person Authentication, pp.: 166-171, March 1999.
47. P. Salembier, A. Oliveras, and L. Garrido. Anti-extensive connected operators for image and sequence processing. IEEE Transactions on Image Processing, 7(4), 555-570, April 1998.
48. R. Sanchez-Reillo, C. Sanchez-Avila, and A. Gonzales-Marcos, Biometric identification through hand geometry measurements, IEEE PAMI, Vol. 22, no. 10, October 2000, pp. 1168-1171.
49. J. Holmes, L. Wright, and R. Maxwell, "A performance evaluation of Biometric identification Devices" Sandia National Laboratories, U.S.A, 1991.
50. W. Shu and D. Zhang, Automated personal identification by palmprint, Optical Engineering, vol. 37, no. 8, pp. 2359-2362, 1998.
51. A.R. Weeks, Fundamentals of Electronic Image Processing, pp. 466-467, SPIE Press, 1996.
52. L. Wong and P. Shi, Peg-free Hand Geometry Recognition Using Hierarchical Geometry and Shape Matching, IAPR Workshop on Machine Vision Applications, Nara, Japan, 281-284, 2002.
53. D.L. Woodard and P.J. Flynn, Finger Surface as a Biometric Identifier, Computer Vision and Image Understanding, vol. 100, 357-384, 2005.
54. X. Wu, K. Wang, and D. Zhang, Fuzzy directional energy element based palmprint identification, Int. Conference on Pattern Recognition, ICPR02, pp. 95-98, Quebec City, Canada.
55. C. Xu and J.L. Prince, Snakes, IEEE Transactions on Image Processing, 7(3), pp. 359-369, March 1998.
56. E. Konukoğlu, E. Yoruk, J. Darbon, and B. Sankur, Shape-Based Hand Recognition, IEEE Trans. on Image Processing, 15(7), 1803-1815, 2006.
57. E. Yoruk, H. Dutagaci, and B. Sankur, Hand Biometrics, Image and Vision Computing, 24(5), 483-497, 2006. 860
58. E. Yoruk, H. Dutagaci, and B. Sankur, Hand-Based Biometry, SPIE Electronic Imaging Conference: Image and Video Communications and Processing, pp. 1106-1115, 6-20 January 2005, San Jose, USA.
59. J. You, W. Li, and D. Zhang, 2002. Hierarchical palmprint identification via multiple feature extraction, Pattern Recognition 35, 847-859, 2002.
60. J. You, W.K. Kong, D. Zhang, and K.H. Cheung On Hierarchical Palmprint Coding with Multiple Features for Personal Identification in Large Database, IEEE Trans. on Circuits and Systems for Video Technology, vol. 14, no. 1, 234-242, January 2004.
61. D. Zhang and W. Shu, Two novel characteristics in palmprint verification: datum point invariance and line feature matching. Pattern Recognition 32, 691-702, 1999.
62. D. Zhang, W. K. Kong, J. You, and M. Wong, Online palmprint identification, IEEE Transactions on Pattern Analysis and Machine Intelligence, 25(9), 1041-1050, 2003.

Chapter 6
Online Handwritten Signature Verification

Sonia Garcia-Salicetti, Nesma Houmani, Bao Ly-Van, Bernadette Dorizzi, Fernando Alonso-Fernandez, Julian Fierrez, Javier Ortega-Garcia, Claus Vielhauer, and Tobias Scheidat

Abstract In this chapter, we first provide an overview of the existing main approaches, databases, evaluation campaigns and the remaining challenges in online handwritten signature verification. We then propose a new benchmarking framework for online signature verification by introducing the concepts of "Reference Systems", "Reference Databases" and associated "Reference Protocols." Finally, we present the results of several approaches within the proposed evaluation framework. Among them are also present the best approaches within the first international Signature Verification Competition held in 2004 (SVC'2004), Dynamic Time Warping and Hidden Markov Models.

All these systems are evaluated first within the benchmarking framework and also with other relevant protocols. Experiments are also reported on two different databases (BIOMET and MCYT) showing the impact of time variability for online signature verification. The two reference systems presented in this chapter are also used and evaluated in the BMEC'2007 evaluation campaign, presented in Chap 11.

6.1 Introduction

Online signature verification is related to the emergence of automated verification of handwritten signatures that allows the introduction of the signature's dynamic information. Such dynamic information is captured by a digitizer, and generates "online" signatures, namely a sequence of sampled points conveying dynamic information during the signing process. Online signature verification thus differs from off-line signature verification by the nature of the raw signal that is captured: off-line signature verification processes the signature as an image, digitized by means of a scanner [25, 24, 8] while online signature is captured through an appropriate sensor sampling at regular time intervals the hand-drawn signal. Such sensors have evolved recently allowing to capture on each point not only pen position but also pen pressure and pen inclination in a three-dimensional space. Other pen-based

D. Petrovska-Delacrétaz et al. (eds.), *Guide to Biometric Reference Systems and Performance Evaluation*, DOI 10.1007/978-1-84800-292-0_6,

interfaces such as those on Personal Digital Assistants (PDAs) and Smartphones operate via a touch screen to allow only a handwritten signature as a time sequence of pen coordinates to be captured.

Actually, signature is the most socially and legally accepted means for person authentication and is therefore a modality confronted with high level attacks. Indeed, when a person wants to bypass a system, he/she will forge the signature of another person by trying to reproduce as close as possible the target signature. The online context is favorable to identity verification because in order to produce a forgery, an impostor has to reproduce more than the static image of the signature, namely a personal and well anchored "gesture" of signing—more difficult to imitate than the image of the signature.

On the other hand, even if a signature relies on a specific gesture, or a specific motor model [24], it results in a strongly variable signal from one instance to the next. Indeed, identity verification by an online signature still remains an enormous challenge for research and evaluation, but signature, because of its wide use, remains a potential field of promising applications [37, 31, 23, 32, 33].

Some of the main problems are related to signature intraclass (intrapersonal) variability and signature's time variability. It is well known that signing relies on a very fast, practiced and repeatable motion that makes signature vary even over a short term. Also, this motion may evolve over time, thus modifying the aspect of the signature significantly. Finally, a person may change this motion/gesture over time, thus generating another completely different signature.

On the other hand, there is also the problem related to the difficulty of assessing the resistance of systems to imposture. Indeed, skilled forgery performance is extremely difficult to compare across systems because the protocol of forgery acquisition varies from one database to another. Going deeper into this problem, it is hard to define what is a good forgery. Some works and related databases only exploit forgeries of the image of the signature while in an online context [12, 22, 16, 4]; few exploit forgeries of the personal gesture of signing, additionally to skilled forgeries of the image of the signature [5, 6, 36, 2]. Finally, some works only exploit random forgeries to evaluate the capacity of systems to discriminate forgeries from genuine signatures [18].

The first international Signature Verification Competition (SVC'2004) [36] was held in 2004, and only 15 academic partners participated to this evaluation, a number far behind the existing approaches in the extensive literature on the field. Although this evaluation allowed for the first time to compare standard approaches in the literature, as Dynamic Time Warping (DTW) and Hidden Markov Models (HMMs), it was carried out on a small database (60 people); with the particularity of containing a mixture of Western and Asian signatures. Indeed, on one hand, this had never been the case in published research works and therefore the participants to SVC'2004 had never been confronted before to this type of signatures. On the other hand, it is still unclear whether a given cultural type of signature may be better suited for a given approach compared to another and thus one may wonder: were all the systems in equal conditions in this evaluation? All these factors still make difficult for the scientific community to assess algorithmic performance and to compare the existing systems of the extensive literature about online signature verification.

This chapter has different aims. First, it aims to make a portrait of research and evaluation in the field nowadays (existing main approaches, databases, evaluation campaigns, and remaining challenges). Second, it aims to introduce the new benchmarking framework for online signature for the scientific community in order to allow future comparison of their systems with standard or reference approaches. Finally, it aims to perform a comparative evaluation (within the proposed benchmarking framework) of the best approaches according to SVC'2004 results, Dynamic Time Warping (DTW) and Hidden Markov Models (HMMs), relatively to other standard approaches in the literature, and that on several available databases with different protocols, some of which have never been considered in the framework of evaluation (with time variability).

The benchmarking experiments (defined on two publicly available databases) can be easily reproduced, following the How-to documents provided on the companion website [11]. In such a way they could serve as further comparison points for newly proposed research systems. As highlighted in Chap. 2, this comparison points are multiple, and are dependent of what we want to study and what we have at our disposal. The comparisons points that are illustrated in this book regarding the signature experiments are the following:

- One possible comparison when using such a benchmarking framework is to compare different systems on the same database and same protocols. In such a way, the advantages of the proposed systems could be pinpointed. If error analysis and/or fusion experiments are done furthermore, the complementarity of the proposed systems could be studied, allowing to a further design of new more powerful systems. In this chapter, five research signature verification systems are compared to the two reference (baseline) systems.
- One comparison point could be obtained by researchers if they run the same open-source software (with the same relevant parameters) on different databases. In such a way the performance of this software could be compared within the two databases. The results of such a comparison are reported in Chap. 11, where the two online signature reference systems are applied on a new database, that has the particularity of being recorded in degraded conditions.
- Comparing the same systems on different databases is an important point in order to test the scalability of the reported results (if the new database is of different size or nature), or the robustness of the tested systems to different experimental conditions (such as robustness to degraded data acquisition situations).

This chapter is organized as follows: first, in Sect. 6.2 we describe the state of the art in the field, including the existing main approaches and the remaining challenges. The existing databases and evaluation campaigns are described in Sects. 6.3 and 6.4, respectively. In Sect. 6.5, we describe the new benchmarking framework for online signature by introducing the concept of "Reference Systems", on "Reference Databases" and associated "Reference Protocols". In Sect. 6.6 several research algorithm are presented and evaluated within the benchmarking framework. The conclusions are given in Sect. 6.7.

6.2 State of the Art in Signature Verification

In order to perform signature verification, there are two possibilities (related to the classification step): one is to store different signatures of a given person in a database and in the verification phase to compare the test signature to these signatures, called "Reference Signatures" by means of a distance measure; in this case a dissimilarity measure is the outcome of the verification system, after combining by a given function the resulting distances. The other is to build a statistical model of the person's signature; in this case, the outcome of the verification system is a likelihood measure—how likely it is that a test signature belongs to the claimed client's model.

6.2.1 Existing Main Approaches

In this section, we have chosen to emphasize the relationship between the verification approach used (the nature of the classifier) and the type of features that are extracted to represent a signature. For this reason, we have structured the description of the research field in two subsections, the first concerning distance-based approaches and the second concerning model-based approaches. Issues related to fusion of the scores resulting from different classifiers (each fed by different features) are presented in both categories.

6.2.1.1 Distance-based Approaches

There are several types of distance-based approaches. First, as online signatures have variable length, a popular way of computing the distance between two signatures is Dynamic Time Warping [26]. This approach relies on the minimization of a global cost function consisting of local differences (local distances) between the two signatures that are compared. As the minimized function is global, this approach is tolerant to local variations in a signature, resulting in a so-called "elastic matching"—or elastic distance—that performs time alignment between the compared signatures.

Among distance-based approaches, an alternative is to extract global features and to compare two signatures therefore described by two vectors of the same length (the number of features) by a classical distance measure (Euclidean, Mahalanobis, etc.). Such approaches have shown rather poor results. In [13], it is shown on a large data set, the MCYT complete database, that a system based on a classical distance measure on dynamic global features performs weakly compared to an elastic distance matching character strings that result from a coarse feature extraction.

Initially, Dynamic Time Warping was used exclusively on time functions captured by the digitizer (no feature extraction was performed) and separately on each time function. Examples of such strategies are the works of Komiya et al. [18] and Hangai et al. [15].

In [18], the elastic distances between the test signature and the reference signatures are computed on three types of signals: coordinates, pressure and pen-inclination angles (azimuth and altitude), and the three resulting scores are fused by a weighted mean. On a private database of very small size (eight people) and using 10 reference signatures which is a large reference set compared to nowadays standards—as established by the first international Signature Verification Competition in 2004 (SVC'2004) [36]—of five reference signatures, an EER of 1.9% was claimed.

In [15], three elastic distances are computed on the raw time functions captured by the digitizer: one on the spherical coordinates associated to the two pen-inclination angles, one on the pressure time function and one on the coordinates time functions. Note that, in this work, the pen-inclination angles were claimed to be the most performing time functions when only one elastic distance measure is considered separately on a private database. The best results were obtained when a weighted sum was used to fuse the three elastic distances.

Other systems based on Dynamic Time Warping (DTW) performing time alignment at another level of description than the point level, were also proposed. On one hand, in [35], the fusion of three elastic distance measures each resulting from matching two signatures at a given level of description, is performed. On the other hand, systems performing the alignment at the stroke level have also appeared [4], reducing the computational load of the matching process. Such systems are described in the following paragraph.

Wirotius et al. [35] fuse by a weighted mean, three complementary elastic distances resulting from matching two signatures at three levels of description: the temporal coordinates of the reference and test signatures, the trajectory lengths of the reference and test signatures, and the coordinates of the reference and test signatures. The data preparation phase consists in the selection of some representative points in the signatures corresponding to the local minimum of speed.

On the other hand, Chang et al. [4] proposed a stroke-based signature verification method based on Dynamic Time Warping and tested the method on Japanese signatures. It is interesting to note that in Asian signatures, stroke information may be indeed more representative than in Western signatures in which intra-stroke variation is more pronounced. The method consists of a modified Dynamic Time Warping (DTW) allowing stroke merging. To control this process, two rules were proposed: an appropriate penalty-distance to reduce stroke merging, and new constraints between strokes to prevent wrong merging. The temporal functions (x and y coordinates, pressure, direction and altitude), and inter-stroke information that is the vector from the center point of a stroke to its consequent stroke, were used for DTW matching. The total writing time was also used as a global feature for verification. Tested on a private database of 17 Japanese writers on skilled forgeries, an Equal Error Rate (EER) of 3.85% was obtained by the proposed method while the EER of the conventional DTW was 7.8%.

Main works in this category of distance-based approaches are those of Kholmatov et al. [3] and Jain et al. [16], both using Dynamic Time Warping.

Jain et al. [16] performed alignment on feature vectors combining different types of features. They present different systems based on this technique, according to which type of feature or which combination of features is used (spatial with a context bitmap, dynamic, etc.) and which protocol is used (global threshold or person-dependent threshold). The main point is that the minimized cost function depends as usual on local differences on the trajectory but also on a more global characteristic relying on the difference in the number of strokes of the test signature and the reference signature. Also, a resampling of the signature is done but only between some particular points, called "critical" (start and end points of a stroke and points of trajectory change) that are kept. The local features of position derivatives, path tangent angle and the relative speed (speed normalized by the average speed) are the best features with a global threshold.

Kholmatov's system [3] is the winning approach of the first online Signature Verification Competition (SVC) in 2004 [36]. Using position derivatives as two local features, it combines a Dynamic Time Warping approach with a score normalization based on client intra-class variability, computed on the eight signatures used for enrollment. On these eight enrollment signatures, three normalization factors are generated by computing pairwise DTW distances among the enrollment signatures: the maximum, the minimum and the average distances. A test signature's authenticity is established by first aligning it with each reference signature for the claimed user. The distances of the test signature to the nearest reference signature, farthest reference signature and the average distance to the eight reference signatures are considered; then these three distances are normalized by the corresponding three factors obtained from the reference set to form a three-dimensional feature vector. Performance reached around 2.8% EER on the SVC test dataset, as described in detail in Sect. 6.4.

6.2.1.2 Model-based Approaches

Model-based approaches appeared naturally in signature verification because Hidden Markov Models (HMMs) have long been used for handwriting recognition [25, 24, 8].

One of the main pioneering and more complete work in the literature is Dolfing's [5, 6]. It couples a continuous left-to-right HMM with a Gaussian mixture in each state with different kinds of features extracted at an intermediate level of description, namely portions of the signature defined by vertical velocity zeros. Also, the importance of each kind of feature (spatial, dynamic, and contextual) was studied in terms of discrimination by a Linear Discriminant Analysis (LDA) on the Philips database (described in Sect. 6.3). Dynamic and contextual features appeared to be much more discriminant compared to spatial features [5]. Using 15 training signatures (that is a large training set compared to nowadays standards of five training signatures) [36], with person-dependent thresholds, an EER of 1.9-2.9% was reached for different types of forgeries (of the image by amateur forgers, of the dynamics, and of the image by professional forgers).

At the same time, discrete HMMs were proposed by Kashi et al. [17] with a local feature extraction using only the path tangent angle and its derivative on a resampled version of the signature. It is a hybrid classifier that is finally used to take the decision in the verification process: another classifier using global features, based on a Mahalanobis distance with the hypothesis of uncorrelated features, is combined to HMM likelihood. The training set is of more limited size (six training signatures) in this work. The performance was evaluated on the Murray Hill database containing signatures of 59 subjects, resulting in an EER of 2.5%. A conclusion of this work is that fusing the scores of the two classifiers using different levels of description of the signature, gives better results than using only the HMM with the local feature extraction.

Discrete HMMs were also proposed for online signature by Rigoll et al. in [29], coupled to different types of features: the low-resolution image ("context bitmap") around each point of the trajectory, the pen pressure, the path tangent angle, its derivative, the velocity, the acceleration, some Fourier features, and some combinations of the previously mentioned features. A performance of 99% was obtained with this model with a given combination of spatial and dynamic features, unfortunately on a private database which is not really described as often in the field.

More recently, other continuous HMMs have been proposed for signature by Fierrez-Aguilar et al. [7] by using a pure dynamic encoding of the signature, exploiting the time functions captured by the digitizer (x and y coordinates, and pressure) plus the path tangent angle, path velocity magnitude, log curvature radius, total acceleration magnitude and their first-order time derivatives to end with 14 features at each point of the signature. In the verification stage, likelihood scores are further processed by the use of different score-normalization techniques in [10]. The best results, using a subset of the MCYT signature database, described in Sect. 6.3, resulted in 0.78% of EER for skilled forgeries (3.36% without score normalization).

Another HMM-based approach, performing fusion of two complementary information levels issued from the same continuous HMM with a multivariate Gaussian mixture in each state, was proposed in [34] by Ly-Van et al. A feature extraction combining dynamic and local spatial features was coupled to this model. The "segmentation information" score derived by analyzing the Viterbi path, that is the segmentation given by the HMM on the test signature by the target model, is fused to the HMM likelihood score, as described in detail in Sect. 6.5.2. This work showed for the first time in signature verification that combining such two sorts of information generated by the same HMM considerably improves the quality of the verification system (an average relative improvement of 26% compared to using only the HMM likelihood score), after an extensive experimental evaluation on four different databases (Philips [5], SVC'2004 development set [36], the freely available subset of MCYT [22], and BIOMET [12]).

Besides, a personalized two-stage normalization, at the feature and score levels, resulted in client and impostor scores distributions that are very close from one database to another. This stability of such distributions resulted in the fact that testing the system on the set composed of the mixture of the four test databases almost does not degrade the system's performance: a state-of-the-art performance of 4.50%

is obtained compared to the weighted average EER of 3.38% (the weighted sum of the EER obtained on each of the four test databases, where the weights are respectively the number of test signatures in each of the four test databases).

Another hybrid approach using a continuous HMM is that of Fierrez-Aguilar et al. [9], that uses additionally to the HMM a nonparametric statistical classifier using global features. The density of each global feature is estimated by means of Parzen Gaussian windows. A feature selection procedure is used by ranking the original 100 global features according to a scalar measure of interuser class separability based on the Mahalanobis distance between the average vector of global features computed on the training signatures of a given writer, and all the training signatures from all other writers. Optimal results are obtained for 40 features selected from the 100 available. Performance is evaluated on the complete MCYT Database [22] of 330 persons. Fusion by simple rules as maximum and sum of the HMM score, based on local features, and the score of the non parametric classifier, based on global features, leads to a relative improvement of 44% for skilled forgeries compared to the HMM alone (EER between 5% and 7% for five training signatures). It is worth noticing that the classifier based on density estimation of the global features outperforms the HMM when the number of training signatures is low (five signatures), while this tendency is inverted when using more signatures in the training phase. This indicates that model-based approaches are certainly powerful but at the price of having enough data at disposal in the training phase.

Another successful model-based approach is that of Gaussian Mixture Models (GMMs) [27]. A GMM is a degenerated version of an HMM with only one state. In this framework, another element appears: a normalization process of the score given by the client GMM by computing a log-likelihood ratio considering also the score given on the test signature by another GMM, the "world-model" or "Universal Background Model" (UBM), representing an "average" user, trained on a given pool of users no longer used for the evaluation experiments.

This approach, widely used in speaker verification, was first proposed in signature verification by Richiardi et al. [28] by building a GMM "world-model" and GMM client models independently, in other words, with no adaptation of the world model to generate the client model. In this work, a local feature extraction of dynamic features was used (coordinates, pressure, path tangent angle, velocity). As experiments were carried out on a very small subset of MCYT [22] of 50 users, the world-model was obtained by pooling together all enrollment data (five signatures per user) and five forgeries per user done by the same forger; thus, the world model was not trained on a separate devoted pool of users. Similar performance was observed in this case with an HMM of two states with 32-Gaussian components per state, and a 64-Gaussian components GMM. More recently, the same authors have evaluated different GMM-based systems [2] (see also Chap. 11), some based only on local features, some based on the fusion of the outputs of GMMs using global features and GMMs using local features—obtaining very good results on the BioSecure signature subcorpus DS3 acquired on a Personal Digital Assistant (PDA).

Furthermore, Martinez-Diaz et al. [21] proposed in signature verification the use of Universal Background Model Bayesian adaptation to generate the client model.

The parameters of the adaptation were studied on the complete MCYT database by using the 40 global features reported in [9]. Results reported show 2.06% of EER with five training signatures for random forgeries, and 10.49% of EER for skilled forgeries.

6.2.2 Current Issues and Challenges

Signatures are highly variable from one instance to another, particularly for some subjects, and highly variable in time. A remaining challenge in research is certainly the study of the influence of time variability on system performance, as well as the possibility of performing an update of the writer templates (references) in the case of distance-based approaches, or an adaptation of the writer model in the case of model-based approaches. Alternatively, the study of personalized feature selection would be of interest for the scientific community since it may help to cope with intraclass variability, usually important in signature (although the degree of such variability is writer-dependent); indeed, one may better characterize a writer by those features that show more stability for him/her.

From the angle of systems evaluation, the previous discussion shows that it is difficult to compare the existing approaches to the different systems in the literature and that few evaluations have been carried out in online signature verification. The first evaluation was SVC'2004 [36], on signatures captured on a digitizer, but on a database of very limited size (60 persons, only one session) mixing signatures of different cultural origins. More recently, the BioSecure Network of Excellence has carried out the first signature verification evaluation on signatures captured on a mobile platform [14], on a much larger database (713 persons, two sessions).

In this respect, the scientific community needs a clear and permanent evaluation framework, composed of publicly available databases, associated protocols and baseline "Reference" systems in order to be able to compare their systems to the state of the art. Section 6.5 introduces such a benchmarking framework.

6.3 Databases

There exist a lot of online handwritten signature databases, but not all of them are freely available. We will describe here some of the most well-known databases.

6.3.1 PHILIPS

The signatures in the Philips database [5, 6] were captured on a digitizer at a sampling rate of up to 200 Hz. At each sampled point, the digitizer captures the coordinates $(x(t), y(t))$, the axial pen pressure $p(t)$, and the "pen-tilt" of the pen in x and y directions, that is two angles resulting from the projection of the pen in each of the coordinate planes xOz and yOz.

This database contains data from 51 individuals (30 genuine signatures of each individual) and has the particularity of containing different kinds of forgeries. Three types of forgeries were acquired: "over the shoulder", "home improved", and "professional." The first kind of forgeries was captured by the forger after seeing the genuine signature being written, that is after learning the dynamic properties of the signature by observation of the signing process. The "home improved" forgeries are made in other conditions: the forger only imitates the static image of the genuine signature, and has the possibility of practicing the signature at home. Finally, the "professional" forgeries are produced by individuals who have professional expertise in handwriting analysis, and that use their experience in discriminating genuine from forged signatures to produce high- quality spatial forgeries.

This database contains 1,530 genuine signatures, 1,470 "over the shoulder" forgeries (30 per individual except two), 1,530 "home improved" forgeries (30 per individual), and 200 "professional" forgeries (10 per individual for 20 individuals).

6.3.2 BIOMET Signature Subcorpus

The signatures in the online signature subset of the BIOMET multimodal database [12] were acquired on the WACOM Intuos2 A6 digitizer with an ink pen, at a sampling rate of 100 Hz. At each sampled point of the signature, the digitizer captures the (x, y) coordinates, the pressure p and two angles (azimuth and altitude), encoding the position of the pen in space. The signatures were captured in two sessions with five months spacing between them. In the first session, five genuine signatures and six forgeries were captured per person. In the second session, ten genuine signatures and six forgeries were captured per person. The 12 forgeries of each person's signature were made by four different impostors (three per impostor in each session). Impostors try to imitate the image of the genuine signature. In Fig. 6.1, we see for one subject the genuine signatures acquired at Session 1 (Fig. 6.1 (a)) and Session 2 (Fig. 6.1 (b)), and the skilled forgeries acquired at each session (Fig. 6.1 (c)). As for certain persons in the database some genuine signatures or some forgeries are missing, there are 84 individuals with complete data. The online signature subset of BIOMET thus contains 2,201 signatures (84 writers $\times$ (15 genuine signatures + 12 imitations) – eight missing genuine signatures – 59 missing imitations).

Fig. 6.1 Signatures from the BIOMET database of one subject: (**a**) genuine signatures of Session 1, (**b**) genuine signatures of Session 2, and (**c**) skilled forgeries

6.3.3 SVC'2004 Development Set

SVC'2004 development set is the database that was used by the participants to tune their systems before their submission to the first international Signature Verification Competition in 2004 [36]. The test database on which the participant systems were ranked is not available.

This development set contains data from 40 people, both from Asian and Western origins. In the first session, each person contributed 10 genuine signatures. In the second session, which normally took place at least one week after the first one, each person came again to contribute with another 10 genuine signatures.

For privacy reasons, signers were advised not to use their real signatures in daily use. However, contributors were asked to try to keep the consistency of the image and the dynamics of their signature, and were recommended to practice thoroughly before the data collection started. For each person, 20 skilled forgeries were provided by at least four other people in the following way: using a software viewer, the forger could visualize the writing sequence of the signature to forge on the computer screen, therefore being able to forge the dynamics of the signature.

The signatures in this database were acquired on a digitizing tablet (WACOM Intuos tablet) at a sampling rate of 100 Hz. Each point of a signature is characterized by five features: x and y coordinates, pressure and pen orientation (azimuth and altitude). However, all points of the signature that had zero pressure were removed.

Therefore, the temporal distance between points is not regular. To overcome this problem, the time corresponding to the sampling of a point was also recorded and included in signature data. Also, at each point of signature, there is a field that denotes the contact between the pen and the digitizer. This field is set to 1 if there is contact and to 0 otherwise.

6.3.4 MCYT Signature Subcorpus

The number of existing large public databases oriented to performance evaluation of recognition systems in online signature is quite limited. In this context, the MCYT Spanish project, oriented to the acquisition of a bimodal database including fingerprints and signatures was completed by late 2003 with 330 subjects captured [22]. In this section, we give a brief description of the signature corpus of MCYT, still the largest publicly available online western signature database.

In order to acquire the dynamic signature sequences, a WACOM pen tablet, model Intuos A6 USB was employed. The pen tablet resolution is 2,540 lines per inch (100 lines/mm), and the precision is 0.25 mm. The maximum detection height is 10 mm (pen-up movements are also considered), and the capture area is 127 mm (width) 97 mm (height). This tablet provides the following discrete-time dynamic sequences: position x_n in x-axis, position y_n in y-axis, pressure p_n applied by the pen, azimuth angle γ_n of the pen with respect to the tablet, and altitude angle ϕ_n of the pen with respect to the tablet. The sampling frequency was set to 100 Hz. The capture area was further divided into 37.5 mm (width) 17.5 mm (height) blocks which are used as frames for acquisition. In Fig. 6.2, we see for each subject the two left signatures that are genuine, and the one on the right that is a skilled forgery. Plots below each signature correspond to the available information—namely: position trajectories, pressure, pen azimuth, and altitude angles.

The signature corpus comprises genuine and shape-based highly skilled forgeries with natural dynamics. In order to obtain the forgeries, each contributor is requested to imitate other signers by writing naturally, without artifacts such as breaks or slowdowns. The acquisition procedure is as follows. User n writes a set of five genuine signatures, and then five skilled forgeries of client $n-1$. This procedure is repeated four more times imitating previous users $n-2, n-3, n-4$ and $n-5$. Taking into account that the signer is concentrated in a different writing task between genuine signature sets, the variability between client signatures from different acquisition sets is expected to be higher than the variability of signatures within the same set. As a result, each signer contributes with 25 genuine signatures in five groups of five signatures each, and is forged 25 times by five different imitators. The total number of contributors in MCYT is 330. Therefore the total number of signatures present in the signature database is $330 \times 50 = 16,500$, half of them genuine signatures and the rest forgeries.

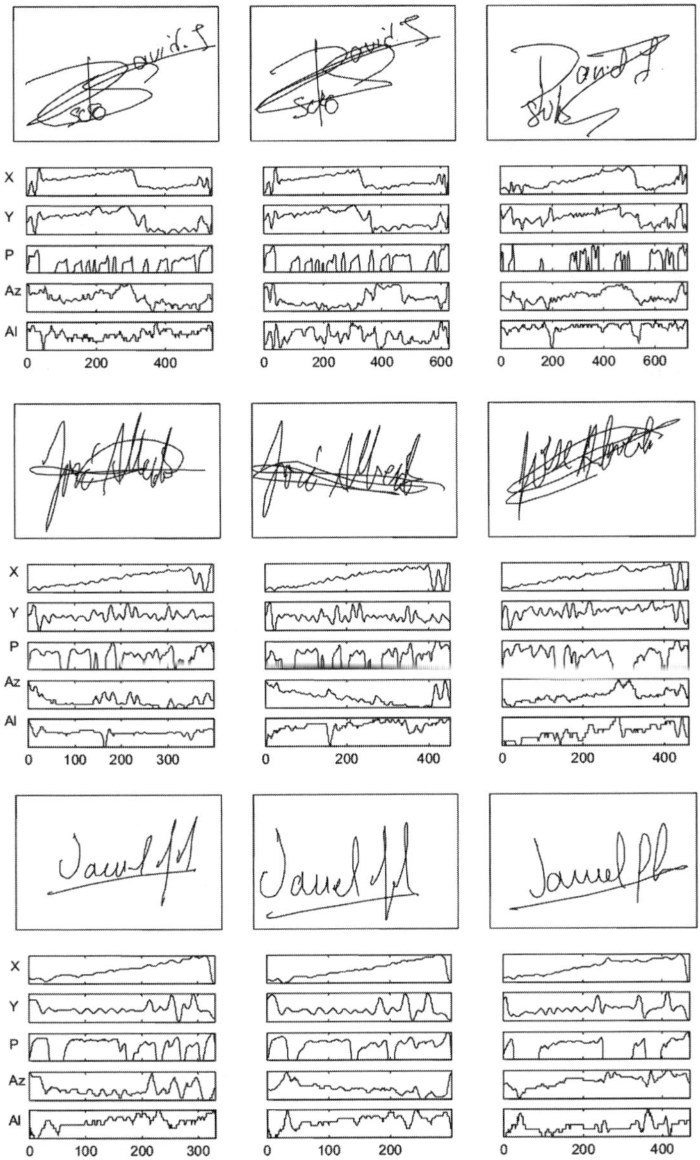

Fig. 6.2 Signatures from MCYT database corresponding to three different subjects. Reproduced with permission from Annales des Telecommunications, source [13]

6.3.5 BioSecure Signature Subcorpus DS2

In the framework of the BioSecure Network of Excellence [1], a very large signature subcorpus containing data from about 600 persons was acquired as part of the multimodal Data Set 2 (DS2). The scenario considered for the acquisition of DS2 signature dataset is a PC-based off-line supervised scenario [2].

The acquisition is carried out using a standard PC machine and the digitizing tablet WACOM Intuos3 A6. The pen tablet resolution is 5,080 lines per inch and the precision is 0.25 mm. The maximum detection height is 13 mm and the capture area is 270 mm (width)×216 mm (height). Signatures are captured on paper using an inking pen. At each sampled point of the signature, the digitizer captures at 100 Hz sampling rate the pen coordinates, pen pressure (1,024 pressure levels) and pen inclination angles (azimuth and altitude angles of the pen with respect to the tablet).

This database contains two sessions, acquired two weeks apart. Fifteen genuine signatures were acquired at each session as follows: the donor was asked to perform, alternatively, three times five genuine signatures and two times five skilled forgeries. For skilled forgeries, at each session, a donor is asked to imitate five times the signature of two other persons (for example client $n-1$ and $n-2$ for Session 1, and client $n-3$ and $n-4$ for Session 2).

The BioSecure Signature Subcorpus DS2 is not yet available but, acquired on seven sites in Europe, it will be the largest online signature multisession database acquired in a PC-based scenario.

6.3.6 BioSecure Signature Subcorpus DS3

The scenario considered in this case relies on a mobile device, under degraded conditions [2]. Data Set 3 (DS3) signature subcorpus contains the signatures of about 700 persons, acquired on the PDA HP iPAQ hx2,790, at the frequency of 100 Hz and a touch screen resolution of 1,280×960 pixels. Three time functions are captured from the PDA: x and y coordinates and the time elapsed between the acquisition of two successive points. The user signs while standing and has to keep the PDA in her/his hand.

In order to have time variability in the database, two sessions between November 2006 and May 2007 were acquired, each containing 15 genuine signatures. The donor was asked to perform, alternatively, three times five genuine signatures and two times five forgeries. For skilled forgeries, at each session, a donor is asked to imitate five times the signature of two other persons (for example client $n-1$ and $n-2$ for Session 1, and client $n-3$ and $n-4$ for Session 2). In order to imitate the dynamics of the signature, the forger visualized the writing sequence of the signature they had to forge on the PDA screen and could sign on the image of such signature in order to obtain a better quality forgery, both from the point of view of the dynamics and of the shape of the signature.

The BioSecure Signature Subcorpus DS3 is not yet available but, acquired on eight sites in Europe, it is the first online signature multisession database acquired in a mobile scenario (on a PDA).

6.4 Evaluation Campaigns

The first international competition on online handwritten signature verification (Signature Verification Competition–SVC [36]) was held in 2004. The disjoint development data set related to this evaluation was described in Sect. 6.3.3. The objective of SVC'2004 was to compare the performance of different signature verification systems systematically, based on common benchmarking databases and under a specific protocol. SVC'2004 consisted of two separate signature verification tasks using two different signature databases: in the first task, only pen coordinates were available; in the second task, in addition to coordinates, pressure and pen orientation were available. Data for the first task was obtained by suppressing pen orientation and pressure in the signatures used in the second task.

The database in each task contained signatures of 100 persons and, for each person there were 20 genuine signatures and 20 forgeries. The development dataset contained only 40 persons and was released to participants for developing and evaluating their systems before submission. No information regarding the test protocol was communicated at this stage to participants, except the number of enrollment signatures for each person, which was set to five.

The test dataset contained the signatures of the remaining 60 persons. For test purposes, the 20 genuine signatures available for each person were divided into two groups of 10 signatures, respectively devoted to enrollment and test. For each user, 10 trials were run based on 10 different random samplings of five genuine enrollment signatures out of the 10 devoted to enrollment. Although samplings were random, all the participant systems were submitted to the same samplings for comparison. After each enrollment trial, all systems were evaluated on the same 10 genuine test signatures and the 20 skilled forgeries available for each person. Each participant system had to give a normalized similarity score between 0 and 1 as an output for any test signature,

Overall, 15 systems were submitted to the first task, and 12 systems were submitted to the second task. For both tasks, the Dynamic Time Warping DTW-based system submitted by Kholmatov and Yanikoglu (team from Sabanci University of Turkey) [3] obtained the lowest average EER values when tested on skilled forgeries (EER = 2.84% in Task 1 and EER = 2.89% in Task 2). In second position, we distinguished the HMM-based systems with Equal Error Rates around 6% in Task 1 and 5% in Task 2, when tested on skilled forgeries. This DTW system was followed by the HMM approach submitted by Fierrez-Aguilar and Ortega-Garcia (team from Universidad Politecnica de Madrid) [7], which outperformed the winner in the case of random forgeries (with EER = 2.12% in Task 1 and EER = 1.70% in Task 2).

6.5 The BioSecure Benchmarking Framework for Signature Verification

The BioSecure Reference Evaluation Framework for online handwritten signature is composed of two open-source reference systems, the signature parts of the publicly available BIOMET and MCYT-100 databases, and benchmarking (reference)

experimental protocols. The reference experiments, to be used for further comparisons, can be easily reproduced following the How-to documents provided on the companion website [11]. In such a way they could serve as further comparison points for newly proposed research systems.

6.5.1 Design of the Open Source Reference Systems

For the signature modality, the authors could identify no existing evaluation platform and no open-source implementation prior to the activities carried out in the framework of BioSecure Network of Excellence [13, 14]. One of its aims was to put at disposal of the community a platform in source code composed of different algorithms that could be used as a baseline for comparison. Consequently, it was decided within the BioSecure consortium to design and implement such a platform for the biometric modality of online signatures. The main modules of this platform are shown in Fig. 6.3.

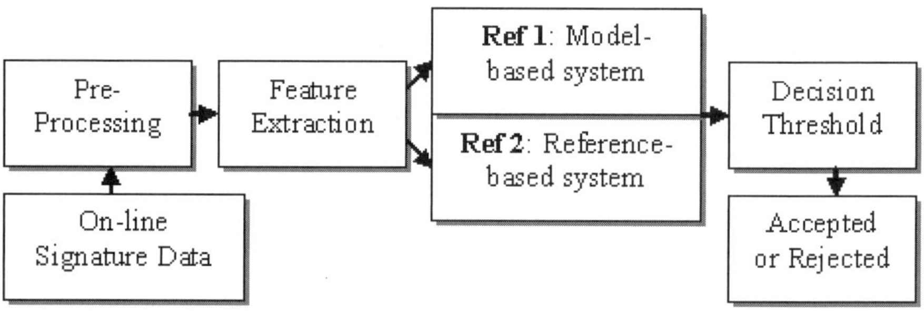

Fig. 6.3 Main modules of the open-source signature reference systems Ref1 and Ref2

The pre-processing module allows for future integration of functions like noise filtering or signal smoothing, however at this stage this part has been implemented as a transparent all-pass filter. With respect to the classification components, the platform considers two types of algorithms: those relying on a distance-based approach and those relying on a model-based approach. Out of the two algorithms integrated in the platform, one falls in the category of model-based methods, whereas the second is a distance-based approach.

In this section these two algorithms are described in further detail. The first is based on the fusion of two complementary information levels derived from a writer HMM. This system is labeled as Reference System 1(Ref1) and was developed by TELECOM SupParis (ex. INT) [34]. The second system, called Reference System 2

(Ref2), is based on the comparison of two character strings—one for the test signature and one for the reference signature—by an adapted Levenshtein distance [19], developed by University of Magdeburg.

6.5.2 Reference System 1 (Ref1-v1.0)

[1] Signatures are modeled by a continuous left-to-right HMM [26], by using in each state a continuous multivariate Gaussian mixture density. Twenty-five dynamic features are extracted at each point of the signature; such features are given in Table 6.1 and described in more detail in [34]. They are divided into two subcategories: gesture-related features and local shape-related features.

The topology of the signature HMM only authorizes transitions from each state to itself and to its immediate right-hand neighbors. The covariance matrix of each multivariate Gaussian in each state is also considered diagonal. The number of states in the HMM modeling the signatures of a given person is determined individually according to the total number T_{total} of all the sampled points available when summing all the genuine signatures that are used to train the corresponding HMM. It was considered necessary to have an average of at least 30 sampled points per Gaussian for a good re-estimation process. Then, the number of states N is computed as:

$$N = \left\lfloor \frac{T_{total}}{4 \times 30} \right\rfloor \tag{6.1}$$

where brackets denote the integer part.

In order to improve the quality of the modeling, it is necessary to normalize for each person each of the 25 features separately, in order to give an equivalent standard deviation to each of them. This guarantees that each parameter contributes with the same importance to the emission probability computation performed by each state on a given feature vector. This also permits a better training of the HMM, since each Gaussian marginal density is neither too flat nor too sharp. If it is too sharp, for example, it will not tolerate variations of a given parameter in genuine signatures or, in other words, the probability value will be quite different on different genuine signatures. For further information the interested reader is referred to [34].

The Baum-Welch algorithm described in [26] is used for parameter re-estimation. In the verification phase, the Viterbi algorithm permits the computation of an approximation of the log-likelihood of the input signature given the model, as well as the sequence of visited states (called "most likely path" or "Viterbi path"). On a particular test signature, a distance is computed between its log-likelihood and

---

[1] This section is reproduced with permission from Annales des Telecommunications, source [13].

Table 6.1 The 25 dynamic features of Ref1 system extracted from the online signature: (**a**) gesture-related features and (**b**) local shape-related features

	N^o	Feature name
	1-2	Normalized coordinates $(x(t) - x_g, y(t) - y_g)$ relatively to the gravity center (x_g, y_g) of the signature
	3	Speed in x
	4	Speed in y
	5	Absolute speed
	6	Ratio of the minimum over the maximum speed on a window of five points
a)	7	Acceleration in x
	8	Acceleration in y
	9	Absolute acceleration
	10	Tangential acceleration
	11	Pen pressure (raw data)
	12	Variation of pen pressure
	13-14	Pen-inclination measured by two angles
	15-16	Variation of the two pen-inclination angles
	17	Angle α between the absolute speed vector and the x axis
	18	Sine(α)
	19	Cosine(α)
	20	Variation of the α angle: φ
b)	21	Sine(φ)
	22	Cosine(φ)
	23	Curvature radius of the signature at the present point
	24	Length to width ratio on windows of size five
	25	Length to width ratio on windows of size seven

the average log-likelihood on the training database. This distance is then shifted to a similarity value—called "Likelihood score"—between 0 and 1, by the use of an exponential function [34].

Given a signature's most likely path, we consider an *N-components segmentation vector*, *N* being the number of states in the claimed identity's HMM. This vector has in the ith position the number of feature vectors that were associated to state i by the Viterbi path, as shown in Fig. 6.4. We then characterize each of the training signatures by a reference *segmentation vector*. In the verification phase (as shown in Fig. 6.5) for each test signature, the City Block Distance between its associated *segmentation vector* and all the reference segmentation vectors are computed, and such distances are averaged. This average distance is then shifted to a similarity measure between 0 and 1 (Viterbi score) by an exponential function [34]. Finally, on a given test signature, these two similarity measures based on the classical likelihood and on the segmentation of the test signature by the target model are fused by a simple arithmetic mean.

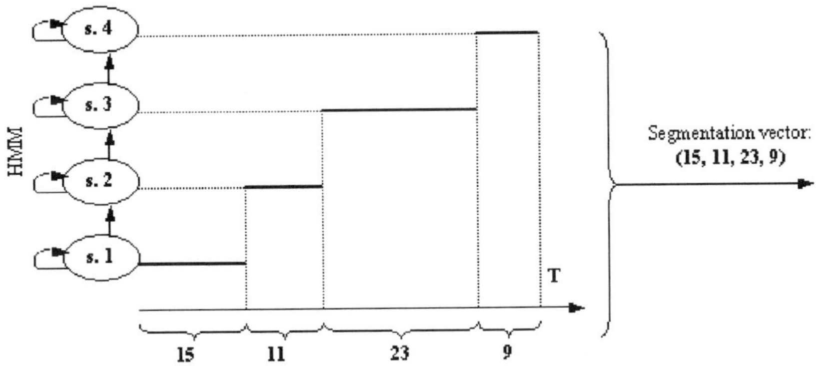

Fig. 6.4 Computation of the segmentation vector of Ref1 system

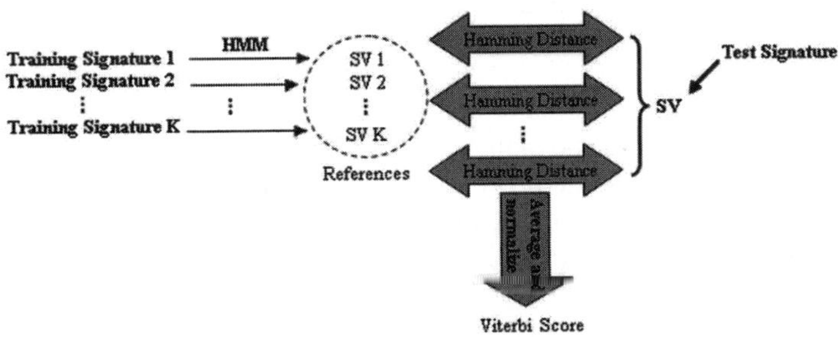

Fig. 6.5 Exploitation of the Viterbi Path information (SV stands for Segmentation Vector) of Ref1 system

6.5.3 Reference System 2 (Ref2 v1.0)

[2]The basis for this algorithm is a transformation of dynamic handwriting signals (position, pressure and velocity of the pen) into a character string, and the comparison of two character strings based on test and reference handwriting samples, according to the Levenshtein distance method [19]. This distance measure determines a value for the similarity of two character strings. To get one of these character strings, the online signature sample data must be transferred into a sequence of characters as described by Schimke et al. [30]: from the handwriting raw data (pen position and pressure), the pen movement can be interpolated and other signals can be determined, such as the velocity. The local extrema (minimum, maximum) of the function curves of the pen movement are used to transfer a signature into a string. The occurrence of such an extreme value is a so-called *event*. Another event type is a gap after each segment of the signature, where a segment is the signal from one pen-down to the subsequently following pen-up. A further type of event is a short segment, where it is not possible to determine extreme points because insufficient

[2] This section is reproduced with permission from Annales des Telecommunications, source [13].

data are available. These events can be subdivided into single points and segments from which the stroke direction can be determined. The pen movement signals are analyzed, then the feature events ε are extracted and arranged in temporal order of their occurrences in order to achieve a string-like representation of the signature. An overview of the described events ε is represented in Table 6.2.

Table 6.2 The possible event types present in the Reference System 2 (Ref2)

E-code	S-code	Description
$\varepsilon_1 \ldots \varepsilon_6$	$xXyYpP$	$x-\min, x-\max, y-\min, y-\max, p-\min, p-\max$
$\varepsilon_7 \ldots \varepsilon_{12}$	$v_xV_xv_yV_yvV$	$v_x-\min, v_x-\max, v_y-\min, v_y-\max, v-\min, v-\max$
$\varepsilon_{13} \ldots \varepsilon_{14}$	$g\ d$	gap, point
$\varepsilon_{15} \ldots \varepsilon_{22}$		short events; directions: $\uparrow$, $\nearrow$, $\rightarrow$, $\searrow$, $\downarrow$, $\swarrow$, $\leftarrow$, $\nwarrow$

At the transformation of the signature signals, the events are encoded with the characters of the column entitled 'S-Code' resulting in a string of events: positions are marked with x and y, pressure with p, velocities with v, v_x and v_y, gaps with g and points with d. Minimum values are encoded by lower case letters and maximum values by capital letters. One difficulty in the transformation is the simultaneous appearance of extreme values of the signals because then no temporal order can be determined. This problem of simultaneous events can be treated by the creation of a combined event, requiring the definition of scores for edit operations on those combination events. In this approach, an additional normalization of the distance is performed due to the possibility of different lengths of the two string sequences [30]. This is necessary because the lengths of the strings created using the pen signals can be different due to the fluctuations of the biometric input. Therefore, signals of the pen movement are represented by a sequence of characters. Starting out with the assumption that similar strokes have also similar string representations, biometric verification based on signatures can be carried out by using the Levenshtein distance.

The Levenshtein distance determines the similarity of two character strings through the transformation of one string into another one, using operations on the individual characters. For this transformation a sequence of operations (insert, delete, replace) is applied to every single character of the first string in order to convert it into the second string. The distance between the two strings is the smallest possible number of operations in the transformation. An advantage of this approach is the use of weights for each operation. The weights depend on the assessment of the individual operations. For example, it is possible to weight the deletion of a character higher than replacing it with another character. A weighting with respect to the individual characters is also possible. The formal description of the algorithm is given by the following recursion:

$$\left.\begin{array}{lll} D(i,j) & := \min[D(i-1,j) & + w_d, \\ & \quad D(i,j-1) & + w_i, \\ & \quad D(i-1,j-1) & + w_r] \\ D(i,0) & := D(i-1,0) & + w_d \\ D(0,j) & := D(0,j-1) & + w_i \\ D(0,0) & := 0 & \end{array}\right\} \forall i,j>0 \tag{6.2}$$

In this description, i and j are the lengths of strings S_1 and S_2 respectively. w_i, w_d and w_r are the weights of the operations insert, delete and replace. If characters $S_1[i] = S_2[j]$ the weight w_r is 0. Smaller distance D between any two strings S_1 and S_2 denotes greater similarity.

6.5.4 Benchmarking Databases and Protocols

Our aim is to propose protocols on selected publicly available databases, for comparison purposes relative to the two reference systems described in Sect. 6.5. We thus present in this section the protocols associated with three publicly available databases: the BIOMET signature database [12], and the two MCYT signature databases [22] (MCYT 100 and the complete MCYT-330) for test purposes.

6.5.4.1 Protocols on the BIOMET Database

On this database, we distinguish two protocols; the first one does not take into account the temporal variability of the signatures; the second exploits the variability of the signatures over time (five months spacing between the two sessions).

In order to reduce the influence of the selected five enrollment signatures, we have chosen to use a cross-validation technique to compute the generalization error of the system and its corresponding confidence level. We have considered 100 samplings (or trials) of the five enrollment signatures on the BIOMET database, as follows: for each writer, five reference signatures are randomly selected from the 10 genuine signatures available of Session 2 and only the genuine test set changes according to the protocol; in the first protocol (Protocol 1), test is performed on the remaining five genuine signatures of Session 2—which means that no time variability is present in data—as well as on the 12 skilled forgeries and the 83 random forgeries. In the second protocol (Protocol 2), test is performed on the five genuine signatures of Session 1—this way introducing time variability in data—as well as on the 12 skilled forgeries and the 83 random forgeries. We repeat this procedure 100 times for each writer.

6.5.4.2 Protocol on the MCYT-100 Data Subset

On MCYT-100 database, we consider in the same way 100 samplings of the five enrollment signatures out of the 25 available genuine signatures. For each sampling, systems were tested on the 20 remaining genuine signatures, the 25 skilled forgeries and the 99 random forgeries available for each person.

6.5.4.3 Protocol on the Complete MCYT Database (MCYT-330)

As MCYT-330 is a much larger database than BIOMET and MCYT-100, for computational reasons, we could not envisage performing 100 samplings of the five enrollment signatures. Therefore, a study on the necessary number of samplings to reach an acceptable confidence on our results was carried out on this complete database. This study was carried out with the two reference systems (Ref1 and Ref2) described in Sect. 6.5.

To that end, we assume that the standard deviation (across samplings) of the Equal Error Rate (EER) (computed on skilled forgeries) is reduced when the number of samplings increases. Thus, we search the number of random samplings that ensures that the standard deviation (across samplings) of the EER is significantly reduced. Figure 6.6 shows results on both reference systems.

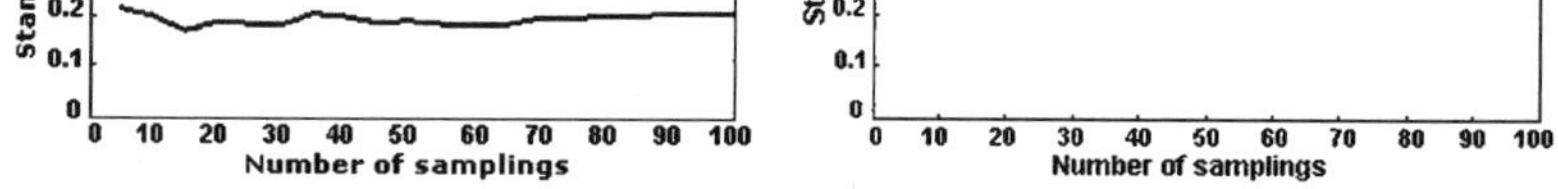

(a) (b)

Fig. 6.6 Standard deviation of the Equal Error Rate (EER) on MCYT-330 database, against the number of random samplings of the five enrollment signatures on skilled forgeries: (**a**) Reference System 1 and (**b**) Reference System 2

According to Fig. 6.6, we notice that at 15 random samplings, the standard deviation lowers for Reference System 1, but that 25 random samplings are required to reach the same result for Reference System 2. Besides, we notice in both cases that a substantial increase in the number of samplings (up to 100 samplings) does not lead to a lower value of the standard deviation of the EER. Given these results, we assumed that 25 random samplings are sufficient to evaluate systems on the complete MCYT database, instead of considering 100 samplings as done on BIOMET and MCYT-100 databases which are smaller.

The resulting protocol is thus the following: five genuine signatures are randomly selected among the 25 available genuine signatures for each writer and this procedure is repeated 25 times. For each person, the 20 remaining genuine signatures, the 25 skilled forgeries and the 329 random forgeries are used for test purposes.

6.5.5 Results with the Benchmarking Framework

We compute the Detection Error Tradeoff (DET) curves [20] of Reference System 1 (Ref1 v1.0) and Reference System 2 (Ref2 v1.0). We report the average values of Equal Error Rate (EER) corresponding to Reference Systems, over 100 samplings on MCYT-100 database according to the protocol described in Sect. 6.5.4.2, and over 100 samplings on BIOMET database with two different protocols. In the first protocol, the test is performed only on the remaining five genuine signatures of Session 2 (Protocol 1, described in Sect. 6.5.4.1). In the second protocol, the test is performed on both the remaining five genuine signatures of Session 2 and the five genuine signatures of Session 1 (Protocol 3). Experimental results of the two Reference Systems on the BIOMET database according to Protocol 2, described in Sect. 6.5.4.1, are presented in Sect. 6.6.6. Two schemes are studied: one considering skilled forgeries, the other one considering random forgeries.

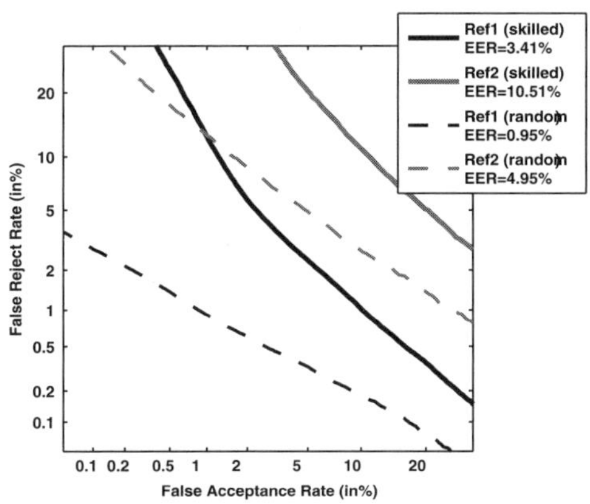

Fig. 6.7 DET curves of the two reference systems—Ref1 v1.0 and Ref2 v1.0—on the MCYT-100 database on skilled and random forgeries

Table 6.3 EERs of the two reference systems—Ref1 v1.0 and Ref2 v1.0—on the MCYT-100 database and their Confidence Interval (CI) of 95%, on skilled and random forgeries

MCYT-100			
Skilled forgeries		**Random forgeries**	
System	EER% CI 95%	System	EER% CI 95%
Ref1	3.41 ± 0.05	Ref1	0.95 ± 0.03
Ref2	10.51 ± 0.13	Ref2	4.95 ± 0.09

Table 6.4 EERs of the two reference systems—Ref1 v1.0 and Ref2 v1.0—on the BIOMET database and their Confidence Interval (CI) of 95%, on skilled and random forgeries

BIOMET				
	Protocol 1		**Protocol 3**	
	Skilled forgeries	**Random forgeries**	**Skilled forgeries**	**Random forgeries**
System	EER% CI 95%	EER% CI 95%	EER% CI 95%	EER% CI 95%
Ref1	2.37 ± 0.06	1.60 ± 0.07	4.93 ± 0.07	4.06 ± 0.06
Ref2	8.26 ± 0.15	6.83 ± 0.16	9.55 ± 0.15	7.80 ± 0.14

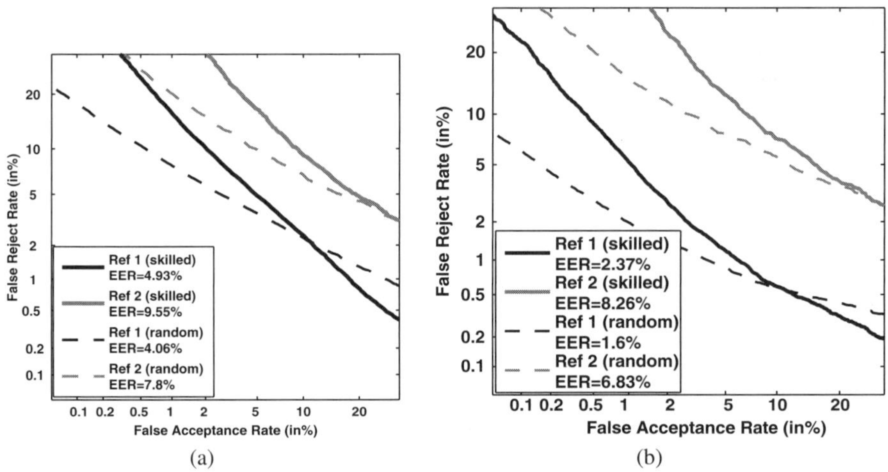

Fig. 6.8 DET curves of the two reference systems—Ref1 v1.0 and Ref2 v1.0—on the BIOMET database according to **(a)** Protocol 3 and **(b)** Protocol 1, on skilled and random forgeries

6.6 Research Algorithms Evaluated within the Benchmarking Framework

In this section, results within the proposal evaluation framework of several research systems are presented. Among them are also present the best approaches within the

SVC'2004 evaluation campaign (DTW and HMM). All these systems are evaluated first with the benchmarking framework and also with other relevant protocols.

6.6.1 HMM-based System from Universidad Autonoma de Madrid (UAM)

[3]This online signature verification system is based on functional feature extraction and Hidden Markov Models (HHMs) [7]. This system was submitted by Universidad Politecnica de Madrid (UPM) to the first international Signature Verification Competition (SVC'2004) with excellent results [36]: in Task 2 of the competition, where both trajectory and pressure signals were available, the system was ranked first when testing against random forgeries. In the case of testing skilled forgeries, the system was only outperformed by the winner of the competition, which was based on Dynamic Time Warping [3]. Below, we provide a brief sketch of the system, and for more details we refer the reader to [7].

Feature extraction is performed as follows. The coordinate trajectories (x_n, y_n) and the pressure signal p_n are the components of the unprocessed feature vectors, where $n = 1, \ldots, N_s$ and N_s is the duration of the signature in time samples. In order to retrieve relative information from the coordinate trajectory (x_n, y_n) and not being dependent on the starting point of the signature, signature trajectories are preprocessed by subtracting the center of mass. Then, a rotation alignment based on the average path tangent angle is performed. An extended set of discrete-time functions is derived from the preprocessed trajectories. The resulting functional signature description consists of the following feature vectors $(x_n, y_n, p_n, \theta_n, v_n, \rho_n, a_n)$ together with their first order time derivatives, where θ, v, ρ and a stand, respectively, for path tangent angle, path velocity magnitude, log curvature radius and total acceleration magnitude. A whitening linear transformation is finally applied to each discrete-time function so as to obtain zero mean and unit standard deviation function values.

Given the parametrized enrollment set of signatures of a user, a continuous left-to-right HMM was chosen to model each signer's characteristics. This means that each person's signature is modeled through a double stochastic process, characterized by a given number of states with an associated set of transition probabilities, and, in each of such states, a continuous density multivariate Gaussian mixture. No transition skips between states are permitted. The Hidden Markov Model (HMM) λ is estimated by using the Baum-Welch iterative algorithm. Given a test signature parametrized as O (with a duration of N_s time samples) and the claimed identity previously enrolled as λ, the similarity matching score s:

$$s = \frac{1}{N_s} \log p(O/\lambda) \tag{6.3}$$

is computed by using the Viterbi algorithm [26].

[3] This section is reproduced with permission from Annales des Telecommunications, source [13].

6.6.2 GMM-based System

This system is based on a coupling of a Gaussian Mixture Model [27] with a local feature extraction, namely the 25 local features used for Reference System 1, described in Sect. 6.5.2. Indeed, it is an interesting question whether the GMM viewed as a degenerate version of an HMM can be compared to an HMM-based approach in terms of performance on the same feature extraction. As for the HMM-based approach of Reference System 1, the number of Gaussians of the writer GMM is chosen in a personalized way, which is set as $4N$ where N is the number of states as computed in (6.1).

6.6.3 Standard DTW-based System

This system is based on Dynamic Time Warping, which compensates for local handwriting variations, and allows to determine the dissimilarity between two time sequences with different lengths [26]. This method, with a polynomial complexity, computes a matching distance by recovering optimal alignments between sample points in the two time series. The alignment is optimal in the sense that it minimizes a cumulative distance measure consisting of "local" distances between aligned samples. In this system, the DTW-distance between two time series $x_1,\ldots,x_M$ and $y_1,\ldots,y_N$, $D(M,N)$ is computed as:

$$D(i,j) = \min \left\{ \begin{array}{l} D(i,j-1) \\ D(i-1,j) \\ D(i-1,j-1) \end{array} \right\} + w_p \times d(i,j) \tag{6.4}$$

where the "local" distance function $d(i,j)$ is the Euclidian distance between i^{th} reference point and j^{th} testing point, with $D(0,0) = d(0,0) = 0$, and equal weights w_p are given to insertions, deletions and substitutions. Of course, in general, the nature of the recurrence equation (which are the local predecessors of a given point), and the "local" distance function $d(i,j)$ may vary [26]. Standard DTW-based system aligns by Dynamic Time Warping (DTW) a test signature with each reference signature and the average value of the resulting distances is used to classify the test signature as being genuine or a forgery. If the final distance is lower than the value of the decision threshold, the claimed identity is accepted. Otherwise it is rejected.

6.6.4 DTW-based System with Score Normalization

This system is also based on Dynamic Time Warping (DTW), calculated according to (6.4). However, a score normalization following the principle of Kholmatov's system [3], the winning system of the first international Signature Verification

Competition [36] (SVC'2004), is introduced. This normalization, previously described in Sect. 6.2.1.2, relies on intraclass variation; more precisely, the system only normalizes the output distance (defined as the average DTW distances between the test signature and the five reference signatures) by dividing the latter by the average of pairwise DTW distances in the enrollment set. This results in a dissimilarity score which is in a range from 0 to 1. If this final score is lower than the value of the threshold, the test signature is authentic, otherwise it is a forgery.

We chose to consider this second version of a DTW-based approach because Kholmatov's system obtained indeed excellent results in SVC'2004 with such intraclass normalization, particularly in comparison to statistical approaches based on HMMs [36].

6.6.5 System Based on a Global Approach

The principle of this system is to compute, from the temporal dynamic functions acquired by the digitizer (coordinates, pressure, pen-inclination angles), 41 global features (described in Table 6.5), and to compare a test signature to a reference signature by the City Block distance.

During enrollment, each user supplies five reference signatures. Global feature vectors are extracted from such five reference signatures, and the average value of all pairwise distances is computed by the City Block distance, to be used as a normalization factor. In the verification phase, a test signature is compared to each reference signature by the City Block distance, providing an average distance. The final dissimilarity measure results from the ratio of this average distance and the normalization factor previously mentioned. If this final value is lower than the value of the decision threshold, the claimed identity is accepted, otherwise it is rejected.

6.6.6 Experimental Results

We compute the Detection Error Tradeoff (DET) curves [20] of the following seven systems: Reference System 1 (*Ref1*), Reference System 2 (*Ref2*), UAM's HMM-based system (*UAM*), a GMM-based system with local features (*GMM*), a standard DTW system (*DTWstd*), the DTW system with the score normalization based on intraclass variance (*DTWnorm*) and, finally, a system based on a global approach and a normalized City Block distance measure (*Globalappr*).

We report the average values of Equal Error Rate (EER) corresponding to the seven systems, over 100 samplings on BIOMET and MCYT-100, and over 25 samplings on the complete MCYT database (according to our previous study on the required number of samplings in Sect. 6.5.4.3). Two schemes are studied: one considering skilled forgeries, the other one considering random forgeries.

Table 6.5 The 41 global features extracted from the online signature

N^o	Feature name
1	Signature Duration
2	Number of sign changes in X
3	Number of sign changes in Y
4	Standard Deviation of acceleration in x by the maximum of acceleration in x
5	Standard Deviation of acceleration in y by the maximum of acceleration in y
6	Standard Deviation of velocity in x by the maximum of velocity in x
7	Average velocity in x by the maximum of velocity in x
8	Standard Deviation of velocity in y by the maximum of velocity in y
9	Average velocity in y by the maximum of velocity in y
10	Root mean square (RMS) of y position by the difference between maximum and minimum of position in y
11	Ratio velocity change
12	Average velocity by the maximum of velocity
13	Root mean square (RMS) of velocity in x by the maximum of the velocity
14-15-16	Coordinates ratio
17	Correlation velocity by square of velocity
18	Root mean square (RMS) of acceleration by maximum of acceleration
19	Average acceleration by the maximum of acceleration
20	Difference between the Root mean square (RMS) and the minimum of x position by the RMS of x position
21	Root mean square (RMS) of x position by the difference between maximum and minimum of position in x
22	Root mean square of velocity in x by the maximum of velocity in x
23	Root mean square of velocity in y by the maximum of velocity in y
24	Velocity ratio
25	Acceleration ratio
26	Correlation coordinates
27	Correlation coordinates by the square of the maximum of acceleration
28	Difference between the Root mean square and the minimum of y position by the Root mean square of y position
29	Difference between the Root mean square and the minimum of velocity in x by the Root mean square of velocity in x
30	Difference between the Root mean square and the minimum of velocity in y by the Root mean square of velocity in y
31	Difference between the Root mean square and the minimum of velocity by the Root mean square of velocity
32	Difference between the Root mean square and the minimum of acceleration in x by the Root mean square of acceleration in x
33	Difference between the Root mean square and the minimum of acceleration in y by the Root mean square of acceleration in y
34	Difference between the mean and the minimum of acceleration by the mean of acceleration
35	Ratio of the time of max velocity over the total time
36	Number of strokes
37-38	Mean of positive and negative velocity in x
39-40	Mean of positive and negative velocity in y

6.6.6.1 On the BIOMET Database

As we mentioned in Sect. 6.5.4.1, two cases are studied, depending on presence of time variability or not.

With no Time Variability In Table 6.6, the performances of the seven systems are presented at the Equal Error Rate (EER) point with a confidence interval of 95%. For more insight, we also report the performance of the two systems based on the two scores that are fused in Ref1 System, the classical score based on Likelihood (the associated system is denoted by *Ref1-Lik*) and the score based on the segmentation of the test signature by the target model (the associated system is denoted by *Ref1-Vit*).

Table 6.6 EERs of the seven systems on the BIOMET database and their Confidence Intervals of 95% in case of no time variability

BIOMET—without time variability			
Skilled forgeries		Random forgeries	
System	EER% CI 95%	System	EER% CI 95%
Ref1	2.37 ± 0.06	Ref1	1.60 ± 0.07
UAM	3.41 ± 0.11	UAM	1.90 ± 0.10
Ref1-Vit	3.86 ± 0.08	Globalappr	3.25 ± 0.09
Globalappr	4.65 ± 0.10	Ref1-Vit	3.42 ± 0.10
Ref1-Lik	4.85 ± 0.11	Ref1-Lik	3.72 ± 0.10
GMM	5.13 ± 0.12	GMM	3.77 ± 0.10
DTWstd	5.21 ± 0.09	DTWstd	5.25 ± 0.09
DTWnorm	5.47 ± 0.11	DTWnorm	5.58 ± 0.10
Ref2	8.26 ± 0.15	Ref2	6.83 ± 0.16

It clearly appears in Table 6.6 and Fig. 6.9 that the best approaches are statistical, particularly those based on Hidden Markov Models (Reference System 1 and UAM's HMM system) for both skilled and random forgeries. Furthermore, at the EER point, the best HMM-based system is Reference System 1, which performs the fusion of two sorts of information corresponding to two levels of description of the signature—the likelihood information that operates at the point level, and the segmentation information that works on portions of the signature, corresponding to an intermediate level of description.

This result is followed at the EER by the performance of UAM's HMM system, whose output score is the Log-likelihood of the test signature given the model. Nevertheless, when analyzing all functioning points in DET curves (see Fig. 6.9), we notice that UAM's HMM system is better than Reference System 1 when the False Acceptance Rate is for skilled forgeries lower than 1% and for random forgeries lower than 0.3%. Also, UAM's HMM system performs better than Ref1's likelihood score alone and Ref1's Viterbi score alone at the EER, particularly on random

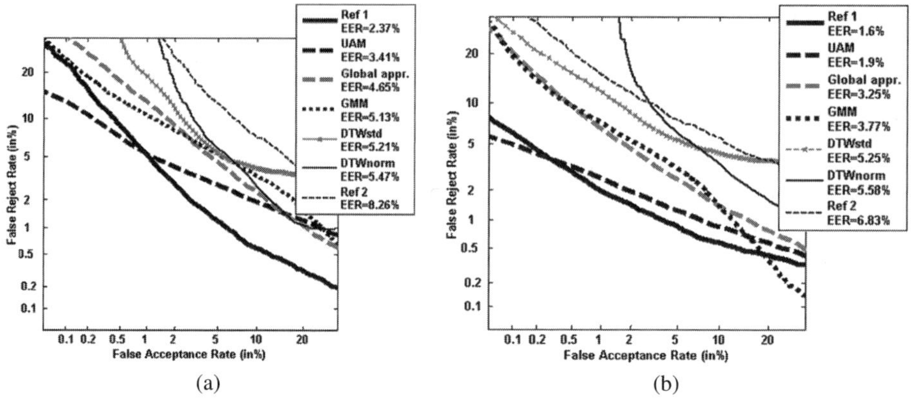

Fig. 6.9 DET curves on the BIOMET database of the seven systems in case of no time variability: (**a**) on skilled forgeries and (**b**) on random forgeries

forgeries with a relative improvement of around 46%. Indeed, although Ref1 and UAM's system are both based on HMMs, their structural differences are important: Reference System 1 uses a variable number of states (between 2 and 15) according to the client's enrollment signatures length, whereas UAM's system uses only two states, and the number of Gaussian components per state is also different (4 in the case of Reference System,1, and 32 in the case of UAM's System). As already shown in a previous study [13], such differences in the HMM architecture lead to complementary systems, simply because the resulting "compression" of the information of a signature (the model) is of another nature.

HMM-based systems are followed in performance first by the distance-based approach using 41 global features, and then by the GMM-based system with local features and a personalized number of Gaussians.

On the other hand, it is clearly shown in Fig. 6.9 that the worst systems are elastic distance-based systems. Indeed, we notice that both DTW-based systems that work at the point level reach an Equal Error Rate (EER) of 5.3% on skilled and random forgeries, and Reference System 2 using Levenshtein distance coupled to a coarse segment-based feature extraction reaches an EER of 8.26% on skilled forgeries and 6.82% on random forgeries. This result is unexpected, particularly for the normalized DTW-based system evaluated in this work that uses the same principles in the Dynamic Time Warping (DTW) implementation as the winning system of SVC'2004 [36] (equal weights for all operations of insertion, destruction and substitutions, score normalization by intraclass variance, see Sect. 6.2.2).

This result may be mainly due to two reasons: a) the DTW winning algorithm of SVC'2004 uses only two position derivatives, whereas our DTW-based system uses 25 features, among which we find the same two position derivatives; and b) particularities of the BIOMET database. Indeed, this database has forgeries that are in general much longer than genuine signatures (by a factor two or three), as well as highly variable genuine signatures from one instance to another. In this configuration of the data, statistical models are better suited to absorb client intraclass variability and, in particular, we remark that the HMM performs better than the GMM, because it performs a segmentation of the signature, which results in an increased detection power of skilled forgeries with regard to the GMM. This phenomenon is clearly illustrated by the good performance of the system based only on the segmentation score (called *Ref1-Vit*), one of the two scores fused by Reference System 1.

Also, the good ranking of the distance-based approach coupled to a global feature extraction (41 global features), behind the two HMM-based systems, is due to a smoothing effect of the holistic feature extraction that helps to characterize a variable signature, and to detect coarse differences between forgeries and genuine signatures, as signature length among others. Moreover, comparing now the two systems based on Dynamic Time Warping, we notice that the DTW system using the normalization based on intraclass variance is outperformed by the standard DTW in the area of low False Acceptance. This can be explained by the high intraclass variability on BIOMET database, since genuine signatures are in general highly variable as already pointed out. On such clients, the personalized normalization factor distorts the scores obtained on forgeries thus producing false acceptances. To go further, if we suppose that the SVC'2004 Test Set (unfortunately not available to the scientific community) is mainly of the same nature as the SVC development set, we may assert that the data configuration in the BIOMET database is completely opposite of that of SVC, which contains stable genuine signatures and skilled forgeries of approximately the same length as this of the genuine signatures. This enormous difference in the very nature of the data impacts systems in a totally different way and explains that the best approaches in one case are no longer the best in another case. We will pursue our analysis of results with this spirit on the other databases as well.

In Presence of Time Variability Table 6.7 reports the experimental results obtained by each system in presence of time variability. First, we notice an important degradation of performance for all systems; this degradation is of at least 200% for the Global distance-based approach and can even reach 360% for Reference System 1. Indeed, we recall that in this case, time variability corresponds to sessions acquired five months apart, thus to long-term time variability.

As in the previous case of no time variability, results in Table 6.7 and Fig. 6.10, show that the best approaches remain those based on HMMs (Ref1 and UAM's systems). Ref1 is still the best system on skilled forgeries, but on random forgeries UAM system is the best. This can be explained by the fact that the score based on segmentation used in Ref1, as mentioned before, helps in detecting skilled forgeries on BIOMET based mainly on a length criterion. This does not occur on random forgeries of course, and thus there is no longer a substantial difference in segmentation between forgeries and genuine signatures.

Table 6.7 EERs of the seven systems on the BIOMET database and their Confidence Interval (CI) of 95%, in case of time variability

BIOMET—with time variability			
Skilled forgeries		**Random forgeries**	
System	EER% CI 95%	System	EER% CI 95%
Ref1	6.63 ± 0.10	UAM	4.67 ± 0.13
UAM	7.25 ± 0.15	Ref1	5.79 ± 0.10
Ref1-Vit	7.61 ± 0.12	Globalappr	6.61 ± 0.14
Globalappr	8.91 ± 0.14	Ref2	8.69 ± 0.18
Ref2	10.58 ± 0.18	Ref1-Vit	8.88 ± 0.17
DTWstd	11.36 ± 0.10	GMM	9.01 ± 0.10
DTWnorm	11.83 ± 0.51	Ref1-Lik	9.90 ± 0.11
Ref1-Lik	12.78 ± 0.15	DTWstd	12.67 ± 0.12
GMM	13.15 ± 0.14	DTWnorm	13.85 ± 0.28

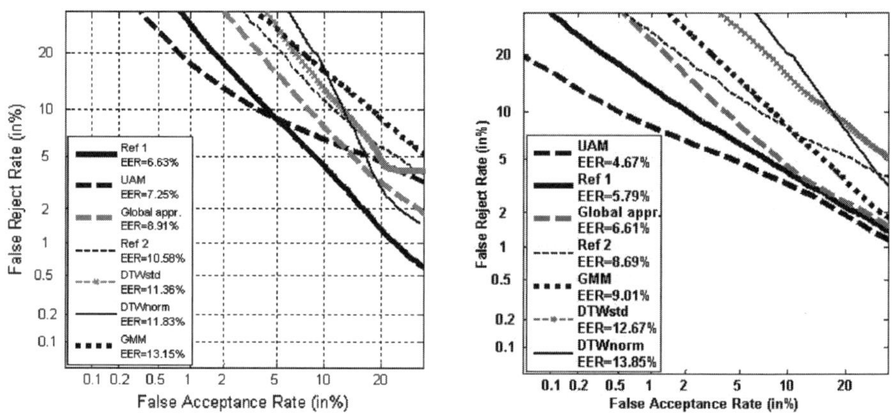

(a) (b)

Fig. 6.10 DET curves on the BIOMET database of the seven systems in case of time variability: (**a**) on skilled forgeries and (**b**) on random forgeries

Taking into consideration time variability, we notice that the system based only on Likelihood score (Ref1-Lik) gives lower results compared to the case without time variability, with degradation around 260% on skilled forgeries (from 4.85% to 12.78%) and random forgeries (from 3.72% to 9.9%). The system based only on the Viterbi score (Ref1-Vit) is however more robust in terms of time variability on skilled forgeries, with a degradation of 190% (from 3.86% to 7.61%). On random forgeries, Ref1-Vit is degraded in the same way as Ref1-Lik (from 3.42% to 8.88%).

The HMM-based systems are followed in performance by the Global distance-based approach as observed without time variability, then by Reference System 2, then by the standard DTW, and finally by the score-normalized-DTW. The GMM-based system, which is the last system on skilled forgeries, behaves differently on random forgeries, but it still remains among the last systems. It is interesting to note that the Global distance-based approach shows the lowest degradation in performance (around 200% on skilled and random forgeries). This approach processes the signature as a whole, and when the signature varies over time, strong local variations appear, but such variations are smoothed by the holistic description of the signature performed by the feature extraction step.

For the same reason, elastic distance works well when coupled to a rough feature extraction detecting "events" and encoding the signature as a string (case of Ref2) while it gives bad results when coupled to a local feature extraction (case of both DTW-based systems).

On the other hand, the same tendencies observed in the previous subsection (without time variability) and due to the characteristics of the BIOMET database, are observed in this case for DTW-based systems and the GMM. The GMM-based system, coupled to a local feature extraction, which gave good results in the previous case, doesn't resist well to time variability and becomes in this case the last system on skilled forgeries. This result is interesting because it suggests that the piecewise stationarity assumption on the signature, inherent to an HMM, may be helpful with respect to a GMM mostly in presence of long-term time variability. Unfortunately, there has been no online signature verification evaluation yet on long-term time variability data that would permit to assess this analysis. Nevertheless, to have a better insight on the contribution of the segmentation information (the fact of modeling a signature by different states) in the presence of time variability, we compared three statistical approaches on the BIOMET database: Ref1, HMM-based, a GMM with a personalized number of Gaussians, and a GMM with different configurations in the Gaussian mixture (2, 4, 8, 16, 32, 64 and 128 Gaussians). Experimental results obtained by such systems are reported in Table 6.8 (a) and (b).

Table 6.8 EERs of the GMM corresponding to different number of Gaussians on the BIOMET database: (**a**) on skilled forgeries and (**b**) on random forgeries

	N° **Gaussians**	**2**	**4**	**8**	**16**	**32**	**64**	**128**	**GMM person**
a)	**Without variab.**	15.88%	12.37%	10.16%	9.16%	**8.92%**	9.95%	13.53%	**5.13%**
	With variab.	26.6%	22.95%	19.9%	18.04%	**17.00%**	17.6%	21.74%	**13.15%**
b)	**Without variab.**	11.96%	9.47%	7.99%	7.02%	**6.71%**	13.69%	11.31%	**3.77%**
	With variab.	20.02%	16.93%	14.59%	12.99%	**12.46%**	13.69%	18.03%	**9.01%**

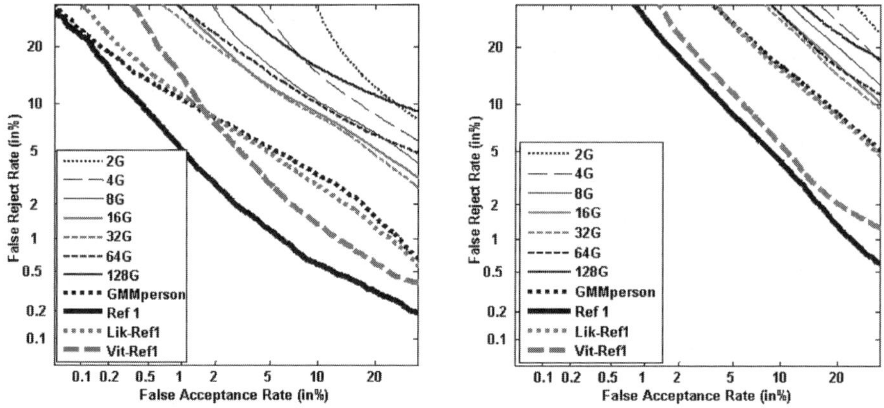

(a) (b)

Fig. 6.11 DET curves on the BIOMET database comparing Ref1 system, a GMM with a personalized number of Gaussians, and a GMM with a different number of Gaussians on skilled forgeries: ((**a**) without time variability and (**b**) with time variability

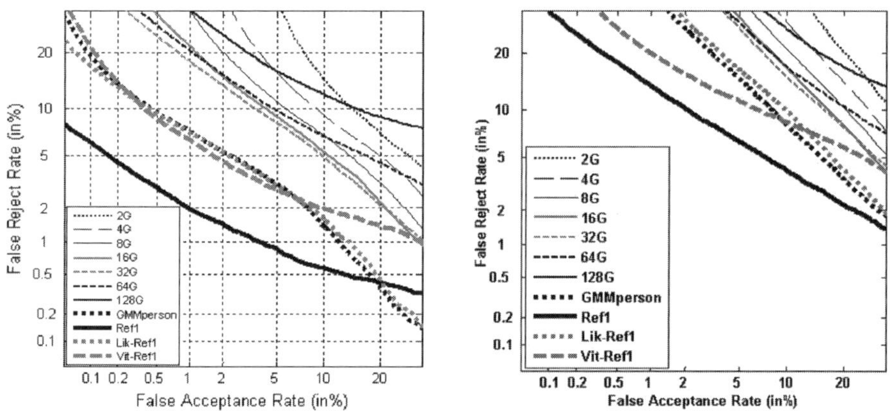

(a) (b)

Fig. 6.12 DET curves on the BIOMET database comparing Ref1 system, GMM with a personalized number of Gaussians, and GMM with a different number of Gaussians on random forgeries: (**a**) without time variability and (**b**) with time variability

Figures 6.11 and 6.12, as well as Tables 6.8 (a) and (b), show that a GMM with a personalized number of Gaussians performs better than a GMM with a common number of Gaussians for all users, even in the best case.

6.6.6.2 On MYCT Database

Tables 6.9 and 6.10 report the experimental results obtained by all systems when tested on the MCYT-100 subset and on the complete MCYT database, with the evaluation protocols described in Sects. 6.5.4.2 and 6.5.4.3, respectively.

Table 6.9 EERs of the seven systems on the MCYT-100 database and their Confidence Interval (CI) of 95%

MCYT-100			
Skilled forgeries		**Random forgeries**	
System	EER% CI 95%	System	EER% CI 95%
Ref1	3.41 ± 0.05	Ref1	0.95 ± 0.03
DTWnorm	3.91 ± 0.07	DTWstd	1.20 ± 0.06
UAM	5.37 ± 0.08	DTWnorm	1.28 ± 0.04
Ref1-Vit	5.59 ± 0.07	Ref1-Lik	2.13 ± 0.05
Ref1-Lik	5.66 ± 0.07	UAM	2.34 ± 0.05
DTWstd	5.96 ± 0.09	Ref1-Vit	2.44 ± 0.04
GMM	6.74 ± 0.09	GMM	2.81 ± 0.05
Globalappr	7.23 ± 0.10	Globalappr	3.15 ± 0.07
Ref2	10.51 ± 0.13	Ref2	4.95 ± 0.09

When comparing DET curves on skilled and random forgeries for each database in Figs. 6.13 and 6.14, it clearly appears that very similar results are obtained on MCYT-100 and MCYT-330. Therefore, we analyze the experimental results only on the MCYT-330 database, as it is the complete database.

As shown in Fig. 6.14, the best system is Reference System 1, for both skilled and random forgeries. The fact that Ref1 is the best system on two different databases, BIOMET and MCYT, having different characteristics (size of the population, sensor resolution, nature of skilled forgeries, stability of genuine signatures, presence or not of time variability, nature of time variability, etc.) that can strongly influence systems performance, shows that Reference System 1 holds up well across databases [34].

Ref1 system is indeed followed at the EER point by the score-normalized DTW system (an increase of EER from 3.91% to 4.4% on skilled forgeries, and from 1.27% to 1.69% on random forgeries). At other functioning points, the gap between Ref1 and the normalized DTW increases. This good result of the score-normalized DTW system can be explained by the fact that this score normalization exploits information about intraclass variability and the nature of the MCYT database in this respect. Indeed, as in this database the genuine signatures do not vary as much as in the BIOMET database, no distortion effects occur on the scores on forgeries when applying the normalization. This result also confirms the tendency of results obtained in SVC'2004 [36] concerning the coupling of a normalization based on

Table 6.10 EERs of the seven systems on the complete MCYT database (MCYT-330) and their Confidence Interval (CI) of 95%

MCYT-330			
Skilled forgeries		**Random forgeries**	
System	EER% CI 95%	System	EER% CI 95%
Ref1	3.91 ± 0.09	Ref1	1.27 ± 0.04
DTWnorm	4.40 ± 0.08	DTWnorm	1.69 ± 0.05
Ref1-Vit	5.81 ± 0.12	DTWstd	1.75 ± 0.08
UAM	6.31 ± 0.11	UAM	1.97 ± 0.05
Ref1-Lik	6.57 ± 0.10	Ref1-Vit	2.91 ± 0.06
DTWstd	7.04 ± 0.09	Ref1-Lik	2.93 ± 0.06
Globalappr	7.45 ± 0.09	Globalappr	3.22 ± 0.06
GMM	7.45 ± 0.09	GMM	3.83 ± 0.07
Ref2	12.05 ± 0.10	Ref2	6.35 ± 0.10

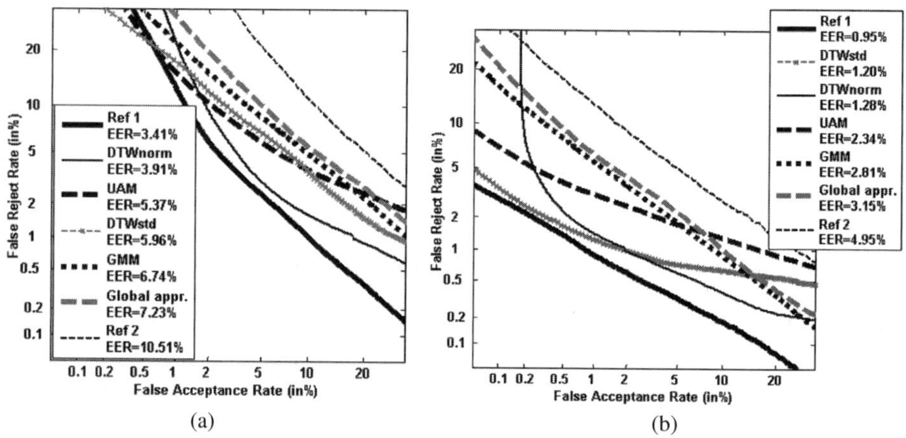

Fig. 6.13 DET curves of the seven systems on the MCYT-100 database: (**a**) on skilled forgeries and (**b**) on random forgeries

intraclass variance and a DTW. To go further, MCYT is more similar in two main characteristics to the SVC Development Set, than it is to the BIOMET database: on one hand more stability in genuine signatures, and on the other hand skilled forgeries not having an important difference in length with respect to genuine signatures. Finally, we notice that on the complete MCYT database, the statistical approach based on the fusion of two sorts of information, Reference System 1, that participated in the SVC'2004 and was then outperformed by this normalized DTW approach, gives the best results in this case. Of course, some other differences in nature between MCYT and SVC databases, like for instance the influence of cultural

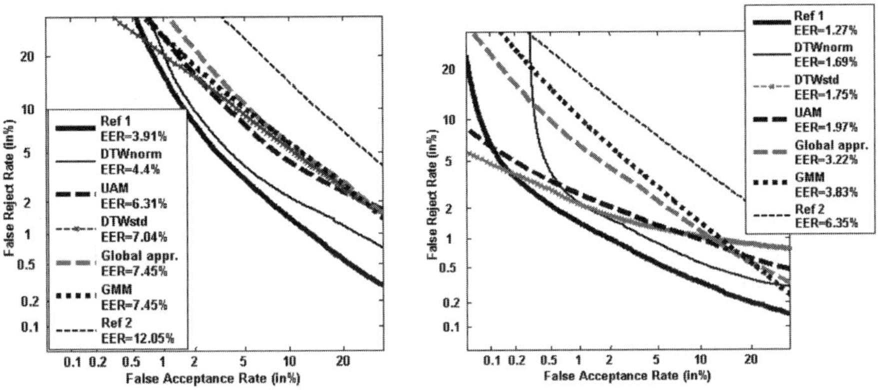

(a) (b)

Fig. 6.14 DET curves of the seven systems on the MCYT-330 database: (**a**) on skilled forgeries and (**b**) on random forgeries

types of signature on approaches (MCYT contains only Western signatures while SVC mixes Western and Asian styles), may be responsible of this result.

Nevertheless, we still notice on MCYT a phenomenon already observed on BIOMET: that the normalization based on intraclass variance coupled to DTW increases considerably the False Rejection Rate in the zone of low False Acceptance Rate. The standard DTW gives lower results but does not show this effect in this zone. This phenomenon also increases significantly on random forgeries.

Although UAM's HMM system was favored on MCYT since it was optimized on the first 50 writers and the test is performed on the totality of the 330 writers, it is ranked behind Ref1 and the DTW with intraclass variance normalization.

On the other hand, we observe that on MCYT the worst system is the Global distance-based approach, followed by Reference System 2, while the GMM with local features remains in between the best model-based approaches (HMM-based) and the worst systems. Indeed, as the database shows less variability in the genuine signatures and less differences in the dynamics between the forgeries and the genuine signatures than BIOMET, a global feature extraction coupled with a simple distance measure, or alternatively an elastic distance with a coarse segment-based feature extraction, are not precise enough to discriminate genuine signatures from forgeries in this case.

6.7 Conclusions

We have made in the present chapter a complete overview of the online signature verification field, by analyzing the existing literature relatively to the main approaches, by recalling the main results of the international evaluations performed, by describing the existing public databases at the disposal of the researcher in the field, and by discussing the main challenges nowadays.

Our experimental work on seven online signature verification systems and three different public databases with different protocols completes the view of the field. We have indeed compared in this work model-based approaches (two HMM-based systems, and a GMM-based system) coupled to local features, and distance-based approaches (two elastic distances coupled to local features, an elastic distance coupled to a segment-based feature extraction, and a standard distance coupled to a holistic feature extraction).

Our experiments lead to the following conclusions. We had three databases but one is a subset of the other, so mainly we are in the presence of two data configurations in terms of acquisition protocol, population, sensor, nature of forgeries, etc. Also, one of the databases allowed to evaluate the seven systems in presence of long-term (several months) time variability, for the first time in the literature.

Moreover, two out of the seven systems considered in our experimental study had already been evaluated at the First International Signature Verification Competition in 2004 [36], SVC'2004, and one of the distance-based approaches compared is based on the same principles as those of the winning algorithm [3]; these facts gave us many elements of comparison in our analysis.

We noticed an important variation of systems' ranking from one database to another and from one protocol to another (concerning the presence of long-term time variability). This ranking also varied with respect to SVC test set [36]. This fact rises many important questions; indeed, when the data configuration in a database is totally at the opposite of that of another, regarding for example stability of genuine signatures and resemblance of skilled forgeries to genuine signatures in terms of dynamics, this will impact the systems and the best approaches in one case will no longer be the best in another case.

Nevertheless, across databases, some tendencies have emerged.

First, HMM-based systems outperformed Dynamic Time Warping systems and GMM-based system; in particular Reference System 1, based on the fusion of two information levels from the signature, has the same behavior across databases and protocols. This system is classified as the first in all cases, and no tuning was performed on a development set in any of such cases, at the opposite of the other HMM-based system. A sophisticated double-stage and personalized normalization scheme is at the origin of these nice properties [34].

Second, the approach that won SVC'2004, Dynamic Time Warping with the intraclass variance normalization, is not always ranked in the same way across databases and protocols. We have shown that the intraclass variability has a distortion effect on forgeries' scores when the normalization factor is high because of high variance in genuine scores (the distance between the forgery and the genuine signature is normalized by the intraclass variance distance). Therefore, this approach is very sensitive to the nature of the data, in terms of genuine signature variability. We have remarked that on MCYT data this approach is ranked second behind Ref1, while it is ranked sixth out of seven on BIOMET without time variability and seventh in the presence of time variability (the Global distance-based approach and Ref2 based on coarse feature extraction and elastic distance perform better in this case, as we explain later).

Third, the distance-based approach using City Block distance coupled to a holistic feature extraction is well ranked on data with high intraclass variability (when the genuine signatures are highly variable from one instance to another) and also when long-term time variability is present in the data.

The Gaussian Mixture Model coupled with the same local feature extraction used by Reference System 1 gives lower results than HMM-based approaches in general and the distance-based approach using City Block distance with a holistic feature extraction. We also obtained an interesting result: the GMM coupled to local features resists poorly to long-term time variability (five months). One open question, given the good results obtained by the GMM-based systems at the BioSecure Evaluation Campaign (BMEC'2007) [2] in the presence of short-term time variability (2-3 weeks), is whether a GMM-based system coupled with a holistic feature extraction would perform better in the same long-term time variability conditions?

More generally, we observed the terrible impact of time variability on systems, causing degradation of at least 200% for the distance-based approach coupled with a holistic feature extraction, and can reach 360% for the best system, Reference System 1. Indeed, we recall that in this case, time variability corresponds to sessions acquired five months apart, thus to long-term time variability. More studies on this are necessary. A remaining challenge in research is certainly the study of the possibility of performing an update of the writer templates (references) in the case of distance-based approaches, or an adaptation of the writer model in the case of model-based approaches. Also, personalized feature selection should be explored by the scientific community since it may help to cope with intraclass variability, which is the main problem in signature and even with time variability. Indeed, one may better characterize a writer by those features that show more stability for him/her.

Finally, the scientific community may find in this work the access to a permanent evaluation framework, composed of publicly available databases, associated protocols and baseline reference systems in order to be able to compare their systems to the state of the art.

Acknowledgments

This work was funded by the IST-FP6 BioSecure Network of Excellence. J. Fierrez-Aguilar and F. Alonso are supported by a FPI Scholarship from Consejeria de Educacion de la Comunidad de Madrid and Fondo Social Europeo (Regional Government of Madrid and European Union).

References

1. http://www.biosecure.info/.
2. www.int-evry.fr/biometrics/bmec2007/.
3. A. Kholmatov and B.A. Yanikoglu. Identity authentication using improved online signature verification method. *Pattern Recognition Letters*, 26(15):2400–2408, 2005.
4. W. D. Chang and J. Shin. Modified dynamic time warping for stroke-based on-line signature verification. In *Proceedings of the 9th International Conference on Document Analysis and Recognition (ICDAR 2007)*, volume 2, pages 724–728, Brazil, 2007.
5. J. G. A. Dolfing. *Handwriting recognition and verification, a Hidden Markov approach.* PhD thesis, Philips Electronics N.V., 1998.
6. J. G. A. Dolfing, E. H. L. Aarts, and J. J. G. M. Van Oosterhout. On-line signature verification with hidden markov models. In *Proc. of the International Conference on Pattern Recognition*, pages 1309–1312, Brisbane, Australia, 1998.
7. J. Fierrez, D.Ramos-Castro, J. Ortega-Garcia, and J.Gonzales-Rodriguez. Hmm-based on-line signature verification: feature extraction and signature modelling. *Pattern Recognition Letters*, 28(16):2325–2334, December 2007.
8. J. Fierrez and J. Ortega-Garcia. On-line signature verification. In A. K. Jain, A. Ross, and P. Flynn, editors, *Handbook of Biometrics*, pages 189–209. Springer, 2008.
9. J. Fierrez-Aguilar, L. Nanni, J. Lopez-Peñalba, J. Ortega-Garcia, and D. Maltoni. An on-line signature verification system based on fusion of local and global information. In *Proc. of 5th IAPR Intl. Conf. on Audio- and Video -based Biometric Person Authentication, AVBPA*, Springer LNCS, New York, USA, July 2005.
10. J. Fierrez-Aguilar, J. Ortega-Garcia, and J. Gonzalez-Rodriguez. Target dependent score normalization techniques and their application to signature verification. *IEEE Transactions on Systems, Man and Cybernetics, part C*, 35(3):418–425, 2005.
11. BioSecure Benchmarking Framework. http://share.int-evry.fr/svnview-eph/.
12. S. Garcia-Salicetti, C. Beumier, G. Chollet, B. Dorizzi, J. Leroux-Les Jardins, J. Lanter, Y. Ni, and D. Petrovska-Delacretaz. Biomet: a multimodal person authentication database including face, voice, fingerprint, hand and signature modalities. In *Proc. of 4th International Conference on Audio and Vidio-Based Biometric Person Authentication*, pages 845–853, Guildford, UK, 2003.
13. S. Garcia-Salicetti, J. Fierrez-Aguilar, F. Alonso-Fernandez, C. Vielhauer, R. Guest, L. Allano, T. Doan Trung, T. Scheidat, B. Ly Van, J. Dittmann, B. Dorizzi, J. Ortega-Garcia, J. Gonzalez-Rodriguez, M. Bacile di Castiglione, and M. Fairhurst. *Biosecure Reference Systems for On-Line Signature Verification: A Study of Complementarity*, pages 36–61. Annals of Telecommunications, Special Issue on Multimodal Biometrics, France, 2007.
14. R. Guest, M. Fairhurst, and C. Vielhauer. Towards a flexible framework for open source software for handwritten signature analysis. In M. Spiliopoulou, R. Kruse, C. Borgelt, A. Nuernberger, and W. Gaul, editors, *From Data and Information Analysis to Knowledge Engineering, Proceedings of the 29 Annual Conference of the German Classification Society GfKl 2005*, pages 620–629. Springer, Berlin, 2006. ISBN 1431-8814.
15. S. Hangai, S. Yamanaka, and T. Hamamoto. Writer verification using altitude and direction of pen movement. In *International Conference on Pattern Recognition*, pages 3483–3486, Barcelona, September 2000.
16. A. K. Jain, F. D. Griess, and S. D. Connell. On-line signature verification. *Pattern Recognition*, 35(12):2963–2972, December 2002.
17. R. Kashi, J. Hu, W. L. Nelson, and W. Turin. A hidden markov model approach to online handwriting signature verification. *International Journal on Document Analysis and Recognition*, 1(2):102–109, Jul 1998.
18. Y. Komiya and T. Matsumoto. On-line pen input signature verification ppi (pen-position/pen-pressure/pen-inclination). *Proc. IEEE International Conference on SMC*, pages 41–46, 1999.

19. V. I. Levenshtein. *Binary codes capable of correcting deletions, insertions and reversals*, volume 10 of *Soviet Physics*. 1966.
20. A. Martin, G. Doddington, T. Kamm, and and M. Przybocki M. Ordowski. The det curve in assessment of detection task performance. In *Proc. Eurospeech '97*, volume 4, pages 1895–1898, Rhodes, Greece, 1997.
21. M. Martinez-Diaz, J. Fierrez, and J. Ortega-Garcia. Universal background models for dynamic signature verification. *Proceedings of the First IEEE International Conference on Biometrics: Theory, Applications and Systems (BTAS)*, September 27-29th 2007.
22. J. Ortega-Garcia, J. Fierrez-Aguilar, D. Simon, J. Gonzalez, M. Faundez-Zanuy, V. Espinosa, A. Satue, I. Hernaez, J.-J. Igarza, C. Vivaracho, D. Escudero, and Q.-I. Moro. Mcyt baseline corpus: A bimodal biometric database. *IEE Proceedings Vision, Image and Signal Processing, Special Issue on Biometrics on the Internet*, 150(6):395–401, December 2003.
23. R. Plamondon, W. Guerfali, and M. Lalonde. Automatic signature verification: a report on a large-scale public experiment. In *Proceedings of the International Graphonomics Society*, pages 9–13, Singapore, June 25 – July 2 1999.
24. R. Plamondon and G. Lorette. Automatic signature verification and writer identification – the state of the art. *Pattern Recognition*, 22(2):107–131, 1989.
25. R. Plamondon and S. Srihari. On-line and off-line handwriting recognition: A comprehensive survey. *IEEE Transactions on Pattern Analysis and Machine Intelligence*, 22(1):63–84, 2000.
26. L. Rabiner and B.H. Juang. *Fundamentals of Speech Recognition*. Prentice Hall Signal Processing Series. 1993.
27. D. A. Raynolds and R. C. Rose. Robust text-independent speaker identification using gaussian mixture speaker models. *IEEE Transactions on Speech and Audio Processing*, 3(1):72–83, Jan 1995.
28. J. Richiardi and A. Drygajlo. Gaussian mixture models for on-line signature verification. In *International Multimedia Conference, Proceedings 2003 ACM SIGMM workshop on Biometrics methods and applications*, pages 115–122, Berkeley, USA, Nov 2003.
29. G. Rigoll and A. Kosmala. A systematic comparison of on-line and off-line methods for signature verification with hidden markov models. In *Proc. of 14th International Conference on Pattern Recognition*, pages 1755–1757, Brisbane, Autralia, 1998.
30. S. Schimke, C. Vielhauer, and J. Dittmann. Using adapted levenshtein distance for on-line signature authentication. In *Proceedings of the ICPR 2004, IEEE 17th International Conference on Pattern Recognition*, 2004. ISBN 0-7695-2128-2.
31. O. Uréche and R. Plamondon. Document transport, transfer and exchange: Security and commercial aspects. In *Proceedings of the Fifth International Conference on Document Analysis and Recognition*, pages 585–588, 1999.
32. O. Uréche and R. Plamondon. Systémes numériques de paiement sur internet. *Pour la science*, 260:45–49, 1999.
33. O. Uréche and R. Plamondon. Digital payment systems for internet commerce: the state of the art. *World Wide Web*, 3(1):1–11, 2000.
34. B. Ly Van, S. Garcia-Salicetti, and B. Dorizzi. On using the viterbi path along with hmm likelihood information for online signature verification. *IEEE Transactions on Systems, Man and Cybernetics-Part B: Cybernetics, Special Issue on Recent Advances in Biometric Systems*, 37(5):1237–1247, October 2007.
35. M. Wirotius, J.-Y. Ramel, and N. Vincent. Selection of points for on-line signature comparison. In *Proceedings of the 9th Int'l Workshop on Frontiers in Handwriting Recognition (IWFHR)*, Tokyo, Japan, September 2004.
36. Dit-Yan Yeung, Hong Chang, Yimin Xiong, Susan George, Ramanujan Kashi, Takashi Matsumoto, and Gerhard Rigoll. Svc2004: First international signature verification competition. In *International Conference on Biometric Authentication (ICBA)*, volume 3072 of *Springer LNCS*, pages 16 – 22, Hong Kong, China, July 15-17 2004.
37. T. G. Zimmerman, G. F. Russell, A. Heilper, B. A.Smith, J. Hu, D. Markman, J. E. Graham, and C. Drews. Retail applications of signature verification. In A. K. Jain and K. Ratha, editors, *Biometric Technology for Human Identification*, volume 5404, pages 206–214. Proceedings of SPIE, Bellingham, 2004.

Chapter 7
Text-independent Speaker Verification

Asmaa El Hannani, Dijana Petrovska-Delacrétaz, Benoît Fauve, Aurélien Mayoue, John Mason, Jean-François Bonastre, and Gérard Chollet

Abstract In this chapter, an overview of text-independent speaker verification is given first. Then, recent developments needed to reach state-of-the-art performances using low-level (acoustic) features as well as how to use complementary high-level information, are presented. The most relevant speaker verification evaluation campaigns and databases are also summarized. The BioSecure benchmarking framework for speaker verification using open-source state-of the-art algorithms, well-known databases, and reference protocols is presented after.

It is also shown how to reach state-of-the-art performances using open-source software with a case study example on the National Institute of Standards and Technology 2005 Speaker Evaluation data (NIST'2005 SRE). The examples of key factors influencing the performances of speaker verification experiments on the NIST'2005 evaluation data are grouped in three parts. The first set of experiments is related to the importance of front-end processing and data selection to fine-tune the acoustic Gaussian Mixture systems. The second set of experiments illustrates the importance of speaker and session variability modeling methods in order to cope with mismatched enrollment/test conditions. The third series of experiments demonstrates the usefulness of data-driven speech segmentation methods for extracting complementary high-level information. The chapter ends with conclusions and perspectives.

7.1 Introduction

Speaker verification consists of verifying a person's claimed identity. Speech is the product of a complex behavior conveying different speaker-specific traits that are potential sources of complementary information. Consequently, humans use several levels of perceptual cues for speaker recognition. The speaker's voice characteristics can be categorized in "high-level" and "low-level" attributes [92, 17].

D. Petrovska-Delacrétaz et al. (eds.), *Guide to Biometric Reference Systems and Performance Evaluation*, DOI 10.1007/978-1-84800-292-0_7,

The first set of information reflects the spectral properties of speech (low-level), which are related to the physical structure of the vocal apparatus. The second set of information reflects the behavioral traits (high-level) such as prosody, phonetic information, pronunciation, idiolectal word usage, conversational patterns, topics of conversations, etc. These behavioral cues are influenced by many factors such as sociolinguistic context, education and socio-economic environment. Usually, more data are needed to capture such high-level information.

Even if all these levels seem to convey useful speaker information, automatic speaker recognition has concentrated, since the beginning and for a long time, only on low-level information via short-term acoustic features. However, in recent years, there is an increasing interest in using high-level sources of information in addition to the acoustic features. Thus, it has been reported in several studies that gains in speaker recognition accuracy are possible by exploiting such high-level information sources (see e.g. [94], [85]).

Gaussian Mixtures Models (GMMs) have become the dominant approach for text-independent speaker verification systems over the past 10 years. Most of the state-of-the-art text-independent speaker verification systems are based on GMMs or use them in combination with other classifiers. In addition, several techniques were developed around the GMMs in order to improve the robustness of the systems. GMMs have the advantage of representing well-understood statistical models, are computationally inexpensive, and are insensitive to the temporal variability of speech. They are used in combination with well-known speech parametrization techniques based on cepstral analysis. Such systems, denoted here as acoustic GMMs, have excellent performances in artificially good conditions, such as quiet environments, high-quality microphones, matched enrollment and test conditions, and with cooperative speakers. When applied to more challenging real world applications, including recordings with background noise, different microphones and transmission channels, the performances of GMMs using spectral-level features are degraded. Normalization techniques can be used at different levels in order to cope with such more challenging situations.

This chapter describes the most recent developments in automatic text-independent speaker verification that lead to state-of-the-art performance as confirmed by the latest National Institute of Standards and Technology Speaker Recognition Evaluations (NIST-SREs). As explained in [36], in order to reach and remain close to the ever moving state of the art, a high level of research and technology is required. In this context, combined effort across sites can clearly help. The simplest and most common example of this is sharing of system's scores with score-level fusion. At the other extreme of such cooperation is open-source software, the potential of which is far more profound. When used within yearly evaluations the usage of state-of-the-art open-source software avoids duplication of efforts and contributes to meaningful improvements in performance.

Regarding algorithmic performance evaluation two complementary approaches emerge:

- *NIST-like Speaker Recognition Evaluations* [71] and [91], are evaluations in which both systems and databases change every year. In such evaluations, the

algorithmic performance of the submitted systems is measured. With the common mandatory task, all the submitted systems can be compared among them. Such an evaluation gives a snapshot of the status of the submitted systems, that is strongly related to the database and protocols used.
- *Benchmarking evaluation methodology*, introduced in this book, is composed of validated state-of-the-art open-source software and well defined and publicly available development and evaluation databases, as well as related benchmarking protocols. The benchmarking databases and protocols define a common denominator with the open-source reference systems and newly developed systems. With this common denominator (benchmarking database and protocols) the new systems can be compared to the open-source system. In the same time, different systems using this same common denominator could be compared among them. This helps in direct evaluation of the underlying technology, neutralizing to some extent database and protocol nuances.

In this chapter these two complementary algorithmic performance evaluation approaches are illustrated and show how to reach up-to-date performances with open-source software.

The outline of this chapter is the following. In Sect. 7.2, an overview of speaker verification is given, including front-end processing, speaker modeling, decision making, and evaluation. Recent developments and results using high-level information for text-independent speaker verification experiments are also summarized. In Sect. 7.3 the most relevant speaker verification evaluation campaigns and databases are summarized. Section 7.4 presents the BioSecure benchmarking methodology using open-source state-of-the-art algorithms, publicly availably databases, and evaluation protocols. In Sect. 7.5, examples of factors influencing the performances of speaker verification experiments are shown. They illustrate the difficulties of text-independent speaker verification systems. The experiments are grouped in three parts. Results presented in Sect. 7.5.1, illustrate the difficulties of fine tuning a variety of parameters in order to achieve well performing GMM based systems. In Sect. 7.5.2 recent developments, including mainly Factor Analysis (FA) in a generative framework and Nuisance Attribute Projection (NAP), are reported. In these approaches the goal is to model the mismatch by estimating the variabilities from a large data set in which each speaker is recorded in multiple sessions. In Sect. 7.5.3, yet another solution to improve GMM based systems, when more enrollment data is available, is to use high-level information extracted with data-driven methods and to combine them with baseline GMM systems. The conclusions and perspectives are given in Sect. 7.6.

7.2 Review of Text-independent Speaker Verification

[1]There are two main tasks of speaker recognition; speaker identification and speaker verification. The difference between these two tasks resides mainly in the type of decision that should be made. Usually, they are both based on the same modeling

[1] This section is reproduced with permission from Springer-Verlag, source [85].

technologies [112, 98]. The **speaker identification** task consists in determining, from a sequence of speech samples, the identity of an unknown person among N recorded speakers, called reference speakers. The identification answers the question "Whose voice is this?". This process gives place to N possible results. In the **automated speaker verification task**, treated in this chapter, the goal is to decide if a person, who claims to be a target speaker[2], is or is not this speaker. The decision will be either an acceptance or a rejection. The verification answers the question "Am I who I claim to be?" If the person is not a target speaker, he is called an impostor.

There are two phases in any speaker verification system: the enrollment (or training) and verification (or recognition or test). The feature extraction, the speaker modeling and the decision making are the three main modules in these two phases. In the feature extraction step (Sect. 7.2.1.1), which should be the same in the enrollment and verification stages, the speech signal is converted into a sequence of vectors. Each vector represents a short window of the waveform with overlapping adjacent windows. The speaker modeling step (Sect. 7.2.2) creates a model for each of the speakers' voices using samples of their speech. The speaker model once trained allows to perform the verification step by scoring the test speech using the model of the reference speaker. Finally, the resulting score is used to decide whether to accept or reject the claimant (Sect. 7.2.4).

Speaker recognition applications can be classified in three major categories according to the textual content of the speech data:

- In *text-dependent* applications (with Personal Identification Numbers-PINs or passwords) the user must reproduce during the testing phase, the same words or sentences that he pronounced during the enrollment step.
- For *text-prompted* scenarios, during the test step, the speaker has to pronounce sentences imposed by the system. The obligation to pronounce different sentences at each time increases the security of the systems, but requires additional speech recognition implementations.
- In *text-independent* (also called free-text) applications the speaker can speak freely during the training and testing phases.

This chapter is focused on text-independent tasks, because they have the biggest actual and potential applications, considering governmental surveillance scenarios, and applications related to automated dialog systems.

The next section summarizes the state of the art in text-independent speaker verification. An overview of front-end processing, speaker modeling, decision making, systems' evaluation, and current issues and challenges is given.

[2] Also referred in the literature as true, reference or client speaker.

7.2.1 *Front-end Processing*

The task of speaker verification is a typical pattern recognition problem. One important step is the extraction of relevant information from the speech data that is used to characterize the speakers. Thus, before applying speaker recognition, a preprocessing step is necessary. This includes the feature extraction and normalization and also the selection of speech frames. In this section we will focus only on the low-level features.

7.2.1.1 Feature Extraction

Low-level feature extraction consists in extracting a time sequence of feature vectors that represents the temporal evolution of the spectral characteristics of a speech signal. This step is crucial because the choice of one or the other feature extraction methods could influence the performance of the whole system. Most of the speech parametrization techniques used for speaker recognition systems rely on a cepstral representation of speech. Although these speech features are currently the most used and successful in speech recognition, it can be argued that they are not the best choice for speaker recognition because they should capture different information. Indeed, speech recognition aims to capture the characteristics of different speech sounds without any consideration of the speaker-specific traits while speaker recognition aims to exploit this distinctive information. In the following section, Linear Prediction Coding and filter-bank cepstral parameters are briefly summarized.

LPC-based Cepstral Features The basic principle of the Linear Prediction Coding (LPC) [79, 35, 80, 69, 93] method is that the speech signal can be modelled by a linear process predicting the signal at each time using a certain number of preceding samples. After preemphasizing and windowing the speech signal, a spectral analysis is applied on each window of speech using an all-pole modeling constraint. Within each window, each sample is approximated with a linear combination of the previous samples. The estimation of the prediction coefficients is done by minimizing the prediction error between the predicted signal and the actual signal. The prediction coefficients can be further transformed into Linear Predictive Cepstral Coefficients (LPCC) using a recursive algorithm (see [93] for more details).

Another variant of LPC analysis is the Perceptual Linear Prediction (PLP) [52] method. The main idea of this technique is to take advantage of some characteristics derived from the psychoacoustic properties of the human ear. The PLP analysis applies three transformations to the speech signal to simulate the perceptual properties of the human ear. These transformations are applied prior to building an all-pole model.

Filter-bank Cepstral Features The second approach is based on a filter-bank model [15, 89, 93, 13]. The steps needed to transform the speech signal to cepstral vectors based on filter banks are the following: preemphasis, windowing, Fast

Fourier Transform (FFT), extraction of the FFT modulus, application of the filter-bank in order to perform smoothing and get the envelope of the spectrum, log transform and discrete cosine transform in order to get the final cepstral parameters. The filter-bank is defined by the shape of the filters and by their frequency localization. The filters could be spaced uniformly according to a linear scale to calculate the Linear Frequency Cepstral Coefficients (LFCCs) or according to a Mel scale to calculate the Mel Frequency Cepstral Coefficients (MFCCs). MFCCs are supposed to exploit auditory principles [22].

As pointed out in [92], an important property of MFCC based parameters is that the discrete cosine transform, which is used for their calculation, has the property of decorrelating the coefficients. Using decorrelated coefficients is important to reduce computational complexity for probabilistic modeling, such as the widely used Gaussian Mixture Models [95].

Additional Features In most speaker verification systems, features representing the dynamics of the speech signal are used in addition to the static cepstral coefficients. These coefficients are often called "dynamic" or "delta" coefficients as they are estimated using the first and second order derivatives (Δ and $\Delta\Delta$) of the cepstral features [40]. Other coefficients such as the log-energy and its first derivative (Δ-log-energy) are also often added to the feature vectors. In practice, the Δ-log-energy is used, whereas the log-energy is discarded, because the log-energy is too dependent on the recording conditions. An example of using these features is given Sect. 7.5.1.2.

Feature Selection Regarding the cepstral parameters and the additional features, a lot of possible configurations can be found. Until today, there is no study showing the systematic advantage of using one or another configuration. Each approach has proven some advantages in special cases but could not be generalized. The multiple choices are related to the kind of features (LPCC, LFCC, MFCC, etc.), the numbers of coefficients, the use or not of the $\Delta\Delta$ coefficients, of the log-energy and of Δ-log-energy, etc. These choices are dependent on different factors such as the characteristics of the speech signal (noise, bandwidth, sampling rate, etc.), the quantity of data available for training, and the speaker modeling method that will be used. A comparison of some of the different features used for speaker recognition can be found in [96, 12].

7.2.1.2 Selection of Speech Frames

Another crucial step in any speaker recognition system is the selection of the frames conveying speaker information (see Sect. 7.5.1.1). One way to separate speech from non-speech or background noise is to compute a bi-Gaussian model of the log-energy coefficients (see for example [68, 116]). Normally, the useful frames will belong to the Gaussian with the highest mean. A threshold dependent on the parameters of this Gaussian can then be used for the selection of the frames. Another possibility to select the useful frames is to use Hidden Markov Models. Such models are used in current speech recognizers, and models can be learned to separate speech from non-speech and noisy data.

7.2.1.3 Feature Normalization

The speaker verification performance varies according to the sample quality and the environment in which the sample was recorded. The feature vectors are indeed affected directly by the recording conditions. The feature normalization techniques aim to reduce the information specific to the recording conditions without affecting the speaker-specific characteristics. This section gives a brief overview of the feature normalization state of the art.

Cepstral Mean Substraction and Variance Normalization Cepstral Mean Substraction (CMS) [39] is one of the widely used normalization methods in speech and speaker recognition. The CMS, also referred to as blind deconvolution, consists of removing the mean cepstral coefficients from each feature over the entire speech duration, which reduces the stationary convolution noises due to the transmission channel effects. The CMS could also be performed over a sliding window in order to take into account the linear channel variation inside the same recording. To compensate for the linear channel variations, CMS was noted as a promising approach. However, under additive noise conditions, the feature estimates degrade significantly. That is why CMS is sometimes supplemented with variance normalization [111, 61]. The coefficients are transformed to fit a zero mean and a unit variance distribution over all the files or using a sliding window. The mean and variance values are usually estimated only on frames belonging to speech to have a better estimate of the transmission channel.

RASTA The RASTA (Relative SpecTrA) [53] is a generalization of the CMS method. It addresses the problem of a slowly time-varying linear channel in contrast to the time-invariant channel attenuated by the CMS technique. Its essence is a cepstral filter that removes low and high modulation frequencies.

Feature Warping The whole distribution of the coefficients and not only the mean and the variance are affected by noise and various channel and transducer effects. Recently, a feature warping [82] method was applied to deal with this problem. This method aims to construct a more robust representation of each cepstral feature distribution. This is achieved by mapping the individual cepstral feature distributions such that they follow a normal distribution over a window of speech frames. In more recent work [115], a variant of the feature warping is presented. This last approach, called short-time gaussianization, is similar but applies a linear transformation to the features before mapping them to a normal distribution. The purpose of this linear transformation is to make the resulting features independent. Results [82, 8] have shown that feature warping slightly outperforms mean and variance normalization, but it is computationally more expensive.

Feature Mapping The feature mapping-approach [94] is another normalization method based on the idea of minimizing the channel variability in the feature domain. This method focuses on mapping features from different channels into a common channel independent feature space. The feature mapping procedure is achieved in the following steps. First, a channel independent GMM is trained using a pool of data from many different channels. Then, channel dependent GMMs are trained by adapting the channel-independent GMM using channel-dependent data. Finally, the feature-mapping functions are learned by examining how the channel independent model parameters change after the adaptation. During the normalization step, and for each utterance, the most likely channel-dependent model is first detected and then each feature vector in the utterance is mapped to the channel independent space using the corresponding feature-mapping functions. This method showed good performances in channel compensation, but its disadvantage is that it requires a lot of data to train the different channel models.

Factor Analysis Another successful approach for modeling channel variability is the joint factor analysis [58, 57]. This method is quite similar to the feature mapping with the exception that in joint factor analysis the channel effect is modelled by a normal distribution of the GMM supervector space, whereas in the feature mapping this effect is modelled by a discrete distribution. The basic assumption in the joint factor analysis is that a speaker and channel-dependent supervector can be decomposed into a sum of two supervectors—one depends on the speaker and the other on the channel. Also it assumes that speaker and channel supervectors are both normally distributed.

Suppose that a speaker S is modeled by GMMs with C mixture components in an P dimensional feature space. That is, a speaker and channel-dependent supervector, denoted by a CP-dimensional random vector M, can be decomposed as:

$$M = sv + c \tag{7.1}$$

where sv is the speaker-dependent supervector and c is the channel-dependent supervector. Thus, the factor analysis model is specified by the hyperparameters of sv and c. To estimate these hyperparameters, first a speaker independent Principal Component Analysis (PCA) model is trained from a large database in which each speaker is recorded in multiple sessions. Then the resulting model is adapted to each target speaker.

Nuisance Attribute Projection (NAP) The Nuisance Attribute Projection (NAP) technique was introduced by Solomonoff et al. in [105] to handle the problem of handset and channel variabilities for an SVM based speaker verification system. This approach consists in modifying the kernel function in order to increase its ability to be invariant to channel effects. For this purpose the authors propose the use of modified kernel matrix which projects out the effects of channel. The criterion for constructing this matrix is to minimize the average distance between cross-channel pairs.

7.2.2 Speaker Modeling Techniques

Once the feature vectors are extracted and the irrelevant frames corresponding to non-speech or noisy data are removed, the remaining data could be used for extracting speaker-specific information. This step is denoted as training (or enrollment) step of the recognition system and the associated speech data used to build the speaker model are called training (or enrollment) data. During the test phase, the same feature vectors are extracted from the waveform of a test utterance and matched against the relevant model.

As the focus of this chapter is on text-independent speaker verification, techniques based on measuring distances between two patterns are only mentioned, leaving more emphasis to statistical modeling techniques. The "distance based" methods were mainly used in systems developed at the beginning of the speaker recognition history. In the beginning (1930–1980), methods like template matching and Dynamic Time Warping and Vector Quantization were used and evaluated on small size databases recorded in "clean conditions," with few speech data and few speakers. With the evolution of storage and computers' calculating capacities, methods using statistical models such as Gaussian Mixture Models, as well as Neural Networks, began to be more widely used. They cover the period from 1980–2003. Last year's developments combine the well-developed statistical models with methods that extract high-level information for speaker characterization

In this section, only statistical approaches are presented. There are several ways to build speaker models using statistical methods. They can be divided into two distinct categories: generative and discriminative models. The difference between the generative and discriminative models is that the former treat the samples of one speaker independently from the samples of the other group, whereas the latter minimize the error on training samples of data belonging to both classes (i.e., targets and impostors).

7.2.2.1 Generative Models

Generative models include mainly Gaussian Mixture Models (GMMs) and Hidden Markov Models (HMMs). These models are probability density estimators that model the acoustic feature vectors. GMMs represent a particular case of HMMs and can be viewed as a single-state HMM where the probability density is defined by a mixture of Gaussians.

Gaussian Mixture Models The use of Gaussian Mixture Models (GMMs) for speaker modeling was introduced by D. Reynolds [95, 99]. Over the past 10 years this approach has become the dominant approach for text-independent speaker verification systems. GMMs are probability density estimators that attempt to capture all of the variations of the speech data. Given a P-dimensional feature vector, x_t, the probability density function $p(x_t|\lambda)$ is approximated as a weighed sum of N multinormal Gaussian densities

$$p(x_t|\lambda) = \sum_{n=1}^{N} w_n \mathcal{N}(x_t, \mu_n, \Sigma_n) \tag{7.2}$$

where $\mathcal{N}(x_t, \mu_n, \Sigma_n)$ is a density function with a $P \times 1$ mean vector, μ_n, and a $P \times P$ covariance matrix[3], Σ_n. w_n is the mixture weights, with the constraint $\sum_{n=1}^{N} w_n = 1$.

A GMM is defined by the set of parameters $\lambda = \{w_n, \mu_n, \Sigma_n\}$. During the training phase, these parameters are iteratively estimated using the Expectation-Maximization (EM) algorithm [24]. Usually, only limited data are available to train the speaker model. Therefore, adaptation techniques are used. The speaker model is then derived by adapting the parameters of the background model with the speaker's enrollment speech data. Different adaptation techniques, such as Maximum a Posteriori (MAP) [43] and Maximum Likelihood Linear Regression (MLLR) estimations [64], can be applied.

By making the assumption of independence of the features, the log-likelihood of a model λ for a sequence of feature vectors $X = \{x_1, \ldots. x_T\}$ is computed as follows:

$$\log p(X|\lambda) = \sum_{t=1}^{T} \log p(x_t|\lambda) \tag{7.3}$$

where $p(x_t|\lambda)$ is computed as stated in equation 7.2. The logarithm is used in equation 7.3 in order to avoid computer precision problems. Note that often the average log-likelihood value $\frac{\log p(X|\lambda)}{T}$ is used in order to normalize out the duration effects from the log-likelihood value.

Conceptually the GMM does not account for temporal ordering of feature vectors. The linguistic and temporal structure of the speech signal is not taken into account, and all sounds are represented using a single model. The temporal and linguistic knowledge can be incorporated by using HMMs.

Hidden Markov Models A Hidden Markov Model (HMM) is a doubly stochastic process in that it has an underlying stochastic process that is not observable (hence the term hidden) but can be observed through another stochastic process that produces a sequence of observations [93]. A Markov chain consists of states and arcs between these states. The arcs, which are associated to transition probabilities, permit to pass from one state to the another, to skip a state, or contrary to remain in a state. In a Markov Model, one knows, at each time of the progression, the states and their probabilities of transitions. Whereas in a Hidden Markov Model, the states sequence is hidden. External observations, such as the vectors resulting from the pre-processing phase, will allow to determine the state sequence that minimize the probability of the observations given the HMM parameters. As explained in [93] there are three fundamental problems for the HMM design: (a) the evaluation of the probability (or likelihood) of a sequence of observations given a specific HMM, (b) the determination of the best sequence of model states, and (c) the adjustment of model parameters so as to best account of the observed signal.

---

[3] Usually, the coefficients of the feature vectors are assumed uncorrelated, so only diagonal covariance matrices are used.

For speaker recognition applications, each state of HMMs may represent phones or other larger units of speech. Temporal information is encoded by moving from one state to another respecting the allowed transitions. In this case, the HMM method consists in determining for each speaker the best alignment between the sequence of speech vectors and the Hidden Markov Model associated with the pronounced word or phrase. The probabilities of the HMM process are accumulated to obtain the utterance likelihood in a similar fashion to the GMM.

Gaussian Mixture Models versus Hidden Markov Models State-of-the-art text-independent speaker verification systems use GMM. Conceptually they do not account for temporal ordering of feature vectors. The linguistic and temporal structure of the speech signal is not taken into account and all sounds are represented using a unique model. The temporal and linguistic knowledge can be incorporated by using HMM. In text-dependent speaker recognition tasks, where there is a prior knowledge of the textual content, HMM [77, 109] are more accurate than GMM since the former can better model temporal variations. In text-independent tasks the GMM have proven their efficiency through consecutive NIST speaker-recognition evaluations. Some recent studies [108, 14, 7] have looked at improving performance for text-independent speaker verification by attempting to convert the task into a text-dependent one. This was achieved by constraining the verification process to a limited set of words. The results were encouraging.

Motivated by research that has shown that voiced phones and fricatives are the most effective broad speech classes for speaker discrimination [81, 28, 78, 86], several studies examined the combination of speech and speaker recognition for text-independent speaker verification, trying to exploit the temporal information of speech data. Most of them are based on GMM, HMM or MultiLayer Perceptrons. The idea behind all these systems is the following: first a sequence of phones is found from a given utterance using speech recognition systems, based on HMM. Then speaker verification is performed separately for each phone to obtain a verification score. Finally, the global utterance score is obtained by combining the weighted results from all phones.

In order to exploit the above ideas for text-independent speaker recognition tasks, more data and the availability of speech recognizers are necessary. Such approaches necessitate the usage of large vocabulary speech recognizers, phone recognizers, or data-driven speech segmentation methods. They can be used in two manners: to compute likelihood values at a finer temporal level or to extract high-level information, as shown in Sect. 7.5.3.

7.2.2.2 Discriminative Models

The discriminative models are optimized to minimize the error on a set of genuine and impostor training samples. They include, among many other approaches, MultiLayer Perceptrons (MLPs) and Support Vector Machines (SVMs). They also include discriminatively trained generative models [67, 90].

MultiLayer Perceptrons MultiLayer Perceptrons (MLP) [50] are feed-forward neural networks usually trained using the back-propagation algorithm. They can be used as binary classifiers for speaker verification systems to separate the speaker and the nonspeaker classes. The MLP is usually composed of several layers, each one with several nodes. Each node computes a linear weighted sum over its input connections, where the weights of the summation are the adjustable parameters. A transfer function is applied to the result to compute the output of that node. The weights of the network are estimated by gradient descent based on the back-propagation algorithm. An MLP for speaker verification would classify speakers' and impostors' access by scoring each frame of the test utterance. The final utterance score is the mean of the MLP's output over all the frames in the utterance. Among the works that used MLPs in text-independent speaker verification tasks, we can mention [73] and [87]. Despite their discriminating power, the MLPs present some disadvantages. The main ones are that their optimal configuration is not easy to select and a lot of data are needed for the training and the cross-validation steps. That could explain why the MLPs are not widely used in speaker-verification systems (as it can be noticed in the yearly NIST speaker recognition evaluations).

Support Vector Machines Support Vector Machines are discriminant and binary classifiers [110]. Their basic principle is to project the nonlinearly separable multidimensional data in a hyperspace, where they can be linearly separated. Given a collection of feature vectors belonging to two classes that are separable by a hyperplane, the SVM will attempt to find the hyperplane with the maximal margin. In other words, the distance between the closest labeled vectors to the hyperplane is maximal. This hyperplane could be further used (during the testing phase) to determine to which class an unknown vector belongs.

In recent years, the SVM-based approach has become one of the best performing discriminant methods [104]. In speaker verification, the use of SVM has taken two directions. The first approach uses SVM in the acoustic features space [103]. The decision score is calculated by averaging the SVM scores over all the frames in the test utterance. This method gave promising results for the speaker-identification task, but proved to be less successful than well-trained GMM for speaker verification.

The second approach consists of combining GMMs and SVMs. Some results are presented in [113, 114, 26, 59, 23, 18]. Wan and Renals incorporate in [113, 114] generative models into a discriminative framework of an SVM so that an entire utterance is classified discriminatively instead of the constituent frames. A similar approach is presented in [26], where discriminative training of GMM is performed. In [59, 23, 18] the SVM was used in order to better separate the GMM scores. All these techniques, which take advantage of both generative and discriminative models, produced better accuracy than either their purely generative or purely discriminative version.

Few attempts have been made to use discriminatively trained generative models [67, 90]. The difference between the generative and discriminative models is that the former treat the samples of one speaker independently from the samples of the other group whereas the latter minimize the error on training samples of data belonging to both classes (i.e., speaker and impostors).

7.2.3 High-level Information and its Fusion

In recent years, research on text-independent speaker verification has expanded from using only the acoustic (low-level) content of speech to trying to exploit high-level information. The former type of information is related to physical traits of the vocal apparatus. However, the latter type includes behavioral cues like dialect, word usage, conversational patterns, topics of conversations, etc. Behavioral cues are generally more difficult to extract by automated systems but they are less sensitive to noise and channel mismatch than the low-level cues.

The above-mentioned information sources for speaker recognition can be categorized, running from low-level features to high-level information sources.

- **Acoustic**: The acoustic features represent the spectral properties of speech and convey information about the shape of the vocal apparatus. They are a direct function of the detailed anatomical structure of the vocal tract and are modelled using very short time windows (typically 10-20 ms).
- **Prosodic**: The prosodic information are derived from the acoustic characteristics of speech and they include pitch, duration, and intensity. All these forms are present in varying quantities in every spoken utterance.
- **Phonetic and pseudo-phonetic**: These features are related to phonetic and data-driven speech units, denoted here as "pseudo-phonetic" units. The phoneme is the atomic speech unit. The phonetic characteristics are related to the way a speaker pronounces different phones.
- **Idiolectal**: Idiolectal information characterizes the speaking style. It is manifested by patterns of word selection and grammar. Every individual has an idiolect, however, it could depend on the context in which the speaker is talking (such as the kind of interlocutor, the subject, the emotional situation, etc.)
- **Dialogic**: Dialogic features are based on the conversational patterns and define the manner in which the speaker communicates. Indeed, every speaker could be characterized by the frequency and the duration of his turns in a conversation. These traits are also dependent on the conversation context.
- **Semantic**: Semantic characteristics of the speech are related to the meaning of the utterance. The kind of subject frequently discussed by the speaker could also provide information on her/his identity.

Recently, there has been a rising interest in computing and modeling high-level features, which start to be used in combination with low-level spectral features. Studies examining the exploitation of high-level information sources have provided strong evidence that gains in speaker recognition accuracy are possible [94, 17, 41, 37]. Among the high-level speaker verification systems that have been largely explored, one could note the phonetic-based systems. The use of prosodic, idiolectal and duration characteristics of speakers was also explored in several studies [1, 25, 19, 37].

The following paragraphs present a summary of the usefulness of high-level information for speaker verification experiments.

Prosodic Information Results published in [106, 1] have shown that prosodic information can be used to effectively improve the performance of speaker verification systems. In [106] the authors appended the prosodic features to a standard spectral based features and used them in a traditional distribution modeling systems. The addition of these dynamic prosodic features improved the performance of the GMM system significantly. Adami et al. proposed in [1] two approaches that use the fundamental frequency and energy trajectories to capture long-term information. The first approach uses bigrams to capture the dynamics of the fundamental frequency and energy trajectories for each speaker. The second approach uses the fundamental frequency trajectories of a pre-defined set of words as the speaker templates and then, using Dynamic Time Warping, computes the distance between the templates and the words from the test message. They also showed that the prosodic approaches improve the performance of systems that use short-term information.

Phonetic Information The phonetic information is also an important aspect of the speech signal that conveys speaker information. Matsui and Furui, in [72], used phoneme-specific HMMs for modeling the target speakers. A speaker verification system based on broad phonetic categories was proposed in [62, 56] and achieved an improvement over the baseline system. Auckenthaler et al. [5], compared GMMs and HMMs across different phonemes, and unlike what is detailed in the above cited works, phonetic information was used only during the scoring phase. Hebert et al. [51] introduced a phonetic class-based GMM system based on a tree-like structure, which outperformed a single GMM system. Closer to what is presented in this last work are the approaches presented in [48] and [45], where phoneme-adapted GMMs were built for each speaker. The authors concluded that the phoneme-adapted GMM system outperformed the phoneme-independent GMM system. Klusacek et al. [60] present a new technique to explicitly model speaker's pronunciations. It uses time-aligned streams of phones and phonemes to model speaker's specific pronunciation.

Idiolectal Information The idiolectal information was explored by several authors. Doddington [25] studied the possibility of using word n-gram statistics for speaker verification. This technique exploited the idiolectal information in a straightforward way and gave encouraging results. Motivated by this work, similar techniques have been applied to phone n-gram statistics [3]. This last approach gave good results and was found to provide features complementary to short-term acoustic features. Another variant of this approach is presented by Campbell et al. [19]. The basic idea of this approach is to use an SVM to combine the phone n-gram scores instead of the log-likelihood ratio method. The SVM based method halved the error rate of the standard phone n-gram approach [3]. Further improvements were reported by using lattice phonetic decoding instead of the 1-best decoding [49].

Data-driven High-level Information Most of the above reported promising methods are, however, based on phonetic transcriptions. Two of the major problems that arise when phone-based systems are being developed are the possible mismatch between the development and evaluation data and the lack of transcribed databases.

Data-driven segmentation techniques provide a potential solution to these problems because they do not use transcribed data and can easily be applied on development data minimizing the mismatches. Their usage for speech recognition is not straightforward, but such methods can be used to extract speaker-specific information, for language identification [83] or for call-type classification [84]. Petrovska-Delacrétaz et al. [88, 87] proposed a speaker verification system, based on an automatic data-driven speech segmentation. The speech data was clustered in eight classes and a per-class MLP were used to model the speaker. This data-driven segmentation is based on Automatic Language Independent Speech Processing (ALISP) tools [21]. More recently, El Hannanni et al. [30, 32, 31] used the same method in combination with Gaussian Mixture Models (GMM). In [30] the performances of a segmental ALISP-based and a global GMM systems were compared. Even though the ALISP classes were not explicitly modeled and the segmental information was used only during the scoring phase, the segmental system provided better performance compared to the global GMM system. In [32] the data-driven ALISP units were explicitly modeled by GMMs. The data-driven segmentation was also used to capture speaker-specific idiolectal information [31]. In this system, speaker specific information is captured only by analyzing sequences of ALISP units like in [3]. This system was fused with an acoustic GMM system and the resulting fused system reduced the error rate of the individual systems. In [33] the authors attempted to analyze the correlation between the automatically aligned phonemes and ALISP units. They also compare the results obtained with a speaker recognition system based on data-driven acoustic units and phonetic speaker recognition systems trained on Spanish and English data. Compared to phone, data-driven units could lead to better speaker recognition results with the additional advantage of not requiring phonetically transcribed speech. On the other hand, further improvements can be achieved by combining both approaches. The results of combining different levels of information using such data-driven methods on NIST'2005 are shown in Sect. 7.5.3.

7.2.4 Decision Making

The speaker verification task involves making the decision whether the speech data collected during the test phase, belongs to the claimed model or not. Given a speech segment X and a claimed identity S the speaker verification system should choose one of the following hypothesis:

H_S: X is pronounced by S
$H_{\bar{S}}$: X is **not** pronounced by S

The decision between the two hypothesis is usually based on a likelihood ratio given by

$$\Lambda(X) = \frac{p(X|H_S)}{p(X|H_{\bar{S}})} \begin{cases} > \Theta & accept\ H_S \\ < \Theta & accept\ H_{\bar{S}} \end{cases} \tag{7.4}$$

where $p(X|H_S)$ and $p(X|H_{\bar{S}})$ are the probability density functions (called also likelihoods) associated with the speaker S and nonspeaker $\bar{S}$, respectively. Θ is the threshold to accept or reject H_S.

In practice, H_S is represented by a model λ_S, estimated using the training speech from the hypothesized speaker S, and $H_{\bar{S}}$ is represented by a model $\lambda_{\bar{S}}$, estimated using a set of other speakers that cover as much as possible the space of the alternative hypothesis. There are two main approaches to selecting this set of other speakers.

The first one consists of choosing, for each speaker S a set of speakers $\bar{S_1},...,\bar{S_N}$, called a cohort [102]. In this case, each speaker will have a corresponding nonspeaker model.

A more practical approach consists of having a unique or gender-dependent set of speakers representing the nonspeakers, where a single (or gender dependent) nonspeaker model is trained for all speakers [97]. This model is usually trained using speech samples from a large number of representative speakers. This model is referred into the literature as world model or Universal Background Model (UBM) [99]. This last approach is the most commonly used in speaker verification systems. It has the advantage of using a single nonspeaker model for all the hypothesized speakers, or two gender-dependent world (background) models.

The likelihood ratio in (7.4) is then rewritten as

$$\Lambda(X) = \frac{p(X|\lambda_S)}{p(X|\lambda_{\bar{S}})} \tag{7.5}$$

Often the logarithm of this ratio is used. The final score is then:

$$S(X) = \log \Lambda(X) = \log p(X|\lambda_S) - \log p(X|\lambda_{\bar{S}}) \tag{7.6}$$

The values of the likelihoods $p(X|\lambda_S)$ and $p(X|\lambda_{\bar{S}})$ are computed using one of the techniques described in Sect. 7.2.4.

Once the model is trained, the speaker verification system should make a decision to accept or reject the claimed identity. This last step consists of comparing the score of the test utterance with a decision threshold. Setting the threshold appropriately for a specific speaker verification application is still a challenging task. The threshold is usually chosen during the development phase, and is speaker-independent. However these kinds of thresholds do not really reflect the speaker peculiarities and the intra-speaker variability. Furthermore, if there is a mismatch between development and test data, the optimal operating point could be different from the pre-set threshold.

There are two main approaches to dealing with the problem of automatic threshold estimation. The first one consists of setting a priori speaker-dependent threshold [66], in such a way that the threshold is adjusted for each speaker in order to compensate the score variability effects. In the second approach, score normalization techniques (see Sect. 7.2.4.1) make the speaker-independent threshold more robust and easy to set.

7.2.4.1 Score Normalization

The score normalization techniques aim, generally, to reduce the scores' variabilities. This normalization is equivalent, from the decision point of view, to the use of a speaker-dependent threshold. However, the score normalization permits the estimation of a unique speaker-independent threshold.

Most of the actual normalization techniques are based on the assumption that the impostors' scores follow a Gaussian distribution where the mean, μ_S, and the standard deviation σ_S, depend on the considered speaker model and/or test utterance. These mean and standard deviation values will then be used to normalize any incoming score $\Lambda(X)$:

$$\tilde{\Lambda}(X) = \frac{S(X) - \mu_S}{\sigma_S} \tag{7.7}$$

In this section, we will briefly describe the score normalization methods used to deal with mismatched enrollment/test conditions.

ZNorm The zero normalization (ZNorm) method [65, 101] normalizes the score distribution using the claimed speaker statistics. In other words, the claimed speaker model is tested against a set of impostors, resulting in an impostor similarity score distribution, which is then used to estimate the normalization parameters μ_S and σ_S. The main advantage of the ZNorm is that the estimation of these parameters can be performed during the training step (off-line).

TNorm The test normalization (TNorm) [4] is another score normalization technique in which the mean and the standard deviation parameters, μ_S and σ_S, are estimated using the test utterance. Thus, during testing, a set of impostor models is used to calculate impostor scores for the given test utterance. μ_S and σ_S are estimated using these scores. The TNorm is known to improve the performances particularly in the region of low false alarm. More details about TNorm can be found in [75]. In contrary to the ZNorm, the TNorm has to be performed online during testing.

Variants of Score Normalization There are several variants of the ZNorm and TNorm that aim to reduce the microphone and transmission channel's effects. Among the variants of ZNorm, are the Handset Normalization (HNorm) [101] and the Channel Normalization (CNorm). In these last approaches, a handset- or channel-dependent normalization parameters are estimated by testing each speaker model against a handset or channel-dependent set of impostors. During testing, the type of handset or channel related to the test utterance is first detected and then the corresponding set of parameters are used for score normalization. The HTNorm, a variant of TNorm, uses basically the same idea as the HNorm. Here, handset-dependent normalization parameters are estimated by testing each test utterance against handset-dependent impostor models. Finally, and in order to improve the speaker verification performance, different normalization methods may be combined, such for the ZTNorm (ZNorm followed by TNorm) or TZNorm (TNorm followed by ZNorm).

DNorm The main issue to be addressed when using TNorm, ZNorm or their variants is the availability of pseudo-impostor's data. Ben et al. proposed in [11] another normalization method, called DNorm, to deal with this problem. In this approach, pseudo-impostor data are generated from the world (background) model using Monte Carlo-based method.

7.2.5 Performance Evaluation Metrics

7.2.5.1 Performance Evaluation on a Single Operating Point

The performance of speaker verification systems is evaluated as a function of the error rates. There are two types of errors that can occur during a verification task: false acceptance when the system accepts an impostor and false rejection when the system rejects a valid speaker. Both types of errors depend on the decision threshold Θ (see Eq. 7.4].

With a high threshold, the system will be highly secured. In other words, the system will make very few false acceptances but a lot of false rejections. If the threshold is fixed to a low value, the system will be more convenient to the users, making few false rejections but lots of false acceptances. The rates of false acceptance, *FAR*, and false rejection, *FRR*, define the operating point of the system. They are calculated as follows:

$$FAR = \frac{number\ of\ false\ acceptances}{number\ of\ impostors\ access} \tag{7.8}$$

$$FRR = \frac{number\ of\ false\ rejections}{number\ of\ targets\ access} \tag{7.9}$$

These rates are normally estimated on the development set and are further used to compute the Detection Cost Function (DCF). This cost function is a weighted measure of both false acceptance and false rejection rates:

$$DCF = C_{FR}P_{tar}FRR + C_{FA}P_{imp}FAR \tag{7.10}$$

where C_{FR} is the cost of false rejection, C_{FA} is the cost of false acceptance, P_{tar} is the a priori probability of targets and P_{imp} is the a priori probability of impostors.

The DCF is the most used measure to evaluate the performances of operational speaker verification systems. The smaller the value of the DCF is, the better the system for the given application and conditions is. Thus, the decision threshold should be optimized in order to minimize the DCF. This optimization is often done during the development of the system on a limited set of data.

Another popular single point performance measure is the Equal Error Rate (EER). It represents the error at the threshold that gives equal false acceptance and false rejection rates, and it is not interpretable in function of the cost. The EER is widely used as a reference indication of the performance of a given system.

7.2.5.2 Detection Error Trade-off (DET) Curve

The measures presented previously indicate the performance of the system at a single operating point. However, representing the performance of the speaker verification system over the whole range of operating points is also useful and can be achieved by using a performance curve. The Detection Error Trade-off (DET) curve [70] is a variant of the Receiver Operating Characteristic (ROC) curve [29], which has been widely used for this purpose. In the DET curve the *FAR* is plotted as a function of the *FRR* and the axis follow a normal deviate scale. The points of the DET curve are obtained by varying the threshold Θ. This representation allows an easy comparison of the performances of the systems at different operating points. The EER appears directly on this curve as the intersection of the DET curve with the first bisectrix.

7.2.6 Current Issues and Challenges

Speaker verification performance is dependent upon many factors that could be grouped in the following categories:

- **Amount of Speech Data**: The amount of speech data available for enrollment is important in order to have good speaker models. Duration of speech that is used during the test phase has also a large impact on the accuracy of the systems. This was confirmed during the NIST-SRE evaluations [76], where it has been shown that the duration and number of sessions of enrollment and verification affect the performance of the speaker verification systems.
- **Intra-speaker Variabilities**: Usually the speaker model is obtained using limited speech data that characterizes the speaker at a given time and situation. However, the voice could change due to aging, illness, emotions, tiredness and potentially other factors. For these reasons, the speaker model may not be representative of the speaker in all his/her potential states. Variabilities may not all be covered, which negatively affects the performance of the speaker verification systems. To deal with this problem, incremental enrollment techniques can be used in order to include the short and long-term evolution of the voice (see for example [9]).
- **Mismatch Factors**: Mismatched recording conditions between enrollment and testing is the main challenge for automatic speaker recognition, especially when the speech signal is acquired over telephone lines. Differences in the telephone handset, in the transmission channel and in the recording devices can, indeed, introduce variabilities over the recordings and decrease the accuracy of the system. This decrease of accuracy is mainly due to the statistical models that capture not only the speaker characteristics but also the environmental ones. Hence, the system decision may be biased if the verification environment is different from the enrollment. Normalization techniques done at a feature level (presented in Sect. 7.2.1.3) and the normalization technique at a score level (presented in

Sect. 7.2.4.1) are necessary to make speaker verification systems more robust to recording conditions. The high-level features introduced in Sect. 7.2.3 are also important because they are supposed to be more robust to mismatched conditions.

7.3 Speaker Verification Evaluation Campaigns and Databases

Because many proposed methods only solve specific problems, it is crucial to clearly understand the potential and limitations of each method. Standard evaluation resources with which one can compare these methods is also a key point when comparing different systems. The goal of this section is to present the most important evaluation campaigns and databases. Regarding the evaluation campaigns, the National Institute of Standards and Technology Speaker Recognition Evaluations (NIST-SRE) are by far the most popular evaluation campaigns, when telephonic speech and text-independent tasks are considered.

Speaker verification can also be done in a text-dependent mode, where the user has to choose his password and pronounce it in order to be recognized. An overview of text-dependent databases can be found in [44, 16].

Important issues for operational systems are the accuracy regarding the acceptance of true clients and the robustness of the system in relation to impostors. Concerning the latter point only random (also called zero effort) impostors are normally considered. The issue of robustness to impostors with prerecorded, transformed, or synthesized speech, has also to be considered. The focus of this overview regarding speaker recognition databases is oriented towards speaker databases that also allow or define evaluation of the biometric systems including other impostures than only random impostures.

7.3.1 National Institute of Standards and Technology Speaker Recognition Evaluations (NIST-SRE)

The speech group of the National Institute of Standards and Technology (NIST) has been organizing evaluations of text-independent speaker verification technologies since 1997, with increasing success over the years [74].

The NIST Speaker Recognition Evaluations (NIST-SRE) are about text-independent speaker verification over telephonic lines. On almost a yearly basis, a unique data-set and a core evaluation protocol are provided to each participating laboratory, so that participants can compare their submitted results and highlight problems that require further research. The data are sent to the subscribed participants. One month later, the participants have to deliver their results, and also participate in a workshop (open only to the participants). This workshop gives the opportunity to present the submitted systems, and to discuss the results and the problems that are still to be solved. Each participant can also submit publications but only related to their own systems.

Usually, the NIST-SRE data are composed of enrollment data using increasing amounts of speech data (from five minutes to an hour), and with mismatched enrollment-test conditions. The duration of test data is about five minutes. There is one common (core) task that each participant has to run, called *1conv-1conv* task (where approximately five minutes of speech is used for enrollment and five minutes for testing). In order to study the influence of more enrollment data, another task called *8conv-1conv* is also present (with approximately one hour of speech data for enrollment and five minutes for testing).

NIST-SRE evaluations are mostly relevant for applications when the interest is to find if speech from a target speaker is present in the test data. Such applications include governmental surveillance applications, as well as applications for speaker segmentation, clustering or database annotations. NIST-SRE represent a unique, challenging and valuable test bed for text-independent speaker verification.

Speaker verification has a potential for commercial applications, but in order to be convenient for the users, such systems need to be functional with short training and testing data, and to resist not only random impostors but also to detect other kind of impostures. In order to ensure secure applications of speaker verification technologies it is important to consider robustness to intentional impostures. Multimodality could bring some advantages, including better accuracy and robustness to impostures. Such evaluations were proposed in the recent BioSecure Multimodal Evaluation Campaign (BMEC'2007) (see Chap. 11) where multimodal biometric systems were tested in the presence of different types of imposture.

7.3.2 Speaker Recognition Databases

For text-independent speaker verification experiments, NIST-SRE databases (described in the previous paragraph) are the most relevant ones. Among the available text-dependent speaker verification databases [44, 16], we will list only some of them, either because they are widely used, or because they could be combined together for new evaluation protocols, or because they address the issue of robustness to impostures.

The BANCA [6], BIOMET [42], MyIDea [27], and IV^2 [55] databases present the unique feature that the acquisition protocols are performed in similar ways, so that new evaluation protocols could be designed with them. They are also presented in a more detailed way in Chap. 11, where other multimodal databases are also described.

Among the available speaker databases, in order to put in practice the BioSecure Benchmarking Evaluation Methodology we have chosen the NIST'2005 evaluation data and the speech part of the BANCA database. One of the NIST databases is chosen because NIST-SRE has the longest evaluation history and experience. NIST-SRE databases are most easily available to participants in the yearly evaluations.

They can also be obtained through the Linguistic Data Consortium (LDC) [63]. As an alternative choice, for laboratories that have not participated in NIST-SRE evaluations, we have chosen the BANCA [6] database. The benchmarking speaker verification experiments which are introduced in the following section, use the BANCA and NIST'2005 speech databases.

7.4 The BioSecure Speaker Verification Benchmarking Framework

There are different factors that affect the performance of a speaker verification system. They can be evaluated using appropriately designed corpora that reflect the reality of the speaker characteristics and the complexity of the foreseen application. Measuring real progress achieved with new research methods and pinpointing the unsolved problems is only possible when relevant publicly available databases and protocols are associated with a benchmarking framework [20]. Such benchmarking framework should be composed of open-source state-of-the-art algorithms defined on publicly available databases and protocols. In this section, we present the Speaker Benchmarking Framework. First, we describe the already existing open-source software that was used as a reference system. Then, the databases used for the evaluation and the corresponding protocols are described along with the associated performance measures and results.

The benchmarking experiments defined in this section can be easily reproduced using some additional material that could be found on the companion website [38]. All the needed material (including pointers to the open-source software and databases, How-to documents, scripts and lists of tests to be done) are available on this website.

7.4.1 Description of the Open Source Software

Two open-source software packages have been tested in the framework of the BioSecure Benchmarking framework:

- The first one is based on the HTK software [54] (used for the feature extraction part) and the BECARS v1.1.9 [10] open-source toolkits. It is also referred as BECARS Reference system throughout this chapter.
- The second one is based on SPro [107] (used for the feature extraction part) and ALIZE v1.04 [2] open-source toolkits. It is also referred as ALIZE Reference system throughout this chapter.

Both systems are composed of three main modules:

- **Feature extraction**: The speech processing is based on the usual cepstral feature vectors (such as Mel Frequency Cepstral Coefficients-MFCC), performed

on 20ms Hamming window frames with 10ms of overlap. From these features first order deltas and delta-energy could be used in addition. The speech activity detection, normally a bi-Gaussian model, is fitted to the energy component of a speech sample. The threshold t used to determine the set of frames to discard is computed as follows: $t = \mu - 2 * \sigma$, where μ and σ are the mean and the variance of the highest Gaussian component, respectively. Using only the frames corresponding to nonsilent portions, the feature vectors are normalized to fit a zero-mean and an unit variance distribution.
- **Model building**: The Gaussian Mixture Model (GMM) approach is used to build models from the speaker data. An Universal gender-dependent Background Model (UBM) is trained with the Expectation Maximization (EM) algorithm. Then, each speaker model is built by adapting the parameters of the UBM using the speaker's training feature vectors and the Maximum A Posteriori (MAP) criterion.
- **Score calculation**: The similarity score is the estimation of the log-likelihood ratio between the target (client) and world models.

7.4.2 The Benchmarking Framework for the BANCA Database

The BioSecure Reference Database is the speech part of the BANCA database [6]. This database is composed by 52 speakers divided into two groups $G1$ and $G2$ of 26 speakers each (13 females and 13 males). Each speaker recorded 12 sessions, each of these sessions containing two recordings: one client access where the speaker pronounces digits and his/her (fake) own address and one impostor access where he/she pronounces digits and the address of another person. The 12 sessions were separated into three different scenarios:

- Controlled for Sessions 1-4
- Degraded for Sessions 5-8
- Adverse for Sessions 9-12

An additional set of 30 other subjects (15 females and 15 males) recorded one session. This set of data is referred to as world data. These speakers claimed two different identities.

7.4.2.1 The BioSecure Reference Protocol for BANCA

The pooled protocol is chosen as the reference protocol. It is one of the eight protocols originally distributed with the BANCA database [6], where:

- True client data from Session 1 are used for enrollment;
- True client data from Sessions 2, 3, 4, 6, 7, 8, 10, 11 and 12 are used for client testing;
- All the impostor attack data from all the sessions are used for impostor data.

Since the BANCA database is made of two disjoint groups $G1$ and $G2$, $G1$ can be used as the development set when tests are performed on $G2$, and vice versa. Furthermore, two microphones have been used to record the BANCA's audio data: a good quality (left channel) and a poor quality one (right channel). The results obtained with these two microphones are reported in the following section. The world model is built using the BANCA's world model data only.

7.4.2.2 The Benchmarking Results on the BANCA Database

Both reference systems have been evaluated on the speech part of the BANCA database according to the pooled P protocol. The results obtained on both channels and with both groups are presented in Table 7.1. Corresponding DET curves are displayed in Figs. 7.1 and 7.2. More details about the experimental configurations are given on the companion URL [38].

Table 7.1 EER performance measures of the reference systems (on the BANCA database) with their Confidence Intervals (CI) for $G1$ and $G2$ test sets, and for both types of microphones. Left-channel (respectively right-channel) results correspond to good-quality (respectively bad-quality) microphones

System	G1 left channel	G2 left channel	G1 right channel	G2 right channel
ALIZE v1.04	10.84% [±3.13]	9.36% [±2.93]	6.03% [±2.40]	4.23% [±2.02]
BECARS v1.1.9	14.70% [±3.56]	13.59% [±3.44]	6.44% [±2.47]	5.89% [±2.36]

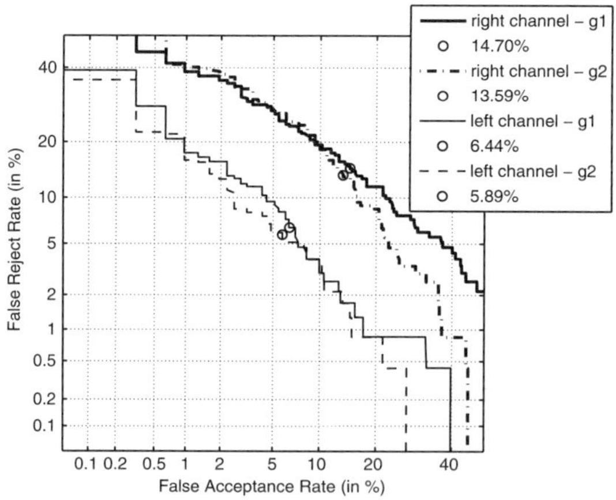

Fig. 7.1 DET curves obtained by applying the BECARS v1.1.9 reference system on the speech part of the BANCA database (with the two types of microphones), according to the pooled P protocol, and with 256 Gaussian mixtures

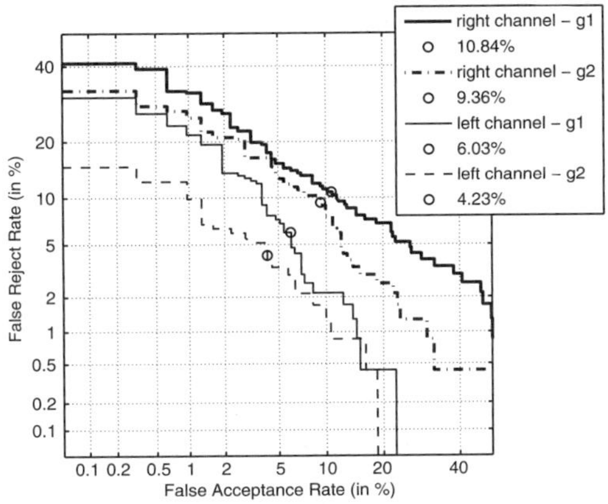

Fig. 7.2 DET curves obtained by applying the ALIZE v.1.04 reference system on the speech part of the BANCA database (with the two types of microphones) according to the pooled *P* protocol, and with 256 Gaussian mixtures

Despite the fact that the two systems use same or similar parameters, the performance of the two systems is different, mainly in the more challenging conditions with the poor quality microphone. Therefore the ALIZE System was chosen for the benchmarking experiments on the NIST database, because in NIST evaluations the speech data is even more degraded, corresponding to telephonic conversations.

7.4.3 The Benchmarking Experiments with the NIST'2005 Speaker Recognition Evaluation Database

Because of the wide success and relevance of the NIST Speaker Recognition Evaluations (NIST-SRE), we have chosen to use the NIST'2005 evaluation data and the core mandatory protocol as a part of the BioSecure benchmarking framework for text-independent speaker verification. The performance of the ALIZE v.1.04 system on NIST'2005 data and core *1conv-1conv* task is reported in this section.

7.4.3.1 NIST Databases and Protocols

The development database is composed of conversational telephone speech data from the speaker recognition evaluations (2003–2004) administered by the NIST. These databases contain mainly English speech, but they may include some speech in several additional languages. The NIST'2005 data and evaluation protocols are used for the benchmarking evaluation experiments. The speech data necessary to carry out the benchmarking speaker verification experiments with the NIST database consist of

- The development data set, denoted as *Devdb*, is composed of data from NIST'2003 and NIST'2004 evaluations. This set is further divided into a world data used for training the gender dependent background models; a tuning set used to tune the system parameters; and a normalization set for pseudo-impostors (77 male and 113 female speakers) used for score normalization.
- *Evaldb* evaluation data set: primary task data (*1conv-1conv*) of the NIST'2005 speaker recognition evaluation campaign, using all trails[4].

7.4.3.2 Benchmarking Results on NIST'2005 Evaluation Data

The parameters of the ALIZE v.1.04 system have been tuned using the development set of the NIST database. These parameters, which are slightly different from the common setup described in Sect. 7.4.1, are the following:

1. Feature extraction:
   - Number of channels (in the filter bank): 24 + no liftering.
   - Frequency range: 300-3400 Hz.
   - Features: 16 LFCCs + first order deltas + delta-energy.
2. Frame removal: the speech activity detector is based on a three Gaussian modeling of the energy of the speech data.
3. Model building:
   - 512 Gaussian mixtures for the World/Speaker models.
4. Score calculation: average log-likelihood ratio (using only the 10 best Gaussian components).
5. Score normalization with TNorm.

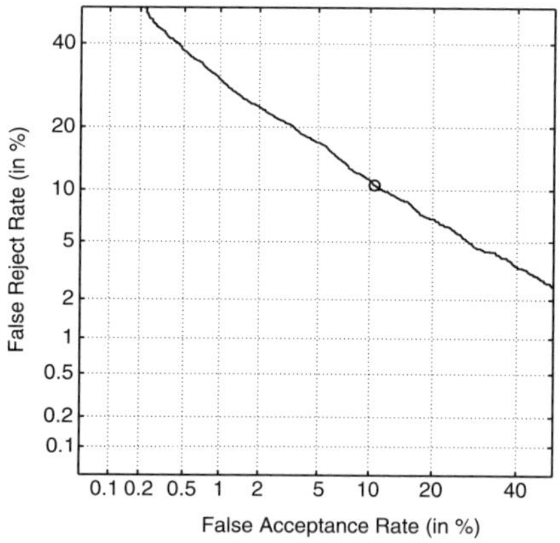

Fig. 7.3 Benchmarking experimental results (DET plot) with the ALIZE v.1.04 reference system on the NIST'2005 data and the core *1conv-1conv* task, with an EER of 10.63% [±0.63]

[4] The NIST'2005 data could also be split in per language trials.

The results reported in this section can be easily reproduced using the material and pointers provided on the companion website of this book [38]. In this precise case, the material is composed of pointers to the ALIZE toolkit, How-to and Read-me documents, lists and scripts that will enable new researchers to run these benchmarking experiments, and that will benefit of the previous precious experiences of the researchers who built the software and run an endless list of experiments in order to achieve satisfactory performance. Using these parameters with the ALIZE v.1.04 reference system gives an EER of 10.63% [±0.63]. The corresponding DET curve is displayed in Fig. 7.3. In such a way this benchmarking experiment could be easily reproduced, and serve as a basis for new developments. In the same time it will be an universal comparison point for future experiments.

At this point one question arises regarding the adjective "state-of-the-art". As already pointed out in [36], the notion of state of the art is somewhat subjective. If we take the example of NIST'2006 evaluations an overview of the submitted systems shows a small number of sites with EER in the region of 5%, with two sites just below it. The performance limits and systems used within the last NIST Speaker Recognition Evaluations (NIST-SRE) could be briefly summarized as follows:

- NIST'2004 SRE: standard GMMs with TNorm were used. We could report the result of the LIA'2004 submission, with an EER of 9.92% obtained with the above described open-source ALIZE software.
- NIST'2005 SRE: new ideas beyond the conventional GMM framework appeared, such as SVM or feature mapping, pushing the best reported results to an EER of 7.2%.
- NIST'2006 and 2007 SRE have seen an effective exploitation of session variability trough Nuisance Attribute Projection and Factor Analysis.
- This analysis only reflects the interpretation of performance of individual systems. The issues and improvements related to multisite score fusion which have appeared during the last years, is out of the scope of this chapter.

In the following section, we will show how the reference system can be pushed up to a state-of-the art performance of 6.02%, on the NIST'2005 evaluation data.

7.5 How to Reach State-of-the-art Speaker Verification Performance Using Open Source Software

In speaker verification, there are quite a lot of factors, such as speaker variability, channel variability, silence detection, or score normalization, that influence the performance of the speaker verification algorithms. The choice of the feature extraction method and speaker modeling often depends on the available resources and on the kind of speaker recognition application. Thus, the performance of the overall system depends on each of these modules independently and combined. There is to date no universally optimal feature set for use in speaker verification. The tendency is to use cepstral features, the choice of which is guided by their widespread usage in speech recognition.

The yearly NIST-SRE evaluations have shown that Gaussian Mixture Models are best suited for text-independent speaker verification experiments. At the same time, they have shown their limitations that occur mainly because of the mismatched train/test conditions using different microphones and transmission lines. In this section, some examples of factors influencing the results and presenting the difficulties of the text-independent speaker verification task are given. The development and evaluation databases as well as evaluation protocols underlying these examples are presented in Sect. 7.4.

The experimental results presented in this section are grouped in three parts. Section 7.5.1 illustrates the difficulties of fine tuning a variety of parameters in order to achieve well performing GMM based systems. Experiments in Sect. 7.5.2 show how new improvements due to Nuisance Attribute Projection and Factor Analysis can be achieved. These experiments are carried out on the core task of the NIST'2005 speaker recognition evaluation. In this task denoted as *1conv-1conv*, one two-channel (four-wire) conversation, of approximately five minutes total duration is used to build the speaker model and another conversation for testing.

Section 7.5.3 shows the improvements that could be achieved when high-level information extracted with data-driven speech segmentation methods are combined with GMM based systems. Such data-driven segmentation techniques are useful for new tasks and new languages, when classical speech-recognizers (based on annotated training data) are not available. The results are also shown on the NIST'2005 data, but using the long training/short test task, which is more suited for extracting high-level speaker-specific information.

With the presented experiments, it is shown how starting with the BioSecure Benchmarking Framework that allows the reproducibility of the benchmarking results (based on open-source software), state-of-the-art performance (as reported in last years NIST-SRE evaluations) can be reached.

7.5.1 Fine Tuning of GMM-based Systems

The experiments presented in this section illustrate the influence of the following factors to fine tune the GMM-based systems:

- Selection of relevant speech frames (known also as silence detection).
- Choice of the configuration of the feature vectors.
- Complexity of the World/Speaker models.
- Score normalization.

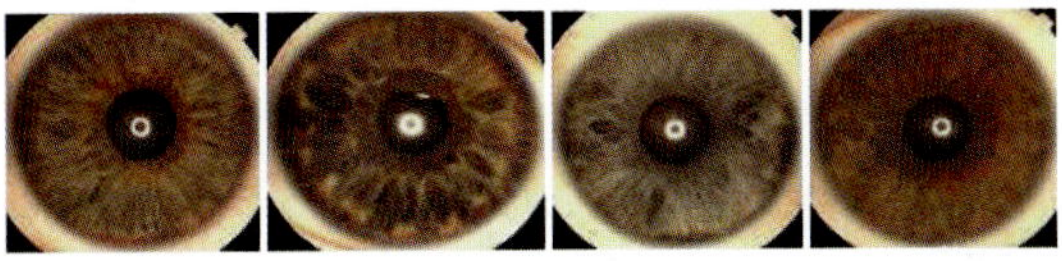

Fig. 1 Examples of iris images from different databases. Color representation of part (d) of Fig. 3.1

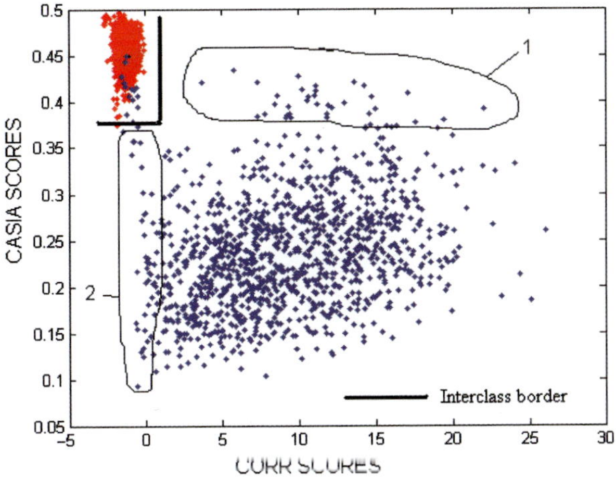

Fig. 2 Intraclass and interclass distances for the CASIA System (*Y axis*) and the Correlation System (*X axis*). Color representation of Fig. 3.11

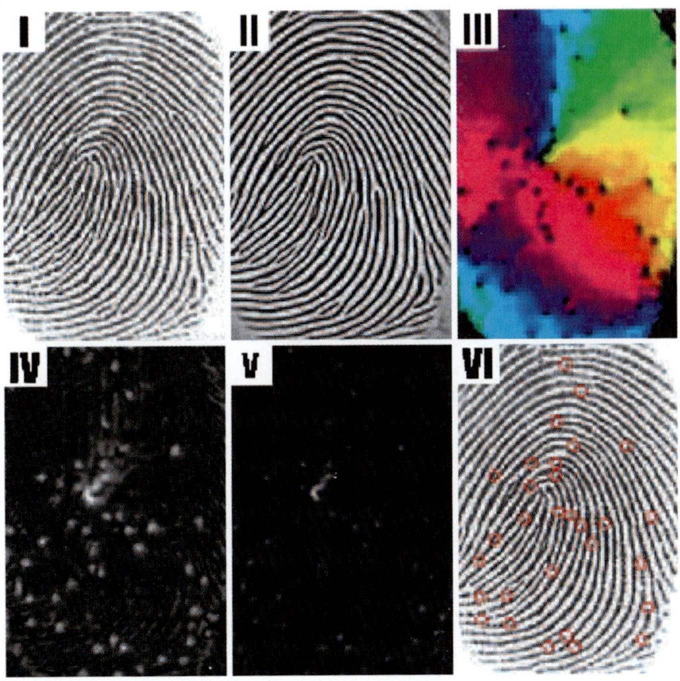

Fig. 3 Local feature extraction using complex filtering (HH system): **(I, II)** show the initial fingerprint and its enhanced version; **(III)** linear symmetry *LS*; **(IV)** parabolic symmetry *PS*; **(V)** sharpened magnitudes $|PSi|$; and **(VI)** the first ordered 30 minutiae. Color representation of Fig. 4.18

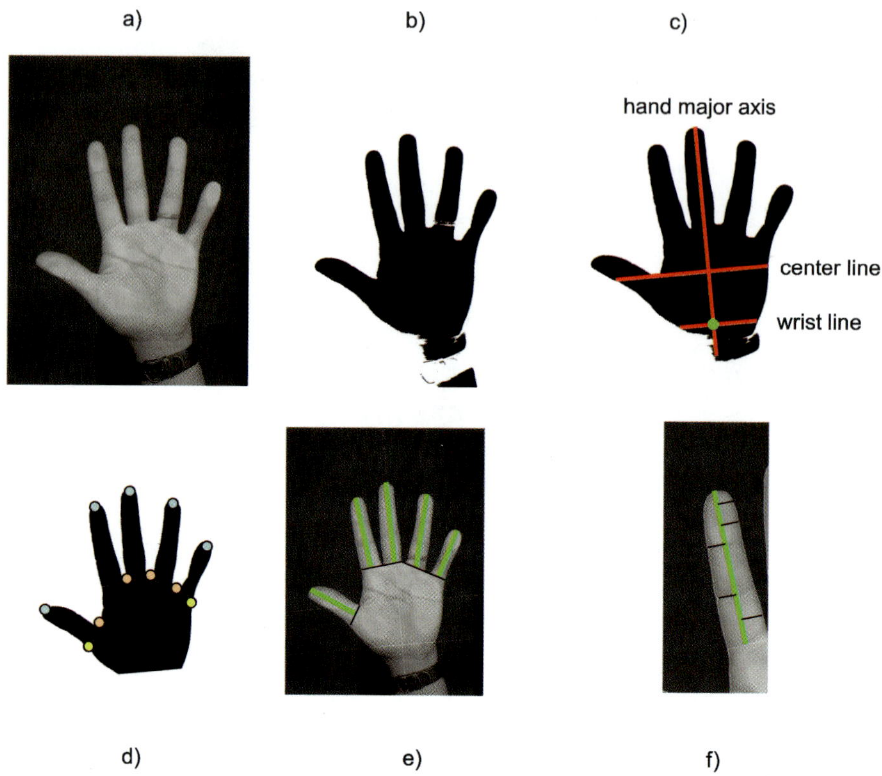

Fig. 4 Processing steps and feature extraction for the geometry-based reference system: (**a**) original image; (**b**) binarized hand with one finger disconnected; (**c**) hand component with reconnected finger, construction lines (hand major axis, centerline and wrist line) and contour starting point at the intersection of the wrist line and the hand major axis; (**d**) hand with removed wrist region, the five tip points, the four valley points extracted from the radial distance curve, and the two estimated valley points; (**e**) segmented fingers and finger major axes; and (**f**) distances from finger contour to finger axis are searched in order to get the distance distribution. Color representation of Fig. 5.3

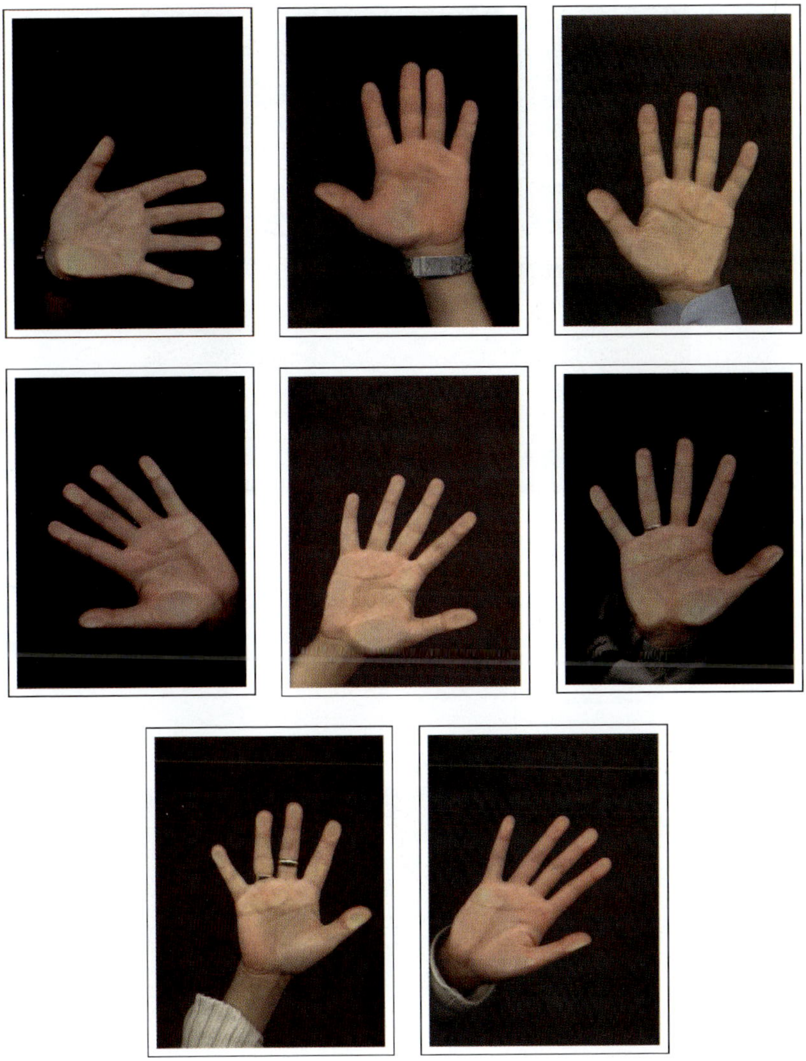

Fig. 5 Sample images of right and left hands from the BIOMET, BU and ENST databases. Color representation of Fig. 5.4

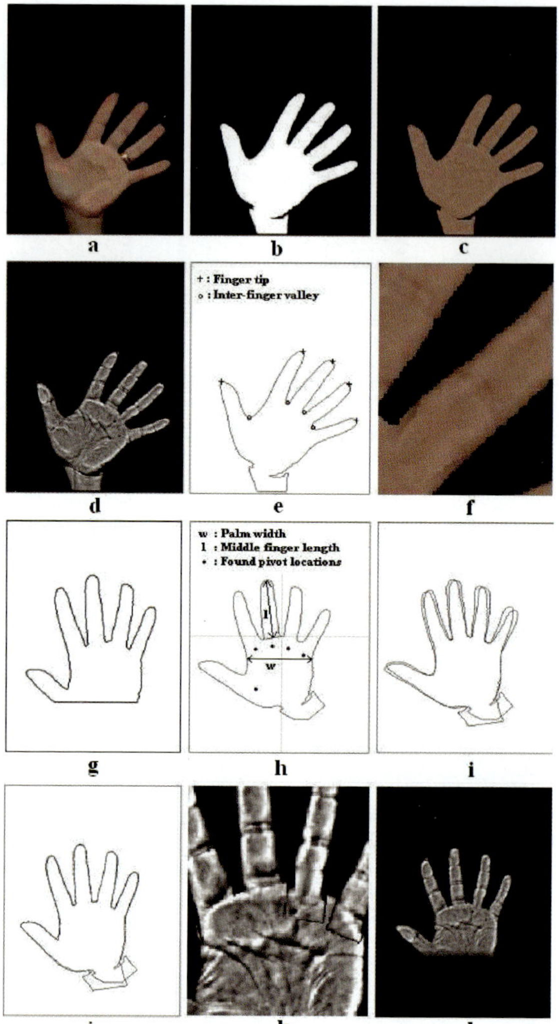

Fig. 6 Processing steps for hand normalization: (**a**) original hand image; (**b**) segmented hand image; (**c**) illumination corrected hand image (ring removed); (**d**) graylevel, texture enhanced hand image; (**e**) determination of finger tips and valleys; (**f**) finger after ring removal; (**g**) hand after wrist-completion; (**h**) initial global registration by translation and rotation: middle finger length and palm width for hand image scaling and derivation of the metacarpal pivots; (**i**) superposed contours taken from different sessions of the same individual with rigid hand registration only; (**j**) superposed contours taken from different sessions of the same individual after finger orientation normalization; (**k**) texture blending around pivot location for finger rotation; (**l**) final grayscale, normalized hand with cosine-attenuated wrist. Color representation of Fig. 5.15

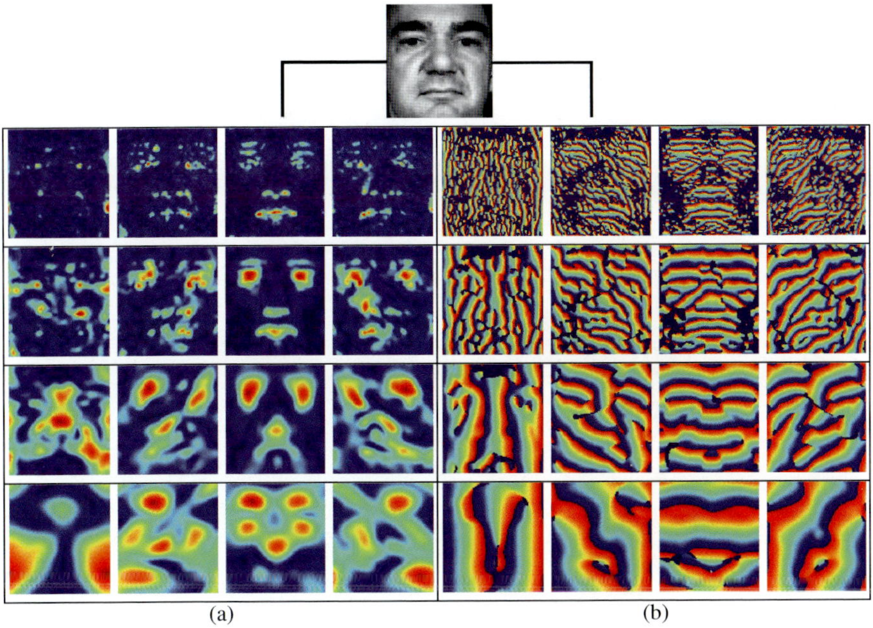

Fig. 7 Result of the convolution of a face image (from FRGC database), with a family of Gabor filters of four horizontal orientations and four vertical scales. (**a**) Gabor magnitude and (**b**) Gabor phase representations. Color representation of Fig. 8.4

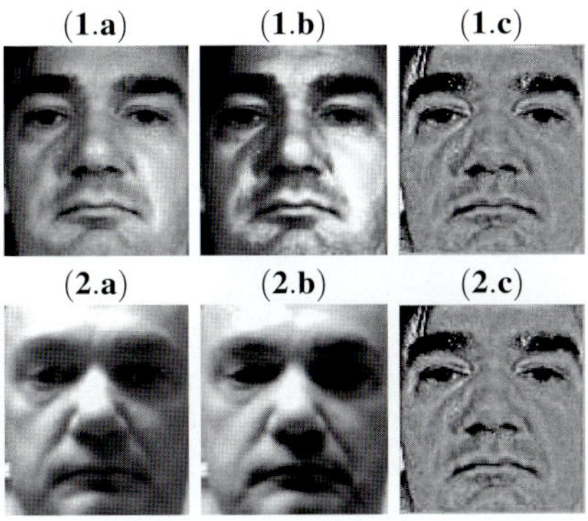

Fig. 8 Face illumination preprocessing on two face images from the FRGC v2 database: (**x.a**) geometric normalization, (**x.b**) histogram equalization, and (**x.c**) anisotropic smoothing. Color representation of Fig. 8.6

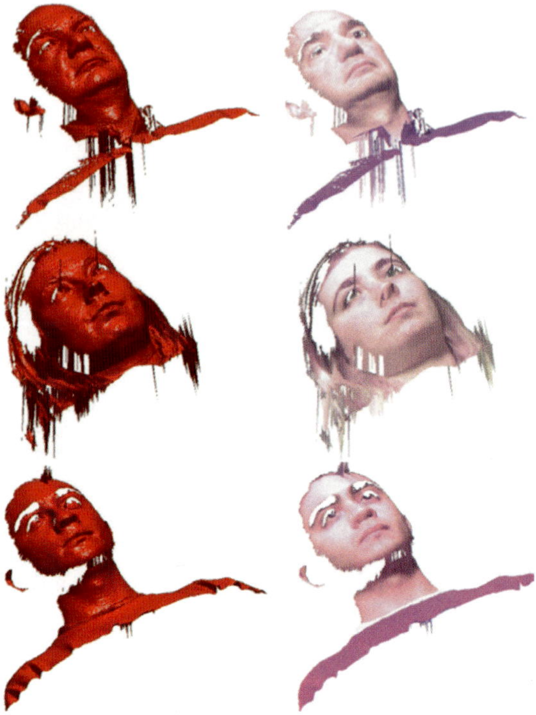

Fig. 9 Sample 3D faces from the UND [30] face database. Color representation of Fig. 9.1

Fig. 10 Two facial surfaces, from FRGC database [9], registered with the Iterative Closest Point (ICP) algorithm. Color representation of Fig. 9.2

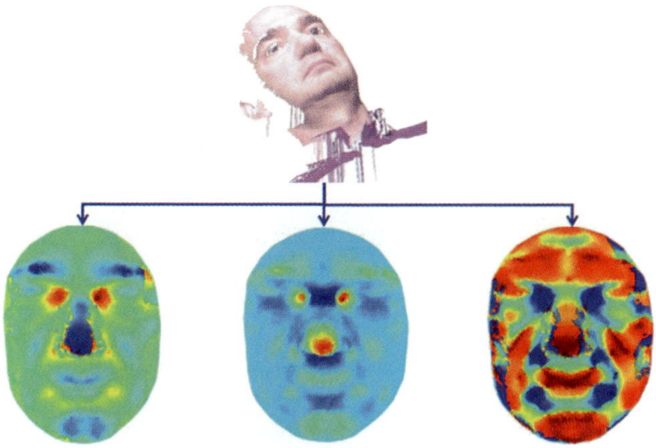

Fig. 11 A sample face from the FRGC database [19] and its mean, Gaussian curvature, and shape index maps (from left to right). Color representation of Fig. 9.4

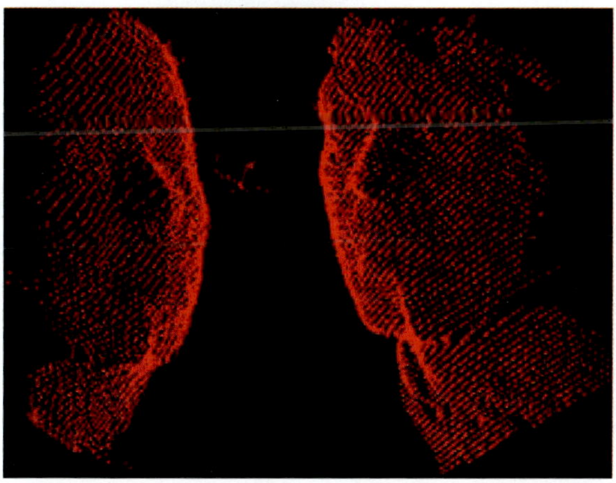

Fig. 12 Two facial point clouds taken from the 3D-RMA database [27]. Color representation of Fig. 9.5

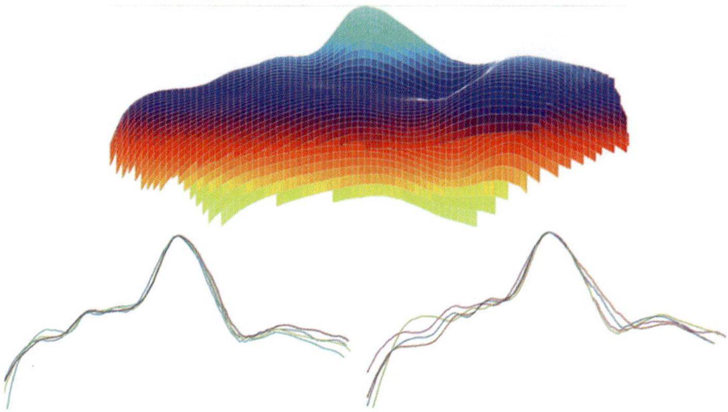

Fig. 13 **Upper image** shows a profile view of a facial surface. **Lower left** image displays central profile curves computed from the same subject. **Lower right** image shows central profiles obtained from different subjects, from the 3D-RMA database [27]. Color representation of Fig. 9.7

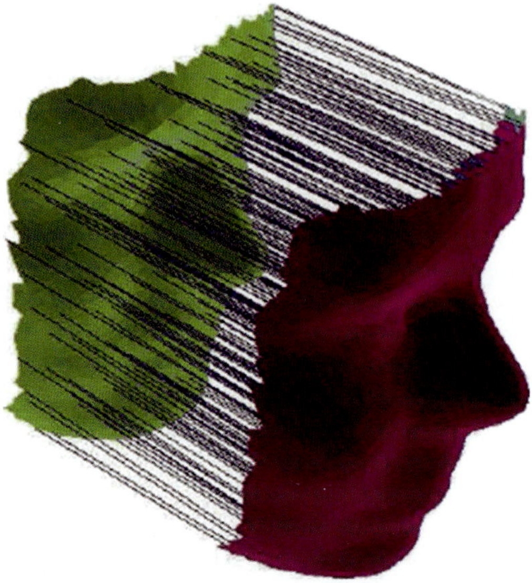

Fig. 14 Dense point-to-point correspondence between two faces (from 3D-RMA database [27]) with the 3D Face Recognition Reference System (3D-FRRS). Color representation of Fig. 9.10

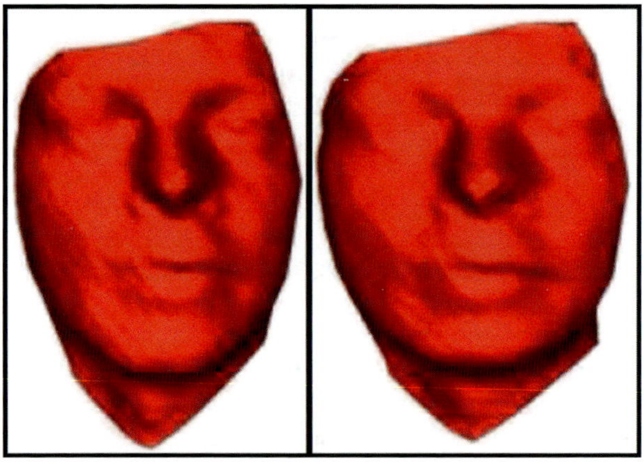

Fig. 15 Original face from 3D-RMA database [27] and its Thin-Plate Spline (TPS) warped version in the 3D Face Recognition Reference System (3D-FRRS). Color representation of Fig. 9.11

7.5.1.1 Selection of Relevant Speech Data

The first set of experiments concerns the study of the influence of frame removal, associated with silence detection. Table 7.2 shows the results using the frame removal procedure implemented in the ALIZE software. For the frame removal, the energy coefficients are first normalized using zero mean and unit variance. Then the normalized energies are used to train a three-component GMM. Finally, $N\%$ of the most energized frames are selected through the GMM with

$$N = w_1 + (g \times \alpha \times w_2) \tag{7.11}$$

where w_1 is the weight of the highest Gaussian component, w_2 is the weight of the middle component, g is an integer ranging form 0 to 1, and α is a weighting parameter.

This frame removal method is compared to the frame removal method using speech transcripts that are produced with an Automatic Speech Recognition (ASR) system, available with the data. These transcripts are errorful, with word error rates typically in the range of 15-30%. Table 7.2 shows that the application of the α-based frame removal improves the performance considerably. The statistics on speech data kept in each case are also given. The best result corresponding to $\alpha = 0$ is retained.

Table 7.2 Percentage of retained speech frames after applying the frame removal procedure and performance of the corresponding speaker verification systems. GMM system with 512 Gaussians, evaluated on NIST'2005 using all trials

Frame removal	% of speech data removed	EER%
NIST transcripts	43	14.66
$\alpha = 0.9$	53	18.73
$\alpha = 0.25$	36	11.01
$\alpha = 0$	28	11.00

7.5.1.2 Selection of Feature Vectors

In the second series of experiments various combinations of static, Δ energy, double Δ, and Δenergy are tested. In Fig. 7.4, $\Delta +$log-energy and/or Δ energy are appended to the cepstral feature vector of dimension 16. Results show that the addition of the $\Delta +$ log-energy to the parameter vectors slightly improves the results in comparison to the use of the cepstral and Δ-cepstral coefficients only. Adding the log-energy to the feature vectors clearly degrades the results. One possible explanation is that the log-energy can be more sensible to the channel effects and some kind of normalization should be used to eliminate this effect. This configuration corresponds to the benchmarking experiment reported in Sect. 7.4.3.2, without TNorm normalization, and is denoted as BioSecure Reference System furthermore.

The influence of using more static dimensions and partial double deltas is also measured. Results of two different configurations are reported: the previously reported feature vector of dimension 33, composed of $16LFCC + 16\Delta + \Delta$ (the BioSecure Ref. System) and a feature vector of dimension 50, composed of $19LFCC + 19\Delta + \Delta ene + 11\Delta\Delta$. The difference in performance using these two configurations is reported in Fig. 7.5. The complete set of double deltas brings no improvement.

7.5.1.3 Parameters Related to the World/Speaker Model

The third set of experiments is related to tuning of the GMM models. Figures 7.6 and 7.7 show the influence of using more data to build the gender dependent background model, and of the number of Gaussians present in the GMMs. Figure 7.6 illustrates the influence of using more appropriate speech data for building the World model. The DET curve of using only data from NIST'2003 and NIST'2004 to build the world GMM model is labelled as "Biosecure Ref. Sys." Adding 600 more speakers form the Fisher data set improves the results. The 600 speakers are balanced by the handset type (cordless, cellular and landline).

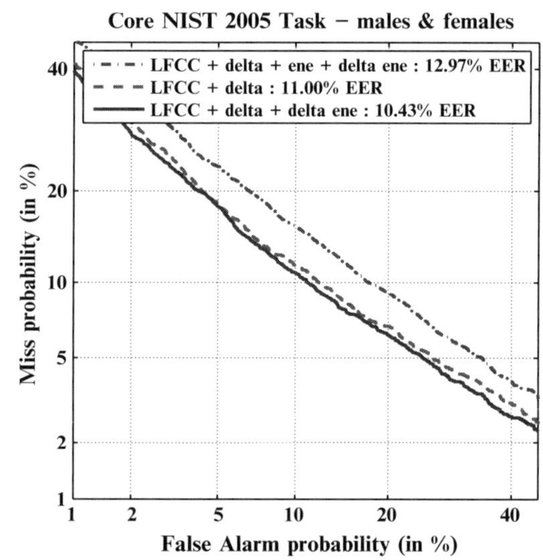

Fig. 7.4 DET plot showing the effect of feature selection. The GMM systems with 512 Gaussians are evaluated on the NIST'2005 core task using all trials. This configuration corresponds to the benchmarking experiment reported in Sect. 7.4.3.2 without TNorm normalization

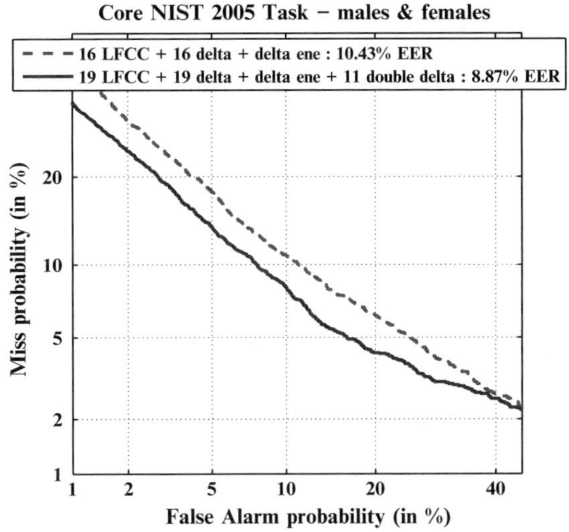

Fig. 7.5 DET plot showing the comparison of performances of the GMM system using feature vectors of size 50 and 33, on the NIST'2005 evaluation data using all trials

The use of 2,048 Gaussians instead of 512 for the speaker modeling (cf. Fig. 7.7) slightly improves the performances. Acknowledging the fact that GMMs with 2,048 Gaussians need more computation, a model with 512 Gaussians is a good compromise.

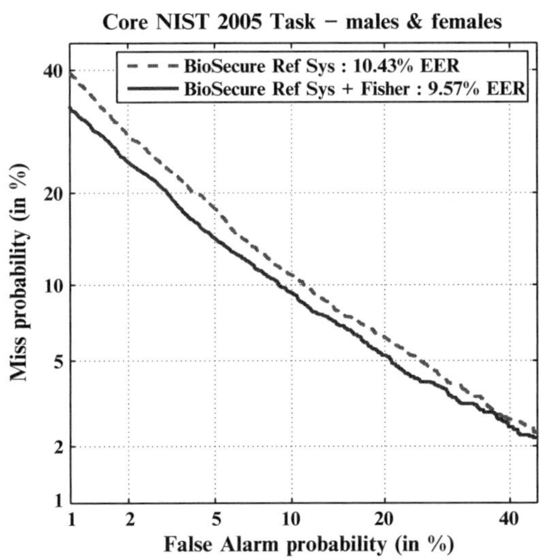

Fig. 7.6 DET plot showing the effect of using more data to train the background (UBM) model. The baseline reference system is defined with $LFCC + \Delta ene + \Delta LFCC$ features, a frame removal parameter with $\alpha = 0$, the reference world model, and a GMM with 512 Gaussians. Results are reported on NIST'2005 using all trials

7.5.1.4 Score Normalization

The problem of mismatched enrollment/test data can be solved in different ways. Score normalization techniques are one solution. Different score normalization methods (explained in Sect. 7.2.4.1) are applied on the best configuration of Fig. 7.5. As expected (see Fig. 7.8), the TNorm improves the performances particularly in the region of low false alarm resulting in an improvement of the minimum DCF. However, no amelioration is observed for the Z and ZTNorm approaches. This is mainly due to the fact that the cohort set used for normalization wasn't explicitly tuned for the ZNorm. Nevertheless, the normalization techniques make the speaker-independent threshold more robust and easy to set. In the next set of experiments all systems are normalized using TNorm approach and the TNormalized GMM will be considered as a baseline for the next series of experiments.

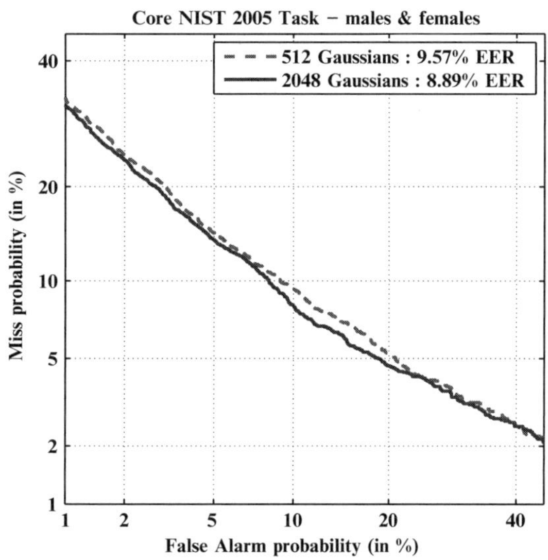

Fig. 7.7 DET plot showing the comparison of performances using 512 and 2,048 Gaussians in the GMM, on the NIST'2005 evaluation data using all trials

7.5.2 Choice of Speaker Modeling Methods and Session's Variability Modeling

NIST-SRE evaluations have also shown over recent years that key factors of improvements in performance relate to approaches that minimize the channel variability due to the mismatched enrollment/test conditions. These recent developments

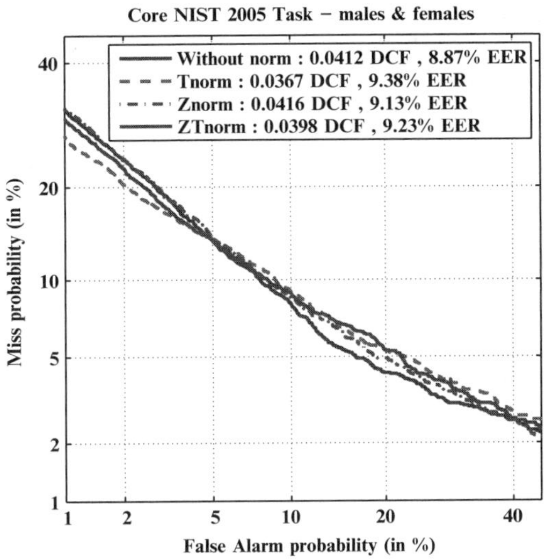

Fig. 7.8 DET plot showing the effect of normalization techniques. The GMM systems with 512 Gaussians are evaluated on the NIST'2005 using all trials

include mainly Factor Analysis (FA) in the generative framework and Nuisance Attribute Projection (NAP) for the SVM framework. In these approaches the goal is to model the mismatch by estimating the variabilities from a large data set in which each speaker is recorded in multiple sessions as described in Sect. 7.2.1.3. More details can be found in [36].

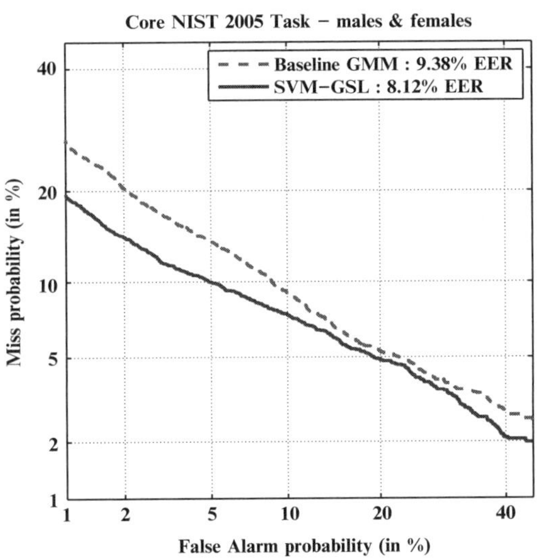

Fig. 7.9 DET plot showing the comparison of performances using GMM and SVM systems, on the NIST'2005 evaluation data using all trials

7.5.2.1 GMM Supervector Linear Kernel (GSL)

As pointed out in Sect. 7.2.2.2, in the last few years the SVM approach started to be used as an alternative classification strategy to the widely used GMM. In the experiment presented in this section, Kullback-Leibler divergence is used to define new sequence kernels based on GMM supervectors. Figure 7.9 shows that the GSL system gives the best performance. The EER was reduced to 8.12% compared to 9.38% of the GMM system. More details can be found in [36].

7.5.2.2 Nuisance Attribute Projection (NAP)

As described in Sect. 7.2.1.3, the goal of NAP is to project out a subspace from the original expanded space, where information has been affected by nuisance effects. This is performed by learning on a background set of recordings, without explicit labeling, from many different speakers' recordings. The most straightforward approach is to use the difference between a given session and the mean across sessions for each speaker.

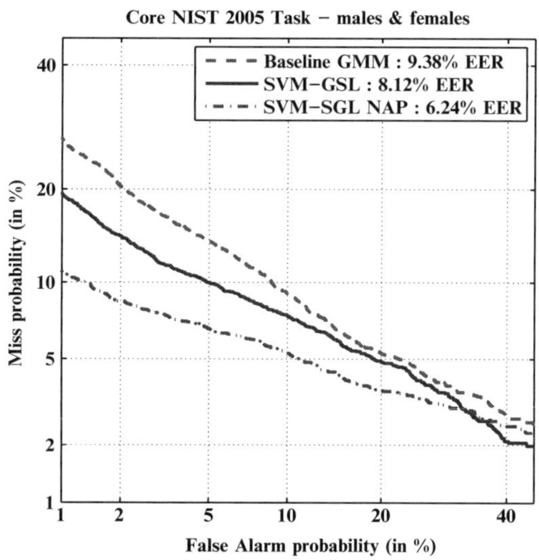

Fig. 7.10 DET plot showing the NAP system performances. Results are shown on the NIST'2005 evaluation data using all trials

The experiments are conducted with exactly the same setup as for the GSL experiments. The NAP matrix is learned on the complete set of NIST'2004 database. For example, in the male case after removing a few speechless files we have 2,938 training sessions for 124 different male speakers, which led to an average of 23.7 recordings per speaker. Figure 7.10 shows the effect of using the NAP approach in comparison with the GSL and GMM systems. A great increase in the performance could be observed.

7.5.2.3 Factor Analysis (FA)

Factor analysis is based on the same concept as NAP except that it operates on generative models. Figure 7.11 shows that like NAP the FA method significantly outperforms the GMM baseline system, improving the results from 9.38% to 6.02%.

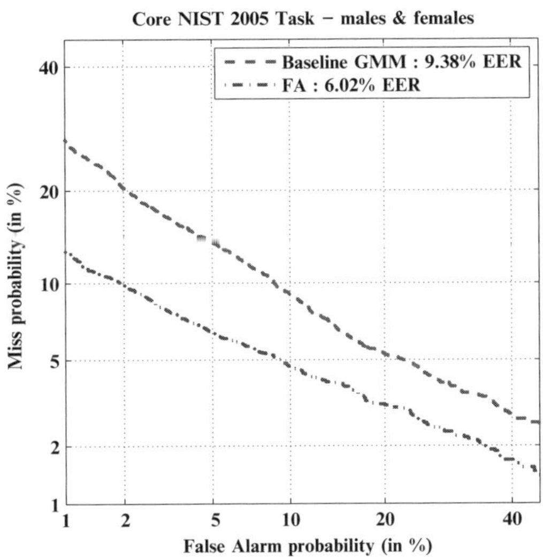

Fig. 7.11 DET plot showing the comparison of performances using GMM and Factor Analysis (FA). Results are shown on the NIST'2005 evaluation data using all trials

7.5.3 *Using High-level Features as Complementary Sources of Information*

The experiments presented in the previous section illustrate a variety of parameters and methods needed in order to have well-performing acoustic (low-level) systems. Another way to improve speaker verification results is to exploit high-level features, as explained in Sect. 7.2.3. High-level information is linked to the textual representation of speech. Such textual information is obtained as an output of a speech recognizer. Speech recognition systems are based on phonetic transcriptions and require transcribed speech databases for the training phase. Therefore such speech recognizers are only available for a small set of languages (including English) for which transcribed speech databases can be found. An alternative when only the segmentation of speech is needed without its semantics and no transcribed databases are available, is to use data-driven speech segmentation methods that require no manually annotated data.

In this section, results with various speaker verification systems using high-level information extracted with a data-driven segmentation method are given. The systems use the Automatic Language Independent Speech Processing (ALISP) tools [21] for the segmentation step. In order to have pseudo-phonetic units, the number of ALISP classes is fixed to 65 (with one class representing silence). Each class is modeled by a left-to-right Hidden Markov Model (HMM) having three emitting states and containing up to eight Gaussians each. The number of Gaussians is determined through a dynamic splitting procedure. The gender dependent ALISP HMMs are trained on subsets from NIST'1999, 2001 and 2003 evaluation data. The average length of the 64 ALISP classes is 75 ms and is very close to the average length of phones (80 ms). The speech parametrization for the data-driven ALISP recognizer is done with Mel Frequency Cepstral Coefficients (MFCC). Mel frequency bands are computed in the $300-3400\ Hz$ range. Cepstral mean substraction is applied to the 15 static coefficients, estimating the mean on the speech-detected parts of the signal. The energy and Δ components are appended, leading to 32 coefficients for each feature vector. The MFCC[5] are chosen for the parametrization of the speech data for practical reasons.

Various speaker verification systems using high-level information were built starting from the data-driven speech segmentation. For the baseline acoustic GMM system the BioSecure Reference System, (based on the ALIZE software [2]) is used with a 32 dimensional feature vector, Fisher data to build the World model, $2,048$ Gaussian mixtures, and TNorm (see Sect.7.5.1). For the *Segmental GMM* system, ALISP tools [21] provide the speech segmentation, and the 64 class-dependent GMM models are built using the ALIZE software. For all the other ALISP-based systems the HTK toolkit [54] is used for all the steps except for the initial data-driven transcription, which is done using the ALISP tools.

The results of all these systems are shown in Table 7.3. Their main characteristics are the fillowing:

- For the *Segmental ALISP-GMM* system the speech data is first segmented. Furthermore, ALISP class-specific background models are built using the feature vectors of the given ALISP class. Then, the speaker models are obtained via adaptation of the background models. Finally, each speaker is modeled by 64 GMMs corresponding each to an ALISP class.
- The systems denoted by *Idiolectal* and *Language models* capture high-level information about the speaking style of each speaker. This speaker-specific information is captured by analyzing sequences of ALISP units produced by the data-driven ALISP recognizer.

[5] They can easily be used with the HTK toolkit.

- Systems denoted by *Segments' duration* and *States' duration* exploit speaker-specific ALISP durations. In this case, the speakers are modeled using only the duration of the ALISP units and HMM states respectively.

Table 7.3 Comparison of baseline GMM (BioSecure Ref. Sys. from Table 7.4 + Fisher + 2,048 GMM + TNorm) and ALISP data-driven high-level systems performances on the 8conv-1conv task of the NIST'2005 SRE

Systems	EER %	Systems	EER %
Baseline GMM	7.04	Idiolectal: 2-gram	17.04
Segmental ALISP-GMM	5.83	Idiolectal: 3-gram	15.43
Segments' duration	16.86	Language models: 1-gram	21.38
States' duration	17.04	Language models: 2-gram	15.21
Idiolectal: 1-gram	20.59	Language models: 3-gram	15.42

More details about all these systems can be found in [31, 33, 47, 34]. The results show that the EER performance of the baseline acoustic GMMs (7.04%) can be improved to 5.83% with the Segmental ALISP GMMs. The individual performance of the only high level systems is as expected lower, and spans from 15.21–21.38%.

It is interesting to compare the performances of the ALISP and phonetic high-level systems. The n-gram ALISP systems' performances compare favorably and are even better then the n-gram system described in [100]. Indeed, the 2-gram phone system described in [100] gave an EER of 20% on the NIST'2004 SRE (8side-1side) data in comparison to 18% of the ALISP 2-gram system. In [46] and [34] the ALISP high-level systems outperformed the phonetic systems trained on NTIMIT.

The complementarity of high-level systems with the baseline GMM can be studied with fusion experiments. The fusion of the ALISP data-driven high-level systems with the baseline GMM system are shown in Fig. 7.12. Improvements of the fused systems on NIST'2005 evaluation data are observed. Nevertheless, the fusion is more effective on English data, illustrating the sensitivity of the fusion to languages (see also [34]). It has to be noted that the ALISP recognizer is trained on English data only. The scores of the different systems are fused with a Support Vector Machine (SVM) trained on NIST'2004 data. Further improvement could be envisioned with ALISP recognizers trained also for different languages.

7.6 Conclusions and Perspectives

In this chapter, an overview of text-independent speaker verification is given, including recent developments needed to reach state-of-the-art performances using low-level (acoustic) features, as well as how to use complementary high-level information.

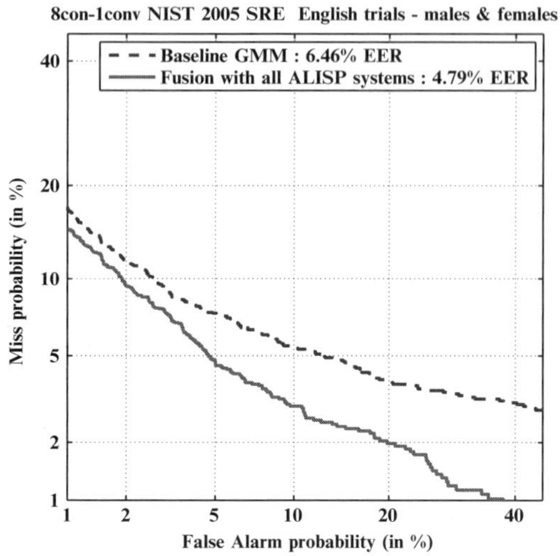

(a)

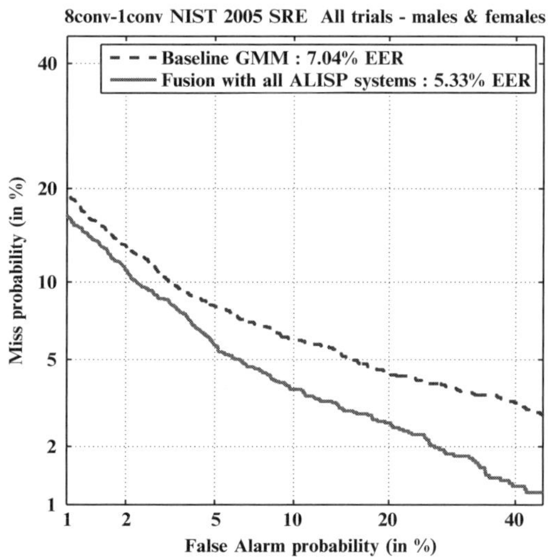

(b)

Fig. 7.12 DET plots showing the performance of the baseline GMM system and its fusion with ALISP systems. The systems are evaluated on the 8conv-1conv task of NIST'2005 SRE using **(a)** English trials only and **(b)** all trials including other languages such as Arabic, Mandarin, Russian, and Spanish

The BioSecure benchmarking framework for speaker verification using open-source state-of-the-art algorithms, well-known databases, and reference protocols is used as a baseline comparison point for the case study experiments.

The examples of key factors influencing the results of speaker verification experiments on the NIST'2005 evaluation data are grouped in three parts. The first set of experiments shows mainly the importance of front-end processing and data selection to fine tune the acoustic Gaussian mixture systems. The second set of experiments illustrates the importance of speaker and session variability modeling methods, in order to cope with mismatched enrollment/test conditions. The third series of experiments demonstrates the usefulness of data-driven speech segmentation methods for extracting complementary high-level information, in the case when more enrollment data is available.

The experiments reported in this chapter, summarized in Table 7.4, illustrate how to improve the results of the widely used Gaussian Mixture Systems in the challenging mismatched enrollment/test conditions from an EER of 10.43% to 6.02%. The experiments summarized in Table 7.5 illustrate the importance of complementary high-level features that can be used to improve the acoustic GMM systems in the case when more enrollment data are available. The particularity of the presented systems is the usage of ALISP data-driven methods for the speech segmentation

Table 7.4 How to improve the EER of the baseline (reproducible) BioSecure Reference System. GMM stands for Gaussian Mixture Model, NAP for Nuisance Attribute Projection, and FA for Factor Analysis; on NIST'2005 core 1conv-1conv task using all trials

BioSecure Ref. Sys. 10.43% + ...			
+ Fisher ⇒ 9.57%	+ 2,048 GMM ⇒ 8.89%		
+ 50 Feat. ⇒ 8.87%	+ ZT Norm ⇒ 9.38%	+ GSL ⇒ 8.12%	+ NAP ⇒ 6.24%
+ 50 Feat. ⇒ 8.87%	+ ZT Norm ⇒ 9.38%	+ FA ⇒ 6.02%	

Table 7.5 How to improve the EER of the baseline (reproducible) BioSecure Reference System. *GMM* stands for Gaussian Mixture Model and ALISP for Automatic Language Independent Speech Processing; on NIST'2005 8conv-1conv task using longer enrollment data

	Baseline GMM	Baseline GMM + ALISP high-level systems
All trials	7.04%	5.33%
English trials	6.46%	4.79%

part. Such systems can be useful in emerging conversational applications, when the user could access the required information and in parallel be verified in order to access to some secure applications.

Acknowledgments

For some of the ALISP segmentation tools, we thank J. Černocký and F. Bimbot. This work was partially funded by the IST-FP6 BioSecure Network of Excellence (IST-2002-507634). A. El Hannani was also supported by the Swiss National Fund for Scientific Research (No. 20002-108024).

References

1. A. Adami, R. Mihaescu, D.A. Reynolds, and J.J. Godfrey. Modeling prosodic dynamics for speaker recognition. *In the proceedings of the IEEE International Conference on Acoustics, Speech, and Signal Processing (ICASSP)*, April 2003.
2. Alize. http://www.lia.univ-avignon.fr/heberges/alize/.
3. W.D. Andrews, M.A. Kohler, J.P. Campbell, and J.J. Godfrey. Phonetic, idiolectal, and acoustic speaker recognition. *In the proceedings of the IEEE Workshop on Speaker and Language Recognition (Odyssey)*, June 2001.
4. R. Auckenthaler, M.J. Carey, and H. Llyod-Thomas. Score normalization for text-independent speaker verification systems. *Digital Signal Processing*, 10, 2000.
5. R. Auckenthaler, E.S. Parris, and M.J. Carey. Improving a gmm speaker verification system by phonetic weighting. *In the proceedings of the IEEE International Conference on Acoustics, Speech, and Signal Processing (ICASSP)*, March 1999.
6. E. Bailly-Baillière, S. Bengio, F. Bimbot, M. Hamouz, J. Kittler, J. Mariéthoz, J. Matas, K. Messer, V. Popovici, F. Porée, B. Ruiz, and J.-P. Thiran. The BANCA Database and Evaluation Protocol. In *4th International Conference on Audio-and Video-Based Biometric Person Authentication (AVBPA'03)*, pages 625–638, Surrey, UK, 2003.
7. B. Baker, R. Vogt, and S. Sridharan. Gaussian mixture modelling of broad phonetic and syllabic events for text-independent speaker verification. *In the proceedings of the European Conference on Speech Communication and Technology (Eurospeech)*, September 2005.
8. C. Barras and J.-L. Gauvain. Feature and score normalization for speaker verification of cellular data. *In the proceedings of the IEEE International Conference on Acoustics, Speech, and Signal Processing (ICASSP)*, April 2003.
9. C. Barras, S. Meignier, and J.-L. Gauvain. Unsupervised online adaptation for speaker verification over the telephone. *In the proceedings of the IEEE Workshop on Speaker and Language Recognition (Odyssey)*, June 2004.
10. BECARS. http://www.tsi.enst.fr/becars/.
11. M. Ben, R. Blouet, and F. Bimbot. A monte-carlo method for score normalization in automatic speaker verification using kullback-leibler distances. *In the proceedings of the IEEE International Conference on Acoustics, Speech, and Signal Processing (ICASSP)*, May 2002.
12. F. Bimbot, M. Blomberg, L. Boves, D. Genoud, H.-P. Hutter, C. Jaboulet, J.W. Koolwaaij, J. Lindberg, and J.-B. Pierrot. An overview of the cave project research activities in speaker verification. *Speech Communication*, 31:158–180, 2000.
13. F. Bimbot, J.F. Bonastre, C.Fredouille, G. Gravier, I. Magrin-Chagnolleau, S. Meignier, T. Merlin, J. Ortega-Garcia, D. Petrovska-Delacretaz, and D. A. Reynolds. A tutorial on text-independent speaker verification. *Eurasip Journal On Applied Signal Processing*, 4:430–451, 2004.
14. K. Boakye and B. Peskin. Text-constrained speaker recognition on a text-independent task. *In the proceedings of the IEEE Workshop on Speaker and Language Recognition (Odyssey)*, pages 129–134, June 2004.
15. R.N. Bracewell. *The Fourier Transform and Its Applications*. McGraw-Hill, New York, NY USA, 1965.

16. J.P. Campbell and D. Reynolds. Corpora for the evaluation of speaker recognition systems. *In the proceedings of the IEEE International Conference on Acoustics, Speech, and Signal Processing (ICASSP)*, March 1999.
17. J.P. Campbell, D. Reynolds, and R. Dunn. Fusing high- and low-level features for speaker recognition. *In the proceedings of the European Conference on Speech Communication and Technology (Eurospeech)*, September 2003.
18. W. Campbell, D. Sturim, D. Reynolds, and A. Solomonoff. Support vector machines using gmm supervectors for speaker verification. *IEEE Signal Processing Letters*, 2006.
19. W.M. Campbell, J.P. Campbell, D. Reynolds, D.A. Jones, and T.R. Leek. Phonetic speaker recognition with support vector machines. *In the proceedings of the Neural Information Processing Systems Conference*, pages 361–388, December 2003.
20. G. Chollet, G. Aversano, B. Dorizzi, and D. Petrovska-Delacrétaz. The first biosecure residential workshop. *4th International Symposium on Image and Signal Processing and Analysis-ISPA2005*, pages 198–212, September 2005.
21. G. Chollet, J. Černocký, A. Constantinescu, S. Deligne, and F. Bimbot. Towards alisp: a proposal for automatic language independent speech processing. *In Keith Ponting, editor, NATO ASI: Computational models of speech pattern processing Springer Verlag*, 1999.
22. S.B. Davies and P. Marmelstein. Comparison of parametric representations for monosyllabic word recognition in continuosly spoken utterances. *In the proceedings of the IEEE International Conference on Acoustics, Speech, and Signal Processing (ICASSP)*, 28(4):357–366, April 1980.
23. N. Dehak and G. Chollet. Support vector gmms for speaker verification. *In the proceedings of the IEEE Workshop on Speaker and Language Recognition (Odyssey)*, June 2006.
24. A. Dempster, N. Laird, and D. Rubin. Maximum likelihood from incomplete data via the em algorithm. *Journal of the Royal Statistical Society*, pages 19–38, 1977.
25. G. Doddington. Speaker recognition based on idiolectal differences between speakers. *In the proceedings of the European Conference on Speech Communication and Technology (Eurospeech)*, 4:2517–2520, September 2001.
26. X. Dong and W. Zhaohui. Speaker recognition using continuous density support vector machines. *Electronics Letters*, 37(17):1099–1101, August 2001.
27. B. Dumas, C. Pugin, J. Hennebert, D. Petrovska-Delacrétaz, A. Humm, F. Evéquoz, R. Ingold, and D. Von Rotz. MyIdea - multimodal biometrics database, description of acquisition protocols. In *Proc. of Third COST 275 Workshop (COST 275)*, pages 59–62, Hatfield UK, October 2005.
28. J.P. Eatock and J.S. Mason. A quantitative assessment of the relative speaker discriminant properties of phonemes. *In the proceedings of the IEEE International Conference on Acoustics, Speech, and Signal Processing (ICASSP)*, 1:133–136, April 1994.
29. J. Egan. *Signal Detection Theory and ROC Analysis*. Academic Press, 1975.
30. A. El Hannani and D. Petrovska-Delacrétaz. Segmental score fusion for alisp-based gmm text-independent speaker verification. *In the book, Advances in Nonlinear Speech Processing and Applications, Edited by G. Chollet, A. Esposito, M. Faundez- Zanuy, M. Marinaro*, pages 385–394, 2004.
31. A. El Hannani and D. Petrovska-Delacrétaz. Exploiting high-level information provided by alisp in speaker recognition. *In the proceedings of the Non Linear Speech Processing Workshop (NOLISP)*, April 2005.
32. A. El Hannani and D. Petrovska-Delacrétaz. Improving speaker verification system using alisp-based specific gmms. *In the proceedings of the International Conference on Audio and Video Based Biometric Person Authentication (AVBPA)*, July 2005.
33. A. El Hannani, D.T. Toledano, D. Petrovska-Delacrétaz, A. Montero-Asenjo, and J. Hennebert. Using data-driven and phonetic units for speaker verification. *In the proceedings of the IEEE Workshop on Speaker and Language Recognition (Odyssey)*, June 2006.
34. A. El Hannani. *Text-independent Speaker Verification based on High Level Information Extracted with Data-driven Methods*. PhD Thesis, Université de Fribourg and Institut National des Télécommunications Evry, 2007.

35. G. Fant. *Acoustic Theory of Speech Production*. Mouton, The Hague, The Netherlands, 1970.
36. B. Fauve, D.Matrouf, N. Scheffer, J.F. Bonastre, and J. Mason. State-of-the-art performance in text-independent speaker verification through open-source software. In *IEEE Transactions on Speech and Audio Processing*, pages 1960–1968, 2007.
37. L. Ferrer, H. Bratt, V.R.R. Gadde, S. Kajarekar, E. Shriberg, K. Sonmez, A. Stolcke, and A. Venkataraman. Modeling duration patterns for speaker recognition. *In the proceedings of the European Conference on Speech Communication and Technology (Eurospeech)*, pages 2017–2020, September 2003.
38. BioSecure Benchmarking Framework. http://share.int-evry.fr/svnview-eph/.
39. S. Furui. Cepstral analysis technique for automatic speaker verification. *IEEE Transactions on Acoustics, Speech and Signal Processing*, 29(2):254–272, April 1981.
40. S. Furui. Comparison of speaker recognition methods using statistical features and dynamic features. *IEEE Transactions on Acoustics, Speech and Signal Processing*, 29(3):342–350, June 1981.
41. D. Garcia-Romero, J. Fierrez-Aguilar, J. Ortega-Garcia, and J. Gonzalez-Rodriguez. Support vector machine fusion of idiolectal and acoustic speaker information in spanish conversational speech. *In the proceedings of the IEEE International Conference on Acoustics, Speech, and Signal Processing (ICASSP)*, April 2003.
42. S. Garcia-Salicetti, C. Beumier, G. Chollet, B. Dorizzi, J. Leroux les Jardins, J. Lunter, Y. Ni, and D. Petrovska-Delacrétaz. BIOMET: a Multimodal Person Authentication Database Including Face, Voice, Fingerprint, Hand and Signature Modalities. In *4th International Conference on Audio and Video Based Biometric Person Authentification (AVBPA)*, Guilford UK, June 2003.
43. J.-L. Gauvain and C.-H. Lee. Maximum a posteriori estimation for multivariate gaussian mixture observations of markov chains. *IEEE Transactions on Speech and Audio Processing*, 29:291–298, April 1994.
44. J. Godfrey, D. Graff, and A. Martin. Public databases for speaker recognition and verification. *ESCA Workshop on Automatic Speaker Recognition Identification and Verification*, pages 39–42, April 1994.
45. D. Gutman and Y. Bistritz. Speaker verification using phoneme-adapted gaussian mixture models. *In the proceedings of the European Signal Processing Conference (EUSIPCO)*, September 2002.
46. A. El Hannani and D. Petrovska-Delacrétaz. Comparing data-driven and pnonetic systems for text-independent speaker verification. *In the proceedings of the IEEE First International Conference on Biometrics: Theory, Application*, September 2007.
47. A. El Hannani and D. Petrovska-Delacrétaz. Fusing acoustic, phonetic and data-driven systems for text-independent speaker verification. *In the proceedings of the International Conference on Speech Communication and Technology (Interspeech)*, August 2007.
48. E.G. Hansen, R.E. Slyh, and T.R. Anderson. Speaker recognition using phoneme-specific GMMs. *In the proceedings of the IEEE Workshop on Speaker and Language Recognition (Odyssey)*, June 2004.
49. A.O. Hatch, B. Peskin, and A. Stolcke. Improved phonetic speaker recognition using lattice decoding. *In the proceedings of the IEEE International Conference on Acoustics, Speech, and Signal Processing (ICASSP)*, March 2005.
50. S. Haykin. *Neural Networks: A Comprehensive Foundation*. IEEE Computer society Press, Macmillan, New York, NY, USA, 1994.
51. M. Hébert and L. P. Heck. Phonetic class-based speaker verification. *In the proceedings of the European Conference on Speech Communication and Technology (Eurospeech)*, September 2003.
52. H. Hermansky. Perceptual linear prediction (plp) analysis of speech. *Journal of the Acoustical Society of America*, 87(4), 1990.
53. H. Hermansky. Rasta processing of speech. *IEEE Transactions on Speech and Audio Processing*, 2(4), 1994.
54. HTK. http://htk.eng.cam.ac.uk/.

55. IV2: Identification par l'Iris et le Visage via la Vidéo. http://iv2.ibisc.fr/pageweb-iv2.html.
56. S.S. Kajarekar and H. Hermanskey. Speaker verification based on broad phonetic categories. *In the proceedings of the IEEE Workshop on Speaker and Language Recognition (Odyssey)*, June 2001.
57. P. Kenny and P. Dumouchel. Experiments in speaker verification using factor analysis likelihood ratios. *In the proceedings of the IEEE Workshop on Speaker and Language Recognition (Odyssey)*, June 2004.
58. P. Kenny and P. Dumouchel. Disentangling speaker and channel effects in speaker verification. *In the proceedings of the IEEE International Conference on Acoustics, Speech, and Signal Processing (ICASSP)*, 1, May 2005.
59. J. Kharroubi, D. Petrovska-Delacrétaz, and G. Chollet. Combining GMM's with support vector machines for text-independent speaker verification. *In the proceedings of the European Conference on Speech Communication and Technology (Eurospeech)*, pages 1761–1764, September 2001.
60. D. Klusacek, J. Navratil, D.A. Reynolds, and J.P. Campbell. Conditional pronunciation modeling in speaker detection. *In the proceedings of the IEEE International Conference on Acoustics, Speech, and Signal Processing (ICASSP)*, April 2003.
61. J. Koolwaaij and L. Boves. Local normalization and delayed decision making in speaker detection and tracking. *Digital Signal Processing*, 10, 2000.
62. J. Koolwaaij and J. de Veth. The use of broad phonetic class models in speaker recognition. *In the proceedings of the International Conference on Spoken Language Processing (ICSLP)*, December 1998.
63. LDC:Linguistic Data Consortium. http://www.ldc.
64. C.J. Leggetter and P.C. Woodland. Maximum likelihood linear regression for speaker adaptation of continuous density hidden markov models. *Computer Speech and Language*, 9(2):171–185, April 1995.
65. K.-P. Li and J.E. Porter. Normalizations and selection of speech segments for speaker recognition scoring. *In the proceedings of the IEEE International Conference on Acoustics, Speech, and Signal Processing (ICASSP)*, 1:595–598, April 1988.
66. J. Lindberg, J. Koolwaaij, H. Hutter, D. Genoud, M. Blomberg, F. Bimbot, and J. Pierrot. Techniques for a priori decision threshold estimation in speaker verification. *In the Proceedings of the Workshop Reconnaissance du Locuteur et ses Applications Commerciales et Criminalistiques (RLA2C)*, pages 89–92, 1998.
67. C. Ma and E. Chang. Comparaison of discriminative training methods for speaker verifiction. *In the proceedings of the IEEE International Conference on Acoustics, Speech, and Signal Processing (ICASSP)*, April 2003.
68. I. Magrin-Chagnolleau, G. Gravier, and R. Blouet. Overview of the 2000-2001 elisa consortium research activities. *In the proceedings of the IEEE Workshop on Speaker and Language Recognition (Odyssey)*, June 2001.
69. J. Makhoul. Linear prediction: A tutorial review. *Proceedings of the IEEE*, 63(4):561–580, 1975.
70. A. Martin, G. Doddington, T. Kamm, M. Ordowski, and M. Przybocki. The det curve in assessment of detection task performance. *In the proceedings of the European Conference on Speech Communication and Technology (Eurospeech)*, 4:1895–1898, September 1997.
71. A. Martin and M. Przybocki. Nist speaker rrecognition evaluation cronicles. In *In the proceedings of the IEEE Workshop on Speaker and Language Recognition (Odyssey)*, pages 15–22, 2004.
72. T. Matsui and S. Furui. Concatenated phoneme models for text-variable speaker recognition. *In the proceedings of the IEEE International Conference on Acoustics, Speech, and Signal Processing (ICASSP)*, pages 133–136, 1993.
73. J.M. Naik and D. Lubenskt. A hybrid hmm-mlp speaker verification algorithm for telephone speech. *In the proceedings of the IEEE International Conference on Acoustics, Speech, and Signal Processing (ICASSP)*, 1, April 1994.
74. NIST: National Institute of Standars and Technology. http://www.nist.gov/speech/tests/spk.

75. J. Navratil and G. N. Ramaswamy. The awe and mystery of t-norm. *In the proceedings of the European Conference on Speech Communication and Technology (Eurospeech)*, September 2003.
76. NIST Speaker Recognition Evaluations. http://www.nist.gov/speech/tests/spk.
77. T. Nordstrm, H. Melin, and J. Lindberg. A comparative study of speaker verification systems using the polycost database. *In the proceedings of the International Conference on Spoken Language Processing (ICSLP)*, December 1998.
78. J. Olsen. A two-stage procedure for phone based speaker verification. *In the proceedings of the International Conference on Audio and Video Based Biometric Person Authentication (AVBPA)*, pages 199–226, March 1997.
79. A.V. Oppenheim and R.W. Schafer. Homomorphic analysis of speech. *IEEE Transactions on Audio and Electroacoustics*, 16(2):221–226, 1968.
80. A.V. Oppenheim and R.W. Schafer. *Discrete-Time Signal Processing*. Prentice-Hall, Englewood Cliffs, NJ, USA, 1989.
81. E.S. Parris and M.J. Carey. Discriminative phonemes for speaker identification. *In the proceedings of the International Conference on Spoken Language Processing (ICSLP)*, pages 1843–1846, September 1994.
82. J. Pelecanos and S. Sridharan. Feature warping for robust speaker verification. *In the proceedings of the IEEE Workshop on Speaker and Language Recognition (Odyssey)*, June 2001.
83. D. Petrovska-Delacrétaz, M. Abalo, A. El Hannani, and G. Chollet. Data-driven speech segmentation for speaker verification and language identification. *In the proceedings of the Non Linear Speech Processing Workshop (NOLISP)*, May 2003.
84. D. Petrovska-Delacrétaz, A.L. Gorin, J.H. Wright, and G. Riccardi. Detecting acoustic morphemes in lattices for speken landuage understanding. *In the proceedings of the International Conference on Spoken Language Processing (ICSLP)*, October 2000.
85. D. Petrovska-Delacrétaz, A. El Hannani, and G. Chollet. Text-independent speaker verification: State of the art and challenges. In Y. Stylianou, M. Faundez-Zanuy, and A. Esposito, editors, *Progress in Nonlinear Speech Processing*, volume 4391, pages 135–169. Springer-Verlag, 2007.
86. D. Petrovska-Delacretaz and J. Hennebert. Text-prompted speaker verification experiments with phoneme specific MLP's. *In the proceedings of the IEEE International Conference on Acoustics, Speech, and Signal Processing (ICASSP)*, pages 777–780, May 1998.
87. D. Petrovska-Delacrétaz, J. Černocký, and G. Chollet. Segmental approaches for automatic speaker verification. *Digital Signal Processing*, 10(1-3):198–212, January/April/July 2000.
88. D. Petrovska-Delacrétaz, J. Černocký, J. Hennebert, and G. Chollet. Text-independent speaker verification using automatically labeled acoustic segments. *In the proceedings of the International Conference on Spoken Language Processing (ICSLP)*, December 1998.
89. J. Picone. Signal modeling techniques in speech recognition. *Proceedings of the IEEE*, 81(9):1214–1247, September 1993.
90. A. Preti, N. Scheffer, and J.-F. Bonastre. Discriminant approches for gmm based speaker detection systems. *In the workshop on Multimodal User Authentication*, 2006.
91. M. Przybocki, A. Martin, and A. Lee. Nist speaker rrecognition evaluation cronicles-part 2. In *In the proceedings of the IEEE Workshop on Speaker and Language Recognition (Odyssey)*, pages 1–6, 2006.
92. Thomas F. Quatieri. *Speech Signal Processing*. Prentice Hall Signal Processing Series, 2002.
93. L. Rabiner and B.H. Juang. *Fundamentals of Speech Recognition*. Prentice Hall, 1993.
94. D. Reynolds, W. Andrews, J.P. Campbell, J. Navratil, B. Peskin, A. Adami, Q. Jin, D. Klusacek, J. Abramson, R. Mihaescu, J. Godfrey, J. Jones, and B. Xiang. The supersid project: Exploiting high-level information for high-accuracy speaker recognition. *In the proceedings of the IEEE International Conference on Acoustics, Speech, and Signal Processing (ICASSP)*, April 2003.
95. D. A. Reynolds. A gaussian mixture modeling approach to text-independent speaker identification. *Ph.D. Thesis, Georgia Institute of Technology*, 1992.
96. D.A. Reynolds. Experimental evaluation of features for robust speaker identification. *IEEE Transactions on Speech and Audio Processing*, 2(3):639–643, 1994.

97. D.A. Reynolds. Automatic speaker recognition using gaussian mixture speaker models. *The Lincoln Laboratory Journal*, 8(2):173–191, 1995.
98. D.A. Reynolds. Speaker identification and verification using gaussian mixture speaker models. *Speech Communication*, 17(1):91–108, August 1995.
99. D.A. Reynolds. Comparison of background normalization methods for text-independent speaker verification. *In the proceedings of the European Conference on Speech Communication and Technology (Eurospeech)*, pages 963–966, September 1997.
100. D.A. Reynolds, W. Campbell, T. Gleason, C. Quillen, D. Sturim, P. Torres-Carrasquillo, and A. Adami. The 2004 mit lincoln laboratory speaker recognition system. *In the proceedings of the IEEE International Conference on Acoustics, Speech, and Signal Processing (ICASSP)*, 1, March 2005.
101. D.A. Reynolds, T.F. Quatieri, and R.B. Dunn. Speaker verification using adapted gaussian mixture models. *Digital Signal Processing*, 10(1-3):19–41, January/April/July 2000.
102. A. E. Rosenberg, J. DeLong, C. H. Lee, B. H. Juang, and F. K. Soong. The use of cohort normalized scores for speaker verification. *In the proceedings of the International Conference on Spoken Language Processing (ICSLP)*, pages 599–602, November 1992.
103. M. Schmidt and H. Gish. Speaker identification via support vector machines. *In the proceedings of the IEEE International Conference on Acoustics, Speech, and Signal Processing (ICASSP)*, May 1996.
104. B. Schölkopf and A. J. Smola. Learning with kernels: Support vector machines, regularization, optimization and beyond. *MIT press*, 2001.
105. A. Solomonoff, C. Quillen, and W. Campbell. Channel compensation for svm speaker recognition. *In the proceedings of the IEEE Workshop on Speaker and Language Recognition (Odyssey)*, June 2004.
106. K. Sönmez, E. Shriberg, L. Heck, and M. Weintraub. Modeling dynamic prosodic variation for speaker verification. *In the proceedings of the International Conference on Spoken Language Processing (ICSLP)*, December 1998.
107. SPro. http://www.irisa.fr/metiss/guig/spro/index.html.
108. D. Sturim, D. Reynolds, R. Dunn, and T. Quatieri. Speaker verification using text-constrained gaussian mixture models. *In the proceedings of the IEEE International Conference on Acoustics, Speech, and Signal Processing (ICASSP)*, 1:677–680, May 2002.
109. N. Tishby. On the application of mixture ar hidden markov models to text-independent speaker recognition. *IEEE Transactions on Signial Processing*, 39(3):563–570, March 1991.
110. V. Vapnik. *The Nature of Statistical Learning Theory*. Springer-Verlag, New York, 1995.
111. O. Viikki and K. Laurila. Cepstral domain segmental feature vector normalization for noise robust speech recognition. *Speech Communication*, 25:133–147, 1998.
112. V. Wan and W. Campbell. Support vector machines for speaker verification and identification. *In proceedings of the IEEE Signal Processing Society Workshop*, 2:775–784, 2000.
113. V. Wan and S. Renals. SVM: Support vector machine speaker verification methodology. *In the proceedings of the IEEE International Conference on Acoustics, Speech, and Signal Processing (ICASSP)*, 2:221–224, April 2003.
114. V. Wan and S. Renals. Speaker verification using sequence discriminant support vector machines. *IEEE Transactions on Speech and Audio Processing*, 13:203–210, 2005.
115. B. Xiang, U. Chaudhari, J. Navratil, G. Ramaswamy, and R. Gopinath. Short-time gaussianization for robust speaker verification. *In the proceedings of the IEEE International Conference on Acoustics, Speech, and Signal Processing (ICASSP)*, 1:681–684, May 2002.
116. R.D. Zilca, J.W. Pelecanos, U.V. Chaudhari, and G.N. Ramaswamy. Real time robust speech detection for text-independent speaker recognition. *In the proceedings of the IEEE Workshop on Speaker and Language Recognition (Odyssey)*, pages 123–128, June 2004.

Chapter 8
2D Face Recognition

Massimo Tistarelli, Manuele Bicego, José L. Alba-Castro, Daniel Gonzàlez-Jiménez, Mohamed-Anouar Mellakh, Albert Ali Salah, Dijana Petrovska-Delacrétaz, and Bernadette Dorizzi

Abstract An overview of selected topics in face recognition is first presented in this chapter. The BioSecure 2D-face Benchmarking Framework is also described, composed of open-source software, publicly available databases and protocols. Three methods for 2D-face recognition, exploiting multiscale analysis, are presented. The first method exploits anisotropic smoothing, combined Gabor features and Linear Discriminant Analysis (LDA). The second approach is based on subject-specific face verification via Shape-Driven Gabor Jets (SDGJ), while the third combines Scale Invariant Feature Transform (SIFT) descriptors with graph matching.

Comparative results are reported within the benchmarking framework on the BANCA database (with Mc and P protocols). Experimental results on the FRGC v2 database are also reported. The results show the improvements achieved with the presented multiscale analysis methods in order to cope with mismatched enrollment and test conditions.

8.1 State of the Art in Face Recognition: Selected Topics

Face recognition (identification and verification) has attracted the attention of researchers for more than two decades and is among the most popular research areas in the field of computer vision and pattern recognition. Several approaches have been proposed for face recognition based on 2D and 3D images. In general, face recognition technologies are based on a two-step approach:

- An off-line enrollment procedure is established to build a unique template for each registered user. The procedure is based on the acquisition of a predefined set of face images (or a video sequence) selected from the input image stream, and the template is built upon a set of features extracted from the image ensemble.
- An online identification or verification procedure where a set of images is acquired and processed to extract a given set of features. From these features a face description is built to be matched against the user's template.

D. Petrovska-Delacrétaz et al. (eds.), *Guide to Biometric Reference Systems and Performance Evaluation*, DOI 10.1007/978-1-84800-292-0_8,

Regardless of the acquisition devices exploited to grab the image streams, a simple taxonomy based on the computational architecture applied to extract powerful features for recognition and to derive a template description for subsequent matching can be adopted. Two main algorithmic categories can be defined on the basis of the relation between the subject and the face model, i.e., whether the algorithm is based on a subject-centered (eco-centric) representation or on a camera-centered (ego-centric) representation. The former class of algorithms relies on a more complex model of the face, which is generally 3D or 2.5D, and it is strongly linked with the 3D structure of the face. These methods require a more complex procedure to extract the features and build the face model, however they have the advantage of being intrinsically pose-invariant. The most popular face-centered algorithms are those based on 3D face data acquisition and on face depth maps. The ego-centric class of algorithms strongly relies on the information content of the gray level structures of the images. Therefore, the face representation is strongly pose-variant and the model is rigidly linked to the face appearance, rather than to the 3D face structure. The most popular image-centered algorithms are the holistic or subspace-based methods, the feature-based methods and the hybrid methods.

Over these elementary classes of algorithms, several elaborations have been proposed. Among them, kernel methods greatly enhanced the discrimination power of several eco-centric algorithms, while new feature analysis techniques such as the local binary pattern representation greatly improved the speed and robustness of Gabor filtering-based methods. The same considerations are valid for eco-centric algorithms, where new shape descriptors and 3D parametric models, including the fusion of shape information with the 2D face texture, considerably enhanced the accuracy of existing methods.

The objective of this survey is not to enumerate all existing face recognition paradigms, for which other publications have already been produced (see for example [16]), but rather to illustrate a few remarkable example categories for which extensive tests have been performed on publicly available datasets. This list is, by its nature, incomplete but directly reflects the experience made along the BioSecure Network of Excellence.

8.1.1 Subspace Methods

The most popular techniques used for frontal face recognition are the subspace methods. The subspace algorithms consider the entire image as a feature vector and their aim is to find projections (bases) that optimize some criterion defined over the feature vectors corresponding to different classes. Then, the original high dimensional image space is projected into a low dimensional one. The classification is usually performed according to a simple distance measure in the final multidimensional space.

Various criteria have been employed in order to find the bases of the low dimensional spaces. Some of them have been defined in order to find projections that best express the population without using the information of how the data are separated to different classes. Another class of criteria is the one that deals directly with the discrimination between classes. Finally, statistical independence in the low dimensional feature space have been used as a criterion to find the linear projections.

One of the oldest and best studied methods for low dimension representation of faces using this type of criteria is the eigenfaces Principal Component Analysis (PCA) approach [51]. This representation was used in [112] for face recognition. The idea behind the Eigenface representation is to choose a dimensionality reduction linear transformation that maximizes the scatter of all projected samples. In [98], the PCA approach was extended to a nonlinear alternative using kernel functions.

Another subspace method that aims at representing the face without using class information is Nonnegative Matrix Factorization (NMF) [59]. This algorithm, like PCA, represents a face as a linear combination of bases. The difference with PCA is that it does not allow negative elements in both the basis vectors and the weights of the linear combination. This constraint results in radically different bases from PCA. The bases of PCA are eigenfaces, some of which resemble distorted versions of the entire face, whereas the bases of NMF are localized features that correspond better to the intuitive notions of face parts [59].

An extension of NMF that gives even more localized bases by imposing additional locality constraints is the so-called local nonnegative matrix Linear Discriminant Analysis. It is one of the most well-studied methods that aim to find low dimensional representations using the information of how faces are separated to classes. In [125, 72], it was proposed to use LDA in a reduced PCA space for facial image retrieval and recognition, the so-called fisherfaces. Fisherface is a two-step dimensionality reduction method. First, the feature dimensionality is reduced using the eigenfaces approach to make the between-class scatter matrix nonsingular. After that, the dimension of the new features is reduced further, using Fisher's Linear Discriminant (FLD) optimization criterion to produce the final linear transformation.

Recently, direct LDA algorithms for discriminant feature extraction were proposed [11, 80, 71] in order to prevent the loss of discriminatory information that occurs when a PCA step is applied prior to LDA [71]. Such algorithms are usually applied using direct diagonalization methods for finding the linear projections that optimize the discriminant criterion [11, 80, 71]. For solving nonlinear problems, the classic LDA has been generalized to its kernel version, namely General Discriminant Analysis (GDA) [78] or Kernel Fisher Discriminant Analysis (KFDA) [79]. In GDA, the original input space is projected using a nonlinear mapping from the input space (the facial image space) to a high-dimensional feature space, where different classes of faces are supposed to be linearly separable. The idea behind GDA is to perform LDA in the feature space instead of the input space. The interested reader can refer to [11, 80, 71, 78, 79] for different versions of KFDA and GDA.

The main drawback of methods that use discriminant criteria is that they may cause over-training. Moreover, large difficulties appear in constructing a discriminant function on small training sample sets, resulting in discriminant functions that have no generalization abilities [48, 91]. That is true in many practical cases where a very limited number of facial images are available in database training sets. The small number of facial images for each face class affects both linear and nonlinear methods where the distribution of the client class should be evaluated in a robust way [79]. This fact was also confirmed in [76], where it was shown that LDA outperforms PCA only when large and representative training datasets are available.

In order to find linear projections that minimize the statistical dependence between its components, the low-dimensional feature space Independent Component Analysis (ICA) has been proposed [7, 65] for face recognition. The nonlinear alternative of ICA using kernel methods has been also proposed in [119].

8.1.2 Elastic Graph Matching (EGM)

Another popular class of techniques used for frontal face recognition is Elastic Graph Matching (EGM), which is a practical implementation of the Dynamic Link Architecture (DLA) for object recognition [56]. In EGM, the reference object graph is created by overlaying a rectangular elastic sparse graph on the object image and calculating a Gabor wavelet bank response at each graph node. The graph matching process is implemented by a stochastic optimization of a cost function that takes into account both jet similarities and node deformation. A two-stage coarse-to-fine optimization procedure suffices for the minimization of such a cost function. Since its invention, EGM for face verification and identification has been a very active research field. In [126], EGM outperformed eigenfaces and autoassociation classification neural networks for face recognition.

In [119], the graph structure was enhanced by introducing a stack-like structure, the so-called bunch graph, and was tested for face recognition. In the bunch graph structure for every node, a set of jets was measured for different facial features (e.g., with mouth opened or closed, eyes opened or closed). That way, the bunch graph representation could cover a variety of possible changes in the appearance of a face.

In [118], the bunch graph structure was used to determine facial characteristics such as beard, presence of glasses or a person's gender. Practical methods for increasing the robustness of EGM against translations, deformations, and changes in background have been presented in [122]. In [118], EGM was applied for frontal face verification, where different choices for the elasticity of the graph have been investigated. A variant of the standard EGM, the so-called Morphological Elastic Graph Matching (MEGM), was proposed for frontal face verification and tested for various recording conditions [54, 53]. In MEGM, the Gabor features were replaced by multiscale morphological features obtained through dilation-erosion of the facial image by a structuring function [54]. In [54], the standard coarse-to-fine approach [119] for EGM was replaced by a simulated annealing method that optimizes a cost function of the jet similarity distances subject to node deformation constraints. It was proven that multiscale morphological analysis is suitable for facial image analysis, and MEGM gave comparable verification results to the standard EGM approach, without the need to compute the computationally expensive Gabor filter bank output.

Another variant of EGM was presented in [110], where morphological signal decomposition was used instead of the standard Gabor analysis [119]. Discriminant techniques were employed in order to enhance the recognition performance of the EGM. The use of linear discriminating techniques on feature vectors for selecting the most discriminating features has been proposed in [119, 54, 110].

Several schemes that aim to weigh the graph nodes according to their discriminatory power were proposed [54, 110, 55, 109]. In [55], the selection of the weighting coefficients was based on a nonlinear function that depends on a small set of parameters. These parameters were determined on the training set by maximizing a criterion using the simplex method. In [54, 110], the set of node weighting coefficients was calculated by using the first and second order statistics of the nodes similarity values. A Bayesian approach for determining which nodes are more reliable was used in [119]. A more sophisticated scheme for weighting the nodes of the elastic graph by constructing a modified class of support vector machines was proposed in [109]. In [109], it was also shown that the verification performance of the EGM can be highly improved by proper node weighting strategies. The subspace of the face recognition algorithms considers the entire image as a feature vector and their aim is to find projections that optimize some criterion defined over the feature vectors corresponding to different classes.

The main drawback of these methods is that they require the facial images to be perfectly aligned. That is, all the facial images should be aligned in order to have all the fiducial points (such as eyes, nose or mouth) represented at the same position inside the feature vector. For this purpose, the facial images are very often aligned manually and moreover they are anisotropically scaled. Perfect automatic alignment is in general a difficult task to be assessed. On the contrary, elastic graph matching does not require perfect alignment in order to perform well. The main drawback of the elastic graph matching is the time required for multiscale analysis of the facial image and for the matching procedure.

8.1.3 Robustness to Variations in Facial Geometry and Illumination

It is a common knowledge that different illumination conditions between the enrollment and test images cause a lot of problems for the face recognition algorithms. How computers conceive individual's face geometry is also a problem that researchers are called to solve in order to increase the robustness and the stability of a face recognition system. In what follows, the latest research on this subject is presented.

In [114], the authors present a general framework for face modeling under varying lighting conditions. They show that a face lighting subspace can be constructed based on three or more training face images illuminated by non-coplanar lights. The lighting of any face image can be represented as a point in this subspace. Second, they show that the extreme rays, i.e. the boundary of an illumination cone, cover the entire light sphere. Therefore, a relatively sparsely sampled face images can be used to build a face model instead of calculating each extremely illuminated face image. Third, a face normalization algorithm is presented, called illumination alignment, that changes the lighting of one face image to that of another face image. The main contribution of this paper is the proposal for a very general framework for analyzing and modeling face images under varied lighting conditions. The concept of face lighting space is introduced, as well as a general face model and a general face imaging model for face modeling under varied lighting conditions. Illumination alignment approach for face recognition is proposed too. The provided experimental results show that the algorithms could render reasonable face images and effectively improve the face recognition rate under varied lighting conditions. Although the authors deduced an approach showing that lighting space can be built from sparsely sampled images with different lighting, the matter of how to construct an optimal global lighting space from these images is still an issue. Whether a global lighting space constructed from one person's images is better than multi persons' images is also an open question. The authors conclude that illumination and pose are two problems that have to be faced concurrently.

In [15], researchers present an experimental study and declare that it is the largest study on combining and comparing 2D and 3D face recognition up to year 2004. They also maintain, that this is the only such study to incorporate significant time lapse between enrollment and test images and to look at the effect of depth resolution. A total of 275 subjects participated in one or more data acquisition sessions. Results are presented for gallery (enrollment) and probe (test) datasets of 200 subjects imaged in both 2D and 3D, with one to thirteen weeks time lapse, yielding 951 pairs of 2D and 3D images. Using a PCA based approach tuned separately for 2D and 3D, they found that 3D outperforms 2D. However, they also found a multimodal rank-one recognition rate of 98.5% in a single-probe study and 98.8% in multi-probe study, which is statistically significantly greater than either 2D or 3D alone. The value of multimodal biometrics with 2D intensity and 3D shape of facial data in the context of face recognition is examined in a single-probe study and a multi-probe study. In the results provided, each modality of facial data has roughly similar value as an appearance-based biometric. The combination of the face data from both modalities results in statistically significant improvement over either individual biometric. In general, the results appear to support the conclusion that the path to higher accuracy and robustness in biometrics involves the use of multiple biometrics rather than the best possible sensor and algorithm for a single biometric.

In their later work [16], authors of [15] make four major conclusions. They use PCA-based methods separately for each modality, and match scores in the separate face spaces that are combined for multimodal recognition. More specifically, researchers have concluded that:

- Similar recognition performance is obtained using a single 2D or a single 3D image.
- Multimodal 2D+3D face recognition performs significantly better than using either 3D or 2D alone.

- Combining results from two or more 2D images using a similar fusion scheme as used in multimodal 2D+3D also improves performance over using a single 2D image.
- Even when the comparison is controlled for the same number of image samples used to represent a person, multimodal 2D+3D still outperforms multisample 2D, though not by as much; also, it may be possible to use more 2D samples to achieve the same performance as multimodal 2D+3D.

The results reported use the same basic recognition method for both 2D and 3D. Researchers report that it is possible that some other algorithms, which exploit information in 2D images in some ideal way that cannot be applied to 3D images, might result in 2D face recognition being more powerful than 3D face recognition, or vice-versa. Overall, researchers conclude that improved face recognition performance will result from the combination of 2D+3D imaging, and also from the representation a person by multiple images taken under varied lighting and facial expressions.

The topic of multiimage representations of a person for face recognition is even less well explored. In [39], an accurate and robust face recognition system was developed and tested. This system exploits the feature extraction capabilities of the Discrete Cosine Transform (DCT) and invokes certain normalization techniques that increase its robustness to variations in facial geometry and illumination. The method was tested on a variety of available face databases, including one collected at McGill University. The system was shown to perform very well when compared to other approaches. The experimental results confirm the usefulness and robustness of DCT for face recognition. The mathematical relationship between the DCT and the Karhunen-Loève Transform (KLT) explains the near-optimal performance of the former. This mathematical relationship particularly justifies the use of DCT for face recognition, because Turk and Pentland have already shown earlier that the KLT performs well in this application [112]. The system also uses an affine transformation to correct for scale, position, and orientation changes in faces. It was seen that tremendous improvements in recognition rates could be achieved with such normalization.

Illumination normalization was also investigated extensively. Various approaches to the problem of compensating for illumination variations among faces were designed and tested, and it was concluded that the recognition rate of the specific system was sensitive to many of these approaches. This sensitivity occurs partly because the faces in the databases used for the tests were uniformly illuminated and partly because these databases contained a wide variety of skin tones. That is, certain illumination normalization techniques had a tendency to make all faces have the same overall gray-scale intensity, and they thus resulted in the loss of much of the information about the individuals' skin tones.

A complexity comparison between DCT and KLT is of interest. In the proposed method, training essentially means computing the DCT coefficients of all the database faces. On the other hand, when using KLT, training entails computing the basis vectors, i.e. the KLT is more computationally expensive with respect to training. However, once the KLT basis vectors have been obtained, it may be argued that computing the KLT coefficients for recognition is trivial. Computing DCT coefficients is also trivial, with the additional provision that DCT may take advantage of very efficient computational algorithms [90]. The authors argue that multiple face models per person might be a simple way to deal with 3D facial distortions. In this regard, the KLT method is not distortion-invariant, so it would suffer from degradation under face distortions.

In [120], a distortion-invariant method is described. This method performs relatively well, but it is based on a Dynamic Link Architecture (DLA), which is not very efficient. Specifically, in this method, matching is dependent on synaptic plasticity in a self-organizing neural network. Thus, to recognize a face, a system based on this method has to first match this face to all models (through the process of map self-organization) and then choose the model that minimizes some cost function. Obviously, simulating the dynamics of a neural network for each model face in a database in order to recognize an input image is computationally expensive. Therefore, it seems that there remains a strong trade-off between performance and complexity in many existing face recognition algorithms.

The system presented in [39] lacks face localization capabilities. It would be desirable to add one of the many reported methods in the literature so that the system could be completely independent of the manual input of the eye coordinates. In fact, the DCT could be used to perform this localization. That is, frequency domain information obtained from the DCT could be used to implement template-matching algorithms for finding faces or eyes in images.

Geometric normalization could also be generalized to account for 3D pose variations in faces. As for illumination compensation, researchers have observed that light-color faces were artificially tinted and darker color faces brightened due to the choice of target face illumination used when applying histogram modification. Thus, being able to categorize individuals in terms of, perhaps, skin color could be used to define different target illuminations, independently tuned to suit various subsets of the population. For example, an average of Caucasian faces would not be very well suited to modify the illumination of black faces, and vice versa. This classification approach would have the advantage of reducing the sensitivity of the system to illumination normalization. Finally, authors of [39] support that they can contemplate other enhancements similar to those attempted for the KLT method. For example, the DCT could be used as a first stage transformation followed by linear discriminant analysis. Also, the DCT could be computed for local facial features in addition to the global computation, which, while moderately enlarging the size of the feature vectors, would most likely yield better performance.

To deal with the problem of illumination in face recognition systems researchers in [88] present a novel illumination normalization approach by relighting faces to a canonical illumination based on harmonic images. Benefit from the observations that the human faces share similar shape of the face surface is quasi-constant, they first estimate the nine low-frequency components of the lighting from the input face image. Then the face image is normalized by relighting it to canonical illumination based on illumination ratio image.

For face recognition purpose, two kinds of canonical illumination, uniform and frontal point lighting, are considered, among which the former encodes merely texture information, while the latter encodes both texture and shading information. With the discovery that the effect of illumination on a diffuse object is low dimensional with analytic analysis, it will not be more difficult to deal with generic illumination than to deal with simple point light source model. Based on these observations, the authors propose a technique for face relighting under generic illumination based on harmonic images, i.e., calibrating the input face image to the canonical illumination to reduce the negative effect of poor illumination in face recognition. A comparison study is performed between two kinds of relit images and original face. The two kinds of canonical illuminations are the uniform, which incorporates texture information, and frontal point lighting, which incorporates texture and shape information. The experimental results show that the proposed lighting normalization method based on face relighting can significantly improve the performance of a face recognition system. The performance of relit images under uniform lighting is a little better than that of frontal point lighting, contrary to what researchers had expected. This indicates that there are risks in using shape information if it is not very accurate. Labeling feature points under good lighting conditions is practical, while results under extreme lighting are not good enough with current technology. Therefore maybe the recovered harmonic base for gallery images under good lighting with the 9D linear subspace [10] is more applicable for face recognition systems under extreme lighting.

In [89], researchers consider the problem of recognizing faces under varying illuminations. First, they investigate the statistics of the derivative of the irradiance images (log) of the human face and find that the distribution is very sparse. Based on this observation, they propose an illumination-insensitive distance measure based on the min operator of the derivatives of two images. The proposed measure for recovering reflectance images is compared with the median operator proposed by Weiss [115]. When the probes are collected under varying illuminations, the experiments of face recognition on the CMU-PIE database show that the proposed measure is much better than the correlation of image intensity and a little better than the Euclidean distance of the derivative of the log image used in [112].

8.1.4 2D Facial Landmarking

Facial feature localization (also called anchor point detection and facial landmarking) is an important component of biometric applications that rely on face data, but also important for facial feature tracking, facial modeling and animation, and expression analysis. Robust and automatic detection of facial features is a difficult problem, suffering from all the known problems of face recognition, such as illumination, pose and expression variations, and clutter. This problem should be distinguished from face detection, which is the localization of a bounding box for the face. The aim in landmark detection is locating selected facial points with the greatest possible accuracy.

Facial landmarks are used in registering face images, normalizing expressions and recognition based on geometrical distribution of landmarks. There is no universal set of landmark points accepted for these applications. Fred Bookstein defines landmarks as "points in one form for which objectively meaningful and reproducible biological counterparts exist in all the other forms of a data set" [14]. Most frequently used landmarks on faces are the nose tip, eye and mouth corners, center of the iris, tip of the chin, the nostrils, the eyebrows, and the nose.

Many landmarking techniques assume that the face has already been detected, and the search area for each landmark is greatly restricted [33, 37, 47, 113, 121]. Similarly, many facial landmarking algorithms are guided by heuristics [4, 13, 37, 41, 47, 103, 121]. Typically, one uses vertical projection histograms to initialize the eye and mouth regions, where one assumes that the first and second histogram valleys correspond to the eye sockets and lips, respectively [17, 18, 37, 57, 103, 106, 131]. Another frequently encountered characteristic of facial landmarking is a serial search approach where the algorithm starts with the easiest landmark, and uses the detected landmark to constrain the search for the rest of the landmarks [4, 13, 37, 38]. For instance in [103], the eyes are the first landmarks to be detected, and then the perpendicular bisecting segment between the two eyes and the information of interocular distance are used to locate the mouth position, and finally the mouth corners.

We can classify facial feature localization as appearance-based, geometric-based and structure-based [96]. As landmarking is but a single stage of the complete biometrics system, most approaches use a coarse-to-fine localization to reduce the computational load [4, 27, 41, 94, 96, 105].

In appearance-based approaches, the face image is either directly processed, or transformed in preprocessing. For direct processing, horizontal, vertical or edge field projections are frequently employed to detect the eye and mouth area through its contrast [9, 121], whereas color is used to detect the lip region [95]. The most popular transformations are principal components analysis [2, 94], Gabor wavelets [27, 96, 103, 105, 113, 121], independent components analysis [2], discrete cosine transform [96, 132] and Gaussian derivative filters [4, 33]. Through these transforms, the variability in facial features is captured, and machine learning approaches like boosted cascade detectors [17, 18, 113], support vector machines [2], mixture models [96], and multilayer perceptrons [94] are used to learn the appearance of each landmark.

In geometric-based methods, the distribution of landmark points on the face is used in the form of heuristic rules that involve angles, distances, and areas [103, 106, 132]. In structure-based methods, the geometry is incorporated into a complete structure model. For instance, in the elastic bunch graph matching approach, a graph models the relative positions of landmarks, where each node represents one point of the face and the arcs are weighted according to expected landmark distances. At each node, a set of templates is used to evaluate the local feature similarity [119]. Since the possible deformations depend on the landmark points (e.g., mouth corners deform much more than the nose tip), landmark-specific information can be incorporated into the structural model [123]. As the jointly optimized constraint set is enlarged, the system runs more frequently into convergence problems and local minima, which in turn makes a good and often manual initialization necessary. Table 8.1 summarizes the facial feature extraction methods in 2D face images. See [96] for more detail.

Table 8.1 Summary of 2D facial landmarking methods

Reference	Coarse Localization	Fine Localization
Antonini et al. [2]	Corner detection	PCA and ICA projections, SVM-based template matching
Arca et al. [4]	Color segmentation + SVM	Geometrical heuristics
Chen et al. [17]	Gaussian mixture based feature model + 3D shape model	
Cristinacce et al. [20]	Assumed given	Boosted Haar wavelet-like features and classifiers
Feris et al. [27]	Hierarchical Gabor wavelet network + template matching on features and faces	
Gourier et al. [33]	Gaussian derivatives + clustering	Not present
Ioannou et al. [47]	SVM	Luminance, edge geometry-based heuristics
Lai et al. [57]	Colour segmentation + edge map	Vertical projections
Salah et al. [96]	Gabor wavelets + mixture models + structural correction	DCT template matching
Shakunaga et al. [101]	PCA on feature positions + structural correction	PCA
Shih et al. [103]	Edge projections + geometrical feature model	Not present
Smeraldi et al. [105]	Gabor wavelets + SVM	
Ryu et al. [94]	Projections of edge map	PCA + MLP
Vukadinovic et al. [113]	Ada-boosted Haar wavelets	Gabor wavelets + Gentle-boost
Zobel et al. [132]	DCT + geometrical heuristics + probabilistic model	Not present

8.1.4.1 Exploiting and Selecting the Best Facial Features

Feature selection for face representation is one of central issues to face classification or detection systems. Appearance-based approaches that generally operate directly on images or appearances of face objects and process the images as 2D holistic patterns provide some of the most promising solutions [72, 111]. Some of the most popular solutions are provided by the eigenfaces [112] and fisherfaces [87] algorithms, and their variants.

The work in [34] introduces an algorithm for the automatic relevance determination of input variables in kernel Support Vector Machines (SVM) and demonstrates its effectiveness on a demanding facial expression recognition problem. The relevance of input features may be measured by continuous weights or scale factors, which define a diagonal metric in input space. Feature selection results then in determining a sparse diagonal metric, and this can be encouraged by constraining an appropriate norm on scale factors. Feature selection is performed by assigning zero weights to irrelevant variables. The metric in the input space is automatically tuned by the minimization of the standard SVM empirical risk, where scale factors are added to the usual set of parameters defining the classifier. As in standard SVMs, only two tunable hyper-parameters are to be set: the penalization of training errors, and the magnitude of kernel bandwidths. In this formalism, an efficient algorithm to monitor slack variables when optimizing the metric is derived. The approximation of the cost function is tight enough to allow large updates of the metric when necessary.

In [40], an algorithm for automatically learning discriminative parts in object images with SVM classifiers is described. This algorithm is based on growing image parts by minimizing theoretical bounds on the error probability of an SVM. This method automatically determines rectangular components from a set of object images. The algorithm starts with a small rectangular component located around a preselected (possibly at random) point in the object image (e.g., in the case of face images, this could be the center of the left eye). The component is extracted from each object image to build a training set of positive examples. In addition, a training set of nonface patterns that have the same rectangular shape as the component is generated. After training an SVM on the component data, the performance of the SVM is estimated, based on the upper bound on the error probability P [117]. Next, the component is grown by expanding the rectangle by one pixel in one of the four directions (up, down, left or right). Again training data are generated, SVM is trained and P is computed. This procedure is iterated for expansions into each of the four directions until P increases. The same greedy process can then be repeated by selecting new seed regions. The set of extracted components is then ranked according to the final value of P and the top N components are chosen. Component-based face classifiers are combined in a second stage to yield a hierarchical SVM classifier. Experimental results in face classification show considerable robustness to rotations in depth and suggest performance at a significantly better level than other face detection systems.

In [50], a learning vector quantization learning method based on combination of weak classifiers is proposed. The weak classifiers are generated using automatic elimination of redundant hidden layer neurons of the network on both the entire face images and the extracted features: forehead, right eye, left eye, nose, mouth, and chin. The output-decision vectors are then combined using majority voting. Also, a ranking of the class labels is used in case the majority of the feature classifiers do not agree upon the same output class. It has been found experimentally that the recognition performance of the network for the forehead is the worst, while the nose yields the best performance among the selected features. The ranking of the features in accordance with the recognition performance is nose, right eye, mouth, left eye, chin, and forehead. The selection of features for the face recognition system to be designed highly depends on the nature of data to be tested on and the feature region itself, especially when luminance variations are severe. Commonly, it is considered that the mouth and eyes are dynamic features as compared to the chin or forehead. However, experimental results show that the percentage of the correct classification rate for eyes is better than the chin or forehead, which are static features. When one region of the face is affected by the variation of the pose or expression, other face regions may be unaffected. Thus, the recognition performance is high for the systems based on feature combination.

More recently, a number of studies have shown that facial features provided by infrared imagery offer a promising alternative to visible imagery as they are relatively insensitive to illumination changes. However, infrared has other limitations, including opaqueness to glass. As a result, it is very sensitive to facial occlusion caused by eyeglasses. In [104], it is proposed to fuse infrared with visible images, exploiting the relatively lower sensitivity of visible imagery to occlusions caused by eyeglasses. Two different fusion schemes have been investigated in this work. The first one is image-based, which operates in the wavelet domain, and yields a fused image capturing important information from both spectra. Fusing multiresolution image representations allows features with different spatial extents to be fused at the resolution that they are most salient. Genetic Algorithms (GAs) are used to decide which wavelet coefficients to select from each spectrum. The second one is feature-based, which operates in the eigenspace domain, and yields a set of important eigenfeatures from both spectra. GAs are used again to decide which eigenfeatures and which eigenspace to use. Results show substantial overall improvements in recognition performance, suggesting that the idea of exploiting/selecting features from both infrared and visible images for face recognition deserves further consideration.

In [107], the authors show that feature selection is an important problem in object detection and demonstrate that genetic algorithms provide a simple, general, and powerful framework for selecting good subsets of features, leading to improved detection rates of faces. As a case study, PCA was considered for feature extraction and support vector machines for classification. The goal is searching the PCA space using genetic algorithms to select a subset of eigenvectors encoding important information about the target concept of interest. This is in contrast to traditional methods selecting some percentage of the top eigenvectors to represent the target concept, independently of the classification task. A wrapper-based approach is used to evaluate the quality of the selected eigenvectors. Specifically, feedback from a support vector machine classifier is used to guide the genetic algorithm's search in selecting a good subset of eigenvectors, improving detection accuracy. Given a set of eigenvectors, a binary encoding scheme is used to represent the presence or absence of a particular eigenvector in the solutions generated during evolution. The proposed framework was tested on the face detection problem, showing significant performance improvements.

8.1.5 Dynamic Face Recognition and Use of Video Streams

Historically, face recognition has been treated as the matching between snapshots containing the representation of a face. In the human visual system, the analysis of visual information is never restricted to a time-confined signal. Much information on the analyzed visual data is contained within the temporal evolution of the data itself. Therefore, a considerable amount of the "neural power" in humans is devoted to the analysis and interpretation of time variations of the visual signal.

On the other hand, processing single images considerably simplifies the recognition process. Therefore, the real challenge is to exploit the added information in the time variation of face images, limiting the added computational burden. An additional difficulty in experimenting with dynamic face recognition is the dimensionality of the required test data. A statistically meaningful experimental test requires a considerable number of subjects (at least 80 to 100) with several views taken at different times. Collecting video streams of 4–5 seconds from each subject and for each acquisition session implies the storage and subsequent processing of a considerable amount (hundreds of Gigabytes) of data.

There are only a few face recognition systems in the literature based on the analysis of image sequences. The developed algorithms generally exploit the following advantages from the video sequence:

- The matching process is repeated over more images and the resulting scores are combined according to some criterion. Several approaches have been proposed to integrate multiple similarity measurements from video streams. Most of the proposed algorithms rely on the concept of data fusion [3] and uncertainty reduction [43].
- The input sequence is filtered to extract the image data best suited for recognition. This method is often coupled with a template representation based on a sequence of face views. An example of this use is the Incremental Refinement of Decision Boundaries [23] where the face representation is dynamically augmented by processing and selecting subsequent frames in the input video stream on the basis of the output of a statistical classifier. Weng et al. [116] proposed to incrementally derive discriminating features from training video sequences.
- The motion in the sequence is used to infer the 3D structure of the face and perform 3D instead of 2D recognition [32]. An interesting and similar approach is based on the generalization of classic single view matching to multiple views [61, 62, 63] and the integration of video into a time-varying representation called "identity surfaces."
- The processing algorithm extends the face template representation from 2D to 3D, where the third dimension is time. There are few examples of this

approach including composite PCA, extended HMM, parametric eigenspaces, multi-dimensional classifiers, neural networks and other, video-oriented, integrated approaches.
- Facial expression is detected and identified either for face renormalization or emotion understanding.

The enclosed bibliography traces a comprehensive view of the actual state of the art related to the use of video streams for face recognition. The use of video for expression analysis and recognition are considered below. In the remainder of this chapter, only the most relevant and novel concepts related to the fourth bullet are addressed.

8.1.5.1 Face Representation from Video Streams

Several approaches have been proposed to generalize classical face representations based on a single-view to multiple-view representations. Examples of this kind can be found in [74, 73] and [93, 92] where face sequences are clustered using vector quantization to identify different facial views and subsequently feed to a statistical classifier. Recently, Krueger, Zhou and Chellappa [129, 130] proposed the "video-to-video" paradigm, where the whole sequence of faces acquired during a given time interval of the video sequence is associated with a class (identity). This concept implies the temporal analysis of the video sequence with dynamical models (e.g., Bayesian models), and the "condensation" of the tracking and recognition problems. These methods are a matter of ongoing research, and the reported experiments were performed without huge variations of pose and face expressions.

In the algorithm of Zhou et al. [129], the joint probability distribution of identity and motion is modeled using sequential importance sampling, yielding the recognition decision by marginalization.

Other face recognition systems based on still-to-still and multiple stills-to-still paradigms have been proposed [63, 42, 62]. However, none of them is able to effectively handle the large variability of critical parameters, like pose, lighting, scale, face expression, some kind of forgery in the subject appearance (e.g., the beard). Effective handling of lighting, pose and scale variations is an active research area. Typically, a face recognition system is specialized on a certain type of face view (e.g., frontal views), disregarding the images that do not correspond to such view. Therefore, a powerful pose estimation algorithm is required. But this is often not sufficient, and an unknown pose can deceive the whole system. Consequently, a face recognition system can usually achieve good performance only at the expense of robustness and reliability.

The use of Multiple Classifier Systems (MCSs) has been recently proposed in [97] to improve the performance and robustness of individual recognizers. Such systems cover a wide spectrum of applications: handwritten character recognition, fingerprint classification and matching, remote sensing images classification, etc. Achermann and Bunke [1] proposed the fusion of three recognizers based on frontal and profile faces. The outcome of each expert, represented by a score (i.e., a level of confidence about the decision) is combined with simple fusion rules (majority voting, rank sum, Bayes' combination rule). Lucas [74, 73] used a n-tuple classifier for combining the decisions of experts based on subsampled images.

Other interesting approaches are based on the extension of conventional, parametric classifiers to improve the "face space" representation. These methods proved to be particularly useful whenever a large variation in pose and/or illumination is present in the face image sequence. Two such examples are the extended HMMs [68], and parametric eigenspaces [3], where the dynamic information in the video sequence is explicitly used to improve the face representation and, consequently, the discrimination power of the classifier. In [60] Lee et al. approximated face manifolds by a finite number of infinite extent subspaces and used temporal information to robustly estimate the operating part of the manifold.

There are fewer methods that recognize from manifolds without the associated ordering of face images. Two algorithms worth mentioning are the Mutual Subspace Method (MSM) of Yamaguchi et al. [124, 30] and the Kullback-Leibler divergence based method of Shakhnarovich et al. [100]. In MSM, infinite extent linear subspaces are used to compactly characterize face sets—i.e., the manifolds that they lie on. The two sets are then compared by computing the first three principal angles between corresponding Principal Component Analysis (PCA) subspaces [92]. Varying recognition results were reported using MCM. The major limitation of this technique is its simplistic modeling of manifolds of face variation. Their high nonlinearity invalidates the assumption that data re well described by a linear subspace. More subtly, the nonlinearity of modeled manifolds means that the PCA subspace estimate is very sensitive to the particular choice of training samples. For example, in the original paper [124] in which face motion videos were used, the estimates are sensitive to the extent of rotation in a particular direction. Finally, MSM does not have a meaningful probabilistic interpretation. The Kullback-Leibler Divergence (KLD) based method [100] is founded on information-theoretic grounds. In the proposed framework, it is assumed that the i-th person's face patterns are distributed according to a prior distribution. Recognition is then performed by finding the distribution that best explains the set of input samples—quantified by the Kullback-Leibler divergence. The key assumption in this approach is that face patterns are normally distributed, which makes divergence computation tractable.

8.1.6 Compensating Facial Expressions

A fully automatic facial expression analyzer should be able to cope with the following tasks:

- Detect the face in a scene.
- Extract the facial expression features.
- Recognize and classify facial expressions according to some classification rules.

We shall focus on the last two issues. Facial expression analysis is usually carried out according to certain facial action coding schemes, using either spatio-temporal or spatial approaches.

Neural networks are often used for facial expression recognition and are used either directly on facial images or combined with Principal Component Analysis (PCA), Independent Component Analysis (ICA) or Gabor wavelets filter. Fasel [25] has developed a system based on convolutional neural networks in order to allow for an increased invariance with regard to translation and scale changes. He uses multi-scale simple feature extractor layers in combination with weight-sharing feature extraction layers. Another neural network is used in [75]. The data are processed in three steps: first the image is filtered by applying a grid of overlapping 2D Gabor filters; the second step is to perform dimensionality reduction by applying PCA; the reduced data are fed into a neural network containing six outputs, one for each of the six basic emotions. Support Vector Machines is another approach used to tackle facial actions classification employed in [99].

Appearance-based methods and geometric feature-based methods are also investigated by several researchers. For appearance-based methods, the fiducial points of the face are selected either manually or automatically. The face images are convolved with Gabor filters and the responses extracted from the face images at fiducial points form vectors that are further used for classification. Alternatively, the Gabor filters can be applied to the entire face image instead of specific face regions. Regarding the geometric feature-based methods, the positions of a set of fiducial points in a face form a feature vector that represents the face geometry. Although the appearance-based methods (especially Gabor wavelets) seem to yield a reasonable recognition rate, the highest recognition rate is obtained when these two main approaches are combined [64].

Two hybrid systems for classifying seven categories of human facial expression are proposed in [45]. The first system combines Independent Component Analysis (ICA) and Support Vector Machines (SVMs). The original face image database is decomposed into linear combinations of several basis images, where the corresponding coefficients of these combinations are fed into SVMs instead of an original feature vector comprised of grayscale image pixel values. The classification accuracy of this system is compared against that of baseline techniques that combine ICA with either two-class cosine similarity classifiers or two-class maximum correlation classifiers. They found that ICA decomposition combined with SVMs outperforms the aforementioned baseline classifiers. The second system proposed operates in two steps: first, a set of Gabor wavelets is applied to the original face image database. After that, the new features obtained are classified by using either SVMs, cosine similarity classifiers, or a maximum correlation classifier. The best facial expression recognition rate is achieved when Gabor wavelets are combined with SVM classifiers.

In [8], a user-independent fully automatic system for real time recognition of basic emotional expressions from video is presented. The system automatically detects frontal faces in the video stream and codes each frame with respect to seven dimensions: neutral, anger, disgust, fear, joy, sadness, and surprise. The face finder employs a cascade of feature detectors trained with boosting techniques [26]. The expression recognizer receives image patches located by the face detector. A Gabor representation of the patch is formed and then processed by a bank of SVM classifiers, which are well suited to this task, because the high dimensionality of the Gabor representation does not affect training time for kernel classifiers. The classification was performed in two stages. First, SVMs performed binary decision tasks. Seven classifiers were trained to discriminate each emotion from the others. The emotion category decision is effected by choosing the classifier with the maximum margin for the test example. Generalization to novel subjects was tested using leave-one-subject-out cross-validation. Linear, polynomial, and Radial Basis Function kernels with Laplacian and Gaussian basis functions were explored. In addition, a novel combination approach that chooses the Gabor features by Adaboost as a reduced representation for training the SVMs was found to outperform the traditional Adaboost methods. The system that is presented is fully automatic and operates in real-time at a high level of accuracy (93% generalization to new subjects on a seven-alternative forced choice). Moreover, the preprocessing does not include explicit detection and alignment of internal facial features. This reduces the processing time, that is important for real-time applications. Most interestingly, the outputs of the classifier change smoothly as a function of time, providing a potentially valuable representation to code facial expression dynamics in a fully automatic and unobtrusive manner.

In [44], a novel hierarchical framework for high resolution, nonrigid facial expression tracking is presented. The high-quality dense point clouds of facial geometry moving at video speeds are acquired using a phase shift-based structured light ranging technique [127]. In order to use such data for the temporal study of the subtle dynamics in expressions and for face recognition, an efficient nonrigid facial tracking algorithm is used to establish intraframe correspondences. This algorithm uses a multiresolution 3D deformable face model, and a hierarchical tracking scheme. This framework can not only track global facial motion that is caused by muscle action, but it also fits to subtler expression details that are generated by highly local skin deformations. Tracking of global deformations is performed efficiently on the coarse level of the face model using a mesh with one thousand nodes, to recover the changes in a few intuitive parameters that control the motion of several deformable regions. In order to capture the complementary highly local deformations, the authors use a variational algorithm for nonrigid shape registration based on the integration of an implicit shape representation and the cubic B-spline based Free Form Deformations. Due to the strong implicit and explicit smoothness constraints imposed by the algorithm, the resulting registration/deformation field is smooth, continuous and gives dense one-to-one intra-frame correspondences. User-input sparse facial feature correspondences can also be incorporated as hard constraints in the optimization process, in order to guarantee high accuracy of the established correspondences. Extensive tracking experiments using the dynamic facial scans of five different subjects demonstrate the accuracy and efficiency of the proposed framework.

In [19], continuous video input is used for the classification of facial expressions. Bayesian network classifiers are used for classifying expressions from video, focusing on changes in distribution assumptions, and feature dependency structures. In particular, Naive-Bayes classifiers are used and the distribution is changed from Gaussian to Cauchy, because of the ability of Cauchy to account for heavy tail distributions. The authors also use Gaussian Tree-Augmented Naive Bayes (TAN) classifiers to learn the dependencies among different facial motion features. Gaussian TAN classifiers are used because they have the advantage of modeling dependencies between the features without much added complexity compared to the Naive-Bayes classifiers. TAN classifiers have an additional advantage in that the dependencies between the features, modeled as a tree structure, are efficiently learned from data and the resultant tree structure is assured to maximize the likelihood function. A facial expression recognition method from live video input using temporal cues is presented. In addition to the static classifiers, the authors also use dynamic classifiers, since dynamic classifiers take into account the temporal pattern in displaying facial expression. A multilevel hidden Markov model classifier is used, combining the temporal information that allows not only to perform the classification of a video segment to the corresponding facial expression, but also to automatically segment an arbitrary long video sequence to different expressions segments without resorting to heuristic methods of segmentation.

8.1.7 Gabor Filtering and Space Reduction Based Methods

As already reported in previous sections, Gabor filters can be used to extract facial features. The Gabor approach for face recognition was first proposed in 1993 by Lades et al. [56]. They proposed a neuronal approach based on the magnitude response of the Gabor family filters (the first version of the Elastic Graph Matching method). The reason for using only the magnitude is that the magnitude provides a monotonic measure of the image property.

Many other works have used the Gabor wavelets since then. Wiskott et al. [119] used Gabor features for the elastic bunch graph matching, and [5] applied rank correlation on Gabor filtered images. Algorithms using space reduction methods (such as PCA, LDA, GDA, or Kernel PCA) applied on Gabor features (on the magnitude response of the filters and also on the combination of the magnitude and real part, are also reported in Sect. 8.4.2.1.

In 2004, Liu has successfully used Kernel PCA (KPCA) with fractional power polynomial kernel applied to face Gabor features [66]. In [67], he used the kernel Fisher analysis applied to the same Gabor features and he succeeded improving the Face Recognition Grand Challenge accuracy from 12% Verification Rate (VR) at False Acceptance Rate (FAR) 0.1% for the baseline PCA method, to 78%. It was by far the most important improvement published for this database. Independent Component Analysis has also been applied to Gabor-based features of the facial images [65].

In [102], many kernel methods (such as GDA or KPCA) with Gabor features were tested and compared to classical space reductions approaches, showing the importance of Gabor features. In Sect. 8.4, further investigations related to Gabor features and space reduction methods are presented.

8.2 2D Face Databases and Evaluation Campaigns

There are several publicly available face databases that can be used for development and evaluation of the profusion of algorithms that are proposed in the literature. Listing all the available face databases is beyond the scope of this chapter. More complete reviews of available face databases can be found in [35] and [29]. Some multimodal databases (including face data) are also described in Chap. 11, related to multimodal evaluations. In this section, some databases are briefly introduced either because they underlie recent evaluation campaigns, because they are new and include multimodal face data, or because they are related to the benchmarking experiments reported in this chapter. A review of evaluation methods in face recognition can be found in [84].

8.2.1 Selected 2D Face Databases

In the *Face Recognition Grand Challenge (FRGC)* database [83, 86], both 3D scans and high resolution still images (taken under controlled and uncontrolled conditions) are present. More then 400 subjects participated to the data collection. The database was collected at Notre Dame within the FRGC/FRVT2006 technology evaluation and vendor test program conducted by National Institute of Standards and Technology (NIST) to assess commercial and research systems for multimodal face recognition.

The *IV^2* database (described in [82] and available at [46]) is a multimodal database, including 2D, 3D face images, audiovisual (talking-face) sequences, and iris data. This database, recorded during the French 2007 TechnoVision Program, is a three-site database. The 2D and 3D faces have expression, pose and illumination variations. A full 3D face model is also present for each subject. The IV^2 database contains 315 subjects with one session data, of which 77 subjects also participated in a second session. A disjoint development dataset of 52 subjects is also part of this database. An evaluation package IV^2 2007 has been defined, allowing new experiments to be reported with the same protocols used in reported results with baseline algorithms.

The *BANCA* database [6] is an audio-visual database that is widely used in publications, which means that it is a good choice for comparing new results with already published ones. In the English part of this database, which is the most widely used set, 52 subjects participated to the data collection. Three acquisition conditions were defined, simulating cooperative, degraded and adverse scenarios. The data were acquired with high- and low-quality cameras and microphones. More details about the experiments used for the 2D face benchmarking framework can be found in Sect. 8.3.2. This database is also chosen for the benchmarking talking-face experiments in Chap. 10, where the audio-video sequences are used.

8.2.2 Evaluation Campaigns

This section summarizes recent evaluation campaigns, including those related to the 2D face modality. The FRGC [83, 86] and FRVT2006 [85] are part of the NIST efforts for technology evaluation and vendor test. Within FRGC, seven experiments are defined in order to assess specific problems. More details about the experiments related to mismatched train/test conditions can be found also in Sect. 8.4.4.1. In Sect. 9.3.2 of Chap. 9 analysis about FRGC and FRVT regarding to the 2D/3D complementarity can be found.

In Chap. 11 related to the BioSecure Multimodal Evaluation Campaign BMEC'-2007, more details about this recent multimodal evaluation, including 2D still images, video sequences and audio-video impostures, are reported.

It should be noted that these three evaluation campaigns (FRGC, IV^2 2007 and BMEC'2007) used or made available open-source baseline algorithms along with evaluation data, which are important for comparisons among different systems. The BioSecure Benchmarking Framework, introduced in Chap. 2, and put in practice for eight biometric modalities in this book, follows such an evaluation methodology.

8.3 The BioSecure Benchmarking Framework for 2D Face

In order to ensure fair comparison of various 2D face verification algorithms, a common evaluation framework has to be defined. In this section, the BioSecure Benchmarking Framework for 2D face verification is presented. First, the reference system that can been used as a baseline for future improvements and comparisons is described. The database and the corresponding protocols that have been chosen are presented next, with the associated performance measures. The relevant material (such as the open-source code of the reference system, pointers to the databases, lists for the benchmarking experiments, and How-to documents) that is needed to reproduce the 2D face benchmarking experiments can be found on the companion URL [81].

8.3.1 The BioSecure 2D Face Reference System v1.0

The BioSecure 2D Face Reference System v1.0 was developed by Boğaziçi University and it uses the standard Eigenface approach [112] to represent faces in a lower dimensional subspace. All the images used by the system are first normalized. The face space is built using a separate development set (part of the development database, denoted as *Devdb*). The dimensionality of the reduced space is selected such that 99% of the variance is explained by the principal components. At the feature extraction step, all the enrollment and test images are projected onto the face space. Then, the L_1 norm is used to measure the distance between the projected vectors of the test and enrollment images.

8.3.2 Reference 2D Face Database: BANCA

The BANCA database [6] is a multimodal database, containing both face and voice. It has been widely used in publications and evaluation campaigns, and therefore it is a good choice for comparing new results with already published ones. For face verification experiments, five frontal images have been extracted from each video recording to be used as true client and impostor attack images. The English part of the database is composed of 52 subjects (26 female and 26 male). Each gender population is itself subdivided into two groups of 13 subjects (denoted in the following as $G1$ and $G2$). Each subject recorded 12 sessions, each of these sessions containing two recordings: one true client access and one impostor attack. The 12 sessions were recorded under three different scenarios:

- Controlled environment for Sessions 1–4.
- Degraded environment for Sessions 5–8.
- Adverse environment for Sessions 9–12.

An additional set of 30 other subjects (15 male and 15 female) recorded one session. This set of data, $30 \times 5 \times 2 = 300$ images, is referred to as world data. These subjects claimed two different identities. They are part of the development set *Devdb*, and can be used to build world models, or face spaces when needed.

Another set of development data is $G1$, when $G2$ is used as evaluation (*Evaldb*), and vice versa. The thresholds are usually set on this dataset.

For the performance measures, three specific operating conditions corresponding to three different values of the cost ratio, $R = FAR/FRR$, namely $R = 0.1$, $R = 1$, and $R = 10$ have been considered. The so-called Weighted Error Rate (WER) given by

$$WER(R) = \frac{FRR + R \cdot FAR}{1 + R} \tag{8.1}$$

could be calculated for the test data of groups $G1$ and $G2$ at the three proposed values of R. The average WER and the Equal Error Rate (EER) could also be reported as final performance measures for the two groups, as well as Detection Error Trade-off (DET) curves. The Confidence Intervals for the EER are calculated with the parametric method, described in the Appendix of Chap. 11.

8.3.3 Reference Protocols

Among the multiple proposed BANCA protocols [6], the Pooled (*P*) and Match Controlled (*Mc*) experiments were chosen as the comparison protocols for the benchmarking framework. The *P* protocol is the most challenging one using controlled images for enrollment, and controlled, adverse and degraded images as a test set. The *Mc* protocol is a subset of the *P* protocol using only the controlled images as a test set. For each individual from *Evaldb*, we describe below the enrollment and tests sets for the two configurations.

Pooled (*P*) Protocol

- *Enrollment set:* Five frontal images of the true client from Session 1.
- *Test set:* Five frontal images of the true client from Sessions 2, 3, 4, 6, 7, 8, 10, 11, and 12, for client tests; and five frontal images of the impostor attacks from all the sessions for the impostor tests.

Match Controlled (*Mc*) Protocol

- *Enrollment set:* Five frontal images of the true client from Session 1.
- *Tests sets:* Five frontal images of the true client from sessions 2, 3, and 4, for the client tests; and five frontal images of the impostor attacks from Sessions 1, 2, and 3 for the impostor tests.

The algorithms should compare each image of the test set to the five images of the enrollment set or to a model constructed from these five images. For each test, only one score is provided by the system. For the *Mc* Protocol and for each group $G1$ and $G2$, there are $26 \times 5 \times 3 = 390$ client tests and $26 \times 5 \times 4 = 520$ impostor tests. For the *P* Protocol and for each group $G1$ and $G2$, there are $26 \times 5 \times 9 = 1,170$ client tests and $26 \times 5 \times 12 = 1,560$ impostor tests.

8.3.4 Benchmarking Results

The main parameters used to obtain the benchmarking results are:

- Database: BANCA.
- Evaluation protocols: *P* and *Mc* protocols from BANCA.
- Preprocessing step: each image is normalized and cropped such that the size of the image is 55×51 pixels.

- Face space building: the 300 images of the BANCA world model are used to build the face space, the dimensionality of the face space is selected such as the 99% of the variance is used.
- Client model: all of the projected vectors of the five enrollment images are used. At the verification step, only the minimum distance between the test image and these five client vectors is selected.
- Distance measure: L_1 norm.

EER results of the reference PCA system are presented in Table 8.2, DET curves are displayed in Fig. 8.1, and WER results are given in Table 8.3.

Table 8.2 Equal Error Rate (EER), and Confidence Intervals (CI), of the 2D Face Reference System V1.0 on the BANCA database, according to the *Mc* and *P* protocols

Protocol	EER% [CI] for *G*1	EER% [CI] for *G*2
Mc	16.38 [±3.43]	8.14 [±2.53]
P	26.67 [±2.36]	24.69 [±2.31]

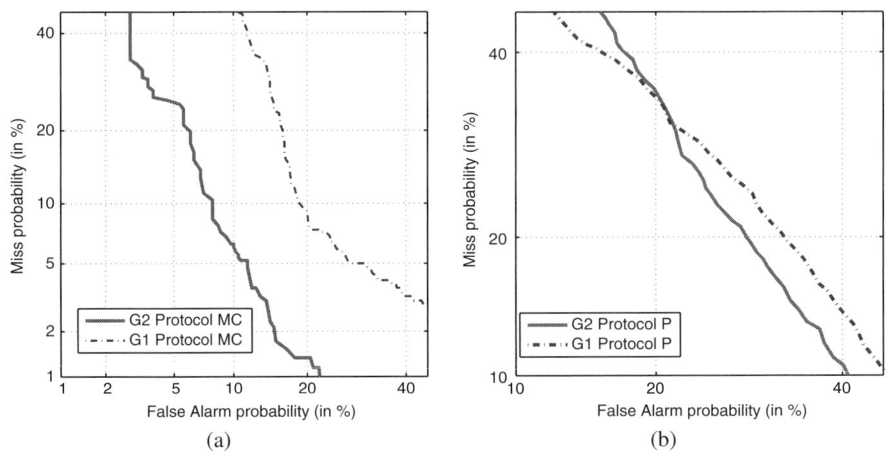

Fig. 8.1 DET curves of the BioSecure reference PCA system v1.0 on the BANCA database with: (**a**) Mc protocol, and (**b**) P protocol

Table 8.3 WER Results of the BioSecure reference PCA system v1.0 on the BANCA database, for *Mc* and *P* protocols

Protocol	WER(0.1) G1	WER(0.1) G2	WER(1) G1	WER(1) G2	WER(10) G1	WER(10) G2	Av. WER %
Mc	15.65	9.59	16.08	8.20	6.56	5.01	**10.18**
P	8.95	10.23	26.85	26.59	8.35	6.62	**14.60**

8.4 Method 1: Combining Gabor Magnitude and Phase Information [TELECOM SudParis]

In this section, a new approach exploiting the fusion of magnitude and phase responses of Gabor filters is presented. It is evaluated on different databases and protocols, including the reference framework described in Sect. 8.3. Results related to Experiments 1 and 4 of the FRGC v2 database (Face Recognition Grand Challenge) are also reported.

8.4.1 The Gabor Multiscale/Multiorientation Analysis

The characteristics of the Gabor wavelets (filters), especially for frequency and orientation representations, are similar to those of the human visual system [22]. They have been found to be particularly appropriate for texture representation and discrimination. The Gabor filters-based features, directly extracted from grayscale images, have been widely and successfully used in fingerprint recognition [58], texture segmentation [49], and especially in iris recognition [21]. As reported in Sect. 8.1.7 they have also been used for face recognition [128, 67, 102].

In the spatial domain, a 2D Gabor filter is a Gaussian kernel function modulated by a complex sinusoidal plane wave

$$G(x,y) = \frac{1}{2\pi\sigma\beta} e^{-\pi\left[\frac{(x-x_0)^2}{\sigma^2}+\frac{(y-y_0)^2}{\beta^2}\right]} e^{i[\xi_0 x+\nu 0 y]} \tag{8.2}$$

where (x_0, y_0) is the center of the filter in the spatial domain, ξ_0 and $\nu 0$ the spatial frequency of the filter, and σ and β the standard deviation of the elliptic Gaussian along x and y.

All filters can be generated from one mother wavelet by dilation and rotation. Each filter has the shape of a plane wave with frequency f, restricted by a Gaussian envelope function with relative standard deviation. To extract useful features from an image (e.g., a face image) a set of Gabor filters with different scales and orientations is required (cf. Fig. 8.3).

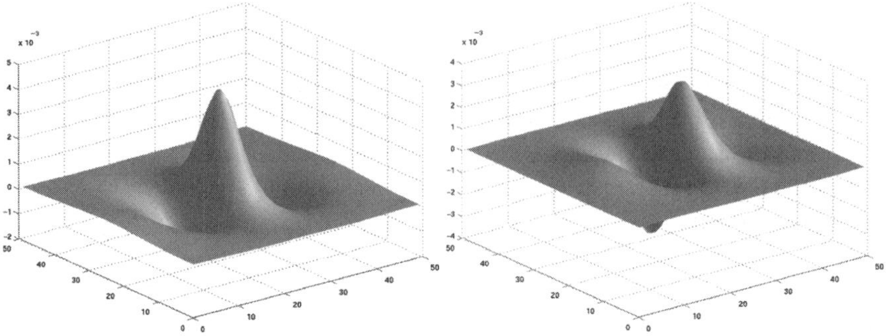

(a) (b)

Fig. 8.2 Complex Gabor filter: (**a**) real part and (**b**) imaginary part (*)

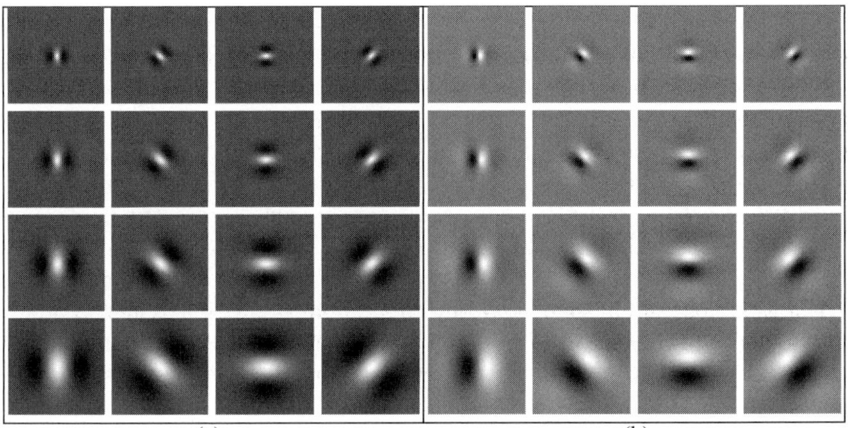

(a) (b)

Fig. 8.3 (**a**) Real and (**b**) imaginary parts of a Gabor filter bank, with four horizontal orientations and four vertical scales

8.4.2 Extraction of Gabor Face Features

The representation of a face image is obtained by the convolution of the face image with the family of Gabor filters, defined by $IG_{s,o} = I \otimes G_{s,o}$, where $IG_{s,o}$ denotes the convolution result corresponding to the Gabor filter at a certain orientation o and scale s. We can note that $IG_{s,o}$ is a complex number. Its magnitude and phase parts are denoted by $M(IG_{s,o})$ and $P(IG_{s,o})$, respectively. Both magnitude and phase part of the convolution results are shown in Fig. 8.4.

(*) Images created by the matlab code from P. D. Kovesi. MATLAB and Octave Functions for computer Vision and Image Processing. School of Computer Science & Software Engineering, The University of Western Australia. Available from: http://www.csse.uwa.edu.au/~pk/research/matlabfns/

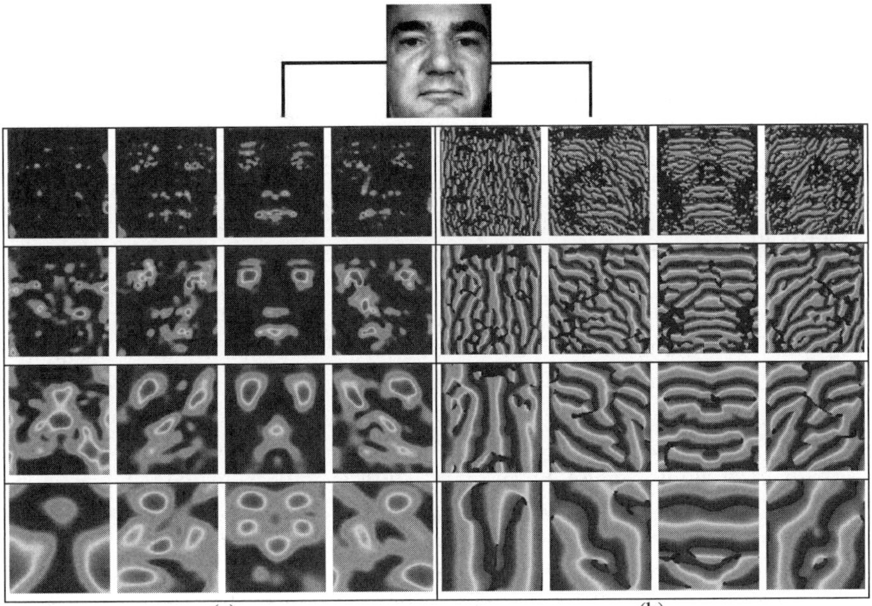

Fig. 8.4 Result of the convolution of a face image (from FRGC database), with a family of Gabor filters of four horizontal orientations and four vertical scales. (**a**) Gabor magnitude and (**b**) Gabor phase representations; (see insert for color reproduction of this figure)

8.4.2.1 Combination of Gabor Magnitude and Phase Representations

As mentioned in Sect. 8.1.7, most of the experiments using Gabor features for face recognition are based on the magnitude part of the Gabor features. In this section, experiments combining the magnitude and phase parts of Gabor filter analysis are presented. They are motivated by the fact that the texture information is mostly located in the phase part of Gabor filter analysis. Indeed, the phase features are widely used in texture analysis and are more robust to global noise than the magnitude. The success of using the phase part in iris recognition [21] is also a good indication of the robustness of the phase response.

In the case of normalized face images (fixed distance between the center of eyes), some parts of the face have no informative texture that could be analyzed by the lower scales of Gabor filters. For these regions, the Gabor analysis gives $Real(IG_{s,o}) \sim 0$ and $Im(IG_{s,o}) \sim 0$. Even if its values are very near to 0, the magnitude part of the convolution is not affected by this problem. The phase part takes an undetermined form for these specific regions. To bypass the undetermined form, we propose to select the informative regions by thresholding the magnitude at each analysis point

$$P(IG_{s,o}(x,y)) = \begin{cases} \arctan(\frac{Im(IG_{s,o}(x,y))}{Real(IG_{s,o}(x,y))}) & \text{if } M(IG_{s,o})(x,y) > Th \\ 0 & \text{else} \end{cases} \tag{8.3}$$

where (x,y) are coordinates of the analysis point. The threshold *Th* is chosen in order to optimize the performance on FRGC v2. This value is used for the experiments on the BANCA database. Figure 8.5 shows the evolution of the verification rate with the threshold *Th*.

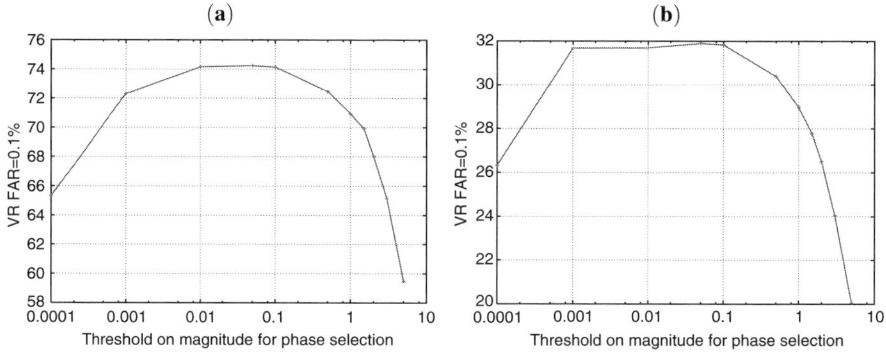

Fig. 8.5 Evolution of the verification rate with the threshold Th for phase selection on FRGC v2 database, for (**a**) Exp1 and (**b**) Exp4

The magnitude ($M(IG_{s,o})$) and the corrected phase (from Eq. 8.3) at each scale/orientation are first down-sampled, then normalized to zero mean and unit variance, and finally transformed to a vector by concatenating the rows. This new feature vector is used as the new representation of face images.

8.4.3 Linear Discriminant Analysis (LDA) Applied to Gabor Features

The purpose of Linear Discriminant Analysis (LDA) is to look for axes in the data space that best discriminate the different classes [28]. In other words, for some given independent parameters, the LDA creates a linear combination of those parameters that maximizes the distances between the means of the different classes and minimizes at the same time the distances between samples of the same class. More precisely, for the classes in the samples space, two kinds of measures are defined. The within-class scatter matrix is defined by

$$S_w = \sum_{j=1}^{c} \sum_{i=1}^{N_j} (x_i^j - \mu_j)(x_i^j - \mu_j)^T \tag{8.4}$$

where x_i^j is the ith sample of the class j, μ_j is the mean of class j, c is the number of classes, and N_j is the number of training samples of class j.

The second measure is the between-class scatter matrix, defined by

$$S_b = \sum_{j=1}^{c} (\mu_j - \mu)(\mu_j - \mu)^T \tag{8.5}$$

where μ_j is the mean of the class j and μ is the mean of all samples.

The purpose of LDA is to determine a set of discriminant basis vectors so that the quotient of the between-class and within-class scatter, $det|S_b|/det|S_w|$, is maximized [87]. This procedure is equivalent to finding the eigenvalues $\lambda > 0$ and eigenvectors V satisfying the equation $\lambda V = S_w^{-1} S_b V$. The maximization of this quotient is possible if the S_w matrix is invertible. In face recognition, the number of training samples is almost always much smaller than the dimension of the feature vectors, which can easily lead to the "small sample size" problem and in this situation S_w is not invertible [28].

To solve this problem, L. Swets [108] proposed the use of the PCA reduction technique before computing the LDA. The idea is first to compute the principal axes using Principal Component Analysis, then to reduce the training samples by projecting them on the computed principal axes, and finally to apply LDA on the reduced set.

8.4.4 *Experimental Results with Combined Magnitude and Phase Gabor Features with Linear Discriminant Classifiers*

The experiments reported in this section show the importance of combining magnitude and phase Gabor features. These features are used with a linear discriminant classifier. Two photometric preprocessing algorithms are also applied to the geometrically normalized face images, namely histogram equalization and anisotropic smoothing (see also [36]). Examples of the two preprocessing algorithms are shown in Fig. 8.6. Results are reported on FRGC v2 and BANCA databases. For the BANCA database, the tests are done with the proposed benchmarking experiments defined in Sect. 8.3.3 in order to be able to compare the results with the other methods, which are described in Sects. 8.5 and 8.6.

8.4.4.1 Performance on the FRGC Database

FRGC (Face Recognition Grand Challenge) is the largest publicly available face database [83]. It contains images from 466 subjects and is composed of 8,024

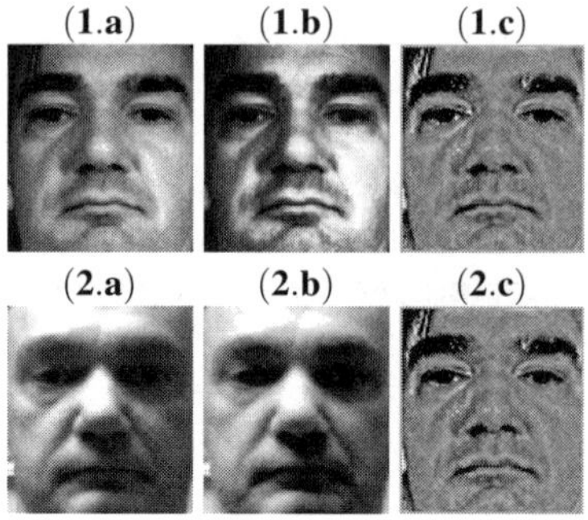

Fig. 8.6 Face illumination preprocessing on two face images from the FRGC v2 database: (**x.a**) geometric normalization, (**x.b**) histogram equalization, and (**x.c**) anisotropic smoothing

non-controlled still images, captured under uncontrolled lighting conditions, and 16,028 controlled still images, captured under controlled conditions. It contains two types of face expressions (smiling and neutral), and a big time variability (from some months to more than a year). Many experiments are designed to evaluate the performances of algorithms on FRGC v2 as a function of different parameters.

In this section, results on two specific tests are presented: Experiment 1 and 4. Exp1 is designed to evaluate tests on controlled illumination conditions. The test and enrollment still images are taken from the controlled sessions. Exp4 is designed to measure the performance of tests done under noncontrolled illumination conditions. The query (test) images are taken from the noncontrolled sessions and the enrollment images are taken from the controlled sessions. With these two experiments, the degradation of performance, related to illumination variability, can be measured. The results on the FRGC data are reported by the Verification Rate (VR) at the False Acceptance Rate (FAR) of 0.1% [83]. The Equal Error Rate (EER) is also calculated. Confidence Intervals (CI) are calculated with the parametric method, described in the Appendix of Chap. 11. It has to be noted that face images are normalized to 110×100 pixels, with a distance of 50 pixels between the eyes. The eye locations are obtained manually.

Influence of Different Features Constructed from Gabor Filters The results of different feature sets constructed from Gabor filters are reported in Tables 8.4 and 8.5. They show the gap in performance between the LDA applied to the magnitude response of the Gabor filters and the LDA applied to the phase response. This gap in performance could be explained by the uniformity of the magnitude response and the high discontinuity of the phase response (cf. Fig. 8.4). Although the phase response is known to be robust against uniform noise, it seems that the monotony of the magnitude allows for better analysis for face verification.

Results related to Exp4 from Tables 8.4, 8.5, and 8.6 show the robustness of the anisotropic smoothing approach in the uncontrolled conditions. For the controlled conditions (Exp1), a simple preprocessing algorithm like histogram equalization is sufficient to obtain good performances. It can be noticed that the improvement in

Table 8.4 Results with Gabor magnitude features and LDA, on FRGC v2 database for Experiments 1 and 4. Results are given for VR@0.1% FAR, and Equal Error Rate (EER)%, with their Confidence Intervals (CI)

Normalization		VR@0.1% FAR[CI]	EER%[CI]
Histogram equalization	Exp1	89.93 [±0.13]	1.83 [±0.06]
–	Exp4	47.12 [±0.31]	7.89 [±0.16]
Anisotropic smoothing	Exp1	87.50 [±0.14]	2.22 [±0.06]
–	Exp4	48.65 [±0.31]	6.71 [±0.15]

Table 8.5 Results corrected Gabor phase features and LDA, on FRGC v2 database for Experiments 1 and 4. Results are given for VR@0.1% FAR, and Equal Error Rate (EER)%, with their Confidence Intervals (CI)

Normalization		VR@0.1% FAR[CI]	EER%[CI]
Histogram equalization	Exp1	79.18 [±0.17]	2.97 [±0.07]
–	Exp4	37.16 [±0.30]	8.99 [±0.17]
Anisotropic smoothing	Exp1	75.31 [±0.19]	2.72 [±0.07]
–	Exp4	36.23 [±0.30]	9.60 [±0.16]

Table 8.6 Results of fusion of Gabor corrected phase and magnitude features and LDA, on FRGC v2 database for Experiments 1 and 4. Results are given for VR@0.1% FAR, and Equal Error Rate (EER)%, with their Confidence Intervals (CI)

System		VR@0.1% FAR[CI]	EER%[CI]
Hist[1]-cGabor[2]-LDA	Exp1	87.41 [±0.13]	1.75 [±0.05]
–	Exp4	47.12 [±0.31]	6.26 [±0.15]
AS[3]-cGabor-LDA	Exp1	87.62 [±0.14]	2.14 [±0.06]
–	Exp4	50.22 [±0.31]	5.31 [±0.14]
FRGC v2 baseline PCA	Exp1	66.00	5.60
–	Exp4	12.00	24.00

[1] histogram, [2] combined Gabor features, and [3] anisotropic smoothing

performance is more outstanding for the EER than for the Verification Rate@0.1% FAR. For comparison, the performance of the baseline FRGC v2 PCA system is also reported.

Figure 8.7 shows the DET curves of the different configurations and illustrates the improvement gained by the combination of Gabor phase and magnitude features.

Influence of the Face Space on the LDA Performance In FRGC v2 database two subsets are defined: Development (*Devdb*) and Evaluation (*Evaldb*). The *Evaldb* is composed of 466 subjects. The *Devdb*, which can be used to construct the LDA Space, is composed of 222 subjects with 12,706 images. All the subjects of this

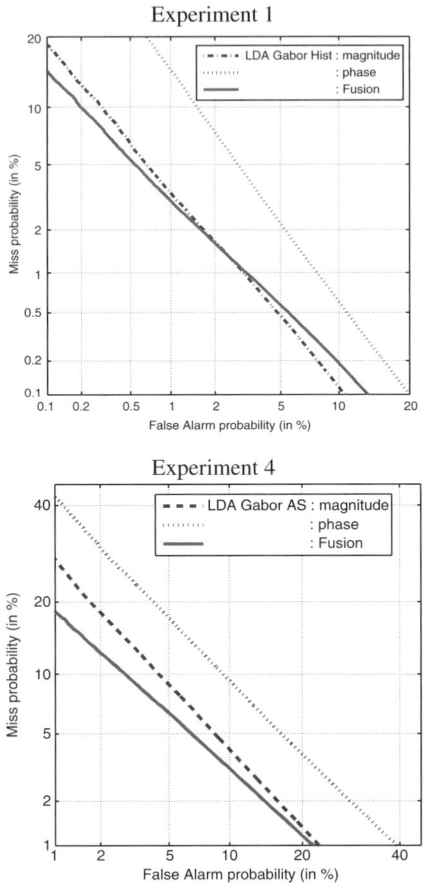

Fig. 8.7 DET curves for Exp. 1 and Exp4. The curves show the LDA applied to different Gabor features (magnitude, phase, and combination of magnitude and phase). Histogram equalization is used for the preprocessing step for Expl and Anisotropic Smoothing for Exp4. to improve the quality of the images

set also belong to the evaluation set. For the experiments presented in this section (because of practical issues), only 216 persons with 8,016 images from the *Devdb* are selected.

An interesting question is: What are generalization capabilities of the LDA? In order to study the influence of the overlap of subjects (classes) between the training set and the evaluation set on the performance, three new experiments from Exp1. of the FRGC v2 database were defined:

- Exp1-same: Evaluation and LDA's training sets are composed of the same persons (216 subjects).
- Exp1-rand: Choose randomly 216 subjects from the available 466 subjects in the evaluation set and repeat this operation 100 times.

- Exp1-diff: Choose randomly 216 subjects from the available 466 subjects in the evaluation set, with the additional condition that they are different from the persons of the training set. Repeat this operation 100 times.

The results of these experiments are reported on Fig. 8.8 and Table 8.7.

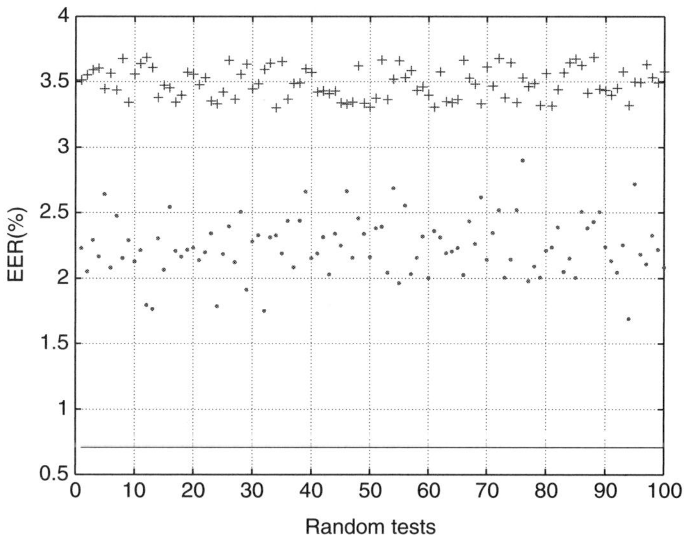

Fig. 8.8 EER% results as a function of the number of random tests for Exp1-diff (+), Exp1-rand (∗), and the line corresponding to the Exp1-same experiment

Table 8.7 Influence of the training set of the LDA on the verification performance, for experiments defined on Exp1 of FRGCž database

EER% [CI]		
Exp1-same	Exp1-rand	Exp1-diff
0.71	2.24 [±0.22]	3.48 [±0.11]

It can be noted that, as expected, the best results are obtained for *Exp1-same* when the LDA axes are learned on the same subjects than those of the evaluation set (0.71% of EER). The performance of *Exp1-rand* decreases when some subjects of the evaluation set are not present in the LDA training set (from 0.71% to 2.24%). Finally, the performance decreases considerably for *Exp1-diff* when the evaluation set and the training set are totally independent (from 0.71% to 3.48%). These results confirm the weakness of LDA as far as generalization capability is concerned.

Influence of the Multiresolution Analysis The experiments reported in Sect. 8.4.4.1 showed that the best Gabor features are obtained when combining the magnitude and the corrected phase information. In this section the influence of the multiresolution analysis is studied. Two types of experiments are considered:

- LDA applied on the face pixels' intensity.
- LDA applied on the Gabor features (combination of the Gabor magnitude and phase).

For the reported results, only the Anisotropic Smoothing (AS) preprocessing was performed. The LDA Space was constructed using the configuration where the same 216 persons (with 10 images/subject) are used to construct the LDA face space and are also present among the 466 subjects in the evaluation set (see also Sect. 8.4.4.1).

Table 8.8 Results (VR with Confidence Intervals-CI) of the LDA method applied to pixels' intensity and to Gabor features using the combination of magnitude and phase on FRGC v2 for Exp1 and 4

	Experiment 1	Experiment 4
AS[1]-LDA	64.09 [±0.21]	28.57 [±0.28]
AS-cGabor[2]-LDA	87.62 [±0.14]	50.22 [±0.31]

[1]anisotropic smoothing and [2]combined Gabor features

Results of Table 8.8 clearly show the importance of using the multiresolution analysis as a representation of face. The relative improvements (40% for Exp1 and 80% for Exp4) show the robustness of the multiresolution approach. The same improvement rates, not reported here, were also observed using the histogram equalization.

8.4.4.2 Performance on the BANCA Database

In order to confirm the generalization capability of the LDA face space constructed with face images from FRGC v2 on a completely different database (BANCA°, the AS-cGabor-LDA configuration (from Table 8.6) is used. It has to be remembered that difficult illumination conditions are also present in the BANCA *P* protocol. The BANCA results are given by the EER on the two test groups *G*1 and *G*2. These results are going to be compared in Sect. refsec-2d:7 with the results reported with the two other algorithms from University of Vigo and University of Sassari groups.

As shown in Tables 8.9-8.11, compared to the BioSecure reference system, the proposed approach performs better (G1[9.63 vs 26.67], G2[16.48 vs 24.69]) using the same illumination pre-processing. Table 8.12 shows the published results extracted from the test report [24], with two additional lines, related to the BioSecure

Table 8.9 EER results with the Confidence Intervals (CI) from the two fusion experiments with Gabor corrected phase and magnitude on BANCA protocol P

System	G1 (EER%[CI])	G2 (EER%[CI])
Hist[1]-cGabor[2]-LDA	9.63 [±1.69]	16.48 [±2.12]
AS[3]-cGabor-LDA	8.56 [±1.60]	13.29 [±1.94]

[1]histogram, [2]combined Gabor features, and [3]anisotropic smoothing

Table 8.10 Results in WER on BANCA protocol P for the two fusion experiments with Gabor corrected phase and magnitude

	WER(0.1)		WER(1)		WER(10)		Av. WER %
	G1	G2	G1	G2	G1	G2	
Hist[1]-cGabor[2]-LDA	4.75	7.13	8.93	16.82	4.62	5.56	**7.97**
AS[3]-cGabor-LDA	4.49	4.66	10.20	12.63	2.85	4.32	**6.52**

[1] histogram [2]combined Gabor features, and [3]anisotropic smoothing

Table 8.11 WER results on BANCA Protocols P and Mc, for the BioSecure baseline (RefSys) and the combined Gabor features and Linear Discriminant Analysis (AS-cGabor-LDA)

		WER(0.1)		WER(1)		WER(10)		Av. WER %
		G1	G2	G1	G2	G1	G2	
P	BioSecure RefSys	8.95	10.23	26.85	26.59	8.35	6.62	**14.60**
	AS-cGabor-LDA	4.49	4.66	10.20	12.63	2.85	4.32	**6.52**
Mc	Biosecure RefSys	15.65	9.59	16.08	8.20	6.56	5.01	**10.18**
	AS-cGabor-LDA	2.51	3.18	3.26	4.26	1.14	1.27	**2.60**

Reference System (RefSys) and to the results reported when Anisotropic Smoothing and combined Gabor Features are used for the LDA classification (AS-cGabor-LDA). The average Weighted Error Rate results of the AS-cGabor-LDA approach on both G1 and G2 show that this method outperforms many popular methods reported in [24].

8.5 Method 2: Subject-Specific Face Verification via Shape-Driven Gabor Jets (SDGJ) [University of Vigo]

In this approach, presented in more details in [31], the selection of points is accomplished by exploiting shape information. Lines depicting face structure are extracted by means of a ridges and valleys detector [69], leading to a binary representation that sketches the face. In order to select a set of points from this sketch,

Table 8.12 Weighted Error Rate (see Eq. 8.1) results on BANCA Protocol P from the evaluation report [24], the BioSecure 2D Face Reference System v1.0 (RefSys v1.0), and the AS-cGabor-LDA method (last two lines)

	WER(0.1)		WER(1)		WER(10)		Av. WER %
	G1	G2	G1	G2	G1	G2	
IDIAP-HMM	8.69	8.15	25.43	20.25	8.84	6.24	**12.93**
IDIAP-FUSION	8.15	7.43	21.85	16.88	6.94	6.06	**11.22**
QUT	7.70	8.53	18.08	16.12	6.50	4.83	**10.29**
UPV	5.82	6.18	12.29	14.56	5.55	4.96	**8.23**
Univ.Nottingham	1.55	1.77	6.67	7.11	1.32	1.58	**3.33**
National Taiwan Univ	1.56	8.22	21.44	27.13	7.42	11.33	**13.85**
UniS	4.67	7.22	12.46	13.66	4.82	5.10	**7.99**
UCL-LDA	8.24	9.49	14.96	16.51	4.80	6.45	**10.08**
UCL-Fusion	6.05	6.01	12.61	13.84	4.72	4.10	**7.89**
NeuroInformatik	6.40	6.50	12.10	10.80	6.50	4.30	**7.77**
Tsinghua Univ	1.13	0.73	2.61	1.85	1.17	0.84	**1.39**
CMU	5.79	4.75	12.44	11.61	6.61	7.45	**8.11**
BioSecure RefSys	8.95	10.23	26.85	26.59	8.35	6.62	**14.60**
AS-cGabor-LDA	4.49	4.66	10.20	12.63	2.85	4.32	**6.52**

a dense rectangular grid ($n_x \times n_y$ nodes) is applied onto the face image and each grid node is moved towards its nearest line of the sketch. Finally, a set of points $\mathcal{P} = \{\mathbf{p_1}, \mathbf{p_2}, \ldots, \mathbf{p_n}\}$, and their corresponding $\{\mathcal{J}_{\mathbf{p}_i}\}_{i=1,\ldots,n}$ jets, with $n = n_x \times n_y$ are obtained.

8.5.1 Extracting Textural Information

A set of 40 Gabor filters $\{\psi_m\}_{m=1,2,\ldots,40}$, with the same configuration as in [119], is used to extract textural information. These filters are convolution kernels in the shape of plane waves restricted by a Gaussian envelope, as it is shown next

$$\psi_m(\mathbf{x}) = \frac{\|\mathbf{k}_m\|^2}{\sigma^2} \exp\left(\frac{-\|\mathbf{k}_m\|^2 \|\mathbf{x}\|^2}{2\sigma^2}\right) \left[\exp(i \cdot \mathbf{k}_m \mathbf{x}) - \exp\left(\frac{-\sigma^2}{2}\right)\right] \tag{8.6}$$

where $\mathbf{k}_m$ contains information about scale and orientation, and the same standard deviation $\sigma = 2\pi$ is used in both directions for the Gaussian envelope. The region surrounding a pixel in the image is encoded by the convolution of the image patch with these filters, and the set of responses is called a jet, $\mathcal{J}$. So, a jet is a vector with 40 complex coefficients, and it provides information about a specific region of the image. At each shape-driven point $\mathbf{p_i} = [x_i, y_i]^T$, we get the following feature vector

$$\{\mathcal{J}_{\mathbf{p}_i}\}_m = \sum_x \sum_y I(x,y)\, \psi_m(x_i - x, y_i - y) \tag{8.7}$$

where $\{\mathcal{J}_{\mathbf{p}_i}\}_m$ stands for the m-th coefficient of the feature vector extracted from $\mathbf{p}_i$. So, for a given face with a set of points $\mathcal{P} = \{\mathbf{p_1}, \mathbf{p_2}, \ldots, \mathbf{p_n}\}$, we get n Gabor jets $\mathcal{R} = \{\mathcal{J}_{\mathbf{p}_1}, \mathcal{J}_{\mathbf{p}_2}, \ldots, \mathcal{J}_{\mathbf{p}_n}\}$ (see Fig. SDGI).

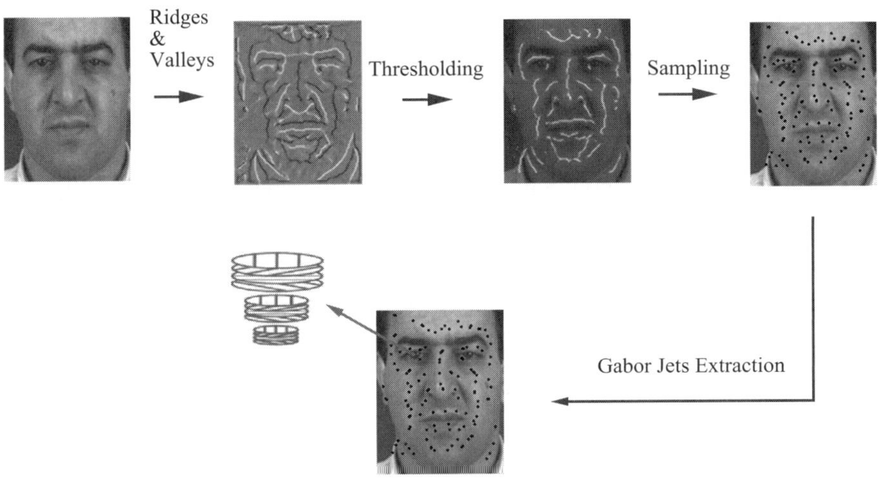

Fig. 8.9 Subject-specific face verification via Shape-Driven Gabor Jets (SDGJ), sample image from client 003 of the XM2VTS database [77]

8.5.2 Mapping Corresponding Features

Suppose that shape information has been extracted from two images, $\mathcal{F}_1$ and $\mathcal{F}_2$. Let $\mathcal{S}_1$ and $\mathcal{S}_2$ be the sketches for these incoming images, and let $\mathcal{P} = \{\mathbf{p_1}, \mathbf{p_2}, \ldots, \mathbf{p_n}\}$ be the set of points for $\mathcal{S}_1$, and $\mathcal{Q} = \{\mathbf{q_1}, \mathbf{q_2}, \ldots, \mathbf{q_n}\}$ the set of points for $\mathcal{S}_2$. In the SDGJ approach, there does not exist any a priori correspondence between points, nor between features (i.e., there is no label indicating which pair of points are matched). In order to compare jets from both faces, we used a point-matching algorithm based on shape contexts [12], obtaining a function ξ that maps each point from $\mathcal{P}$ to a point within $\mathcal{Q}$

$$\xi(i) : \mathbf{p_i} \Longrightarrow \mathbf{q}_{\xi(i)} \tag{8.8}$$

with an associated cost denoted by $C_{\mathbf{p}_i \mathbf{q}_{\xi(i)}}$ [31]. Finally, the feature vector from $\mathcal{F}_1$, $\mathcal{J}_{\mathbf{p}_i}$, will be compared to $\mathcal{J}_{\mathbf{q}_{\xi(i)}}$, extracted from $\mathcal{F}_2$.

8.5.3 Distance Between Faces

Let $\mathcal{R}_1 = \{\mathcal{J}_{\mathbf{p}_1}, \mathcal{J}_{\mathbf{p}_2}, \ldots, \mathcal{J}_{\mathbf{p}_n}\}$ be the set of jets for $\mathcal{F}_1$ and $\mathcal{R}_2 = \{\mathcal{J}_{\mathbf{q}_1}, \mathcal{J}_{\mathbf{q}_2}, \ldots, \mathcal{J}_{\mathbf{q}_n}\}$ the set of jets extracted from $\mathcal{F}_2$. Before computing the distance between faces, every jet $\mathcal{J}$ is processed such that each complex coefficient is replaced by its modulus, obtaining $\mathbf{J}$. For the sake of simplicity, we will maintain the name of jet. The distance function between the two faces, $\mathcal{DF}(\mathcal{F}_1, \mathcal{F}_2)$, is given by

$$\mathcal{DF}(\mathcal{F}_1, \mathcal{F}_2) = \Upsilon_{i=1}^{n} \left\{ \mathcal{D}\left(\mathbf{J}_{\mathbf{p}_i}, \mathbf{J}_{\mathbf{q}_{\xi(i)}}\right) \right\} \tag{8.9}$$

where $\mathcal{D}\left(\mathbf{J}_{\mathbf{p}_i}, \mathbf{J}_{\mathbf{q}_{\xi(i)}}\right)$ represents the distance used to compare corresponding jets, and $\Upsilon_{i=1}^{n}\{\ldots\}$ stands for a generic combination rule of the n local distances $\mathcal{D}\left(\mathbf{J}_{\mathbf{p}_1}, \mathbf{J}_{\mathbf{q}_{\xi(1)}}\right), \ldots, \mathcal{D}\left(\mathbf{J}_{\mathbf{p}_n}, \mathbf{J}_{\mathbf{q}_{\xi(n)}}\right)$.

Following [119], a normalized dot product to compare jets is chosen, i.e.,

$$\mathcal{D}(X,Y) = -\cos(X,Y) = -\frac{\sum_{i=1}^{n} x_i y_i}{\sqrt{\sum_{i=1}^{n} x_i^2 \sum_{i=1}^{n} y_i^2}} \tag{8.10}$$

Moreover, the median rule has been used to fuse the n local Gabor distances, i.e., $\Upsilon_{i=1}^{n}\{\ldots\} \equiv$ median.

8.5.4 Results on the BANCA Database

The experiments were carried out on the BANCA database, on protocols P and Mc (see Sect. 8.3.2 for more details). Table 8.13 shows the obtained results for the SDGJ approach.

Table 8.13 SDGJ results on the BANCA database for protocols Mc and P

	WER(0.1)		WER(1)		WER(10)		Av. WER %
	G1	G2	G1	G2	G1	G2	
Protocol Mc	4.23	3.22	11.03	4.68	4.28	1.89	**4.89**
Protocol P	7.73	8.60	18.95	16.47	7.39	6.24	**10.90**

The lowest error rates obtained with an implementation of the Elastic Bunch Graph Matching (EBGM) approach developed by Colorado State University are 8.79% and 14.21% for protocols Mc and P, respectively, confirming the benefits of the SDGJ approach that reaches much lower error rates.

8.6 Method 3: SIFT-based Face Recognition with Graph Matching [UNISS]

For the method proposed in [52], the face image is first photometrically normalized by using histogram equalization. Then, rotation-, scale-, and translation-invariant SIFT features are extracted from the face image. Finally, a graph-based topology is used for matching two face images. Three matching techniques, namely, gallery image-based match constraint, reduced point-based match constraint and, regular grid-based match constraint, are developed for experimental purposes.

8.6.1 Invariant and Robust SIFT Features

The Scale Invariant Feature Transform, called a SIFT descriptor, has been proposed by Lowe [70] and proven to be invariant to image rotation, scaling, translation, partly illumination changes, and projective transform. The basic idea of the SIFT descriptor is detecting feature points efficiently through a staged filtering approach that identifies stable points in the scale-space. This is achieved by the following steps:

1. Select candidates for feature points by searching peaks in the scale-space from a difference of Gaussian (DoG) function.
2. Localize the feature points by using the measurement of their stability.
3. Assign orientations based on local image properties.
4. Calculate the feature descriptors which represent local shape distortions and illumination changes. After candidate locations have been found, a detailed fitting is performed to the nearby data for the location, edge response, and peak magnitude. To achieve invariance to image rotation, a consistent orientation is assigned to each feature point based on local image properties. The histogram of orientations is formed from the gradient orientation at all sample points within a circular window of a feature point. Peaks in this histogram correspond to the dominant directions of each feature point.

For illumination invariance, eight orientation planes are defined. Towards this end, the gradient magnitude and the orientation are smoothed by applying a Gaussian filter and then sampled over a 4×4 grid with eight orientation planes.

8.6.2 Representation of Face Images

In this approach, each face is represented with a complete graph drawn on feature points extracted using the SIFT operator [70]. Three matching constraints are proposed: gallery image-based match constraint, reduced point-based match constraint and regular-grid based match constraint. These techniques can be applied to find the corresponding subgraph in the probe face image given the complete graph in the gallery image.

8.6.3 Graph Matching Methodologies

Each feature point is composed by four types of information: spatial coordinate, key point descriptor, scale and orientation. A key point descriptor is a vector of 1×128 values.

8.6.3.1 Gallery Image-Based Match Constraint

It is assumed that matching points will be found around similar positions—i.e., fiducial points on the face image. To eliminate false matches a minimum Euclidean distance measure is computed by means of the Hausdorff metric. It may be possible that more than one point in the first image corresponds to the same point in the second image. Let $N =$ number of interest points on the first image; $M =$ number of interest points on the second image. Whenever $N \leq M$, many interest points from the second image are discarded, while if $N \geq M$, many repetitions of the same point match in the second image. After computing all the distances, only the point with the minimum distance from the corresponding point in the second image is paired. The mean dissimilarity scores are computed for both the vertices and the edges. A further matching index is given by the dissimilarity score between all corresponding edges. The two distances are then averaged.

8.6.3.2 Reduced Point-Based Match Constraint

After completing the previous phase, there can still be some false matches. Usually, false matches are due to multiple assignments, which exist when more than one point is assigned to a single point in the other image, or to one-way assignments. The false matches due to multiple assignments are eliminated by pairing the points with the minimum distance. The false matches due to one-way assignments are eliminated by removing the links that do not have any corresponding assignment from the other side. The dissimilarity scores on reduced points between two face images for nodes and edges, are computed in the same way as for the gallery-based constraint. Lastly, the average weighted score is computed. Since the matching is done on a very small number of feature points, this graph matching technique proved to be more efficient than the previous match constraint.

8.6.3.3 Regular Grid-Based Match Constraint

In this technique, the images are divided in subimages, using a regular grid with overlaps. The matching between a pair of two face images is done by computing distances between all pairs of corresponding subimage graphs, and finally averaging them with dissimilarity scores for a pair of subimages. From an experimental evaluation, subimages of dimensions 1/5 of width and height represent a good compromise between localization accuracy and robustness to registration errors. The overlap was set to 30%. The matching score is computed as the average between the matching scores computed on the pairs of image graphs.

8.6.4 Results on the BANCA Database

The proposed graph-matching technique is tested on the BANCA database. For this experiment, the Matched Controlled (*Mc*) protocol is followed, where the images from the first session are used for training, whereas second, third, and fourth sessions are used for testing and generating client and impostor scores. Results are presented in Tables 8.14 and 8.15.

Table 8.14 Prior EER on G1 and G2, and their average, on the BANCA database, P protocol, for the three graph matching methods: Gallery Image-Based Match Constraint (GIBMC), Reduced Point-Based Match Constraint (RPBMC), and Regular Grid-Based Match Constraint (RGBMC)

	GIBMC	RPBMC	RGBMC
Prior EER on G1	10.13%	6.66%	4.65%
Prior EER on G2	6.92%	1.92%	2.56%
Average	8.52%	4.29%	3.6%

8.7 Comparison of the Presented Approaches

The results of the three algorithmic methods studied in this chapter are summarized in Table 8.16. The experiments were carried out on the BANCA database with the Pooled and the Match controlled protocols. For these comparisons, the PCA-based BioSecure Reference System v1.0 is considered as a baseline.

Table 8.15 WER on BANCA database, for the three graph matching methods: Gallery Image-Based Match Constraint (GIBMC), Reduced Point-Based Match Constraint (RPBMC), and Regular Grid-Based Match Constraint (RGBMC)

	WER(0.1)		WER(1)		WER(10)		Av. WER %
	G1	G2	G1	G2	G1	G2	
GIBMC	10.24	6.83	10.13	6.46	10.02	6.09	**8.29**
RPBMC	7.09	2.24	6.66	1.92	6.24	1.61	**4.29**
RGBMC	4.07	3.01	4.60	2.52	4.12	2.02	**2.89**

From the first method (presented in Sect. 8.4), exploiting different image normalizations, Gabor features and Liner Discriminant Analysis (LDA), four experimental configurations are reported. The Hist-LDA configuration, is based on histogram equalization and LDA. The configuration denoted as AS-LDA, is based on Anisotropic Smoothing and LDA. The Hist-cGabor-LDA experiments are based on histogram equalization, combined Gabor features and LDA. For the experiments denoted as AS-cGabor-LDA, anisotropic smoothing and combined Gabor features are used as an input to the LDA classifier.

The results of the subject-specific face verification via Shape-Driven Gabor Jets (SDGJ) method presented in Sect. 8.5 are also given in Table 8.16.

For the third method, SIFT-based face recognition with graph matching, presented in Sect. 8.6, the results of the best configuration with Regular Grid-Based Match Constraint, (denoted as SIFT-RGBMC), are reported for comparison purposes.

Table 8.16 Results on BANCA protocols P and Mc, given in Avg. WER%

Algorithms	Avg. WER% for P	Avg. WER% for Mc
Biosecure RefSys	14.60	10.18
Hist-LDA	12.36	7.54
AS-LDA	11.05	6.54
SDGJ	10.90	4.89
Hist-sGabor-LDA	7.97	2.91
SIFT-RGBMC	NA	2.89
AS-cGabor-LDA	6.53	2.66

Figure 8.10 shows the relative improvements of the different algorithms compared to the baseline. Note that using multiscale analysis improves the recognition performance substantially. Indeed, LDA applied to Gabor features, the Shape-Driven Gabor Jet (SDJS) method and the SIFT-based face recognition method are

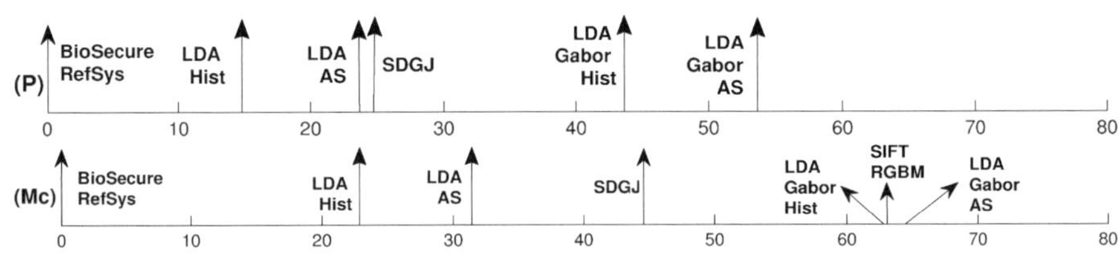

Fig. 8.10 Diagrams of relative percentage improvements of different methods compared to the BioSecure baseline RefSysǏ.0 on BANCA database for the pooled (P) and match-controlled (Mc) protocols

based on the multiscale analysis of the whole image for the first method (LDA on Gabor feature) and multiscale analysis on some specific landmarks for SDGJ and SIFT method.

Local and global approaches show similar performances for this database. In general, local approaches relying on landmark detection are sensitive to environment and personal variability (poses, illumination or expressions). The methods presented in this chapter rely on a good landmark detection, particularly in adverse conditions, which explains the high quality of the reported results.

8.8 Conclusions

In this chapter, we have explored some important issues regarding the state of the art in 2D face recognition, followed by the presentation and comparison of three methods that exploit multiscale analysis of face images. The first method uses Anisotropic Smoothing, combined Gabor features and Linear Discriminant Classifiers (AS-cGabor-LDA). Results of the AS-cGabor-LDA method were reported on two databases. In such a way the generalization ability of the proposed method is also evaluated. The second approach is based on subject-specific face verification via Shape-Driven Gabor Jets (SDGJ), while the third one combines Scale Invariant Feature Transform (SIFT) descriptors with Graph Matching. The BioSecure 2D-face Benchmarking Framework, composed of open-source software, publicly available database and protocols, is also described. Comparative results are reported on the BANCA database (with *Mc* and *P* protocols). The results show the improvements achieved under illumination variability with the presented multiscale analysis methods.

Acknowledgments

We would like to thank the Italian Ministry of Research (PRIN framework project), a special grant from the Italian Ministry of Foreign Affairs under the India-Italy mutual agreement and to the European sixth framework program under the Network of Excellence BioSecure (IST-20026507604).

References

1. B. Achermann and H. Bunke. Combination of classifiers on the decision level for face recognition. *Technical Report IAM-96-002*, 1996.
2. G. Antonini, V. Popovici, and J. Thiran. Independent Component Analysis and Support Vector Machine for Face Feature Extraction. In *4th International Conference on Audio- and Video-Based Biometric Person Authentication, Guildford, UK*, volume 2688 of *Lecture Notes in Computer Science*, pages 111–118, Berlin, 2003. IEEE.
3. Ognjen Arandjelovic and Roberto Cipolla. Face recognition from face motion manifolds using robust kernel resistor-average distance. In *CVPRW '04: Proceedings of the 2004 Conference on Computer Vision and Pattern Recognition Workshop (CVPRW'04) Volume 5*, page 88, Washington, DC, USA, 2004. IEEE Computer Society.

4. Stefano Arca, Paola Campadelli, and Raffaella Lanzarotti. A face recognition system based on automatically determined facial fiducial points. *Pattern Recognition*, 39(3):432–443, 2006.
5. O. Ayinde and Y.H. Yang. Face recognition approach based on rank correlation of Gabor-filtered images. *Pattern Recognition*, 35(6):1275–1289, June 2002.
6. E. Bailly-Baillière, S. Bengio, F. Bimbot, M. Hamouz, J. Kittler, J. Mariéthoz, J. Matas, K. Messer, V. Popovici, F. Porée, B. Ruiz, and J.-P. Thiran. The BANCA Database and Evaluation Protocol. In *4th International Conference on Audio-and Video-Based Biometric Person Authentication (AVBPA'03), volume 2688 of Lecture Notes in Computer Science*, pages 625–638, Guildford, UK, January 2003. Springer.
7. A. Bartlett and JR Movellan. Face recognition by independent component analysis. *IEEE Trans. Neural Networks*, 13:303–321, November 2002.
8. M. Bartlett, G. Littlewort, I. Fasel, and J. Movellan. Real time face detection and facial expression recognition: Development and application to human-computer interaction. *In Computer Vision and Pattern Recognition for Human-Computer Interaction*, 2003.
9. Selin Baskan, M. Mete Bulut, and Volkan Atalay. Projection based method for segmentation of human face and its evaluation. *Pattern Recognition Letters*, 23(14):1623–1629, 2002.
10. R. Basri and D. Jacobs. Lambertian reflectance and linear subspaces. *IEEE Transactions on Pattern Analysis and Machine Intelligence*, pages 383–390, 2003.
11. G. Baudat and F. Anouar. Generalized discriminant analysis using a kernel approach. *Neural Comput.*, 12(10):2385–2404, 2000.
12. S. Belongie, J. Malik, and J. Puzicha. Shape matching and object recognition using shape contexts. *Transactions on Pattern Analysis and Machine Intelligence*, 24(4):509–522, Apr 2002.
13. Chris Boehnen and Trina Russ. A fast multi-modal approach to facial feature detection. In *WACV-MOTION '05: Proceedings of the Seventh IEEE Workshops on Application of Computer Vision (WACV/MOTION'05)*, volume 1, pages 135–142, Washington, DC, USA, 2005. IEEE Computer Society.
14. F.L. Bookstein. Principal warps: Thin-Plate Splines and the decomposition of deformations. *IEEE Transactions on Pattern Analysis and Machine Intelligence*, 11(6):567–585, 1989.
15. K.I. Chang, K.W. Bowyer, and P.J. Flynn. Face recognition using 2D and 3D facial data. *Workshop in Multimodal User Authentication*, pages 25–32, 2003.
16. K.I. Chang, K.W. Bowyer, and P.J. Flynn. An evaluation of multimodal 2D+3D face biometrics. *IEEE Trans. Pattern Anal. Mach. Intell.*, 27(4):619–624, 2005.
17. Longbin Chen, Lei Zhang, Hongjiang Zhang, and Abdel-Mottaleb M. 3D shape constraint for facial feature localization using probabilistic-like output. *Automatic Face and Gesture Recognition, 2004. Proceedings. Sixth IEEE International Conference on*, pages 302–307, 17-19 May 2004.
18. Longbin Chen, Lei Zhang, Long Zhu, Mingjing Li, and Hongjiang Zhang. A novel facial feature point localization algorithm using probabilistic-like output. *Proc. Asian Conference on Computer Vision (ACCV)*, 2004.
19. I. Cohen, N. Sebe, L. Chen, A. Garg, and T. Huang. Facial expression recognition from video sequences: Temporal and static modeling. *in Computer Vision and Image Understanding*, 91:160–187, 2003.
20. D. Cristinacce, T. Cootes, and I. Scott. A multi-stage approach to facial feature detection. In 15th *British Machine Vision Conference, London, England*, pages 277–286, 2004.
21. J. Daugman. How iris recognition works. *Circuits and Systems for Video Technology, IEEE Transactions on*, 14(1):21–30, Jan. 2004.
22. John G. Daugman. Uncertainty relation for resolution in space, spatial frequency, and orientation optimized by two-dimensional visual cortical filters. *Journal of the Optical Society of America*, 2(7):1160, 1985.
23. O. Déniz, Modesto Castrillón Santana, Javier Lorenzo, and Mario Hernández. An incremental learning algorithm for face recognition. In *ECCV '02: Proceedings of the International ECCV 2002 Workshop Copenhagen on Biometric Authentication*, pages 1–9, London, UK, 2002. Springer-Verlag.

24. Kieron Messer et al. Face authentication test on the BANCA database. In *ICPR '04: Proceedings of the Pattern Recognition, 17th International Conference on (ICPR'04) volume 4*, pages 523–532, Washington, DC, USA, 2004. IEEE Computer Society.
25. B. Fasel. Multiscale facial expression recognition using convolutional neural networks. *in Proc. of the third Indian Conference on Computer Vision (ICVGIP)*, 2002.
26. I. Fasel and J. R. Movellan. Comparison of neurally inspired face detection algorithms. *in Proc. of Int. Conf. on Artificial Neural Networks (ICANN)*, 2002.
27. R.S. Feris and V. Krüger. Hierarchical wavelet networks for facial feature localization. In *FGR '02: Proceedings of the Fifth IEEE International Conference on Automatic Face and Gesture Recognition*, page 125, Washington, DC, USA, 2002. IEEE Computer Society.
28. R.A Fisher. The use of multiple measures in taxonomic problems. *Ann. Eugenics*, 7:179–188, 1936.
29. Patrick J. Flynn. Biometrics databases. In A.K. Jain, A. Ross, and P. Flynn, editors, *Handbook of Biometrics*, pages 529–540. Springer, 2008.
30. K. Fukui and O. Yamaguchi. Face recognition using multiview point patterns for robot vision. In *Robotics ResearchThe Eleventh International Symposium*, pages 260–265. Springer, 2003.
31. D. Gonzalez-Jimenez and J. L. Alba-Castro. Shape-driven Gabor jets for face description and authentication. *Information Forensics and Security, IEEE Transactions on*, 2(4):769–780, Dec. 2007.
32. G. Gordon and M. Lewis. Face recognition using video clips and mug shots. *Proceedings of the Office of National Drug Control Policy (ONDCP) International Technical Symposium (Nashua, NH)*, October 1995.
33. N. Gourier, D. Hall, and J.L. Crowley. Facial features detection robust to pose, illumination and identity. *Systems, Man and Cybernetics, 2004 IEEE International Conference on*, 1:617–622 vol.1, 10-13 Oct. 2004.
34. Yves Grandvalet and Stéaphane Canu. Adaptive scaling for feature selection in SVMs. *Neural Information Processing Systems*, 2002.
35. Ralph Gross. Face databases. In Stan Z. Li and Anil K. Jain, editors, *Handbook of Face Recognition*, pages 301–327. Springer, 2005.
36. Ralph Gross and Vladimir Brajovic. An image preprocessing algorithm for illumination invariant face recognition. In *4th International Conference on Audio- and Video-Based Biometric Person Authentication (AVBPA)*. Springer, June 2003.
37. H. Gu, G. Su, and C. Du. Feature points extraction from faces. In *Image and Vision Computing*, pages 154–158, 2003.
38. H. Gunduz, A. Krim. Facial feature extraction using topological methods. *Image Processing, 2003. ICIP 2003. Proceedings. 2003 International Conference on*, 1:I–673–6 vol.1, 14-17 Sept. 2003.
39. Ziad M. Hafed and Martin D. Levine. Face recognition using the discrete cosine transform. *Int. J. Comput. Vision*, 43(3):167–188, 2001.
40. B. Heisele, T. Serre, M. Pontil, T. Vetter, and T. Poggio. Categorization by learning and combining object parts. *Advances In Neural Information Processing Systems*, 2002.
41. R. Herpers, M. Michaelis, K. H. Lichtenauer, and G. Sommer. Edge and keypoint detection in facial regions. In *FG '96: Proceedings of the 2nd International Conference on Automatic Face and Gesture Recognition (FG '96)*, page 212, Washington, DC, USA, 1996. IEEE Computer Society.
42. A. J. Howell and H. Buxton. Towards unconstrained face recognition from image sequences. In *FG '96: Proceedings of the 2nd International Conference on Automatic Face and Gesture Recognition (FG '96)*, page 224, Washington, DC, USA, 1996. IEEE Computer Society.
43. K.S. Huang and M.M. Trivedi. Streaming face recognition using multicamera video arrays. *Pattern Recognition, 2002. Proceedings. 16th International Conference on*, 4:213–216 vol.4, 2002.
44. Xiaolei Huang, Song Zhang, Yang Wang, Dimitris Metaxas, and Dimitris Samaras. A hierarchical framework for high resolution facial expression tracking. In *CVPRW '04: Proceedings of the 2004 Conference on Computer Vision and Pattern Recognition Workshop (CVPRW'04) Volume 1*, page 22, Washington, DC, USA, 2004. IEEE Computer Society.

45. Buciu I., Kotropoulos C., and Pitas I. ICA and Gabor representation for facial expression recognition. *Image Processing, 2003. ICIP 2003. Proceedings. 2003 International Conference on*, 2:II–855–8 vol.3, 14-17 Sept. 2003.
46. IV2: Identification par l'Iris et le Visage via la Vidéo. http://iv2.ibisc.fr/PageWeb-IV2.html.
47. Spiros Ioannou, George Caridakis, Kostas Karpouzis, and Stefanos Kollias. Robust feature detection for facial expression recognition. *J. Image Video Process.*, 2007(2):5–5, 2007.
48. A.K. Jain and B. Chandrasekaran. Dimensionality and sample size considerations in pattern recognition practice. *IEEE Trans. Pattern Anal. Mach. Intell.*, 2:835–855, 1987.
49. F. Jain, A.K. Farrokhnia. Unsupervised texture segmentation using Gabor filters. *Systems, Man and Cybernetics, 1990. Conference Proceedings., IEEE International Conference on*, pages 14–19, 4-7 Nov 1990.
50. G.A. Khuwaja. An adaptive combined classifier system for invariant face recognition. *Digital Signal Processing*, 12:2146, 2001.
51. M. Kirby and L. Sirovich. Application of the Karhunen-Loeve procedure for the characterization of human faces. *IEEE Trans. Pattern Analysis and Machine Intelligence*, 12:103–108, Jan 1990.
52. D.R. Kisku, A. Rattani, E. Grosso, and M. Tistarelli. Face identification by SIFT-based complete graph topology. *Automatic Identification Advanced Technologies, 2007 IEEE Workshop on*, pages 63–68, 7-8 June 2007.
53. C. Kotropoulos, A. Tefas, and I. Pitas. Morphological elastic graph matching applied to frontal face authentication under optimal and real conditions. In *ICMCS '99: Proceedings of the IEEE International Conference on Multimedia Computing and Systems Volume II*, page 934, Washington, DC, USA, 1999. IEEE Computer Society.
54. C.L. Kotropoulos, A. Tefas, and I. Pitas. Frontal face authentication using discriminating grids with morphological feature vectors. *Multimedia, IEEE Transactions on*, 2(1):14–26, Mar 2000.
55. Norbert Krüger. An algorithm for the learning of weights in discrimination functions using a priori constraints. *IEEE Trans. Pattern Anal. Mach. Intell.*, 19(7):764–768, 1997.
56. J. Lange, C. von den Malsburg, R.P. Wurtz, and W. Konen. Distortion invariant object recognition in the dynamic link architecture. *Transactions on Computers*, 42(3):300–311, Mar 1993.
57. JianHuang Lai, Pong C. Yuen, WenSheng Chen, Shihong Lao, and Masato Kawade. Robust facial feature point detection under nonlinear illuminations. In *RATFG-RTS '01: Proceedings of the IEEE ICCV Workshop on Recognition, Analysis, and Tracking of Faces and Gestures in Real-Time Systems (RATFG-RTS'01)*, page 168, Washington, DC, USA, 2001. IEEE Computer Society.
58. C.-J. Lee and S.-D. Wang. Fingerprint feature extraction using Gabor filters. *Electronics Letters*, 35(4):288–290, 18 Feb 1999.
59. D. D. Lee and H. S. Seung. Learning the parts of objects by non-negative matrix factorization. *Nature*, 401(6755):788–791, October 1999.
60. Kuang-Chih Lee, Jeffrey Ho, Ming-Hsuan Yang, and David Kriegman. Video-based face recognition using probabilistic appearance manifolds. *Proc. IEEE CVPR*, 01:313, 2003.
61. Y. Li, S. Gong, and H. Liddell. Video-based online face recognition using identity surfaces. *Recognition, Analysis, and Tracking of Faces and Gestures in Real-Time Systems, 2001. Proceedings. IEEE ICCV Workshop on*, pages 40–46, 2001.
62. Yongmin Li, Shaogang Gong, and H. Liddell. Support vector regression and classification based multi-view face detection and recognition. *Automatic Face and Gesture Recognition, 2000. Proceedings. Fourth IEEE International Conference on*, pages 300–305, 2000.
63. Yongmin Li, Shaogang Gong, and H. Liddell. Modelling faces dynamically across views and over time. *Computer Vision, 2001. ICCV 2001. Proceedings. Eighth IEEE International Conference on*, 1:554–559 vol.1, 2001.
64. Ying li Tian, Takeo Kanade, and Jeffrey F. Cohn. Evaluation of Gabor-wavelet-based facial action unit recognition in image sequences of increasing complexity. In *FGR '02: Proceedings of the Fifth IEEE International Conference on Automatic Face and Gesture Recognition*, page 229, Washington, DC, USA, 2002. IEEE Computer Society.

65. C. Liu and H. Wechsler. Independent component analysis of Gabor features for face recognition. *IEEE Trans. Neural Networks*, 14(4):919–928, July 2003.
66. Chengjun Liu. Gabor-based kernel PCA with fractional power polynomial models for face recognition. *IEEE Trans. Pattern Anal. Mach. Intell.*, 26(5):572–581, 2004.
67. C.J. Liu. Capitalize on dimensionality increasing techniques for improving face recognition grand challenge performance. *IEEE Transactions on Pattern Analysis and Machine Intelligence*, 28(5):725–737, May 2006.
68. Xiaoming Liu and Tsuhan Cheng. Video-based face recognition using adaptive hidden markov models. *Computer Vision and Pattern Recognition, 2003. Proceedings. 2003 IEEE Computer Society Conference on*, 1:I–340–I–345 vol.1, 18-20 June 2003.
69. A.M. Lopez, F. Lumbreras, J. Serrat, and J.J. Villanueva. Evaluation of methods for ridge and valley detection. *Transactions on Pattern Analysis and Machine Intelligence*, 21(4):327–335, Apr 1999.
70. D.G. Lowe. Object recognition from local scale-invariant features. *Computer Vision, 1999. The Proceedings of the Seventh IEEE International Conference on*, 2:1150–1157 vol.2, 1999.
71. J Lu and KN Plataniotis. Face recognition using kernel direct discriminant analysis algorithms. *IEEE Trans. on Neural Networks*, pages 117–126, January 2003.
72. J. Lu, K.N. Plataniotis, and A.N. Venetsanopoulos. Face recognition using LDA-based algorithms. *IEEE Transactions on Neural Networks*, 14(1):195–200, Jan 2003.
73. Simon M. Lucas and Tzu-Kuo Huang. Sequence recognition with scanning n-tuple ensembles. In *ICPR '04: Proceedings of the Pattern Recognition, 17th International Conference on (ICPR'04) Volume 3*, pages 410–413, Washington, DC, USA, 2004. IEEE Computer Society.
74. S.M. Lucas. Continuous n-tuple classifier and its application to real-time face recognition. *IEE Proceedings - Vision, Image, and Signal Processing*, 145(5):343–348, 1998.
75. C. Padgett M. N. Dailey, W. C. Cottrell and R. Adolphs. EMPATH: a neural network that categorizes facial expressions. *Journal of Cognitive Science*, pages 1158–1173, 2002.
76. AM Martinez and AC Kak. PCA versus LDA. *IEEE Trans. Pattern Analysis and Machine Intelligence*, 23:228–233, 2001.
77. K. Messer, J. Matas, J. Kittler, J. Luettin, and G. Maitre. XM2VTSDB: The extended M2VTS database. In *Proc. Second International Conference on Audio- and Video-based Biometric Person Authentication (AVBPA)*, 1999.
78. S. Mika, G. Rätsch, J. Weston, B. Schölkopf, and K.R. Mullers. Fisher discriminant analysis with kernels. *Neural Networks for Signal Processing IX, 1999. Proceedings of the 1999 IEEE Signal Processing Society Workshop*, pages 41–48, Aug 1999.
79. S. Mika, G. Rätsch, J. Weston, B. Schölkopf, A. Smola, and K. Müller. Invariant feature extraction and classification in kernel spaces. *Advances in Neural Information Processing Systems 12*, pages 526–532, 2000.
80. K.-R. Muller, S. Mika, G. Rätsch, K. Tsuda, and B. Schölkopf. An introduction to kernel-based learning algorithms. *IEEE Trans. on Neural Networks*, 12(2):181–201, Mar 2001.
81. BioSecure NoE. http://share.int-evry.fr/svnview-eph/.
82. D. Petrovska-Delacrétaz, S. Lelandais, J. Colineau, L. Chen, B. Dorizzi, E. Krichen, M.A. Mellakh, A. Chaari, S. Guerfi, J. DHose, M. Ardabilian, and B. Ben Amor. The iv^2 multimodal (2d, 3d, stereoscopic face, talking face and iris) biometric database, and the iv^2 2007 evaluation campaign. In *In the proceedings of the IEEE Second International Conference on Biometrics: Theory, Applications (BTAS)*, Washington DC USA, September 2008.
83. Jonathon Phillips and Patrick J Flynn. Overview of the face recognition grand challenge. *Proc. IEEE CVPR*, June 2005.
84. P. Jonathon Phillips, Patrick Groether, and Ross Micheals. Evaluation methods in face recognition. In Stan Z. Li and Anil K. Jain, editors, *Handbook of Face Recognition*, pages 329–348. Springer, 2005.
85. P. Jonathon Phillips, W. Todd Scruggs, Alice J. O Toole, Patrick J. Flynn, Kevin W. Bowyer, Cathy L. Schott, and Matthew Sharpe. *FRVT 2006 and ICE 2006 Large-Scale Results (NISTIR 7408)*, March 2007.

86. P.J. Phillips, P.J. Flynn, T. Scruggs, K.W. Bowyer, and W. Worek. Preliminary face recognition grand challenge results. In *Proceedings 7th International Conference on Automatic Face and Gesture Recognition*, pages 15–24, 2006.
87. Belhumeur PN, Hespanha JP, and Kriegman DJ. Eigenfaces vs fisherfaces: Recognition using class specific linear projection. *Proc of the 4th European Conference on Computer Vision*, pages 45–58, April 1996.
88. Laiyun Qing, Shiguang Shan, and Xilin Chen. Face relighting for face recognition under generic illumination. *Acoustics, Speech, and Signal Processing, 2004. Proceedings. (ICASSP '04). IEEE International Conference on*, 5:V–733–6 vol.5, 17-21 May 2004.
89. Laiyun Qing, Shiguang Shan, and Wen Gao. Face recognition under varying lighting based on derivates of log image. In *SINOBIOMETRICS*, pages 196–204, 2004.
90. K. R. Rao and P. Yip. *Discrete cosine transform: algorithms, advantages, applications*. Academic Press Professional, Inc., San Diego, CA, USA, 1990.
91. Sarunas J. Raudys and Anil K. Jain. Small sample size effects in statistical pattern recognition: Recommendations for practitioners. *IEEE Trans. Pattern Anal. Mach. Intell.*, 13(3):252–264, 1991.
92. B. Raytchev and H. Murase. Unsupervised face recognition from image sequences. *Image Processing, 2001. Proceedings. 2001 International Conference on*, 1:1042–1045 vol.1, 2001.
93. Bisser Raytchev and Hiroshi Murase. Unsupervised recognition of multi-view face sequences based on pairwise clustering with attraction and repulsion. *Comput. Vis. Image Underst.*, 91(1-2):22–52, 2003.
94. Yeon-Sik Ryu and Se-Young Oh. Automatic extraction of eye and mouth fields from a face image using eigenfeatures and ensemble networks. *Applied Intelligence*, 17(2):171–185, 2002.
95. M. Sadeghi, J. Kittler, and K. Messer. Modelling and segmentation of lip area in face images. *IEE Proceedings on Vision, Image and Signal Processing*, 149(3):179–184, Jun 2002.
96. A.A. Salah, H. Cinar, L. Akarun, and B. Sankur. Robust facial landmarking for registration. *Annals of Telecommunications*, 62(1-2):1608–1633, 2007.
97. August-Wilhelm M. Scheer, Fabio Roli, and Josef Kittler. *Multiple Classifier Systems: Third International Workshop, MCS 2002, Cagliari, Italy, June 24-26, 2002. Proceedings (Lecture Notes in Computer Science)*. Springer, August 2002.
98. B Schölkopf, A Smola, and KR Muller. Nonlinear component analysis as a kernel eigenvalue problem. *Technical Report No 44*, December 1996.
99. M. Schulze, K. Scheffler, and K.W. Omlin. Recognizing facial actions with support vector machines. *in Proc. PRASA*, pages 93–96, 2002.
100. Gregory Shakhnarovich, III John W. Fisher, and Trevor Darrell. Face recognition from long-term observations. In *ECCV '02: Proceedings of the 7th European Conference on Computer Vision-Part III*, pages 851–868, London, UK, 2002. Springer-Verlag.
101. T. Shakunaga, K. Ogawa, and S. Oki. Integration of eigentemplate and structure matching for automatic facial feature detection. In *FG '98: Proceedings of the 3rd. International Conference on Face & Gesture Recognition*, page 94, Washington, DC, USA, 1998. IEEE Computer Society.
102. L.L. Shen and L. Bai. Gabor feature based face recognition using kernel methods. In *AFGR04*, pages 170–175, 2004.
103. Frank Y. Shih and Chao-Fa Chuang. Automatic extraction of head and face boundaries and facial features. *Inf. Sci. Inf. Comput. Sci.*, 158(1):117–130, 2004.
104. S. Singh, A. Gyaourova, G. Bebis, and I. Pavlidis. Infrared and visible image fusion for face recognition. *in Proc. of Int. Society for Optical Engineering (SPIE)*, 2004.
105. F. Smeraldi and J. Bigun. Retinal vision applied to facial features detection and face authentication. *Pattern Recogn. Lett.*, 23(4):463–475, 2002.
106. Karin Sobottka and Ioannis Pitas. A fully automatic approach to facial feature detection and tracking. In *AVBPA '97: Proceedings of the First International Conference on Audio- and Video-Based Biometric Person Authentication*, pages 77–84, London, UK, 1997. Springer-Verlag.

107. Z. Sun, G. Bebis, and Miller R. Object detection using feature subset selection. *Pattern Recognition*, 37:2165–2176, 2004.
108. Daniel L. Swets and John (Juyang) Weng. Using discriminant eigenfeatures for image retrieval. *IEEE Transactions on Pattern Analysis and Machine Intelligence*, 18(8):831–836, 1996.
109. Anastasios Tefas, Constantine Kotropoulos, and Ioannis Pitas. Using support vector machines to enhance the performance of elastic graph matching for frontal face authentication. *IEEE Transactions on Pattern Analysis and Machine Intelligence*, 23(7):735–746, 2001.
110. Anastasios Tefas, Constantine Kotropoulos, and Ioannis Pitas. Face verification using elastic graph matching based on morphological signal decomposition. *Signal Processing*, 82(6):833–851, 2002.
111. M. Turk. A random walk through eigenspace. *IEICE Transactions on Information and Systems (Special Issue on Machine Vision Applications)*, 84(12):1586–1595, 2001.
112. M. Turk and A. Pentland. Eigenfaces for recognition. *Journal of Cognitive Neuroscience*, 3(1):71–86, 1991.
113. M. Vukadinovic, D. Pantic. Fully automatic facial feature point detection using Gabor feature based boosted classifiers. *Systems, Man and Cybernetics, 2005 IEEE International Conference on*, 2:1692–1698 Vol. 2, 10-12 Oct. 2005.
114. Haitao Wang, Stan Z. Li, Yangsheng Wang, and Weiwei Zhang. Illumination modeling and normalization for face recognition. In *AMFG '03: Proceedings of the IEEE International Workshop on Analysis and Modeling of Faces and Gestures*, page 104, Washington, DC, USA, 2003. IEEE Computer Society.
115. Y. Weiss. Deriving intrinsic images from image sequences. *Computer Vision, 2001. ICCV 2001. Proceedings. Eighth IEEE International Conference on*, 2:68–75 vol. 2, 2001.
116. Juyang Weng, C.H. Evans, and Wey-Shiuan Hwang. An incremental learning method for face recognition under continuous video stream. *Automatic Face and Gesture Recognition, 2000. Proceedings. Fourth IEEE International Conference on*, pages 251–256, 2000.
117. J. Weston, S. Mukherjee, O. Chapelle, M. Pontil, T. Poggio, and V. Vapnik. Feature selection for support vector machines. *in Advances in Neural Information Processing Systems*, 13, 2001.
118. L. Wiskott. Phantom faces for face analysis. In *ICIP '97: Proceedings of the 1997 International Conference on Image Processing (ICIP '97) 3-Volume Set-Volume 3*, page 308, Washington, DC, USA, 1997. IEEE Computer Society.
119. Laurenz Wiskott, Jean-Marc Fellous, Norbert Krüger, and Christoph von der Malsburg. Face recognition by elastic bunch graph matching. *IEEE Trans. on Pattern Analysis and Machine Intelligence*, 19(7):775–779, 1997.
120. Laurenz Wiskott and Christoph von der Malsburg. Recognizing faces by dynamic link matching. In Axel Wismüller and Dominik R. Dersch, editors, *Symposion über biologische Informationsverarbeitung und Neuronale Netze-SINN '95*, volume 16, pages 63–68, München, 1996.
121. K.W. Wong, K.M. Lam, and W.C. Siu. An efficient algorithm for human face detection and facial feature extraction under different conditions. *Pattern Recognition*, 34(10):1993–2004, October 2001.
122. Rolf P. Würtz. Object recognition robust under translations, deformations, and changes in background. *IEEE Trans. Pattern Anal. Mach. Intell.*, 19(7):769–775, 1997.
123. Zhong Xue, Stan Z. Li, and Eam Khwang Teoh. Bayesian shape model for facial feature extraction and recognition. *Pattern Recognition*, 36(12):2819–2833, 2003.
124. O. Yamaguchi, K. Fukui, and K.-I. Maeda. Face recognition using temporal image sequence. *Automatic Face and Gesture Recognition, 1998. Proceedings. Third IEEE International Conference on*, pages 318–323, 1998.
125. Hua Yu and Jie Yang. A direct LDA algorithm for high-dimensional data – with application to face recognition. *Pattern Recognition*, 34(10):2067–2070, 2001.
126. J. Zhang, Y. Yan, and M. Lades. Face recognition: Eigenface, elastic matching, and neural nets. *PIEEE*, 85(9):1423–1435, September 1997.

127. S. Zhang and S.-T. Yau. High-resolution, real-time 3D absolute coordinate measurement based on a phase-shifting method. *Opt. Express 14*, pages 2644–2649, 2006.
128. M. Zhou and H. Wei. Face verification using Gabor wavelets and AdaBoost. In *ICPR*, pages 404–407, 2006.
129. S.H. Zhou, V. Krueger, and R. Chellappa. Probabilistic recognition of human faces from video. *CVIU*, 91(1-2):214–245, July 2003.
130. S.K. Zhou and R. Chellappa. Probabilistic identity characterization for face recognition. *Computer Vision and Pattern Recognition, 2004. CVPR 2004. Proceedings of the 2004 IEEE Computer Society Conference on*, 2:II–805–II–812 Vol. 2, 27 June-2 July 2004.
131. X. Zhu, J. Fan, and A.K. Elmagarmid. Towards facial feature extraction and verification for omni-face detection in video/images. *In Proc. ICIP*, 2:II–113–II–116 vol. 2, 2002.
132. M. Zobel, A. Gebhard, D. Paulus, J. Denzler, and H. Niemann. Robust facial feature localization by coupled features. *Proc. Fourth IEEE Int. Conf. Automatic Face and Gesture Recognition*, pages 2–7, 2000.

Chapter 9
3D Face Recognition

Berk Gökberk, Albert Ali Salah, Lale Akarun, Remy Etheve, Daniel Riccio, and Jean-Luc Dugelay

Abstract Three-dimensional human facial surface information is a powerful biometric modality that has potential to improve the identification and/or verification accuracy of face recognition systems under challenging situations. In the presence of illumination, expression and pose variations, traditional 2D image-based face recognition algorithms usually encounter problems. With the availability of three-dimensional (3D) facial shape information, which is inherently insensitive to illumination and pose changes, these complications can be dealt with efficiently.

In this chapter, an extensive coverage of state-of-the-art 3D face recognition systems is given, together with discussions on recent evaluation campaigns and currently available 3D face databases. Later on, a fast Iterative Closest Point-based 3D face recognition reference system developed during the BioSecure project is presented. The results of identification and verification experiments carried out on the 3D-RMA database are provided for comparative analysis.

9.1 Introduction

Face recognition is the preferred mode of identity recognition by humans: it is natural, robust and unintrusive. However, automatic face recognition techniques have failed to match up to expectations: variations in pose, illumination and expression limit the performance of 2D face recognition techniques. In recent years, using 3D information has shown promise for overcoming these challenges. With the availability of cheaper acquisition methods, 3D face recognition can be a way out of these problems, both as a standalone method, and as a supplement to 2D face recognition.

In Sect. 9.2, we review the relevant work on 3D face recognition, and discuss the merits of different representations and recognition algorithms. Currently available 3D face databases and evaluation campaigns are reviewed in Sect. 9.3. In Sect. 9.4, the 3D face benchmarking framework developed for the BioSecure project is explained and the results of the benchmarking experiments are given. In Sect. 9.5, more experimental results and comparisons with the reference system are given. Section 9.6 ends with conclusions.

D. Petrovska-Delacrétaz et al. (eds.), *Guide to Biometric Reference Systems and Performance Evaluation*, DOI 10.1007/978-1-84800-292-0_9,

9.2 State of the Art in 3D Face Recognition

Two factors make face recognition especially attractive for biometrics. The acquisition of the face information is easy and nonintrusive, as opposed to iris and retina scans for example, which is important if the system is going to be used frequently, and by a large number of users. The second point is the relatively low privacy of the information: we expose our faces constantly, and if the stored information is compromised, it does not lend itself to improper use like signatures and fingerprints would. The drawbacks of 3D face recognition compared to 2D face recognition include high cost and decreased ease-of-use for sensors, low accuracy for other acquisition types, and the lack of sufficiently powerful algorithms.

3D face recognition represents an improvement over 2D face recognition in some respects. Recognition of faces from still images is a difficult problem, because the illumination, pose and expression changes in the images create great statistical differences, and the identity of the face itself becomes shadowed by these factors. Humans are very capable in this modality, precisely because they learn to deal with these variations.

3D face recognition has the potential to overcome feature localization, pose and illumination problems, and it can be used in conjunction with 2D systems, in which case we deal with a *multimodal* system.

This survey on 3D face recognition is divided into three sections. In Sect. 9.2.1, we talk about acquisition and preprocessing. Section 9.2.2 deals with the registration of 3D data, which is very important for the subsequent recognition stage. The 3D face recognition literature is reviewed in Sect. 9.2.3, where we focus on different representations of 3D information, and the fusion of different sources of information.

9.2.1 3D Acquisition and Preprocessing

We distinguish between a number of range data acquisition techniques. The acquisition method, cost, accuracy, and the usability of the resulting systems differ greatly. They are summarized in this section as are the main preprocessing issues.

9.2.1.1 3D Acquisition

Three main acquisition techniques are presented in this section. In the *stereo camera* technique, two or more calibrated cameras are employed to acquire simultaneous snapshots of the subject. Camera calibration is a well-studied problem, and correct calibration is important for the accuracy of the representation [88]. The depth information for each point can be computed from geometrical models and by solving a correspondence problem. If the exact camera locations are unknown, the correspondence problem is hard due to the smoothness (lack of features) of the faces.

The second approach uses *structured light* patterns projected on the face. The distortion of the pattern reveals depth information. This setup is relatively cheap, and allows a single standard camera to produce 3D information. The acquisition is fast, and the texture information can be obtained by taking another shot in normal light. The obtained images will not be full 3D, as there is a single perspective. Structured light is used frequently in the literature to create some of the most frequently used 3D databases [3, 10, 65]. Chang et al. [20] use a range scanning camera that uses structured light and provides depth and intensity values for all points on the acquired image. Batlle et al. [7] present a survey of different coded structured light methods.

The third approach uses *laser sensors*, which are more accurate, but also more expensive and slower to use. In the context of face recognition, they are also used to produce accurate head models [43, 95]. Lee et al. [56] use silhouettes obtained from laser scans and establish correspondence between vertices. Tsutsumi et al. [91] combine a fiber grating vision sensor (made up of a fiber grating, a laser diode and a CCD camera) with an infrared sensor to acquire range data with graylevel image data. The Minolta Vivid 700^{TM} uses a laser in conjunction with a CCD camera. The positions of the light emitter and sensor are used to calculate the range to the surface through triangulation. The Face Recognition Grand Challenge (FRGC) [19] dataset was acquired with a Minolta 910^{TM} scanner, which produces a 3D depth map with its registered 2D texture image. The relatively slow scanning speed of the scanner gives rise to poor correspondences for some of the acquisitions. Blais [12] gives a thorough survey of commercial sensors and their range and accuracy characteristics. The calibration of these systems is discussed in [35]. See [54] for a survey of 3D assisted face recognition techniques that especially pertains to sensor technology.

There are commercial systems for all three approaches, although the trend with later structural light systems is to use multiple cameras as well. Genex Technologies^{TM} produces 3D FaceCam^{TM}, where three sensors acquire the face image simultaneously [50]. Similarly, Geometrix's FaceVision^{TM} employs a two-camera stereo system. In both systems, high-resolution 2D images are used for constructing 3D shape [51]. *A*4 Vision^{TM} [48] uses near-infrared light to produce a 3D model with accompanying standard 2D texture, but their internal representation is not available as an output. The Minolta Vivid 910^{TM} [71] and Cyberware 3030^{TM} [49] are examples for the third approach, although the former is not specific to facial images. These acquisition methods can be extended to capture 3D video. In [92], a structural light system is described that can acquire 3D scene information with 30 frames per second.

9.2.1.2 Preprocessing

Face recognition systems have to cope with a number of traditional difficulties: different illumination conditions, expression changes, affine changes, background clutter, and face-specific changes like glasses, beard, etc. For 3D acquisition, a number of other problems are added to the list. Depending on the type of sensor, there might be holes and spikes (artifacts) in the range data (see Fig. 9.1). Eyes and hair do not reflect the light appropriately, and the structured light approaches have trouble correctly registering those portions. Illumination still affects the 3D acquisition, unless accurate laser scanners are employed [16]. Some of the scanners acquire 2.5D information, i.e., depth information taken from a single viewpoint. In [61], five such images are combined to produce a true 3D model of the face.

Fig. 9.1 Sample 3D faces from the UND [30] face database (see insert for color reproduction of this figure)

For patching the holes, missing points can be filled by interpolation or by looking at the other (potentially close to symmetrical) side of the face [62, 89]. Gaussian smoothing and linear interpolation are used for both texture and range information [3, 17, 20, 42, 45, 62, 69, 86]. Clutter is usually removed manually [13, 17, 45, 69, 57, 61, 75, 86] and sometimes parts of the data are completely omitted where the acquisition leads to noise levels that cannot be coped with algorithmically [20, 61, 93]. Median filter is also employed to reduce noise [2, 20]. To help distance calculation, mesh representations can be regularized [52, 98], or a voxel discretization can be used [2]. Intensity values can be thresholded for robustness [55, 57]. For costly registration techniques, subsampling the data by a factor of up to 16 speeds up registration significantly, and helps smooth out the surface irregularities [33]. Sampling the 3D data from a regular grid is also beneficial for the latter purpose [32, 53, 84].

9.2.2 *Registration*

Detection of the face is the first step of registration. In most of the scenarios, the background is automatically eliminated, or assumed to be absent. Most of the algorithms start by aligning the detected faces, either by their centers of mass [17, 75], nose tip [45, 57, 58, 62, 73, 86], the eyes [42, 55], or by fitting a plane to the face and aligning it with that of the camera [2]. Registration of the images is important for all local similarity metrics.

The key idea in registration is to define a similarity metric and a set of possible transformations, where the aim is to find the transformation to maximize the similarity. The similarity is measured by point-to-point or point-to-surface distances, or cross correlation between more complex features. The transformations can be rigid, or deformation-based. The rigid transformation of a 3D object involves a 3D rotation and translation (i.e., six degrees of freedom) but the nonlinearity of the problem calls for iterative methods [22]. As the quality of registration directly influences the recognition accuracy, more elaborate registration schemes use facial landmarks as guides.

9.2.2.1 Landmarking

Landmark locations used in registration are either found manually [8, 13, 20, 55, 58, 61, 70, 81, 89, 94] or automatically [4, 24, 52, 83, 84, 100]. The correct localization of the landmarks is crucial to many algorithms, and it is usually not possible to judge the sensitivity of an algorithm to localization errors from its description. Nevertheless, fully automatic landmark localization remains an unsolved problem.

Most registration or coarse facial landmarking algorithms are guided by heuristics [5, 14, 97]. For example, in 3D, the biggest protrusion is usually taken as the tip of the nose; although, depending on the pose, a chin or a streak of hair can be labeled erroneously as such [60]. Another typical characteristic of facial landmarking is the serial search approach, where the localization of one landmark depends on the localization of other landmarks [5, 14]. For example, one often starts with one prominent landmark, say tip of the nose in 3D, and based on this ground truth, proceeds to identify the other features [25]. Some rigid registration methods, most notably the Iterative Closest Point (ICP) method, are robust to landmarking errors, but it has been shown that locating multiple landmarks results in better registration than supplying just the nose tip [84].

3D information is not commonly used in finding facial fiducial points, since 3D face imaging and handling of the resulting data volume are still not mainstream techniques. Furthermore, outlier noise makes reliable processing difficult. In [93] the bunch graph method that uses 2D Gabor jet features introduced in [96] is extended to a 324-dimensional 3D jet method that simultaneously locates facial landmarks. Colbry et al. [25] employ surface curvature-based shape indices under geometrical constraints to locate features on frontal 3D faces. Their method has been generalized to the multipose case with the aid of 2D information, such as the output of Harris corner detector on the grayscale information and related geometrical constraints. Conde et al. [26] use Support Vector Machine (SVM) classifiers trained on spin images for a purely 3D approach. As their proposed method requires great computational resources, they constrain the search for the landmarks by using a priori knowledge about the face. In [14], 3D information plays a secondary or support role in filtering out the background, and in computing intrafeature distances in geometry-based heuristics. In [4], 3D information is used to assist 2D in filtering out the background, and a comparison between 2D and 3D landmarking methods under controlled illumination conditions indicates superiority of the 2D approaches. However, 3D methods are more robust under adverse illumination conditions [83].

9.2.2.2 Registration

The most frequently used registration technique is the Iterative Closest Point (ICP) algorithm [9, 22, 23, 36, 52, 58, 61, 62, 74, 75], which requires the test samples to be in point cloud representation. ICP is a rigid registration technique that iteratively minimizes the sum of distances for each point in the test sample to the registered surface. Scale normalization needs to be done first, and often a good initial coarse registration is necessary. A number of variants are developed for ICP (see [82] for a review). Ayyagari et al. [6] developed a registration method based on Gaussian fields that has better convergence characteristics.

The advantage of rigid registration is that the registered surface is not deformed, hence discriminatory information is preserved. Figure 9.2 shows two facial surfaces registered via the ICP method. Warping and deforming the models (nonrigid registration) for better alignment helps in colocating the landmarks. An important method is the Thin-Plate Spline (TPS) algorithm, which establishes perfect correspondence for a subset of points [15, 52, 59]. This subset is generally formed by the facial landmarks. The warping that forces the landmark to fixed positions may be detrimental to the recognition performance, as discriminatory information is lost proportional to the number of anchor points. Lu and Jain [59] also distinguish between intersubject and intrasubject deformations, which is found useful for classification. For a review of other registration methods, especially for a number of 3D images in temporal sequence, see [85].

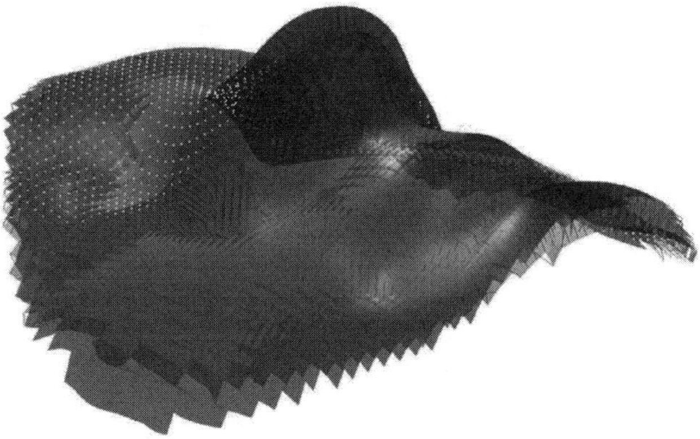

Fig. 9.2 Two facial surfaces, from FRGC database [19], registered with the Iterative Closest Point (ICP) algorithm (see insert for color reproduction of this figure)

9.2.3 3D Recognition Algorithms

We summarize relevant work in 3D face recognition. We classified each work according to the primary representation used in the recognition algorithm, much in the spirit of [16]. Figure 9.3 shows a general view of different types of 3D face recognition algorithms according to the representation methods they use. The most frequently used representations for the acquired 3D data can be listed as:

- *Point clouds and mesh structure:* where a large number of 3D points that are sampled from the surface of the face are stored. Meshes impose a structure, often triangles, and can be considered as a higher-level representation scheme.
- *Range (depth) images:* one or more 2D range images can be stored, especially in multiview systems and several features such as depth and/or color histograms or subspace projection coefficients (from Principal Component Analysis-PCA or Linear Discriminant Analysis-LDA) can be used.
- *Feature sets:* there are different features that one can derive and store for each face. Typical features are coordinates of landmark locations (nose tip, eyes, corners of the mouth, etc.) or their geometrical properties, surface normals, curvatures, profile features, shape indices, and edges.

More than one representation may be used in a single algorithm. Texture information, if available, is generally stored for each 3D point or triangle.

9.2.3.1 Curvatures and Surface Features

In one of the early 3D face papers, Gordon [42] proposed a curvature-based method for face recognition from 3D data, kept in a cylindrical coordinate system. Since the curvatures involve second derivatives, they are very sensitive to noise. An adaptive

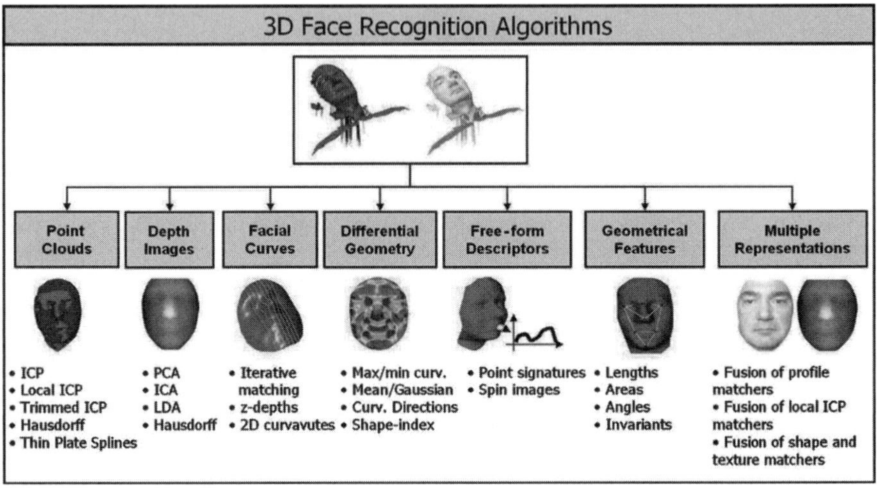

Fig. 9.3 Types of 3D face recognition systems according to the representation schemes used

Gaussian smoothing is applied so as not to destroy curvature information. Figure 9.4 shows mean, Gaussian curvatures and shape indices computed from a sample 3D face. In [87], principal directions of curvatures are used. Moreno et al. [69] extracted a number of features from 3D data, and found that curvature and line features perform better than area features. In [81], 3D geometric invariants are computed from control points on faces and used for recognition. Gokberk et al. [41] have compared different representations on the 3D-RMA dataset [10]: point clouds, surface normals, shape-index values, depth images, and facial profile sets. Surface normals are reported to be more discriminative than others, and LDA is found very useful in extracting discriminative features. In their later work [38], the authors confirm that using a two-stage hierarchical fusion scheme can outperform parallel fusion schemes. Wang and Chua [94] extract 3D Gabor features from the face surface to accommodate rotations in depth. In the absence of good registration, template-based approaches fail under rotations as much as $\pm 60^{\circ}$. See Table 9.1 for a summary of 3D face recognition systems that use curvature features.

9.2.3.2 Point Clouds and Meshes

Point cloud is the most primitive 3D representation for faces (see Fig. 9.5). When the data are in the point cloud representation, Iterative Closest Point (ICP) algorithm is the most widely used registration technique. The similarity of two point sets that is calculated at each iteration of the ICP algorithm is frequently used in point cloud-based face recognizers. Medioni and Waupotitsch [64] present a verification system that acquires the 3D image of the subject with two calibrated cameras and ICP algorithm is used to define similarity between two face meshes. Lu et al. [58] use a

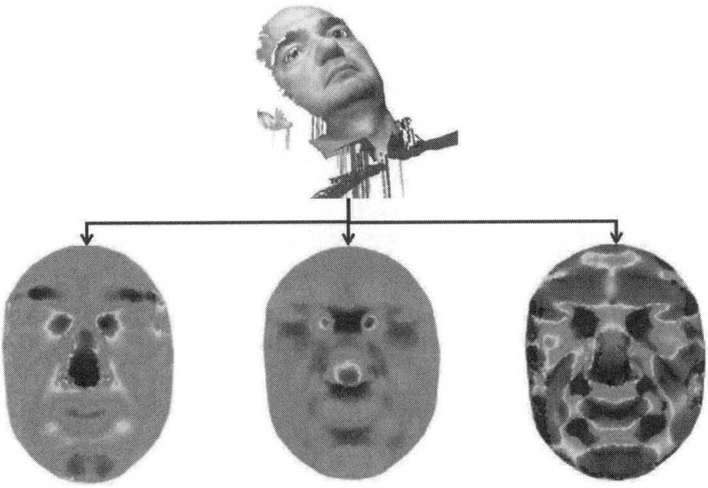

Fig. 9.4 A sample face from the FRGC database [19] and its mean, Gaussian curvature, and shape index maps (from left to right) (see insert for color reproduction of this figure)

Table 9.1 3D face recognition systems that use surface features, where NN stands for Nearest Neighbor, EGI for Enhanced Gaussian Image, and HD for Hausdorff Distance

Group	**Representation**	**Database**	**Algorithm**
Gordon [42]	Curvatures	26 training 24 test	Euclidean NN
Tanaka et al. [87]	Curvature based EGI	NRCC	Fisher's spherical correlation
Moreno et al. [69]	Curvature, line, region features	7 img. × 60 subj.	Euclidean NN
Wang et al. [94]	3D Gabor features	12 img. × 80 subj.	Least Trimmed Square HD
Riccio et al. [81]	3D geometric invariants	3 img. × 50 subj.	NN and voting

hybrid ICP-based registration using Besl's method and Chen's method successively. The base mesh is also used for alignment in [98], where features are extracted from around landmark points, and nearest neighbor after Principal Component Analysis (PCA) is used for recognition. Lu and Jain [59] use ICP for rigid deformations, but they also propose to use Thin-Plate Spline (TPS) warping for intrasubject and intersubject nonrigid deformations, with the purpose of handling expression variations. Deformation analysis and combination with appearance-based classifiers both increase the recognition accuracy. Achermann and Bunke [2] employ Hausdorff distance for matching the point clouds. They use a voxel discretization to speed up matching, but it causes some information loss. Lao et al. [55] discard matched points with large distances as noise. In [76], an annotated mesh is aligned with the test face via a deformable variant of ICP, and Haar coefficients from particular points are used for recognition. This work is later extended in [53]. Table 9.2 summarizes 3D face recognition systems that use point clouds and meshes.

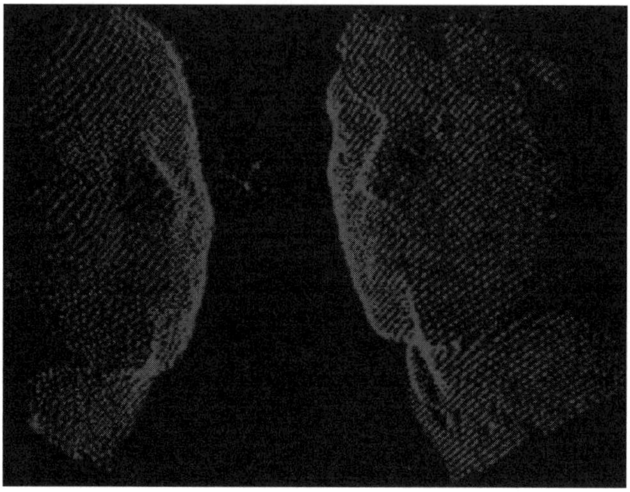

Fig. 9.5 Two facial point clouds taken from the 3D-RMA database [27] (see insert for color reproduction of this figure)

Table 9.2 3D face recognition systems that use point clouds and meshes. Enroll. stands for enrollment, PCA for Principal Component Analysis, ICP for Iterative Closest Point, TPS for Thin-Plate Spline, and NN for Nearest Neighbor

Group	Representation	Database	Algorithm
Achermann et al. [2]	Point cloud	120 enroll., 120 test	Hausdorff NN
Lao et al. [55]	Curve segments	36 img. × 10 subj.	Euclidean NN
Medioni et al. [64]	Mesh	7 img. × 100 subj.	Normalized cross-correlation
İrfanoğlu et al. [52]	Point cloud	3D-RMA [27]	Point set difference
Lu et al. [58]	Mesh	90 enroll., 113 test	Hybrid ICP and cross-correlation
Xu et al. [98]	Regular mesh	3D-RMA	Feature extraction, PCA and NN
Lu and Jain [59]	Deformation points	500 enroll., 196 test	ICP + TPS, NN
Passalis et al. [76]	Mesh	FRGC v.2 [19]	Haar wavelets

9.2.3.3 Depth Map

Depth maps are generally used in conjunction with subspace methods, since most of the existing 2D techniques are suitable for processing the depth maps. The depth map construction consists of selecting a viewpoint, and smoothing the sampled depth values. Figure 9.6 shows a sample depth map images. In [45], PCA and Independent Component Analysis (ICA) were compared on the depth maps. ICA was found to perform better, but PCA degraded more gracefully with declining numbers of training samples. In Srivastava et al. [86], the set of all k-dimensional subspaces of the data space is searched with a simulated annealing algorithm for the optimal linear subspace. The optimal subspace method performed better than PCA, Linear Discriminant Analysis (LDA) or ICA. Achermann et al. [3] compare an eigenface method with a five-state left-right Hidden Markov Model (HMM) on a database of depth maps. They show that the eigenface method outperforms the HMM, and the smoothing effects the eigenface method positively, while its effect on the HMM is detrimental.

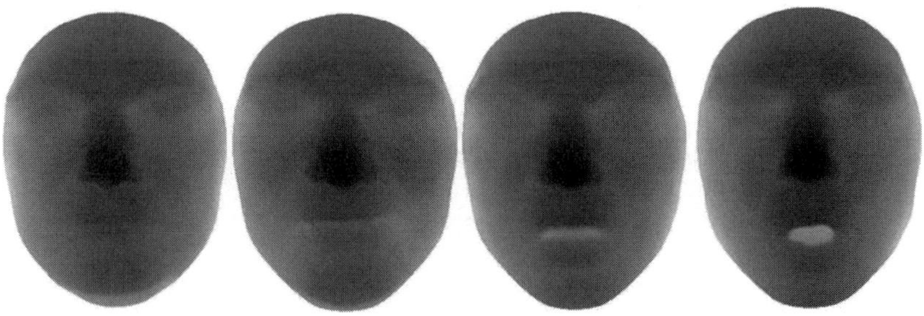

Fig. 9.6 Sample depth images of faces from FRGC database [19]

The 3D data are usually more suitable for alignment, and should be preferred if available. In Lee et al. [57], the 3D image is thresholded after alignment to obtain the depth map, and a number of small windows are sampled from around the nose. The statistical features extracted from these windows are used in recognition. Summary of 3D face recognition systems that use depth maps is given in Table 9.3.

Table 9.3 3D face recognition systems that use depth map

Group	Representation	Database	Algorithm
Achermann et al. [3]	Depth map	120 training 120 test	Eigenface vs. HMM
Hesher et al. [45]	Mesh	FSU	ICA or PCA + NN
Lee et al. [57]	Depth map	2 img. × 35 subj.	Feature extraction + NN
Srivastava et al. [86]	Depth map	6 img. × 67 subj.	Subspace projection + SVM

9.2.3.4 Facial Profile

The most important problem for the profile-based schemes is the extraction of the profile. In an early paper, Cartoux et al. [18] use an iterative scheme to find the symmetry plane that cuts the face into two similar parts. The nose tip and a second point are used to extract the profiles. Nagamine et al. [70] use various heuristics to find feature points and align the faces by looking at the symmetry. Then, the faces are intersected with different kinds of planes (vertical, horizontal or cylindrical around the nose tip), and the intersection curve is used in recognition. Vertical planes around ±20 mm. of the central region and selecting a cylinder with 20–30 mm.

radius around the nose (crossing the inner corners of the eyes) produced the best results. Beumier and Acheroy [10] detail the acquisition of the popular 3D-RMA dataset with structural light and report profile-based recognition results. In addition to the central profile, they use the average of two lateral profiles in recognition. Figure 9.7 shows several central profile contours.

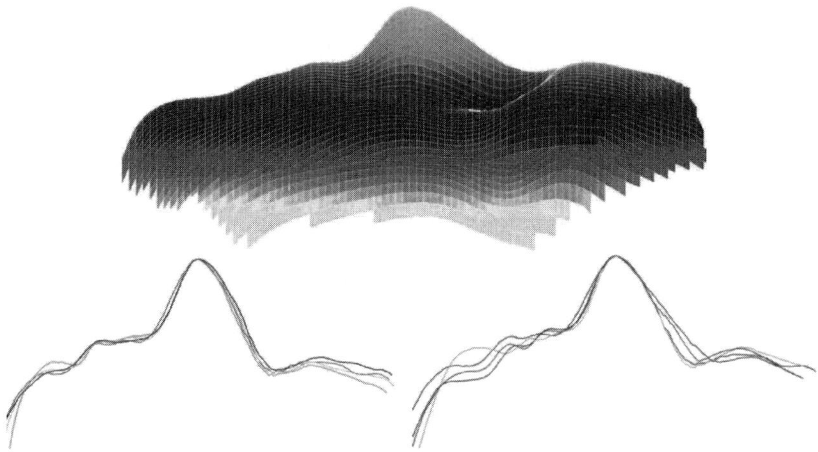

Fig. 9.7 **Upper image** shows a profile view of a facial surface. **Lower left** image displays central profile curves computed from the same subject. **Lower right** image shows central profiles obtained from different subjects, from the 3D-RMA database [27] (see insert for color reproduction of this figure)

Once the profiles are obtained, there are several ways of matching them. In [18], corresponding points of two profiles are selected to maximize a matching coefficient that uses the curvature on the profile curve. Then, a correlation coefficient and the mean quadratic distance is calculated between the coordinates of the aligned profile curves, as two alternative measures. In [10], the area between the profile curves is used. In [41], distances calculated with L_1 norm, L_2 norm, and generalized Hausdorff distance are compared for aligned profiles, and the L_1 norm is found to perform better. In Table 9.4 3D face recognition systems that use profiles are summarized.

Table 9.4 3D face recognition systems that use profiles (NN stands for Nearest Neighbor)

Group	Representation	Database	Algorithm
Cartoux et al. [18]	Profile	3/4 img. × 5 subj.	Curvature based NN
Nagamine et al. [70]	Vert., horiz., circular profiles	10 img. × 16 subj.	Euclidean NN
Beumier et al. [10]	Vertical profiles	3D-RMA [27]	Area based NN

9.2.3.5 Analysis by Synthesis

In [13], the analysis-by-synthesis approach that uses morphable models is detailed. A morphable model is defined as a convex combination of shape and texture vectors of a number of samples that are placed in dense correspondence. A single 3D face model is used to render an image similar to the test image, which leads to the estimation of viewpoint parameters (pose angles, 3D translation, and focal length of the camera), illumination parameters (ambient and directed light intensities, direction angles of the light, color contrast, gains and offsets of the color channels), and deformation parameters (shape and texture).

In [62], a system is proposed to work with 2D color images and corresponding 3D depth maps. The idea is to synthesize a pose and illumination corrected image pair for recognition. The depth images performed significantly better (by 4–7%) than color images, and the combination increased the accuracy as well (by 1–2%). Pose correction is found to be more important than illumination correction. In [101], a morphable model is used to recover 3D information from a 2D image. The illumination is assumed to be Lambertian, and the basis images for illumination space are found by spherical harmonics. Table 9.5 summarizes the 2D face recognition systems that use 3D analysis-by-synthesis method.

Table 9.5 2D face recognition systems that use 3D via analysis by synthesis

Group	Representation	Database	Algorithm
Blanz et al. [13]	2D + viewpoint	CMU-PIE [29], FERET [28]	Analysis by synthesis
Malassiotis et al. [62]	Texture + depth map	110 img.× 20 subj.	Embedded HMM + fusion
Zhang et al. [101]	Illumination basis images	CMU-PIE [29]	Morphable model + spherical harmonics

9.2.3.6 Combinations of Representations

Most of the work that use 3D face data use a combination of representations [39]. The enriched variety of features, when combined with classifiers with different statistical properties, produce more accurate and more robust results. In [91], surface normals and intensities are concatenated to form a single feature vector, and the dimensionality is reduced with PCA. Adding perturbed versions of training images reduces sensitivity of the PCA. In [93], the 3D data are described by point signatures, and the 2D data by Gabor wavelet responses, respectively. 3D information may have missing elements around the eyes and the eyebrows, and the mouth area is sensitive to expressions. These are omitted for robustness. 3D intensities and texture were combined to form the 4D representation in [75]. Bronstein et al. [17] point to the nonrigid nature of the face, and to the necessity of using a suitable similarity metric that takes this deformability into account. For this purpose, they use a multidimensional scaling projection algorithm for both shape and texture information.

Apart from techniques that fuse the representations at the feature level, there are a number of systems that employ combinations at the decision level. Chang et al. propose in [20] to use Mahalanobis distance-based nearest-neighbor classifiers on the 2D intensity and 3D range images separately, and fuse the decisions with a rank-based approach at the decision level. In [90] the depth map and color maps (one for each YUV colorspace channel) are projected via PCA and the distances in four subspaces are combined by multiplication. In [89] the depth map and the intensity image are processed with embedded HMMs separately, and weighted score summation is proposed for the combination. Lu and Jain [61] combine texture and surface (point-to-plane distance) with weighted sum rule. In [8], texture and depth maps are fused at the feature level for classification with LDA, but a decision-level fusion scheme that relies on local feature analysis was found to be more successful. In [46], hierarchical graph matching is applied on 2D and 3D separately. A score-level fusion is shown to be of marginal use. In [44], 17 different surface feature maps are computed using different, mostly curvature-based properties of the surface, and LDA is used on a combination of features obtained from these maps.

Profiles are also used in conjunction with other features. In [11], 3D central and lateral profiles, grayscale central and lateral profiles were evaluated separately, and then fused with Fisher's method. In [73], a surface-based recognizer and a profile-based recognizer are combined at the decision level. Surface-matcher's similarity is based on a point cloud distance approach, and profile similarity is calculated using Hausdorff distance. In [74], a number of methods are tested on the depth map (eigenface, fisherface, and kernel fisherface), and the depth map expert is fused with three profile experts with Max, Min, Sum, Product, Median and Majority Vote rules, out of which the Sum rule was selected.

9.2.3.7 Dealing with Expressions

There are two ways of dealing with expression variations in 3D faces. One way is to take a deformation-based approach and smooth out the effects due to expressions. For this purpose, facial landmarks need to be localized accurately, which is difficult as we assume that there are changes due to expressions. The alternative to accurate landmarking is an iterative approach, which improves the registration step by step. In Kakadiaris et al. [53], an annotated face model is fit to the test scan with an iterative deformable approach, and the surface is resampled to produce a 2D geometrical representation of the 3D surface.

The second way is to base the recognition on patches of the faces that are more resilient to expression variations, e.g., the nose area. For neutral expressions, this approach may have reduced accuracy, as part of the face is not used at all. However, the gain from eliminating expression effects may be greater, depending on the dataset. This approach is successfully applied in [33] and [67], where in each case the outputs from individual rigid regions are combined to give a more robust decision. A more general way of determining local discriminative regions over the

3D facial surface is presented in [37] where facial parts are selected automatically to improve the identification accuracy.

9.2.3.8 Comparative Results on the 3D-RMA Database

We performed a series of experiments to assess the effects of registration and representation on classification accuracy. The accuracies reported in the literature are often difficult to compare, as results are obtained under different assumptions and with different data sets.

In [52], ICP is used to automatically locate facial landmarks in a coarse alignment step, and then faces are warped using a TPS algorithm to establish dense point-to-point correspondences. The use of an average face model significantly reduces the complexity of similarity calculation, and the point cloud representation of registered faces is more suitable for recognition than depth image-based methods, point signatures, and implicit polynomial-based representation techniques. Also, the point set difference is found to be more accurate than PCA on the depth map for recognition. In a follow-up study, Gökberk et al. [41] analyze the effect of registration methods on the classification accuracy. To inspect side effects of warping on discrimination, an ICP-based approximate dense registration algorithm is designed that allows only rotation and translation transformations. Experimental results confirmed that ICP without warping leads to better recognition accuracy.

A single average face model can be replaced by a number of average models that represent different face morphologies. We performed a series of experiments with different average face models that were either automatically generated by a clustering in the shape space, or were based on gender and face morphology [84]. Interestingly, the groups generated by automatic clustering also show intuitive groupings, as separate groups emerge for males and females, and for Asian face morphology.

Table 9.6 summarizes the classification accuracies of different feature extractors for both TPS-based and ICP-based registration algorithms on the 3D-RMA dataset. The superiority of the ICP-based registration technique is visible for all feature extraction methods, except the shape index.

Gökberk et al. [41, 38] propose two combination schemes that use 3D facial shape information. In the first scheme, called *parallel fusion*, different pattern classifiers are trained using different features such as point clouds, surface normals, facial profiles, and PCA/LDA of depth images. The outputs of these pattern classifiers are merged using a rank-based decision-level fusion algorithm. Combination rules, consensus voting, a nonlinear variation of a rank-sum method, and a highest rank majority method are used.

Table 9.7 shows the recognition accuracies of individual pattern recognizers together with the accuracies of the parallel ensemble methods for the 3D-RMA dataset. It is seen that while the best individual pattern classifier (depth-LDA) can accurately classify 96.27% of the test examples, a nonlinear rank-sum fusion of depth-LDA, surface normals, and point cloud classifiers improves the accuracy to

Table 9.6 Average classification accuracies (and standard deviations) of different face recognizers for TPS warping-based and ICP-based face representation techniques

Method	TPS	ICP
Point Cloud	92.95 ± 1.01	96.48 ± 2.02
Surface Normals	97.72 ± 0.46	99.17 ± 0.87
Shape Index	90.26 ± 2.21	88.91 ± 1.07
Depth PCA	45.39 ± 2.15	50.78 ± 1.10
Depth LDA	75.03 ± 2.87	96.27 ± 0.93
Central Profile	60.48 ± 3.78	82.49 ± 1.34
Profile Set	81.14 ± 2.09	94.30 ± 1.55

99.07%. Paired t-test [31] results indicate that all of the accuracies of the parallel fusion schemes are statistically better than individual classifier's performances. The second scheme is called *serial fusion* where the class outputs of a filtering first classifier is passed to a second, more complex classifier. The ranked output lists of these classifiers are fused. The first classifier in the pipeline should be fast and accurate. Therefore a point cloud-based pattern classifier was selected. As the second classifier, depth-LDA was chosen because of its discriminatory power. This system has 98.14% recognition accuracy, which is significantly better than the single best classifier.

Table 9.7 Classification accuracies (Acc.) in %, of single face classifiers (**top part**), and combined classifiers (**bottom part**)

Method	Dimensionality	Acc. in %
Point Cloud	$3{,}389 \times 3$	95.96
Surface Normals	$3{,}389 \times 3$	95.54
Depth PCA	300	50.78
Depth LDA	30	96.27
Profile Set	1,557	94.30

Fusion method	Classifiers	Acc. in %
Consensus Voting	LDA, PC, SN	98.76
Nonlinear Rank-Sum	Profile, LDA, SN	99.07
Highest Rank Majority	Profile, LDA, SN, PC	98.13
Serial Fusion	PC, LDA	98.14

In their later work, Gökberk et al. [40] extend their experiments by employing more base classifiers (point clouds, surface normals, shape index values, facial profiles, LDA of depth images, and LDA of surface normals), and by employing different fusion schemes (sum/product rules, consensus voting, Borda count method, improved consensus voting, and highest confidence rule) for both identification and verification scenarios. They also propose a confidence-assisted serial fusion scheme, where the second classifier is only consulted if the confidence of the first classifier is below a certain threshold. This scheme is significantly faster than forwarding the nearest classes found by the first classifier. By looking at the experimental results on the 3D-RMA database, the following observations are made:

- With strong (i.e., accurate) classifiers in the fused ensemble, the fusion performance improvement is marginal, but with classifiers of moderate strength, the improvement is significantly better.
- The best fusion performances are obtained with improved consensus voting, highest confidence rule, and product rule.
- The idea of confidence-assisted fusion scheme is beneficial, i.e., selecting only the most confident classifier is as good as fusing all base classifiers.
- Serial fusion methods reach the best fusion performances and confidence-based serial fusion is found to be both faster and more accurate than standard serial fusion scheme.

A summary of 3D face recognition systems that use combination of representations is given in Table 9.8.

9.3 3D Face Databases and Evaluation Campaigns

In this section, the most important 3D face datasets are first listed. Discussions on recent evaluation campaigns are given next.

9.3.1 3D Face Databases

- **3D-RMA [27]**: is a structural light based database of 120 individuals, where six images are collected in two different sessions for each individual. Although used frequently in early 3D face research, the quality of acquisition is relatively low.
- **GavabDB [68]**: contains 427 facial meshes with pose and expression variations collected from 61 subjects.
- **University of Surrey, Extended M2VTS Database (XM2VTS) [65]**: four 3D head models of 295 subjects taken over a period of four months are included in this database.
- **FRGC datasets [19]**: was collected at University of Notre Dame. Version 1.0 a of this dataset contains 943 near-frontal acquisitions from 277 subjects [80]. For each acquisition there is a range image and the corresponding registered 2D texture, taken under controlled indoor lighting conditions. Due to slow acquisition, the correspondence between 2D and 3D images are poor for some of the samples. Version 2.0 subsumes version 1.0a, and contains 4,007 frontal scans from 466 subjects recorded at 22 sessions with minor pose, but difficult illumination and

Table 9.8 3D face recognition systems that use combination of representations

Group	Representation	Database	Algorithm
Tsutsumi et al. [91]	Texture + depth map	35 img.× 24 subj.	Concatenated features + PCA
Beumier et al. [11]	2D and 3D vertical profiles	3D-RMA	NN + fusion
Wang et al. [93]	Point signature, Gabor features	6 img. × 50 subj.	Concatenation after PCA + SVM
Bronstein et al. [17]	Texture + depth map	157 subj.	Concatenation after PCA + 1-NN
Chang et al. [20]	Texture + depth map	278 training, 166 test	Mahalanobis NN
Pan et al. [73]	Profile + point clouds	3D-RMA	ICP + Hausdorff + fusion
Tsalakanidou et al. [90]	Texture + depth map	XM2VTS	NN +
Tsalakanidou et al. [89]	Texture + depth map	60 img. × 50 subj.	Embedded HMM + fusion
Pan et al. [74]	Depth map + profile	6 img. × 120 subj.	Kernel Fisherface + Eigenface + fusion
Papatheodorou et al. [75]	Texture + dense mesh	2 img. × 62 subj.	NN + fusion
BenAbdelkader et al. [8]	Texture + depth map	4 img. × 185 subj.	PCA + LDA + fusion
Lu et al. [61]	Mesh + texture	598 test	ICP(3D), LDA(2D) + fusion
Gökberk et al. [41]	Surface normals, profiles, depth map, point cloud	3D-RMA	PCA, LDA, NN, rank based fusion
Hüsken et al. [46]	Texture + depth map	FRGC v.2	Hierarchical graph matching

expression variations. It comes with an infrastructure for evaluating biometrics experiments in an effort to evaluate the myriad of approaches under comparable training and testing conditions.

- **York University 3D Face Databases [72]**: fifteen images with expression and pose variations are recorded from approximately 350 subjects.
- **MIT-CBCL Face Recognition Database [95]**: contains acquired and synthesized (324 images per subject) training sets for 10 subjects, and a test set of 200 images. Illumination, pose and background changes are present.
- **BJUT-3D Large-scale Chinese Face Database [1]**: contains 3D laser scans of 250 male and 250 female Chinese subjects. There is no hair (acquisition with a swim cap) and no facial accessories.
- **IV^2 (described in [77] and available at [47])**: is a multimodal database, including 2D and 3D face images, and iris data. 3D faces have expression and illumination variations. A full 3D face model is also present for each subject. Two pairs of stereoscopic high-resolution cameras provide data for 3D reconstruction also. The IV^2 database contains 315 subjects with one session data where 77 of them

also participated in a second session. A disjoint development data of 52 subjects is also part of the IV^2 database. An evaluation package has been defined, allowing new experiments to be reported with the protocols defined in this evaluation package.

9.3.2 3D Evaluation Campaigns

The increasing number of different algorithms for 3D face recognition systems makes it necessary to design independent benchmarks to evaluate state-of-the-art systems. Main motivations for these evaluations are two fold: 1) compare competitive 3D face recognition algorithms, and 2) compare the performance of 3D systems with other biometric modalities such as high-resolution 2D still imagery and iris scans. Face Recognition Grand Challenge (FRGC) [80] and Face Recognition Vendor Test 2006 (FRVT'06) [78] are the two important evaluations where the 3D face modality is present.

9.3.2.1 Face Recognition Grand Challenge

FRGC is the first evaluation campaign that focuses on the 3D face modality [80, 79]. The aim of the FRGC benchmark is to evaluate the performance of face recognition systems for high resolution 2D still imagery and 3D faces taken under controlled and uncontrolled conditions. The FRGC data corpus contains 50,000 images where the 3D part is divided into two sets: *Development* (943 images) and *Evaluation* (4,007 images collected from 466 subjects). The evaluation set is composed of *target* and *query images*. Images in the target set are to be used for enrollment, whereas images in the query set represent the test images. Images were taken under controlled illumination conditions via Minolta Vivid 900/910 sensor, which is a structured light sensor that takes registered color and range pictures of size 640×480.

FRGC splits 3D verification experiments into three cases: shape and texture (Experiment 3), shape only (Experiment 3s), and texture only (Experiment 3t). The baseline algorithm for the 3D shape and texture experiment consists of PCA performed on the shape and texture channels separately. The scores obtained from these two channels are then fused to obtain the final score. At the FAR rate of 0.1%, the verification rate of the baseline system is found to be 54%. The best reported performance is 97% at FAR rate of 0.1% [80, 79]. Table 9.9 also shows several published results in the literature for a FAR rate of 0.001% using FRGC v.2 database. Conclusions drawn from FRGC 3D experiments can be summarized as follows:

- Fusing shape and texture channels is better than using only shape or texture.
- Individual performance of the texture channel is better than the shape channel.
- High-resolution 2D images obtain slightly better verification rates than 3D modality.

Table 9.9 Verification rates in % of various algorithms at FAR rate of 0.001% on the FRGC v.2 dataset

	Neutral vs All		Neutral vs Neutral		Neutral vs Non-neutral	
System	3D	3D+2D	3D	3D+2D	3D	3D+2D
Mian et al. [66]	98.5	99.3	99.4	99.7	97.0	98.3
Kakadiaris et al. [53]	95.2	97.3	NA	99.0	NA	95.6
Husken et al. [46]	89.5	97.3	NA	NA	NA	NA
Maurer et al. [63]	86.5	95.8	97.8	99.2	NA	NA
FRGC baseline	45.0	54.0	NA	82.0	40.0	43.0

9.3.2.2 Face Recognition Vendor Test 2006

The FRVT'2006 is an independent large-scale evaluation campaign that aims to look at performance of high-resolution 2D and 3D modalities [78]. It was open to universities, research institutes, and companies. Submitted algorithms were tested on sequestered data collected from 330 subjects (3,589 3D scans). The participants of the 3D part were *Cognitec*, *Viisage*, *Tsinghua University*, *Geometrics* and *University of Houston*. The best performers for 3D have a FRR interquartile range of 0.005 to 0.015 at a FAR of 0.001 for the *Viisage* normalization algorithm and a FRR interquartile range of 0.016 to 0.031 at a FAR of 0.001 for the *Viisage* 3D one-to-one algorithm. In FRVT'2006, it has been concluded that a) 2D, 3D and iris biometrics are all comparable in terms of verification rates, and b) there is a decrease in the error rate by at least an order of magnitude over what was observed in the FRVT'2002. This decrease in error rate was achieved by 2D still and by 3D face recognition algorithms.

9.4 Benchmarking Framework for 3D Face Recognition

In this section, the 3D Face Recognition Reference System (3D-FRRS) that is used in the BioSecure project is described in detail. The relevant material (such as open-source code, pointers to the database, lists of enrollment and test images for each experiment, and How-to documents) that is needed to reproduce the experiments described in this section can be found on the URL [34].

9.4.1 3D Face Recognition Reference System v1.0 (3D-FRRS)

The 3D-FRRS v1.0 uses a 3D-to-3D matching algorithm where only shape information is incorporated. The main components of the 3D-FRRS v1.0 are as follows:

- Average face model construction
- Dense correspondence establishment
- Recognition/matching

The algorithm employed in the 3D-FRRS is basically a variant of the ICP-based face matcher, where the crucial phase is the establishment of dense point-to-point correspondence between any two faces. However, the 3D-FRRS can handle non-rigid facial deformations in finding the dense correspondences in contrast to standard ICP-based approaches. 3D-FRRS requires facial landmarks, but the number and type of these landmarks are flexibly defined. For the experiments in this section, an automatic landmark-finding algorithm is used that is explained in [52]. A landmarking algorithm is also provided in the benchmarking framework for reproducing the same experiments. The overall structure of the 3D-FRRS v1.0 system is illustrated in Fig. 9.8.

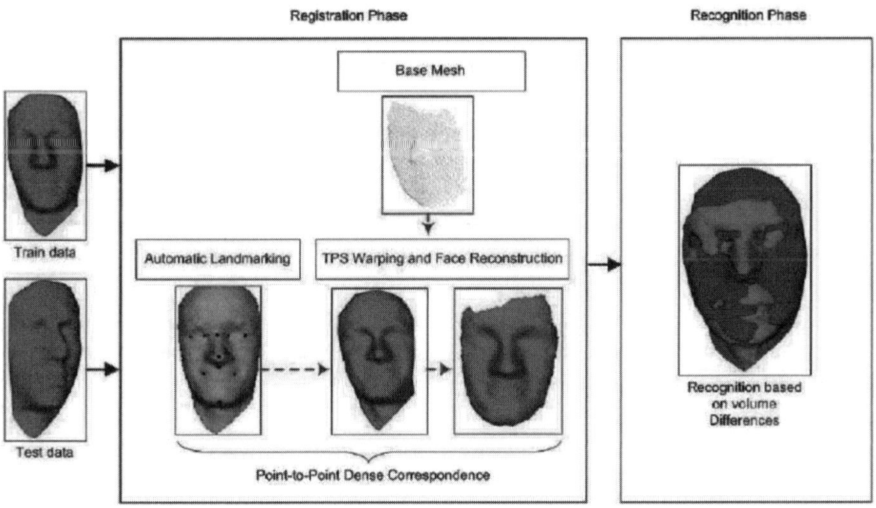

Fig. 9.8 Main modules of the 3D Face Recognition Reference System (3D-FRRS)

The remainder of this section is organized as follows. Section 9.4.1.1 describes the Average Face Model (AFM) construction algorithm. Dense correspondence establishment is explained in Sect. 9.4.1.2. The classification part is treated in Sect. 9.4.1.3.

9.4.1.1 Average Face Model Construction

The 3D-FRRS requires an Average Face Model (AFM) in order to define the similarity between any two faces. This model is constructed once at the off-line training phase, and it is used to normalize and register faces in the later stages of the

3D-FRRS. The average face construction module requires a set of training images together with the locations of several facial features. The main motivation here is to construct a typical canonical face template. Figure 9.9 shows an illustration of the AFM construction algorithm. The fundamental steps of the Average Face Construction algorithm are as follows:

1. *Triangulation*: the first step is to triangulate the 3D points of faces with Delaunay triangulation algorithm in order to obtain a continuous surface. The triangulation is required for interpolation of corresponding points in the registered faces.
2. *Manual Landmarking*: 10 facial landmarks (inner/outer eye corners, mouth corners, nose tip, upper point of the nose bridge, lower point of the nose, chin point) are manually located (see Fig. 9.9).
3. *Computing Mean Landmark Locations*: since the manually located facial feature coordinates of different 3D facial images have different rotation, translation, and scale variations, it is required to transform these coordinates into a common coordinate system. In order to perform this transformation, Procrustes analysis is used. After Procrustes analysis, mean landmark coordinates can be found by averaging.
4. *Thin-Plate Spline (TPS) warping onto the mean landmarks*: in this step, all of the training faces are TPS warped onto the mean landmarks so that all of these faces have approximately the same translation, rotation and scale parameters. Additionally, they undergo a nonlinear transformation via warping.
5. *Average Face Model (AFM) Construction*: among all of the TPS-warped training faces, one candidate face is selected as the AFM. In order to remove noise, the vertices of the candidate AFM are eliminated if their distance to some other training image is more than a threshold.

9.4.1.2 Dense Point-to-Point Correspondence Establishment

The core of the face matcher in the 3D-FRRS is the dense point-to-point correspondence establishment phase. The main idea is to find the corresponding points of a face in all other faces and represent the faces with these corresponding points, as shown in Fig. 9.10.

This procedure is not an easy task, due to the large amount of variance in human faces and nonrigid expression differences. The ICP algorithm, which linearly transforms a shape so that it has the same translation, rotation and scale with another shape, is frequently used to establish dense correspondence. However, ICP works well under the condition that the faces are in similar scales, and it may fail to establish dense correspondences between significantly different faces or facial regions. Therefore, a procedure for warping the faces without changing their personal characteristics is required. Thin-Plate splines (TPS) model a nonlinear transformation as a sum of smaller deformations, under several strict correspondence constraints that

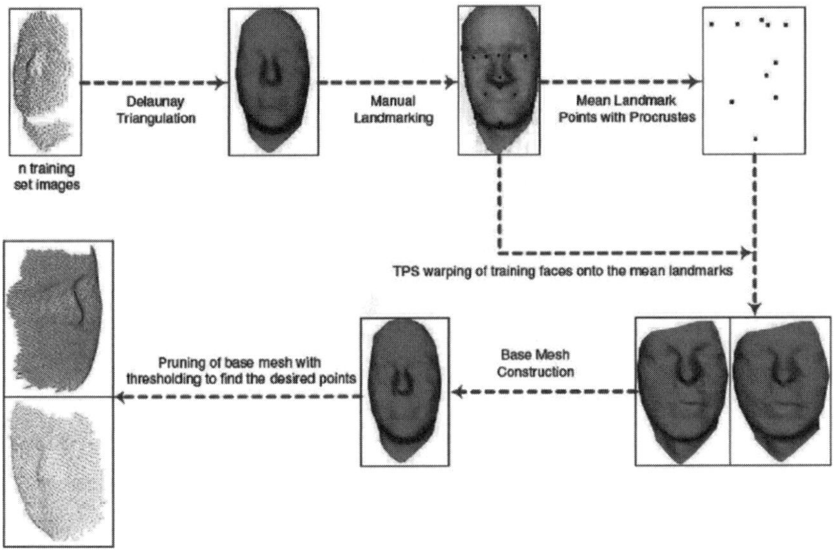

Fig. 9.9 Average face model construction algorithm

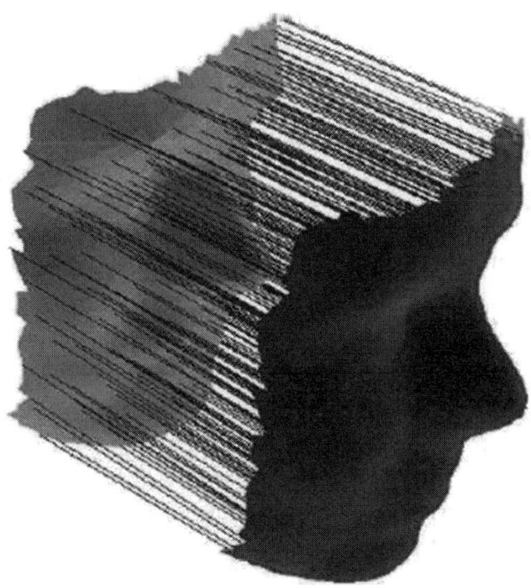

Fig. 9.10 Dense point-to-point correspondence between two faces (from 3D-RMA database [27]) with the 3D Face Recognition Reference System (3D-FRRS); (see insert for color reproduction of this figure)

are usually associated with the landmarks. By using TPS, the test face's landmark points are exactly transformed onto the AFM landmarks, and the rest of the points are interpolated accordingly. Figure 9.11 shows a test face on the left and its TPS warped version on the right.

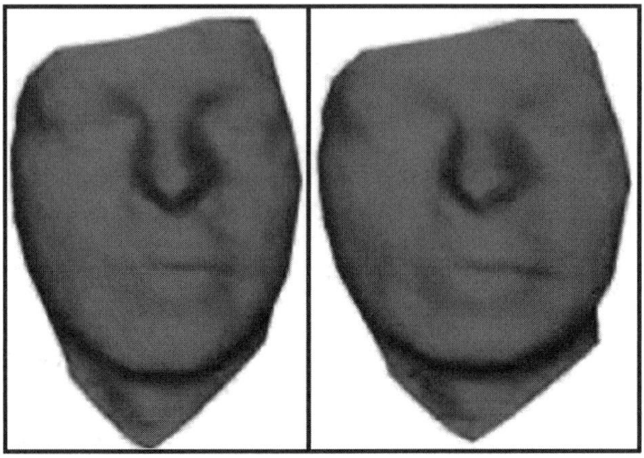

Fig. 9.11 Original face from 3D-RMA database [27] and its Thin-Plate Spline (TPS) warped version in the 3D Face Recognition Reference System (3D-FRRS); (see insert for color reproduction of this figure)

After warping the test face to the AFM, we can easily find the closest points of each vertex in the AFM in the test face. More formally, if there are m points (vertices) in the AFM, we can select m points from the test face, that are the closest points to each AFM vertex. Using this methodology, every test or training face is represented by m correspondent points. In practice, this means that we use the AFM model to infer correspondence between any two faces.

9.4.1.3 Recognition/Matching

Once the point-to-point dense correspondence is established among two faces, the dissimilarity between two facial surfaces can be measured by the total distance of the point sets. This measure is similar to the one used in the ICP matching algorithm. The classification of a test face is performed by selecting the training face that produces the minimum dissimilarity. In general, we use the k-nearest neighbor algorithm as a pattern classifier. Mathematically, the similarity between face A and face B is expressed as

$$d(A,B) = \sum_{i=1}^{m} \|A_i - B_i\| \tag{9.1}$$

where m is the total number of points in correspondence, A_i is the 3D (x,y,z) coordinate of the ith point of the face A, and $\|.\|$ denotes the Euclidean norm.

With the 3D Face Recognition Reference System, identification (one-to-many) and verification (one-to-one) experiments can be done. In the following paragraphs, the proposed benchmarking experimental protocols and results are presented.

9.4.2 Benchmarking Database

The 3D-RMA [27] database is chosen for the benchmarking experiments. It is a structural light-based database of 120 individuals, where six images are collected in two different sessions for each individual. Due to errors in the acquisition steps, some of the faces contain a significant amount of noise. There are slight pose variations in the 3D-RMA for left/right and up/down directions. Although faces are generally neutral, some subjects have smiling expressions. Some artifacts such as glasses, hair, beard and mustache are also present. All of the faces have almost uniform scale. On the average, faces contain about 4,000 3D points. Preprocessing reduces this number to 2,239. The low acquisition quality is an additional challenge when working with this database.

9.4.3 Benchmarking Protocols

With six shots recorded for each subject, different experimental protocols can be defined. Experimental protocols related to verification and identification tasks are defined, denoted as *Verif.* and *Identif. Exp.*. For the benchmarking verification experiments, only protocols using one image for the enrollment are considered. The results of experiments using more shots at the enrollment stage are shown in Sect. 9.5. For each of the 106 subjects, the database has been divided into two different sets:

- An enrollment data set that contains only one shot for each person.
- A test data set that contains the remaining shots for each person.

In order to have statistically significant results, five-fold experiments are defined, each fold representing a different combination of enrollment and test samples. A verification system should compare each 3D shot of the test set to the shots of the training set. For each fold, the total number of trials is

- $87 \times 5 + 19 \times 4 = 511$ genuine trials
- $87 \times (86 \times 5 + 19 \times 4) + 19 \times (18 \times 4 + 87 \times 5) = 53{,}655$ impostor trials

The benchmarking $(1-5$ fold) verification protocols, are denoted as *Verif. Fold 1–5*. The mean result is denoted as *Verif. Fold 1–5 (mean)*. For the identification experiments, two benchmarking experiments are proposed (denoted as *Identif. E1* and *Identif. E4*), which illustrate the influence of the number of enrollment images.

9.4.4 Benchmarking Verification and Identification Results

The recognition results (split in their verification and identification parts) of the benchmarking system are presented in this section.

9.4.4.1 Benchmarking Verification Results

A summary of the reproducible benchmarking verification results is given in Table 9.10. The corresponding DET curves are displayed in Fig. 9.12.

Table 9.10 Equal Error Rates (EER) in %, with their Confidence Intervals (CI), of the 3D reference system (3D-FRRS v1.0) in verification mode, for experiments Verif. Fold 1–5, and their average Verif. Fold 1–5(mean)

Verification folds	EER %	CI
1	12.32	[±1.31]
2	12.72	[±1.33]
3	12.32	[±1.31]
4	11.18	[±1.26]
5	12.48	[±1.32]
Verif. Fold 1–5 (mean)	12.21	[±1.31]

9.4.4.2 Benchmarking Identification Results

For the identification experiments, two benchmarking experiments are proposed (denoted as *Identif. E1* and *Identif. E4*), which illustrate the influence of the number of enrollment images. In *E1* and *E4* experiments, training (enrollment) set contains one and four samples per person, respectively. The mean identification results are presented in Table 9.11.

Besides the proposed benchmarking experiments, other experimental protocols are defined and tested. They are also compared to other published results using the same database. They are presented in the following section.

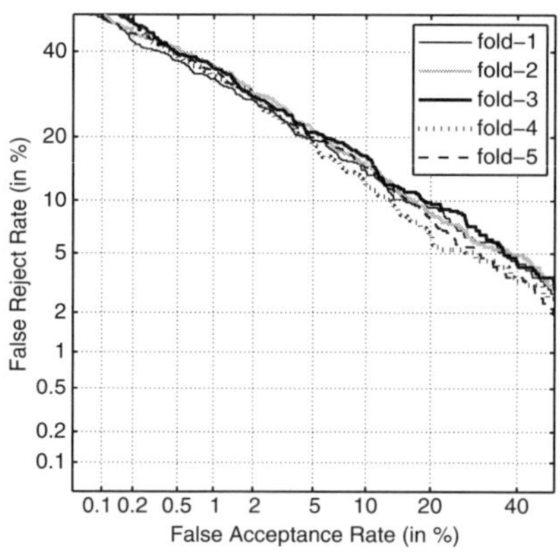

Fig. 9.12 DET curves of the 3D Face Reference System (3D-FRRS v1.0) in verification mode, for the benchmarking experiments Verif. Fold 1-5

Table 9.11 Correct Identification Rates (IR) of the 3D-FRRS v1.0 in identification mode, for experiments Identif. E1 and E4

Experiment	IR %
Identif. E1	72.33
Identif. E4	92.54

9.5 More Experimental Results with the 3D Reference System

The 3D-RMA face database is commonly used as a performance benchmark database in other publications. Table 9.12 and Table 9.13 present some of the verification and identification performance for the 3D-RMA found in the literature, respectively. However, since there is no standard experimental evaluation methodology for the 3D-RMA database, it is difficult to compare the algorithms. This is largely due to: a) the different number of samples per person used in the (enrollment) training set, b) the different number of subjects used in the experiments, and c) different manual cropping and landmarking. The benchmarking framework proposed in this chapter will avoid more research work done with incomparable reported results. For further comparisons, the proposed benchmarking protocols described in Sect. 9.4, can assure comparable reported results with the benchmarking protocols.

In order to measure the influence of the number of images used at the enrollment more precisely, the following set of experiments are defined. In the first experiment, *E1*, only one shot for each person is put into the training set, and in *E2*, *E3* and *E4*, there are two, three, and four shots per person in the training set, respectively. For

Table 9.12 Comparisons of reported Equal Error Rate (EER) Verification results on the 3D-RMA database and the proposed benchmarking framework (3D-FFRS v1.0)

Method	Subjects	Enrollment images	EER %
Central profile [74]	120	One sample	13.76
SDM [74]	120	One sample	8.79
Profile and surface fusion [74]	120	One sample	7.93
Facial profile [10]	30	N/A	9.50
3D-FRRS v1.0	106	One sample	12.56

Table 9.13 Comparison of reported correct identification rates (IR) in % on the 3D-RMA database, and the proposed benchmarking framework (3D-FRRS)

Method	Configuration	Enrollment Images	IR in %
3D Eigenfaces [99]	120 subjects	Five	71.10
3D Eigenfaces [99]	91 subjects	Five	80.20
3D-FRRS	106 subjects	Four	92.95

each experimental setup, we perform k-fold runs. Each fold represents a different combination of training and test set samples. In *E1*, *E2*, *E3*, and *E4*, the number of folds are 5, 10, 10, and 5, respectively.

The identification power of the 3D-FRRS algorithm is also compared to other techniques. As comparative methods, statistical feature extraction methods were selected as in the FRGC evaluations. 3D face images can be converted to 2D depth images (range images). In this work, we apply Principal Component Analysis (PCA) and Linear Discriminant Analysis (LDA) to the depth images. The distance between two faces is calculated as the Euclidean distance between extracted PCA/LDA coefficients. The resolution of depth images formed in this way is 99×77 pixels.

Table 9.14 presents the correct identification rates of the 3D-FRRS algorithm on the experimental configurations E1, E2, E3, and E4 (second row). On the third and fourth rows, the identification rates of the LDA and PCA-based depth image methods are presented. We only present the identification performance of the depth-image PCA algorithm on the E4 experiment since its accuracy is significantly lower than the other methods. Moreover, since there is only a single training image per person in the E1 experiment, depth-image LDA performance is not available for this experiment. By looking at the performance figures presented in Table 9.14, we see that 3D-FRRS performs better than depth-image based algorithms.

Table 9.14 Comparative analysis of correct Identification Rates (IR) in %, with their confidence intervals

Method	E1	E2	E3	E4
3D-FRRS	72.56 [±2.38]	84.42 [±3.58]	89.50 [±2.94]	92.95 [±1.01]
Depth-image LDA	N/A	47.48 [±3.28]	63.51 [3±.76]	70.67 [±2.06]
Depth-image PCA	N/A	N/A	N/A	45.39 [±3.29]

9.6 Conclusions

Advances in sensing technology and the availability of sufficient computing power has made 3D face recognition one of the main modalities for biometrics. Variability in faces is one of the unsolved challenges in 2D face recognition. Illumination and pose variations are handled to a large degree by using 3D information. For expression recognition, 3D deformation analysis offers a promising alternative [21].

There are a number of questions 3D face recognition research needs to address. In acquisition, the accuracy of cheaper and less-intrusive systems needs to be improved, and temporal sequences should be considered. For registration, automatic landmark localization, artifact removal, scaling, and elimination of errors due to occlusions, glasses, beard, etc., need to be worked out. Ways of deforming the face without losing discriminative information will be beneficial.

It is obvious that information fusion is essential for 3D face recognition. There are many ways of representing and combining texture and shape information. We also distinguish between local and configural processing, where the ideal face recognizer makes use of both. For realistic systems, single training instance cases should be considered, which is a great hurdle to some of the more successful discriminative algorithms. Expression variations can be found in recent databases like FRGCv2, but pose variations also need to be considered. Publicly available 3D datasets and precisely defined experimental protocols are necessary to encourage further research on these topics.

References

1. *The BJUT-3D Large-Scale Chinese Face Database, MISKL-TR-05-FMFR-001*, 2005.
2. B. Achermann and H. Bunke. Classifying range images of human faces with Hausdorff distance. In *Proc. Int. Conf. on Pattern Recognition*, pages 809–813, 2000.
3. B. Achermann, X. Jiang, and H. Bunke. Face recognition using range images. In *Proc. Int. Conf. on Virtual Systems and MultiMedia*, pages 129–136, 1997.
4. H. Çınar Akakın, A.A. Salah, L. Akarun, and B. Sankur. 2d/3d facial feature extraction. In *Proc. SPIE Conference on Electronic Imaging*, 2006.
5. S. Arca, P. Campadelli, and R. Lanzarotti. A face recognition system based on automatically determined facial fiducial points. *Pattern Recognition*, 39:432–443, 2006.
6. V.R. Ayyagari, F. Boughorbel, A. Koschan, and M.A. Abidi. A new method for automatic 3d face registration. In *IEEE Conference on Computer Vision and Pattern Recognition*, 2005.
7. J. Batlle, E. Mouaddib, and J. Salvi. Recent progress in coded structured light as a technique to solve the correspondence problem: a survey. *Pattern Recognition*, 31(7):963–982, 1998.
8. C. BenAbdelkader and P.A. Griffin. Comparing and combining depth and texture cues for face recognition. *Image and Vision Computing*, 23(3):339–352, 2005.
9. P. Besl and N. McKay. A method for registration of 3-d shapes. *IEEE Transactions on Pattern Analysis and Machine Intelligence*, 14(2):239–256, 1992.
10. C. Beumier and M. Acheroy. Automatic 3d face authentication. *Image and Vision Computing*, 18(4):315–321, 2000.
11. C. Beumier and M. Acheroy. Face verification from 3d and grey level cues. *Pattern Recognition Letters*, 22:1321–1329, 2001.
12. F. Blais. Review of 20 years of range sensor development. *Journal of Electronic Imaging*, 13(1):231–240, 2004.
13. V. Blanz and T. Vetter. Face recognition based on fitting a 3d morphable model. *IEEE Transactions on Pattern Analysis and Machine Intelligence*, 25(9):1063–1074, 2003.
14. C. Boehnen and T. Russ. A fast multi-modal approach to facial feature detection. In *Proc. 7th IEEE Workshop on Applications of Computer Vision*, pages 135–142, 2005.
15. F.L. Bookstein. Principal warps: thin-plate splines and the decomposition of deformations. *IEEE Transactions on Pattern Analysis and Machine Intelligence*, 11:567–585, 1989.
16. K. Bowyer, Chang K., and P. Flynn. A survey of approaches and challenges in 3d and multimodal 3d + 2d face recognition. *Computer Vision and Image Understanding*, 101:1–15, 2006.
17. A.M. Bronstein, M.M. Bronstein, and R. Kimmel. Expression-invariant 3d face recognition. In J. Kittler and M.S. Nixon, editors, *Proc. of. Audio- and Video-Based Person Authentication*, pages 62–70, 2003.
18. J.Y. Cartoux, J.T. LaPreste, and M. Richetin. Face authentication or recognition by profile extraction from range images. In *Proc. of the Workshop on Interpretation of 3D Scenes*, pages 194–199, 1989.
19. Face Recognition Grand Challenge-FRGC-2.0. Url: http://face.nist.gov/frgc/.
20. K. Chang, K. Bowyer, and P. Flynn. Multi-modal 2d and 3d biometrics for face recognition. In *Proc. IEEE Int. Workshop on Analysis and Modeling of Faces and Gestures*, 2003.

21. Y. Chang, M. Vieira, M. Turk, and L. Velho. Automatic 3d facial expression analysis in videos. In *Proc. IEEE Int. Workshop on Analysis and Modeling of Faces and Gestures*, 2005.
22. Y. Chen and G. Medioni. Object modeling by registration of multiple range images. *Image and Vision Computing*, 10(3):145–155, 1992.
23. C.S. Chua, F. Han, and Y.K. Ho. 3d human face recognition using point signature. In *Proc. IEEE International Conference on Automatic Face and Gesture Recognition*, pages 233–238, 2000.
24. D. Colbry, X. Lu, A. Jain, and G. Stockman. *Technical Report MSU-CSE-04-39: 3D face feature extraction for recognition*, 2004.
25. D. Colbry, G. Stockman, and A.K. Jain. Detection of anchor points for 3d face verification. In *Proc. IEEE Workshop on Advanced 3D Imaging for Safety and Security*, 2005.
26. C. Conde, A. Serrano, L.J. Rodríguez-Aragón, and E. Cabello. 3d facial normalization with spin images and influence of range data calculation over face verification. In *IEEE Conf. Computer Vision and Pattern Recognition*, 2005.
27. 3D RMA database. http://www.sic.rma.ac.be/~beumier/DB/3d_rma.html.
28. FERET database. Url: http://www.itl.nist.gov/iad/humanid/feret.
29. PIE Database. Url: http://www.ri.cmu.edu/projects/project_418_text.html.
30. UND database. Url: http://www.nd.edu/
31. T.G. Dietterich. Approximate statistical tests for comparing supervised classification learning algorithms. *Neural Computations*, 10:18951923, 1998.
32. H.K. Ekenel, H. Gao, and R. Stiefelhagen. 3-d face recognition using local appearance-based models. *IEEE Trans. Information Forensics and Security*, 2(3/2):630–636, 2007.
33. T. Faltemier, K. Bowyer, and P. Flynn. 3d face recognition with region committee voting. In *Proc. Third Int. Symp. on 3D Data Processing Visualization and Transmission*, pages 318–325, 2006.
34. The BioSecure Benchmarking Framework for Biometrics. http://share.int-evry.fr/svnview-eph/.
35. J. Forest and J. Salvi. A review of laser scanning three dimensional digitisers. *Intelligent Robots and Systems*, pages 73–78, 2002.
36. E. Garcia, J.L. Dugelay, and H. Delingette. Low cost 3d face acquisition and modeling. In *Proc. International Conference on Information Technology: Coding and Computing*, pages 657–661, 2001.
37. B. Gökberk and L. Akarun. Selection and extraction of patch descriptors for 3d face recognition. In *Proc. of Computer and Information Sciences LNCS*, volume 3733, pages 718–727, 2005.
38. B. Gökberk and L. Akarun. Comparative analysis of decision-level fusion algorithms for 3d face recognition. In *Proc. of International Conference on Pattern Recognition*, 2006.
39. B. Gökberk, H. Dutağacı, Aydin Ulaş, L. Akarun, and B. Sankur. Representation plurality and fusion for 3d face recognition. *IEEE Transactions on Systems Man and Cybernetics-Part B: Cybernetics*, 38(1), 2008.
40. B. Gökberk, M.O. İrfanoğlu, and L. Akarun. 3d shape-based face representation and feature extraction for face recognition. *Image and Vision Computing*, 24(8):857–869, 2006.
41. B. Gökberk, A.A. Salah, and L. Akarun. Rank-based decision fusion for 3d shape-based face recognition. In T. Kanade, A. Jain, and N.K. Ratha, editors, *Lecture Notes in Computer Science*, volume 3546, pages 1019–1028, 2005.
42. G. Gordon. Face recognition based on depth and curvature features. In *SPIE Proc.: Geometric Methods in Computer Vision*, volume 1570, pages 234–247, 1991.
43. C. Gu, B. Yin, Y. Hu, and S. Cheng. Resampling based method for pixel-wise correspondence between 3d faces. In *Proc. International Conference on Information Technology: Coding and Computing*, volume 1, pages 614–619, 2004.
44. T. Heseltine, N. Pears, and J. Austin. Three-dimensional face recognition using combinations of surface feature map subspace components. *Image and Vision Computing*, 26:382–396, 2008.

45. C. Hesher, A. Srivastava, and G. Erlebacher. A novel technique for face recognition using range imaging. In *Proc. 7th Int. Symposium on Signal Processing and Its Applications*, pages 201–204, 2003.
46. M. Hüsken, M. Brauckmann, S. Gehlen, and C. von der Malsburg. Strategies and benefits of fusion of 2d and 3d face recognition. In *Proc. IEEE Conf. Computer Vision and Pattern Recognition*, 2005.
47. IV2: Identification par l'Iris et le Visage via la Vidéo. http://iv2.ibisc.fr/PageWeb-IV2.html.
48. A4vision Inc. http://www.a4vision.com/.
49. Cyberware Inc. http://www.cyberware.com/products/scanners/ps.html.
50. Genex Technologies Inc. http://www.genextech.com/.
51. Geometrics Inc. http://www.geometrics.com/.
52. M.O. İrfanoğlu, B. Gökberk, and L. Akarun. 3d shape-based face recognition using automatically registered facial surfaces. In *Proc. Int. Conf. on Pattern Recognition*, volume 4, pages 183–186, 2004.
53. I. Kakadiaris, G. Passalis, G. Toderici, N. Murtuza, Y. Lu, N. Karampatziakis, and T. Theoharis. 3d face recognition in the presence of facial expressions: an annotated deformable model approach. *IEEE Trans. Pattern Analysis and Machine Intelligence*, 29(4):640–649, 2007.
54. J. Kittler, A. Hilton, M. Hamouz, and J. Illingworth. 3d assisted face recognition: A survey of 3d imaging, modelling and recognition approaches. In *Proc. IEEE Conf. Computer Vision and Pattern Recognition*, 2005.
55. S. Lao, Y. Sumi, M. Kawade, and F. Tomita. 3d template matching for pose invariant face recognition using 3d facial model built with iso-luminance line based stereo vision. In *Proc. Int. Conf. on Pattern Recognition*, volume 2, pages 911–916, 2000.
56. J. Lee, B. Moghaddam, H. Pfister, and R. Machiraju. *Silhouette-Based 3D Face Shape Recovery*, 2003.
57. Y. Lee, K. Park, J. Shim, and T. Yi. 3d face recognition using statistical multiple features for the local depth information. In *Proc. ICVI*, 2003.
58. X. Lu, D. Colbry, and A.K. Jain. Three-dimensional model based face recognition. In *Proc. Int. Conf. on Pattern Recognition*, 2004.
59. X. Lu and A.K. Jain. Deformation analysis for 3d face matching. In *Proc. IEEE WACV*, 2005.
60. X. Lu and A.K. Jain. *Multimodal Facial Feature Extraction for Automatic 3D Face Recognition Technical Report MSU-CSE-05-22*, 2005.
61. X. Lu, A.K. Jain, and D. Colbry. Matching 2.5d face scans to 3d models. *IEEE Transactions on Pattern Analysis and Machine Intelligence*, 28(1), 2006.
62. S. Malassiotis and M.G. Strintzis. Pose and illumination compensation for 3d face recognition. In *Proc. International Conference on Image Processing*, 2004.
63. T. Maurer, D. Guigonis, I. Maslov, B. Pesenti, A. Tsaregorodtsev, D. West, and G. Medioni. Performance of Geometrix ActiveId 3d face recognition engine on the FRGC data. In *Proc. IEEE Workshop Face Recognition Grand Challenge Experiments*, 2005.
64. G. Medioni and R. Waupotitsch. Face recognition and modeling in 3d. In *IEEE Int. Workshop on Analysis and Modeling of Faces and Gestures*, pages 232–233, 2003.
65. K. Messer, J. Matas, J. Kittler, J. Luettin, and G. Maitre. XM2VTSDB: The extended M2VTS database. In *Proc. 2nd International Conference on Audio and Video-based Biometric Person Authentication*, 1999.
66. Ajmal S. Mian, Mohammed Bennamoun, and Robyn Owens. An efficient multimodal 2d-3d hybrid approach to automatic face recognition. *IEEE Transactions on Pattern Analysis and Machine Intelligence*, 29(11):1927–1943, 2007.
67. A.S. Mian, M. Bennamoun, and R. Owens. Three-dimensional model-based object recognition and segmentation in cluttered scenes. *IEEE Trans. Pattern Analysis and Machine Intelligence*, 28(10):1584–1601, 2006.
68. A.B. Moreno and Á. Sánchez. Gavabdb: A 3d face database. In *Proc. 2nd COST275 Workshop on Biometrics on the Internet*, 2004.
69. A.B. Moreno, Á. Sánchez, J.F. Vélez, and F.J. Díaz. Face recognition using 3d surface-extracted descriptors. In *Proc. IMVIPC*, 2003.

70. T. Nagamine, T. Uemura, and I. Masuda. 3d facial image analysis for human identification. In *Proc. Int. Conf. on Pattern Recognition*, pages 324–327, 1992.
71. Minolta Vivid 910 non-contact 3D laser scanner. http://www.minoltausa.com/vivid/.
72. University of York 3D Face Database. http://www-users.cs.york.ac.uk/~tomh/ 3dface-database.html.
73. G. Pan, Y. Wu, Z. Wu, and W. Liu. 3d face recognition by profile and surface matching. In *Proc. IJCNN*, volume 3, pages 2169–2174, 2003.
74. G. Pan and Z. Wu. 3d face recognition from range data. *Int. Journal of Image and Graphics*, 5(3):573–583, 2005.
75. T. Papatheodorou and D. Rueckert. Evaluation of automatic 4d face recognition using surface and texture registration. In *Proc. AFGR*, pages 321–326, 2004.
76. G. Passalis, I.A. Kakadiaris, T. Theoharis, G. Toderici, and N. Murtuza. Evaluation of 3d face recognition in the presence of facial expressions: an annotated deformable model approach. In *Proc. IEEE Conf. Computer Vision and Pattern Recognition*, 2005.
77. D. Petrovska-Delacrétaz, S. Lelandais, J. Colineau, L. Chen, B. Dorizzi, E. Krichen, M.A. Mellakh, A. Chaari, S. Guerfi, J. DHose, M. Ardabilian, and B. Ben Amor. The iv^2 multi-modal (2d, 3d, stereoscopic face, talking face and iris) biometric database, and the iv^2 2007 evaluation campaign. *In Proc. IEEE Second International Conference on Biometrics: Theory, Applications (BTAS)*, Washington DC USA, September 2008.
78. P. Jonathon Phillips, W. Todd Scruggs, Alice J. OToole, Patrick J. Flynn, Kevin W. Bowyer, Cathy L. Schott, and Matthew Sharpe. *FRVT 2006 and ICE 2006 Large-Scale Results (NISTIR 7408)*, March 2007.
79. P.J. Phillips, P.J. Flynn, T. Scruggs, K.W. Bowyer, and W. Worek. Preliminary face recognition grand challenge results. In *Proceedings 7th International Conference on Automatic Face and Gesture Recognition*, pages 15–24, 2006.
80. P.J. Phillips, P.J. Flynn, W.T. Scruggs, K.W. Bowyer, J. Chang, K. Hoffman, J. Marques, J. Min, and W.J. Worek. Overview of the face recognition grand challenge. In *Proc. IEEE Conf. Computer Vision and Pattern Recognition*, volume 1, pages 947–954, 2005.
81. D. Riccio and J.L. Dugelay. Asymmetric 3d/2d processing: a novel approach for face recognition. In 13th *Int. Conf. on Image Analysis and Processing LNCS*, volume 3617, pages 986–993, 2005.
82. S. Rusinkiewicz and M. Levoy. Efficient variants of the ICP algorithm. In *Proc. of 3DIM01*, pages 145–152, 2001.
83. A. A. Salah and L. Akarun. 3d facial feature localization for registration. In *Proc. Int. Workshop on Multimedia Content Representation, Classification and Security LNCS*, volume 4105/2006, pages 338–345, 2006.
84. A.A. Salah, N. Alyüz, and L. Akarun. Registration of 3d face scans with average face models. *Journal of Electronic Imaging*, 17(1), 2008.
85. J. Salvi, C. Matabosch, D. Fofi, and J. Forest. A review of recent range image registration methods with accuracy evaluation. *Image and Vision Computing*, 25(5):578–596, 2007.
86. A. Srivastava, X. Liu, and C. Hesher. Face recognition using optimal linear components of range images. *Image and Vision Computing*, 24:291–299, 2006.
87. H. Tanaka, M. Ikeda, and H. Chiaki. Curvature-based face surface recognition using spherical correlation. In *Proc. ICFG*, pages 372–377, 1998.
88. R. Y. Tsai. An efficient and accurate camera calibration technique for 3d machine vision. In *IEEE Computer Vision and Pattern Recognition*, pages 364–374, 1987.
89. F. Tsalakanidou, S. Malassiotis, and M. Strinzis. Integration of 2d and 3d images for enhanced face authentication. In *Proc. AFGR*, pages 266–271, 2004.
90. F. Tsalakanidou, D. Tzovaras, and M. Strinzis. Use of depth and colour eigenfaces for face recognition. *Pattern Recognition Letters*, 24:1427–1435, 2003.
91. S. Tsutsumi, S. Kikuchi, and M. Nakajima. Face identification using a 3d gray-scale image-a method for lessening restrictions on facial directions. In *Proc. AFGR*, pages 306–311, 1998.
92. M. B. Vieira, L. Velho, A. Sa, and P. C. Carvalho. A camera-projector system for real-time 3d video. In *Proc. IEEE Computer Society Conference on Computer Vision and Pattern Recognition*, page 96, 2005.

93. Y. Wang, C. Chua, and Y. Ho. Facial feature detection and face recognition from 2d and 3d images. *Pattern Recognition Letters*, 23(1191-1202), 2002.
94. Y. Wang and C.-S. Chua. Face recognition from 2d and 3d images using 3d Gabor filters. *Image and Vision Computing*, 23(11):1018–1028, 205.
95. B. Weyrauch, J. Huang, B. Heisele, and V. Blanz. Component-based face recognition with 3d morphable models. In *Proc. First IEEE Workshop on Face Processing in Video*, 2004.
96. L. Wiskott, J.-M Fellous, N. Krüger, and C. von der Malsburg. Face recognition by elastic bunch graph matching. *IEEE Transactions on Pattern Analysis and Machine Intelligence*, 19(7):775–779, 1997.
97. K. Wong, K. Lam, and W. Siu. An efficient algorithm for human face detection and facial feature extraction under different conditions. *Pattern Recognition*, 34:1993–2004, 2001.
98. C. Xu, Y. Wang, T. Tan, and L. Quan. Automatic 3d face recognition combining global geometric features with local shape variation information. In *Proc. AFGR*, pages 308–313, 2004.
99. C. Xu, Y. Wang, T. Tan, and L. Quan. A new attempt to face recognition using eigenfaces. In *Proc. of the Sixth Asian Conf. on Computer Vision*, volume 2, pages 884–889, 2004.
100. Y. Yacoob and L. S. Davis. Labeling of human face components from range data. *CVGIP: Image Understanding*, 60(2):168–178, 1994.
101. L. Zhang and D. Samaras. Face recognition under variable lighting using harmonic image exemplars. In *Proc. IEEE Conf. Computer Vision and Pattern Recognition*, volume 1, pages 19–25, 2003.

Chapter 10
Talking-face Verification

Hervé Bredin, Aurélien Mayoue, and Gérard Chollet

Abstract This chapter addresses the relatively new area of identity verification based on talking faces. This biometric modality is intrinsically multimodal. Indeed, not only does it contain both voice and face modalities, but it also integrates the combined dynamics of voice and lip motion. First, an overview of the state of the art in the field of talking faces is given. The benchmarking evaluation framework for talking-face modality is then introduced. This framework (which is composed of reference systems, the well-known BANCA database, and its associated Pooled protocol P) aims to ensure a fair comparison of various talking-face verification algorithms. Next, research prototypes, whose main innovation is the use of a globally defined audiovisual synchrony, are evaluated within the benchmarking framework.

10.1 Introduction

Numerous studies have exposed the limits of biometric identity verification based on a single modality (such as fingerprint, iris, handwritten signature, voice, face). The talking face modality, which includes both face recognition and speaker verification, is a natural choice for multimodal biometrics. Talking faces provide richer opportunities for verification than does any ordinary multimodal fusion. The signal contains not only voice and image but also a third source of information: the simultaneous dynamics of these features. Natural lip motion and the corresponding speech signal are synchronized.

However, this specificity is often forgotten and most of the existing talking-face verification systems are based on the fusion of the scores of two separate modules of face verification and speaker verification. Even though this prevalent paradigm may lead to the best performance on widespread evaluation frameworks based on random impostor scenarios, the question of its performance against real life impostor attacks has to be studied.

D. Petrovska-Delacrétaz et al. (eds.), *Guide to Biometric Reference Systems and Performance Evaluation*, DOI 10.1007/978-1-84800-292-0_10,

10.2 State of the Art in Talking-face Verification

In the existing literature, talking-face identity verification is often referred to as audio-visual biometrics [1], which mostly consists of the fusion at score level of two modalities: speaker and face verification. It is not the purpose of this chapter to look deeply into the fusion process: it has already been widely and exhaustively covered in the literature [60]. Furthermore, the problem of speaker and face verification are also covered in Chaps. 7 and 8. This state of the art will focus on what makes the talking-face modality special and worth a look.

10.2.1 Face Verification from a Video Sequence

The most obvious specificity of face verification through talking face is the availability of a sequence of frames where *classical* face verification is only allowed to use one or a few pictures of a face. A face verification algorithm (whether it makes use of still pictures or a video sequence) is usually made of three different modules: one for face detection, another one for features extraction, and the last one dedicated to comparison between features. Each of these three modules can benefit from the additional pieces of information (which may sometimes be redundant) carried by video sequences.

10.2.1.1 Face Detection

Motion information is particularly useful to improving the face detection module. It was originally computed by Turk et al. [69] as a raw difference of pixel value between two successive frames, and to narrow down the region of interest where to look for a face. However, this simple approach is very sensitive to background noise that can happen behind the person to be identified. The association of color and motion information [22] leads to a more robust detection of candidate regions of interest for face. Nevertheless, this kind of method still relies on classical *still* face detection algorithms in the final step [70]. Face detection can also be performed through the frames of a video sequence by detecting the face on the first frame and then performing tracking for the following frames. This can be done by many methods: CAMshift [8] or particle filtering combined with appearance model for instance [73].

10.2.1.2 Feature Extraction

Preliminary work on face verification from video sequences consider the latter as a collection of independent pictures and features are extracted from one or a few randomly chosen frames or from every single frame of the sequences, in the way it is classically done for *still* face verification [72]. An improvement of this approach consists in keeping only the *best* frames according to a pre-defined criteria. As a matter of fact, a nonfrontal pose, bad lighting conditions or a nonneutral face expression can lead to degraded overall performance of the system. Thus, the Distance From Face Space (DFFS) is used as a measure of *faceness* of a face candidate and allows to reject frames that are likely to produce incorrect results [69]. As shown in Fig. 10.1, DFFS is the distance between the face and its projection on the eigenface principal components.

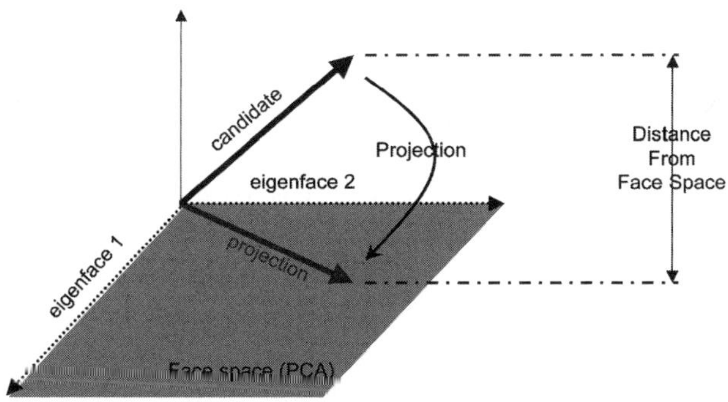

Fig. 10.1 Distance From Face Space (DFFS)

More recently, variations in pose of the face through a video sequence are used in order to perform a 3D reconstruction of the face [23] allowing to proceed with 3D features extraction [72]. A generic 3D model is used in [22] in order to estimate the pose and the orientation of the face and artificially reconstruct a neutral frontal view of the face for each frame of the sequence. Finally, the availability of video sequence of moving face allows for the extraction of dynamic information related to the motion of the face and facial parts. In [61] for instance, the orientation of the face, the blinking of eyes and the openness of the mouth are used as dynamic face features.

10.2.1.3 Model Creation and Comparison

The abundance of biometric samples available from the video sequence leads to new approaches for comparison and modeling. Classical still face verification algorithms do not use any model. Test features are usually directly compared to features extracted from the enrollment data. A direct extension of this principle to video sequences is to use a voting scheme: the n frames extracted from the test video sequence are compared, one by one, to the m frames extracted from the enrollment video sequence. Each of the $n \times m$ comparisons can lead to a decision (accepted or rejected) and a majority vote gives the final decision. Other voting schemes can be used, such as minimum or average distance, for instance. It is shown in [46] that the overall performance is improved when more samples are used. While statistical modeling is not reliable with only one sample, it is possible to learn statistical models from a large collection of samples from the same person. Thus, in [6], a one-class SVM is trained using all the frames of the enrollment sequence. Extending the classical speaker verification approach to face verification, we proposed in [9, 12] to model the face of a person by a Gaussian mixture model using the EM algorithm. Pseudo-hierarchical hidden Markov models are proposed by the authors of [7], where the number of states is determined automatically depending on the motion of the face.

10.2.2 Liveness Detection

As previously mentioned, most of the talking-face biometric systems are only based on the fusion of the scores produced by a speaker verification algorithm and a face verification algorithm. Therefore, if no verification of the actual presence of a real person in front of the camera is performed, such a system would be easily fooled by an impostor who shows a picture of the face of his/her target while playing a recording of his/her voice. These kind of attacks (called replay attacks) are rarely considered in the literature even though they can be considered as the most dangerous threat for audiovisual biometric systems.

10.2.2.1 Random Utterance

The first barrier against this type of attack could also be used for a speaker verification system. It consists of asking the person to pronounce a random utterance, and an automatic speech recognizer allows checking the correctness of what is pronounced. This simple method prevents the use of an audio recording of the voice of the target by an impostor.

10.2.2.2 Motion

Another solution (which is specific to face verification from video sequences) consists of the analysis of the motion of the face and its parts in order to verify it is not a fake one (a picture, for instance). In [45], the motion of some parts of the face (nose, ears, eyes, ...) is compared, and depending on whether they are close to each other or not, the access is decided to be a fake (the motion of each part of a face are nearly identical in case of a picture) or a real access. In [43], the regions of the two eyes are detected and their variation allows the authors to decide if the access is real.

10.2.3 Audiovisual Synchrony

A third solution that benefits from the multimodal status of a talking face is to evaluate the degree of synchrony between the voice acquired by the microphone and the motion of the lip of the person in front of the camera. Note that the notion of synchrony is used here in a special way—referring to the global temporal coherence between the visual and audio information channels instead of the local coherence between visual and audio events.

In this section[1], an overview of the acoustic and visual front-end processing is first given. They are often very similar to the one used for speech recognition and speaker verification, though a tendency to simplify them as much as possible has been noticed. Moreover, linear transformations aiming at improving joint audiovisual modeling are often performed as a preliminary step before measuring the audiovisual correspondence: they are discussed in Sect. 10.2.3.2 and the correspondence measures proposed in the literature are finally presented in Sect. 10.2.3.3.

10.2.3.1 Front-end Processing

This section reviews the speech front-end processing techniques used in the literature for audio-visual speech processing in the specific framework of audiovisual speech synchrony measures. They all share the common goal of reducing the raw data in order to achieve a good subsequent modeling.

Acoustic Speech Processing Acoustic speech parametrization is classically performed on overlapping sliding windows of the original audio signal.

Short-time Energy The raw amplitude of the audio signal can be used as is. In [37], the authors extract the average acoustic energy on the current window as their one-dimensional audio feature. Similar methods such as root mean square amplitude or log-energy were also proposed [4, 13].

Periodogram In [31], a [0–10 kHz] periodogram of the audio signal is computed on a sliding window of length $2/29.97$ s (corresponding to the duration of two frames of the video) and directly used as the parametrization of the audio stream.

Mel-Frequency Cepstral Coefficients (MFCC) The use of MFCC parametrization is very frequent in the literature [63, 24, 54, 41, 18]. There is a practical reason for that: it is the state-of-the-art [59] parametrization for speech processing in general, including speech recognition and speaker verification.

Linear-Predictive Coding (LPC) and Line Spectral Frequencies (LSF) Linear-Predictive Coding, and its derivation Line Spectral Frequencies [67], have also been widely investigated. The latter are often preferred because they are directly related to the vocal tract resonances [71].

[1] This section is reproduced with permission from Hindawi, source [11].

A comparison of these different acoustic speech features is performed in [63] in the framework of the *FaceSync* linear operator, which is presented in the next section. To summarize, in their specific framework, the authors conclude that MFCC, LSF and LPC parametrization lead to a stronger correlation with the visual speech than spectrogram and raw energy features. This result is coherent with the observation that these features are the ones known to give good results for speech recognition.

Visual Speech Processing In this section, we will refer to the grayscale mouth area as the region of interest. It can be much larger than the sole lip area and can include jaw and cheeks. In the rest of the chapter, it is assumed that the detection of this region of interest has already been performed. Most visual speech features proposed in the literature are shared by studies in audiovisual speech recognition. However, some much more simple visual features are also used for synchronization detection.

Raw Intensity of Pixels This is the visual equivalent of the audio raw energy. In [37] and [41], the intensity of gray-level pixels is used as is. In [13], their sum over the whole region of interest is computed, leading to a one-dimensional feature.

Holistic Methods Holistic methods consider and process the region of interest as a whole source of information. In [54], a two-dimensional Discrete Cosine Transform (DCT) is applied on the region of interest and the most energetic coefficients are kept as visual features: it is a well-known method in the field of image compression. Linear transformations taking into account the specific distribution of grayscale in the region of interest were also investigated. Thus, in [14], the authors perform a projection of the region of interest on vectors resulting from a principal component analysis: they call the principal components "eigenlips" by analogy with the well-known "eigenfaces" [68] principle used for face recognition.

Lip-shape Methods Lip-shape methods consider and process lips as a deformable object from which geometrical features can be derived, such as height, width openness of the mouth, position of lip corners, etc. They are often based on fiducial points that need to be automatically located. In [4], videos are recorded using two cameras (one frontal, one from side) and the automatic localization is made easier by the use of face make-up: both frontal and profile measures are then extracted and used as visual features. Mouth width, mouth height and lip protrusion are computed in [36] jointly with what the authors call the relative teeth count, which can be considered as a measure of the visibility of teeth. In [29] [28], a deformable template composed of several polynomial curves follows the lip contours: it allows the computation of the mouth width, height and area. In [18], the lip shape is summarized with a one-dimensional feature: the ratio of lip height and lip width.

Dynamic Features In [19] the authors underline that, though it is widely agreed that an important part of speech information is conveyed dynamically, dynamic features extraction is rarely performed: this observation is also verified for correspondence measures. However, some attempts to capture dynamic information within the extracted features do exist in the literature. Thus, the use of time derivatives is investigated in [33]. In [24], the authors compute the total temporal variation (between two subsequent frames) of pixel values in the region of interest, following the equation

$$v_t = \sum_{x=1}^{W} \sum_{y=1}^{H} |I_t(x,y) - I_{t+1}(x,y)| \quad (10.1)$$

where $I_t(x,y)$ is the grey-level pixel value of the region of interest at position (x,y) in frame t.

Frame Rates Audio and visual sample rates are classically very different. For speaker verification, for example, MFCCs are usually extracted every 10 ms, whereas videos are often encoded at a frame rate of 25 images per second. Therefore, it is often required to down-sample audio features or up-sample visual features in order to equalize audio and visual sample rates. However, though the extraction of raw energy or periodogram can be performed directly on a larger window, down-sampling audio features is known to be very bad for speech recognition. Therefore, up-sampling visual features is often preferred (with linear interpolation, for example). One could also think of using a camera able to produce 100 images per second. Finally, some studies (like the one presented in Sect. 10.2.3.4) directly work on audio and visual features with unbalanced sample rates.

10.2.3.2 Audiovisual Subspaces

In this section, we overview transformations that can be applied on audio, visual and/or audiovisual spaces, with the aim of improving subsequent measure of correspondence between audio and visual clues.

Principal Component Analysis (PCA) PCA is a well-known linear transformation that is optimal for keeping the subspace that has largest variance. The basis of the resulting subspace is a collection of principal components. The first principal component corresponds to the direction of greatest variance of a given dataset. The second principal component corresponds to the direction of second greatest variance, and so on. In [21], PCA is used in order to reduce the dimensionality of a joint audiovisual space (in which audio speech features and visual speech features are concatenated), while keeping the characteristics that contribute most to its variance.

Independent Component Analysis (ICA) ICA was originally introduced to deal with the issue of source separation [38]. In [65], the authors use visual speech features to improve separation of speech sources. In [64], ICA is applied on an audiovisual recording of a piano session: the camera frames a close-up on the keyboard when the microphone is recording the music. ICA allows the authors to clearly find a correspondence between the audio and visual data. However, to our knowledge,

ICA has never been used as a transformation of the audiovisual speech feature space (as in [64] for the piano). A Matlab implementation of ICA [39] is available on the Internet.

Canonical Correlation Analysis (CANCOR) CANCOR is a multivariate statistical analysis allowing to jointly transform the audio and visual feature spaces while maximizing their correlation in the resulting transformed audio and visual feature spaces. Given two synchronized random variables X and Y, the *FaceSync* algorithm presented in [63] uses CANCOR to find canonic correlation matrices $\mathbf{A}$ and $\mathbf{B}$ that whiten X and Y under the constraint of making their cross-correlation diagonal and maximally compact.

Let $\mathcal{X} = (X - \mu_X)^T \mathbf{A}$, $\mathcal{Y} = (Y - \mu_Y)^T \mathbf{B}$ and $\Sigma_{\mathcal{X}\mathcal{Y}} = \mathbb{E}\left[\mathcal{X}\mathcal{Y}^T\right]$. These constraints can be summarized as follows:

- Whitening: $\mathbb{E}\left[\mathcal{X}\mathcal{X}^T\right] = \mathbb{E}\left[\mathcal{Y}\mathcal{Y}^T\right] = I$.
- Diagonal: $\Sigma_{\mathcal{X}\mathcal{Y}} = \mathrm{diag}\{\sigma_1, \ldots, \sigma_M\}$ with $1 \geq \sigma_1 \geq \ldots \geq \sigma_m > 0$ and $\sigma_{m+1} = \ldots = \sigma_M = 0$.
- Maximally compact: for i from 1 to M, the correlation $\sigma_i = \mathrm{corr}(\mathcal{X}_i, \mathcal{Y}_i)$ between $\mathcal{X}_i$ and $\mathcal{Y}_i$ is as large as possible.

The proof of the algorithm for computing $\mathbf{A} = [\mathbf{a}_1, \ldots, \mathbf{a}_m]$ and $\mathbf{B} = [\mathbf{b}_1, \ldots, \mathbf{b}_m]$ is described in [63]. One can show that the $\mathbf{a}_i$ are the normalized eigenvectors (sorted in decreasing order of their corresponding eigenvalue) of matrix $C_{XX}^{-1} C_{XY} C_{YY}^{-1} C_{YX}$ and $\mathbf{b}_i$ is the normalized vector which is collinear to $C_{YY}^{-1} C_{YX} \mathbf{a}_i$, where $C_{XY} = \mathrm{cov}(X, Y)$. A Matlab implementation of this transformation [16] is also available on the Internet.

Co-Inertia Analysis (CoIA) CoIA is quite similar to CANCOR. However, while CANCOR is based on the maximization of the correlation between audio and visual features, CoIA relies on the maximization of their covariance $\mathrm{cov}(\mathcal{X}_i, \mathcal{Y}_i) = \mathrm{corr}(\mathcal{X}_i, \mathcal{Y}_i) \times \mathrm{var}(\mathcal{X}_i) \times \mathrm{var}(\mathcal{Y}_i)$. This statistical analysis was first introduced in biology and is relatively new in our domain. The proof of the algorithm for computing $\mathbf{A}$ and $\mathbf{B}$ can be found in [26]. One can show that the $\mathbf{a}_i$ are the normalized eigenvectors (sorted in decreasing order of their corresponding eigenvalue) of matrix $C_{XY} C_{XY}^t$ and $\mathbf{b}_i$ is the normalized vector that is collinear to $C_{XY}^t \mathbf{a}_i$.

Remark Comparative studies between CANCOR and CoIA are proposed in [36, 29, 28]. The authors of [36] show that CoIA is more stable than CANCOR: the accuracy of the results is much less sensitive to the number of samples available. The *liveness* score proposed in [29, 28] is much more efficient with CoIA than CANCOR. The authors of [29] suggest that this difference is explained by the fact that CoIA is a compromise between CANCOR (where audiovisual correlation is maximized) and PCA (where audio and visual variances are maximized) and therefore benefits from the advantages of both transformations.

10.2.3.3 Correspondence Measures

This section overviews the correspondence measures proposed in the literature to evaluate the synchrony between audio and visual features resulting from audiovisual front-end processing and transformations described in Sect. 10.2.3.1 and Sect. 10.2.3.2.

Pearson's Product-moment Coefficient: Let X and Y be two independent random variables which are normally distributed. The square of their Pearson's product-moment coefficient $R(X,Y)$ (defined in Eq. 10.2) denotes the portion of total variance of X that can be explained by a linear transformation of Y (and reciprocally, since it is a symmetrical measure).

$$R(X,Y) = \frac{\mathrm{cov}\,(X,Y)}{\sigma_X \sigma_Y} \tag{10.2}$$

In [37], the authors compute the Pearson's product-moment coefficient between the average acoustic energy X and the value Y of the pixels of the video to determine which area of the video is more correlated with the audio. This approach permits to decide which of two people appearing in a video is talking.

Mutual Information In information theory, the mutual information $MI(X,Y)$ of two random variables X and Y is a quantity that measures the mutual dependence of the two variables. In the case of X and Y as discrete random variables, it is defined as

$$MI(X,Y) = \sum_{x \in X} \sum_{y \in Y} p(x,y) \log \frac{p(x,y)}{p(x)p(y)} \tag{10.3}$$

It is non-negative ($MI(X,Y) \geq 0$) and symmetrical ($MI(X,Y) = MI(Y,X)$). One can demonstrate that X and Y are independent if and only if $MI(X,Y) = 0$. The mutual information can also be linked to the concept of entropy H in information theory following the equations

$$MI(X,Y) = H(X) - H(X|Y) \tag{10.4}$$

$$MI(X,Y) = H(X) + H(Y) - H(X,Y) \tag{10.5}$$

As shown in [37], in the special case where X and Y are normally distributed monodimensional random variables, the mutual information is related to $R(X,Y)$ via the equation

$$MI(X,Y) = -\frac{1}{2} \log \left(1 - R(X,Y)^2\right) \tag{10.6}$$

In [37, 32, 54, 41], the mutual information is used to locate the pixels in the video that are most likely to correspond to the audio signal—the face of the person who is speaking clearly corresponds to these pixels. However, one can notice that the mouth area is not always the part of the face with the maximum mutual information with the audio signal: it is very dependent on the speaker.

Remark In [14], the mutual information between audio X and time-shifted visual Y_t features is plotted as a function of their temporal offset t. It shows that the mutual information reaches its maximum for a visual delay of between 0 and 120 ms. This observation led the authors of [29, 28] to propose a liveness score $L(X,Y)$ based on the maximum value R_{ref} of the Pearson's coefficient for short-time offset between audio and visual features.

$$R_{\text{ref}} = \max_{-2 \leq t \leq 0} [R(X, Y_t)] \tag{10.7}$$

10.2.3.4 Joint Audiovisual Models

Although the Pearson's coefficient and the mutual information are good at measuring correspondence between two random variables even if they are not linearly correlated (which is what they were primarily defined for), some other methods do not rely on this linear assumption.

Gaussian Mixture Models Lets consider two discrete random variables $X = \{x_t, t \in \mathbb{N}\}$ and $Y = \{y_t, t \in \mathbb{N}\}$ of dimension d_X and d_Y, respectively. Typically, X would be acoustic speech features and Y visual speech features [66, 18]. One can define the discrete random variable $Z = \{z_t, t \in \mathbb{N}\}$ of dimension d_Z where z_t is the concatenation of the two samples x_t and y_t, such as $z_t = [x_t, y_t]$ and $d_Z = d_X + d_Y$.

Given a sample z, the Gaussian Mixture Model λ defines its probability distribution function as follows

$$p(z|\lambda) = \sum_{i=1}^{N} w_i \mathcal{N}(z; \mu_i, \Gamma_i) \tag{10.8}$$

where $\mathcal{N}(\bullet; \mu, \Gamma)$ is the normal distribution of mean μ and covariance matrix Γ. $\lambda = \{w_i, \mu_i, \Gamma_i\}_{i \in [1,N]}$ are parameters describing the joint distribution of X and Y. Using a training set of synchronized samples x_t and y_t concatenated into joint sample z_t, the Expectation-Maximization algorithm (EM) allows the estimation of λ.

Given two sequences of test $X = \{x_t, t \in [1,T]\}$ and $Y = \{y_t, t \in [1,T]\}$, a measure of their correspondence $C_\lambda(X,Y)$ can be computed as

$$C_\lambda(X,Y) = \frac{1}{T} \sum_{t=1}^{T} p([x_t, y_t]|\lambda) \tag{10.9}$$

Then the application of a threshold θ decides on whether the acoustic speech X and the visual speech Y correspond to each other (if $C_\lambda(X,Y) > \theta$) or not (if $C_\lambda(X,Y) \leq \theta$).

Remark λ is well-known to be speaker-dependent: GMM-based systems are the state of the art for speaker verification. However, there are often not enough training samples from speaker S to correctly estimate the model λ_S using the EM algorithm. Therefore, one can adapt the world model λ_Ω (estimated on a large set of training samples from a population as large as possible) using the few samples available from speaker S into a model λ_S. It is not the purpose of this chapter to review adaptation techniques, the reader can refer to [59] for more information.

Hidden Markov Models Like the Pearson's coefficient and the mutual information, time offset between acoustic and visual speech features is not modeled using GMMs. Therefore, the authors of [54] propose to model audio-visual speech with Hidden Markov Models (HMMs). Two speech recognizers are trained, one classical audio only recognizer [58], and an audiovisual speech recognizer as described in [57]. Given a sequence of audiovisual samples $([x_t, y_t], t \in [1, T])$, the audio-only system gives a word hypothesis W. Then, using the HMM of the audiovisual system, what the authors call a measure of plausibility $P(X,Y)$ is computed as follows:

$$P(X,Y) = p([x_1, y_1]...[x_T, y_T]|W) \tag{10.10}$$

An Asynchronous Hidden Markov Model (AHMM) for audio-visual speech recognition is proposed in [5]. It assumes that there is always an audio observation x_t and sometimes a visual observation y_s at time t. It intrinsically models the difference of sample rates between audio and visual speech, by introducing the probability that the system emits the next visual observation y_s at time t. AHMM appears to outperform HMM in the task of audio-visual speech recognition [5] while naturally resolving the problem of different audio and visual sample rates.

Nonparametric Models The use of Neural Networks (NN) is investigated in [24]. Given a training set of both synchronized and not synchronized audio and visual speech features, a neural network with one hidden layer is trained to output one when the audiovisual input features are synchronized and zero when they are not. Moreover, the authors propose to use an input layer at time t consisting of $[X_{t-N_X}, \ldots, X_t, \ldots, X_{t+N_X}]$ and $[Y_{t-N_Y}, \ldots, Y_t, \ldots, Y_{t+Y}]$ (instead of X_t and Y_t), choosing N_X and N_Y such that about 200 ms of temporal context is given as an input. This proposition is a way of solving the well-known problem of coarticulation and the already mentioned lag between audio and visual speech. It also removes the need for down-sampling audio features (or up-sampling visual features).

10.2.4 Audiovisual Speech

The last specificity of talking-face biometrics is the *talking* part of it. Indeed, lip motion can be used as a complementary source of information to acoustic speech. Fusion of audio and visual speech classically falls in one of those three categories: at score level, feature level, or classifier level [19].

Score Fusion The vast majority of audiovisual speaker verification systems are based on score fusion of one acoustic-only and one visual-only speaker verification systems. Acoustic speaker verification is described in Chap. 7, therefore we will only focus on the description of the visual-only speaker verification systems, which are often a direct application of acoustic speaker verification systems to visual features. Speaker-dependent visual-only hidden Markov models are trained using lip shape features in [44], eigenlips in [25] and DCT coefficients of the mouth are in [62]. The authors of [34] conclude that Gaussian mixture modeling might be as efficient as hidden Markov modeling since the best performance is obtained with a one-state HMM. Most of these works have in common the conclusion that score fusion of unimodal acoustic and visual-only verification systems is a simple yet efficient way of improving the overall error rate of recognition, especially in noisy environments.

Feature Fusion Feature fusion consists of the combination of two or more monomodal feature vectors into one multimodal features vector to be used as the input of a common multimodal identity verification algorithm. Audio and visual frame rates are different. Typically, 100 audio feature vectors are extracted per second whereas only 25 video frames are available during the same period. Therefore, one solution is to perform linear interpolation of the visual feature vectors [62, 9]. Another one is to downsample the audio features to reach the video frame rate [2]. Concatenated acoustic and visual features are used as the input for a MultiLayer Perceptron (MLP) in [20] and GMM in [2]. The curse of dimensionality is evoked and one proposed solution is to apply Principal Component Analysis (PCA) or Linear Discriminant Analysis (LDA) on audiovisual features [20] in order to achieve a better modeling and improved performance. In [62], canonical correlation analysis is used to extract acoustic and visual features with lower dimensions and higher cross-correlation, thus allowing better joint HMM modeling. As for score fusion, feature fusion is efficient especially in noisy environments.

Classifier Fusion In classifier fusion, classifiers are intrinsically designed to deal with the bimodal nature of audiovisual speech. Thus, coupled-HMM can be described as two parallel HMM where transition probabilities depend on the states of both of them. They are used in [53] with LDA-transformed eigenlips as visual features and classical MFCC coefficients as acoustic features. Product HMM [47] takes into account the asynchrony between acoustic and visual speech: an acoustic transition does not necessarily correspond to a visual transition. Finally, asynchronous HMM [5] intrinsically models the difference of sampling rates between acoustic and visual features, by considering the probability of the existence of a visual feature vector.

10.3 Evaluation Framework

In order to ensure a fair comparison of various talking-face verification algorithms, a common evaluation framework has to be defined. First, we describe the reference system that can be used as a baseline for future improvements. The database used for the evaluation and the corresponding protocols are then described along with the associated performance measures.

10.3.1 Reference System

The BioSecure talking-face reference system, described also in [9] is based on the fusion of two modalities: face and speech. The face module uses the standard eigenface approach to represent face images (extracted from a given video) in a lower dimensional subspace. The speech module uses the GMM-UBM approach. The fusion module is based on the min-max approach.

10.3.1.1 Face Verification

It is based on the standard eigenface approach [68] to represent face images in a lower dimensional subspace. First, 10 frames are extracted from the video at regular intervals. Using the eye positions detected automatically, each face image is normalized, cropped and projected onto the face space (the face space was built using the 300 images from the BANCA world model and the dimensionality of the reduced space is selected, such as 99% of the variance is explained by the PCA analysis). In this way, 10 feature vectors are produced for a given video. Next, the L1 norm distance measure is used to evaluate the similarity between 10 target and test feature vectors. Finally, the face score is the minimum of these 100 distances.

10.3.1.2 Speaker Verification

The speech processing is performed on 20 ms Hamming windowed frames, with 10 ms overlap. For each frame, a 16-element cepstral vector is computed and appended with first-order deltas. The delta-energy is used in addition. For speech activity detection, a bi-Gaussian model is fitted to the energy component of a speech sample. The threshold t used to determine the set of frames to discard is computed as follows: $t = \mu - 2 * \sigma$, where μ and σ are the mean and the variance of the highest Gaussian component, respectively. Using only the frames corresponding to nonsilent portions, the MFCC-feature vectors are normalized to fit a zero-mean and a unit variance distribution.

The GMM approach is used to build models from the speaker data. An universal background model (UBM) with 256 components has been trained with the EM algorithm using all genuine data of the development database. Then, each speaker model is built by adapting the parameters of the UBM using the speaker's training feature vectors and the maximum a posteriori criterion. At the score calculation step, the MFCC-feature vectors extracted from the test sequence are compared to both the client GMM and the UBM. The speech score is the average log-likelihood ratio.

Note Two open-source systems are used for the speaker verification part of the talking-face reference system: BECARS v1.1.9[2] (with HTK[3]) or ALIZE v1.04 [4]

[2] http://www.tsi.enst.fr/becars/

[3] http://htk.eng.cam.ac.uk/

[4] http://www.lia.univ-avignon.fr/heberges/ALIZE/

(with SPro[5]). In the rest of this chapter, the *BECARS reference system* will refer to the use of BECARS v1.1.9 for the speech module whereas the *ALIZE reference system* will refer to the use of ALIZE v1.04 . It is noted that both reference systems have exactly the same fusion and face verification modules.

10.3.1.3 Fusion Module

The min-max approach [42] is used to fuse the face and speech scores. The fusion parameters have been estimated using all development data.

10.3.2 Evaluation Protocols

10.3.2.1 The Reference Database: BANCA

Several audiovisual databases designed for the evaluation of talking-face verification systems are available. A brief *description* follows, related only to the audiovisual part of the databases:

- BT-DAVID [15]—30 clients recorded on five sessions spaced over several months;
- XM2VTSDB [51]—four recordings (digits and a short sentence) of 295 subjects taken over a period of four month.
- CUAVE [55]—36 different speakers (also contains video with two speakers for speaker localization evaluation).
- BANCA [3]—*described* below.
- Biomet [35]—the audiovisual part is not yet distributed, around 100 people in one or two sessions (a few sentences in French).
- MyIDea [27]—not yet distributed, similar to and compatible with the BANCA and BIOMET databases (in English and French).
- SecurePhone [52]—60 speakers (digits and a short sentence) recorded on three sessions using a PDA.
- IV^2 [40, 56]—315 subjects with one session (77 with two sessions).

We chose to use the well-known BANCA database in order to evaluate the reference systems.

The BANCA database (*Biometric Access control for Networked and e-Commerce Applications*) is an audiovisual database designed to help the development and evaluation of audiovisual authentication algorithms [3]. Audiovisual sequences were acquired in four European languages: each person pronounces ten digits followed by name and address. The constitution of the English part of the BANCA database (the one we used for the reported experiments) is summarized in Fig. 10.2.

[5] http://www.irisa.fr/metiss/guig/spro/index.html

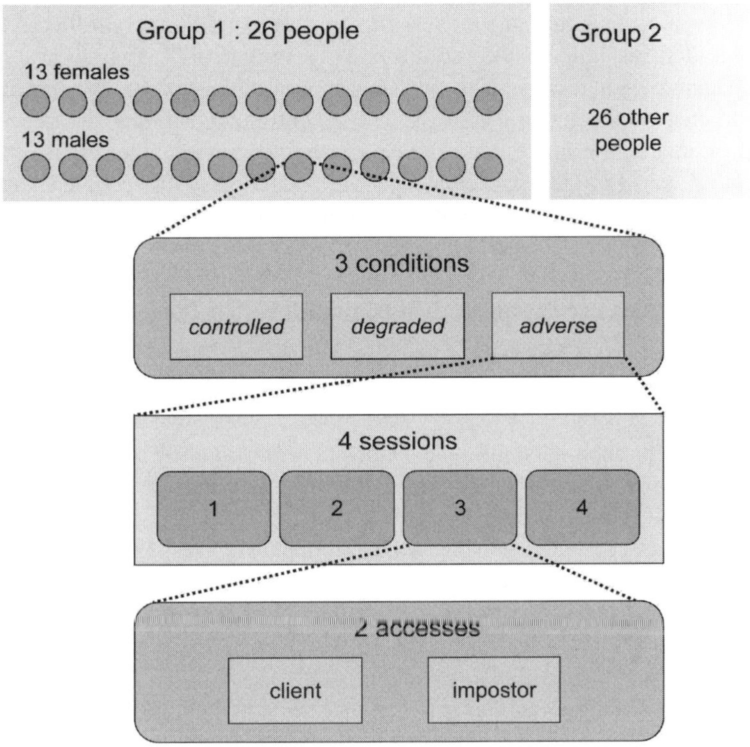

Fig. 10.2 The BANCA database

It is divided into two disjoint groups, hereafter called G1 and G2. Each group contains 26 people (13 females and 13 males). Three recording conditions were used, as shown in Fig. 10.3. In the *controlled* condition, the person appears in a frontal view with a blue background and the acquisition is performed using a DV camera. In the *degraded* condition, the acquisition takes place in an office, using a lower quality webcam. Finally, sequences of the *adverse* condition were acquired in a restaurant where people are walking and talking in the background. In parallel, two microphones, a poor quality one and a good quality one were used for each recording condition.

Fig. 10.3 Example images from the controlled, degraded, and adverse conditions from the BANCA database

Each person participated in four sessions of each condition: controlled sessions (1–4), degraded sessions (5–8), and adverse sessions (9–12). Two accesses were recorded during each session. The first access is a client access: the person pronounces his/her own name and address. The second one is an impostor access: the person pronounces the name and address of another person (the target). A third group (called world model) participated to the collection of 60 sequences from 30 different people and is available for development purpose.

10.3.2.2 The Reference Protocol: the Original BANCA Pooled Protocol

The Pooled protocol is one of the eight protocols originally distributed with the BANCA database [50].

- Enrollment: for each person λ, the sequence corresponding to the client access of the controlled Session 1 may be used as the enrollment biometric sample to build the identity model of person λ.
- Client accesses: for each person λ, the sequences corresponding to the client accesses of the controlled sessions 2–4, degraded sessions 6–8, and adverse sessions 10–12, are compared to the identity model of person λ. Thus, nine client accesses are performed for each person, which makes 234 client accesses per group.
- Impostor accesses: for each person λ, every sequence corresponding to the impostor accesses of person λ (sessions 1–12) is compared to the identity model of the person ε whose name and address is pronounced by person λ ($\varepsilon \neq \lambda$). It appears that each identity model λ is actually compared to every other person ε of the same group and gender. Thus, 12 impostor accesses are performed for each person, which makes 312 impostor accesses per group.

Since the BANCA database is made of two disjoint groups, G1 and G2, G1 can be used as the development set when tests are performed on G2, and vice versa. In the experiments reported herein, only the audio data recorded with the good quality microphone have been used.

10.3.2.3 The Deliberate Impostor Attacks Protocol

The only information about his/her target that is known by the impostor is his/her name and address. No real effort is performed by the impostor while trying to impersonate his/her target. Therefore, these impostor accesses (that we will refer to as random impostor accesses afterwards) appear to be quite unrealistic. Only a fool would attempt to imitate a person knowing so little about them.

In real life, an impostor would have acquired some information about his/her target before trying to impersonate him/her. In the case of audiovisual biometrics, it should be very easy to acquire a picture of the face of the target and a recording of his/her voice (thanks to a telephone call, for example). Showing the picture of the face of the target while playing the audio recording of his/her voice would then be enough to completely fool a talking-face authentication system based on the score fusion of two modules of face and speaker verification.

Such deliberate impostor attacks were simulated. Every original BANCA false claim access was modified according to the following principle: the combination of an audio recording and a video sequence showing a moving picture (as shown in Fig. 10.4), both corresponding to the claimed identity. We will refer to these new impostor accesses as deliberate impostor accesses afterwards.

Fig. 10.4 Deliberate impostor attack

10.3.3 Detection Cost Function

Although DET curves and equal error rates allow comparison of various systems during their development, they cannot be used to evaluate their real-life performance. As a matter of fact, in real working situations, a decision threshold θ (to which verification scores are compared) has to be set once and for all according to a given development set and to expected False Acceptance Rate (FAR) and False Rejection Rate (FRR); the test set being unknown, obviously.

That is why the Detection Cost Function (DCF) will be used in the rest of this chapter in order to compare performances of the various proposed algorithms. It is defined as the weighted sum of FAR and FRR [49]

$$\mathrm{DCF}(\hat{\theta}) = C_a \cdot \mathrm{FAR}(\hat{\theta}) + C_r \cdot \mathrm{FRR}(\hat{\theta}) \tag{10.11}$$

where C_a and C_r are the costs associated with a false acceptance and a false rejection, respectively, and where the decision threshold $\hat{\theta}$ has been optimized a priori by minimizing DCF on a development set. In our particular case, where the main objective is to stay robust to (both random and deliberate) impostor attacks, weights are set to $C_a = 0.99$ and $C_r = 0.10$ [49]: it is therefore more costly to falsely accept an impostor than to reject a true claim.

$$\mathrm{DCF}(\hat{\theta}) = 0.99 \cdot \mathrm{FAR}(\hat{\theta}) + 0.10 \cdot \mathrm{FRR}(\hat{\theta}) \tag{10.12}$$

In the specific framework of the BANCA database, two test sets are available (G1 with development on G2, and G2 with development on G1). However, only one value of FAR, FRR and DCF is reported later on. It is computed as follows

$$\mathrm{FAR} = (\mathrm{NFA}_1 + \mathrm{NFA}_2)/(\mathrm{NI}_1 + \mathrm{NI}_2) \tag{10.13}$$

$$\mathrm{FRR} = (\mathrm{NFR}_1 + \mathrm{NFR}_2)/(\mathrm{NC}_1 + \mathrm{NC}_2) \tag{10.14}$$

$$\mathrm{DCF} = 0.99 \cdot \mathrm{FAR} + 0.10 \cdot \mathrm{FRR} \tag{10.15}$$

where NFA_i (respectively NFR_i) is the number of false acceptance (respectively false rejection) when testing on group Gi; and NI_i (respectively NC_i) is the number of impostor accesses (respectively client accesses) in group Gi.

10.3.4 Evaluation

Figures 10.5 and 10.6 summarize the performance of the proposed reference systems on both random and deliberate impostor scenarios.

For the BECARS v1.1.9 (respectively ALIZE v1.04) reference system, DCF jumps from 4.87% (respectively 3.57%) for random imposture up to 97.6%

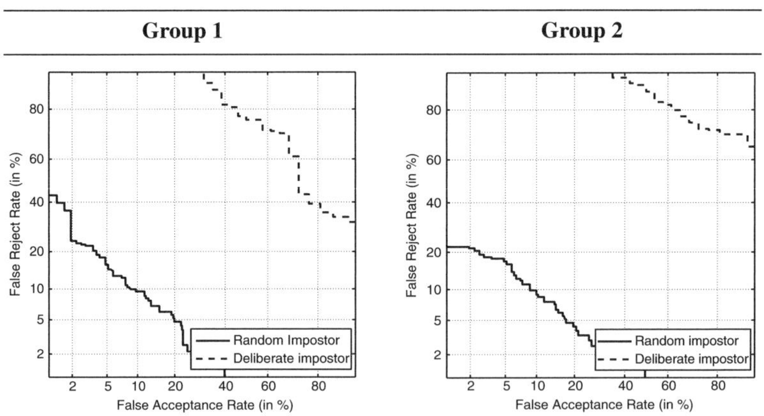

	DCF	FAR	FRR
Random imposture	$4.87 \pm 1.25\%$	$2.40 \pm 1.20\%$	$24.89 \pm 3.92\%$
Deliberate imposture	$97.6\% \in [72\%, 100\%]$	$96.1\% \in [71\%, 100\%]$	$24.8 \pm 3.92\%$

Fig. 10.5 Performance of the BECARS v1.1.9 reference system

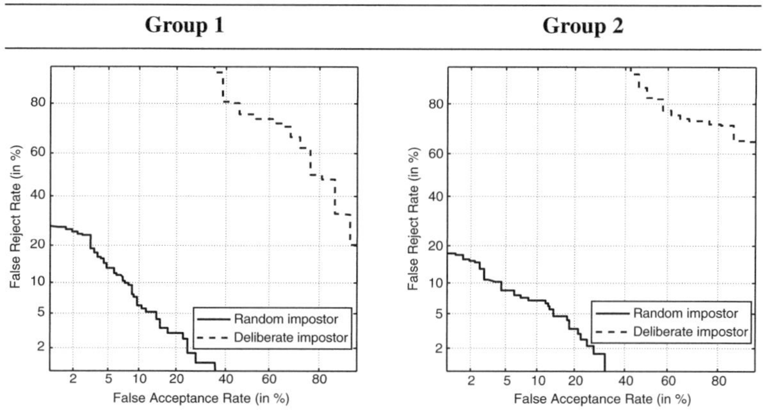

	DCF	FAR	FRR
Random imposture	$3.57 \pm 0.85\%$	$0.96 \pm 0.76\%$	$26.18 \pm 3.99\%$
Deliberate imposture	$94.0\% \in [69\%, 100\%]$	$92.3\% \in [68\%, 100\%]$	$26.1 \pm 3.99\%$

Fig. 10.6 Performance of the ALIZE v1.04 reference system

(respectively 94.0%) for deliberate imposture! While it accepts only 2.40% (respectively 0.96%) of random impostor attacks, it falsely accepts more than 90% (respectively 90%) of deliberate impostor attacks. In a word, both reference systems are completely fooled by an attack as simple as presenting a picture of the target in front of the camera while playing back an audio recording of his/her voice: they are not designed to deal with this kind of attacks and therefore cannot be used as it is in a real life unsupervised scenario.

10.4 Research Systems

In the following paragraphs, we present research prototypes with new modules designed to be robust to deliberate impostures, which appears to be the main weakness of the reference systems.

10.4.1 Face Recognition

The classical eigenface approach, combined with the Mahalanobis distance, is used for the implementation of the face verification module [68].

We propose to benefit from the large number of face samples available in a video sequence to improve the robustness of the system. While both (ALIZE and

BECARS) reference systems make use of only 10 images to compare a person to a model, we intend to use every reliable detected face. The definition of a "reliable face" is given in the next paragraph.

Once face detection is applied on each frame of the video sequence (using Fasel et al. algorithm [30]), the Distance From Face Space (DFFS) is computed for every detected face as the distance between the face and its projection on the face space (obtained via Principal Component Analysis) [68]. A reliability coefficient r is defined as the inverse of the DFFS ($r = 1/\text{DFFS}$). The higher r is, the more reliable the detected face is. Finally, a detected face is kept as correct if its r coefficient is higher than a threshold $\theta_r = 2/3 \cdot r_{\max}$, where $r_{\max}$ is the maximum value of r on the current video sequence. Figure 10.7 shows (from left to right) the face corresponding to $r = r_{\max}$, an example of correctly detected face and an example of rejected face.

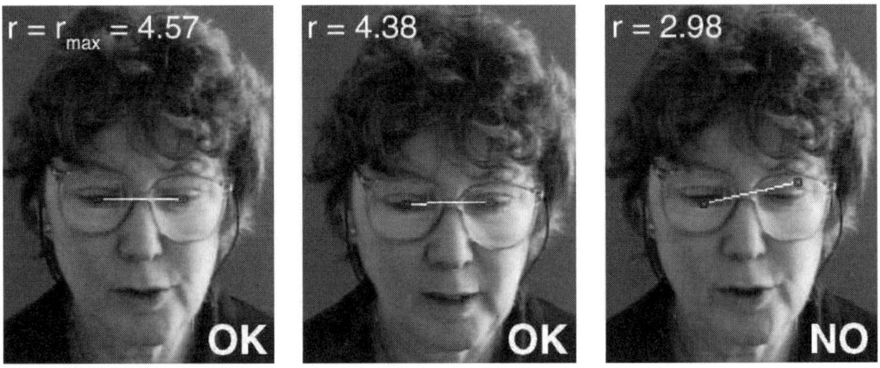

Fig. 10.7 Selection of reliable faces

Only eigenface features corresponding to correctly detected faces are kept to describe the face appearing in the video sequence. Finally, at test time, the Mahalanobis distance (instead of the $L1$ distance in the reference systems) is computed between the eigenface features (of dimension 80, in our case) of each of the N correctly detected faces of the enrollment video sequence and each of the M correctly detected face of the test video sequence, leading to $N \times M$ distances [48]. The opposite of the mean of these $N \times M$ distances is taken as the score S_{f} of the face verification module, which is very similar to what is done in the reference systems.

10.4.2 Speaker Verification

The speaker verification module is also based on a very classical approach: Gaussian Mixture Model with Universal Background Model (GMM-UBM) [59], using 36-dimensional Mel-Frequency Cepstral Coefficients (12 MFCC with first and second derivatives). It is very similar to the reference system speaker verification module. It uses the same tools as the BECARS v1.1.9 reference system: HTK for MFCC feature extraction and BECARS v1.1.9 GMM toolkit; the main difference being in the number of MFCC coefficients (16 MFCC with first derivatives vs. 12 MFCC with first and second derivatives).

First, silence detection is performed, based on a bi-gaussian modeling of the acoustic energy distribution. Then, MFCC features are extracted on a 20 ms long window every 10 ms, while only keeping the features corresponding to nonsilent windows. Using the Expectation-Maximization (EM) algorithm, a 256 Gaussians mixture model (GMM)—called Universal Background Model (UBM)—is trained using a set of recordings of numerous speakers in order to maximally cover the variability among speakers. These speakers are extracted from the world model part of the BANCA database, which is a third set disjoint with G1 and G2. Using the MFCC features extracted from the enrollment sequence, Maximum A Posteriori (MAP) adaptation is applied in order to get a client-dependent GMM from the UBM [59]. At test time, MFCC features are extracted from the test sequence and are compared to both the client-dependent GMM and the UBM: the likelihood ratio is finally taken as the score S_S of the speaker verification module.

10.4.3 Client-dependent Synchrony Measure

So far as can be seen in Fig. 10.11 (page 321), these new modules do not bring any improvements in robustness against deliberate impostor attacks. Similarly to the reference systems, this new Face+Speaker algorithm is completely fooled by these simple attacks: the FAR jumps from 2% up to 94%!

There are many ways of dealing with these kinds of deliberate impostor attacks. The first solution is to ask for the enunciation of a different utterance (chosen randomly) for each new access, thus preventing the prior recording of the voice of the target. An alternative is to analyze the motion of the detected face and look for a suspicious behavior [45, 43]. The third solution is to study the degree of correspondence between the shape and motion of the lip and the acoustic signal [18].

In [10], we introduced a new biometric modality based on a client-dependent measure of the synchrony between acoustic and visual speech features. Its main principles and performance can be summarized as follows. Every 10 ms, a 24-dimensional acoustic feature vector (12 MFCC coefficients and their first derivatives) is extracted and will be denoted as $X \in \mathbb{R}^n$ in the rest of the paper. As far as visual feature vectors are concerned, we chose to extract Discrete Cosine Transform (DCT) of the mouth area (as it is classically used in audiovisual speech processing applications [57]). Figure 10.8 summarizes this process. For each frame of the sequence, the face is detected and a Viola and Jones mouth detector is applied to locate the mouth area [17], from which 28 DCT coefficients corresponding to the low spatial frequencies are computed. In order to equalize the sample rates of acoustic and visual features (initially 100 Hz and 25 Hz, respectively), visual features are linearly interpolated. First derivatives are then appended, leading to 56-dimensional visual feature vectors $Y \in \mathbb{R}^m$.

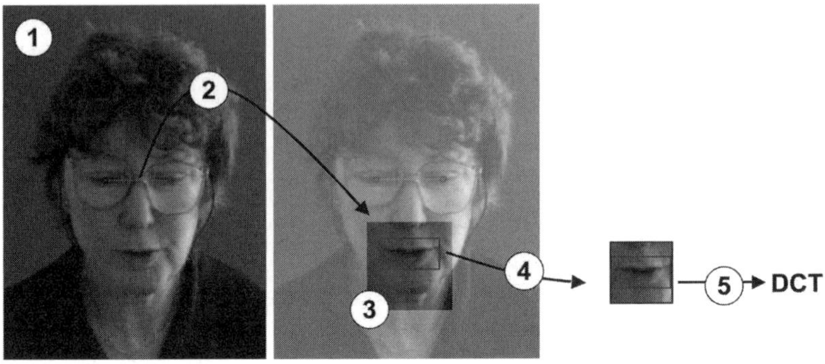

Fig. 10.8 Visual feature extraction

Using the acoustic and visual features X and Y extracted from the enrollment sequence, co-inertia analysis (CoIA) is applied in order to compute the client-dependent synchrony model $(\mathbf{A},\mathbf{B})$. The columns of matrices $\mathbf{A}$ and $\mathbf{B}$ are vectors $\mathbf{a}_k$ and $\mathbf{b}_k$ ($k \in [1, \min(n,m)]$) that are defined recursively as the projection vectors maximizing the covariance between X and Y

$$(\mathbf{a}_1, \mathbf{b}_1) = \underset{(a,b)}{\operatorname{argmax}} \operatorname{cov}\left(a^t X, b^t Y\right) \tag{10.16}$$

The same maximization in the orthogonal subspaces to $\mathbf{a}_1^t X$ and $\mathbf{b}_1^t Y$ allows the computation of $\mathbf{a}_2$ and $\mathbf{b}_2$, and so on for the other $\mathbf{a}_k$ and $\mathbf{b}_k$. More information on CoIA can be found in [26].

At test time, acoustic and visual feature vectors X^Γ and Y^Γ of the test sequence Γ are extracted and a measure S_c of their synchrony is computed using the synchrony model $\left(\mathbf{A}^\lambda, \mathbf{B}^\lambda\right)$ of the claimed identity λ:

$$S_\text{c} = \frac{1}{D} \sum_{k=1}^{D} \operatorname{corr}\left(\mathbf{a}_k^{\lambda^t} X^\Gamma, \mathbf{b}_k^{\lambda^t} Y^\Gamma\right) \tag{10.17}$$

where D is the number of dimensions actually used to compute the correlation.

As can be seen in Fig. 10.10 and 10.11, although it is a weak biometric modality (DCF = 8.6% against random impostor, where the Face+Speaker system yields DCF = 5.8%), the client-dependent synchrony measure is very robust to deliberate imposture (DCF = 7.6% and FAR = 0%): it rejects every single attack.

10.4.4 Two Fusion Strategies

The two systems (the Face+Speaker system and the one based on the client-dependent synchrony measure) are therefore complementary: while Face+Speaker system yields good performance against random imposture but is completely fooled by deliberate impostor attacks, the synchrony modality has poor raw performance but is intrinsically robust to attacks. Thus, we propose two fusion strategies that try to benefit from this complementarity.

The first fusion strategy is the direct extension of the one used in the reference systems. As shown in Eq. 10.18, the fused score S_1 is a weighted sum of three normalized monomodal scores (those weights being optimized on the development set in order to minimize the DCF)

$$S_1 = w_s S_s + w_f S_f + w_c S_c \text{ with } \sum w = 1 \tag{10.18}$$

However, the weight estimation process leads to $w_C = 0$ for both groups G1 and G2. This fusion strategy is therefore equivalent to a Face+Speaker fusion.

As seen in Fig. 10.9, impostor synchrony scores (either random or deliberate) are globally lower than true claim scores. The second fusion strategy uses this property and is designed to benefit from the complementarity of the first fusion strategy and the synchrony verification module—the former being very sensitive to deliberate impostors but more efficient against random impostors, while the latter is very robust to attacks, though it is less efficient against random impostors

$$S_2 = \alpha(S_c) S_1 + [1 - \alpha(S_c)] S_c \tag{10.19}$$

where α is the cumulative distribution function of true claims synchrony scores

$$\alpha(S_c) = p(s \leq S_c | \text{true claim}) \tag{10.20}$$

The function α is drawn as a thick black line in the top right corner of Fig. 10.9. It is estimated using the true claims synchrony scores of the training set. As shown in

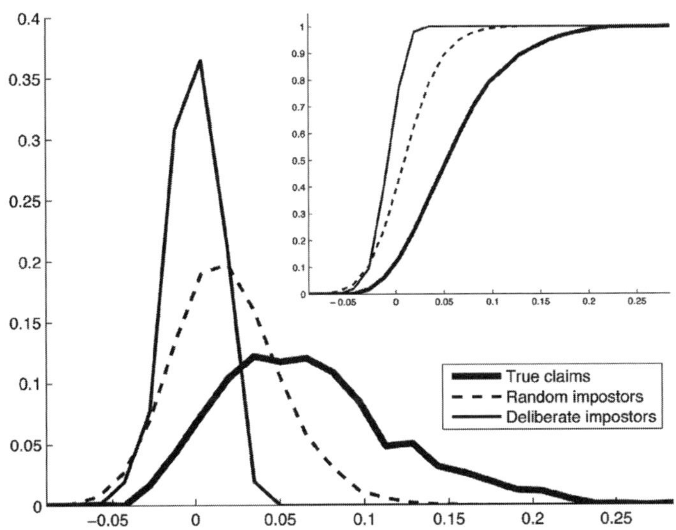

Fig. 10.9 Synchrony scores distributions and their corresponding cumulative distribution functions (in the top right corner)

Eq. 10.19, this last strategy is based on an adaptive weighted sum of (normalized) scores. More weight is given to the synchrony verification module if the synchrony measure is low; and reciprocally its weight is decreased when the synchrony measure is higher and the first strategy fusion can actually be trusted.

10.4.5 Evaluation

Figures 10.10 and 10.11 allow comparison of the performance of the reference systems and the research prototypes.

As far as random imposture is concerned, the performance of the reference systems and the Face+Speaker system are close taking into account the confidence intervals. The final fusion strategy leads to similar raw performance as that of the Face+Speaker system on random impostures.

However, the main difference appears when looking at performance against deliberate imposture. While both the reference systems and the Face+Speaker research prototypes are completely fooled by simple deliberate impostor attacks, the adaptive weighted fusion benefits from the robustness to attacks of the synchrony-based system: it rejects almost every attack (FAR = 2%).

Group 1	Group 2

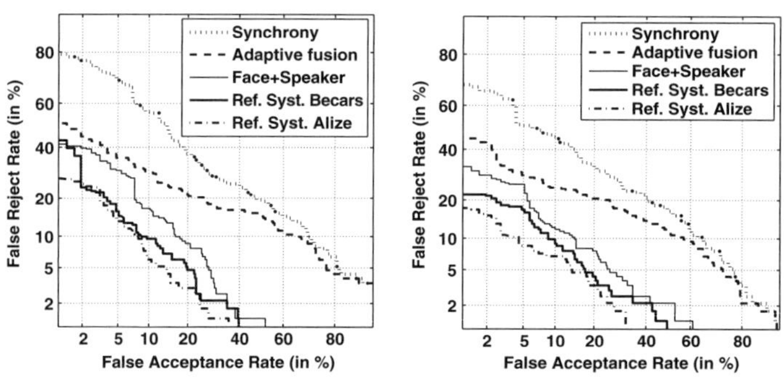

	DCF	FAR	FRR
BECARS v1.1.9 Reference system	4.87 ± 1.25%	2.40 ± 1.20%	24.89 ± 3.92%
ALIZE v1.04 Reference system	3.57 ± 0.85%	0.96 ± 0.76%	26.18 ± 3.99%
Face+Speaker	5.8 ± 1.2%	2.0 ± 1.1%	37.5 ± 4.4%
Synchrony	8.6 ± 0.8%	0.9 ± 0.7%	76.6 ± 3.8%
Adaptive weighted fusion	6.0 ± 0.7%	0.6 ± 0.6%	53.6 ± 4.5%

Fig. 10.10 Performances of the research prototypes against random imposture

10.5 Conclusion

Despite all efforts for improving their raw verification performance, it has been highlighted that current talking-face verification systems (classically based on the fusion at scores level of two modules of face and speaker verification) can be easily fooled by simple deliberate impostor attacks where the impostor would show a picture of his/her target in front of the camera while playing a prior recording of his/her voice. The talking-face reference system (using ALIZE v1.04 or BECARS v1.1.9) is one of those systems and we have therefore proposed research prototypes aiming at solving this issue.

First, a client-dependent audiovisual synchrony measure is introduced that aims at modeling for each client their own way of synchronizing their lips and voice. It is a biometric modality in itself that has weak raw verification performance but is intrinsically robust to deliberate impostor attacks. It is then adaptively fused with an improved Face+Speaker classical verification module so that more importance is given to the latter when it is unlikely that the system is under deliberate attack, and more importance to the synchrony-based module when there is a high probability of attacks. This new approach allows us to build a system that has better verification performance than the reference systems and strongly reduces its vulnerability against attacks.

Group 1	Group 2

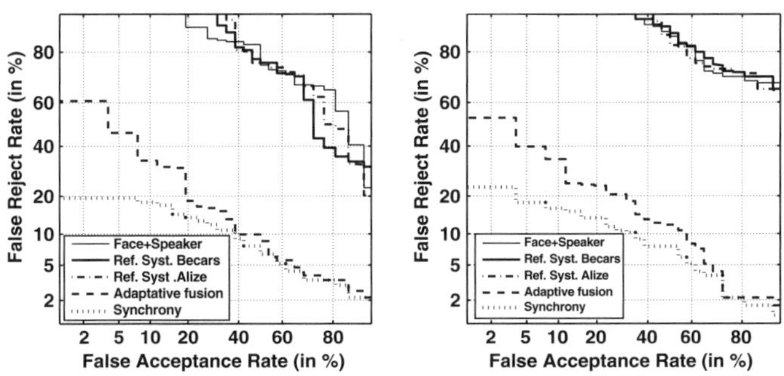

	DCF	FAR	FRR
BECARS v1.1.9 Reference system	97.6% ∈ [72%, 100%]	96.1% ∈ [71%, 100%]	24.8 ± 3.92%
ALIZE v1.04 Reference system	94.0% ∈ [69%, 100%]	92.3% ∈ [68%, 100%]	26.1 ± 3.99%
Face+Speaker	97.0% ∈ [72%, 100%]	94.2% ∈ [69%, 100%]	37.5 ± 4.4%
Synchrony	7.6% ∈ [7%, 15%]	0%	76.6 ± 3.8%
Adaptive weighted fusion	7.2% ∈ [5%, 16%]	1.9% ∈ [0%, 11%]	53.6 ± 4.5%

Fig. 10.11 Performance of the research prototypes against deliberate imposture

Acknowledgments

This work was partially supported by the European Commission through the BioSecure NoE and the KSpace NoE.

References

1. Petar S. Aleksic and Aggelos K. Katsaggelos. Audio-Visual Biometrics. In *Proceedings of the IEEE*, volume 94, pages 2025–2044, November 2006.
2. Ivana Arsic, Roger Vilagut, and Jean-Philippe Thiran. Automatic Extraction of Geometric Lip Features with Application to Multi-Modal Speaker Identification. In *IEEE International Conference on Multimedia and Expo (ICME'06)*, pages 161–164, 2006.
3. Enrique Bailly-Baillière, Samy Bengio, Frédéric Bimbot, Miroslav Hamouz, Josef Kittler, Johnny Mariéthoz, Jiri Matas, Kieron Messer, Vlad Popovici, Fabienne Porée, Belen Ruiz, and Jean-Philippe Thiran. The BANCA Database and Evaluation Protocol. In *4th International Conference on Audio-and Video-Based Biometric Person Authentication (AVBPA'03)*, volume 2688 of *Lecture Notes in Computer Science*, pages 625–638, Guildford, UK, January 2003. Springer.
4. Jon P. Barker and François Berthommier. Evidence of Correlation between Acoustic and Visual Features of Speech. In *14th International Congress of Phonetic Sciences (ICPhS'99)*, pages 199–202, San Francisco, USA, August 1999.
5. Samy Bengio. An Asynchronous Hidden Markov Model for Audio-Visual Speech Recognition. In S. Becker, S. Thrun, and K. Obermayer, editors, *Advances in Neural Information Processing Systems 15*, pages 1213–1220. MIT Press, 2003.
6. Manuele Bicego, Enrico Grosso, and Massimo Tistarelli. Face Authentication using One-Class Support Vector Machines. In Stan Z. Li, Tieniu Tan, Sharath Pankanti, Gérard Chollet, and David Zhang, editors, *International Workshop on Biometric Recognition Systems*, volume 3781 of *Lecture Notes in Computer Science*, page 15, 2005.
7. Manuele Bicego, Enrico Grosso, and Massimo Tistarelli. Person Authentication from Video of Faces: a Behavioral and Physiological Approach using Pseudo Hierarchical Hidden Markov Models. In *International Conference on Biometrics*, volume 3832 of *Lecture Notes in Computer Science*, pages 113–120, Hong-Kong, January 2006.
8. Gary R. Bradski. Real-Time Face and Object Tracking as a Component of a Perceptual User Interface. In *4th IEEE Workshop on Applications of Computer Vision (WACV'98)*, pages 214–219, Princeton, NJ, USA, October 1998.
9. Hervé Bredin, Guido Aversano, Chafic Mokbel, and Gérard Chollet. The Biosecure Talking-Face Reference System. In *2nd Workshop on Multimodal User Authentication (MMUA'06)*, Toulouse, France, May 2006.
10. Hervé Bredin and Gérard Chollet. Audio-Visual Speech Synchrony Measure for Talking-Face Identity Verification. In *32nd IEEE International Conference on Acoustics, Speech, and Signal Processing (ICASSP'07)*, Honolulu, USA, April 2007.
11. Hervé Bredin and Gérard Chollet. Audiovisual speech synchrony measure: Application to biometrics. *EURASIP Journal on Advances in Signal Processing*, 2007:Article ID 70186, 11 pages, 2007. doi:10.1155/2007/70186.
12. Hervé Bredin, Najim Dehak, and Gérard Chollet. GMM-based SVM for Face Recognition. In *18th International Conference on Pattern Recognition (ICPR'06)*, pages 1111–1114, Hong-Kong, August 2006.
13. Hervé Bredin, Antonio Miguel, Ian H. Witten, and Gérard Chollet. Detecting Replay Attacks in Audiovisual Identity Verification. In *31st IEEE International Conference on Acoustics, Speech, and Signal Processing (ICASSP'06)*, volume 1, pages 621–624, Toulouse, France, May 2006.

14. Christoph Bregler and Yochai Konig. “Eigenlips” for Robust Speech Recognition. In *19th IEEE International Conference on Acoustics, Speech, and Signal Processing (ICASSP’94)*, volume 2, pages 19–22, Adelaide, Australia, April 1994.
15. BT-DAVID. http://eegalilee.swan.ac.uk/, 1996.
16. Canonical Correlation Analysis. http://people.imt.liu.se/∼magnus/cca.
17. M. Castrillón Santana, J. Lorenzo Navarro, O. Déniz Suárez, and A. Falcón Martel. Multiple Face Detection at Different Resolutions for Perceptual User Interfaces. In *2nd Iberian Conference on Pattern Recognition and Image Analysis*, Estoril, Portugal, June 2005.
18. Girija Chetty and Michael Wagner. “Liveness” Verification in Audio-Video Authentication. In *10th Australian International Conference on Speech Science and Technology (SST’04)*, pages 358–363, Sydney, Australia, December 2004.
19. Claude C. Chibelushi, Farzin Deravi, and John S.D. Mason. A Review of Speech-Based Bimodal Recognition. *IEEE Transactions on Multimedia*, 4(1):23–37, 2002.
20. Claude C. Chibelushi, John S.D. Mason, and Farzin Deravi. Feature-Level Data Fusion for Bimodal Person Recognition. In *Sixth International Conference on Image Processing and its Applications*, volume 1, pages 399–403, 1997.
21. Claude C. Chibelushi, John S.D. Mason, and Farzin Deravi. Integrated Person Identification Using Voice and Facial Features. In *IEE Colloquium on Image Processing for Security Applications*, number 4, pages 1–5, London, UK, March 1997.
22. Tanzeem Choudhury, Brian Clarkson, Tony Jebara, and Alex Pentland. Multimodal Person Recognition using Unconstrained Audio and Video. In *2nd International Conference on Audio-Video Based Person Authentication*, pages 176–180, Washington, USA, March 1999.
23. A.R. Chowdhury, Rama Chellappa, S. Krishnamurthy, and T. Vo. 3D Face Reconstruction from Video using a Generic Model. In *IEEE International Conference on Multimedia and Expo (ICME’02)*, volume 1, pages 449–452, Lausanne, Switzerland, August 2002.
24. Ross Cutler and Larry Davis. Look Who’s Talking: Speaker Detection using Video and Audio Correlation. In *IEEE International Conference on Multimedia and Expo (ICME’00)*, volume 3, pages 1589–1592, New-York, USA, July 2000.
25. David Dean, Patrick Lucey, Sridha Sridharan, and Tim Wark. Comparing Audio and Visual Information for Speech Processing. In *Eighth International Symposium on Signal Processing and its Applications*, volume 1, pages 58–61, August 2005.
26. Sylvain Dolédec and Daniel Chessel. Co-Inertia Analysis: an Alternative Method for Studying Species-Environment Relationships. *Freshwater Biology*, 31:277–294, 1994.
27. B. Dumas, C. Pugin, J. Hennebert, D. Petrovska-Delacrétaz, A. Humm, F. Evéquoz, R. Ingold, and D. Von Rotz. MyIdea - Multimodal Biometrics Database, Description of Acquisition Protocols. In *Third COST 275 Workshop (COST 275)*, pages 59–62, Hatfield, UK, October 2005.
28. Nicolas Eveno and Laurent Besacier. A Speaker Independent Liveness Test for Audio-Video Biometrics. In *9th European Conference on Speech Communication and Technology (Interspeech’2005 - Eurospeech)*, pages 3081–3084, Lisboa, Portugal, September 2005.
29. Nicolas Eveno and Laurent Besacier. Co-Inertia Analysis for “Liveness” Test in Audio-Visual Biometrics. In *4th International Symposium on Image and Signal Processing and Analysis (ISISPA’05)*, pages 257–261, Zagreb, Croatia, September 2005.
30. Ian Fasel, Bret Fortenberry, and J. R. Movellan. A Generative Framework for Real-Time Object Detection and Classification. *Computer Vision and Image Understanding – Special Issue on Eye Detection and Tracking*, 98(1):182–210, 2004.
31. John W. Fisher and Trevor Darell. Speaker Association With Signal-Level Audiovisual Fusion. *IEEE Transactions on Multimedia*, 6(3):406–413, June 2004.
32. John W. Fisher, Trevor Darrell, William T. Freeman, and Paul Viola. Learning Joint Statistical Models for Audio-Visual Fusion and Segregation. In T. K. Leen, T. G. Dietterich, and V. Tresp, editors, *Advances in Neural Information Processing Systems 13*, pages 772–778. MIT Press, 2001.
33. Niall Fox and Richard B. Reilly. Audio-Visual Speaker Identification Based on the Use of Dynamic Audio and Visual Features. In *4th International Conference on Audio-and Video-Based Biometric Person Authentication (AVBPA’03)*, volume 2688 of *Lecture Notes in Computer Science*, pages 743–751, Guildford, UK, January 2003. Springer.

34. Niall A. Fox, Ralph Gross, Jeffrey F. Cohn, and Richard B. Reilly. Robust Biometric Person Identification using Automatic Classifier Fusion of Speech, Mouth and Face Experts. *IEEE Transactions on Multimedia*, 9(4):701–714, June 2007.
35. S. Garcia-Salicetti, C. Beumier, G. Chollet, B. Dorizzi, J.-L. Jardins, J. Lunter, Y. Ni, and D. Petrovska-Delacretaz. BIOMET: a Multimodal Person Authentication Database including Face, Voice, Fingerprint, Hand and Signature Modalities. In *International Conference on Audio- and Video-Based Biometric Person Authentication (AVBPA'03)*, pages 845 – 853, Guildford, UK, June 2003.
36. Roland Goecke and Bruce Millar. Statistical Analysis of the Relationship between Audio and Video Speech Parameters for Australian English. In *ISCA Tutorial and Research Workshop on Audio Visual Speech Processing (AVSP'03)*, pages 133–138, Saint-Jorioz, France, September 2003.
37. John Hershey and Javier Movellan. Audio-Vision: Using Audio-Visual Synchrony to Locate Sounds. In Michael S. Kearns, Sara A. Solla, and David A. Cohn, editors, *Advances in Neural Information Processing Systems 11*, pages 813–819. MIT Press, 1999.
38. Aapo Hyvärinen. Survey on Independent Component Analysis. *Neural Computing Surveys*, 2:94–128, 1999.
39. ICA. http://www.cis.hut.fi/projects/ica/fastica/.
40. IV2: Identification par l'Iris et le Visage via la Vidéo. http://iv2.ibisc.fr/PageWeb-IV2.html.
41. G. Iyengar, H.J. Nock, and Chalapathy Neti. Audio-Visual Synchrony for Detection of Monologues in Video Archives. In *IEEE International Conference on Multimedia and Expo (ICME'03)*, volume 1, pages 329–332, Baltimore, USA, July 2003.
42. Anil Jain, Karthik Nandakumar, and Arun A. Ross. Score Normalization in Multimodal Biometric Systems. *Pattern Recognition*, 38(12):2270–2285, 2005.
43. Hyung-Keun Jee, Sung-Uk Jung, and Jang-Hee Yoo. Liveness Detection for Embedded Face Recognition System. *International Journal of Biomedical Sciences*, 1(4):235–238, 2006.
44. Pierre Jourlin, Juergen Luettin, Dominique Genoud, and Hubert Wassner. Acoustic-Labial Speaker Verification. In *First International Conference on Audio- and Video-based Biometric Person Authentication*, volume 18, pages 853–858, Crans-Montana, Switzerland, 1997.
45. K. Kollreider, H. Fronthaler, and Josef Bigun. Evaluating Liveness by Face Images and the Structure Tensor. In *Fourth IEEE Workshop on Automatic Identification Advanced Technologies (AutoID'05)*, pages 75–80, 2005.
46. Volker Krueger and Shaohua Zhou. Exemplar-based Face Recognition from Video. In *7th European Conference on Computer Vision*, volume 4, page 732, Copenhagen, Denmark, May 2002.
47. Simon Lucey, Tsuhan Chen, Sridha Sridharan, and Vinod Chandran. Integration Strategies for Audio-Visual Speech Processing: Applied to Text-Dependent Speaker Recognition. *IEEE Transactions on Multimedia*, 7(3):495–506, June 2005.
48. Prasanta Chandra Mahalanobis. On the Generalised Distance in Statistics. In *Proceedings of the National Institute of Science of India 12*, pages 49–55, 1936.
49. Alvin F. Martin and Mark A. Przybocki. The NIST Speaker Recognition Evaluation – an Overview. *Digital Signal Processing*, 10:1–18, 2000.
50. Kieron Messer, Josef Kittler, Mohammad Sadeghi, Miroslav Hamouz, Alexey Kostin, Fabien Cardinaux, Sébastien Marcel, Samy Bengio, Conrad Sanderson, Norman Poh, Yann Rodriguez, Jacek Czyk, Luc Vandendorpe, Chris McCool, Scott Lowther, Sridha Sridharan, Vinod Chandran, Roberto Parades Palacios, Enrique Vidal, Li Bai, LinLin Shen, Yan Wang, Chiang Yueh-Hsuan, Liu Hsien-Chang, Hung Yi-Ping, Alexander Heinrichs, Marco Mueller, Andreas Tewes, Christoph von der Malsburg, Rolf Wurtz, Zhenger Wang, Feng Xue, Yong Ma, Qiong Yang, Chi Fang, Xiaoqing Ding, Simon Lucey, Ralph Goss, and Henry Schneiderman. Face Authentication Test on the BANCA Database. In *17th International Conference on Pattern Recognition (ICPR'04)*, volume 4, pages 523–532, Cambridge, UK, August 2004.
51. Kieron Messer, Jiri Matas, Josef Kittler, Juergen Luettin, and G. Maitre. XM2VTSDB: The Extended M2VTS Database. In *International Conference on Audio- and Video-Based Biometric Person Authentication (AVBPA'99)*, pages 72–77, Washington, USA, March 1999.

52. Andrew C. Morris, Jacques Koreman, Harin Sellahewa, Johan-Hendrik Ehlers, Sabah Jassim, Lorene Allano, and Sonia Garcia-Salicetti. The SecurePhone PDA Database, Experimental Protocol and Automatic Test Procedure for Multi-Modal User Authentication. Technical report, Saarland University, Institute of Phonetics, 2006.
53. Ara V. Nefian and Lu Hong Liang. Bayesian Networks in Multimodal Speech Recognition and Speaker Identification. In *Conference Record of the Thirty-Seventh Asilomar Conference on Signals, Systems and Computers*, volume 2, pages 2004–2008, 2003.
54. H. J. Nock, G. Iyengar, and Chalapathy Neti. Assessing Face and Speech Consistency for Monologue Detection in Video. In *10th ACM International Conference on Multimedia*, pages 303–306, Juan-les-Pins, France, 2002.
55. E. Patterson, S. Gurbuz, Z. Tufekci, and J.N. Gowdy. CUAVE: a new Audio-Visual Database for Multimodal Human-Computer Interface Research. In *IEEE International Conference on Acoustics, Speech, and Signal Processing (ICASSP'02)*, volume 2, pages 2017–2020, Orlando, Florida, May 2002.
56. D. Petrovska-Delacrétaz, S. Lelandais, J. Colineau, L. Chen, B. Dorizzi, E. Krichen, M.A. Mellakh, A. Chaari, S. Guerfi, J. DHose, M. Ardabilian, and B. Ben Amor. The iv^2 multimodal (2d, 3d, stereoscopic face, talking face and iris) biometric database, and the iv^2 2007 evaluation campaign. In *In the proceedings of the IEEE Second International Conference on Biometrics: Theory, Applications (BTAS)*, Washington DC USA, September 2008.
57. Gerasimos Potamianos, Chalapathy Neti, Juergen Luettin, and Iain Matthews. Audio-Visual Automatic Speech Recognition: An Overview. In G. Bailly, Eric Vatikiotis-Bateson, and P. Perrier, editors, *Issues in Visual and Audio-Visual Speech Processing*, chapter 10. MIT Press, 2004.
58. Lawrence R. Rabiner. A Tutorial on Hidden Markov Models and Selected Applications in Speech Recognition. In *Proceedings of the IEEE*, volume 77, pages 257–286, February 1989.
59. Douglas A. Reynolds, Thomas F. Quatieri, and Robert B. Dunn. Speaker Verification using Adapted Gaussian Mixture Models. *Digital Signal Processing*, 10:19–41, 2000.
60. Arun A. Ross, Karthik Nandakumar, and Anil K. Jain. *Handbook of Multibiometrics*. Springer, 2006.
61. Usman Saeed, Federico Matta, and Jean-Luc Dugelay. Person Recognition based on Head and Mouth Dynamics. In *IEEE International Workshop on Multimedia Signal Processing (MMSP'06)*, Victoria, Canada, October 2006.
62. Mehmet Emre Sargin, Engin Erzin, Yucel Yemez, and A. Murat Tekalp. Multimodal Speaker Identification using Canonical Correlation Analysis. In *31st IEEE International Conference on Acoustics, Speech, and Signal Processing (ICASSP'06)*, volume 1, pages 613–616, Toulouse, France, May 2006.
63. Malcolm Slaney and Michele Covell. FaceSync: A Linear Operator for Measuring Synchronization of Video Facial Images and Audio Tracks. In *Advances in Neural Information Processing Systems 13*. MIT Press, 2000.
64. Paris Smaragdis and Michael Casey. Audio/Visual Independent Components. In *4th International Symposium on Independent Component Analysis and Blind Signal Separation (ICA'03)*, pages 709–714, Nara, Japan, April 2003.
65. David Sodoyer, Laurent Girin, Christian Jutten, and Jean-Luc Schwartz. Speech Extraction based on ICA and Audio-Visual Coherence. In *7th International Symposium on Signal Processing and its Applications (ISSPA'03)*, volume 2, pages 65–68, Paris, France, July 2003.
66. David Sodoyer, Jean-Luc Schwartz, Laurent Girin, Jacob Klinkisch, and Christian Jutten. Separation of Audio-Visual Speech Sources: A New Approach Exploiting the Audio-Visual Coherence of Speech Stimuli. *EURASIP Journal on Applied Signal Processing*, 11:1165–1173, 2002.
67. Noboru Sugamura and Fumitada Itakura. Speech Analysis and Synthesis Methods developed at ECL in NTT–From LPC to LSP. *Speech Communications*, 5(2):199–215, June 1986.
68. Matthew Turk and Alex Pentland. Eigenfaces for Recognition. *Journal of Cognitive Neuroscience*, 3(1):71–86, 1991.

69. Matthew Turk and Alex Pentland. Face Recognition using Eigenfaces. In *IEEE Computer Society Conference on Computer Vision and Pattern Recognition (CVPR'91)*, pages 586–591, Maui, USA, June 1991.
70. M.H. Yang, D. Kriegman, and N. Ahuja. Detecting Faces in Images: a Survey. *IEEE Transactions on Pattern Analysis and Machine Intelligence*, 24:34–58, 2002.
71. Hani Yehia, Philip Rubin, and Eric Vatikiotis-Bateson. Quantitative Association of Vocal-Tract and Facial Behavior. *Speech Communication*, (28):23–43, 1998.
72. Wen-Yi Zhao, Rama Chellappa, P.J. Phillips, and Azriel Rosenfeld. Face Recognition: a Literature Survey. *ACM Computing Surveys*, 35(4):399–458, 2003.
73. Shaohua Zhou, Rama Chellappa, and Baback Moghaddam. Visual Tracking and Recognition using Appearance-Adaptive Models in Particle Filters. *IEEE Transactions on Image Processing*, 13(11):1491–1506, 2004.

Chapter 11
BioSecure Multimodal Evaluation Campaign 2007 (BMEC'2007)

Aurélien Mayoue, Bernadette Dorizzi, (in alphabetical order) Lorène Allano, Gérard Chollet, Jean Hennebert, Dijana Petrovska-Delacrétaz, and Florian Verdet

Abstract This chapter presents the experimental results from the mobile scenario of the BioSecure Multimodal Evaluation Campaign 2007 (BMEC'2007). This competition was organized by the BioSecure Network of Excellence (NoE) and aimed at testing the robustness of monomodal and multimodal biometric verification systems to degraded acquisition conditions. The database used for the evaluation is the large-scale multimodal database acquired in the framework of the BioSecure NoE in mobility conditions. During this evaluation, the BioSecure benchmarking methodology was followed to enable a fair comparison of the submitted algorithms. In this way, we believe that the BMEC'2007 database and results will be useful both to the participants and, more generally, to all practitioners in the field as a benchmark for improving methods and for enabling evaluation of algorithms.

11.1 Introduction

One of the key aspirations of the BioSecure NoE [6] is to investigate in depth the potential and merits of multimodal biometrics. This problem is difficult to tackle by any research team individually, because it requires expertise in several biometric modalities, as well as suitable large-scale multimodal biometric databases, and both requirements are normally beyond the scope of a typical research team to meet. In order to create the conditions that would enable such studies to be undertaken in a meaningful way, the NoE has organized three major events during the BioSecure project:

- The consortium brought together the expertise in a wide range of biometric modalities to develop several biometric verification systems during the Paris Residential Workshop in August 2005. These systems are known as BioSecure Reference Systems.

D. Petrovska-Delacrétaz et al. (eds.), *Guide to Biometric Reference Systems and Performance Evaluation*, DOI 10.1007/978-1-84800-292-0_11,

- From November 2006 to May 2007, several BioSecure members collected a substantial multimodal biometric database. This database is known as BioSecure multimodal database.
- The NoE has launched the BMEC [5] in March 2007. This campaign, which was the last step of the BioSecure project, had to enable institutions to easily assess the performance of their own monomodal and multimodal algorithms and to compare them to others. Two predefined scenarios have been planned by the consortium: access control and mobile scenarios. This chapter focuses on the mobile scenario.

This chapter is divided into five main parts. Section 11.2 summarizes the scientific objectives of the mobile scenario. Section 11.3 recapitulates the existing multimodal databases while Sect. 11.4 describes in details the database used for the evaluation. In Sect. 11.5, the criteria and the procedures used for performance evaluation are presented. Finally, Sect. 11.6 reports the overall performance of the participant algorithms.

11.2 Scientific Objectives

The main objective of the mobile scenario is to test the robustness of monomodal and multimodal biometric systems to degraded acquisition conditions. Such conditions can be found when the biometric verification of identity is done either indoor or outdoor using a webcam, a PDA or a mobile phone. The mobile scenario is composed of monomodal and multimodal evaluations.

11.2.1 Monomodal Evaluation

This evaluation is a continuation of the work started during the Paris Residential Workshop. Through the BMEC, the consortium wants to pursue comparative evaluations of monomodal biometric algorithms. This evaluation permits testing and evaluation of the three next points:

1. Robustness to degraded conditions (sensors, environment).
2. Robustness to forgeries.
3. Robustness to elapsed time ($\sim$one month) between sessions.

The modalities used for to evaluation are fingerprint, signature, talking-face and 2D face on video sequences.

11.2.2 Multimodal Evaluation

Multimodality is often presented as a way to improve the performance of monomodal systems, especially in the case of degraded conditions and to improve resistance to forgeries. To validate such assessments, participants should fuse scores provided by the fingerprint, signature and 2D face reference systems (see Sect. 11.4 for the description of these scores and reference systems). In this way, this evaluation permits testing and evaluation of the two next points:

1. Enhancement of performance in degraded conditions (in relation to those obtained with monomodal systems).
2. Robustness to forgeries.

Through both evaluations of the mobile scenario, the organizers believe that the analysis of the experimental results will help to identify remaining challenging issues aiming at improving biometric verification systems in degraded conditions.

11.3 Existing Multimodal Databases

Databases assembled to support research and evaluations in multimodal biometric applications have begun to appear over the last several years. A key requirement for such databases is that they represent real multimodal samples. Several multimodal biometric databases are currently available, mainly as a result of collaborative European or national projects. The most significant ones are shortly described in this section.

BANCA The BANCA database [3] has face video and speech samples (captured simultaneously). 208 subjects were captured (52 subjects in each of four European languages). Each subject participated in 12 sessions, of which four represented a controlled (cooperative) scenario, four a degraded scenario and four an adversarial scenario. A high-quality camera was used in the controlled and adversarial scenario and a webcam was used in the degraded scenario. In parallel, two microphones, a poor quality one, and a good quality one were used in all scenarios. Each session contained both a genuine identity claim and an impostor claim. This database was collected within the BANCA project, which involved 10 partners from four European countries.

BIOMET The BIOMET database [21] has five different modalities: audio, (2D and 3D) face, hand, fingerprint and signature. The fingerprint images were acquired with an optical and a capacitive sensor. For the face images, in addition to a conventional digital camera, an infrared camera was used to suppress the influence of the ambient light. The database consists of three different acquisition sessions (with eight months between the first and the third) and comprises 91 subjects who completed the three sessions.

BioSec The BioSec database [18] has fingerprint images (acquired with three different sensors), frontal face images (from a webcam), iris images and voice utterances (acquired with a close-talk headset and a distant webcam microphone). The baseline corpus comprises 200 subjects with two acquisition sessions per subject. This database was collected within the BIOSEC project, which involved over 20 partners from nine European countries.

BioSecure The BioSecure database was collected by 11 university institutes across Europe in the framework of the BioSecure Network of Excellence. This database is comprised of three different datasets, namely:

- *Internet Dataset (DS1)*: still face images and talking-face recorded through the Internet and under uncontrolled situations. About 1,000 volunteers have participated in two sessions.
- *Desktop Dataset (DS2)*: laboratory dataset with (high/low quality) 2D face, iris, talking-face, signature, (high/low quality) fingerprint and hand modalities. It is PC-based, off-line and supervised data acquisition. About 600 donors were acquired in two sessions.
- *Mobile Dataset (DS3)*: mobile devices under degraded conditions were used to build this dataset. 2D face and talking-face sequences were acquired in both indoor and outdoor environments. Signature and fingerprint modalities were acquired using the sensor of a PDA. About 700 donors have participated in two sessions.

BiosecurID The BioSecurID database [20] has speech, iris, 2D face and talking face, signature, handwriting, fingerprint, hand and keystroking. Data have been collected in an office-like uncontrolled environment (in order to simulate a realistic scenario). The database consists of four different acquisition sessions and comprises 400 subjects. The data were collected in the framework of the BiosecurID project funded by the Spanish Ministry of Education and Science.

FRGC The FRGC database [35] including both 3D scans and high-resolution still images (taken under controlled and uncontrolled conditions). The data corpus contains 50,000 images (acquired during many sessions). The database was collected at Notre Dame within the FRGC/FRVT2006 technology evaluation and vendor test program conducted by NIST to assess commercial and research systems for multimodal face recognition.

IV^2 The IV^{2}database (described in [34] and available at [26]) has talking-face sequences, 2D stereoscopic data acquired with two pairs of synchronized cameras, 3D facial data and iris images. The database is composed of 430 records from 315 different subjects, of which 219 have only one session, 77 subjects have two sessions and 19 subjects have three sessions. The data collection was realized during the Techno Vision program and was supported by the French Research Ministry and the Ministry of Defense.

MCYT The MCYT database [33] has both fingerprint and signature. The fingerprint images were acquired with an optical and a capacitive sensor. The database comprises data from 330 subjects acquired during a single session. The database acquisition process was launched in 2001 by four Spanish academic institutions within the MCYT project.

MyIDea The MyIDea database [14] has talking-face, audio, fingerprint, palmprint, signature, handwriting and hand geometry (pictures of dorsal and lateral sides). Synchronized signature+voice and handwriting+voice were also acquired. Sensors of different quality (digital camera and webcam for talking face, optical and thermal sensor for fingerprint,...) and various scenarios with different levels of control were considered in the acquisition. The database consists of three acquisition sessions and comprises approximately 100 subjects. The data were collected in the framework of the MyIDea project, that involved three European partners.

Smartkom The Smartkom database [39] resulted from the publicly funded German SmartKom project. The SmartKom (SK) consortium consists of seven industrial and three academic partners, and two subcontractors. The goal of the SK project is the development of an intelligent computer-user interface that allows almost natural interaction by the user. The system recognizes natural speech, gestures and facial expression. For database collection, 96 subjects are recorded during 172 sessions of 4.5 minutes length while they are interacting with a simulated version of the SK system. The database was recorded in public places (cinema and restaurant) and includes audio, video recorded by an infrared camera, and two standard DV cameras (one for the facial expression and one for the side view of the subject), hand/finger gesture (captured by the SIVIT system) and pen gesture (captured by a graphical tablet).

XM2VTS The XM2VTS database [32] was collected to support 2D and 3D face recognition, voice recognition, face recognition in video sequences, and various combinations of these modalities. The data was collected at the University of Surrey. The database consists of four different acquisition sessions (with one month interval between each session) and comprises data from 295 subjects.

11.4 BMEC Database

The database used for the mobile scenario of the BMEC is composed of four monomodal databases (fingerprint, signature, talking face and 2D face video sequences) and one fusion database.

The data used to build the monomodal databases come from the mobile dataset (DS3) of the BioSecure multimodal database (see Sect. 11.3) collected in the framework of the NoE. It is reminded that two sessions separated by about a one month interval were recorded. Furthermore, some realistic forgeries have been created a posteriori and included in the signature and talking-face databases.

The fusion database contains exclusively scores provided by applying the fingerprint, signature and 2D face reference systems on the monomodal databases.

Data and scores from 50 donors were selected to build the five development databases that were distributed to participants (who could use them in order to develop their systems), whereas data and scores from 430 different donors have been selected to build the five test databases. The test databases were kept sequestered (not distributed to participants) and where used by the organizers to evaluate the submitted algorithms.

In Sect. 11.4.1, the data and scores contained in the monomodal and fusion databases are described. Some statistics about the development and the test databases are given in Sect. 11.4.2.

11.4.1 Data

in this part, the data and score files that compose the monomodal and fusion databases are described. Furthermore, we mention the devices and the biometric reference systems used to acquire the data and to produce the scores, respectively.

11.4.1.1 2D Face Video Sequences

The device used to record the video sequences ($\sim 4s$) is a SAMSUNG Q1 with a webcam. For each individual enrolled in the database, four video files (in AVI format) without sound are available:

- Two indoor video files acquired during the first session.
- Two outdoor video files acquired during the second session.

11.4.1.2 Fingerprint

The device used to record fingerprints is an HP iPAQ hx2790. For each individual enrolled in the database, four right index fingerprint images (in BMP format) are available:

- Two right index fingerprints acquired during the first session.
- Two right index fingerprints acquired during the second session.

11.4.1.3 Signature

The device used to record signatures is an HP iPAQ hx2790. For each individual enrolled in the database, 40 online signature files (in text format) are available:

- Five genuine signatures acquired during the first session.
- 15 genuine signatures acquired during the second session.

- 20 skilled forgeries acquired during both sessions. These forgeries were produced manually by asking the subjects of the database to perform signature imitations based on a signature dynamic blueprint of another subject.

Each signature file mentioned below is composed of three columns (see Fig. 11.1):

1. The first column contains the x coordinate of each point.
2. The second column contains the y coordinate of each point.
3. The third column contains the time (in ms) elapsed between the acquisition of two successive points.

When the x and y coordinates equal 0.0, it means that the acquisition process did not work.

147	651	0
0	0	10
0	0	10
150	660	11
150	680	9
152	689	12
152	697	10
153	710	218
233	799	10
236	808	10
...		

Fig. 11.1 A sample of a signature file (x coordinates on the first column, y coordinates on the second column and acquisition time on the third column)

For this evaluation, we have also created five so-called "regained" forgeries [25] per user. In this scenario, we assume that the forger has got access to a static version of the genuine signature. He has a dedicated software to automatically recover dynamics of the signature and then he uses these regained signatures to break the verification system. Figure 11.2 illustrates the regain procedure with, on the right-hand part of the figure, a typical example of the signature information that is recovered. It is noticed that the x and y coordinates of such signatures are never equal to 0.0 because the software used to create the dynamics of these signatures does not simulate the acquisition errors (i.e, failure to record a point).

11.4.1.4 Talking Face

The device used to record the video sequences ($\sim 10s$) is a SAMSUNG Q1 with a webcam. For each individual enrolled in the database, four video files (in AVI format), in which a short phrase in English is pronounced, are available:

- Two indoor video files acquired during the first session and containing each a random phrase in English.

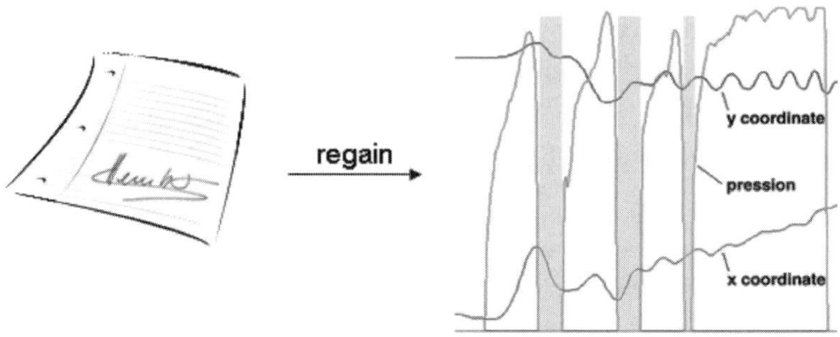

Fig. 11.2 Regained procedure: starting from a static version of the signature stolen from the genuine user, the regain procedure automatically recovers the dynamics

- Two outdoor video files acquired during the second session and containing each a random phrase in English.

The submitted systems are challenged against different types of forgeries ranging from the simplest random forgeries to more sophisticated ones.

Random forgeries (imp1RND) These forgeries are simulated by using video files from other users as input to a specific user model. This category actually does not denote intentional forgeries, but rather accidental accesses by non-malicious users. For the BMEC evaluation, we use the video files from 10 other users taken randomly from the database to perform these tests.

Genuine picture animation (imp2PA) The assumption is the following: the forger has captured a static picture of the genuine user, which is currently realistic. He is then using a commercial software to animate this picture as if the genuine user would be talking. Such commercial software is now available from different vendors (see for example [16]). It is finally assumed that the resulting *avi* file is played back to the verification system. The procedure is illustrated in Fig. 11.3. The animation of the picture is performed automatically by the software that moves parts of the face according to acoustic events detected in the waveform. To produce such forgeries, an annotation work is required to position some reference points on the genuine face image. For example, lips, nostrils and eyes contour have to be tuned. The quality of the final animation is variable and depends on the quality of the original image, on the number of reference points that are used to define the mesh and on the automatic detection of acoustic events such as plosive sounds. As time was limited for producing these forgeries, we limited ourselves to the definition of about 20 reference points and let the software automatically analyze the sound waveform to animate the face. More fine-tuning could of course lead to better animation, but we limited ourselves to a maximum of 5–10 minutes of work per forgery. The speech part here was automatically generated using a freely available Text-To-Speech (TTS) software [41], [42]. The gender of the voice is chosen according to the gender of the user to forge. We produced one such imposture per user for a total of 430 face animation forgeries.

Genuine picture presentation (imp3PP) The assumption here is that a static picture of the target user has been stolen and is simply presented to the verification system. The forger moves the picture in front of the camera to attempt to break the livens detection system, if any. To avoid the burden of recording many such picture presentations, software is used to automate the production of the AVI-files, simply gluing the picture at given coordinates of each frame of the video sequence. Figure 11.4 shows an example of the kind of input the verification system will have to treat. For the speech part, a TTS is also used to generate the voice.

Audio replay attack (imp4AR) We assume here that an audio waveform was recorded from the genuine user and is played back to the system with the forger moving his lips (unsynchronously) on top of the audio playback. The audio part is assumed to have been stolen in outdoor conditions. In practice, we realize these forgeries by ripping the audio part from the outdoor recordings of the genuine user and gluing the waveform in the video of randomly chosen forgers.

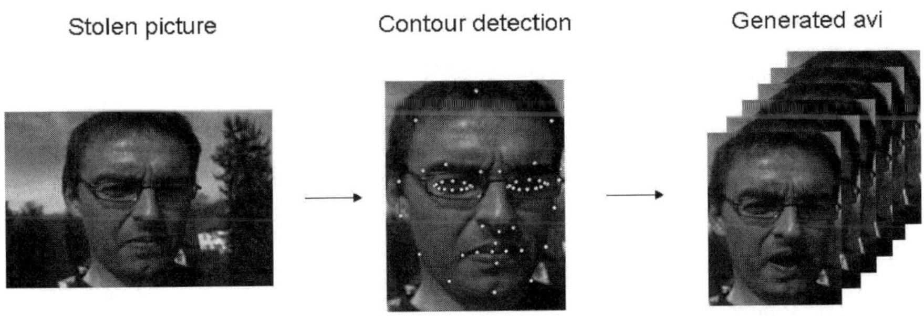

Fig. 11.3 Procedure to generate a genuine picture animation when a picture is stolen from the genuine user: (left) the picture is imported in a face animation tool, (middle) lips, eyes and face contour are detected, and (right) the video sequence is automatically generated from a sound waveform

11.4.1.5 Fusion

The fusion database is exclusively composed of scores provided by three BioSecure reference systems (fingerprint, signature and 2D face) applied on the corresponding BioSecure monomodal databases according to the monomodal protocols (see Sect. 11.6). These systems are the following:

- The 2D face reference system (described in Chap. 8 (page 234)) was developed by Bogaziçi University and is based on the standard eigenface approach [46]. To manage video sequences, it has been decided to extract five frames at regular intervals. The scores provided by this system are distance measures.
- The fingerprint reference system is based on the use of the NIST Fingerprint Image Software 2 [48] in which a standard minutiae approach is available. The scores provided by this system are similarity scores. The same system is used for the fingerprint benchmarking experiments given in Chap. 4 (page 69).

Fig. 11.4 Example of a picture presentation forgery: an AVI file is automatically generated from this picture, simulating the hand movement of the forger

- The signature reference system [47], [22] has been developed by TELECOM SudParis (ex GET-INT) and is based on Hidden Markov Models. The scores provided by this system are similarity scores. The same system is used for the online handwritten benchmarking experiments given in Chap. 6 (page 139).

For each individual enrolled in the database, 44 accesses are available (an access is a set of three scores; one per modality):

- Four client accesses.
- 20 impostor accesses for which the impostor scores were obtained using random forgeries for each modality.
- 20 impostor accesses for which the impostor scores were obtained using skilled forgeries for signature and random forgeries for the other modalities.

It is noted that the only differences between the two sets of impostor accesses are the signature scores.

11.4.2 Statistics

The different acquisition sites have made some statistics about the donors of the development and the test databases. They refer to the following criteria:

- Gender (male / female).
- Age.
- Handedness (right / left).
- Visual aids (glasses / lenses / none).

Furthermore, statistics about scores of the fusion databases are also available.

11.4.2.1 Development Database

The development database is composed of 50 donors. Table 11.1 shows statistics about donors while Table 11.2 gives some pieces of information about scores.[1]

11.4.2.2 Test Database

The test database is composed of 430 donors. Table 11.3 shows statistics about donors while Table 11.4 gives some pieces of information about scores.[2]

The statistics that have been made on the development and test databases prove that these databases are very similar, except for the visual aids. As there are more people wearing glasses in the test database (42.6%), we can suppose that the 2D face and talking-face test databases are "more difficult" than the corresponding development databases (in which there are only 28.0% of donors wearing glasses). For the other modalities (fingerprint, signature and fusion), the results obtained by a system on the development and test databases can be expected to be very close.

11.5 Performance Evaluation

In this section, we describe the tools and criteria used by the organizers of the BMEC to evaluate and compare the performance of the biometric verification systems submitted by the participants.

11.5.1 Evaluation Platform

To produce client and impostor scores for each algorithm, the organizers have run the submitted executables on a Linux cluster using the sequestered test database. It is noted that a test machine was put at participants' disposal during the development step. The goal of this machine was to permit participants to compile and test their systems on the same machines as those used by the organizers at the test step. So, it was hoped that no problems would be encountered by the organizers to run the submitted systems.

---

[1] A score of the fusion development database is meant to be either a similarity score or a distance measure.

[2] A score of the fusion test database is meant to be either a similarity score or a distance measure.

Table 11.1 Statistics about donors of the development database: (**a**) gender, (**b**) age, (**c**) handedness, and (**d**) visual aids

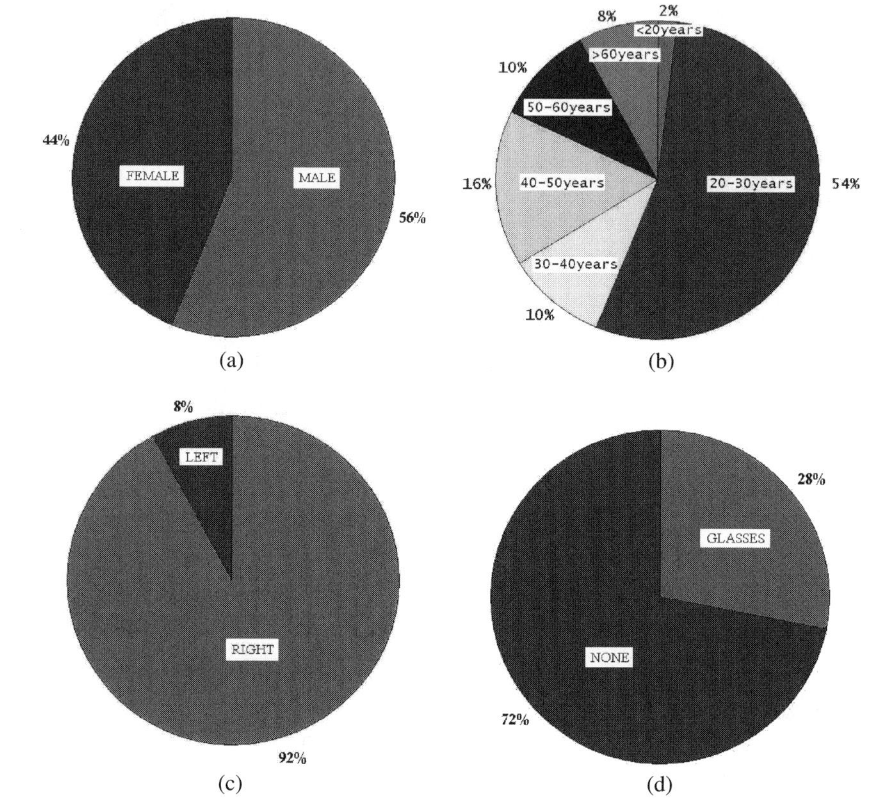

Table 11.2 Statistics about the scores of the fusion development database

Type	Client			Random forgeries			Skilled forgeries
Modality	Fingerprint	2D face	Signature	Fingerprint	2D face	Signature	Signature
Mean	50.8	250.4	0.72	8.4	299.9	0.30	0.45
Standard deviation	42.9	57.5	0.11	4.4	46.6	0.11	0.15

11.5.2 Criteria

The organizers have selected the next criteria to evaluate the performance of the biometric verification systems.

Detection Error Trade-off (DET) curve This curve is used to summarize the performance of a biometric verification system. A DET [31] curve plots error rates on both axes (False Acceptance Rate (FAR) on the x-axis against false rejection rate (FRR) on the y-axis) giving uniform treatment to both types of error.

Table 11.3 Statistics about donors of the test database: (**a**) gender, (**b**) age, (**c**) handedness, and (**d**) visual aids

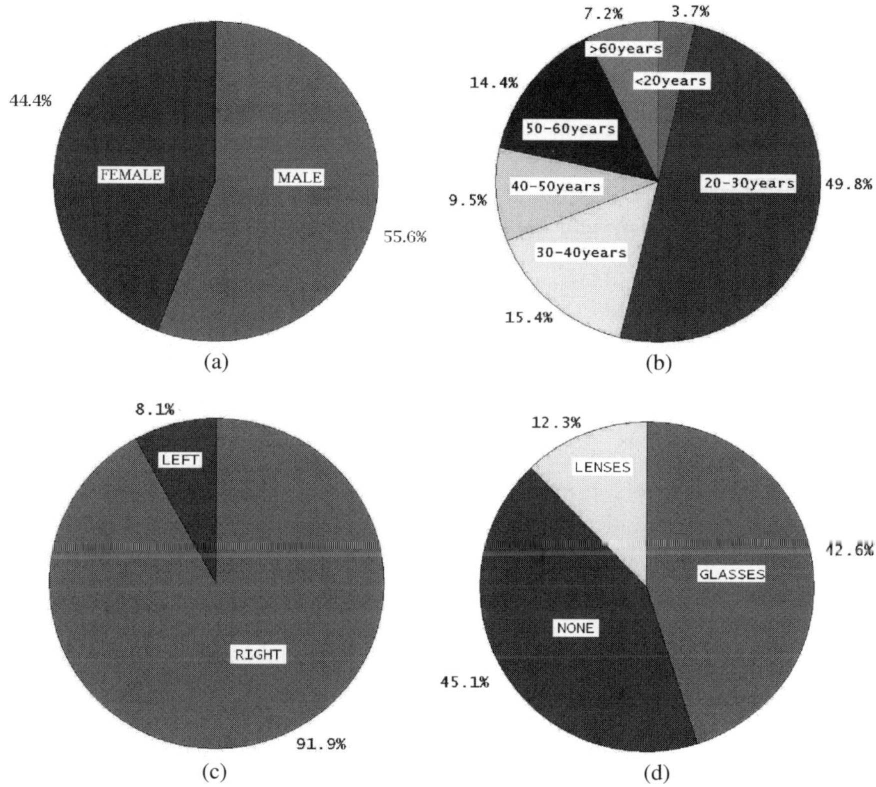

Table 11.4 Statistics about the scores of the fusion test database

Type	Client			Random forgeries			Skilled forgeries
Modality	Fingerprint	2D face	Signature	Fingerprint	2D face	Signature	Signature
Mean	44.4	269.5	0.71	8.3	308.8	0.31	0.46
Standard deviation	37.2	63.0	0.12	4.7	50.7	0.10	0.14

Equal Error Rate (EER) The equal error rate is computed as the point where $FAR(t) = FRR(t)$. In practice, the score distributions are not continuous and a crossover point might not exist. In this case, an interpolation is done to estimate the EER value (see Sect. 11.8).

Operating Point (OP) In practice, biometric systems operate at a low FAR instead of the EER in order to provide high security. This operating point is defined in terms of FRR (%) achieved for a fixed FAR. The fixed value α of FAR depends on the modality. In practice, the OP is computed as follows:

$$OP_{\{FAR=\alpha\}} = FRR(t_{OP}) \mid t_{OP} = \max_{t \in S}\{t|\alpha \leqslant FAR(t)\}$$

where S is the set of thresholds used to calculate the score distributions.

Failure to Match Rate (FMR) The FMR is the proportion of client and impostor tests for which the system is unable to produce scores because of one of the following reasons:

- The system is unable to extract features.
- The system is unable to create the client model.
- The system is so resource-consuming that the processing is not supported by our cluster.

The tests, for which the scores cannot be provided by the system, are systematically considered as errors. It means that a client test for which the system is unable to produce score is considered to be a false rejection for all thresholds, whereas an impostor test is considered to be a false acceptance.

11.5.3 Confidence Intervals

A 90% interval of confidence is provided for the Equal Error Rate (EER) and the Operating Point (OP) value. This allows for determining whether accuracy differences between systems are really statistically significant.

Using a parametric method [7], we could calculate error margins on $FAR(t)$ and $FRR(t)$ at some threshold t (see Sect. 11.9), such as:

- $FAR(t) \in [\hat{\text{FAR}}(t) - err_{\hat{\text{FAR}}(t)}, \hat{\text{FAR}}(t) + err_{\hat{\text{FAR}}(t)}]$ where $\hat{\text{FAR}}$(t) is an estimation of FAR at threshold t and $err_{\hat{\text{FAR}}(t)}$ is the error margin on this value.
- $FRR(t) \in [\hat{\text{FRR}}(t) - err_{\hat{\text{FRR}}(t)}, \hat{\text{FRR}}(t) + err_{\hat{\text{FRR}}(t)}]$ where $\hat{\text{FRR}}$(t) is an estimation of FRR at threshold t and $err_{\hat{\text{FRR}}(t)}$ is the error margin on this value.

In this way, a confidence interval on the EER value is

- $EER \in [\hat{\text{EER}} - err_{\hat{\text{EER}}}, \hat{\text{EER}} + err_{\hat{\text{EER}}}]$ where $\hat{\text{EER}} = \frac{\hat{\text{FAR}}(t_{EER}) + \hat{\text{FRR}}(t_{EER})}{2}$ and $err_{\hat{\text{EER}}} = \frac{err_{\hat{\text{FAR}}(t_{EER})} + err_{\hat{\text{FRR}}(t_{EER})}}{2}$ and t_{EER} is the threshold at which the EER has been evaluated (see Sect. 11.8).

11.6 Experimental Results

For each experiment (2D face on video sequences, fingerprint, signature, talking face and fusion), we present the participants (see also Sect. 11.10), we describe the protocol and we report the experimental results. Furthermore, for each monomodal experiment, the results obtained with the reference systems used for the BioSecure benchmarking framework for 2D Face, fingerprint and online handwritten signature (described in Chaps. 8, 4, and 6) are reported because they permit the calibration of the difficulty of the monomodal databases used for the evaluation. Thus, the performance of the reference systems enable to measure the improvements acquired with each submitted system.

11.6.1 Monomodal Evaluations

The modalities used for the monomodal evaluation are 2D face (Sect. 11.6.1.1), fingerprint (Sect. 11.6.1.2), signature (Sect. 11.6.1.3) and talking face (Sect. 11.6.1.4).

11.6.1.1 2D Face Video Sequences

Participants Three universities have registered to this experiment: GET-ENST, UNIFRI and UVIGO. Overall, nine systems have been submitted by the participants. These systems (+ the reference system) are summarily described below.

Ref. Syst. The BioSecure 2D-face reference system (see Chap. 8 page 234) uses the standard Eigenface approach [46] to represent face images (extracted from a given video) in a lower dimensional subspace. The face space is built using the 300 images from the BANCA world model and the dimensionality of the reduced space is selected such as 99% of the variance is explained by the PCA analysis. To manage video sequences, five frames are extracted at regular intervals. Using the eye positions detected automatically, each face image is then normalized and projected onto the face space. At the matching step, the L1-norm distance measure is used to evaluate the similarity between the five target feature vectors and the five test feature vectors. The final score corresponds to the minimum of these 25 distances.

GET-ENST The system uses the standard Eigenface approach to represent face images (extracted from a given video) in a lower dimensional subspace. The face space is built using 2,200 images from five different databases. Only the 100 first dimensions are kept (where the three very first are left aside). To manage video sequences, the 100 faces with lowest distance to the eigenspace are selected. Then, each face image is projected onto the face space. At the matching step, the distances of Mahalanobis between the 100 feature vectors extracted from target and test video are calculated. Finally, the score is equal to the opposite of the mean of the 10 smallest distances.

UNIFRI1: The system uses the Gaussian Mixtures Models (GMM) approach. First, frames are extracted from the video sequence at intervals of 1 second. Using automatically detected eye position, each image is cropped and resized to 120×160. Then, each image is chopped with a window of size 12×12 and 39 DCT features are extracted. The client model is built by adapting the parameters of the Universal Background Model (UBM) using the maximum a posteriori (MAP) criterion (the UBM has been trained using all genuine data of the BMEC development database). At the matching step, a log-likelihood ratio is calculated for each frame extracted from the test video sequence given the client model and the UBM. The final score is the mean of the scores obtained for all frames.

UNIFRI2 The system is the same as UNIFRI1 except for the calculation of the final score. The final score is here equal to the maximum of the scores obtained for all frames.

UNIFRI3 The system is the same as UNIFRI1. The only difference is that the images are put to gray level and normalized before being resized.

UNIFRI4 The system is the same as UNIFRI3 except for the calculation of the final score. The final score here is equal to the maximum of the scores obtained for all frames.

UNIFRI5 The system is the same as UNIFRI1. The only difference is that the images are put to gray level and equalized before being resized.

UNIFRI6 The system is the same as UNIFRI5 except for the calculation of the final score. The final score here is equal to the maximum of the scores obtained for all frames.

UVIGO1 The system uses the Gabor filters. First, all frames of the video are extracted and OpenCV facilities are used to find the face in these images. Using the eyes and mouth positions, each face image is then normalized. Gabor jets (five different scales and eight orientations) are next extracted in every node of a rigid 10×10 rectangular grid placed on the normalized face. Features are the absolute values of the filter responses. At the matching step, each face of the test video is matched against all faces of the target video using their corresponding jets. Hence, a matrix S of similarity values is obtained

$$\mathbf{S} = \begin{pmatrix} s_{1,1} & s_{1,2} & \cdots & s_{1,N_2} \\ s_{2,1} & \ddots & & \vdots \\ \vdots & & \ddots & \vdots \\ s_{N_1,1} & \cdots & \cdots & s_{N_1,N_2} \end{pmatrix}$$

where N_1 and N_2 stand for the number of processed frames for the test and target video, respectively; $s_{i,j}$ is the similarity value between the face in frame i of the target video and the face in frame j of the test video. Finally, the score is obtained as score $= \text{median}_i\{\max_j[s_{i,j}]\}$.

UVIGO2 The system uses the Gabor filters and it is based on the GMM approach. First, all frames of the video are extracted and OpenCV facilities are used to find the face in these images. Using the eyes and mouth positions, each face image is then normalized. Gabor jets (five different scales and eight orientations) are next extracted in every node of a rigid 10×10 rectangular grid placed on the normalized face. Features are the absolute values of the filter responses. The Universal Background Model (UBM) has been built for each node in the rectangular grid using the whole data set of the BMEC development database. Then, this location-specific model is adapted (by the MAP adaptation technique) to the client features, obtaining a client model for each node. The matching is performed by evaluating the loglikelihood ratio between the user models and the UBMs. We suppose the models to be independent and then, the total loglikelihood ratio for a single frame is the sum of the loglikelihood ratios for each node. We also assume the frames are independent and then, the whole face video sequence loglikelihood ratio is the sum of all the frame loglikelihood ratios.

Protocol The database used for this evaluation is the 2D face monomodal database described in Sect. 11.4.1.1. For each individual enrolled in this database, we describe below the enrollment and test sets:

- Enrollment set: two indoor video files acquired during the first session.
- Test set: two outdoor video files acquired during the second session.

Submitted systems should compare a video of test to each video of enrollment set, hence, the next matching tests (per individual) should be done:

- Four client tests.
- 10×4 random impostor tests (for each client, the two test video files of ten randomly chosen persons are compared to his/her two enrollment video files).

Experimental results The experimental results of each participant systems are shown by a DET curve (Fig. 11.5) and are reported in Table 11.5.

Results analysis Through a very first rough analysis of the results, we try to answer to the next questions.

What is the best method to manage the video sequences? The three most impressive systems (UVIGO1, UVIGO2 and GET-ENST) extract and process all frames from the video sequence whereas the other systems work with only few frames extracted at regular intervals. Furthermore, by comparing performance (in terms of EER) of the GET-ENST system (27.03%) and the reference system (37.12%), which both use the PCA approach, it seems clear that the best way to manage the video sequence is to take into account all frames (or select some of them intelligently).

What are the most adequate features to verify the identity of the users from the BMEC database? By comparing performance (in terms of EER) of the GET-ENST (27.03%) and UVIGO1 (21.92%) systems which both process all frames of the video sequence, it confirms that the Gabor jets are more adequate to cope with the huge illumination variability of the database than the PCA approach.

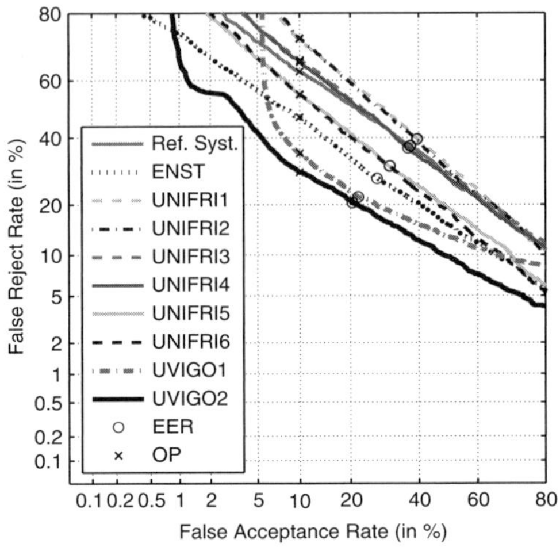

Fig. 11.5 DET curves for the 2D face experiment, with video sequences

Table 11.5 Experimental results for the 2D face experiment, with video sequences [EER = Equal Error Rate; OP = Operating Point; FMR (ct/it) = Failure to Match Rate (client tests/impostor tests)]

Systems	EER in %	$OP_{FAR=10\%}$ in %	FMR (ct/it) in %
Ref. Syst.	37.12 [±1.26]	62.91 [±1.92]	0.0/0.0
GET-ENST	27.03 [±1.16]	47.10 [±1.98]	0.0/0.0
UNIFRI1	39.54 [±1.28]	73.14 [±1.76]	0.17/0.32[1]
UNIFRI2	39.42 [±1.28]	73.31 [±1.75]	0.52/0.26[1]
UNIFRI3	37.29 [±1.26]	66.63 [±1.87]	0.29/0.28[1]
UNIFRI4	36.50 [±1.26]	66.05 [±1.88]	0.29/0.22[1]
UNIFRI5	30.71 [±1.20]	55.06 [±1.97]	0.29/0.26[1]
UNIFRI6	30.81 [±1.21]	55.23 [±1.97]	0.41/0.25[1]
UVIGO1	21.92 [±1.08]	34.83 [±1.89]	5.17/5.49[2]
UVIGO2	20.50 [±1.05]	28.90 [±1.80]	0.81/0.83[2]

[1] The system is so resource-consuming that the processing is not supported by our cluster.
[2] The system is unable to extract features for several persons.

Does the use of a statistic model improve performance? Both systems submitted by UVIGO extract the same features using all frames. But, UVIGO2 uses a GMM approach to integrate the different faces of the person, whereas UVIGO1 compares all feature vectors of the client images to all feature vectors of the test images. By comparing performance in terms of EER of both systems (21.92% for UVIGO1 and 20.50% for UVIGO2), and taking into account the Failure to Match Rate (see Table 11.5), we are not able to claim that the use of a model improves (or not) performance.

11.6.1.2 Fingerprint

Participants Two universities have registered for this experiment. But, both have decided to withdraw from the competition before the deadline for algorithm submission. Finally, only the reference system has been evaluated on the test database:

Ref. Syst. The BioSecure fingerprint baseline system uses a minutiae based matcher (see also Chap. 4 page 69) to verify a person's identity. First, the minutiae detection algorithm relies on binarization of each grayscale input image to locate all minutiae points (ridge ending and bifurcation). Then, the matching algorithm computes a match score between the minutiae pairs from any two fingerprints using the location and orientation of two minutiae points. The matching algorithm is rotation and translation invariant.

Protocol The database used for this evaluation is the fingerprint database described in Sect. 11.4.1.2. For each individual enrolled in this database, we describe below the enrollment and test sets:

- Enrollment set: two right index fingerprints acquired during the first session.
- Test set: two right index fingerprints acquired during the second session.

Submitted systems should compare a fingerprint image of test to a fingerprint of enrollment set, hence, the next matching tests (per individual) should be done:

- Four client tests.
- 10×4 random impostor tests (for each client, the two test fingerprints of ten randomly chosen persons are compared to his/her two enrollment fingerprints).

Experimental results The experimental results obtained for the BioSecure Reference System are shown by a DET curve (Fig. 11.6) and are reported in Table 11.6.

Table 11.6 Experimental results for the fingerprint experiment [EER = Equal Error Rate; OP = Operating Point; FMR (ct/it) = Failure to Match Rate (client tests/impostor tests)]

Systems	EER in %	$OP_{FAR=1\%}$ in %	FMR (ct/it) in %
Ref. Syst.	11.85 [±0.85]	34.42 [±1.88]	0.0/0.0

Results analysis The low performance of the reference system can be explained by the low quality of the images due to the type of sensors (swiping) used on the acquisition device.

11.6.1.3 Signature

Participants Six universities have registered for this experiment: AMSL, EPFL, GET-INT, UNIFRI, University of Tours and UAM. Overall, 11 systems have been

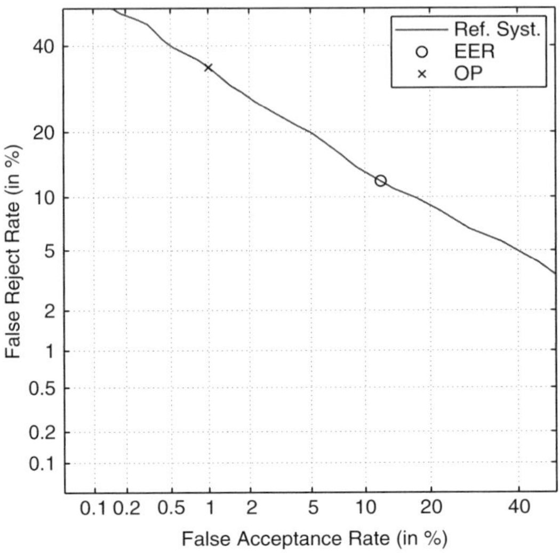

Fig. 11.6 DET curve for the fingerprint experiment

submitted by the participants. These systems (+ the reference system) are summarily described below:

Ref. Syst. The BioSecure reference system (see also Chap. 6 page 139) uses a continuous left-to-right Hidden Markov Model (HMM) to model each signer's characteristics. For each signature, the spatial coordinates are linearly interpolated. 21 dynamic features are then extracted at each point of the signature. Two complementary pieces of information derived from a writer's HMM (likelihood and Viterbi score) are fused to produce the matching score [47], [22].

AMSL The system is based on the Adapted Levenshtein Distance algorithm for handwriting verification [40]. From the raw pen data (pen position and time), the pen movement is firstly estimated using interpolation. An event-string modeling of features derived from pen movement is then used to represent each signature. In order to achieve such a string-like representation, the sample signal is analyzed to extract the feature events (local and global extrema of the pen position in x-axis and y-axis, pen-up event,...) which are coded with single characters and arranged in temporal order of their occurrences leading to an event string (which is simply a sequence of characters). At the matching step, the Levenshtein distance [28] is used to evaluate the similarity between a test and a reference event string.

EPFL1 The system uses the Gaussian Mixtures Models (GMM) approach. For each signature, the raw pen data are preprocessed using linear interpolation and rotation normalization. Then, six local features are extracted. The client model is built using 24 Gaussian components. At the matching step, the likelihood ratio is estimated given the client model and a world model (four Gaussian components) trained on the BMEC development database.

EPFL2 The system uses the Gaussian Mixtures Models (GMM) approach. For each signature, the raw pen data are preprocessed using B-spline interpolation. Then, six local features are extracted. The client model is built using 36 Gaussian components. At the matching step, the likelihood ratio is estimated given the client model and a world model (four Gaussian components) trained on the BMEC development database.

EPFL3 The system is a multiple-classifier system, containing seven basic classifiers. All classifiers are based on the Gaussian Mixtures Models (GMM) approach. The first five classifiers use local features, while the last two classifiers use global features. For each classifier, at the matching step, the likelihood ratio is estimated given the client model and a world model trained on the BMEC development database. To obtain the final similarity score, all likelihood ratios are fused using the mean rule.

EPFL4 The system is a multiple-classifier system, containing six basic classifiers. All classifiers are based on the Gaussian Mixtures Models (GMM) approach. The first five classifiers use local features, while the last classifier uses global features. In all cases, at the matching step, the likelihood ratio is estimated given the client model and a world model trained on the BMEC development database. Furthermore, six quality measures per client model are estimated. Finally, to obtain the final similarity score, the likelihood ratios and quality measures are fused using a model trained on the BMEC development database. It is noted that this system produces a binary output and not a score.

GET-INT The system uses a continuous left-to-right Hidden Markov Model (HMM) to model each signer's characteristics. For each signature, the raw pen data are preprocessed using B-spline interpolation. Nineteen features are then extracted at each point of the signature. At the matching step, we fuse complementary information derived from a writer's HMM: likelihood and Viterbi score. The model is largely inspired by the reference system. A personalized score normalization based on intraclass variance and especially tuned on skilled forgeries was performed.

UAM1 The system is a global-feature based system which uses features such as signature duration, number of pen-ups or direction histograms among others. A feature selection process is carried out using floating search algorithms to select a subset of features that gives the best performance. The similarity score is computed using Mahalanobis distance between the client model (computed from the five training signatures) and the test signatures. This system has been especially tuned for random forgeries.

UAM2 The system is the same as UAM1. The only difference is that this system has been tuned for skilled forgeries.

UNIFRI1 The system uses a Hidden Markov Model (HMM) to model each signer's characteristics. For each signature, the coordinates are linearly interpolated. 19 features are then extracted at each point of the signature. At the matching step, the similarity score is normalized using a world model (which has been trained using all genuine data of the BMEC development database).

UNIFRI2 The system uses the Gaussian Mixtures Models (GMM) approach. For each signature, the coordinates are linearly interpolated. Nineteen features are then extracted at each point of the signature. The client model is built by adapting the parameters of the Universal Background Model (UBM) using the Maximum A Posteriori (MAP) estimation and all target features vectors (the UBM has been trained using all genuine data of the BMEC development database). At the matching step, the similarity score is normalized using the UBM.

UniTOURS In order to compute the dissimilarity measure between signatures, the system uses a selection of representative points to describe an online signature. A point is considered representative if it corresponds to a local minimum for the velocity. Next, the matching uses three variations of dynamic time warping algorithm (one classical, one temporal and one based on curvilinear distance). We then fuse the three scores given by the DTW using the sum rule with weights. The final score is the minimum score given by the five reference signatures.

Protocol The database used for this evaluation is the signature monomodal database described in Sect. 11.4.1.3. For each individual enrolled in this database, we describe below the enrollment and test sets:

- Enrollment set: five genuine signatures acquired during the first session.
- Test set: 15 genuine signatures acquired during the second session.
  20 skilled forgeries acquired during both sessions.
  five regained signatures created *a posteriori*.

Submitted systems should compare each signature of the test set to the five signatures of the enrollment set or to a model constructed from these five signatures. For each test, only one score should be provided by the system and the next matching tests (per individual) should be done:

- 15 client tests.
- 25 intentional impostor tests (using the 20 skilled forgeries and the five regained signatures).
- 20 random impostor tests (using genuine signatures from the test set of randomly chosen persons).

Experimental results The experimental results obtained using random forgeries, skilled forgeries and regained dynamic forgeries have been separated.

Random forgeries The experimental results of each participant system obtained with random forgeries are shown by a DET curve (Fig. 11.7) and are reported in Table 11.7.

Skilled forgeries The experimental results of each participant system obtained with skilled forgeries are shown by a DET curve (Fig. 11.8) and are reported in Table 11.8.

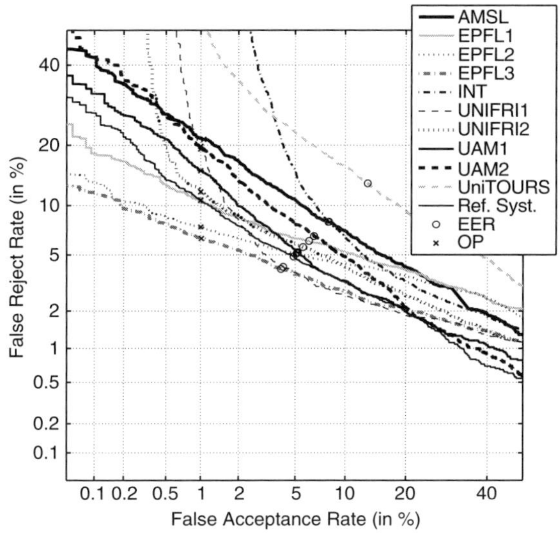

Fig. 11.7 DET curves for the signature experiment with random forgeries

Table 11.7 Experimental results for the signature experiment using random forgeries [EER = Equal Error Rate; OP = Operating Point; FMR (ct/it) = Failure to Match Rate (client tests/impostor tests)]

Systems	EER in %	$OP_{FAR=1\%}$ in %	FMR (ct/it) in %
Ref. Syst.	4.88 [±0.41]	10.74 [±0.63]	0.0/0.0
AMSL	8.00 [±0.52]	21.24 [±0.84]	0.0/0.0
EPFL1	6.14 [±0.46]	10.67 [±0.63]	0.0/0.0
EPFL2	5.12 [±0.42]	7.52 [±0.54]	0.0/0.0
EPFL3	4.03 [±0.38]	6.37 [±0.50]	0.0/0.0
EPFL4[3]	11.24		0.0/0.0
GET-INT	8.07 [±0.52]	76.11 [±0.87]	0.0/0.0
UNIFRI1	4.17 [±0.38]	19.26 [±0.81]	0.42/0.35[1]
UNIFRI2	5.61 [±0.44]	11.88 [±0.66]	0.25/0.34[1]
UAM1	5.18 [±0.42]	15.21 [±0.74]	0.0/0.0
UAM2	6.58 [±0.47]	19.77 [±0.82]	0.0/0.0
UniTOURS	13.14 [±0.65]	52.98 [±1.02]	0.23/0.23[2]

[1] The system is so resource-consuming that the processing is not supported by our cluster.
[2] The system is unable to create a model for one person.
[3] As this system produces a binary output (1 means impostor whereas 2 means client), only the EER value ($\equiv HTER(1.5) = \frac{FAR(1.5)+FRR(1.5)}{2}$) is sensible.

Regained dynamic forgeries The experimental results of each participant system obtained with regained forgeries are shown by a DET curve (Fig. 11.9) and are reported in Table 11.9. It is noticed that no regain forgeries have been distributed to participants for the development of their systems.

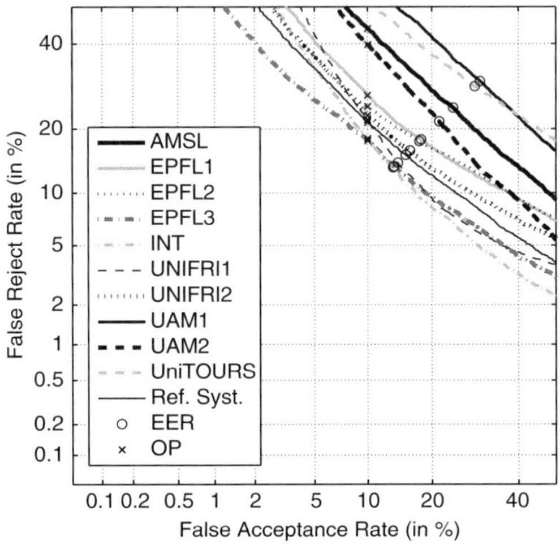

Fig. 11.8 DET curves for the signature experiment with skilled forgeries

Table 11.8 Experimental results for the signature experiment using skilled forgeries [EER = Equal Error Rate; OP = Operating Point; FMR (ct/it) = Failure to Match Rate (client tests/impostor tests)]

Systems	**EER in %**	$OP_{FAR=10\%}$ in %	**FMR (ct/it) in %**
Ref. Syst.	15.36 [±0.69]	21.24 [±0.84]	0.0/0.0
AMSL	24.31 [±0.82]	44.06 [±1.02]	0.0/0.0
EPFL1	18.03 [±0.73]	27.02 [±0.91]	0.0/0.0
EPFL2	17.72 [±0.73]	24.56 [±0.88]	0.0/0.0
EPFL3	13.58 [±0.65]	17.78 [±0.78]	0.0/0.0
EPFL4[3]	17.48		0.0/0.0
GET-INT	13.43 [±0.65]	18.19 [±0.79]	0.0/0.0
UNIFRI1	14.14 [±0.67]	21.77 [±0.85]	0.42/0.44[1]
UNIFRI2	16.09 [±0.70]	22.68 [±0.86]	0.25/0.34[1]
UAM1	30.39 [±0.88]	58.06 [±1.01]	0.0/0.0
UAM2	21.45 [±0.78]	39.77 [±1.00]	0.0/0.0
UniTOURS	29.15 [±0.87]	51.58 [±1.02]	0.23/0.23[2]

[1] The system is so resource-consuming that the processing is not supported by our cluster.
[2] The system is unable to create a model for one person.
[3] As this system produces a binary output (1 means impostor whereas 2 means client), only the EER value ($\equiv HTER(1.5) = \frac{FAR(1.5)+FRR(1.5)}{2}$) is sensible.

Results analysis The submitted systems can be differentiated depending of the type of features extracted, the nature of the information they use in their final score and also on the nature of the classifier.

Features can be local (i.e, extracted at each point of the trajectory) (Ref. System, GET-INT, EPFL1, EPFL2, EPFL3, EPFL4, UNIFRI1, UNIFRI2), intermediary (i.e, extracted at special points of trajectories) (AMSL, UniTOURS) or global (UAM1, UAM2). Some systems produce scores which result of the fusion of local and global information (Ref. System, GET-INT, EPFL3, EPFL4). The 'classifier' used is either a statistical model generated using the five available signatures (Ref. system, GET-INT, EPFL1, EPFL2, EPFL3, EPFL4, UNIFRI1, UNIFRI2) or a simple function (summation, max, min) of the five 1-to-1 distances between the test signature and the five available signatures (AMSL, UniTOURS, UAM1, UAM2). EPFL4 is rather different from the other systems: it not only fuses different systems using local and global informations but it also integrates quality information on data. It also distinguishes from other due to the fact that it only gives one operating point leading to difficulties in comparing systems using ROC curves or EER points.

Skilled forgeries were the forgeries distributed in the development dataset. On those data we observe significant differences of performance between the systems using a model as classifier and those using distances as classifier. Indeed the four systems using distances are the four last systems with a significant difference compared to the other systems that are quite close from each other.

Random forgeries were not explicitly provided as forgeries in the development dataset but it was still possible to train the system on this type of data because they are made using other clients data. On those forgeries, ranks are different from those on skilled forgeries. Although it is an 'easier' task, some systems working well on skilled forgeries have less good performance on random forgeries as it is the case for the GET-INT system, which was not explicitly trained on this type of forgeries. On the other hand, some systems that were not very good on skilled forgeries are performing well on random forgeries, especially UAM1 that was specifically tuned on random forgeries opposed to UAM2 which is the same system tuned on skilled forgeries.

On random forgeries the differences between model and distances approaches are not as clear as on skilled forgeries. However, the four first systems are still using model and local features or a combination of local and global features such as EPFL3.

Regained forgeries were not distributed to participants as development data nor described. Participants were therefore not able to optimize their systems considering this kind of data. Two remarks are important at this point:

1. There were no missing data introduced in regained forgeries, whereas there were missing points in real data as explained in Sect. 11.4.1.3.
2. The five more probable regained signatures were used as forgeries. We have to analyze if those five signatures are of the same level of quality. Because the first is the more reliable and probably the closer to the original signature but the other signatures may not be of good quality in terms of similarity to the original signature.

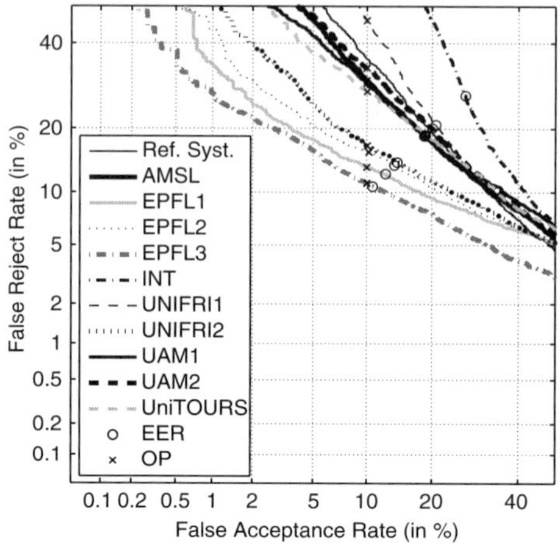

Fig. 11.9 DET curves for the signature experiment with regained forgeries

The first point particularly helps systems that are not doing any interpolation of data to recover missing data. In particular UniTOURS that is not using interpolation has very poor results on skilled and random forgeries probably due to this point. But it has average performance on regained forgeries probably due to the fact that in this experiment, clients and forgeries signatures have very different structure when not considering interpolation of missing data. The influence of the second point has not been analyzed at this stage. It will be the subject of a further study.

Table 11.9 Experimental results for the signature experiment using regained forgeries [EER = Equal Error Rate; OP = Operating Point; FMR (ct/it) = Failure to Match Rate (client tests/impostor tests)]

Systems	EER in %	$OP_{FAR=10\%}$ in %	FMR (ct/it) in %
Ref. Syst.	19.81 [±1.12]	35.98 [±0.98]	0.0/0.0
AMSL	18.53 [±1.08]	30.53 [±0.94]	0.0/0.0
EPFL1	12.41 [±0.92]	13.38 [±0.70]	0.0/0.0
EPFL2	13.67 [±0.96]	15.74 [±0.75]	0.0/0.0
EPFL3	10.73 [±0.87]	11.15 [±0.64]	0.0/0.0
EPFL4[3]	16.46		0.0/0.0
GET-INT	26.97 [±1.24]	78.45 [±0.84]	0.0/0.0
UNIFRI1	20.78 [±1.14]	46.16 [±1.02]	0.42/0.42[1]
UNIFRI2	14.10 [±0.97]	16.85 [±0.77]	0.25/0.37[1]
UAM1	18.76 [±1.09]	29.88 [±0.94]	0.0/0.0
UAM2	20.10 [±1.12]	33.61 [±0.97]	0.0/0.0
UniTOURS	18.80 [±1.09]	27.95 [±0.92]	0.23/0.23[2]

[1] The system is so resource-consuming that the processing is not supported by our cluster.
[2] The system is unable to create a model for one person.
[3] As this system produces a binary output (1 means impostor whereas 2 means client), only the EER value ($\equiv HTER(1.5) = \frac{FAR(1.5)+FRR(1.5)}{2}$) is sensible.

11.6.1.4 Talking Face

Participants Four universities have registered to this experiment: University of Balamand, GET-ENST, UNIFRI and University of Swansea. Overall, 11 systems have been submitted by the participants as well as the BioSecure reference system. These systems are briefly described below.

Reference System The BioSecure reference system is based on the fusion of face and speaker verification scores. **Face verification**: It is based on the standard eigenface approach [46] to represent face images in a lower dimensional subspace. First, 10 frames are extracted from the video at regular intervals. Using the eye positions detected automatically, each face image is normalized, cropped and projected onto the face space (the face space was built using the 300 images from the BANCA world model and the dimensionality of the reduced space was selected such that 99% of the variance is explained by the PCA analysis). In this way, 10 feature vectors are produced for a given video. Next, the L1-norm distance measure is used to evaluate the similarity between 10 target and test feature vectors. Finally, the face score is the minimum of these 100 distances. **Speaker verification**: it is developed using HTK [43] and BECARS [29] open source toolkits. The speech processing is performed on 20 ms Hamming windowed frames, with 10 ms overlap. For each frame, 15 MFCC coefficients (+energy) and their first-order deltas are extracted. For speech activity detection, a bi-Gaussian model is fitted to the energy component of a speech sample. The threshold t used to determine the set of frames to discard is computed as follows: $t = \mu - 2 * \sigma$, where μ and σ are the mean and the variance of the highest Gaussian component, respectively. Next, a cepstral mean substraction (CMS) is applied to the static coefficients. An universal background model (UBM) with 256 components has been trained with the EM algorithm using all genuine data of the development database. A speaker model is built by adapting the parameters of the UBM using the speaker's training feature vectors and the Maximum A Posteriori (MAP) criterion. At the calculation step, the MFCC-feature vectors from the test sequence are compared to both the client GMM and the UBM. The speech score is the average log-likelihood ratio. **Fusion module**: the min-max approach [27] is used to fuse the face and speech scores. The fusion parameters have been estimated using all development data.

GET-ENST1 The system uses the standard Eigenface approach to represent face images (extracted from the video) in a lower dimensional subspace, the standard UBM/GMM approach for speaker verification and finally co-inertia analysis of acoustic and visual speech features to evaluate audiovisual speech synchrony. It then performs score fusion in two steps: (1) synchro and speaker scores are fused, (2) previous results are fused with a face. **Pre-processing**: eyes and mouth detection is performed on every frame of the video using the MPT toolbox and a Viola-Jones mouth detector. **World models**: for the face space, 2,200 images are used (ATT, BANCA world model, BIOMET, CALTECH, GeorgiaTech). The 100 first dimensions are used (where the three very first are left aside). For the speech UBM, the BMEC development data are used to compute a 32 Gaussians GMM. **Feature extraction**:

the distance from face space (of dimension five) is computed for each detected face. The 100 faces with lowest distance from face space are kept, from which eigenface features are extracted (of dimension $100 - 3 = 97$). For the speech part, MFCC extraction with silence removal (based on a bi-Gaussian model of energy distribution) is used to compute 12 MFCC + Delta + DeltaDelta (36 dimensional features). For the synchrony: MFCC+Delta and DCT of mouth area+Delta. **Model creation**: no model is used for the space part; MAP adaptation of the UBM for the speech part and co-inertia analysis for the synchrony (two linear transformation matrices (one for acoustic and one for visual features). **Matching**: for the face part, the distance of Mahalanobis between the 100 vectors extracted from model and test video is computed. Then, the opposite of the mean of the 10 smallest distances is used as the score. For the speech part, we compute the ratio of the client model likelihood and the UBM likelihood. For the synchrony, we use correlation between transformed acoustic and visual features.

GET-ENST2 Same as GET-ENST1 excepted for the fusion step that is performed using a weighted sum of normalized scores (sigma-mu).

GET-ENST3 Same as GET-ENST2 without speech synchrony measures.

GET-ENST4 Same as GET-ENST2 without the speech modeling part.

GET-ENST5 Same as GET-ENST2 without the face modeling part.

GET-ENST6 Only the face part of GET-ENST2.

GET-ENST7 Only the speech part of GET-ENST2.

GET-ENST8 Only the synchrony part of GET-ENST2.

Swansea The Swansea system is a speech-only system based on an LFCC front-end and a GMM system for speaker adaptation and testing [36]. It was developed using SPro [44] and ALIZE [1] open source toolkits. The GMM system is as described in [9] and the front-end is an adaptation from the mean-based feature extraction described in [17], found to perform well on short duration tasks. A UBM with only 64 components is trained from all development data. Score normalization is applied with a TNorm cohort made of 100 models coming from development data. All details not mentioned here can be found in [9]. The systems in previous publications have been optimized on NIST speaker recognition evaluation [15] databases, where the recordings come from telephony speech sample at 8 kHz, but in BMEC talking face evaluation the acoustic signal is sampled at 44.2 kHz. In [17] the features are calculated from 24 filterbanks taken between 300 Hz and 3.4 kHz (telephony band). After experiments on the development data, we retain a front-end where the filterbank width is kept similar to the original configuration by considering 72 linear bands between 300 Hz and 12 kHz. Out of the potential 72 LFCC coefficients, we take only the first 29. The new feature size is 59 with 29 LFCC+29 deltas+delta energy.

UNIFRI The system presented by UNIFRI independently models the speech and face modalities, performing fusion at the score level. Both modalities use GMMs trained with a MAP adaptation procedure from UBMs. **Face verification**: face images are firstly extracted every second from the video sequence. Cropping, resizing to 120×160 pixels, grayscale transformations and intensity/contrast normalization are applied consecutively to each face image. A DCTmod2 feature extraction is then applied on 15×15 pixels windows shifted along the x and y axis (50% overlapping) [37]. The feature vectors are then composed of the 25 first DCT coefficients from which the three first ones are replaced by delta values computed from the adjacent windows along the x and y directions. The background GMM is trained using parts of the data of all genuine users from the development set. To make the impact of illumination uniform, all face images are horizontally flipped. The EM algorithm is used to train this model up to 128 Gaussians using a binary splitting procedure. The client models are obtained using a MAP adaptation from this UBM. **Speaker verification**: the feature extraction is classically based on MFCC features with 13 coefficients. Delta features are not included. A speech activity detection module based on a bi-Gaussian model is used to discard the silence part of the speech signal. The speech detection parameters (essentially the threshold) have been tuned on the development data. Similarly as for the face part, a 32-component background GMM is trained on the development set using the EM algorithm. The client models are obtained using a MAP adaptation from this background model. **Fusion Module**: log-likelihood ratio scores are computed from the face and speech part and are normalized using a ZNorm procedure where normalization coefficients are computed using a cohort composed of users from the development set [4]. A simple sum of normalized scores for each modality is used, without any weighting.

Balamand/GET-ENST This system is the result of a collaboration between University of Balamand and GET-ENST. The system uses both the speech and the visual modalities for speaker verification. On the visual side, faces are tracked in every frame of the video sequence through a machine learning approach based on a boosted cascade of Haar-like features for visual object detection [30]. Faces are then scaled, cropped, gray-scaled, and histogram equalized. Feature extraction is based on orthogonal 2D DCT basis functions of overlapping blocks of the face [37]. On the speech side, the feature extraction module calculates relevant vectors from the speech waveform. On a signal "FFT" window shifted at a regular rate, cepstral coefficients are derived from a filter bank analysis with triangular filters. A Hamming weighting window is used to compensate for the truncation of the signal. The SPro [44] open source toolkit is used. Classification for both modalities uses GMMs to model the distribution of the feature vectors for each identity. GMM client training and testing is performed using the speaker verification toolkit, BECARS [29]. A final decision on the claimed identity of a talking face relies on fusing the scores of both modalities. The speech and face scores are personalized (ZNorm) with mean and variance estimated on the development set.

Protocol The database used for this evaluation is the talking-face database described in Sect. 11.4.1.4. For each individual enrolled in this database, we build two models trained respectively on the first and second English phrases of Session 1, indoor conditions. The genuine tests are performed against both models using the first and second English phrases of Session 2, outdoor conditions. The total number of genuine tests is then equal to 430users × 2models × 2accesses = 1,720tests. As described in Sect. 11.4.1.4, we have different types of forgeries for which the total number of tests are summarized in Table 11.10.

Table 11.10 Number of tests according to the type of forgery for the talking face evaluation

Type of forgery	# genuine users	# models	# forgeries	# accesses	total
Random	430	2	10	2	17,200
Picture animation	430	2	1	1	860
Picture presentation	430	2	1	2	1,720
Audio replay	430	2	1	2	1,720

Experimental results The experimental results obtained using the different types of forgeries (see Sect. 11.4.1.4) have been separated. It is noted that no forgery examples (except random forgeries) have been distributed to participants for the development of their systems.

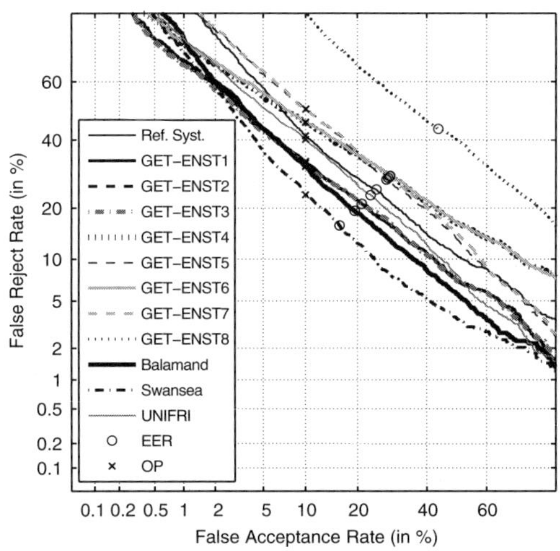

Fig. 11.10 DET curves for the talking-face experiment with random forgeries

Random forgeries (imp1RND) The experimental results of each participant system obtained with random forgeries are shown by a DET curve (Fig. 11.10) and are reported in Table 11.11.

Table 11.11 Experimental results for the talking-face experiment using random forgeries [EER = Equal Error Rate; OP = Operating Point; FMR (ct/it) = Failure to Match Rate (client tests/impostor tests)]

Systems	EER in %	$OP_{FAR=10\%}$ in %	FMR (ct/it) in %
Ref. Syst.	24.80 [±1.13]	41.40 [±1.95]	0.0/0.0
GET-ENST1	21.03 [±1.06]	33.02 [±1.87]	0.0/0.0
GET-ENST2	21.01 [±1.06]	32.56 [±1.86]	0.0/0.0
GET-ENST3	21.05 [±1.06]	31.45 [±1.84]	0.0/0.0
GET-ENST4	28.55 [±1.18]	46.05 [±1.98]	0.0/0.0
GET-ENST5	27.57 [±1.17]	50.58 [±1.98]	0.0/0.0
GET-ENST6	28.67 [±1.18]	46.16 [±1.98]	0.0/0.0
GET-ENST7	28.06 [±1.17]	50.70 [±1.98]	0.0/0.0
GET-ENST8	43.84 [±1.30]	80.23 [±1.58]	0.0/0.0
Balamand	19.36 [±1.03]	31.63 [±1.84]	0.0/0.0
Swansea	16.06 [±0.96]	23.37 [±1.68]	0.0/0.0
UNIFRI	23.28 [±1.10]	40.12 [±1.94]	0.0/0.0

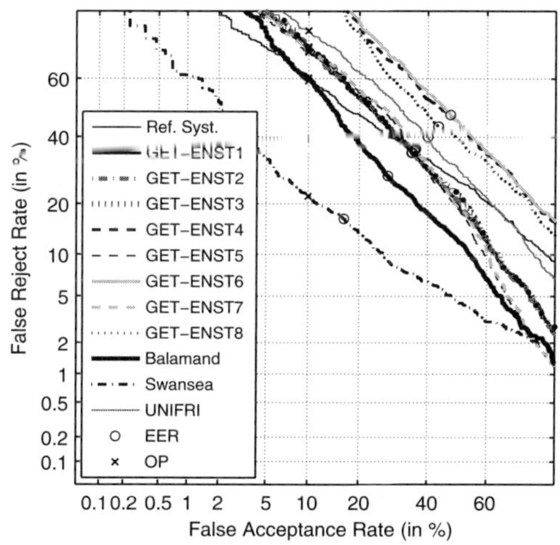

Fig. 11.11 DET curves for the talking-face experiment in which the forger animates a genuine picture

Genuine picture animation (imp2PA) The experimental results of each participant system obtained with this kind of forgery are shown by a DET curve (Fig. 11.11) and are reported in Table 11.12.

Genuine picture presentation (imp3PP) The experimental results of each participant system obtained with this kind of forgery are shown by a DET curve (Fig. 11.12) and are reported in Table 11.13.

Audio replay attack (imp4AR) The experimental results of each participant system obtained with this kind of forgery are shown by a DET curve (Fig. 11.13) and are reported in Table 11.14.

Table 11.12 Experimental results for the talking-face experiment using the genuine picture animation as forgery [EER = Equal Error Rate; OP = Operating Point; FMR (ct/it) = Failure to Match Rate (client tests/impostor tests)]

Systems	**EER in %**	$OP_{FAR=10\%}$ in %	**FMR (ct/it) in %**
Ref. Syst.	34.77 [±2.28]	59.24 [±1.95]	0.0/0.0
GET-ENST1	34.88 [±2.28]	69.83 [±1.82]	0.0/0.0
GET-ENST2	34.91 [±2.28]	70.17 [±1.81]	0.0/0.0
GET-ENST3	35.67 [±2.29]	69.83 [±1.82]	0.0/0.0
GET-ENST4	47.53 [±2.39]	87.62 [±1.31]	0.0/0.0
GET-ENST5	35.61 [±2.29]	68.55 [±1.84]	0.0/0.0
GET-ENST6	47.56 [±2.39]	88.78 [±1.25]	0.0/0.0
GET-ENST7	36.05 [±2.30]	69.01 [±1.83]	0.0/0.0
GET-ENST8	43.55 [±2.37]	88.37 [±1.27]	0.0/0.0
Balamand	27.56 [±2.14]	60.23 [±1.94]	0.0/0.0
Swansea	16.54 [±1.78]	21.92 [±1.64]	0.0/0.0
UNIFRI	40.03 [±2.35]	73.83 [±1.72]	0.0/0.0

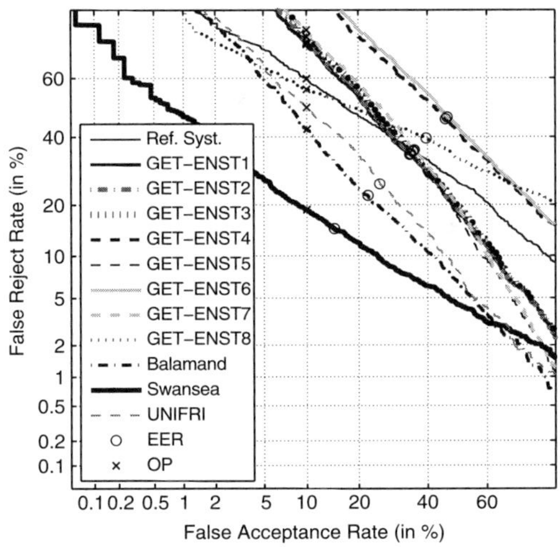

Fig. 11.12 DET curves for the talking-face experiment in which the forger presents a genuine picture in front of the camera

Results analysis Considering the little amount of development data available, the general level of performance on the usual impostor attack (random forgeries) is quite good. Noticeably, Swansea speech-only system shows promising results when compared to EERs usually observed on (telephony) NIST short duration tasks [17]. Optimization of the speech frontend seems to be fundamental on the BMEC type of data.

Exploitation of the face information proved difficult. Here the adopted PCA approaches (Reference System and GET-ENST) proved inadequate to cope with the huge illumination variability.

Table 11.13 Experimental results for the talking-face experiment using the genuine picture presentation as forgery [EER = Equal Error Rate; OP = Operating Point; FMR (ct/it) = Failure to Match Rate (client tests/impostor tests)]

Systems	EER in %	$OP_{FAR=10\%}$ in %	FMR (ct/it) in %
Ref. Syst.	35.35 [±1.90]	59.83 [±1.94]	0.0/0.0
GET-ENST1	34.24 [±1.88]	70.64 [±1.81]	0.0/0.0
GET-ENST2	34.33 [±1.88]	70.93 [±1.80]	0.0/0.0
GET-ENST3	35.20 [±1.89]	72.91 [±1.76]	0.0/0.0
GET-ENST4	46.08 [±1.98]	86.05 [±1.37]	0.0/0.0
GET-ENST5	34.48 [±1.89]	71.22 [±1.80]	0.0/0.0
GET-ENST6	46.60 [±1.98]	87.62 [±1.31]	0.0/0.0
GET-ENST7	35.70 [±1.90]	74.77 [±1.72]	0.0/0.0
GET-ENST8	39.56 [±1.94]	56.22 [±1.97]	0.0/0.0
Balamand	22.30 [±1.65]	42.61 [±1.96]	0.0/0.0
Swansea	14.74 [±1.41]	18.84 [±1.55]	0.0/0.0
UNIFRI	25.44 [±1.73]	50.00 [±1.98]	0.0/0.0

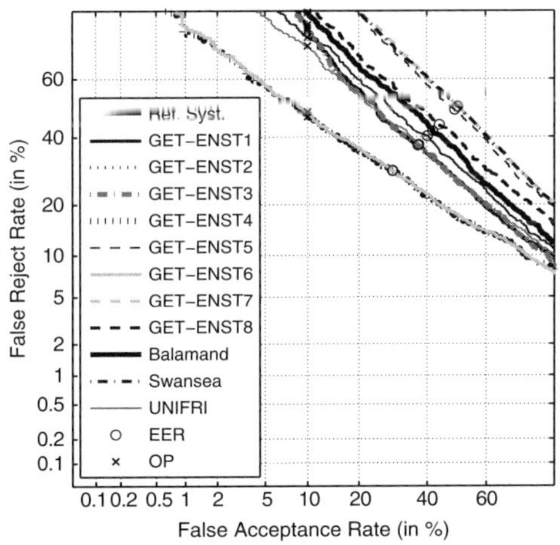

Fig. 11.13 DET curves for the talking-face experiment with audio replay attacks

The ENST-GET8 system, which uses new techniques introduced in [10], gave overall poor results. One reason could be the problem of lack of synchrony between video and speech in this database.

It seems very difficult to resist all types of forgeries with a single system. If a system resists well to a given type of imposture (Swansea on imp2PA/imp3PP and GET-ENST6 on imp4AR), it obtains poor results on another (Swansea on imp4AR and GET-ENST6 on imp2PA/imp3PP).

Table 11.14 Experimental results for the talking-face experiment using audio replay attacks [EER = Equal Error Rate; OP = Operating Point; FMR (ct/it) = Failure to Match Rate (client tests/impostor tests)]

Systems	EER in %	$OP_{FAR=10\%}$ in %	FMR (ct/it) in %
Ref. Syst.	40.23 [±1.95]	73.02 [±1.76]	0.0/0.0
GET-ENST1	37.21 [±1.92]	76.40 [±1.68]	0.0/0.0
GET-ENST2	37.38 [±1.92]	75.64 [±1.70]	0.0/0.0
GET-ENST3	37.18 [±1.92]	75.00 [±1.72]	0.0/0.0
GET-ENST4	29.27 [±1.80]	47.03 [±1.98]	0.0/0.0
GET-ENST5	49.42 [±1.98]	89.94 [±1.19]	0.0/0.0
GET-ENST6	29.16 [±1.80]	48.66 [±1.98]	0.0/0.0
GET-ENST7	50.49 [±1.98]	90.58 [±1.16]	0.0/0.0
GET-ENST8	44.19 [±1.97]	82.09 [±1.52]	0.0/0.0
Balamand	41.98 [±1.96]	79.65 [±1.60]	0.0/0.0
Swansea	50.49 [±1.98]	89.77 [±1.20]	0.0/0.0
UNIFRI	37.21 [±1.92]	70.47 [±1.81]	0.0/0.0

11.6.2 Multimodal Evaluation

Participants Six universities have registered to this experiment: AMSL, EPFL, GET-INT, UNIS, UAM and UVIGO. Overall, nine systems have been submitted by the participants. These systems are briefly described below:

AMSL The fusion score is obtained as a weighted sum of matching scores from individual modalities. The weight represents the importance of the corresponding modality in the mutual decision. The calculation of the weights is based on the estimation of equal error rates provided by the individual modalities on the development set. The smaller the EER of a fusion component, the higher the weight assigned to it. Out of a set of weight calculation strategies proposed in [38] the "linear weighting strategy 2" is selected for Experiment 1 and "quadratic weighting strategy" for Experiment 2. In order to consider the matching scores of all modalities evenly, the fusion is prefaced by normalization, where the normalization coefficients are also calculated on the development set.

EPFL1 The system is based on the independence assumption between the basic classifiers in the ensembles. Each score stream is modelled as a mixture of Gaussian densities, which are then combined by a naive Bayes scheme.

EPFL2 The system is based on multivariate logistic regression with a softmax density. The parameters are trained using iteratively reweighted least squares [24].

EPFL3 The system is based on a mixture of multivariate logistic regression with softmax densities. The regression parameters are trained using iteratively reweighted least squares [24], and the mixture weights are learned via Expectation-Maximization (EM) algorithm.

GET-INT1 The system is based on a weighted sum of multiple scores. Firstly, each score is normalized independently using the Min-Max method. Then, a weighted sum of the three normalized scores (2D face, fingerprint and signature) is used to obtain the final fused score. Weights and normalization parameters have been optimized on the BMEC development database.

GET-INT2 The system is based on the normalization of the three scores (2D face, fingerprint and signature) using the Bayes rule. For each modality, the client and impostor distributions ($P(s/C)$ and $P(s/I)$) are estimated independently on the BMEC development database assuming Gaussian distributions. Then, we can estimate the posterior probability ($P(C/s)$) that the score belongs to the client class using the Bayes rule with equal prior probabilities:

$$P(C/s) = \frac{P(s/C)}{P(s/C) + P(s/I)}$$

The three posterior probabilities are then averaged [23], [2] to obtain the final fused score.

UAM This system first performs a TNorm normalization of the scores of each modality, and then combines the three normalized scores using a linear classifier:

$$f_j = a_0 + a_1 * s_{1j} + a_2 * s_{2j} + a_N * s_{3j},$$

where (s_{1j}, s_{2j}, s_{3j}) are the normalized scores given by each modality for a detection trial j. Weights of the linear fusion are trained using the linear logistic regression fusion implemented in the toolkit FoCal [45]. Using this fusion scheme, the scores are fused in such a way as to encourage good calibration of the output score. Calibration means that output scores are mapped to log-likelihood ratios, that is, the logarithm of the ratio between the posteriori probability of being the client and the posteriori probability of being the impostor. Let $[s_{ij}]$ be an $N \times K$ matrix of scores that each of the $N = 3$ component systems calculated for each of K genuine scores, let $[r_{ij}]$ be an $N \times L$ matrix of scores that each of the $N = 3$ component systems calculated for each of L impostor scores, and given the prior probability $P = P(\text{target})$, it can be demonstrated that minimizing the following cost objective tends to produce a good calibration of the fused scores [11], [12]

$$C_{wlr} = \frac{P}{K} \sum_{j=1}^{K} \log\left(1 + e^{-f_j - \log\left(\frac{P}{1-P}\right)}\right) + \frac{1-P}{L} \sum_{j=1}^{L} \log\left(1 + e^{-g_j - \log\left(\frac{P}{1-P}\right)}\right)$$

where the fused target and non-target scores are respectively

$$f_j = \alpha_0 + \sum_{i=1}^{N} \alpha_i s_{ij}, \quad g_j = \alpha_0 + \sum_{i=1}^{N} \alpha_i r_{ij}$$

UNIS The system is based on the logistic regression (LR) algorithm, which is defined as

$$y_{LR} = \frac{1}{1+\exp(-g(\mathbf{y}))},$$

where y_{LR} is the output score, $\mathbf{y}$ is a vector of input scores, and

$$g(\mathbf{y}) = \sum_{i=1}^{M} \beta_i y_i + \beta_0$$

The weight parameters β_i are optimized using gradient ascent to maximize the likelihood of the data given the LR model [13].

UVIGO The system uses an AdaBoost ensemble of MultiLayer Perceptrons (MLPs). The AdaBoost implementation is the standard one, described in [19]. The MLPs have three inputs (the z-normalized scores), one hidden layer with two neurons and one output.

Protocol The database used for this evaluation is the fusion database described in Sect. 11.4.1.5. The multimodal evaluation is composed of two experiments for which each participant should submit a corresponding system (which could be the same). For both experiments, submitted systems should take as input a set of three scores provided by the fingerprint, signature and 2D face reference systems (i.e., an access) and should output a fusion score.

The first experiment will test the score improvement which can be obtained through the combination of those three modalities. The available scores for each individual enrolled in the database are

- Four client accesses.
- 20 impostor accesses for which the impostor scores were obtained using random forgeries for each modality.

The objective of the second experiment is to test the interest of multimodality in terms of robustness to forgeries. In this case, the impostor scores provided for the signature modality were obtained using skilled forgeries. So, the available scores for each individual enrolled in the database are

- Four client accesses.
- 20 impostor accesses for which the impostor scores were obtained using skilled forgeries for signature and random forgeries for the other modalities.

Experimental results The multimodal evaluation results related to multimodal Experiment 1 and 2 are presented next.

Experiment 1 The results of each participant system obtained for this experiment are shown by a DET curve (Fig. 11.14) and are reported in Table 11.16. To evaluate how multimodality improves performance of the verification monomodal systems, we give (in Table 11.15) the EERs of each modality calculated from the scores of the fusion database.

We can first see that all systems enhance the performance compared to monomodal systems alone. The best system was the signature system with EER of 5.03%. Fusion systems enhance by 40% to 60% compared to the signature system alone.

Systems have rather similar performance in terms of EER. Even if we can see a small difference between the first and the last system, we cannot consider the ranking as very informative. However, at the operating point corresponding to

Table 11.15 EER of each modality calculated from the scores of the fusion test database for Experiment 1

Modality	Fingerprint	2D face	Signature
EER (in %)	12.04	37.04	5.03

Table 11.16 Experimental results for Experiment 1 of the multimodal evaluation [EER = Equal Error Rate; OP = Operating Point]

Systems	**EER in %**	$OP_{FAR=0.1\%}$ **in %**
AMSL	2.67 [±0.46]	11.45 [±1.28]
EPFL1	3.08 [±0.50]	32.56 [±1.86]
EPFL2	2.09 [±0.41]	13.66 [±1.36]
EPFL3	2.09 [±0.41]	13.95 [±1.37]
GET-INT1	1.92 [±0.39]	7.85 [±1.07]
GET-INT2	2.50 [±0.45]	21.22 [±1.62]
UNIS	2.27 [±0.43]	9.13 [±1.14]
UAM	1.93 [±0.39]	8.00 [±1.08]
UVIGO	2.44 [±0.44]	22.27 [±1.65]

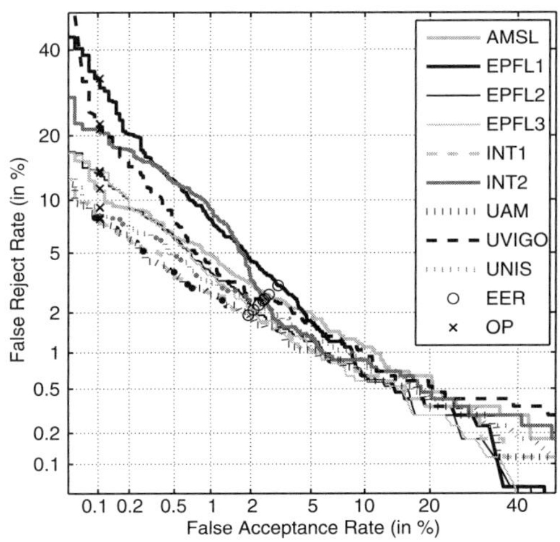

Fig. 11.14 DET curves for Experiment 1 of the multimodal evaluation

FAR = 0.1%, differences are significant and ranking is different from the one of the EER where performance were very close.

Table 11.17 Monomodal EER calculated from the scores of the fusion test database for Experiment 2

Modality	Fingerprint	2D face	Signature
EER (in %)	12.04	37.04	15.19

Table 11.18 Experimental results for Experiment 2 of the multimodal evaluation [EER = Equal Error Rate; OP = Operating Point]

Systems	**EER in %**	$OP_{FAR=1\%}$ in %
AMSL	6.47 [±0.71]	18.31 [±1.53]
EPFL1	6.62 [±0.71]	19.19 [±1.56]
EPFL2	5.85 [±0.67]	15.35 [±1.43]
EPFL3	5.63 [±0.66]	15.58 [±1.44]
GET-INT1	5.92 [±0.68]	15.29 [±1.43]
GET-INT2	6.87 [±0.73]	21.74 [±1.64]
UNIS	5.82 [±0.67]	15.35 [±1.43]
UAM	5.66 [±0.66]	15.41 [±1.43]
UVIGO	10.12 [±0.87]	30.58 [±1.83]

Experiment 2 The results obtained for this experiment are shown by a DET curve (Fig. 11.15) and are reported in Table 11.18. To evaluate how multimodality improves performance of the verification monomodal systems, we give (in Table 11.17) monomodal EERs calculated from the scores of the fusion database.

We can first see that all systems enhance the performance compared to monomodal systems alone. The best system was the fingerprint system with EER of 12.04%. Fusion systems enhance by 15% to 55% compared to the fingerprint system alone.

We can observe approximately three groups of performance, in terms of EER as well as at FAR = 0.1%. The first group contains five systems, the second group contains three systems and the last group contains one system.

As a general conclusion concerning this multimodal evaluation, it seems that there were not enough data in the development set in order to obtain good estimation of the densities or of the separatrix between the classes. For this reason, the systems using such estimations (estimation of posterior probabilities for INT2 or GMM for EPFL1 or estimation of MLPS for UVIGO) did not obtain good performance compared to more simple schemes.

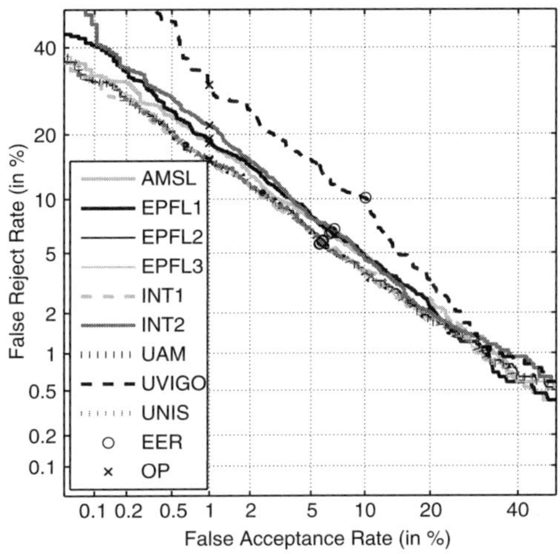

Fig. 11.15 DET curves for Experiment 2 of the multimodal evaluation

11.7 Conclusion

The experimental results of the BMEC'2007 were presented during the final BioSecure workshop on 26–27 September 2007 in Fribourg, Switzerland. On this occasion, all participants have presented their algorithm. At this point, three main remarks can be made:

- Multimodality enhances the performance of the monomodal systems, independently of the "reasonable" fusion method considered. Moreover, it seems that the number of the development data/scores limits the improvement that could be obtained through the use of density estimation methods or any method that needs a learning stage.
- Through the talking-face and signature experiments, we have shown that deliberate well designed impostures are a real threat for state-of-the-art systems. There is a call here for more research work on forgery scenarios in general.
- It has been proved that the use of the Reference Systems is useful to calibrate both the difficulty of the monomodal experiments and the performance of the submitted systems.

Now that the BioSecure project is over, a nonprofit organization called Association BioSecure has been set up to carry on the effort (in particular, release the databases for distribution) and eventually organize other evaluations, this way putting at disposal of the biometric community validated tools for benchmarking.

Acknowledgements

BioSecure is a project of the 6th Framework Programme of the European Union. We thank in particular all the sites that participated in the hard task of data collection, annotation and preparation for the evaluation campaign, and we thank of course all the participants to the BMEC'2007.

Appendix

11.8 Equal Error Rate

The equal error rate is computed as the point where $FAR(t) = FRR(t)$ (Fig. 11.16 a). In practice, the score distributions are not continuous and a crossover point might not exist. In this case (Fig. 11.16 b, c), the EER value is computed as follows

$$EER = \begin{cases} \frac{FAR(t_1)+FRR(t_1)}{2} & \text{if } FAR(t_1) - FRR(t_1) \leqslant FRR(t_2) - FAR(t_2) \\ \frac{FAR(t_2)+FRR(t_2)}{2} & \text{otherwise} \end{cases}$$

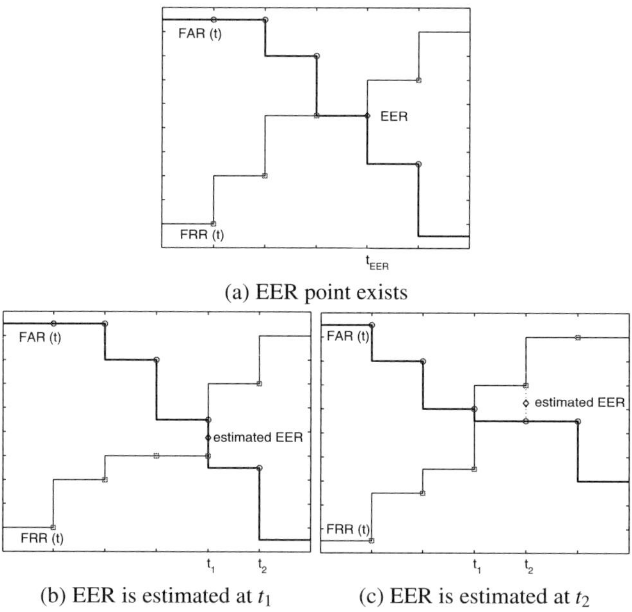

Fig. 11.16 FAR vs FRR curve: (**a**) example where EER point exists, (**b**) and (**c**) examples where EER point does not exist

where

$$t1 = \max_{t \in S}\{t|FRR(t) \leqslant FAR(t)\},\ t2 = \min_{t \in S}\{t|FRR(t) \geqslant FAR(t)\}$$

and S is the set of thresholds used to calculate the score distributions.

11.9 Parametric Confidence Intervals

In this section, we present the parametric method used to estimate the confidence intervals on the FRR and FAR values. This method has already been explained by R.M. Bolle et al. [8].

Suppose we have M client scores and N impostor scores. We denote these sets of scores by $\mathbf{X} = \{X_1, \ldots, X_M\}$ and $\mathbf{Y} = \{Y_1, \ldots, Y_N\}$ respectively. In the following, we suppose that available scores are similarity measures.

Let $\mathbf{S}$ be the set of thresholds used to calculate the score distributions. For the set of client scores, $\mathbf{X}$, assume that this is a sample of M numbers drawn from a population with distribution F, that is, $F(x) = Prob(X \leqslant x), x \in \mathbf{S}$.

Let the impostor scores $\mathbf{Y}$ be a sample of N numbers drawn from a population with distribution $G(y) = Prob(Y \leqslant y), y \in \mathbf{S}$. In this way, $FRR(x) = F(x)$ and $FAR(y) = 1 - G(y)$, x and $y \in \mathbf{S}$.

From now, we have to find an estimate of these distributions at some threshold $t_0 \in \mathbf{S}$ and then, we have to estimate the confidence interval for these estimations.

- The estimate of $F(t_0)$ using data $\mathbf{X}$ is the unbiased statistic:

$$\hat{\mathrm{F}}(t_0) = \frac{1}{M}\sum_{i=1}^{M} \mathbf{1}(X_i \leqslant t_0) \tag{11.1}$$

  $\hat{\mathrm{F}}(t_0)$ is so obtained by simply counting the $X_i \in \mathbf{X}$ that are smaller than t_0 and dividing by M.
  In the same way, the estimate $G(t_0)$ using data $\mathbf{Y}$ is the unbiased statistic:

$$\hat{\mathrm{G}}(t_0) = \frac{1}{N}\sum_{i=1}^{N} \mathbf{1}(Y_i \leqslant t_0) \tag{11.2}$$

- In the following, let us concentrate on the distribution F. For the moment, let us keep $x = t_0$ and let us determine the confidence interval for $\hat{\mathrm{F}}(t_0)$.
  First define Z as a binomial random variable, the number of successes, where success means $(X \leqslant t_0)$ is true, in M trials with probability of success $F(t_0) = Prob(X \leqslant t_0)$. This random variable Z has binomial probability mass distribution:

$$P(Z = z) = \binom{M}{z} F(t_0)^z (1 - F(t_0))^{M-z},\ z = 0, \ldots, M \tag{11.3}$$

The expectation of Z is $E(Z) = MF(t_0)$ and the variance is $\sigma^2(Z) = MF(t_0)(1-F(t_0))$.
From this, it follows that the random variable Z/M has expectation $F(t_0)$ and variance $F(t_0)(1-F(t_0))/M$. When M is large enough, using the law of large numbers, Z/M is distributed according to a normal distribution—i.e., $Z/M \sim N(F(t_0), F(t_0)(1-F(t_0))/M)$.
It now can be seen that $\hat{Z}/M$=$\hat{F}(t_0)$. Hence, for large M, $\hat{F}(t_0)$ is normally distributed, with an estimate of the variance given by:

$$\hat{\sigma}(t_0) = \sqrt{\frac{\hat{F}(t_0)(1-\hat{F}(t_0))}{M}} \tag{11.4}$$

So, confidence intervals can be determined. For example, a 90% interval of confidence is

$$F(t_0) \in [\hat{F}(t_0) - 1.645\hat{\sigma}(t_0), \hat{F}(t_0) + 1.645\hat{\sigma}(t_0)] \tag{11.5}$$

Estimates $\hat{G}(t_0)$ for the probability distribution $G(t_0)$ using a set of impostor scores **Y** can be obtained in a similar fashion. Parametric confidence intervals are computed by replacing $\hat{F}(t_0)$ with $\hat{G}(t_0)$ in Eqs. 11.4 and 11.5.

11.10 Participants

AMSL Otto-von-Guericke-Universitaet Magdeburg
Advanced Multimedia and Security Lab, Biometrics Group
PO Box 4120, Universitaetsplatz 2
39106 Magdeburg - Deutschland

Balamand University of Balamand
Deir El-Balamand, El-Koura, North Lebanon

EPFL Ecole Polytechnique Fédérale de Lausanne
Speech Processing and Biometrics Group
Ecublens, 1015 Lausanne - Switzerland

Swansea University of Wales Swansea, Speech and Image Lab.
Singleton Park - SA2 8PP, Swansea - United Kingdom

TELECOM-ParisTech (formerly GET-ENST), Département TSI
46 rue Barrault, 75013 Paris - France

TELECOM SudParis (formerly GET-INT), Département Electronique et Physique
9 rue Charles Fourier, 91011 Evry Cedex 11 - France

UAM (formerly UPM), Universidad Autonoma de Madrid
Biometrics Research Lab., Ctra. Colmenar, km. 15, E-28049 Madrid - Spain

UNIFRI University of Fribourg, Informatics Department, DIVA group
Chemin du Musée 3, 1700 Fribourg - Switzerland

UNIS University of Surrey, Centre for Vision, Speech and Signal Processing
GU2 7XH Guildford - United Kingdom

UniTOURS Université François Rabelais de Tours, Laboratoire d'informatique
64 avenue Jean Portalis, 37200 Tours - France

UVIGO Universidad de Vigo, Teoria de la Senal y Comunicaciones
ETSI Telecomunicacion, Campus Universitario, 36310 Vigo - Spain

References

1. ALIZE: a free and open tool for speaker recognition. http://www.lia.univ-avignon.fr/heberges/ALIZE/.
2. L. Allano, A.C. Morris, H. Sellahewa, S. Garcia-Salicetti, J. Koreman, S. Jassim, B. Ly Van, D. Wu, and B. Dorizzi. Non intrusive multi-biometrics on a mobile device: a comparison of fusion techniques. In *Proceedings of SPIE 2006, conference on Biometric Techniques for Human Identification III*, Orlando, Florida, USA, April 2006.
3. E. Bailly-Baillière, S. Bengio, F. Bimbot, M. Hamouz, J. Kittler, J. Mariéthoz, J. Matas, K. Messer, V. Popovici, F. Porée, B. Ruiz, and J.-P. Thiran. The BANCA Database and Evaluation Protocol. In *4th International Conference on Audio-and Video-Based Biometric Person Authentication (AVBPA'03)*, pages 625–638, Surrey, UK, 2003.
4. C. Barras and J.-L. Gauvain. Feature and Score Normalization for Speaker Verification of Cellular Data. In *Proceedings of the IEEE International Conference on Acoustics, Speech and Signal Processing (ICASSP 2003)*, Hong Kong, China, 2003.
5. BioSecure Mutimodal Evaluation Campaign 2007 (BMEC2007). http://www.biometrics.it-sudparis.eu/BMEC2007/.
6. BioSecure Network of Excellence. http://biosecure.info/.
7. R.M. Bolle, N.K. Ratha, and S. Pankanti. Evaluation techniques for biometrics-based authentication systems (FRR). In *Proc. 15th Internat. Conf. Pattern Recogn.*, pages 835–841, 2000.
8. R.M. Bolle, N.K. Ratha, and S. Pankanti. Error analysis of pattern recognition systems - the subsets bootstrap. *Computer Vision and Image Understanding*, 93:1–33, 2004.
9. J.-F. Bonastre, N. Scheffer, C. Fredouille, and D. Matrouf. NIST'04 speaker recognition evaluation campaign: new LIA speaker detection plateform based on ALIZE toolkit. In *2004 NIST SRE'04 Workshop: speaker detection evaluation campaign*, Toledo, Spain, 2004.
10. H. Bredin and G. Chollet. Audio-Visual Speech Synchrony Measure for Talking-Face Identity Verification. In *IEEE International Conference on Acoustics, Speech and Signal Processing ICASSP*, 2007.
11. N. Brummer, L. Burget, J. Cernocky, O. Glembek, F. Grezl, M. Karafiat, D.A. van Leeuwen, P. Matejka, P. Scwartz, and A. Strasheim. Fusion of heterogeneous speaker recognition systems in the STBU submission for the NIST speaker recognition evaluation 2006. In *IEEE Transactions on Audio, Speech and Signal Processing*, 2007. To appear.
12. N. Brummer and J. du Preez. *Application independent evaluation of speaker detection.* Computer Speech and Language, 20, pp.230-275, 2006.

13. A.J. Dobson. *An Introduction to Generalized Linear Models*. CRC Press, 1990.
14. B. Dumas, C. Pugin, J. Hennebert, D. Petrovska-Delacrétaz, A. Humm, F. Evquoz, R. Ingold, and D. Von Rotz. MyIdea - multimodal biometrics database, description of acquisition protocols. In *Proc. of Third COST 275 Workshop (COST 275)*, pages 59–62, Hatfield UK, October 2005.
15. NIST Speaker Recognition Evaluation. http://www.nist.gov/speech/tests/spk/.
16. CrazyTalk face animation from Reallusion. http://crazytalk.reallusion.com/.
17. B. Fauve, N.W.D. Evans, and J.S.D. Mason. Improving the Performance of Text-Independent Short Duration GMM- and SVM-Based Speaker Verification. In *Odyssey the Speaker and Language Recognition Workshop*, 2008. To appear.
18. J. Fierrez, J. Ortega-Garcia, D.T. Toledano, and J. Gonzalez-Rodriguez. Biosec baseline corpus: A multimodal biometric database. *Pattern Recognition*, 40(4):1389–1392, 2007.
19. Y. Freund and R.E. Schapire. A Decision-Theoretic Generalization of On-Line Learning and an Application to Boosting. *Journal of Computer and System Scences*, 55(1):119–139, 1997.
20. J. Galbally, J. Fierrez, J. Ortega-Garcia, M.R. Freire, F. Alonso-Fernandez, J.A. Siguenza, J. Garrido-Salas, E. Anguiano-Rey, G. Gonzalez de Rivera, R. Ribalda, M. Faundez-Zanuy, J.A. Ortega, V. Cardenoso-Payo, A. Viloria, C.E. Vivaracho, Q.I. Moro, J.J. Igarza, J. Sanchez, I. Hernaez, and C. Orrite-Urunuela. BiosecurID: a Multimodal Biometric Database. In *Proc. MADRINET Workshop*, pages 68–76, November 2007.
21. S. Garcia-Salicetti, C. Beumier, G. Chollet, B. Dorizzi, J. Leroux les Jardins, J. Lunter, Y. Ni, and D. Petrovska-Delacrétaz. BIOMET: a Multimodal Person Authentication Database Including Face, Voice, Fingerprint, Hand and Signature Modalities. In *4th International Conference on Audio and Video Based Biometric Person Authentification (AVBPA)*, Guilford UK, June 2003.
22. S. Garcia-Salicetti, J. Fierrez-Aguilar, F. Alonso-Fernandez, C. Vielhauer, R. Guest, L. Allano, T. Doan Trung, T. Scheidat, B. Ly Van, J. Dittmann, B. Dorizzi, J. Ortega-Garcia, J. Gonzalez-Rodriguez, M. Bacile di Castiglione, and M. Fairhurst. Biosecure Reference Systems for On-line Signature Verification: a study of complementarity. *Annales des Télécommunications, Special Issue on Multimodal Biometrics*, pages 36–61, January-February 2007.
23. S. Garcia-Salicetti, M.A. Mellakh, L. Allano, and B. Dorizzi. Multimodal biometric score fusion: the mean rule vs. support vector classifiers. In *Proceedings of EUSIPCO 2005*, Antalya, Turkey, September 2005.
24. T. Hastie, R. Tibshirani, and J. Friedman. *The Elements of Statistical Learning*. Springer, section 4.1, 2001.
25. J. Hennebert, R. Loeffel, A. Humm, and R. Ingold. A New Forgery Scenario Based On Regaining Dynamics Of Signature. pages 366–375, Seoul, Korea, 2007.
26. IV2: Identification par l'Iris et le Visage via la Vidéo. http://iv2.ibisc.fr/PageWeb-IV2.html.
27. A. K. Jain, K. Nandakumar, and A. Ross. Score normalization in multimodal biometric systems. *Pattern Recognition*, 38(12):2270–2285, December 2005.
28. V.I. Levenshtein. *Binary codes capable of correcting deletions, insertions and reversals*. Soviet Physics, 10, pp. 707-710, 1966.
29. BECARS Library and Tools for Speaker Verification. http://www.tsi.enst.fr/becars/index.php.
30. R. Lienhart and J. Maydt. An Extended Set of Haar-like Features for Rapid Object Detection. *IEEE ICIP*, 1:900–903, 2002.
31. A. Martin, G.R. Doddington, T. Kamm, M. Ordowski, and M.A. Przybocki. The DET curve in assessment of detection task performance. In *Proceedings of Eurospeech*, pages 1895–1898, Rhodes, Greece, 1997.
32. K. Messer, J. Matas, J. Kittler, J. Luettin, and G. Maitre. XM2VTSDB: The extended M2VTS database. In *Proc. Second International Conference on Audio- and Video-based Biometric Person Authentication (AVBPA)*, 1999.
33. J. Ortega-Garcia, J. Fierrez-Aguilar, D. Simon, M.F.J. Gonzalez nad V. Espinosa, A. Satue, I. Hernaez, J.J. Igarza, C. Vivaracho, D. Escudero, and Q.I. Moro. MCYT baseline corpus: a bimodal biometric database. *IEE Proceedings Vision, Image and Signal Processing*, 150(6):391–401, 2003.

34. D. Petrovska-Delacrétaz, S. Lelandais, J. Colineau, L. Chen, B. Dorizzi, E. Krichen, M.A. Mellakh, A. Chaari, S. Guerfi, J. DHose, M. Ardabilian, and B. Ben Amor. The iv^2 multimodal (2d, 3d, stereoscopic face, talking face and iris) biometric database, and the iv^2 2007 evaluation campaign. *In the proceedings of the IEEE Second International Conference on Biometrics: Theory, Applications (BTAS)*, Washington DC, USA, September 2008.
35. P.J. Phillips, P.J. Flynn, T. Scruggs, K.W. Bowyer, J. Chang, K. Hoffman, J. Marques, J. Min, and W.Worek. Overview of the Face Recognition Grand Challenge. In *IEEE Computer Society Conference on Computer Vision and Pattern Recognition*, pages 947–954, Seoul, Korea, 2005.
36. D.A. Reynolds, T.F. Quatieri, and R. Dunn. Speaker Verification Using Adapted Gaussian Mixture Models. *Digital Signal Processing*, 10(1-3):19–41, 2000.
37. C. Sanderson and K.K. Paliwal. Fast Feature Extraction Method for Robust Face Verification. *IEE Electronics Letters*, 38(25):1648–1650, 2002.
38. T. Scheidat, C. Vielhauer, and J. Dittmann. Distance-Level Fusion Strategies for Online Signature Verification. In *Proceedings of the IEEE International Conference on Multimedia and Expo (ICME)*, Amsterdam, The Netherlands, 2005.
39. F. Schiel, S. Steininger, and U. Trk. The SmartKom multimodal corpus at BAS. In *Proc. Intl. Conf. on Language Resources and Evaluation*, 2002.
40. S. Schimke, C. Vielhauer, and J. Dittmann. Using Adapted Levenshtein Distance for On-Line Signature Authentication. In *Proceedings of the ICPR 2004, IEEE 17th International Conference on Pattern Recognition, ISBN 0-7695-2128-2*, 2004.
41. Festival Text-To-Speech System. http://www.cstr.ed.ac.uk/projects/festival/.
42. Faculté Polytechnique de Mons TCTS MBrola voices. http://tcts.fpms.ac.be/synthesis/mbrola.html.
43. The Hidden Markov Model Toolkit (HTK). http://htk.eng.cam.ac.uk/.
44. Speech Signal Processing (SPro) Toolkit. http://www.irisa.fr/metiss/guig/spro/index.html.
45. Tools for Fusion and Calibration of automatic speaker detection systems (FoCal). http://www.dsp.sun.ac.za/~nbrummer/focal/.
46. M. Turk and A. Pentland. Eigenfaces for recognition. *Journal of Cognitive Neuroscience*, 3(1):71–86, 1991.
47. B. Ly Van, S. Garcia-Salicetti, and B. Dorizzi. On using the Viterbi Path along with HMM Likelihood Information for On-line Signature Verification. In *Proceedings of the IEEE Transactions on Systems, Man and Cybernetics, Part B*, to appear.
48. C. Watson, M. Garris, E. Tabassi, C. Wilson, R. McCabe, and S. Janet. User's Guide to Fingerprint Image Software 2 - NFIS2 (http://fingerprint.nist.gov/NFIS/). NIST 2004.

Index

C

Printed in the United States of America